Explanation of Plate I (*Frontispiece*)

Lower Old Red Sandstone volcanic rocks form the Ochil Hills (background) and are separated by the Ochil Fault from the Carboniferous sedimentary rocks of the Clackmannan Syncline (low ground in the middle distance). The Stirling quartz-dolerite sill forms the crags below Stirling Castle (foreground) and at Abbey Craig (behind, left).

Geology of Stirling (Mem. Geol. Surv.)

PLATE I (Frontispiece)

AERIAL VIEW OF THE OCHIL FAULT-LINE SCARP AND THE STIRLING
SILL FROM THE WEST

Photograph by Aerofilms Ltd.

NATURAL ENVIRONMENT RESEARCH COUNCIL

INSTITUTE OF GEOLOGICAL SCIENCES

MEMOIRS OF THE GEOLOGICAL SURVEY OF GREAT BRITAIN

SCOTLAND

The Geology
of the
Stirling District

(Explanation of One-inch Geological Sheet 39)

By

E. H. FRANCIS, D.SC., F.R.S.E., I. H. FORSYTH, B.SC.,
W. A. READ, B.SC., AND M. ARMSTRONG, B.SC., PH.D.

with contributions by

J. Dawson, B.Sc., R. W. Elliot, B.Sc., A. L. Harris, B.Sc., Ph.D.,
R. McQuillin, M.Sc., J. Taylor, B.Sc., A.M.I.M.M., and
R. B. Wilson, D.Sc., F.R.S.E.

EDINBURGH: HER MAJESTY'S STATIONERY OFFICE

1970

SBN 11 880410 3

PREFACE

THE DISTRICT covered by the Stirling (39) Sheet of the one-inch geological map of Scotland was originally surveyed on the six-inch scale by B. N. Peach and R. L. Jack and the one-inch map was published in 1882. In 1896 C. T. Clough made a detailed study of the Highland Border rocks near Callander and a partial resurvey, related mainly to the Stirling and Clackmannan Coalfield, was carried out between 1905 and 1924 by E. B. Bailey, C. B. Crampton, C. H. Dinham, D. Haldane and H. H. Read. The district was completely resurveyed on the six-inch scale between 1950 and 1961, under the supervision of J. B. Simpson, Mr. J. Knox and Dr. J. R. Earp as District Geologists. The officers concerned, and the areas surveyed by them, are detailed in the list of six-inch maps on p. x. Staff of the Geophysical Department provided valuable assistance in the investigation of specific field problems, notably in locating, or de-limiting, fault lines and igneous intrusions beneath superficial deposits. Seven bore-holes designed to assist the mapping of a heavily drift-covered area west of Stirling were put down under contract for the Geological Survey in 1961–62; the results are discussed in this memoir and the borehole logs are given in Appendix II. The many new industrial boreholes, upon which our knowledge of Upper Carboniferous stratigraphy is largely based, were examined mainly by Messrs. W. Manson, J. M. Dean, E. H. Francis and W. A. Read, together with Mr. C. J. C. Ewing and Mr. F. C. Black of the National Coal Board. 'Solid' and 'Drift' editions of the one-inch map are published.

The original one-inch map was not accompanied by a sheet explanation but in 1932 a memoir entitled 'The economic geology of the Stirling and Clackmannan Coalfield' was published under the authorship of C. H. Dinham and D. Haldane. Subsequently this was supplemented by two Coalfield Papers, the first, by Dr. E. H. Francis, dealing with the area north of the River Forth (published 1956), and the second, by Mr. W. A. Read, covering the area south of the river (published 1959). Well sections and information on the hydrogeology of the Stirling district are given in a Geological Survey Water Supply Paper entitled 'Records of wells in the areas of Scottish one-inch geological sheets Loch Lomond (38), Stirling (39) and Crieff (47)', by Miss N. P. D. Colleran (published 1965).

The present memoir has been written mainly by Dr. E. H. Francis, Mr. I. H. Forsyth, Mr. W. A. Read and Dr. M. Armstrong. Dr. A. L. Harris prepared the chapter on the Dalradian rocks and the chapter on Carboniferous palaeontology is by Dr. R. B. Wilson. Mr. R. W. Elliot contributed an account of the petrography of the Calciferous Sandstone Measures lavas and Mr. J. Dawson of the Atomic Energy Division assisted Dr. Francis in preparing the account of the Ochil Hills mineral veins. The investigations by the Geophysical Department are summarized in Appendix I by Mr. R. McQuillin and the radiometry of the Geological Survey Stirling boreholes is discussed by Mr. J. Taylor of the Atomic Energy Division in Appendix III. The authorship of the various sections is in general indicated by appended initials. The Carboniferous fossils, collected by Mr. W. G. E. Graham and Mr. P. J. Brand, were identified by Dr. R. B. Wilson, with the exception of the goniatites which were named by the late Ethel D. Currie. Our thanks are due to Mr. A. R. Waterston of the Royal Scottish Museum, who identified shells from late-Glacial and post-Glacial marine sediments. Petrographic determinations were made by the surveyors and by Mr. R. W. Elliot. Chemical analyses of igneous rocks and carbonate-rocks were made by staff of the Laboratory of the Government Chemist. The photographs, a list of which is given in Appendix IV, were taken by R. Lunn, Mr. W. Manson and Mr. W. D. Fisher. The memoir was prepared under the supervision of Dr. J. R. Earp and was edited by Mr. T. R. M. Lawrie.

We gratefully acknowledge the information and assistance generously provided by officials of the National Coal Board and the willing co-operation of local landowners, mine and quarry operators at the time of the resurvey.

K. C. DUNHAM
Director

Institute of Geological Sciences.
Exhibition Road,
South Kensington,
London, S.W.7.
6th August 1968

CONTENTS

(References are listed at the end of each chapter)

ILLUSTRATIONS

TEXT-FIGURES

vii

PLATES

LIST OF SIX-INCH MAPS

Geological six-inch maps included wholly or in part in the Stirling (39) Sheet of the one-inch geological map of Scotland are listed below together with the initials of the surveyors and the dates of the survey. The surveyors were: M. Armstrong, A. C. Bishop, A. L. Harris, I. H. Forsyth, E. H. Francis and W. A. Read. The maps marked with an asterisk have been published and are obtainable through Ordnance Survey Agents and most booksellers. The others, in manuscript form, are available for public reference at the Institute of Geological Sciences, 19 Grange Terrace, Edinburgh 9; photostat copies can be purchased on application at the same address.

NN 60 NW	I.H.F.	1957–60	NS 69 NE	W.A.R., I.H.F.	1958–60
NE	I.H.F.	1956–58	SW	W.A.R., I.H.F.	1959–60
SW	I.H.F.	1957–60	SE	W.A.R.	1959–61
SE	I.H.F.	1956–60	78 NW	W.A.R.	1955–61
70 NW	I.H.F.	1956–58	NE	W.A.R.	1952–61
NE	I.H.F.	1955–58	79 NW	W.A.R., I.H.F.	1956–60
SW	I.H.F.	1955–58	NE	W.A.R., E.H.F.,	
SE	I.H.F., E.H.F.	1952–57		I.H.F.	1952–60
80 NW	M.A., I.H.F.	1955–58	SW	W.A.R.	1953–60
NE	M.A., E.H.F.	1958–59	SE	W.A.R., E.H.F.	1952–60
SW	A.C.B., M.A.,		88 NW*	W.A.R.	1952–54
	E.H.F., I.H.F.	1952–58	NE*	W.A.R., E.H.F.	1952
SE	E.H.F., A.C.B.,		89 NW*	E.H.F., W.A.R.	1952
	M.A.	1952–59	NE*	E.H.F.	1951–52
81 SW	M.A., I.H.F.	1958	SW*	W.A.R., E.H.F.	1952
SE	M.A.	1958–59	SE*	E.H.F., W.A.R.	1951–52
90 NW	M.A., E.H.F.	1959–60	98 NW*	E.H.F., W.A.R.	1951–52
NE	M.A., E.H.F.	1960–61	NE*	E.H.F.	1950–51
SW	E.H.F.	1952–60	99 NW*	E.H.F.	1950–59
SE	E.H.F.	1956–60	NE*	E.H.F.	1950–59
91 SW	M.A.	1959–60	SW*	E.H.F.	1950–51
SE	M.A.	1959–61	SE*	E.H.F.	1950–51
NS 68 NW	W.A.R.	1960–61	NT 08 NW*	E.H.F.	1950–51
NE	W.A.R.	1959–61	09 NW*	E.H.F.	1950–56
69 NW	I.H.F., W.A.R.	1959–60	SW*	E.H.F.	1950

The north-western part of Sheet 39 (for which National Grid six-inch topographic maps are not available) is covered on the six-inch scale by sheets of the County series or by special National Grid maps compiled from County series sheets:

PERTH 105 SW	A.L.H., I.H.F.	1959–60	NN 61 SE	I.H.F., A.L.H.	1957–60
SE	I.H.F., A.L.H.	1959	71 SW	I.H.F.	1957–59
115 NW	I.H.F., A.L.H.	1957–59	SE	I.H.F.	1958–59
SW	I.H.F.	1957–60			

Chapter I

INTRODUCTION

AREA AND PHYSICAL FEATURES

THE STIRLING DISTRICT, which comprises the area covered by Sheet 39 of the One-inch Geological Map of Scotland, lies mainly in south Perthshire and Stirlingshire, but includes the county of Clackmannan and small adjoining portions of Kinross-shire and Fife in the south-east. The main features of the geology and topography are shown on Fig. 1.

The relief is dominated by three tracts of high ground, two of which are about 12 miles long and include hills over 2000 ft high. The most northerly of these lies on either side of the Highland Border north and north-east of Callander and comprises a group of hills composed of Dalradian rocks and Lower Old Red Sandstone sediments, mostly conglomerates, which rise to a height of 2181 ft O.D. at Uamh Bheag. These hills are bounded to the south and south-east by the valleys of the River Teith and of the Allan Water, both eroded in relatively soft Lower Old Red Sandstone sediments. The low ground of Strathallan gives way in the eastern and north-eastern part of the district to a second upland tract—the Ochil Hills—where Lower Old Red Sandstone volcanic rocks rise to 2363 ft O.D. at Ben Clach (Cleuch), the highest point in the Stirling district. The Ochil Hills taper off south-westwards, and at Stirling almost meet the third tract of high ground, which extends for about 8 miles in the south-western part of the district. This tract comprises the Fintry, Gargunnock and Touch hills, formed by the northernmost of the Lower Carboniferous lavas of the Clyde Plateau and rising to 1677 ft O.D. at Stronend. The low ground east of the Touch Hills and south of the Ochils (Plate I, frontispiece), which lies for the most part below 400 ft O.D., is underlain by drift-covered Carboniferous strata downfolded along a north–south axis to form the Clackmannan Syncline.

The main river is the Forth, which enters the area from the west, at Flanders Moss, and flows eastward across Old Red Sandstone sediments before turning towards the south-east to cross the Carboniferous. It is joined on the north by the rivers Teith, Allan Water, Devon and Black Devon, and on the south by the Bannock Burn. The main Forth valley and the lower reaches of some of the tributary valleys are floored by the flat, low-lying areas of marine and estuarine alluvium known as the 'Carse'. This forms a tract $2\frac{1}{2}$ to 3 miles wide in the west, narrowing to one mile near Stirling where the crags of the Stirling sill partly block the gap between the volcanic uplands, then opening out south-eastward to a width of about 4 miles.

Population is most dense in the south-east where industry followed the mining of coal and iron in the Carboniferous rocks. The growth of the largest settlement, the city of Stirling, owes much to its situation on the lowest ford on the Forth near the gap between the Gargunnock and Ochil hills which since very early times has provided the easiest passage for traffic between the Scottish Lowlands and Highlands. Alloa, which is next in size, has declined as a coal port but now supports textile, engineering, brewing and distilling industries which depend, in part, on water obtained from borings into Passage Group strata. Blairlogie,

1

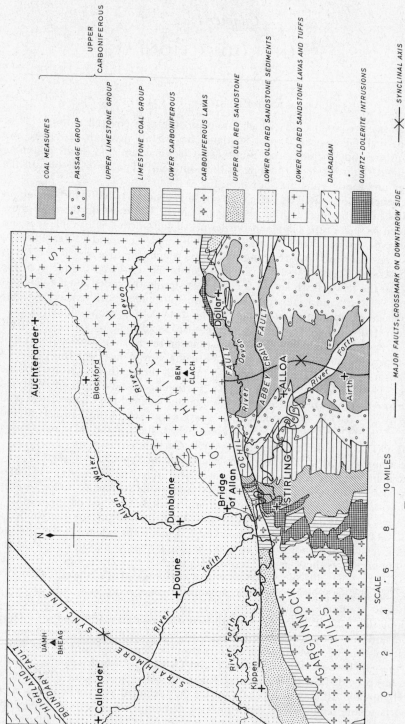

FIG. 1. *Geological sketch-map of the Stirling district*

Menstrie, Alva, Tillicoultry and Dollar are situated along the northern margin of the coalfield: all have been built on alluvial cones which accumulated where fast-running streams from the steep southern scarp of the Ochils were checked on reaching the flat 'carse' of the Devon valley. Other towns and villages in the south and east are Plean, Airth, Cowie, Bannockburn and St. Ninians south of the Forth, and Cambus, Clackmannan, Culross, Coalsnaughton, Blairingone, Kincardine-on-Forth, Tullibody and Sauchie north of the Forth. The area north and west of Stirling is almost entirely rural. Where it has been drained the flat ground of the Carse makes good agricultural land, and the comparatively low ground of the Teith valley and Strathallan is also good, especially for cattle rearing. The higher ground, however, provides much poorer pasture and can support only a low density of sheep per acre; extensive peat-covered tracts are grouse moors and deer forests. The main towns and villages are Kippen, Thornhill, Bridge of Allan, Callander, Doune, Dunblane, Braco, Blackford and Auchterarder.

GEOLOGICAL SEQUENCE

The geological formations occurring within the area are summarized below.

SUPERFICIAL DEPOSITS (DRIFT)

RECENT AND PLEISTOCENE

Landslips
Peat
Freshwater alluvium
Marine and estuarine alluvium (post-Glacial and late-Glacial)
Glacial and fluvio-glacial sand and gravel
Morainic drift
Boulder clay

SOLID FORMATIONS

		Thickness in feet
CARBONIFEROUS		
UPPER CARBONIFEROUS		
Upper Coal Measures:	not exposed or proved by boring estimated	700
Middle Coal Measures:	sandstones, mudstones, siltstones, seatearths and coals	500
Lower Coal Measures:	sandstones, mudstones, siltstones, seatearths and coals	300–500
Passage Group:	sandstone with subordinate fireclays and up to 16 marine bands	740–1100
(The Passage Group was formerly classed as Millstone Grit in Scotland)		
Upper Limestone Group:	sandstones, mudstones, siltstones and marine limestones with mainly thin coals	1020–1980
Limestone Coal Group:	sandstones, mudstones, siltstones and coals	700–1800

*Thickness
in feet*

LOWER CARBONIFEROUS

Lower Limestone Group: sandstones, mudstones, siltstones and marine limestones   300–450

Calciferous Sandstone Measures

 (c) sandstones, mudstones, siltstones and marine limestones: volcanic detritus at base   70–120+

 (b) basaltic lavas with subordinate beds of volcanic detritus and tuff   700–1400+

 (a) cementstones, mudstones and shales with subordinate sandstones and volcanic detritus   950–1600

OLD RED SANDSTONE

UPPER OLD RED SANDSTONE

Cornstone Beds: white and red sandstones, red and purple siltstones and mudstones with cornstones   600–1300

Gargunnock Sandstones: uniform brick-red sandstones underlain by basal conglomerates   1200–2000

unconformity

LOWER OLD RED SANDSTONE

Uamh Bheag Conglomerate: conglomerate with pebbles of quartz, lava, etc.   400

Teith Formation: sandstones, purple, brown and grey, locally coarse   3000

Cromlix Formation[1]: mudstones, red and purple, silty   2500

Dunblane Formation[1]: sandstones, purple and brown, cross-bedded   2600

Buttergask Formation[1]: (presumed correlative of Ruchill Formation) fine-grained sandstones, siltstones and shales   900

Sheriffmuir Formation[1]: sandstones, grey and brown   1400

'Mixed conglomerates'[2] conglomerate with pebbles of quartz, lava etc.   3500

Ruchill Formation[2]: siltstones, shales and flaggy sandstones, purple and brown   3000

Volcanic Conglomerate: conglomerate derived from lavas; partly interleaved with Sheriffmuir Formation and lavas   up to 3000

Volcanic group: basalts, andesites, trachyandesites, rhyodacites, tuffs and agglomerates   up to 10 000

Highland Boundary Fault

CAMBRO-ORDOVICIAN

? Arenig: shales, grey-green and black, with chert and dolomitized, silicified serpentine

[1] Confined to the south-east limb of the Strathmore Syncline
[2] Confined to the north-west limb of the Strathmore Syncline

fault

DALRADIAN (in part Lower Cambrian)
  Leny and Ben Ledi Grits: mainly grits with slate bands
  Aberfoyle Slates: cleaved mudstones and siltstones

INTRUSIONS

Quartz-dolerite sills and dykes of late Carboniferous or early Permian age.
Teschenite and basanite sills of Upper Carboniferous age.
Tuff and agglomerate in necks of Upper Carboniferous age.
Basaltic sills, dykes, etc., of Lower Carboniferous age.
Diorite stocks and consanguineous minor intrusions of Caledonian age.

OUTLINE OF GEOLOGICAL HISTORY

The earliest geological record in the district is provided by the Dalradian rocks which crop out in the north-west. These belong to the upper part of a varied assemblage of sediments deposited in a rapidly sinking geosyncline. The oldest members of the Dalradian assemblage in the district are the mudstones and siltstones which are now represented by the Aberfoyle Slates. These were succeeded by a thick accumulation of grits which were probably introduced by turbidity currents. The rocks deposited in the geosyncline were subjected to powerful earth movements during the Caledonian orogeny and as a result were deformed and metamorphosed. The ?Arenig rocks also were probably deformed at this time.

By the beginning of Old Red Sandstone times the Highland area had emerged as a mountainous tract bordered to the south-east by the subsiding trough of the Midland Valley. In this trough there accumulated a great thickness of Lower Old Red Sandstone sediments and volcanic rocks, the former derived in large measure from the denudation of the Highland mountain chain. The base of the Lower Old Red Sandstone in the Stirling district is nowhere seen and the lowest rocks exposed are the lavas and tuffs of the volcanic group, which reaches a thickness of about 10 000 ft in the Ochil Hills. During the later stages of volcanism, diorites and minor intrusions were emplaced among the lavas. The Caledonian intrusions in the Dalradian are very similar and may well be of the same age. The last of the lavas are interdigitated with conglomerates, sandstones and mudstones, which continued to accumulate until by the end of Lower Old Red Sandstone times they were over 10 000 ft thick.

This sedimentary phase was followed by earth movements of Middle Old Red Sandstone age, as a result of which the older rocks were folded along Caledonoid axes. The formation of the Strathmore Syncline dates from this period, as does the main movement along the Highland Boundary Fault. After a period of erosion, sandstones and cornstones of Upper Old Red Sandstone age were deposited unconformably on the older sediments and lavas. In the western part of the Stirling district, as in many other parts of Scotland, the sandstones and cornstones may be interdigitated with cementstones and mudstones of Lower Carboniferous facies and the junction between the formations then appears to be transitional and conformable. In the east, however, there is some evidence of unconformity at the base of the Carboniferous facies.

It is usually supposed that the earliest Carboniferous sediments were deposited in relatively shallow and possibly enclosed tracts of water, the northern limit of which lay only a short distance to the north of the present Carboniferous outcrop. The deposition of cementstones and mudstones was interrupted in the south-western part of the district by outpourings of flood-basalts forming the northern part of the Clyde Plateau and amounting in thickness to more than 1400 ft in the Fintry and Gargunnock hills. The highest beds of the Calciferous Sandstone Measures are sediments. The lowest of these contain detritus derived from erosion of the lavas, but near the top three limestones appear which can be regarded as forerunners of a major marine transgression which is usually associated with the Hurlet Limestone.

Thereafter, throughout Lower Limestone Group times and on into the Upper Carboniferous, sedimentation was dominantly cyclic. Different lithological members of the cycle characterize the different groups. Thus marine limestones and shales are most important within the Lower and Upper Limestone groups, coals within the Limestone Coal Group and Coal Measures, and sandstones within the Passage Group. The Clackmannan Syncline was initiated at least as early as the first of the cyclic deposits and it continued to function as a depositional basin into Coal Measures times. Upper Carboniferous volcanism was restricted to the south-eastern part of the district where, during Limestone Coal Group and Upper Limestone Group times, a number of small necks were drilled and an alkali-dolerite sill complex was intruded.

Towards the end of the Carboniferous period the sediments were subjected to folding and major east–west faulting and this was accompanied, or closely followed, by emplacement of quartz-dolerite and tholeiite as dykes, sill-complex and fault-intrusions. Geological history during Mesozoic and Tertiary times is obscure as there are no corresponding deposits preserved in the district. It is believed, however, that some of the mineralization which is associated with faults, particularly in the Ochil Hills, is of Tertiary age.

It is probable that the main features of present-day relief and drainage were already in being by the end of the Tertiary, but they were considerably modified by glaciation during the Quaternary period. The deeper valleys became filled with boulder clay and with outwash sands and gravels; and similar deposits give rise to drumlins and hummocky country respectively in the lower ground throughout the district. Some of the most impressive features of ice-retreat are glacial drainage-channels which are particularly numerous in Strathallan.

The late-Glacial sea stood at levels up to about 120 ft O.D. and the deposits of this age are believed to have originated as glacial outwash deltas. Then and in post-Glacial times there was movement of land relative to sea which was partly eustatic and partly isostatic in origin and was probably accompanied by tilting. By Boreal times the sea had fallen below its present level and the newly-exposed land took on a cover of vegetation now preserved locally as a layer of peat beneath younger ('Carse') clays. These clays are the deposits of the final marine transgression during Atlantic times when the sea stood at about 40 ft above O.D. in the neighbourhood of Stirling.   E.H.F.

Chapter II

DALRADIAN AND SUPPOSED ARENIG ROCKS

DALRADIAN rocks occupy an area, some six square miles in extent, on the north-west side of the Highland Boundary Fault north of Callander. They consist entirely of metasediments of low metamorphic grade, comprising a slate group (the 'Aberfoyle Slates'), flanked to the north-west and south-east by predominantly grit groups, the Ben Ledi Grits and the Leny Grits respectively. In the south-eastern part of the Leny Grit outcrop, a thin series of shales with limestone bands, the Leny Limestone and Shales, crops out near the Highland Boundary Fault. Shales and cherts, possibly of Arenig age, form a lenticular outcrop along the fault and are associated at one locality with dolomitized serpentine. The stratigraphy and structure of these rocks have been discussed in a paper by Harris (1962), on which the following summary is based.

DALRADIAN

The existence of a major fold—the Aberfoyle fold—along the Highland Border has been known since Henderson (1938) demonstrated that the Leny and Ben Ledi grit groups between Loch Lubnaig and Loch Lomond both young away from the Aberfoyle Slates which separate them. Anderson (1947) interpreted this fold as an anticline. On the other hand, Shackleton (1956; 1958) produced evidence suggesting that the fold closes downwards and he advanced the hypothesis that it forms the down-bent hinge zone of a recumbent anticline (the 'Tay Nappe') which has its roots far to the north-west. In the Callander area, evidence provided by sedimentary structures confirms the view (Shackleton 1956; 1958; Stone 1957) that the Aberfoyle Fold has a core of older rocks (the slates) and an envelope of younger (the grits). The evidence of tectonic minor structures, however, indicates that the fold is a synform and this accords with Shackleton's view that it is a downward-facing anticline. The plunge of the associated minor folds suggests that the major structure plunges at about 28° towards the west-south-west.

The rocks of the slate belt consist essentially of cleaved mudstones and siltstones. Previous workers in the area assigned the whole belt to the Aberfoyle Slates but detailed work by Harris showed that the slates could be separated into two subdivisions with differing lithology. To the south-west of the Allt an Dubh Choirein, the south-eastern part of the belt is made up of grey, green and, less commonly, purple slates with thin irregular grit bands. These rocks, which Harris regards as the true equivalents of the Aberfoyle Slates, occupy the whole width of the slate belt south-west of Sgiath an Dobhrain, but north-eastwards their outcrop narrows and is interpreted as closing a short distance beyond the Allt an Dubh Choirein. The remainder of the slate belt consists of bluish-grey and greenish-grey slates which show a characteristic rhythmic banding associated with graded bedding; they contain numerous intercalations of grit, some of considerable thickness. These slates form the bulk of the slate belt in the north-eastern part of the area but south-westwards they pass laterally along the strike

B

into typical grits of the Ben Ledi group. This is well seen on the eastern slopes of Sgiath an Dobhrain where the thick slate succession becomes split up into individual bands interdigitated with the grits. From this and other evidence Harris concluded that the rhythmically banded slates, which he called the Ben Ledi Slates, are probably equivalent in age to the Ben Ledi Grits. Thus the

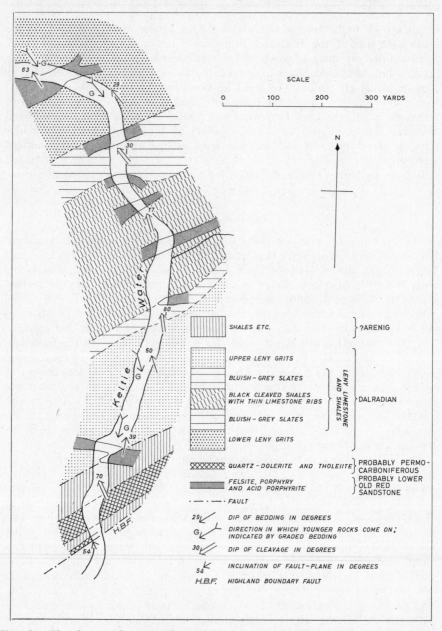

SCALE

| 0 | 100 | 200 | 300 YARDS |

SHALES ETC. } ?ARENIG

UPPER LENY GRITS

BLUISH – GREY SLATES

BLACK CLEAVED SHALES WITH THIN LIMESTONE RIBS } LENY LIMESTONE AND SHALES

BLUISH – GREY SLATES

LOWER LENY GRITS

} DALRADIAN

QUARTZ - DOLERITE AND THOLEIITE } PROBABLY PERMO-CARBONIFEROUS

FELSITE, PORPHYRY AND ACID PORPHYRITE } PROBABLY LOWER OLD RED SANDSTONE

· — · — · FAULT

29 ∠ DIP OF BEDDING IN DEGREES

G ∟ DIRECTION IN WHICH YOUNGER ROCKS COME ON; INDICATED BY GRADED BEDDING

30 ∠ DIP OF CLEAVAGE IN DEGREES

54 ∟ INCLINATION OF FAULT-PLANE IN DEGREES

H.B.F. HIGHLAND BOUNDARY FAULT

Fig. 2. *Sketch-map showing relationships between the Leny Grits and the Leny Limestone and Shales in the Keltie Water*

Aberfoyle Fold in this area is envisaged as having a core of Aberfoyle Slates which closes to the east-north-east, and an envelope consisting of Ben Ledi Grits and Slates to the north, and Leny Grits to the south (Harris 1962, plate i; the slate belt has not been subdivided on the one-inch geological map). Such an interpretation, based on large-scale facies variation, would account in large measure for the lack of symmetry of formations on the two sides of the fold but it seems probable from the position of the axial trace of the fold (*see* Harris 1962, plate i) that there has also been some tectonic attenuation of the southern limb during the formation of the nappe folds.

The grit groups are broadly similar in lithology, consisting essentially of bedded grits with subordinate pelitic bands. The Ben Ledi Grits are in general considerably more deformed than the Leny Grits and they are characterized by a widespread development of cleavage parallel or sub-parallel to bedding. Graded bedding and current-bedding are prevalent in both groups but are commonly less well preserved in the Ben Ledi Grits. The Leny Grits are divisible into a lower and an upper group, separated by the Leny Limestone and Shales (Fig. 2). Within the area of the Stirling Sheet the latter consist mainly of lustrous, graphitic cleaved shales which are commonly calcareous and contain thin limestones and siliceous bands; the shales are overlain and underlain by horizons of bluish-grey, well-cleaved slates. The latter in particular are highly contorted by both fault and fold movements. The way-up evidence, and the absence of any stratigraphical break, confirms Anderson's conclusion (1947) that this group is an intercalation in the Leny Grits. As no similar horizon has been recognized in the Ben Ledi Grits, the Leny Limestone and Shales must be presumed to die out towards the north-west.

In the neighbourhood of the diorite intrusions (p. 11) the slates have been thermally metamorphosed and in a few localities spotted slate and cordierite-hornfels have been recorded. The grits do not appear to have been affected.

Trilobites found by Pringle (1940) in Leny Quarry, west of the area under review, indicate that the Leny Limestone and Shales are of late Lower Cambrian age (Stubblefield, in discussion of Brown and others 1965, p. 133). As there is no evidence of any stratigraphical or structural break between these rocks and the adjacent grits, there is a strong implication that the Upper Leny Grits, and part at least of the Lower Leny and the Ben Ledi grits, are also of Cambrian age.

The Supposed Arenig Rocks

Rocks of possible Arenig age, which belong to the so-called Black Shale and Chert Series of the Highland Border, are preserved in a fault-bounded slice along the Highland Boundary Fault. They are best seen in the Keltie Water (Fig. 2), where about 20 ft of shale, contorted by fold and fault movements, are exposed. Chert and contemporaneous igneous rocks have also been recorded at this locality. In a right-bank tributary of the Keltie Water, about 950 yd north-north-east of Braeleny Farm, carbonaceous shales are associated with a small body of dolomitized and silicified serpentine.

The Black Shale and Chert Series has long been regarded as Arenig in age, partly because of its similarity to known Arenig strata at Ballantrae, and partly because in the Aberfoyle area it yielded fossils which were taken to indicate an Upper Cambrian–Lower Ordovician age (Jehu and Campbell 1917). A re-examination of the fossils suggests, however, that they do not provide precise evidence of age and that their range may be considerably more extended than was previously thought, possibly even Lower Cambrian to Silurian (Summ. Prog. 1963, p. 57). Johnson and Harris (1967) have recently suggested that the so-called 'Arenig' rocks of the Highland Border are of Middle Cambrian age.

A.L.H.

References

ANDERSON, J. G. C. 1947. The geology of the Highland Border: Stonehaven to Arran. *Trans. R. Soc. Edinb.*, **61**, 479–515.

BROWN, P. E., MILLER, J., SOPER, N. J. and YORK, D. 1965. Potassium–argon age patterns of the British Caledonides. *Proc. Yorks. geol. Soc.*, **35**, 103–38.

HARRIS, A. L. 1962. Dalradian geology of the Highland Border near Callander. *Bull. geol. Surv. Gt Br.*, No. 19, 1–15.

HENDERSON, S. M. K. 1938. The Dalradian succession of the Southern Highlands. *Rep. Br. Ass. Advmt Sci.* (*Cambridge* 1938), 424.

JEHU, J. T. and CAMPBELL, R. 1917. The Highland Border rocks of the Aberfoyle district. *Trans. R. Soc. Edinb.*, **52**, 175–212.

JOHNSON, M. R. W. and HARRIS, A. L. 1967. Dalradian–?Arenig relations in parts of the Highland Border, Scotland, and their significance in the chronology of the Caledonian orogeny. *Scott. J. Geol.*, **3**, 1–16.

PRINGLE, J. 1940. The discovery of Cambrian trilobites in the Highland Border rocks near Callander, Perthshire. *Advmt Sci.*, **1**, No. 2, 252.

SHACKLETON, R. M. 1956. Downward-facing structures of the Highland Border. *Proc. geol. Soc.*, No. 1540, 111–4.

—— 1958. Downward-facing structures of the Highland Border. *Q. Jl geol. Soc. Lond.*, **113**, 361–92.

STONE, M. 1957. The Aberfoyle Anticline, Callander, Perthshire. *Geol. Mag.*, **94**, 265–76.

SUMM. PROG. 1963. *Mem. geol. Surv. Summ. Prog.* for 1962.

Chapter III

CALEDONIAN IGNEOUS ROCKS NORTH OF THE HIGHLAND BORDER

INTRODUCTON

THE DALRADIAN rocks in the north-western part of the Stirling district are cut by two small plutons of diorite—the Dubh Choirein diorite and the Meall Odhar diorite—and by the numerous irregular dykes and sheets which constitute the Dubh Choirein swarm of minor intrusions. All these intrusions post-date the folding and metamorphism of the country rocks. Because of their age-relationships, and their similarity to other post-orogenic intrusions of the South-West Highlands of Scotland, they are considered to have been emplaced during the Caledonian phase of igneous activity between the late-Silurian and the mid-Devonian.

The Dubh Choirein swarm is abruptly truncated by the Highland Boundary Fault and its south-eastern portion presumably lies at depth, as a result of the mid-Devonian movements of the fault. None of its members cuts the Lower Old Red Sandstone strata now exposed on the south-eastern side of the fault, but this does not necessarily imply any age-relationship as the upper limit of intrusion may lie below the present level of erosion. The Dubh Choirein diorite is cut by several intrusions of the Dubh Choirein swarm, at least some of whose members are therefore younger than the diorite.

Previous research. The existence of the Dubh Choirein diorite and swarm was discovered during the original survey of the area, but since then they have attracted attention only from Anderson (1947, p. 495), who noted that no other swarm of intrusions occurs in the Highland Border region. He described them as mostly felsites and porphyries with some microdiorites. In the Allt an Dubh Choirein he found 45 dykes averaging 10 ft in thickness within a mile of the Highland Boundary Fault. He described the Dubh Choirein diorite as a medium-grained pyroxene-mica-diorite with partially serpentinized olivine, similar to diorites from other Caledonian complexes and having affinities to the kentallenite suite.

DIORITE STOCKS

Dubh Choirein diorite. The Dubh Choirein diorite is emplaced mainly in Leny Grits, but to some extent also in Aberfoyle Slates, in which it produces considerable thermal metamorphism. Its outcrop, determined partly by surface mapping and partly by magnetic survey, is roughly rectangular in shape with a length of almost $1\frac{1}{2}$ miles in a north-easterly direction and a width of about three-quarters of a mile. The pronounced irregularity in the shape of the outcrop is caused by the preservation, on the Tom Odhar ridge, of part of the roof of the intrusion which is there very gently inclined. The contacts at the sides are seen only in the Allt an Dubh Choirein, where they appear to be more or less vertical.

The only good exposures of the Dubh Choirein diorite are in the Allt an Dubh Choirein itself, where it was originally noted. Over the rest of its outcrop it is

11

at best very poorly exposed, as on Druim nan Eilid, or completely hidden by peat, moraine, etc. The extent of its outcrop had therefore to be determined by geophysical means (*see* p. 310). Three varieties have been distinguished in the Dubh Choirein diorite (*see* Table 1). The first, here termed the normal diorite, is generally non-porphyritic and occurs in the north-western part of the section in the Allt an Dubh Choirein. The second variety, referred to as the fine-grained porphyritic diorite, is very similar to the first in bulk composition (*cf.* Table 1) but is distinguished from it by textural differences. It has been found to contain rhombic as well as monoclinic pyroxene and locally some fresh olivine. In the south-eastern part of the section in the Allt an Dubh Choirein this variety is apparently mingled with the third type of diorite, which is distinguished by its richness in orthoclase. All three types have been observed away from the stream, but exposures are too poor to give any indication of their distribution.

Meall Odhar diorite. The Meall Odhar diorite, first detected during the resurvey, is a much smaller body than the Dubh Choirein diorite. It crops out on the north-west slopes of the hill and is roughly rectangular in shape, with its longer axis, about 350 yd long, extending approximately north–south. The shorter axis measures some 250 yd.

There are two apophyses projecting from the northern end, a westerly one about 350 yd long and an easterly one of about 250 yd. A number of exposures of porphyrite occur on the east side of the diorite with no sign of any intervening country rock: they probably belong to an intrusion of porphyrite, marginal to the diorite and comparable to it in size of outcrop.

Details

Dubh Choirein diorite. The best, and hitherto only known, exposures of the Dubh Choirein diorite are in the Allt an Dubh Choirein [NN 668152–672149][1]. The outcrop is now known to be about 480 yd in length, nearly twice as long as was previously thought. The exposures are confined to the immediate vicinity of the stream and are extensive but not continuous, there being gaps particularly west of the centre of the outcrop. Both contacts are well exposed and appear to be approximately vertical. The north-western one, with slates, is highly complicated, with much brecciation and horn-felsing of the country rock; the general trend of the junction is north-north-westerly. The south-eastern contact, with grits, is much simpler and has an east-north-easterly trend.

The exposures show generally dark-grey and rather fine-grained diorite which does not vary much in grain size or appearance along the outcrop, though locally coarser-grained, mottled varieties occur. The eastern part of the diorite outcrop in the Allt an Dubh Choirein (Fig. 3) is cut by a number of minor intrusions, mostly dykes with a general north-easterly trend and ranging in composition from porphyry to porphyrite. The western part is cut by a later dyke of quartz-dolerite.

Diorite is not seen at the surface north-east of the Allt an Dubh Choirein, and exposures of Dalradian strata only about 100 yd from the stream limit the extent of its outcrop in this direction; the diorite here is probably cut off by one of the north-westerly lines of faulting for which evidence has been found in the Dalradian area.

The south-western slopes of Gleann an Dubh Choirein are heavily mantled in peat and moraine and there is only one small exposure, of grits, in a small stream [NN 669148]. The extent of the diorite could not therefore be ascertained by means of surface mapping.

---

[1] National Grid References are given in this form throughout the Memoir.

There is a small exposure [NN 668145] of diorite, similar to that seen in the Allt an Dubh Choirein, close to the Dalradian rocks which cap the eastern end of the Tom Odhar ridge. Near the Comrie–Callander path [NN 668141] there is a small outcrop of rather weathered diorite in which abundant biotite can be readily distinguished. Further west along the path numerous diorite blocks were noted during the original survey (*see also* Anderson 1947, p. 495), but no undoubted exposure of diorite in place has been found in the vicinity; a small exposure [NN 655141] of fine-grained diorite in a runnel flowing southwards off Tom Odhar may, however, represent part of the top of the pluton or of an apophysis from it.

On Druim nan Eilid, a long, low somewhat hummocky hill to the south of the path, there is a prominent exposure [NN 658133] of cordierite-hornfels (*see* p. 9) whose presence suggested that a sizeable body of igneous rock must occur close by. No actual exposures were found, but a number of diggings were made and in each more or less weathered diorite was proved below peat and soil.

Field evidence thus indicated that the diorite outcrop was much larger than had previously been suspected, but left considerable uncertainty as to its full extent, e.g. continuity of outcrop between the Allt an Dubh Choirein and Druim nan Eilid seemed likely but was unproved. Recourse was therefore made to geophysical methods to determine the extent of the diorite, and a magnetic survey was carried out by the Geophysical Department of the Geological Survey under Mr. R. McQuillin in June 1961. Although the outcrop could not be precisely delimited because diorite at the surface could not be distinguished from diorite beneath a very thin cover of country rock, the results enabled a much more accurate map to be prepared than would otherwise have been the case. In particular it was shown that the diorite does not reach the Highland Boundary Fault at the surface (though it may do so at depth), that the Dubh Choirein and Druim nan Eilid exposures all belong to one body, that the southern slopes of Tom Odhar and the south-western slopes of lower Gleann an Dubh Choirein consist largely of diorite, and that only a thin cap of generally metamorphosed and much intruded Dalradian is present on top of the Tom Odhar ridge.

Meall Odhar diorite. Scattered exposures of diorite occur on the north-western slopes of Meall Odhar and these together with exposures of hornfelsed Dalradian enable the extent of the intrusion to be determined within quite narrow limits. The western apophysis from the diorite mass can be traced by means of exposures in the head-waters [NN 639151] of a tributary of the Keltie Water.

East of the diorite outcrop there are scattered exposures of biotite-porphyrite, mostly on or near the summit ridge of Meall Odhar. The abundance of these exposures, the absence of Dalradian rocks among them (apart from two small remnants of the original roof), and the uniformity of rock type all suggest that they form part of a single intrusion marginal to the diorite, an interpretation that is supported by the geophysical evidence. The age-relations of the two bodies are not known. There are very few exposures of Dalradian rocks to the east and south, and consequently the outcrop of the porphyrite could not be accurately delimited in these directions by surface mapping alone. Geophysical evidence, however, showed that it does not extend far beyond the area of porphyrite exposures.

DUBH CHOIREIN SWARM OF MINOR INTRUSIONS

The minor intrusions of the Dubh Choirein swarm, which lies almost entirely within the area covered by the Stirling (39) Sheet, range in type from basalts to quartz-porphyries. About 240 separate intrusions are exposed and many more doubtless lie beneath the widespread superficial cover. Intermediate types (mostly porphyrites) comprise about a third of the total and another third are acid porphyrites and porphyries. About a quarter are basic types (basalts, basic porphyrites and a single lamprophyre), and the remainder are quartz-porphyries.

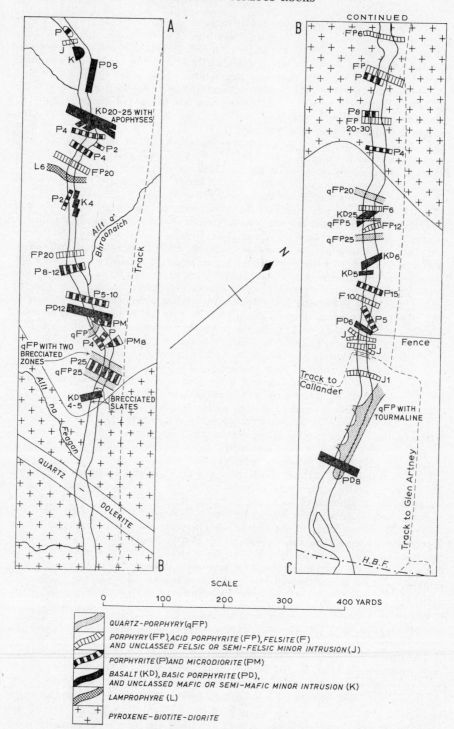

FIG. 3. *Sketch-map showing minor intrusions in the Allt an Dubh Choirein*

The average thickness of the basic and intermediate types is about 7 ft and the maximum is 25 ft; the acid porphyrites and porphyries average over 10 ft and the quartz-porphyries over 20 ft. Some of the porphyries reach 50 ft (e.g. in the Allt Breac-nic [NN 631129] and in the Keltie Water [NN 645124]. Two of the thickest quartz-porphyries also reach 50 ft in thickness, and are remarkable for the presence of tourmaline which occurs as locally abundant small blue dots. The sill on the southern slopes of Tom Odhar was analysed (Anal. IV, Table 3).

The intrusions are rather irregular dykes and steeply inclined sheets, with a few sills. One acid porphyrite dyke has been traced for half a mile and one quartz-porphyry sill for a quarter of a mile, but these are exceptional, for rarely can the others be traced for more than a few yards. This is in part due to the cover of vegetation, peat, etc., but the marked variations in thickness and frequent changes of horizon which are commonly exhibited, e.g. in the Allt an Dubh Choirein section (Fig. 3), suggest that individual members rarely persist for any great distance. Anderson (1947, fig. 8, p. 494) showed some of them extending for about 4 miles, but no evidence has been found to justify this.

The number of intrusions generally increases inwards from the margins of the swarm towards a maximum in the Allt an Dubh Choirein (Fig. 3) near the Dubh Choirein diorite, but there is a secondary maximum near the Meall Odhar diorite. The distribution of the different types appears to be largely random, but there is some tendency for acid intrusions to be more abundant on the western side, in the Keltie valley, and for basic and intermediate types to cluster round the two diorite masses.

Petrography

DIORITE STOCKS

The modal analyses (Table 1) of specimens from the Dubh Choirein diorite show that it falls within the granodiorite family or more specifically the monzotonalite family in the classification of Johannsen (1932), but since granodiorite commonly connotes a higher quartz content the term diorite is retained for this intrusion. Johannsen limited the latter term to rocks with less than 5 per cent. of this mineral, but other authors put the limit at 10 per cent., below which the modal analyses in Table 1 and also the norm (Table 2) all come. Even if there had been less than 5 per cent. of quartz in the rock, Johannsen would have classified it as a syenodiorite or a monzodiorite, on the basis of the amount of orthoclase present, but he limited the term diorite to rocks with very little potashfeldspar, and it is considered better in this account to acknowledge its monzonitic affinities by indicating the characteristic minerals thus: pyroxene-biotite-diorite.

Bailey (1958, p. 3; 1960, p. 203) drew the dividing line between basic and intermediate rocks at a silica percentage of 55, and in doing so grouped some rocks described as diorites with the basic rocks. The Dubh Choirein diorite would also be grouped as a basic rock if the silica percentage were used for classification in this way. Indeed Bailey (1960, p. 213) in describing some biotite-augite-diorites from Argyllshire, which are clearly very similar to the Dubh Choirein intrusion, indicated that they 'had better perhaps be referred to as monzonitic gabbros'. However, he retained (1958, p. 1) the name augite-diorite provisionally and the writer considers that it is better not to use the term gabbro for the Dubh Choirein mass, for the following reasons. The average composition

TABLE 1

Modal analyses of the Dubh Choirein and Meall Odhar diorites and of comparable rocks

Mineral	DUBH CHOIREIN DIORITE					MEALL ODHAR DIORITE		GLEN FALLOCH DIORITE (Anderson 1937b, p. 463)	GARABAL HILL DIORITE (Nockolds 1941, p. 464)
	normal diorite	fine-grained porphyritic diorite			orthoclase-rich diorite				
	S 48167	S 45822	S 45826 (II in Table 3)	S 45521	S 45522	S 45218	S 45220		
Quartz	5·4	6·1	8·0	8·2	7·3	12·8	7·9	—	2·6
Orthoclase	10·5	7·8	9·0	9·7	15·1	11·1	13·3	9·3	3·5
Micropegmatite	—	—	—	—	—	—	4·8	—	—
Plagioclase	47·0	46·5	45·1	45·6	41·9	50·6	49·5	47·7	47·6
Pyroxene	21·7	24·5	24·4	15·8	29·8	16·4	17·7	34·1	27·2
Olivine	1·6	2·9	2·8	1·8	—	—	—	1·1	1·1
Primary hornblende	—	—	—	—	—	2·0	1·1	—	—
Biotite	12·4	7·6	8·0	15·9	3·4	4·8	3·6	7·8	15·9
Iron ore	1·3	4·5	2·6	3·0	2·5	2·4	2·2	—	2·1

TABLE 2

Norms of analysed rocks, with comparative norm

	DUBH CHOIREIN DIORITE (II in Table 3)	PYROXENE-MICA-DIORITE, GARABAL HILL (Nockolds 1941, table vii facing p. 510)	BASALT MINOR INTRUSION (XII in Table 3)
Quartz	6·24	–	4·93
Orthoclase	14·56	11·68	5·67
Albite	26·50	29·87	29·27
Anorthite	21·72	20·29	27·73
Diopside	10·05	15·60	6·15
Hypersthene	15·92	14·64	19·53
Olivine	–	2·50	–
Magnetite	2·71	1·39	4·04
Ilmenite	1·76	2·43	2·10
Apatite	0·55	0·34	0·58

of the plagioclase, which is the major constituent (*see* Tables 1 and 2), lies within the andesine range; olivine is scarce or absent whereas quartz is present in significant amount; and the colour index is less than 40.

The chemical analysis (Anal. II, Table 3), the norm calculated therefrom (Table 2) and microscopic examination including modal analyses (Table 1) all tend to confirm Anderson's (1947, p. 495) allocation of the Dubh Choirein diorite to the kentallenite suite. It is clearly one of the 'little basic bosses' which as Bailey (1958, p. 1) indicated are abundant in the South-West Highlands. He described them as 'augitic with biotite' and stated that they 'often carry olivine and sometimes rhombic pyroxene'.

The chemical analysis compares closely with one (Anal. C, Table 3) quoted by Anderson (1935, p. 279) from one of these bosses near Arrochar, which from his description is a pyroxene-mica-diorite of very similar mineralogical composition. It is also very similar to the analyses given by MacGregor (*in* Richey and others 1930, p. 42) for a basic hypersthene-diorite near Darvel, Ayrshire and that given by Nockolds (1941, table vii facing p. 510) for a pyroxene-mica-diorite (Anal. D, Table 3) in the Garabal Hill–Glen Fyne complex. Nockolds also prepared a modal analysis of this rock (reproduced in Table 1), which shows that the Dubh Choirein diorite is richer in quartz and orthoclase and slightly poorer in biotite and pyroxene. The chemical analysis of a diorite in the Etive complex provided by Anderson (1937a, table 3, p. 518) is also very similar, but his description shows that mineralogically the resemblance is less close in that hornblende is more abundant than augite in the Etive rock. The Dubh Choirein diorite is richer in potash than any of these four analysed rocks and therefore has stronger monzonitic affinities. The Tillicoultry diorite (Anal. III, Table 3) on the other hand is even richer in the alkalis, especially soda, and also in water, and as would be expected carries much secondary amphibole (p. 56).

Anderson (1937b, pp. 462–3) also described from the Glen Falloch area rocks similar to the Dubh Choirein diorite. He quoted one modal analysis (Table 1) which is very similar to that of the latter except that it has appreciably more pyroxene. The Comrie diorite, which lies about 7 miles north-east of the Dubh Choirein diorite, was described by Allan (1940, pp. 189–90) as a quartz-mica-diorite with acid plagioclase and generally decomposed green hornblende. Examination of slices (S 31728[1], 31730) from this intrusion in the Geological Survey collection suggests, however, that the altered material may have been mostly pyroxene, possibly with a little olivine. If this is correct the two intrusions were originally very similar. The Carn Chois diorite, some 4 miles further north, was referred to by Tilley (1924, p. 25) as a hornblende-biotite-diorite locally containing much pyroxene. Nockolds (1941, table iv, p. 497) quoted a previously unpublished analysis, recalculated on a water-free basis, of pyroxene-mica-diorite from this intrusion. It is very similar to the analysis of the Dubh Choirein diorite.

The Meall Odhar diorite (*see* Table 1) is coarser-grained and more felsic than the Dubh Choirein diorite, and the amount of quartz present makes quartz-diorite an appropriate term for it, though on Johannsen's classification (see above) it also is a granodiorite. There appears to have been more primary hornblende present than was found in the latter intrusion, but augite and biotite were probably the principal primary mafic minerals. If so, this intrusion also belongs to the kentallenite suite, of which it is probably one of the most acid members. Numerous intrusions, whose chemical compositions must be similar to that of the Meall Odhar diorite, have been reported in the South-West Highlands, but most of them have much more primary hornblende and belong to the appinite suite. The occurrence of micropegmatite of quartz and orthoclase, locally to the extent of almost 5 per cent., is a feature of note in this body.

DETAILS

Dubh Choirein diorite. The normal diorite (S 44648, 45212, 45233, 45240, 45785, 45823–4, 48167) is generally non-porphyritic and has as its most abundant constituent (*see* Table 1) plagioclase in tabular crystals usually between 0·75 and 1·00 mm in length. They are generally zoned from an acid labradorite core outwards to andesine and are almost entirely fresh, even in slices where the pyroxene is altered, with one exception (S 45785) in which partial alteration to carbonate has taken place. The only pyroxene identified is augite, which is the most abundant ferromagnesian mineral. It forms subhedral or euhedral crystals up to 1·00 mm in size, which in one slice (S 45212) have a tendency to occur in clusters. In some slices (S 44648, 45233, 48167) the augite is mostly fresh, but in general it is largely (S 45824) or completely (S 45785, 45823) altered to secondary minerals including turbid carbonate, iron ore, fibrous amphibole, chlorite, saponite and other viriditic material. Many of the fresh crystals contain much fine dust which in some cases is arranged in zones parallel to the crystal surfaces.

Biotite is the only other abundant primary dark mineral. It occurs mostly in small ragged crystals, pleochroic from chestnut-brown to pale straw-yellow, which were not affected at all by the processes which altered the augite. A few anhedral poikilitic crystals were noted in one slice (S 45212). Pseudomorphs after olivine are rare or absent: they reach 1·5 mm in size (S 48167) and form the only phenocrysts in the normal diorite except in rare instances (S 45233) where augite crystals are large enough to be

---

[1] Numbers preceded by S refer to rock slices in the Geological Survey Scottish collection.

included in this category. A little primary hornblende occurs locally. Orthoclase and quartz are mostly interstitial. Apatite, magnetite and ilmenite are the most abundant accessory minerals.

The fine-grained, porphyritic variety of the Dubh Choirein diorite (S 45223, 45521, 45786, 45821–2, 45825–7) includes the analysed specimen (Anal. II, Table 3). As the modal analyses (Table 1) show there is no great difference between it and the normal diorite in mineralogical composition. It appears to include a sub-variety (S 45521) rich in biotite and deficient in pyroxene. The groundmass in the fine-grained porphyritic variety includes abundant laths of fresh plagioclase (acid labradorite zoned to andesine) with many grains of augite and, in some slices (S 45223, 45822, 45826), of hypersthene. Both pyroxenes are locally altered to chlorite, carbonate, iron ore, etc. Flakes of biotite also occur, with subordinate quartz and orthoclase and accessory ilmenite, magnetite and apatite.

The phenocrysts, which generally are not plentiful, consist, in order of abundance, of pyroxene, olivine and (S 45223, 45821) plagioclase. The pyroxene phenocrysts are mostly augite, but hypersthene also occurs (S 45223, 45822). The crystals are generally euhedral and about 1·0 mm in length with a maximum of 2·0 mm (S 45521). There is a general tendency for the pyroxene phenocrysts to occur in clusters, e.g. one composed of hypersthene crystals (S 45822) is 3 mm long and is rimmed by augite, magnetite and biotite. The pyroxene crystals are generally fresh, but partial or complete alteration has occurred locally to chlorite, amphibole, carbonate, iron ore, etc. Some of them carry zones with much dust similar to those noted above in the normal diorite.

The olivine phenocrysts are rare and generally do not exceed 1·0 mm in length. Most of them are completely replaced by serpentine and iron ore, but in some slices (S 45822, 45826–7) the alteration is only partial. Reaction rims of pyroxene occur round some of them. In two slices (S 45786, 45826) there are discrete fine-grained aggregates about 1·0 mm in size, composed of iron ore, biotite, chlorite and pyroxene, which are believed to represent xenoliths of pelite.

The abundance of orthoclase, which is the most notable feature of the third variety (S 45213, 45234, 45522) of the Dubh Choirein diorite, is shown in Table 1; the mineral occurs mostly in large poikilitic plates which locally enclose biotite and plagioclase and are particularly abundant in one slice (S 45522). Pseudomorphs in chlorite, saponite, amphibole, carbonate and iron ore are presumed to be after originally abundant pyroxene: by contrast biotite is rather scarce and is unaltered. Olivine is doubtfully represented in one slice (S 45234) by a few pseudomorphs. Plagioclase (andesine-labradorite) is abundant and generally fresh, and quartz is widespread. The principal accessory minerals are apatite, magnetite and ilmenite.

Meall Odhar diorite. Plagioclase (*see* Table 1) is the most abundant constituent of all three slices (S 45218, 45220, 45520) from the Meall Odhar diorite. It has been altered to some extent but was determined in one slice (S 45520) as labradorite zoned outwards to andesine. A maximum length of 2 mm was noted (S 45220). The orthoclase, which also has been altered, occurs mainly interstitially and in places (S 45220) has formed micropegmatite with the quartz, whose abundance amply justifies the term quartz-diorite being applied to this intrusion.

Augite, biotite and hornblende all occur as primary ferromagnesian minerals, but no trace of olivine was found. The biotite is generally fresh, but locally has suffered some marginal chloritization. The augite is locally euhedral and partly (S 45218, 45220) or completely (S 45520) replaced; the alteration products include carbonate, iron ore, chlorite, hornblende and fibrous amphibole. These secondary minerals have been included with the pyroxene in the mode in Table 1, although in a few cases they may have come from primary biotite or hornblende. Apatite is the most abundant accessory mineral.

Thermal metamorphism of diorite. The occurrence of secondary amphibole associated with chlorite, serpentine, etc. in pseudomorphs after pyroxene has been noted in all three varieties of the Dubh Choirein diorite and in the Meall Odhar diorite. The material, which is fibrous and locally pleochroic from green to colourless, is probably referable to the tremolite-actinolite group. In a number of specimens (S 45213, 45218, 45220, 45223, 45521, 45822, 48167) the amphibole appears to have replaced the chlorite, serpentine, etc. in a manner similar to that described by MacGregor (*in* Richey and others 1930, p. 41) in both diorite and minor intrusions from the Distinkhorn complex, Ayrshire, and ascribed by him to thermal metamorphism. The peculiar cloudiness of the feldspars, especially the plagioclase, which he described (p. 36) as a parallel effect of thermal metamorphism, usually at a more advanced stage, was noted in only one specimen (S 45223). Epidote also was noted in only one specimen (S 45220): MacGregor (p. 35) found that this mineral replaced pyroxene 'probably through the medium of a pseudomorph' at the first stage of metamorphism in the minor intrusions. If the phenomena described above are indeed the results of thermal metamorphism, then it seems likely that below the diorites there exists a large intrusion, probably granitic in composition.

DUBH CHOIREIN SWARM OF MINOR INTRUSIONS

Most of the swarms of minor intrusions in the South-West Highlands, e.g. the Ben Nevis and Etive swarms (Bailey 1960), are composed largely of intermediate types; acid types are subordinate and the basic members are lamprophyres. The Dubh Choirein swarm on the other hand has only one recorded lamprophyre, the rest of the basic intrusions being basalts or basic porphyrites. One of the basalts has been analysed (Anal. XII, Table 3) and found to be very similar to a basalt dyke in the Ochil Hills (Anal. XIII, Table 3). Few other comparable analyses have been traced, but two of basic andesite lavas of Lower Old Red Sandstone age, one from the Sidlaw Hills (Anal. S, Table 3) and one from Glen Coe (Bailey 1960, table 2, analysis 5, p. 206) are fairly similar. According to Bailey's definition based on silica percentage (*see* p. 15) analysis XII represents a basic rock: on the other hand the norm (Table 2) shows it to be slightly oversaturated, and intermediate as regards both the composition of the plagioclase (basic andesine) and the colour index, which is less than 40.

A few of the basalts carry olivine pseudomorphs and hypersthene has been noted as well as augite. Fresh primary hornblende is rare throughout the swarm, but secondary fibrous amphiboles are common. Biotite is generally present in all but the most acid members and is the major ferromagnesian mineral in the solitary lamprophyre and some of the porphyrites: in general it has been more resistant to alteration than the other dark minerals, whose proneness to change contrasts with the general freshness of the plagioclase, especially in the basic members of the swarm. Two of the quartz-porphyries are rendered notable by the occurrence of tourmaline (p. 22).

DETAILS

Lamprophyre. Only one intrusion (S 44569) sufficiently mafic to be classed as a lamprophyre has been found in the Dubh Choirein swarm. It is a porphyritic rock with abundant small phenocrysts of rather pale biotite, many of them darker brown at the margins. This is the only unaltered primary mineral in the slice, except for iron ore granules in the groundmass. There are some much larger phenocrysts, up to 2 mm long, which may originally have been olivine, but are now completely altered to carbonate, serpentine, etc. There are also a few pseudomorphs in carbonate, possibly after plagioclase. The groundmass is composed of biotite flakes, iron ore granules, quartz and carbonated feldspar.

Basalts. The most striking feature of the basalts, including the analysed rock (S 45787; Anal. XII, Table 3), is the abundance of euhedral plagioclase crystals (mostly of basic labradorite) which are generally fresh, whereas the ferromagnesian minerals are almost always partly, and in many cases completely, altered to chlorite, serpentine, tremolite-actinolite, iron ore, carbonate, etc. Many of the plagioclase crystals are markedly zoned, locally in oscillatory fashion, from a basic labradorite core to an acid labradorite or andesine margin. Some fresh augite has survived in a few slices (S 44571, 45225, 45232, 45237, 45787-8) and some hypersthene in one (S 44644). The augite locally shows zones of dust similar to those noted in slices from the Dubh Choirein diorite (p. 18). The presence of pseudomorphs probably after olivine was noted in several slices (S 44571, 44646, 45237, 45787): in the analysed rock they locally exceed 1·0 mm in length. Iron ore is ubiquitous as an accessory mineral, and hornblende, biotite, apatite, quartz and alkali-feldspar have also been noted.

The fibrous tremolite-actinolite which occurs in some of the pyroxene pseudomorphs appears in some cases at least (S 45214, 45227, 45232, 45236) to be replacing chlorite, serpentine, etc. rather than the pyroxene directly. This process has been tentatively ascribed (pp. 19–20) to thermal metamorphism, and supporting evidence is provided by the occurrence in one slice (S 45236) of epidote in some of the pseudomorphs. All the basalt and basic porphyrite (see below) intrusions affected are in hornfelsed sediments (mostly on Tom Odhar) close to the Dubh Choirein diorite, which is presumed to have caused the changes.

Most of the basalts are conspicuously porphyritic, both in regard to the number of phenocrysts and the difference in grain size between phenocrysts and groundmass; the feldspar phenocrysts are, however, much smaller than those in the basalts from the Ochil Hills described on p. 60. Plagioclase forms most of the phenocrysts, with a maximum size usually between 1·0 and 1·5 mm. Pyroxene phenocrysts are generally fewer in number but their maximum size in most slices exceeds that of the feldspars. The overall maximum, however, is about the same at 1·5 mm. The olivine pseudomorphs where present tend to be smaller but reach 1·0 mm (S 44646). In a few slices (S 45232, 45235) the grain size is variable and there is no clear separation into phenocrysts and groundmass: in others (S 45457, 45460) phenocrysts are few in number but are clearly distinguished in size from the groundmass.

Basic porphyrites. Closely allied to the basalts are the basic porphyrites, which have somewhat more sodic plagioclase, rather more primary hornblende, biotite and quartz, and little or no olivine. Plagioclase forms abundant phenocrysts which are generally fresh and euhedral. They are usually zoned outwards from an acid labradorite core, with a composition about $Ab_{45}An_{55}$, to an andesine rim; they vary a good deal in size from slice to slice but reach a maximum of 2 mm in length (S 45237). In several slices (e.g. S 45239) the augite is partly fresh, but in others it is wholly altered to chlorite, serpentine, carbonate, iron ore, etc. It also forms phenocrysts which attain 2 mm in length (S 44586). In one slice (S 45224) some at least of the pseudomorphs in serpentine rimmed with iron ore are probably after olivine. Both primary and secondary (see below) amphiboles have been noted; among the former is a brown hornblende which occurs in a few slices (S 44586, 45239). Biotite is a common accessory and is quite abundant in one slice (S 44586). Quartz, iron ore and alkali-feldspar also occur.

The texture is generally porphyritic but the abundance and size distinction of the phenocrysts is rather variable. Parallelism of the plagioclase laths in the groundmass is well marked in one slice (S 44643).

Several slices (S 45224, 45228, 45237-8) show replacement of chlorite and serpentine by secondary amphibole, probably mainly tremolite-actinolite, and by biotite (S 45228). This replacement is similar to that noted above in a few of the basalts and is likewise tentatively attributed to thermal metamorphism. The occurrence of epidote in some of the pseudomorphs (S 45224) supports this.

Porphyrites. The use of the term 'porphyrite' is discussed on p. 59: the slices here described represent a varied group of rocks which, while showing differences in detail, are all porphyritic in texture and intermediate in composition. They are all altered to some extent, some of them considerably. Plagioclase phenocrysts are almost invariably present, and are especially conspicuous in some intrusions. Included with the porphyrites is the marginal intrusion (S 45216–7) on the eastern side of the Meall Odhar diorite, which is a biotite-porphyrite with plagioclase phenocrysts reaching about 3 mm in length and biotite plates 1·5 mm across. The groundmass is brown and turbid. Biotite normally remains fresh both in the diorites and the minor intrusions in this suite, even where other ferromagnesian minerals have been altered, but in one slice (S 45193) it is largely chloritized. Most of the other slices probably represent rather basic porphyrites but the degree of alteration is too great for this to be determined. Almost invariably the augite is completely altered to either carbonate or chlorite, serpentine and other viriditic material; hornblende likewise is altered except in two specimens (S 45458–9) where it is only partly affected. The groundmass consists of a mesh of feldspar laths with some biotite, quartz, alkali-feldspar, various secondary minerals, and accessory apatite, zircon and sphene.

Microdiorites and plagiophyres. Very few of the intermediate members of the Dubh Choirein swarm are sufficiently even-grained to be classed as microdiorites. The two which have been sliced (S 44585, 44641) are both rather highly altered. They consist of networks of feldspar laths with pseudomorphs in carbonate, chlorite and serpentine after pyroxene or amphibole. Fresh biotite flakes are present in both slices and are abundant in one (S 44585). Iron ore and quartz grains also occur. Plagiophyres are also of rare occurrence: the only sliced representative (S 44578) is somewhat similar to the microdiorites, but is more felsic and more highly altered.

Acid porphyrites. In hand specimen the groundmass of the acid porphyrites is usually pink or cream in colour: under the microscope it is seen to consist of a very fine granular aggregate of quartz and feldspar with some muscovite and secondary minerals. The phenocrysts include kaolinized and sericitized feldspars, up to 3 mm long (S 44567), chloritized biotite and possibly amphibole, and quartz crystals which are corroded and surrounded by reaction rims, and may be xenocrysts.

Porphyries. The feldspar phenocrysts, which reach 3 mm in length, are mostly of plagioclase, which is generally cloudy but in one case (S 44572) could be determined as andesine. Small quartz grains are also present locally (S 44584, 44588); in one slice (S 44588) they are surrounded by reaction rims and may be xenocrysts. Small muscovite flakes also occur in this slice. Pseudomorphs in iron ore, carbonate and a colourless mineral possibly of the montmorillonite group which occur in two slices (S 44572, 44584) are probably after biotite and hornblende. Some biotite has survived locally (S 44584). Increase in amount of these pseudomorphs would make these rocks very similar to the acid porphyrites. The groundmass consists of iron ore, feldspar laths, quartz and small flakes of muscovite with accessory apatite and zircon.

Quartz-porphyries. The quartz-porphyries are distinguished by the presence of abundant phenocrysts of quartz, which locally exceed 1·0 mm in diameter. Feldspar crystals, invariably altered, are ubiquitous and some exceed 1·0 mm in length. Small flakes of muscovite are the only other phenocrysts. The same three minerals in a granular aggregate constitute the bulk of the groundmass. The analysis (Anal. IV, Table 3) shows that one of the sills is a highly acid rock, so much so as to suggest that secondary enrichment in silica has occurred: no comparable analysis of an unaltered igneous rock has been found.

Two of the quartz-porphyry sills (S 45222, 45230, 45789) are rendered conspicuous by the presence of tourmaline, which occurs in spongy subhedral crystals, clusters of small grains and rosettes. The crystals are pleochroic from dull prussian blue to pale yellow or almost colourless and have been identified as the schorlite member of the tourmaline group. In one specimen (S 45222) the mineral is quite absent from one part of the slice, while in the other part it is both disseminated throughout and concentrated along veinlets; this suggests that the tourmaline, as in so many cases, is a secondary or late-stage mineral.

Records of tourmaline associated with intrusions of Old Red Sandstone age are few. MacGregor (*in* Eyles and others 1949, p. 44) recorded tourmalinization, locally intense, in the Fore Burn complex, in south Ayrshire, which is largely composed of quartz-diorite with some albite-porphyry. Thomas and Anderson (*in* Carruthers and others 1932, pp. 94–5) found that tourmaline has a wide distribution as an accessory mineral in the Cheviot granite, and that patches of blue or green tourmaline are particularly associated with quartzose areas in the marginal fine-grained granite. They attributed the tourmalinization to late-stage pneumatolytic activity which affected certain dykes (including two of quartz-porphyry) and crush-lines which cut the granite. Gardiner and Reynolds (1932, p. 20) recorded tourmaline in one of the aplite minor intrusions in the Loch Doon area.   I.H.F.

REFERENCES

ALLAN, D. A. 1940. The geology of the Highland Border from Glen Almond to Glen Artney. *Trans. R. Soc. Edinb.*, **60**, 171–93.

ANDERSON, J. G. C. 1935. The Arrochar intrusive complex. *Geol. Mag.*, **72**, 263–83.

—— 1937a. The Etive granite complex. *Q. Jl geol. Soc. Lond.*, **93**, 487–533.

—— 1937b. Intrusions of the Glen Falloch area. *Geol. Mag.*, **74**, 458–68.

—— 1947. The geology of the Highland Border: Stonehaven to Arran. *Trans. R. Soc. Edinb.*, **61**, 479–515.

BAILEY, E. B. 1958. Some chemical aspects of South-West Highland Devonian igneous rocks. *Bull. geol. Surv. Gt Br.*, No. 15, 1–20.

—— 1960. The geology of Ben Nevis and Glen Coe. 2nd edit. *Mem. geol. Surv. Gt Br.*

CARRUTHERS, R. G., BURNETT, G. A. and ANDERSON, W. 1932. The geology of the Cheviot Hills. *Mem. geol. Surv. Gt Br.*

EYLES, V. A., SIMPSON, J. B. and MACGREGOR, A. G. 1949. The geology of central Ayrshire. *Mem. geol. Surv. Gt Br.*

GARDINER, C. I. and REYNOLDS, S. H. 1932. The Loch Doon 'granite' area, Galloway. *Q. Jl geol. Soc. Lond.*, **88**, 1–34.

JOHANNSEN, A. 1932. *A descriptive petrography of the igneous rocks.* Vol. 2. Chicago.

NOCKOLDS, S. R. 1941. The Garabal Hill–Glen Fyne igneous complex. *Q. Jl geol. Soc. Lond.*, **96**, 451–511.

RICHEY, J. E., ANDERSON, E. M. and MACGREGOR, A. G. 1930. The geology of North Ayrshire. *Mem. geol. Surv. Gt Br.*

TILLEY, C. E. 1924. Contact metamorphism in the Comrie area of the Perthshire Highlands. *Q. Jl geol. Soc. Lond.*, **80**, 22–71.

C

Chapter IV

LOWER OLD RED SANDSTONE
LOWER DIVISION

INTRODUCTION

WITHIN THE AREA of the Stirling Sheet the lower part of the Lower Old Red Sandstone consists mainly of volcanic rocks with subordinate sedimentary intercalations. These rocks form narrow, elongate outcrops in the vicinity of the Highland Boundary Fault north and north-east of Callander, but their main outcrop is in the Ochil Hills, in the north-eastern part of the district. Here they occupy an area of about 220 square miles which extends northwards from the Ochil Fault to the northern slopes of the hills between Bridge of Allan and Auchterarder. The southern face of the Ochils is a steep fault-line scarp (Plate I, frontispiece) and the lavas rise abruptly from the low ground south of the fault; gradients are as high as 1 in 1·5 between 50 and 1500 ft O.D., thereafter inclining less steeply to summits 2000 ft or more above sea-level. Ben Clach at 2363 ft O.D. is the highest point in the district.

The Ochil Hills outcrop consists mainly of lavas intercalated with beds of tuff and agglomerate, which form part of the north-western flank of a broad north-easterly anticlinal arch, the axis of which extends from Muckart, at the eastern margin of the district, towards Bridge of Earn. Except for a few local variations the dip averages about 15° towards the north-west, swinging round to west or even west-south-west in the Glendevon area.

It can be seen from Fig. 4 that the volcanic pile reaches its maximum to the north of Tillicoultry where a stratigraphic thickness of 8000 ft is apparent. This estimate may be increased to at least 10 000 ft if it is assumed that the older beds forming the core of the anticline further east persist beneath Tillicoultry.

The lavas and clastic rocks are cut by intrusions of several types. These include the large stock-like masses of diorite and related rocks at Tillicoultry and Glendevon; a group of intrusions consisting mainly of dykes, which is genetically associated with the diorites; and a less prominent group comprising sills, dykes and chonoliths which appears to be related to the lavas. It is assumed that all are approximately contemporaneous with the volcanism since they do not cut the overlying Lower Old Red Sandstone sediments of the Strathmore Syncline to the west and north. Later Permo-Carboniferous dykes of quartz-dolerite, however, cut sediments and volcanic rocks alike: they are described in Chapter XV.

E.H.F.

In the north-western part of the district up to about 1000 ft of nearly vertical lavas with some sediments lie between components of the Highland Boundary Fault. The outcrop in the Keltie Water area consists mainly of lavas with thin intercalations of sediments. In upper Glen Artney both sandstones and lavas are present.

I.H.F.

24

Lavas and Intercalated Rocks

Lavas. The lavas of the Ochil Hills consist mainly of varieties of basalt, pyroxene-andesite and hornblende-andesite with subordinate flows of trachy-andesite and rhyodacite. With a few exceptions it is not possible to distinguish between basalts and andesites in the field, but the more acid rocks are easier to recognize. This has important applications in mapping since although there is intermittent lava-scarp featuring on Berry, Craigentaggart, Tambeth, Tarmangie and Wether hills, most slopes are smooth and grass-covered, and north of the Ochil scarp exposures are mainly intermittent and restricted to the partly drift-filled stream courses.

The distribution of the various lavas is so much at random both laterally and vertically (Fig. 4) that no simple pattern of magmatic trend is apparent. It is notable, however, that no specimen of hornblende-andesite has been found among any of the lavas sectioned from the upper part of the pile, that is above the horizon of the rocks forming Bank Hill, near Dollar.

Individual lava flows, as well as pyroclastic bands, are demonstrably imper-sistent and there can be little doubt that here, as in the Sidlaws (Harry 1956, p. 45) the volcanic pile 'is composed of lenticular interdigitating sheets'. If the lavas had been produced by large central-type volcanoes like those of the modern andesite fields of Central America the dip in the Ochils would be variable, rather than virtually constant, in direction and amount. This, and other evidence advanced in the next section, suggests strongly that though there may have been small centres of explosive activity, most of the lavas were extruded as sheets, possibly fed from fissures.   E.H.F.

The lavas of the north-western outcrop are best exposed in the Keltie Water (*see* Fig. 7). They are mainly basalts with a few basic andesites. Most of the flows, which number at least eleven, are porphyritic; some have plagioclase phenocrysts up to 5 mm in length. They are significantly affected by the fault movements only in the immediate vicinity of the Highland Boundary and Eas Dearg faults (p. 241). In upper Glen Artney the lavas are probably either basalts or andesites but they are too highly brecciated and altered by percolating fluids to permit classification.   I.H.F.

Tuffs and agglomerates. Most of the clastic rocks intercalated with the lavas of the Ochil Hills range in grade from coarse tuff to agglomerate. As remarked by Geikie (1900, p. 17) many of them owe their accumulation not only 'to volcanic explosion, but partly also to the denudation of previous eruptions'. Thus, while it is possible to recognize on the one hand a few beds which appear to be wholly pyroclastic in origin and on the other volcanic sandstones and conglomerates (p. 70) which are apparently wholly sedimentary, most of the 'tuffs' and 'agglo-merates' of the Ochils lie somewhere between the two (*see also* Read 1927, p. 89).

Most of the fragmentary material in the tuffs and agglomerates is crystalline and magmatic, representing accidental ejecta derived from lower levels in the volcanic pile. Much of it is basic or intermediate like the lavas in composition, but there are also some fragments which have a felsitic appearance. They may indicate that, as in Kincardineshire (Campbell 1913), northern Forfarshire (Allan 1928) and near Perth (Davidson 1932), the earliest extrusions were acid. Alternatively they may have 'been derived from the explosion of a felsitic magma which may not always have reached the surface in streams of lava'

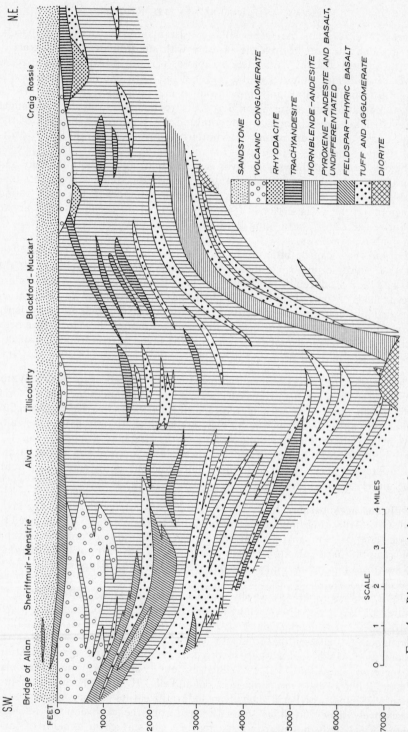

Fig. 4.   Diagrammatic horizontal section showing lateral variation in the volcanic sequence in the Ochil Hills

(Geikie 1900, p. 17). Yet another possibility is that this pale material represents originally more basic rock which has been altered by juvenile or secondary processes.

The pyroclastic beds are thickest, coarsest and most numerous in the south alongside the Ochil Fault. In the absence of any recognizable neck this fact led Peach (unpublished MS.) to conclude that 'the centre or centres of distribution . . . . . . lie buried beneath the Carboniferous Rocks to the south'. It is tempting to expand this idea and postulate a row of vents marking a line of weakness that was later to become the Ochil Fault. This theory, however, does not fully explain the present distribution of volcanic rocks; in the upper reaches of the River Devon and in the valley of the Coul Burn, for instance, there are agglomerates which seem too localized and too coarse to have been derived from the Ochil Fault zone four miles or more to the south. It seems likely, therefore, that there were centres of eruption in other parts of the Ochils, and the discovery, during the recent resurvey, of one small neck (p. 36) and various neck-marginal features as well as intrusions which may have been feeders (p. 39) supports this view. Compared to the volume of lavas and intercalated pyroclastic rocks these are on a small scale and do not give rise to any distinctive topographic featuring. This may account for the well-known sparseness of records of eruptive foci both in the Ochils and in other Lower Old Red Sandstone volcanic fields in Scotland.

Intra-volcanic sediments. In the Ochil Hills, as in virtually every other centre of Lower Old Red Sandstone volcanism, many of the lavas contain fissures filled with purple, green or yellow sandstone and siltstone. A few lavas contain inclusions of sediment which appear to have been still in a plastic state when caught up by flow (p. 36). In the upper part of the succession a few lavas are interbedded with beds of sandstone and volcanic conglomerate, the latter consisting mainly of rounded blocks of previously-erupted rocks with pockets of finer sediment. These beds become thicker towards the western end of the hills where they take the place of up to 1000 ft of lava. Lower in the succession there are rare occurrences of tuff and agglomerate which contain small lenses of sandstone and siltstone.   E.H.F.

In the north-western outcrop sandstone occurs between two components of the Highland Boundary Fault in upper Glen Artney, and there are thin intercalations of sandstone, mudstone and volcanic conglomerate between the lava flows in the Keltie Water area.   I.H.F.

Conditions of deposition. As elsewhere in the Midland Valley, the Lower Old Red Sandstone sediments of the Strathmore Syncline probably accumulated under semi-arid conditions, mostly on flood plains but in part perhaps in temporary lakes (*see* pp. 69–70). Since pillow-structure is unknown in the lavas, volcanism appears to have been essentially subaerial in character, though lava may occasionally have flowed into temporary shallow pools. Local sedimentary intercalations in the lavas indicate that fine sediment was washed by rain or flood into such pools and into cracks or cavities in lava tops. The volcanic conglomerates represent torrential deposits derived from local lavas and pyroclasts.

Some amplification of this concept is prompted by consideration of the Ochil rocks. The local reddening of lavas, particularly trachyandesites (p. 34), certainly suggests some degree of subaerial oxidation, but the almost total absence of bole or of widespread reddening, on the other hand, indicates that conditions suitable for such oxidation seldom persisted for more than brief periods. This was probably due to relatively rapid covering of the tops of flows by new extrusive layers, implying rapid accumulation of the volcanic pile as a whole. While much of the detritus in the sedimentary intercalations is derived locally from the volcanic rocks, some, including the quartz in the sandstones, is not. This suggests that from time to time the area was receiving sediment from a more distant, presumably Highland, source and thus the volcanic pile must have been sub-siding at a rate which barely kept pace with its growth by eruption.

This balance between eruption and subsidence was further affected by rapid local erosion and transport of the volcanic rocks. It may be supposed, therefore, that when volcanism was most active during the early and middle period, these local processes contributed to the formation of some of the 'agglomerates' and 'tuffs'. When eruptive activity slackened in later stages, regional sedimentary processes gained ascendancy so that sandstone intercalations became more frequent and a greater rounding of the locally derived material in the volcanic conglomerates became possible.

DIORITE STOCKS

A group of diorite stocks occurs within an area of contact-altered lavas and tuffs to the north of Tillicoultry; another, smaller group is found to the north of Glendevon and an isolated boss [NN 974111] 120 yd across occurs 1100 yd south of Upper Coul. At Tillicoultry there are four masses in line, 35 to 150 yd apart, and each cut off to the south by the Ochil Fault. The smallest and western-most is about 200 yd in diameter and is patchily exposed on the steep slopes north-west of the town. The next diorite to the east, in the lower part of Mill Glen, Tillicoultry, is about the same size and has a westward dyke-like extension about 400 yd long by 30 yd wide. The Wester Kirk Craig mass, a short distance further east, is about half a mile in diameter and the fourth body, at Elistoun Hill, is three-quarters of a mile across; the last is deeply dissected by Harviestoun Glen.

The diorites in the area north of Glendevon comprise a stock and four small bosses. The stock, crossing Borland Glen and Black Creich Hill, measures 1100 by 250 yd, elongated from west to east. One of the bosses, 200 yd farther south, measures 100 by 70 yd; another, in Lamb Burn, is only about 50 yd in diameter, and two bosses on the south side of Corb Glen are each less than 20 yd across.

The diorites range in grade and colour from fine-grained and grey to coarse-grained and pink mottled with green or blue-grey. Transitions from fine to coarse may take place within only a few feet and while there is a tendency for the fine grey rocks to be marginal varieties, their distribution is, in many places, unrelated to the margins. The impression of heterogeneity is heightened by the abundance of country-rock xenoliths, particularly near the edges of each mass and in the case of the Elistoun Hill diorite by the inclusion of several strips of vaguely defined hornfelsed country-rock cropping out at intervals along the floor of Harviestoun Glen.

By contrast there are a few localities at which the diorite margins are sharp and are either vertical or highly inclined outwards, suggesting that some of the apparently discrete masses converge at depth. In places it is difficult to recognize the junction between diorite with partly digested xenoliths on the one side and hornfels with pods of diorite on the other, but the hybridized zone is usually narrow enough to form a topographical feature by means of which the diorite margin can be mapped. The jointing and weathering of the diorites, particularly of the coarser varieties, give these rocks a massive, rounded granitic aspect which contrasts with the more angular outlines of the lava crags. It is therefore notable that lava scarps on White Creich Hill continue into the small boss of diorite, and that at Elistoun Hill and Harviestoun Glen the diorites display a 'ghost' scarp-featuring dipping to north-west at about 10° in conformity with the regional lavas and tuffs. Moreover, in the last-mentioned locality the diorite shows differences in composition from one layer to another (p. 38).

This evidence, taken in conjunction with the gradational contacts, hybridization and petrographic characters (p. 56), supports Peach's contention (unpublished MS.) that some of the diorites represent lavas and tuffs metasomatized in situ, while others, such as the dyke crossing the Mill Glen, are intrusive.

In general this is reflected in the petrography since those diorites which from field relations and texture seem most likely to have been formed by metamorphism of country rocks also tend to be richer in pyroxene and olivine than obviously intrusive rocks like the Mill Glen dyke. Rocks of the latter type, moreover, are relatively rich in quartz and potash-feldspar—the principal minerals of the aplite veins in diorites and aureole—suggesting that the source magma tends more towards granodiorite in composition than most of the dioritic rocks now exposed.

METAMORPHIC AUREOLES

Each of the groups of diorite stocks is surrounded by a metamorphic aureole. That of the Tillicoultry group is about a quarter of a mile wide to the west and north, but to the east it forms a belt half a mile wide which extends approximately alongside the Ochil Fault for $3\frac{1}{2}$ miles. This easterly extension corresponds approximately to the presence of a thick quartz-dolerite intrusion along the plane of the Ochil Fault and it is possible that the metamorphism at this locality may be caused by the dolerite. This, however, is thought to be unlikely in view of the relatively minor degree of contact alteration caused by similar intrusions in Carboniferous sediments of the Midland Valley. The presence of diorite underlying the area at no great depth seems more probable.

The aureole surrounding the group of Glendevon diorites has similar features. It is a quarter to half a mile wide around the White Creich Hill–Borland Glen stocks, but extends north-eastwards in a belt a mile wide and $2\frac{1}{2}$ miles long. In this belt there is no possibility of a late quartz-dolerite metamorphism and the presence of underlying diorite is indicated by the small bosses exposed in Lamb Burn and Corb Glen.

Within the aureoles the degree of alteration depends not only on the distance from the nearest diorite mass, but also on the permeability of the extrusive country-rock. In general the tuffs and autobrecciated lavas are more permeable and they alter to pale pink, grey or even greenish, partly amorphous rocks which weather with a yellow, soft outer shell. The discrete component fragments lose their angular outlines at an early stage of alteration, and with the development of pink feldspar porphyroblasts a vaguely heterogeneous appearance is all that remains of the original texture. Certain of the lavas, especially those originally containing amygdales, show ill-defined pink recrystallized patches. Others take on a hackly fracture as a first stage in alteration through hornfels to fine-grained grey diorite. In places transition can be seen from such lavas to diorites without any sharp break between stages.

All the metamorphic and dioritic rocks are traversed by veins of pink, commonly granular, aplitic material which fade into the host rock without sharp junctions and which seem to be intimately related to the metamorphism. In the case of some of the less permeable lavas this material has entered by way of high-angled joint planes which are locally so abundant as to divide the rocks into slices only a few inches wide. Even where there has been no intrusion of pink material along these fracture planes, the lavas adjacent to them show a noticeably higher degree of alteration than elsewhere. Moreover, in the more highly hornfelsed rocks the outlines of the fracturing become blurred as though the metamorphism had been superimposed upon it.

At any particular locality the joints have a single dominant alignment, but this varies from place to place, often in conformity with the trend of local porphyrite dykes. The pattern of fracturing is essentially radial to the diorites, suggesting that it is related in some way to the mechanical emplacement of these bodies. It may be envisaged that intrusion at depth caused the radial fracturing without significant up-doming of the roof of the magma chamber and that the diorite made its way up from below partly by simple intrusion and assimilation and partly by replacement ('dioritization') of country rock.

MINOR INTRUSIONS

The minor intrusions of Lower Old Red Sandstone age in the Ochils consist mainly of dykes with only a few sills and chonoliths and even fewer bosses. Petrographically they comprise basalts, andesites, porphyrites, plagiophyres and quartz-albite-porphyries ranging in colour from pale or dark grey to green, purple or salmon-pink. Most contain phenocrysts orientated parallel to the walls of the intrusion; elongated greenish amygdales are in some cases similarly flow-aligned. Some paler dykes contain melanocratic xenoliths of basalt and andesite derived from the wall rocks.

The dykes range in thickness from 18 in to 80 ft and weather out to form gullies, some of which extend for long distances and control courses of streams. The basalts and the andesites are sufficiently like the lavas to be taken for feeders. Most dykes, however, are highly albitized porphyrites, acid porphyrites and plagiophyres; these increase in number and thickness as they converge upon the diorite stocks.

Of the dykes cutting the diorites only one is marginally chilled and thus significantly younger. The others, as well as some which stop at the diorite margins, make ragged, unchilled and even gradational contacts suggesting contemporaneity; dykes of this kind, moreover, are microscopically similar to the aplitic veins which permeate both diorites and aureole rocks (p. 58). These lines of evidence suggest that the emplacement of the diorites was attended by a release of aplite-porphyrite material which became chilled only where it intruded ground outside the aureoles. The dykes must have been emplaced either in several phases or over an extended period, for some follow fractures which cut and displace earlier dykes of the same suite.

It is worth noting here that although there is a distinctly radial element in the disposition of the dykes around the diorites (Fig. 5) there is a marked tendency for preferred orientation along north-north-west and north-north-east lines—a preference noted also in the Cheviot dyke swarms (Anderson *in* Carruthers and others 1932, p. 97). Since these lines coincide with the main fault trends throughout the Ochils it thus seems that this fracture pattern throughout

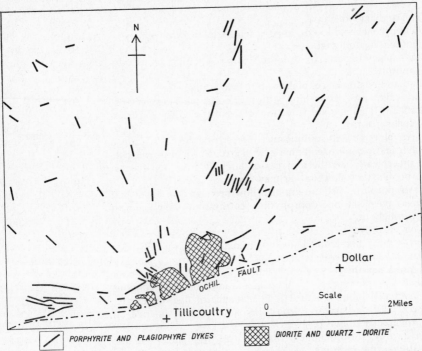

FIG. 5. *Sketch-map showing radial disposition of porphyrite and plagiophyre dykes relative to diorite stocks in the Ochil Hills*

the lava country was initiated either before or during diorite emplacement. This may explain why such faults can seldom be traced northward and westward into the overlying sediments.

DETAILS: OCHIL HILLS

SEQUENCE

The following section, measured from the summit down the eastern slopes of Dumyat and down Menstrie Glen, exemplifies the sequence within the volcanic pile:

	Thickness ft	Total thickness ft
Feldspar-phyric olivine-basalt (north of summit)	?100	100
Basalt, fluidal	35	135
Basalt, purple, earthy, autobrecciated	30	165
Basalt, fluidal	35	200
Tuff and agglomerate	40	240
Lava, blue-grey, microporphyritic, with green amygdales ..	40	280

	Thickness ft	Total thickness ft
Tuff and agglomerate	40	320
Lava, blue-grey, fine-grained, locally flow-banded, with scattered phenocrysts of plagioclase	60	◦380
Tuff and agglomerate	50	430
Acid pyroxene-andesites, impersistent, grey-brown, flaggy ..	70	500
Tuff and agglomerate	50	550
Lava, blue-grey, microporphyritic, with red 'iddingsite' pseudomorphs	25	575
Tuff and agglomerate, bombs up to 3 ft in diameter	350	925
Lava, blue-grey, crystalline, with plagioclase phenocrysts ..	60	985
Tuff and agglomerate (junction of Menstrie Glen and First Inchna Burn) .. .. up to	300	1285
Lava, blue-grey, crystalline, microporphyritic, hematite-stained	20	1305
Lava, feldspar-pyroxene-phyric, with green amygdales; massive, spheroidally weathering; passes laterally into flow-breccia (possibly two flows rather than one)	?40	1345
Lava, purplish, medium-grained, flow-brecciated in lower half	20	1365
Lava, purplish, microporphyritic, earthy and slaggy almost throughout	10	1375
Lava, as above	10	1385
Lava, grey, fine-grained, fresh, crystalline, microporphyritic, with hematitic streaks and mottling; seems to pass laterally into an earthy rock like the underlying flow .. .. about	20	1405
Lava, purple-blue, flow-brecciated and earthy; contains hardened lumps up to 3 ft in diameter of fine, chocolate-coloured micaceous sandstone and green siltstone–all apparently caught up by flow	23	1428
Lava, grey, fresh, splintery, microporphyritic, with hematitic streaks and mottling	20	1448
Lava, purplish, medium-grained, aphyric, with a 3-ft red slaggy band at top	18	1466
Lava, purplish, medium-grained, aphyric, vesicular throughout	12	1478
Lava, purplish, medium-grained, with hematitic streaks; 2-ft vesicular band at top and 6-ft slaggy base	28	1506
Obscured	6	1512
Acid pyroxene-andesite, brown, fine-grained base with plagioclase phenocrysts; massive, block-jointed, with poorly defined ropy layers 30 ft and 50 ft from base	80	1592
Agglomerate, rudely bedded with an irregular base; unsorted, with bombs up to 3½ ft (average 1 ft) which are sub-rounded or, more commonly, angular, in a matrix of green coarse tuff	60	1652
Trachyandesite, flow-banded, grey with red spots (analysed rock of Lipney; see p. 33 and Table 3, Anal. ix) .. .. up to	100	1752
Agglomerate containing massive blocks 2–3 ft across; irregular top and base	150	1902
Lava, fine-grained, microporphyritic, with a thin slaggy layer at top	19	1921
Siltstone, green, bedded in topmost 6 in only; extends down into fissures in underlying lava	3	1924
Lava, purplish, fine-grained, microporphyritic, with vesicles containing carbonate, chlorite and pink agate; a 4-ft slaggy band at centre and a thin slaggy band at top; base not seen	20+	1944

LAVAS

Basalt and andesite. Most varieties of basalt and andesite contain phenocrysts or microphenocrysts of plagioclase and of one or more ferromagnesian mineral, but there are also a few aphanitic rocks, some of which, like a lava near the summit of Dumyat (p. 31), are fluidal. It is seldom possible to distinguish andesites from basalts in the field for many rocks are transitional between the two. Moreover within each type colours range from pale to dark greys or purples with red hematitic streaking or mottling. Some of the mottling simulates red 'iddingsite' which is the most common pseudomorph after olivine in the Ochil suite, but even if 'iddingsite' is recognized it is not diagnostic since it is present in some of the basic andesites and missing in some of the basalts.

This difficulty in distinguishing between basalt and andesite in the field is exemplified by lavas at the western end of the hills. Near Bridge of Allan they consist mainly of distinctive feldspar-phyric rocks determined by extensive sectioning as basalts. They can be traced north-eastwards without any apparent break, but further sampling in the Old Wharry Burn shows all except the topmost flow there to be andesite. Other flows of feldspar-phyric basalt occur sporadically throughout the area. A less common type of basalt containing large phenocrysts of fresh augite crops out along the lower slopes of Castleton and Seamab hills, north-east of Dollar.

Some andesitic rock-types are sufficiently distinctive to be recognized in the field. An example is a leucocratic pyroxene-poor andesite having a fine-grained pale-brown or brownish-purple base. One such rock forms a lenticular outcrop on the western flanks of Dumyat, a second occurs above the prominent Lipney trachyandesite (p. 32) and a third can be traced for $3\frac{1}{2}$ miles from the Second Inchna Burn eastward, forming characteristic carious-weathering, massively block-jointed crags at Bengengie Hill, Calf Craigs and The Law. Another distinctive type of andesite is a black glassy rock which contains fresh phenocrysts of labradorite, hypersthene and augite. Rocks of this kind are exposed in a stream on the north side of Common Hill [NN 944053], midway up the northern slopes of Peat Hill [NN 975042] and in the River Devon at Black Linn [NN 994042]. The field relationships at these localities are uncertain, but the rocks are assumed to be lavas, like similar types in the Cheviot Hills (Carruthers and others 1932, pp. 12–4), though a petrographically identical rock (Flett 1897) from above Blairlogie (pp. 60–1) is sill-like.

In the thick band of hornblende-andesites between Bank Hill, Dollar, and Glendevon, feldspar-phyric varieties are dominant at the former locality, but more easily recognized hornblende-phyric rocks appear farther north, particularly on the eastern slopes of Whitewisp Hill, in Glen Quey [NN 965013], on the south bank of the River Devon, 300 yd south of Glendevon Castle [NN 975052] and north of Cleugh Hill, up the west bank of the Westplace Burn [NN 972062].

At many localities some degree of flow-brecciation is apparent in the lavas; the rocks so affected can be mistaken for agglomerate, particularly where exposure is poor. Moreover, where breccia occurs between central crystalline portions of successive flows it is not always possible to determine whether it forms the top of one flow or the base of the other. During excavations at the Upper Glendevon Reservoir one lava was seen to pass laterally from fresh crystalline rock to a flow-breccia which probably marks the outer edge of the flow. It is more difficult to find an explanation for the thick sequence of wholly brecciated flows cropping out farther downstream in the Cleugh Burn and on the hill slopes south of the River Devon at Glendevon. These flows are mainly hornblende-andesites and may, perhaps, have been more viscous than the more basic andesites and basalts. A striking example in this area is exposed on a hill 500 yd north-north-east of Glendevon Castle [NN 977058] where large blocks of crystalline lava set in a similar matrix weather out like agglomerate. Other notable flow-brecciated lavas occur west and south-west of Bankfold, along the Coul Burn south-east of Coulshill, and on the western slopes of Glen Eagles above St. Mungo's.

Vesicles, drawn out in the direction of flow, are most commonly filled with green earthy material and carbonate, occurring either separately or together. Pink and white agates are particularly abundant along the Frandy Burn and are to be found in smaller quantities in the Balquharn, Menstrie, Alva and Tillicoultry burns; in the lavas along the fault-line scarp between Airthrey and Alva; on the north-west slopes of Ben Shee; on the north slope of The Shank; on the southern face of Common Hill, along Glen Sherup and on the hillside south of Upper Coul. Larger agates were obtained from a steam cavity filled with soft yellow steatitic material, which was exposed by quarrying in the east bank of the Broich Burn [NN 912038] during construction of the Upper Glendevon Reservoir. There are no localities as well known for collection of agates, however, as Path of Condie and Rossie Ochil, about 4 miles beyond the eastern limit of the district.

Local reddening or purpling at the tops of some lavas indicates some degree of subaerial oxidation but true boles are rare. One layer, 2 in thick, forms a capping to a lava in the Finglen Burn [NN 883024].

Trachyandesite. In the field, the trachyandesites can usually be distinguished from the more basic lavas by their colour. Earthy varieties of trachyandesite, which are rare, are very pale blue-grey rocks with scattered vesicles, but even the freshest rocks are paler than the basalts and andesites. They are distinctively fine-grained and have a prominent flow-banding which gives rise to platy jointing with a scaly feldspar shimmer on the joint surfaces parallel to the banding and hackly fracture at right-angles to it. In some places the flow-banding gives the rock a marked fissility and this is not always parallel to the tops and bottoms of individual lavas. On Green Maller [NN 959102] and on the west side of Eastbow Hill, for instance, flow-banding with very variable inclination is markedly discordant to the general dip of the lava beds; and on the north side of Common Hill [NN 938060] the fissility is arcuate, suggesting some rolling during flow. A few lavas near the top of the succession carry feldspar phenocrysts.

The lava which forms the outliers capping Crodwell (Grodwell) Hill [NN 915020] and Middle Hill [NN 928022] shows fluxion structure parallel to top and base, dipping to north-west at both localities in conformity with the regional dip. In an intervening outlier on the northern spur of Skythorn Hill, however, the dip is steep towards the south-west, but this is likely to be a tectonic feature rather than the result of flow down a penecontemporaneous slope since agglomerates, a short distance upstream, display a similar aberrant south-westerly dip.

A remarkable trachyandesite forms an oval outcrop capping Ben Shee. The centre of the oval is grassed over, but peripherally the flow-banding dips inwards at a consistent 60° to 70°. This is a difficult structure to interpret. Analogy with Carboniferous neck structures at Dunbar (Francis 1962) would suggest that the inward dip is a vent-marginal feature, rimming either a cryptovolcanic structure (i.e. an incipient neck which did not surface) or a post-volcanic subsidence. In either case the trachyandesite should be regarded not as a plug but as a flow which predated the formation of the neck structure. Geikie (1897, p. 308) described both the Ben Shee mass and the trachyandesite of Black Maller, near Auchterarder, as bosses penetrating the volcanic pile, but offered no evidence for this view. His locality, Black Maller, may be an error for the adjacent Green Maller, where the trachyandesite exhibits an incomplete ring of inward-dipping flow-banding less perfect than that on Ben Shee, but possibly of similar origin.

A certain amount of hematitic streaking and spotting is apparent in all the trachyandesites, but in the upper part of the lava succession there is patchy reddening which is most intense where the flow-banding lies at high angles and therefore provides readier access to oxidizing agents presumed to come from above (pp. 27–8). At exposures of this kind the weathered surfaces take on a pale porcellanous aspect and the rocks are so fissile as to superficially resemble red shales. Good examples can be seen on Core Hill and Berry Hill and best of all on Bald Hill [NN 934038] where, within a single flow, transition can be seen from a fresh grey to a highly altered state.   E.H.F.

Rhyodacite. The rhyodacites are restricted to the area south and east of Auchterarder where they occupy stratigraphical positions high in the volcanic pile. The lava forming Craig Rossie and extending as an outlier to Ben Effry is the most important of the rhyodacites, though not the youngest lava in the Ochils as thought by Geikie (1900, p. 25) for it is overlain by the trachyandesite of Thorny Hill. Typically it consists of pale phenocrysts of feldspar set in a fine-grained brown or pink matrix, but in places the whole rock has a bleached appearance due to alteration. Flow-banding is a notable feature and is conspicuously displayed on the hillside south-east of Pairney and in the neighbourhood of Castle Craig [NN 976127] and Kay Craig [NN 974128]. The banding is usually very even, simulating stratification, but here and there it is folded and even overturned.

Even where there is no folding the flow-banding is seldom parallel to the base of the rhyodacite. This is illustrated in the north-western part of the Craig Rossie outcrop, where the rhyodacite base, with grey amygdaloidal basalt beneath, can be traced from the Pairney Burn [NN 974127] up the north-east side of a gully eroded along a south-easterly fault; if this junction were parallel to the flow-banding in the area, the underlying basalt should reappear along the strike in a deeply-cut glacial channel a short distance to the north-east. Since it does not it is deduced that the rhyodacite base must descend north-eastwards from the visible outcrops in a manner discordant to the flow-banding. Presumably the rhyodacite occupies a depression in the pre-existing lavas and is of lenticular form, thinning out both eastwards and westwards.

An exposure [NN 976124] north-east of Upper Coul shows rhyodacite very nearly in contact with the underlying amygdaloidal lava. The rhyodacite here contains small patches of fine sediment (p. 55).

A decomposed brown porphyritic rock with numerous amygdales containing calcite and red chalcedony is exposed beside the Pairney Burn [NN 973131] west of Pairney. This exposure probably lies near the upper surface of the Craig Rossie rhyodacite.

South of Craig Rossie, rhyodacites at two stratigraphically lower levels crop out on the west and south-west slopes of Beld Hill. Further west, on the north-west slopes of Eastbow Hill above Glen Eagles, the acid lavas again occur near the top of the volcanic sequence.

M.A.

BEDDED TUFF AND AGGLOMERATE

The pyroclastic rocks of the Ochils fall within three of the categories defined by Wentworth and Williams (1932), namely coarse tuffs, lapilli-tuffs and agglomerates; fine tuffs are virtually unknown. The coarse tuffs and lapilli-tuffs, mottled blue, pink and purple, are found mainly in the central part of the area where also there are a few beds of agglomerate, containing blocks up to 3 or 4 ft wide, exposed in the Coul Burn north-east of Bankfold, in Fin Glen, along the Frandy Burn, in Glen Quey and north of the road 600 yd east-south-east of Glendevon Castle [NN 971053].

The agglomerates are thickest, and coarsest, in the south, along the Ochil scarp, and reach a maximum on the steep slopes above Blairlogie, where there is an uninterrupted thickness of more than 1000 ft of agglomerate which has been intensely mineralized (Fig. 31). To the north-east a few thin, impersistent lavas appear within the mass on the south slopes of Dumyat, and nearer Menstrie there is a group of thicker lavas interdigitated with the agglomerates. Some of the included blocks in the agglomerates are 'as large as a Highland crofter's cottage' (Geikie 1897, p. 310) though diameters of between 2 and 4 ft are more common. There is little sign of sorting in this mass or in any of the other thick beds of agglomerate along the scarp and the originating necks cannot therefore be far away (p. 27). Some agglomerates, however, show rude bedding and on the north-western slopes of Elistoun Hill, on the eastern flank of Seamab Hill and on Fire Hill, east of Muckart, this gives rise to scarp featuring.

AGGLOMERATE IN NECKS

South of Craigentaggart Hill, at a locality [NN 908046] now under the waters of the Upper Glendevon Reservoir, agglomerate containing bombs up to 3½ ft across extends for about 100 ft along the north bank of the old course of the River Devon. Apart from another small outcrop of agglomerate 120 yd to the north-west, exposures to west and north are obscured by drift. To the east, however, the margin of the agglomerate mass is seen to be inclined inwards at 70° to 80°. It has a curved trace following the river bed so that there is no outcrop of agglomerate on the south bank. Outside the margin a slaggy-topped lava is turned down towards the agglomerate at an angle of about 45°, being inclined westward and northward on the north and south banks respectively. This marginal structure is reminiscent of the down-folding frequently remarked in the strata around necks in the Scottish Carboniferous. The agglomerate is therefore interpreted as filling a vent; it is shown on the map as having an oval outcrop, 200 by 150 yards, elongated to the south-east.

About 1000 yd south-east of the vent, on the east bank of the Broich Burn [NN 913037], there is agglomerate containing ragged-edged bombs, up to 2 ft across, of greenish, decomposed juvenile basalt or andesite set in a fine-grained blue-grey matrix. It is lithologically unique among the Ochil rocks, but resembles many Carboniferous neck-fillings. If there is a neck located here or nearby, however, field relations are too obscure for the structure to be mapped.

The only other locality at which there may be a neck is at the summit of Ben Shee where a ring-like outcrop of trachyandesite displays inward dips (p. 34). No agglomerate is exposed at this locality.

INTRA-VOLCANIC SEDIMENTS

Veins and xenoliths. Sedimentary fillings of fissures in lavas are almost ubiquitous, but three localities may be singled out as better exposed and more readily accessible than others. One is on the south face of White Hill [NS 808976], on the west side of the road from Bridge of Allan to Sheriffmuir, another is at the foot of Menstrie Glen [NS 849972] and a third lies at the spillway of the Lower Glendevon Dam, a few yards north of Frandy farmhouse [NN 940044]. A group of sedimentary dykes cutting a lava in the Wharry Burn [NN 828016] is unusual in containing so much carbonate in veins and cement as to approach sandy limestone in composition.

During construction of the Upper Glendevon Dam [NN 914045] the cut-off trench traversed an andesite that is interpreted as a lava which flowed into a bed of soft sediment. The andesite is slaggy and brecciated, intermingled with, and chilled against, marginally-baked discrete fragments of green siltstone and sandstone in which bedding, where preserved, is disorientated with respect to the flow of the lava and to the bedding in other fragments. A 4-ft mass of sandstone in a lava cropping out in Cleugh Burn, 550 yd south-south-west of Kaim Knowe [NN 956049], also probably represents sediment caught up by lava flow.

Sandstone and siltstone. Grey micaceous sandstone, containing scattered pebbles of lava up to half an inch across, crops out alongside the Bridge of Allan to Sheriffmuir road: it is up to 30 ft thick in an old quarry [NS 808974] 750 yd west-north-west of Parkhead. About 400 yd farther south flaggy grey and purple sandstone forms lenses between the top of a pyroxene-andesite and the base of an overlying agglomerate. At a bend [NS 806970] in the Sheriffmuir road one lens up to 4 ft thick wedges out eastward; another in Hermitage Wood [NS 811971], farther east, is 10 to 20 ft thick and is shifted by a north-north-westerly fault.

In the Danny Burn 10 ft of finely laminated yellow and chocolate-coloured sandstone with mottled layers containing volcanic detritus crops out on the west bank, 1200 yd upstream from Whaick [NN 882058]. Its base is not seen, but it is overlain successively by 13 ft of volcanic conglomerate and by porphyritic lava. One and a half miles up-stream another lava rests on 3 ft or more of fine red sandstone.

In the River Devon, west of the mouth of the Glenmacduff Burn [NN 887039], about 6 ft of fine, hard, flaggy, brown sandstone are overlain by green and white mottled tuffaceous sandstone which passes up into coarse tuff and agglomerate. At the head of the Greenhorn Burn [NN 898024] 2 ft of fine, flaggy, patchily red and green sandstone separate flows of trachyandesite, and a band of chocolate-brown sandstone of indeterminate thickness crops out among andesites and basalts high up on the south-west bank of the Broich Burn, 1500 yd upstream from the River Devon.

Nearly a mile up Alva Glen [NS 881989] a lava with a vesicular top is separated from an overlying agglomerate by a 2-ft band of tuff containing lenses of red, green and purple siltstone.

DIORITE STOCKS

Castle Craig. The westernmost diorite is intermittently exposed on the steep slopes north-west of Tillicoultry; it has an ill-defined edge and is assumed to be about 200 yards square. The rock is fine- to medium-grained with scattered melanocratic xeno-liths showing various stages of transition from hornfelsed lava to diorite.

Mill Glen. The Mill Glen diorite is a coarse and handsomely mottled pink and bluish-green rock throughout and has been quarried on a small scale on the east bank of the glen close above the Ochil Fault quartz-dolerite intrusion. Alongside the stream, a few yards to the north, it comes against hornfelsed tuffs, the contact being marked by a vertical band, 1 to 2 ft wide, of pink aplitic rock. This passes into the diorite without a sharp margin and both rocks locally contain melanocratic xenoliths of partly-digested country-rock. Similar inclusions are seen inside the vertical or steeply outward-dipping margin of the diorite as it is followed upstream along the east bank, and are particularly well-exposed in and around an old trial adit [NS 912978].

The central and eastern parts of the diorite form massive crags higher up the hill. In the northern part, which is crossed by the steep track leading from Tillicoultry to Blackford, two lobes of diorite are linked by a dyke of pink aplite or acid porphyrite. This cuts the hornfelsed tuff between the lobes, but appears to merge into the diorites without chilled contacts.

A dyke-like apophysis of diorite extends westwards from the mass for about 400 yd and crosses the Mill Glen about 50 yd up from the Ochil Fault. A good section is seen alongside the path on the west bank where the dyke is about 100 ft wide. The southern margin dips south at about 70°, parallel with jointing within the country rock from which the diorite is separated by a pink aplitic zone 6 to 9 in wide. This rock is soft and partly crushed as though affected by later fault movements but merges without chilling into medium-grained diorite which in turn becomes coarse towards the centre of the dyke. As it is followed up the hill the dyke becomes finer-grained and grey and is terminated against fractured hornfels.

An exposure of diorite on the south bank of the Gannel Burn about 160 yd upstream from the Daiglen confluence may be part of another dyke emanating from the northern edge of the stock. It cannot be traced back to the latter, however, nor is it seen to cross to the north bank of the Gannel Burn. Faulting may be responsible for this, but it may be, on the other hand, that the exposure is merely a local dioritized pod like some of the local hybrids (p. 39).

Wester Kirk Craig. The western and north-western margin of the Wester Kirk Craig diorite forms a marked topographic feature inside which hybrid rocks are abundant. In the north and west the diorites inside the hybridized margin are mainly compact, fine- to medium-grained rocks whereas elsewhere they are coarser and mottled pink and blue-grey. At some localities the coarser rocks are deeply weathered to a soft brownish sand and one band of this softer rock on the southern slopes of the hill is sandwiched between two layers of hard blue-grey rock. Impersistent veins of pink granular rock, 2 to 3 in wide, are ubiquitous in both diorite and hybrid marginal rocks, but are particularly prominent where they cut the diorite to the north-east and south. Near the centre of the stock, 120 yd east of the trigonometrical point, there is a dyke of aplitic material or porphyrite, up to 25 ft thick, which shows no sign of marginal chilling: instead it forms an intricate, ill-defined junction with the diorite, suggesting approximate contemporaneity of the two rocks. A porphyrite dyke cutting the north-western edge of the mass, by contrast, is certainly younger since it is chilled against the diorite (pp. 40–1, Fig. 6).

Elistoun Hill. In the Elistoun Hill mass fine- to medium-grained diorite occurs near the western margin and also, more centrally, to the east of Harviestoun Glen, where it forms a prominent crag surrounded by coarser types. As in the Wester Kirk Craig stock the rest of the mass consists of coarse diorite with deeply weathered patches. Near the western margin and, more especially, in the north [NS 925992] there are good examples of rapid transition from hornfels to coarse diorite, with or without inter-mediate finer-grained stages: the angular outlines of jointed blocks show a corres-ponding softening.

The stock is deeply incised by Harviestoun Glen along which there are several poorly-defined 'windows' of hornfelsed lava and a good deal of hybridization, parti-cularly at the indented northern and southern margins. These features lie well below the topographic level of extensive outcrops of unhybridized coarse diorite and this suggests some degree of layering within the mass. This finds support in the corres-pondence between joint planes in the diorite and the regional dip (10° to 15° to north-west) of bedding planes in the surrounding lavas, especially as midway along Harvies-toun Glen there appears to be a macroscopic variation in the diorite from one 'layer' to another.

The indentation of the northern edge of the stock by Harviestoun Glen is crossed by two dykes. One is an aplite or acid porphyrite which, like the dyke in the Mill Glen mass, seems penecontemporaneous with the diorite since it links the lobes on either side without any marginal chilling. The other, farther upstream, is a north-westerly apophysis of coarse diorite. A notable broad dyke of acid porphyrite, like the one described above, extends eastward for about half a mile along the southern slopes of King's Seat Hill.

Borland Glen and Creich Hills. The largest of the diorite masses near Glendevon is best exposed north of the summit of White Creich Hill, where it is a coarse grey rock with pink felsic veinlets. Similar diorite with associated hybrid varieties is inter-mittently exposed on the west side and the floor of Borland Glen and again on the south side of a path in the forestry plantation on Black Creich Hill [NN 997063].

On the south slopes of White Creich Hill [NN 994058] coarse diorite forms a boss measuring 100 by 70 yards, elongated north to south, within hornfelsed lavas. Promi-nent scarp featuring in the lavas continues into the diorite.   E.H.F.

Lamb Burn. The diorite in the Lamb Burn [NO 007073] is a grey rock with pink patches; the small outcrops of dioritic rock [NO 00320833 and 00370840] on the south side of Corb Glen and the isolated boss [NN 974111] south of Upper Coul (Summ. Prog. 1962, p. 47) are more uniform in appearance.   M.A.

METAMORPHIC AUREOLES

Tillicoultry Burn. In and around Mill Glen, as far upstream as the Daiglen–Gannel confluence, there is intensive hornfelsing of lavas and tuffs. The hornfelsed rocks have a characteristic hackly fracture and are generally grey, becoming white on weathering. Recrystallization of the tuffs gives rise to a fine-grained patchy rock similar in appear-ance to some of the lavas—particularly those containing pink felsitic patches, some of which may represent reconstituted amygdales. Irregular veins of pink aplitic material up to 2 ft thick permeate all rock types. There is intensive local fracturing and jointing with north-north-west trend on the hill slopes west and north of Mill Glen, and with northerly trend to the east.

In the Gannel Burn about 100 yd up from the Daiglen confluence, on the opposite bank from a possibly dyke-like apophysis of diorite (p. 37), there is a zone, 50 yd wide, of hybrid rock. This shows, patchily, all stages of transition between lava and coarse diorite, without any evidence of intrusion of the one by the other. Even the coarsest varieties of diorite, for example, occur in apparently quite disconnected pockets or blebs. The zone of hybridization does not continue at higher topographic levels of the gorge. Similar hybridization occurs patchily between the Mill Glen and Wester Kirk Craig stocks where, at one locality, transition from hornfelsed tuff to diorite is seen to occur within a distance of only 3 ft.

Kirk Burn. In the upper part of the Kirk Burn and along Kirk Craigs there is a thick flow, or series of flows, of fresh, compact pyroxene-andesite. It is traversed by belts of high-angled north-north-east fractures, alternating with zones of massive, relatively unbroken lava. The rock is much less metamorphosed where it is massive than where broken: along the lines of fracture it is particularly notable that there is alteration to a pink or purplish rock. Farther down the burn, where metamorphosed tuff appears to be faulted against diorite, both rocks are extensively 'soaked' in pink aplitic material forming irregular dykes and sills.

Dollar Burn. Although nearly 2 miles from the nearest diorite on Elistoun Hill the rocks in the Dollar Burn are highly altered, especially towards the Ochil Fault. Along this lower part of the glen and gorge they consist mainly of rotten earthy, pale pink, grey and green, yellow-weathering rocks of patchy appearance. They contain pink feldspar porphyroblasts and thus bear a superficial resemblance to some of the altered lavas, but northwards up the glen an original tuff texture becomes gradually more obvious as the outlines of angular clastic fragments become less blurred. There are similar pink porphyroblasts in the altered hornblende-andesite lava higher upstream around Castle Campbell, where there is repetition by faulting. To the east, on Gloom Hill, agglomerates are similarly intensely altered and partly recrystallized.

Borland Glen and Creich Hills. Around the Glendevon stocks and bosses the metamorphic rock types are similar to those of the Tillicoultry area. Fresh hackly lavas crop out around the diorites on White Creich Hill and impersistently in the forested area on Black Creich. But in Borland Glen, on Fanny Hill and in the Fanny Burn, bands of tuff or lava breccia have been altered to rotten, yellow-weathering rocks veined by pink or purple xenolithic aplitic material.   E.H.F.

Lamb Burn. In the Lamb Burn the volcanic rocks, including fragmental types which are probably lava breccias, are extensively hornfelsed and recrystallized and a small boss of the associated diorite is exposed in the stream. Farther north lavas cropping out at a higher topographic level on the ridge east of Sim's Hill are less altered. Exposures in the burn to the east of John's Hill and at the east end of Corb Glen are in altered lavas, commonly rotten and yellow-weathering.   M.A.

MINOR INTRUSIONS

Dykes. A few of the Ochil dykes are petrographically so similar to the lavas as to be regarded either as feeders or as 'blind' dykes contemporaneous with extrusion of the lavas. They include a 6-ft olivine-basalt in Fin Glen [NN 882027], a trachyandesite in the Middle Hill Burn [NN 934029] and a vertical dyke of earthy purplish andesite narrowing downward and eastward as it crosses Menstrie Glen [NS 848974]. On the map, the trachyandesite has been grouped with the plagiophyres and the andesite with the porphyrites. Another probable feeder is the most spectacular of all the Ochil dykes —a hornblende-andesite similar in type to the lavas in the Glendevon area. It is up to 80 ft wide and extends for a mile and a half in an east-north-easterly direction across Hillkitty, Cleugh Hill, Westplace Burn and Long Craig.

D

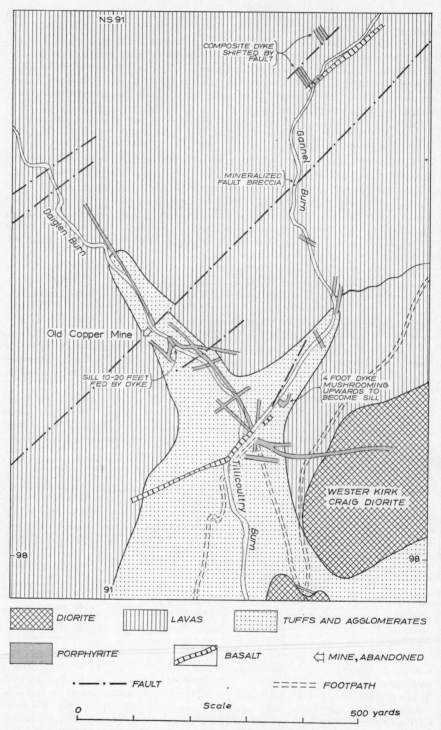

FIG. 6. *Sketch-map showing dykes and faults in relation to diorite stocks north of Tillicoultry*

Most of the dykes, however, are porphyrite and plagiophyre members of the swarms associated with the diorites and these are most numerous in the tributaries to the Tillicoultry Burn (Fig. 6) and the Burn of Sorrow. These dykes usually weather out to form gullies, some of which can be followed for long distances, as on the slopes above Blairlogie and Alva. Some gullies in the Glendevon area, like one on Gled's Nose [NN 967040], look like dyke features, but contain no exposures. Differential weathering along dykes frequently results in stream control, as can be seen in the Daiglen and Gannel burns (Fig. 6) and in the Burn of Sorrow tributaries.

Examples of dykes cut and displaced by faults are seen in West Cameron Burn [NN 862006], Alva Glen [NS 885976], Daiglen Burn [NS 911984] and Gannel Burn [NS 913988]. Dykes which, on the other hand, follow fault lines are exposed at the confluence of the Daiglen and Gannel burns [NS 912982] and in Glen Sherup [NN 946022].

Only one dyke is demonstrably later than the diorites. It crops out high above the east bank of the Tillicoultry Burn [NS 914982: Fig. 6] and consists of 7 to 8 ft of pink porphyrite marginally chilled against medium-grained grey diorite. Dykes apparently contemporaneous with the diorites include one joining the two lobes of the Mill Glen stock (p. 37), a 25-ft red porphyrite on Wester Kirk Craig [NS 919983] and two porphyrites in Harviestoun Glen: all have irregular, ill-defined margins and pass into the enclosing diorites without chilling. There may be a similar relationship between the diorites and the many acid porphyrite and porphyrite members of the dyke swarm which stop at the margins of the stocks, for nowhere have any of the diorites been observed to cut or be chilled against these dyke rocks.

One of the basic dykes, however, appears to be older than the nearest diorites. It crops out [NS 906978] in a burn half a mile west of Mill Glen and lies parallel to, and 100 yd south of, the dyke at the confluence of the Daiglen and Gannel burns mentioned above. The rock is epidotized and it may be supposed that this has been brought about during the emplacement of either the Castle Craig diorite stock, 300 yd to the south-east, or the diorite dyke 350 yd to the east, as some of the lavas of the aureole (p. 59) are also epidotized: similar epidotization has been recorded in contact-altered basic dykes in Ayrshire (MacGregor in Richey and others 1930, p. 35).

A north-westerly composite dyke crops out [NS 913987] on the north bank of the Gannel Burn, 600 yd upstream from the Tillicoultry Burn: it comprises, from west to east, acid porphyrite, porphyrite and plagiophyre, 5, 7 and 5 ft thick respectively. Each member has chilled edges and the dyke as a whole dips to the south-west. Farther up the bank it is shifted eastward by faulting (Fig. 6). An acid porphyrite 11 ft thick, cropping out in the Garchel Burn [NN 971017], simulates a multiple dyke: it is green and red at the centre, and becomes flow-banded, pink and albitized for a distance of 18 inches from the margins.

Sills. Sills are comparatively rare in the Ochils. The thickest is a felsitic acid porphyrite which attains a maximum thickness of more than 300 ft on the foothills north-west of Blairlogie, where it forms pink-weathering crags and screes. At the centre of the mass it is a dark pink to purplish rock containing scattered microphenocrysts of acid plagioclase in a fine-grained groundmass, but marginally it becomes pale, non-porphyritic and blotchy, showing some resemblance to the autobrecciated lavas. It is shifted by faulting to the higher slopes west of Dumyat, where it thins out rapidly to east and west and shows signs of minor transgression across the lava–tuff sequence. A second sill of similar blotchy rock occurs between two faults still farther west, midway between Dumyat and the Sheriffmuir road.

A short distance to the north of the blotchy rock is the glassy hypersthene-andesite described by Flett (1897, p. 291) as 'strikingly beautiful . . . pitch-black in colour, with a velvety lustre and frequent veins of brilliant red'. Peach found evidence that the rock bakes and hardens the shaly bed overlying it (op. cit., p. 294) and the recent resurvey has confirmed Flett's observation that the body is transgressive and that its western margin is nearly vertical. More important, it is now apparent that the black glassy

D*

rock is a marginal, chilled version of a more widespread brownish, platy porphyritic andesite which can be traced to the east and north-east, its outcrop shifted by faulting, as far as the north-west slopes of Dumyat. The groundmass of this brown rock is less glassy than that of the black andesite and the rock, as a whole, is less fresh. This accords with the correlation between freshness and compactness (permeability) which has frequently been expressed with regard to very similar pitchstone-andesites in the Cheviots (Carruthers and others 1932, p. 14).

The other sills of the area are porphyrites. One crops out as a thin sheet in Yellow-craig Wood [NS 820973]; another in the Daiglen Burn [NS 911982] is an offshoot, 10 to 20 ft thick, from a 15-ft dyke running along the bottom of the valley (Fig. 6). A short distance to the east, in the Gannel Burn [NS 913983], a dyke-like intrusion, 4 ft wide, spreads out upwards to become sill-like. In the bed of the River Devon, 170 yd downstream from its confluence with the Greenhorn Burn [NN 898044], there is a transgressive sheet of porphyrite, 8 ft thick, dipping at 45° upstream, and in the Reacleugh Burn a porphyrite sheet of uncertain thickness dips concordantly towards the north-west.

Bosses. Three small bosses of fine-grained andesitic rock occur on the south slopes of Dumyat, about half a mile west-north-west of Blairlogie. One has a circular outcrop, 50 to 60 ft in diameter; a second—the most southerly—is about 100 by 500 ft and is elongated east to west; the third, comparable in size to the second, has been cut and shifted by a large fault [NS 836972].

Chonoliths. In the Glendevon area there are several intrusions of quartz-albite-porphyry and acid porphyrite which are highly irregular in form. The largest extends for two miles between the Westrig Burn and Borland Glen and is a pink or buff, earthy-looking rock with phenocrysts of white turbid plagioclase and flecks of black resorbed hornblende and biotite. In the Westplace Burn [NN 975066] it is dyke-like and 70 to 80 ft wide, with pale-green, flinty chilled margins; it broadens both to east and west, reaching a maximum width of over 500 yd in the Westrig Burn. Rocks of similar appearance form smaller intrusions of indefinite shape on the east flank of Wether Hill [NN 934062], in the Hodyclach Burn [NN 985077] south-south-east of Coulshill, south-east of Glendevon House [NN 981043] and on the south slopes of King's Seat Hill [NS 935991], Whitewisp Hill [NN 953001] and Seamab Hill [NN 995011].

E.H.F.

DETAILS: KELTIE WATER AND GLEN ARTNEY

In the Keltie Water (Fig. 7), between the Highland Boundary Fault and the Eas Dearg Fault, there is an almost complete section in which 1000 ft or more of basic lavas with intercalated bands of sediment are exposed. At least eleven flows are represented in the succession. Locally the slaggy tops of flows or sedimentary partings which provide the main criteria for separating individual flows may be completely sheared out, bringing the more resistant parts of two flows into contact. As petrographically similar flows would be very difficult to differentiate in such circumstances it is possible that some of the thicker lavas (e.g. 3 and 7, Fig. 7) may in fact comprise more than one flow.

The lowest flow (1) occurs near the Highland Boundary Fault [NN 645123] and is consequently much sheared into lenses. Both it and the highly vesicular second flow have feldspar phenocrysts up to 5 mm long but are too highly altered to permit classification. Between them there is a band of red shaly sandstone and sandy shale, and another sedimentary band, made up of purple and grey sandstones, lies between flows 2 and 3. The latter consists of fine-grained vesicular olivine-basalt and forms both the stack of Caisteal Corrach [NN 644121] and the walls of the gorge of Cnoc na Faing. Interbanded purple shales and volcanic sandstones lie below flow 4, which is separated in turn by highly altered sediments from flow 5, a coarse-grained olivine-basalt. An impersistent band of very soft volcanic sandstone occurs at the base of flow 6, another

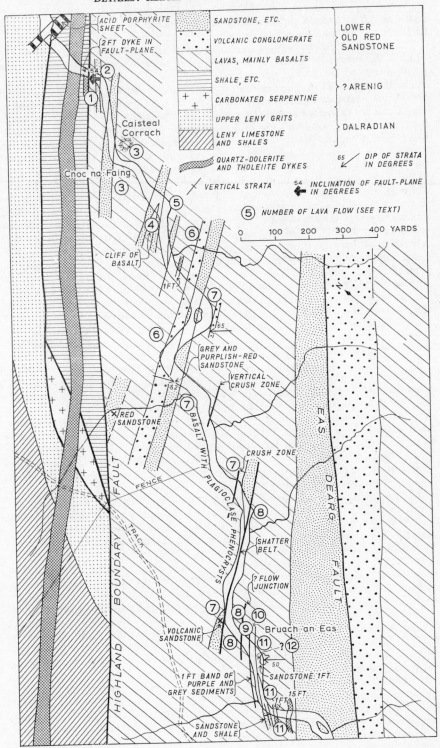

FIG. 7. *Sketch-map showing Lower Old Red Sandstone lavas exposed in the Keltie Water*

basalt, which is rendered conspicuous by the presence of large plates of plagioclase up to 5 mm in length, and which has a highly vesicular top.

The thickest of the sedimentary intercalations overlies flow 6. It is well exposed at a bend in the stream [NN 642118] and consists of volcanic conglomerate overlain by purplish-red and grey sandstones.

The thickest 'flow' in the sequence (7) is probably multiple. It consists of uniform porphyritic basalt with plagioclase phenocrysts. Its top is marked partly by a band of purple and red sandstone and mudstone (see Fig. 7) and partly by a shatter belt which the Keltie Water follows for some distance. The overlying flow (8) is a vesicular basalt which carries both feldspar and ferromagnesian phenocrysts; it is not separated from flow 9 by a band of sediments, but a line of contact between vesicular and non-vesicular material can be discerned at the north end of Bruach an Eas [NN 639115].

The Keltie Water flows through Bruach an Eas parallel to the flow margins, of which at least two can be made out by means of sedimentary partings. The lower parting is purple and grey in colour and is locally absent. The upper is exposed at the south-west end of the outcrop and consists of purplish-red, grey and yellow sandstone and shale, mashed and possibly sheared out, and lying approximately vertically. The lava flow (10) between them is a vesicular andesite with andesine phenocrysts up to 5 mm long. Flow 11 is a highly vesicular olivine-basalt and is much smashed. At one point the steep south-east wall of Bruach an Eas is breached to show a 1-ft band of purplish-red shaly sandstone between this flow and harder, less vesicular lava which possibly represents a twelfth flow. This sedimentary parting, however, is not recogniz-able between flow 11 and the Eas Dearg Fault further downstream, where the strata are so sheared and smashed that their original nature is not everywhere determinable. They include some lava, but probably consist mainly of volcanic sandstone with volcanic conglomerate.

The lavas form a group of hillocks stretching south-westwards from the Keltie Water past Drumardoch [NN 631110] to the western limit of the district. The most prominent are Tom a'Bhranndaidh [NN 637114] on which the lower flows are seen, and Creag na Cuthaige [NN 628106], where the higher flows are exposed. A thick intercalation of sediments, mainly volcanic sandstone with some volcanic conglom-erate and red shale, is exposed in the stream which flows along the northern flank of Creag na Cuthaige. It must lie near the middle of the lava succession but cannot with certainty be identified with any of those in the Keltie Water. Above this intercalation several flows are exposed further down the same stream. The two lowest carry large feldspar phenocrysts and are overlain by a highly vesicular flow. All are too altered to allow exact classification. A band of purple and grey sandstone, 3 to 4 ft thick, occurs above the vesicular flow. It is followed by a considerable thickness of microporphyritic lava, some at least of which is basalt, in which no definite flow junctions have been detected. Further downstream highly smashed and sheared lavas and sediments are exposed near the line of the Eas Dearg Fault.

East of the Keltie Water there are several exposures of purple lavas with plagioclase phenocrysts in the head-waters of the Allt na Mna Ruaidhe.

South-east of the Eas Dearg Fault, the basalt lava intercalated near the base of the volcanic conglomerates can be traced north-eastwards over Druim Buidhe to the small stream 200 yd south of Braeleny, and to the Keltie Water where it forms the cliff of Creag a' Choin on the east bank. The best exposures are on Tom a'Ghobhainn [NN 639111], north-east of which the basalt is not seen for about half a mile. It is exposed at several localities on the north-west side of Druim Meadhoin but it apparently dies out farther to the north-east.

On the moors about half a mile south-west of Glenartney Lodge [NN 688155], there are several exposures of sandstone between the volcanic conglomerates and the Dalradian rocks to the north-west; they probably lie in a fault slice within the High-land Boundary Fault Zone. In the stream which flows northwards round Monadh Odhar to join the Water of Ruchill [NN 696156], basic or intermediate lavas, too much

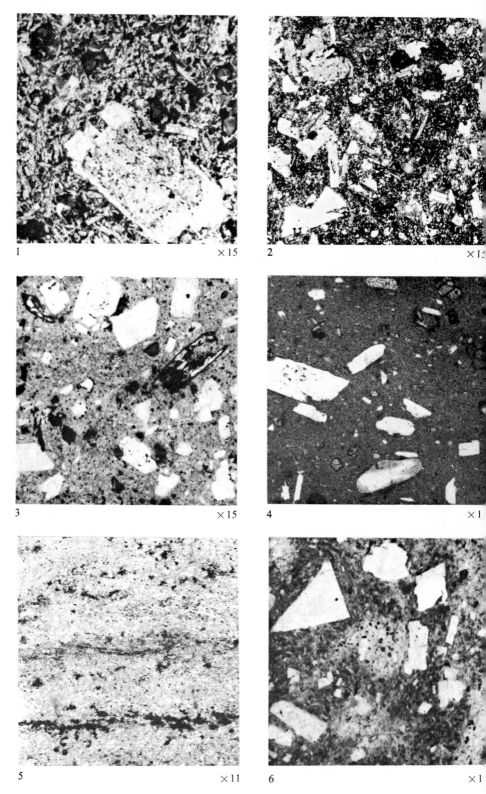

1   ×15   2   ×1

3   ×15   4   ×1

5   ×11   6   ×1

smashed for classification and also heavily veined by carbonate, occur in association with volcanic sandstone; these rocks also probably form part of a fault slice.

A belt of brecciated and carbonated material, about 180 yd wide, is exposed in the Allt Srath a'Ghlinne north-west of Auchinner. The exposures actually lie beyond the northern limit of Sheet 39 but part of the outcrop, too small to be shown on the 1-inch map, probably falls within the area of the sheet. The rock is orange-weathering, more or less brecciated, and is made up of carbonate with purple patches presumed to be relics of the original material. Slices from these patches show them to be altered lavas, possibly with some tuffs, comparable to the basalts and andesites of Lower Old Red Sandstone age. This suggests that the carbonated rocks belong to the Lower Old Red Sandstone volcanic assemblage rather than to the Serpentine Belt, to which they were assigned by Anderson (1947, p. 493). It is thought likely that they lie in a fault slice, within the Highland Boundary Fault Zone, which has been subjected to strong impregnation by carbonate-bearing fluids. I.H.F.

PETROGRAPHY

LAVAS OF THE OCHIL HILLS

Comparison of the petrographical characters of lavas from the Ochils and from other Lower Old Red Sandstone volcanic fields shows that from one field

---

PLATE II

PHOTOMICROGRAPHS OF LOWER OLD RED SANDSTONE LAVAS AND SILL

FIG. 1. Feldspar-phyric olivine-basalt. Lava. Wharry Burn, 550 yd W.3°S. of Cauldhame. Corroded phenocrysts of labradorite, with microphyric euhedral olivine pseudomorphed in bowlingite rimmed with 'iddingsite' and iron ore, set in a groundmass of plagioclase laths, granular colourless augite, iron ores and interstitial chloritic minerals. S 40664. Plane polarized light. Magnification × 15.

FIG. 2. Leucocratic pyroxene-andesite. Lava. 1110 yd N.4°W. of Jerah. Tablets of albitized andesine and of pyroxene pseudomorphed in carbonate, bastite and bowlingite, set in a hyalopilitic groundmass. S 45020. Crossed nicols. Magnification × 15.

FIG. 3. Hornblende-andesite. Lava. 1140 yd E.5°S. of trigonometrical point on Whitewisp Hill summit. Phenocrysts of idiomorphic greenish-brown hornblende rimmed with iron ore, and of andesine with oscillatory zoning, in a hyalopilitic groundmass of andesine microlites and ore dust. S 45154. Plane polarized light. Magnification × 15.

FIG. 4. Glassy pyroxene-andesite. Sill. East of Sheriffmuir road, 680 yd N.37°E. of Parkhead. Phenocrysts of labradorite, hypersthene and augite in a matrix of fresh, pale-brown glass containing microlites of plagioclase, granular pyroxene and specks of ore. S 45150. Plane polarized light. Magnification × 15.

FIG. 5. Trachyandesite. Lava. Alva Glen, west bank, 500 yd upstream from Glenwinnel Burn confluence. Small fluxioned laths of oligoclase, with a little iron ore and with veins of hematite and quartz parallel to the banding. S 40172. Plane polarized light. Magnification × 11.

FIG. 6. Rhyodacite. Lava. 950 yd E.41°S. of Upper Coul. Phenocrysts of oligoclase-albite, fox-red biotite and corroded quartz in a glassy matrix containing small laths of plagioclase, ragged areas of quartz and patchily distributed hematite dust. S 46132. Plane polarized light. Magnification × 15.

to another there is a remarkably close similarity in rock types. This is not always apparent in the published accounts as the similarity has been to some extent obscured, particularly among the acid rocks, by the use of differing nomenclatures.

The main lava types represented in the Ochils comprise feldspar-phyric olivine-basalt, aphyric basalt, andesitic basalt, pyroxene-andesite, hornblende-andesite, trachyandesite and rhyodacite. In addition there are transitional rocks which are less easy to classify. The distinction between basalt and pyroxene-andesite is particularly difficult since the plagioclase in both is zoned from labradorite to andesine or oligoclase; in classifying these rocks the proportion of mafic minerals and the texture have been used as additional criteria.

DETAILS

Feldspar-phyric olivine-basalt. Most of the olivine-basalts contain phenocrysts of plagioclase which in the coarser varieties approach, but seldom exceed, 4·0 mm in length (Plate II, fig. 1). They have an average composition of about An_{55-60} at the core and are frequently zoned to andesine, in some instances in oscillatory fashion (S 44737, 44744). Corrosion or replacement by carbonate is common; in some rocks the plagioclase is albitized (S 39420, 40326, 40328) or penetrated by veinlets of hematite (S 40649). Only one specimen (S 44191) is flow-banded.

Olivine is ubiquitous, forming euhedral crystals which are usually 0·1 to 0·5 mm long, becoming occasionally porphyritic (S 44201, 45022, 45026, 45266). In common with similar rocks of this age from other parts of Scotland the olivine is nowhere fresh: the most common pseudomorphs are in a reddish-brown or yellow pleochroic 'iddingsite' rimmed with iron ore and these can usually be identified macroscopically. Other replacement minerals include carbonate or quartz rimmed with ore.

Augite forms colourless to pale-brown subhedral phenocrysts or glomeroporphyritic aggregates up to 3·0 mm diameter (S 40185, 44790, 45280, 46989) which are occasionally replaced by carbonate. It is accompanied by subordinate phenocrysts of orthopyroxene which in some rocks (S 40327, 40656, 44181, 44770, 44937, 45281) is fresh enough to determine as hypersthene, but in others (S 39434, 40177, 40328, 40652) is pseudomorphed in bastite. In many basalts the only pyroxene is granular augite disseminated through the groundmass (S 39426, 39433, 40649, 40650, 40662, 40664) and in still others it is absent or, possibly, represented only by pseudomorphs in ore minerals (S 44735, 44739, 46085). Subophitic augite as described in the Sidlaw Hills by Harry (1956; 1958) has not been recognized in a fresh state, but it occurs in altered form as chloritic material partially enclosing plagioclase in three coarse, decomposed rocks (S 39431, 40329, 45284). In rare instances pyroxene is associated with or is rimmed by biotite (S 46989).

The groundmass of these basalts consists of laths and microlites of plagioclase set in a fine devitrified glassy residuum, turbid with iron ore, some of which is hematite. Amygdaloidal minerals include carbonate, quartz, chalcedony and fibrous or spherulitic viriditic minerals.

Similar feldspar-phyric basalts from the central Ochils (Kinross (40) Sheet) include analysed rocks described by Sabine (S 36411, 37267 *in* Guppy 1956, pp. 25–7). Other comparable rocks occur at Moncreiffe Hill, near Perth (Davidson 1932, pp. 461–2) and the Sidlaw Hills (Harry 1956, pp. 46–57), but none of the Ochil rocks contain such large phenocrysts of feldspar as the Carnethy Porphyry of the Pentland Hills (Mykura 1960, p. 142) or the Crawton Basalt of Kincardineshire (Campbell 1913, p. 939; analysis of S 30692 quoted in Guppy 1956, pp. 26–7).

Aphyric basalt. Aphyric basalts comprise a small group consisting of fluxioned laths of basic labradorite (An_{60-70}) with granular augite and iron ores, including hematite. Pseudomorphs after olivine are present as insets in some rocks (S 44734, 44747, 44749, 44778) but are absent in others (S 39422, 44207).

The analysed basalt (S 45165; Anal. XIV, Table 3), which is a member of this group, contains glomeroporphyritic granular augite with a few euhedral microphenocrysts. A finer-grained specimen of the same lava (S 45147) is traversed by impersistent carbonate veinlets parallel to the flow and containing flakes of biotite up to 1·5 mm long.

One of the two analysed rocks (Guppy 1956, pp. 25–6) obtained from the ground farther east (Kinross (40) Sheet) is quoted for comparison in Table 3 (Anal. U), together with an olivine-free two-pyroxene basalt (Anal. Y) from the western Sidlaws (Harry 1956, pp. 49–51). Other aphyric basalts of this kind are recorded from Moncreiffe Hill (Davidson 1932, pp. 457–61).

Andesitic basalt. Basalts transitional to andesites form an ill-defined group. One variety, exemplified by S 44761, consists of abundant olivine, andesine-labradorite and iron ore, but contains no pyroxene. In others the feldspar is labradorite, but the proportion of olivine or pyroxene is lower than in the more normal basalts.

Andesitic basalts among other Old Red Sandstone lavas have been recognized by Robson (1948, p. 132) and Harry (1956, pp. 50–2; 1958, p. 109), but precise comparison is difficult since it is not clear whether classification in each case is based on similar criteria.

Pyroxene-andesite. Nearly all pyroxene-andesites contain stout lath-like phenocrysts of plagioclase which in megaphyric varieties (S 40651, 40666) are seriate up to 6·0 mm long. They consist mainly of labradorite zoned to about oligoclase, some of the zoning being markedly oscillatory (S 44745). Corrosion (S 44212) and albitization (S 40651, 45283) are common, but flow-banding (S 44197, 45023) is rare.

Orthopyroxene, present in all but a few rocks, forms prisms of characteristic outline which are usually about 0·5 to 1·0 mm long, though exceptionally megaphyric (S 40325, 45277). Where fresh it is usually identified as weakly pleochroic hypersthene, but some may be referred to enstatite (S 39425). In one instance (S 44745) the orthopyroxene has a reaction rim of green hornblende. It is more usual for the orthopyroxene to be wholly or partly pseudomorphed either in bastite (S 31661, 44751) or a highly birefringent pleochroic mineral which is probably bowlingite (S 40666, 44212), or even a mixture of both (S 40668). The clinopyroxene is a colourless to pale-brown augite which is either granular or microphyric and displays twinning and hourglass structure. Where microphyric it occasionally forms glomeroporphyritic aggregates either alone or with orthopyroxene around which it may form a rim (S 44933). Although less susceptible to alteration than the orthopyroxene it is replaced partly or wholly by carbonate in some rocks (S 44751, 45020, 45274).

The groundmass of the pyroxene-andesites is usually brownish and turbid, consisting of more or less devitrified glass so that textures range from intersertal, with laths of andesine and idiomorphic iron ore (S 40179, 40325), to hyalopilitic or hyalophitic (S 36314, 40173, 45286). Both glass and the cryptocrystalline feldspar, into which glass may be partly resolved, have refractive indices below 1·54. In addition to black opaque iron ore and hematite the accessory minerals include olivine (S 31661, 40668, 46145) and apatite, which may be colourless and acicular (S 40182) or purple, striated, pleochroic and microphyric (S 44197, 46086). Quartz is present in the groundmass of many rocks, but it is at least partly hydrothermal.

Amygdaloidal minerals include quartz, chalcedony, opal, calcite and various fibrous or spherulitic green minerals. Hematite rims (S 44776) to amygdales and elongation with flow (S 44932) are only occasionally found. In one slice (S 44746) there is an impersistent veinlet of quartz and hornblende with a little biotite.

There is a small group of more feldspathic andesites, distinguished in hand specimen by a pale brownish or purplish colour, which contain only small quantities of pyroxene. They are exemplified by S 44746, 45020 (Plate II, fig. 2), the former from the distinctive Calf Craigs rock (p. 33). Another specimen (S 45019), from half a mile north-north-east of Jerah, contains abundant sphene.

TABLE 3 *Analyses of Lower Old Red Sandstone igneous rocks*

	DIORITES								PORPHYRIES, PORPHYRITES AND PLAGIOPHYRES									
	I	II	III	A	B	C	D	E	IV	V	VI	VII	F	G	H	J	K	L
SiO_2	59·17	54·67	52·53	64·39	57·15	53·75	54·07	52·90	80·58	67·36	64·75	60·17	66·71	65·20	64·54	63·31	57·40	53·50
Al_2O_3	15·97	15·02	17·68	14·68	18·39	16·20	15·36	13·02	12·72	15·96	15·29	17·50	15·33	15·88	15·83	15·91	19·64	17·22
Fe_2O_3	2·87	1·75	2·76	1·71	1·42	0·83	0·98	0·93	0·58	3·47	1·48	1·97	1·46	0·26	1·75	1·68	0·46	0·54
FeO	3·67	4·71	4·18	3·24	4·25	7·42	6·76	7·01	0·13	0·08	1·98	3·07	2·26	2·62	2·80	3·07	4·96	5·74
MgO	2·92	5·51	6·88	1·96	3·54	6·55	6·44	10·85	0·16	0·45	1·32	2·62	1·53	1·00	1·01	2·18	2·41	3·80
CaO	4·09	6·77	4·26	3·22	5·75	7·90	8·09	8·00	0·04	0·36	3·13	2·01	2·72	2·62	2·13	4·32	5·70	3·95
Na_2O	4·30	2·98	4·37	3·65	3·81	3·25	3·54	3·10	0·12	5·26	3·70	4·72	3·67	4·54	5·25	3·48	3·60	3·43
K_2O	2·76	2·34	2·89	3·79	2·99	1·46	1·96	2·35	1·54	4·87	3·79	3·79	3·96	4·32	2·95	3·38	2·65	3·01
H_2O+	1·53	1·24	2·37	1·18	0·20	0·55	0·75	0·45	3·17	0·77	1·94	2·18	0·28	0·45	1·39	1·03	1·10	2·50
H_2O-	0·32	0·48	0·29	0·17	0·80	0·45	0·40	0·15	0·30	0·44	0·40	0·32	0·88	0·70	0·42	0·13	0·55	0·60
TiO_2	1·18	0·88	1·08	1·03	0·75	1·05	1·30	1·02	0·02	0·36	0·42	0·63	0·69	0·37	1·09	1·07	1·10	1·06
P_2O_5	0·37	0·24	0·22	0·44	0·22	0·15	0·24	0·20	0·03	0·15	0·16	0·32	0·19	0·13	n.d.?	0·19	0·26	0·34
MnO	0·08	0·12	0·17	0·19	0·15	0·25	0·14	0·15	0·02	0·05	0·08	0·11	0·18	tr.	0·26	0·29	tr.	tr.
CO_2	0·58	3·01	0·17	0·46	0·55	—	—	—	0·41	—	1·61	0·59	0·15	1·75	0·27	0·11	—	4·30
B_2O_3	—	—	—	—	tr.	—	—	—	—	—	—	—	—	—	0·15	—	—	0·12
Total S as FeS_2	—	—	—	—	—	—	—	—	—	—	—	—	—	—	0·15	—	—	—
Allow for minor constituents	0·19	0·36	0·22	—	—	—	—	—	0·06	0·19	0·16	0·23	—	—	—	—	—	—
Other constituents	—	—	—	0·03†	—	—	—	—	—	—	—	—	0·10†	—	0·07†	0·01†	—	—
Totals	100·00	100·08	100·07	100·14	99·97	99·81	100·03	100·13	99·88	99·77	99·99	100·23	100·11	99·84	99·91	100·16	99·83	100·11
	p.p.m.	p.p.m.	p.p.m.						p.p.m.	p.p.m.	p.p.m.	p.p.m.						
*Ba	800	1000	550						250	1000	800	750						
*Cr	10	250	90						n.d.	10	10	10						
*Co	10	30	20						n.d.	5	3	9						
*Cu	40	30	40						<1	10	10	10						
*Ga	20	15	15						n.d.	10	15	15						
Li	—	—	—						95	—	—	—						
*Ni	tr.	150	60						n.d.	tr.	n.d.	n.d.						
*Sr	450	950	700						10	450	250	750						
*V	100	150	100						n.d.	25	45	150						
*Zr	150	150	200						n.d.	150	200	200						
S	—	—	—						200	—	—	—						

TABLE 3 (continued)

Analyses of Lower Old Red Sandstone igneous rocks

	RHYODACITE	RHYOLITE	TRACHYANDESITES			ANDESITES						BASALTS						
	VIII	M	IX	N	O	X	XI	P	Q	R	S	XII	XIII	XIV	T	U	W	Y
SiO_2	71·23	72·78	62·78	63·02	54·01	63·60	61·21	62·09	60·58	56·80	53·35	53·37	52·90	52·10	55·58	53·13	52·28	48·80
Al_2O_3	14·92	12·86	15·56	15·50	15·10	15·35	16·93	17·30	12·25	18·51	15·22	16·41	17·53	16·42	17·93	17·95	17·65	18·03
Fe_2O_3	1·75	3·14	2·42	4·81	3·98	1·29	4·08	3·74	1·01	2·56	2·14	4·92	4·91	4·60	4·81	2·32	3·69	3·96
FeO	0·10	0·26	1·74	0·13	3·39	3·12	0·69	0·92	2·86	3·55	7·42	6·52	5·22	5·83	4·34	4·06	2·56	4·28
MgO	0·33	0·83	3·87	0·62	3·34	1·96	2·90	2·41	4·40	5·70	6·81	7·21	6·70	8·47	6·32	7·32	4·98	4·74
CaO	1·15	0·92	2·21	2·67	6·37	4·37	3·67	3·94	3·61	3·76	2·92	3·36	3·50	3·32	3·81	4·35	8·86	8·02
Na_2O	4·46	2·31	4·34	4·46	5·58	4·47	5·23	4·27	2·19	2·21	0·76	0·93	1·22	1·49	2·06	1·78	3·73	3·26
K_2O	4·31	4·14	3·00	3·96	2·61	2·16	2·16	1·10	—	0·75	1·98	1·97	2·18	1·24	1·10	0·71	1·30	0·82
H_2O+	0·60	1·89	2·11	1·49	1·18	2·10	1·22	0·69	—	1·85	3·27	0·57	0·39	1·87	1·40	1·74	1·00	1·72
H_2O-	0·39	1·05	0·69	1·00	1·77	0·45	0·78	0·65	—	1·20	1·16	1·07	1·46	1·13	1·20	1·24	1·21	3·88
TiO_2	0·18	0·19	0·63	0·43	1·38	0·76	0·75	0·39	—	0·23	0·21	0·25	0·30	0·21	0·25	0·44	0·31	1·77
P_2O_5	0·12	0·14	0·18	0·16	0·67	0·18	0·21	0·05	0·15	—	0·43	0·27	0·11	0·23	tr.	0·20	0·10	0·26
MnO	0·04	0·09	*0·08	0·10	0·30	0·09	0·06	tr.	tr.	tr.	tr.	0·34	0·65	0·29	tr.	0·12	0·53	0·23
CO_2	0·06	0·00	—	1·82	0·05	—	0·08	0·02	—	—	—	—	—	—	—	0·02	0·01	n.d.
Total S as FeS_2	0·02	n.d.	0·03	0·03	—	—	—	—	—	—	—	—	—	—	—	—	—	—
Allow for minor constituents	0·19	—	—	—	—	0·25	0·18	—	—	—	—	0·23	0·19	—	—	—	—	—
Other constituents	—	0·08	0·20†	—	—	—	—	0·06†	2·70†	—	—	—	—	0·22†	—	0·05†	0·04†	—
Totals	99·85	100·68	99·84	100·20	99·73	100·15	100·15	100·59	93·88	100·09	100·23	100·10	100·12	100·15	99·88	100·08	100·36	99·77
	p.p.m.					p.p.m.	p.p.m.	p.p.m.				p.p.m.	p.p.m.	p.p.m.				
*Ba	1200					1000	600	—				350	450	150				
*Cr	15					10	55	tr.				200	30	30		tr.	tr.	
*Co	n.d.					9	15	—				30	30	30				
*Cu	10					15	20	—				50	35	30				
*Ga	15					15	20	—				20	15	15				
*Li	—					—	—	—				90	—	—				
*Ni	tr.					tr.	10	n.d.				80	50	65		tr.	tr.	
*Sr	300					350	550	tr.				600	600	700		tr.	tr.	
*V	n.d.					70	70	n.d.				200	150	200				
*Zr	150					200	200	n.d.				150	200	150				

*Spectrographical determination. † Other constituents given in full in original analysis. n.d. not detected. p.p.m. parts per million. tr. trace.

DETAILS OF ANALYSED ROCKS OF TABLE 3

I. Quartz-pyroxene-diorite (fine-grained). 340 yd W.20°S. of Wester Kirk Craig Trigonometrical Station. [NS 91569815]. S 45149. Lab. No. 1838. Anal. P. R. Kiff, G. A. Sergeant and L. J. Lionnel, spectrographic work by K. L. H. Murray and R. E. Mortlock. *Mem. geol. Surv. Summ. Prog.* for 1962, 1963, p. 62.

II. Pyroxene-biotite-diorite (fine-grained). Allt an Dubh Choirein, 330 yd upstream from footbridge. [NN 67251482]. S 45826. Lab. No. 1898. Anal. P. R. Kiff and W. H. Evans, spectrographic work by K. L. H. Murray. *Mem. geol. Surv. Summ. Prog.* for 1963, 1964, p. 68.

III. Uralitized diorite (coarse-grained). Mill Glen, Tillicoultry, 2130 yd S.10°E. of The Law Trigonometrical Station. [NS 91329770]. S 45151. Lab. No. 1840. Anal. P. R. Kiff, G. A. Sergeant and L. J. Lionnel, spectrographic work by K. L. H. Murray and R. E. Mortlock. *Mem. geol. Surv. Summ. Prog.* for 1962, 1963, p. 62.

A. Hornblende-biotite-granodiorite. Dubs Burn, Tulloch Hill, Darvel, Ayrshire. Anal. E. G. Radley. Richey and others 1930, p. 42.

B. Augite-biotite-quartz-diorite. Margin of Priestlaw intrusion, Faseny Water, East Lothian. Anal. W. H. Herdsman. Walker 1928, p. 161.

C. Pyroxene-mica-diorite (medium-grained). Allt Coiregrogain, 1 mile S.E. of summit of Ben Vane. Anal. W. H. Herdsman. Anderson 1935b, p. 279.

D. Pyroxene-mica-diorite. West of Garabal Farm. Anal. W. H. Herdsman. Nockolds 1941, table vii facing p. 510.

E. Kentallenite. $\frac{1}{4}$ mile S.S.E. of A'Chrois, Argyll. Anal. W. H. Herdsman. Anderson 1935b, p. 279.

IV. Quartz-porphyry; sill. 950 yd E.N.E. of Arivurichardich. [NN 65111401]. S 45789. Lab. No. 1897. Anal. P. R. Kiff and W. H. Evans, spectrographic work by K. L. H. Murray. *Mem. geol. Surv. Summ. Prog.* for 1963, 1964, p. 68.

V. Quartz-albite-hornblende-porphyry; chonolith. On E. bank of Westrig Burn 1650 yd N.5°W. of Kaimknowe. [NN 94570018]. S 45166. Lab. No. 1845. Anal. P. R. Kiff, W. H. Evans and L. J. Lionnel, spectrographic work by K. L. H. Murray and R. E. Mortlock. *Mem. geol. Surv. Summ. Prog.* for 1962, 1963, p. 63.

VI. Acid porphyrite; dyke. Burn of Sorrow, 1110 yd E.27°N. of the Trigonometrical Station on King's Seat Hill. [NN 94570018]. S 45148. Lab. No. 1837. Anal. P. R. Kiff, G. A. Sergeant and L. J. Lionnel, spectrographic work by K. L. H. Murray and R. E. Mortlock. *Mem. geol. Surv. Summ. Prog.* for 1962, 1963, p. 62.

VII. Porphyrite; dyke. Silver Glen, 1905 yd S.23°E. of The Nebit Trigonometrical Station. [NS 89179773]. S 45152. Lab. No. 1841. Anal. P. R. Kiff, G. A. Sergeant and L. J. Lionnel, spectrographic work by K. L. H. Murray and R. E. Mortlock. *Mem. geol. Surv. Summ. Prog.* for 1962, 1963, p. 62.

F. Hornblende-porphyrite; dyke. Glen Etive. Anal. E. G. Radley. Bailey and Maufe 1916, p. 183.

G. Oligoclase-biotite-porphyrite; chonolith. Ninewells, Dundee. Anal. W. H. Herdsman. Harris 1928a, p. 66.

H. Plagiophyre; sill. Pap Craig, Tinto, Lanarkshire. Anal. B. E. Dixon. Guppy 1931, p. 22.

J. Porphyrite; dyke. $\frac{1}{2}$ mile N. E. of Barbeth, Darvel, Ayrshire. Anal. E. G. Radley. Richey and others 1930, p. 42.

K. Quartz-biotite-hypersthene-porphyrite. East margin of Cockburnlaw intrusion, River Whiteadder, Berwickshire. Anal. W. H. Herdsman. Walker 1928, p. 161.

L.   Plagiophyre; dyke. Ninewells railway cutting, Dundee. Anal. W. H. Herdsman.
         Harris 1928a, p. 66.
VIII.   Rhyodacite; lava. Near summit of Ben Effrey, 2850 ft E.41°S. of Upper Coul.
         [NN 98001150]. S 46132. Lab. No. 1872. Anal. P. R. Kiff and G. A. Sergeant,
         spectrographic work by K. L. H. Murray.
M.   Rhyolite; lava. Quarry, ¼ mile W.S.W. of Woodhouselee House, Pentland
         Hills, Edinburgh. Anal. W. Pollard. Peach and others 1910, p. 39.
IX.   Trachyandesite; lava. Alva Glen, west bank, 500 yd upstream from confluence
         with Glenwinnel Burn. [NS 87969906]. S 42142. Lab. No. 1739. Anal. A. D.
         Wilson and J. Palframan, spectrographic work by C. O. Harvey and K. L. H.
         Murray. *Mem. geol. Surv. Summ. Prog.* for 1958, 1959, p. 52.
N.   Trachyte; lava. Mortonhall Golf Clubhouse quarry, Braid Hills, Edinburgh.
         Anal. W. H. Pollard. Peach and others 1910, p. 37.
O.   Trachyandesite; lava. Craighead Quarry, Sidlaws, Perthshire. Anal. R. Phillips.
         Harry 1956, p. 51.
X.   Glassy pyroxene-andesite; sill. Between Sheriffmuir road and Dumyat, 680 yd
         N.37°E. of Parkhead. [NS 81469788]. S 45150. Lab. No. 1839. Anal. P. R.
         Kiff, G. A. Sergeant and L. J. Lionnel, spectrographic work by K. L. H. Murray
         and R. E. Mortlock. *Mem. geol. Surv. Summ. Prog.* for 1962, 1963, p. 62.
XI.   Hornblende-andesite; lava. 1140 yd E.5°S. of the Trigonometrical Station on
         Whitewisp Hill summit. [NN 96560126]. S 45154. Lab. No. 1842, Anal. P. R.
         Kiff, G. A. Sergeant and L. J. Lionnel, spectrographic work by K. L. H.
         Murray and R. E. Mortlock. *Mem. geol. Surv. Summ. Prog.* for 1962, 1963,
         p. 62.
P.   Hornblende-andesite; lava. Quarry 800 yd E.S.E. of Middle Third, Dunning,
         central Ochils, Perthshire. Anal. W. F. Waters, spectrographic work by J. A. C.
         McClelland. Guppy 1956, p. 17.
Q.   Glassy pyroxene-andesite; lava. Bowmont Water, Yetholm, Cheviots, Rox-
         burghshire. Anal. J. S. Grant Wilson. Geikie 1897, vol. i, p. 275.
R.   Glassy hypersthene-augite-andesite; lava. Stannergate, Dundee. Anal. W. H.
         Herdsman. Harris 1928a, p. 66; 1928b, p. 110.
S.   Basic andesite; lava. Over Fingask, Sidlaws, Perthshire. Anal. W. H. Herdsman.
         Harry 1956, p. 51.
XII.   Basalt; sheet. 1450 yd E. by S. of Meall Odhar Trigonometrical Station.
         [NN 66001433]. S 45787. Lab. No. 1896. Anal. P. R. Kiff and W. H. Evans,
         spectrographic work by K. L. H. Murray. *Mem. geol. Surv. Summ. Prog.* for
         1963, 1964, p. 68.
XIII.   Basalt; dyke. Gannel Burn, north bank, 1590 yd S.8°E. of The Law Trigono-
         metrical Station. [NS 91239820]. S 45164. Lab. No. 1843. Anal. P. R. Kiff,
         W. H. Evans and L. J. Lionnel, spectrographic work by K. L. H. Murray and
         R. E. Mortlock. *Mem. geol. Surv. Summ. Prog.* for 1962, 1963, p. 63.
XIV.   Aphyric olivine-basalt; lava. Frandy Burn, north bank, 1350 yd N.43°W. of
         Scad Hill Trigonometrical Station. [NN 93070306]. S 45165. Lab. No. 1844.
         Anal. P. R. Kiff, W. H. Evans and L. J. Lionnel, spectrographic work by
         K. L. H. Murray and R. E. Mortlock. *Mem. geol. Surv. Summ. Prog.* for 1962,
         1963, p. 63.
T.   Hypersthene-quartz-dolerite; intrusion. Balgay Hill, Dundee. Anal. W. H.
         Herdsman. Harris 1928a, p. 66.
U.   Aphyric olivine-basalt; lava. Arngask, central Ochils, Perthshire. Anal. W. F.
         Waters, spectrographic work by J. A. C. McClelland. Guppy 1956, p. 26.
W.   Feldspar-phyric olivine-basalt; lava. Leden Urquhart, Arngask, central Ochils,
         Perthshire. Anal. W. F. Waters, spectrographic work by J. A. C. McClelland.
         Guppy 1956, p. 26.
Y.   Olivine-free two-pyroxene basalt. Guardwell Hill, Sidlaws, Perthshire. Anal.
         W. H. Herdsman. Harry 1956, p. 51.
E

The ophitic textures found in Forfarshire andesites (Robson 1948, p. 133) are absent from the Ochil rocks and are approached only in some glassy varieties (S 44933, 44943) containing glomeroporphyritic aggregates of feldspar and pyroxene which are to a minor degree intergrown. Such glassy rocks, where fresh, resemble the intrusive hypersthene-andesite described by Flett (1897) and the pitchstone-andesites of the Cheviots (Carruthers and others 1932, pp. 12–4) where they are more abundant than in the Ochils. Glassy hypersthene-andesites in Kincardineshire (Campbell 1913, p. 944) and the Dundee area (Harris 1928b, p. 109) are also comparable.

Hornblende-andesite. The hornblende-andesites (Plate II, fig. 3) are microphyric or macrophyric rocks, with seriate plagioclase insets that tend to be more stumpy and idiomorphic than those in the more basic lavas. They display spectacular, often oscillatory, zoning and range in composition from andesine or, rarely, acid labradorite, to oligoclase. In some rocks extensively corroded basic plagioclase cores are mantled by fresh andesine-oligoclase; in others corrosion is restricted to outer margins. Albitization is common, especially in the autobrecciated flows.

Hornblende is mainly idiomorphic and elongated, being pleochroic in shades of cinnamon-brown and greenish-brown. In some rocks it is seriate; in others it occurs only as phenocrysts. It is invariably rimmed with iron ore and, in many rocks, is completely resorbed, being then outlined in turbid iron ore with, in some cases, a little carbonate and chloritic material at the centre.

In about half of the slides of hornblende-andesites examined there are subordinate amounts of tabular orthopyroxene, usually pseudomorphed in bastite, and of augite which is usually fresh, but may occasionally be replaced by carbonate. Remnants of augite appear as cores in some hornblende phenocrysts (S 45273). Accessory minerals include silicified pseudomorphs after olivine (S 36313, 44200) and dusky, pleochroic apatite, striated parallel to the c-axis, and occasionally microphyric (S 44800). The groundmass is almost invariably pale-brown and hyalopilitic with finely disseminated ore. Some rocks are hematitized in streaks which cross the line of flow (S 44793). Amygdales are formed by quartz, chalcedony, spherulitic viriditic minerals and carbonate.

A few rocks transitional to pyroxene-andesite (S 44190, 44792, 44953) contain equal quantities of hornblende and pyroxene and in these rocks plagioclase phenocrysts are correspondingly more basic; scattered pseudomorphs after olivine also occur. The few hornblende-andesites which are fluxioned (S 44200, 44793) also fall within the more basic end of the group.

The analysed rock (S 45154; Anal. XI, Table 3) comprises seriate plagioclase up to 3·0 mm long, zoned from andesine-labradorite at the core to oligoclase, and elongated ore-rimmed yellow-brown hornblende, up to 2·0 mm long, partly replaced by biotite, set in a hyalopilitic base containing disseminated octahedra of ore. In thin section it resembles two analysed rocks from Glen Coe (Bailey 1960, p. 206) and one from the central Ochils quoted in Table 3 (Anal. P).

Hornblende-andesites appear to be absent from the Lower Old Red Sandstone lavas in the Sidlaws (Harry 1956; 1958) and eastern Forfarshire (Robson 1948), but they are recorded farther north along the Highland Boundary Fault (Campbell 1913, pp. 942–3; Allan 1928, p. 67; 1940, p. 174) and at Ben Nevis and Glen Coe (Bailey 1960).

Trachyandesite. The trachyandesites (Plate II, fig. 5) are formed mainly of fluxioned laths of acid plagioclase ranging in composition from oligoclase to andesine. The laths, which are about 0·05 mm long in the fine-grained rocks (S 39429, 44938) and up to 0·15 mm long in the coarser (S 40670), are set in a residuum of alkali-feldspar containing a good deal of finely divided ore. Some rocks contain phenocrysts, 0·5 to 1·5 mm long, of acid andesine which may be replaced by albite and carbonate; they are usually sparsely scattered but occasionally are so abundant (S 44204, 44773, 46138) as to be microphyric. Sporadic small insets of ore-rimmed pseudomorphs after hornblende, and of bastite, chlorite or carbonate after pyroxene are common; rarely these are aggregated (S 40172). Hematite occurs in ragged patches and as a lining to quartzo-feldspathic stringers which occasionally contain small flakes of biotite. These stringers are usually aligned parallel to the flow-banding, but some also lie at an angle to it (S 39429) and cut other stringers (S 44209). A little carbonate appears in some stringers and occurs patchily in the groundmass of one rock (S 38351). Vesicles are filled with carbonate or chalcedony, but are rare.

A rock transitional to hornblende-andesite (S 38352) contains phenocrysts of corroded labradorite, carbonated hornblende and clinopyroxene, and bastite pseudomorphs after orthopyroxene, set in a fluxioned trachyandesitic groundmass. A more acid variant, tending towards rhyodacite (S 44766), contains small plates of biotite and a good deal of groundmass quartz, some of which is, however, secondary.

The trachyandesites of the western Ochils are very similar to those from the Sidlaws described by Harry (1956, p. 52), to the oligoclase-trachytes of the Cheviots described by Thomas (*in* Carruthers and others 1932, pp. 14–5, 40) and to two analysed rocks, trachyte (Anal. N, Table 3) and andesite, from the Edinburgh area which were described by Flett (*in* Peach and others 1910, pp. 34, 37). Similar rocks have been identified also in the central part of the Ochils where they have been grouped with trachytes and rhyolites on the published map (Kinross (40) Sheet). An analysed specimen of trachyandesite from the central Ochils (Guppy 1956, p. 16) closely resembles that from Alva Glen (Anal. IX, Table 3), but both show slightly more silica than the trachyandesite from Craighead Quarry in the Sidlaws (Harry 1956, p. 57; see also Anal. O, Table 3).

A specimen (S 46015) obtained from the last locality differs from the Ochil rocks in being coarser and devoid of the quartz-rich stringers.

Rhyodacite. The red, banded megaphyric lava of Craig Rossie is the most important of the rhyodacites. It was originally described as rhyolite by Macnair (1908, pp. 74–5, fig. 39), but Geikie (1900, p. 259) regarded it as 'intermediate in character between andesite and rhyolite with affinities to dacite and trachyte'. The feldspar phenocrysts are up to 2·0 mm long and in the freshest state (S 46132) display oscillatory zoning between andesine and albite (Plate II, fig. 6). In most specimens there is also extensive albitization occasionally accompanied by sericitization and in these rocks the composition of the plagioclase seems to lie between albite and oligoclase. Some of the feldspar phenocrysts are simply twinned and were described as orthoclase in earlier accounts. Staining tests show, however, that they are acid plagioclase so that the potash indicated by the analysis (Anal. VIII, Table 3) must be restricted to the groundmass feldspar and biotite.

Biotite is the main ferromagnesian mineral; it forms chunky flakes which display various stages of resorption, becoming in some rocks (S 46122) completely replaced by turbid iron ore. Rare pseudomorphs in ore, occasionally accompanied by chloritic material, have outlines suggestive of hornblende (S 8883, 46123).

Corroded phenocrysts of quartz with rounded outlines appear in most slices, though amounts vary. Quartz also accompanies alkali-feldspar in the groundmass where it is occasionally micropoikilitic. In some of the fine-grained, fresher rocks the subcrystalline groundmass feldspar occurs in radiating sheaf-like aggregates, in which hematite has grown, and colour spreading out from these gives the rock its patchy red appearance. In the paler, altered varieties (S 8886, 46137) biotite or its alteration products is less abundant and the quartzo-feldspathic groundmass encloses a good deal of cryptocrystalline viriditic material. Apatite and, less commonly, zircon are accessory minerals.

A lithologically very similar rock is the trachyte from the northern part of the Cheviots (Geikie 1897, p. 276), though its analysis shows it to be less acid than the Craig Rossie rock. The analysis of the latter compares better with that (Anal. V, Table 3) of the macroscopically similar quartz-albite-porphyry (p. 62), thus suggesting that some of the chonolithic intrusions represent feeder channels for the rhyodacite lavas. E.H.F.

E*

LAVAS OF THE KELTIE WATER AND GLEN ARTNEY

Three of the types of lavas from the Ochil Hills described above have been recognized in the Keltie Water, namely feldspar-phyric olivine-basalt, aphyric basalt and pyroxene-andesite. They are all more highly altered than their Ochil counterparts. Pyroxene, olivine, and locally also plagioclase are completely replaced, so that some of the flows cannot be classified. The lavas in Glen Artney are all much too highly smashed and carbonated to be classified.

DETAILS

Feldspar-phyric olivine-basalt. Flows 1, 2, 6 and 7 in the Keltie Water are all probably of this type: they have phenocrysts of plagioclase up to 5 mm long (S 44533, 44536, 46608–9), all too altered for determination. Olivine pseudomorphs in 'iddingsite' and iron ore are generally present. The lava flow which lies near the base of the volcanic conglomerate is a member of this group.

Aphyric basalt. Flows 3, 4, 5, 8, 9 and 11 of the Keltie Water section appear to fall into this group. Pseudomorphs after olivine occur in several of these flows and reach 3 mm in length in flow 5 (S 44532), which is a coarse-grained olivine-basalt with abundant laths of labradorite up to 2 mm long.

Pyroxene-andesite. Flow 10 (S 44539, 45247) is classed with the andesites rather than the basalts because of the presence of abundant phenocrysts of andesine; these are up to 5 mm long and are set in a dark fine-grained groundmass. A specimen (S 43330) from the exposures near the source of the Allt na Mna Ruaidhe has a similar texture.

I.H.F.

TUFFS

All the tuffs contain angular to sub-rounded fragments of crystalline lava texturally resembling the Ochil suite though they are invariably too turbid and decomposed for identification; feldspars are albitized and kaolinized and ferromagnesian minerals are replaced by viriditic minerals or carbonate. In some rocks (S 38353, 44187, 44803) the proportion of such fragments is sufficiently high to warrant their description as lithic tuffs (Pirsson 1915).

Most rocks also contain fragments of highly altered plagioclase, pyroxene or olivine and where these are as abundant as the lava fragments the rocks may be termed crystal-lithic tuffs (S 44180, 44185, 44203, 44781). Glassy material is also present in various proportions, and it too is generally altered to greenish or brown turbid material (S 44206) though some yellowish isotropic fragments may represent glass which is nearly fresh (S 44777, 44942). Cusp-shapes and vitroclastic textures are rare (S 44188) among this group.

The groundmass of the tuffs is turbid and obscure: it includes some possibly kaolinitic material, viriditic minerals and a little hydrothermal quartz (partly chalcedony). Carbonate occurs extensively as a replacement mineral in some rocks and hematitization is also common (S 44184, 44767).

INTRA-VOLCANIC SEDIMENTS

Intra-volcanic sediments range in grain size from mudstone to sandstone (0·4 mm). Grading is usually crude or absent, except in one rock (S 44771) which shows prominent load-casting at the base of the sandstone layers. The coarser constituents are mainly detrital grains of quartz with rarer accessory zircons, garnets and sphenes. Volcanic debris is abundant, but is highly decomposed to brownish turbid masses. In these masses glassy textures are not preserved at all, and even the lath-structures are obliterated in the smaller fragments of crystalline rock detritus. Brownish and colourless micas and green chloritic flakes are aligned along bedding planes in the finer layers.

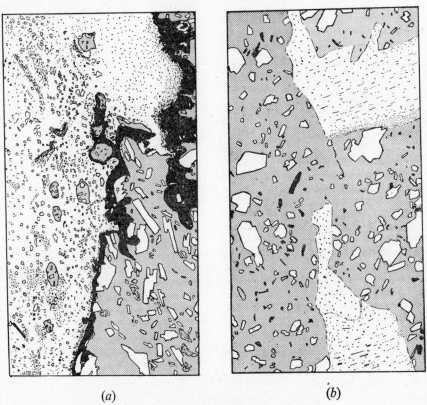

(a)   (b)

FIG. 8.   *Sediments enclosed in lavas*
(Drawn from photomicrographs. Magnification ×5)

(a) Sediment of heterogeneous texture, with disorientated remnants of bedding, caught up in slaggy andesite lava. Upper Glendevon Dam. S 38357
(b) Sediment, showing bedding orientation of micas, etc., filling fissures in rhyodacite lava. 1200 ft N.44°E. of Upper Coul. S 46136

There is a marked contrast in texture between sediment caught up by lava on the one hand and sediment filling fissures in previously solidified lava on the other. A specimen of the first kind (Fig. 8a) consists of quartz sand with pockets of silt and with much highly decomposed volcanic debris; some of the silt pockets show traces of a rude bedding which has been highly disturbed and dislocated. By contrast the elements of bedding in sediments filling fissures are relatively undisturbed and have the same orientation throughout the rock

(Fig. 8b). In sediments of this kind there are also, in places, segregations of finer particles along the fissure walls. This feature has been described elsewhere (Ewing and Francis 1960, p. 55) as possibly resulting from some kind of electrolytic attraction exerted by the walls of the fissures.

DIORITE STOCKS

The stocks of Tillicoultry and Glendevon are formed by rocks consisting mainly of plagioclase with varying proportions of ferromagnesian minerals and with sufficient quartz to warrant their classification as quartz-diorites.

DETAILS

Fine-grained diorites. The fine-grained diorites are grey saccharoidal rocks sharing many of the characteristics of both hornfelsed country-rocks and coarse diorites. Indeed it is this group which offers some of the most convincing evidence of the formation of some of the diorites by metamorphism of country-rock lavas.

In varieties most nearly related to hornfels (S 38363–4) some of the plagioclase is still turbid and of tabular habit even where there has been an outer growth of fresh clear plagioclase. In these rocks biotite, in poikilitic plates, is the only fresh ferromagnesian mineral; pyroxenes and amphiboles of the original lavas are replaced by carbonate, penninite and other viriditic minerals. In varieties representing more completely dioritized lavas (such as the analysed rock S 45149; Anal. I, Table 3. Also S 44148, 44159) the plagioclase is pellucid andesine which has the appearance of having been cleared of inclusions, partly fused and partly replaced by albite (Plate III, fig. 2). Tabular habit is apparent only in occasional porphyroblasts which enclose granular, colourless clinopyroxenes. Other subhedral clinopyroxenes, together with hypersthene, are rimmed with colourless to pale-green amphibole and biotite and form, with quartz and plagioclase, a crystalloblastic mosaic texture. Apart from texture there is other evidence to show that these pyroxenes were formed during an advanced stage of metamorphism; in one of the hybrid rocks (S 44143; Plate III, fig. 3) a narrow impersistent zone containing abundant granular pyroxene in a crystalloblastic groundmass separates hornfelsed lava from coarse diorite.

In all these rocks clear apatite and varying proportions of sphene are common accessories.

Coarse-grained diorites. The coarse-grained diorites can be subdivided into four groups:

    i. A granodioritic variant with no pyroxene and a relatively high proportion of pink turbid potash-feldspar forming, with quartz, interstitial micropegmatite; this variant is restricted to parts of the dyke and stock in the Mill Glen, Tillicoultry (S 44133, 45016).

    ii. Variants with abundant uralitic amphibole, but with little or no pyroxene; rocks of this group occur in several of the Tillicoultry stocks (S 44134, 44146, 44156, 44165, 44179) and include the analysed rock (S 45151; Anal. III, Table 3; Plate III, fig. 1).

    iii. Two-pyroxene diorites with subordinate amphibole; such rocks occur within the Tillicoultry stocks (S 44149, 44152, 44153, 44159, 44166).

    iv. Varieties allied to kentallenite, containing two pyroxenes and appreciable amounts of olivine pseudomorphed in iron ore and carbonate or bastite; this variety seems to be restricted to the Glendevon stocks (S 45264, 45271, 45752).

All these rocks have in common a holocrystalline texture in which the plagioclase is labradorite or andesine zoned to oligoclase or albite and is either clear, or clouded

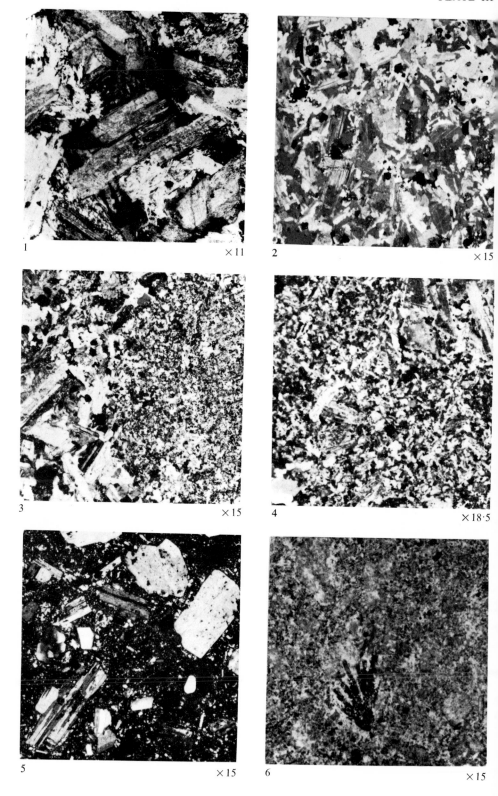

1 ×11

2 ×15

3 ×15

4 ×18·5

5 ×15

6 ×15

with small flakes of sericite. There is some replacement by water-clear albite both marginally and along cleavage, and there is also a good deal of turbid orthoclase rimming the plagioclase.

Orthopyroxene is represented by hypersthene, some of which is fresh and rimmed with clinopyroxene or amphibole, while some is replaced wholly or partly by bastite or bowlingite. The clinopyroxene is either turbid and altered along the cleavage in a manner analogous to schiller structure or is replaced by carbonate; it is commonly rimmed with amphibole or biotite.

The amphibole is pale to buff with maximum extinction angle $Z: c = 18°$, indicating tremolite-actinolite. It is in two generations, of which the earlier forms large fibro-lamellar plates while the later, a slightly paler variety, forms sheaf-like aggregates which may marginally replace the older. Both forms are associated with various chloritic minerals, including penninite, but the relationships between these minerals and the amphiboles are usually difficult to determine. In some cases early amphibole is clearly replaced by a fibrous yellowish mineral of low polarization; in others the second generation amphibole seems to have replaced chlorite. There is evidence too that some of the first generation tremolite-actinolite has grown as a uralitic replacement of an earlier altered, turbid pyroxene.

Biotite occurs in plates which are either associated with aggregates of iron ore and pyrite or, less commonly, are moulded around amphibole, and have replaced it along

---

PLATE III

PHOTOMICROGRAPHS OF DIORITES, HORNFELS AND MINOR INTRUSIONS

FIG. 1. Coarse uralitized diorite. Mill Glen, Tillicoultry, 2130 yd S.10°E. of trigonometrical point on The Law. Large laths of sericitized andesine-oligoclase rimmed by albite, with pale-green sheaf-like amphibole growing out of uralitized pyroxene, and with accessory biotite, iron ores and interstitial potash-feldspar. S 45151. Crossed nicols. Magnification × 11.

FIG. 2. Fine-grained quartz-diorite. 340 yd W.20°S. of trigonometrical point on Wester Kirk Craig, near Tillicoultry. Pellucid andesine partly replaced by albite in a crystalloblastic mosaic texture with clinopyroxene and hypersthene (both rimmed by green hornblende) and with biotite and quartz. S 44148A. Partially crossed nicols. Magnification × 15.

FIG. 3. Hybrid rock. 400 yd N.70°E. of the confluence of the Daiglen and Gannel burns, north of Tillicoultry. A zone rich in granular pyroxene separates hornfelsed lava from coarse diorite. S 44143. Crossed nicols. Magnification × 15.

FIG. 4. Hornfels. 1360 yd S.2°W. of trigonometrical point on King's Seat Hill, Tillicoultry. Phenocrysts of acid plagioclase, partly replaced by viriditic minerals, partly clear, in a xenoblastic mosaic of quartz, pink turbid alkali-feldspar, biotite, carbonate, iron ores and accessory sphene. S 44170. Crossed nicols. Magnification × 18·5.

FIG. 5. Quartz-albite-hornblende-porphyry. Chonolith crossing Westrig Burn, Glendevon, 1650 yd N.5°W. of Kaimknowe. Stumpy prisms of albite and resorbed idiomorphic hornblende in a pale hyalopilitic groundmass of quartz, small laths of acid plagioclase, longulites of iron ore and accessory apatite and zircon. S 45153. Crossed nicols. Magnification × 15.

FIG. 6. Tourmalinized aplite. Dyke. 120 yd E.10°S. of trigonometrical point on Wester Kirk Craig, near Tillicoultry. Sheaf-like green tourmaline and granular sphene with phenocrysts of turbid albite, partly replaced by carbonate and penninite in a fine-grained crystalloblastic quartzo-feldspathic groundmass. S 44151. Plane polarized light. Magnification × 15.

the cleavage. The biotite is locally altered to chlorite minerals, including penninite, indicating some degree of retrograde metamorphism. Carbonate occurs in clear plates or in turbid areas replacing chlorites. Quartz occurs in all rocks, but in smaller quantities in the kentallenitic varieties than in the granodioritic ones. There is abundant accessory apatite, some of it microporphyritic (up to 2·0 mm), with sphene and rare epidote and zircon.

Two small stocks of diorite south-west of Glenfarg in the central Ochils (Kinross (40) Sheet) are composed of kentallenitic rocks like the Glendevon masses. Farther northeast a small quartz-diorite mass at Glenduckie Hill, in north Fife, would seem from Walker's (1939) description to resemble the coarse two-pyroxene rocks of Tillicoultry.

Aplitic rocks. The pink aplitic rocks occur in segregation patches or in veins, ranging in thickness from a few millimetres to several feet, which cut diorites and aureole rocks alike; they also occur at some of the diorite margins. In hand specimen most of them appear to have a granular texture, but in thin section many are seen to carry plagioclase phenocrysts. These are occasionally fresh enough at the core to determine as andesine or oligoclase, but they are more commonly either rimmed with turbid potash-feldspar or altered, wholly or in part, to turbid material so that in extreme cases (e.g. S 45267) only shadowy outlines of the original phenocrysts remain.

There are sporadic pseudomorphs in penninite or other chloritic minerals with iron ores and epidote, but the only fresh ferromagnesian mineral is biotite. The groundmass, which in some specimens forms the bulk of the rock, consists mainly of turbid alkali-feldspar and quartz, commonly granular (S 44141), rarely graphically intergrown (S 44147) or forming micropegmatite (S 44132). Sphene, apatite, epidote and carbonate are accessory and, in some rocks (e.g. S 44172) the last two occur together in irregular veins and pockets. A less common accessory is tourmaline, pleochroic from colourless or straw-yellow to dark blue-green and forming radiate sheaf-like aggregates of elongate prisms which partly replace feldspars (S 44151, 44173; Plate III, fig. 6).

Diorites cut by aplitic veins show signs of contact-alteration as evidenced by replacement of ferromagnesian minerals by epidote and chlorite (S 44140); the veins, however, are not chilled, but have a gradational, intergrown contact with the host rock. Similar gradational contacts appear between some of the hornfelsed rocks and the included segregation pods and patches of pink aplite. In some cases the pink material appears to have 'soaked' into the hornfels (S 44141); in others there is abundant iron ore with accessory sphene occurring at the irregular contact between aplite pod and hybrid rock (S 44129).

Other specimens of aplitic rocks are: S 44138, 44150, 44157, 44167, 44759, 44962 and 45260.

CONTACT-ALTERED ROCKS

The country rocks in the vicinity of the diorite stocks show varying degrees of contact-alteration. In the less altered rocks the original lava or tuff textures are still well-preserved, but where the metamorphic grade is higher the rocks have been hornfelsed and original textures have been largely obliterated. The degree of metamorphism is not directly related to the distance from the diorite margin; some slightly altered rocks are virtually in contact with coarse diorite while some of the hornfelses are hundreds of feet from diorite margins.

Low-grade metamorphism of lavas. In some of the less altered lavas (S 44135, 44139, 45263, 45272), the plagioclase remains fresh, but the pyroxene is first made turbid then uralitized with accessory carbonate and chlorite, while iron ores, including those originally pseudomorphing olivine and hornblende, become slightly dispersed to form small ore-rich aggregates which give the rocks a dark spotted appearance in hand specimen. The groundmass is clouded by growth of finely-shredded uralite and chlorite with possibly some mica.

In other, perhaps more highly altered, rocks (S 40186, 44144, 44163, 44168, 45261, 45269) in which the lava textures are still preserved, the feldspars are completely heat-clouded, and partly sericitized. Chlorites, including penninite, occur in the ground-mass and in one rock (S 44155) appear also as a replacement to plagioclase, being accompanied by small granules of clear pyroxene—probably diopside—which also occurs in the groundmass. In many of these rocks the only remnants of the original ferromagnesian minerals are aggregates of finely divided ore which give rise to a macro-scopic black spotted appearance. In some rocks too there has been extensive replace-ment by carbonate.

Specimens transitional to hornfels show a growth of fresh micropoikilitic quartz (S 45270) or patchy intergrowths of clear acid plagioclase and quartz with a little biotite, chlorite, granular iron ore and a little epidote (S 44131, 44162).

Low-grade metamorphism of tuffs. As in the lavas, the earliest stages in the alteration of the tuffs are represented by heat-clouding and sericitization of plagioclase, partial dispersion of the iron ores originally pseudomorphing ferromagnesian minerals and varying degrees of replacement of all components by carbonate (S 44177). In addition there is loss of definition of the lithic fragments and this is apparent both in hand specimen (pp. 38–9) and under the microscope where the groundmass of the original fragments is seen to merge with the matrix of the tuff to form a turbid, cryptocrystalline, low-polarizing aggregate, so that the fragments themselves are distinguished only by the grouping (sometimes flow-aligned) of the plagioclase phenocrysts.

With further alteration new minerals appear either in the form of a xenoblastic groundmass of quartz and acid plagioclase with flecks of uralite and chlorite (S 44130, 45259) or as fresh euhedral plagioclase growing out of the older, heat-clouded pheno-crysts (S 44964, 44966).

Hornfelses. In the hornfelses the heat-clouding noted in the lower-grade rocks has become wholly or partially cleared and the feldspars have a marginal growth of clear, fresh acid plagioclase. Alignment of some of these feldspars in a few specimens (S 38362, 44162) is the only remaining palimpsest structure; the rocks are otherwise xenoblastic or granoblastic in texture and contain abundant interstitial and poikiloblastic quartz with a good deal of fresh, dark-brown biotite (S 38361, 44164, 44170; Plate III, fig. 4). Some of the biotite has replaced chlorites; some is associated with ore minerals. Accessory minerals include iron ores and apatite. Epidote is also accessory and is usually sparse except in one specimen (S 44161) where it forms a wide green vein in association with uralitic hornblende and chloritic minerals and also occurs in abundance throughout the adjacent rock.

MINOR INTRUSIONS

For descriptive purposes the minor intrusions are subdivided into basalt, andesite, porphyrite, acid porphyrite, plagiophyre and quartz-albite-porphyry. With few exceptions there is a general correlation between these subdivisions and the field relations of the rocks, the basalts, andesites and porphyries being intrusive equivalents of lavas, while the porphyrites and plagiophyres form the dyke-swarms around the diorites.

Some authors (Hatch and others 1949, p. 264; Tocher 1961, p. 238) would classify most of the intrusions of intermediate composition as 'microdiorite', but there may be some objection to using this term since other authors have used it in various senses (e.g. Anderson 1935a, p. 259; Bailey 1960, pp. 228–9). In this memoir, therefore, porphyrite and plagiophyre are preferred and are used broadly in the sense defined by MacGregor (1939; and *in* Macgregor and MacGregor 1948, pp. 25–8). Thus porphyrites comprise rocks of andesitic aspect (sometimes altered) with abundant phenocrysts of plagioclase and of pyroxene or hornblende. With the addition of quartz in the groundmass they grade into acid porphyrites or with the addition of numerous phenocrysts of quartz become quartz-albite-porphyries. The plagiophyres are altered rocks allied to acid porphyrite but without porphyritic feldspar.

DETAILS

Basalt. Two types of basalt are represented among the minor intrusions. One is identical with the lavas and is exemplified by a 6-ft feldspar-phyric dyke in Fin Glen (p. 39). It consists of phenocrysts of decomposed plagioclase, up to 3·0 mm long, with fresh microphyric augite and euhedral 'iddingsite' after olivine in a groundmass of fluxioned plagioclase, granular augite, 'iddingsite' and viriditic material (S 46991).

The other basalts are less certainly identified with lavas. They are dark grey where fresh, becoming green if decomposed, and are characterized by large orientated feldspar phenocrysts which have a platy appearance on surfaces parallel to the flow-banding. These phenocrysts may occur as single crystals up to 7·0 mm across (S 44757) or form glomeroporphyritic groups (S 45288); they consist of labradorite ranging in composition from about An_{50} to An_{60}. In most rocks the principal ferromagnesian mineral is augite, forming fresh subhedral phenocrysts (S 44174, 44757) or pseudo-morphs in chloritic minerals (S 39955, 45288, 45289). Other ragged pseudomorphs in bastite and iron ore appear to have replaced orthopyroxene and some of these are rimmed with fresh augite (S 44174). Ore-rimmed pseudomorphs after olivine are less common (S 45017). The groundmass consists of plagioclase, granular pyroxene and octahedral iron ore in a glassy, and in some instances chloritized, residuum. In the analysed rock (S 45164; Anal. XIII, Table 3) there is also a fair amount of interstitial and amygdaloidal material with a moderately high birefringence and a refractive index below that of balsam; this may be one of the saponite minerals. A little quartz may be present but it is not clear what proportion of this is primary. The pyroxenes of one dyke of this group are replaced by epidote and pale-green fibrous amphibole (S 45290).

The suite is closely related to the basalt minor intrusions in the Dalradian rocks north of Callander (p. 21). They also appear to be allied to some of the sub-basic intrusions of north Ayrshire (MacGregor *in* Richey and others 1930, p. 31) and to the somewhat coarser rocks described as hypersthene-dolerite and quartz-dolerite in the Dundee area (Harris 1928a, pp. 59–68). Analyses are given in Table 3 (Anals. XII, XIII, T).

Andesite. The pyroxene-andesite dykes closely resemble the pyroxene-andesite lavas and call for little individual description. They contain phenocrysts of labradorite zoned to andesine, some of which are chloritized, with pseudomorphs after ortho-pyroxene and clinopyroxene in green minerals and carbonate respectively. The ground-mass consists of andesine laths, in some cases fluxioned, with a little quartz and micro-phyric apatite. Examples from the Blairlogie district are S 40176 and S 40181: others, farther north, are S 44743 (Glenwinnel Burn), S 44202 (Birken Glen) and S 44783 (Frandy Burn). The sill in Yellowcraig Wood (S 40180) and one of the bosses above Blairlogie (S 40174) are similar, but another boss (S 40182) consists of a coarse-grained grey rock containing phenocrysts of labradorite (3·0 mm), hypersthene partly altered to bowlingite (1·0 mm) and fresh augite (0·75 mm) in a groundmass comprising laths of andesine zoned to albite, granular augite, octahedral ore, interstitial quartz, acicular apatite and brownish microlitic residuum.

An intrusion of pyroxene-andesite requiring special mention is the strikingly fresh rock forming a sill west of Dumyat (pp. 41–2). A detailed description by Flett (1897) lists phenocrysts of fresh labradorite, hypersthene and augite set in a glassy base (S 7146, 9078, 31755, 36030–4, 45150; Plate II, fig. 4). Brown, more decomposed varieties of the rock in which the labradorite is albitized and the pyroxenes altered to bastite and chlorite are represented by S 44732–3 and S 45286. The groundmass in these is slightly more devitrified and the flow structure of the feldspar microlites more prominent than is the case in the black marginally chilled rocks to which Flett's description relates. As recognized by Flett, the rock is very similar to the pitchstone-andesites of the Cheviots, though the latter are all described as lavas (Teall 1883, pp. 102–7; Barrow *in* Carruthers and others 1932, pp. 12–4). A new analysis has been made to supplement Flett's petrographic description and it is quoted in Table 3 (Anal. X) with comparative analyses of one of the Cheviot rocks (Anal. Q) and one of a similar rock from Dundee (Anal. R). The analysis shows a higher percentage of silica than is normal in pyroxene-andesites and indicates that the glassy residuum is acid in character.

The wide hornblende-andesite dyke in the Glendevon area (p. 39) differs from the local lavas only in being somewhat coarser at the centre. Under the microscope (S 44951) it is seen to contain phenocrysts of pinkish albitized plagioclase 0·5 to 1·5 mm long with ore-rimmed euhedral hornblende (up to 1·5 mm), pleochroic from straw-yellow to greenish-brown, set in a finely granular groundmass of acid plagioclase with a little quartz, interstitial green minerals and aggregates of finely divided iron ores.

Porphyrite. The porphyrites are grey, green, purple or pink and tend to be paler in more acid varieties, though the latter cannot be certainly identified without microscopic examination. Plagioclase is usually turbid and altered in porphyritic and fluxioned groundmass laths. The main ferromagnesian pseudomorphs are after hornblende but those after pyroxenes becomes more abundant in the basic varieties of porphyrite (S 44158, 44192, 44764). The analysed rock (S 45152; Anal. VII, Table 3) contains phenocrysts of turbid altered plagioclase (2·0 mm) and sparse microphyric pseudomorphs in carbonate after clinopyroxene (0·5 mm) set in a groundmass of fluxioned, cloudy pink acid plagioclase, octahedral iron ore, carbonate and chloritic material, the last of which, together with traces of quartz, may be hydrothermal.

Other typical examples are S 39435, 44163, 44182, 44748, 44755, 44763 and 44936.

Acid porphyrite. In the acid porphyrites plagioclase forms turbid, albitized phenocrysts up to 3 mm in diameter and these are seriate (S 44171) or glomeroporphyritic (S 44736, 44741, 44758). Pinker, more turbid rims in some rocks (S 44758) appear to be alkali-feldspar. Elongated phenocrysts of hornblende are pseudomorphed in carbonate and ore (S 44183) or carbonate and viriditic minerals (S 44961, 45279) and these may also replace pyroxene (S 44199, 44741, 44754, 44758). In most specimens the groundmass consists of fluxioned laths of altered turbid plagioclase with iron ores and interstitial carbonate and chloritic material (S 44171, 44736) and accessory apatite. Quartz forms small aggregates, in some cases associated with chloritic minerals, and it is difficult to assess how much of it is primary. It is more certainly primary where it is interstitial and particularly where micropoikilitic (S 44742, 44758). Amygdales consist of carbonate rimmed with 'green earths' (S 44736) or with spherulitic penninite (S 44199).

The analysed acid porphyrite (Anal. VI, Table 3), from a dyke in the Burn of Sorrow, contains rare quartz phenocrysts. Some of the quartz, corroded and mantled by felted laths of turbid alkali-feldspar, is probably primary, but other ragged patches may be secondary. In addition the rock contains phenocrysts of turbid acid plagioclase rimmed with pink potash-feldspar, biotite and hornblende pseudomorphed in carbonate, set in a groundmass of pink felted turbid feldspar laths with a little quartz, iron ore and accessory clear apatite. Aggregates of spherulitic penninite are also seen. A second specimen from the same dyke (S 44186) incorporates a xenolith 10 mm in diameter of greenish altered andesite containing euhedral pseudomorphs in iron ore after hornblende, and much viriditic material, some of which may have replaced pyroxene.

The large sill at Blairlogie and Dumyat (p. 41) is grouped with the acid porphyrites, but differs from the dyke rocks in texture. It has a cryptocrystalline to felsitic matrix of pink turbid alkali-feldspar intergrown with micropoikilitic quartz (S 7142, 40332,

46083) enclosing phenocrysts of corroded, albitized plagioclase with dark reaction rims, resorbed hornblende and, less commonly, microphyric bastite after orthopyroxene. At one locality specimens (S 7143, 46083) contain abundant subhedral grains of zircon associated with the iron ore. Some patchy pink and grey rocks (S 7142, 40178) have a fragmental aspect which tends to confirm the impression of marginal brecciation gained in the field (p. 41). The rock is similar to the analysed rhyolite from the Pentland Hills (Anal. M, Table 3) but is finer in grain.

Plagiophyre. The rocks here described as plagiophyre (S 44175, 44176, 44740) are pink to purplish-grey and non-porphyritic, and compare well with specimens in Geological Survey Collections described by MacGregor (1939, p. 101). They consist of pink turbid albitized and fluxioned laths of plagioclase, 0·2 to 0·3 mm long, with bright green chloritic minerals, some of which are nearly isotropic while others have a blue polarization. These partly pseudomorph ferromagnesian minerals, but also occur interstitially and as fillings to vesicles where they are associated with carbonate, iron ores and, in places, with a little quartz. Included in this group is a microphyric rock (S 44756) transitional to acid porphyrite.

Quartz-albite-porphyry. The main intrusion of quartz-albite-porphyry is an elongate body, partly dyke, partly chonolith, which extends for about two miles eastwards from the Westrig Burn, north of Glen Devon (p. 42). It is a buff to pink, earthy rock except at the chilled margins where it becomes green or brown and flinty. Albite and acid andesine zoned to albite are the most abundant phenocrysts (Plate III, fig. 5) and these are commonly corroded or partially replaced by carbonate. They tend to be stumpy and idiomorphic. Hornblende, the principal ferromagnesian mineral, is both euhedral and partly or wholly resorbed, being pseudomorphed in aggregates of ore with flakes of biotite. In a marginal glassy rock (S 44956) biotite occurs also, forming thick ore-rimmed flakes. Quartz occurs plentifully in the groundmass and also forms corroded phenocrysts, though in a few samples from the same intrusion these may be absent (S 44947). Some graphic intergrowths of quartz and carbonate appear to be secondary (S 44947). The groundmass texture is usually microgranular, but at the margins of the intrusion it is a brown devitrified glass having a refractive index higher than 1·54. The analysed rock (S 45166; Anal. V, Table 3) contains phenocrysts of albite and corroded quartz with pseudomorphs in ore after hornblende and microphyric brown, stumpy, striated apatite, set in a pale-brown felsitic matrix containing ragged patches of quartz with lazulites, speculites, and microlites of iron ore.

The rocks which form the chonoliths on Wether Hill and Whitewisp Hill (p. 42), and those further east in the central Ochils (Kinross (40) Sheet), are similar to the Glen Devon mass described above, as are some of the larger intrusions of the Dundee area (Harris 1928a, pp. 62–3, plate xv, fig. 4). But the rocks of some of the other chonoliths in the western Ochils, though macroscopically similar in being dull and earthy, lack quartz phenocrysts and should thus be classed perhaps with the acid porphyrites.

E.H.F.

REFERENCES

ALLAN, D. A. 1928. The geology of the Highland Border from Tayside to Noranside. *Trans. R. Soc. Edinb.*, **56**, 57–88.

—— 1940. The geology of the Highland Border from Glen Almond to Glen Artney. *Trans. R. Soc. Edinb.*, **60**, 171–93.

ANDERSON, J. G. C. 1935a. The marginal intrusions of Ben Nevis, the Coille Lianachain complex and the Ben Nevis dyke swarm. *Trans. geol. Soc. Glasg.*, **19**, 225–69.

—— 1935b. The Arrochar intrusive complex. *Geol. Mag.*, **72**, 263–83.

—— 1947. The geology of the Highland Border: Stonehaven to Arran. *Trans. R. Soc. Edinb.*, **61**, 479–515.

BAILEY, E. B. 1960. The geology of Ben Nevis and Glen Coe. 2nd edit. *Mem. geol. Surv. Gt Br.*

—— and MAUFE, H. B. 1916. The geology of Ben Nevis and Glen Coe. *Mem. geol. Surv. Gt Br.*

CAMPBELL, R. 1913. The geology of south-eastern Kincardineshire. *Trans. R. Soc. Edinb.*, **48**, 923–60.

CARRUTHERS, R. G., BURNETT, G. A. and ANDERSON, W. 1932. The geology of the Cheviot Hills. *Mem. geol. Surv. Gt Br.*

DAVIDSON, C. F. 1932. The geology of Moncreiffe Hill, Perthshire. *Geol. Mag.*, **69**, 452–64.

EWING, C. J. C. and FRANCIS, E. H. 1960. No. 3 Off-Shore Boring in the Firth of Forth (1956–1957). *Bull. geol. Surv. Gt Br.*, No. 16, 48–68.

FLETT, J. S. 1897. A hypersthene-andesite from Dumyat (Ochils). *Trans. Edinb. geol. Soc.*, **7**, 290–7.

FRANCIS, E. H. 1962. Volcanic neck emplacement and subsidence structures at Dunbar, south-east Scotland. *Trans. R. Soc. Edinb.*, **65**, 41–58.

GEIKIE, A. 1897. *The ancient volcanoes of Great Britain*, vol. 1. London.

—— 1900. The geology of central and western Fife and Kinross-shire. *Mem. geol. Surv. Gt Br.*

GUPPY, EILEEN M. 1931. Chemical analyses of igneous rocks, metamorphic rocks and minerals. *Mem. geol. Surv. Gt Br.*

—— 1956. Chemical analyses of igneous rocks, metamorphic rocks and minerals, 1931–1954. *Mem. geol. Surv. Gt Br.*

HARRIS, J. W. 1928a. The intrusive igneous rocks of the Dundee district. *Trans. Edinb. geol. Soc.*, **12**, 53–68.

—— 1928b. Notes on the extrusive rocks of the Dundee district. *Trans. Edinb. geol. Soc.*, **12**, 105–10.

HARRY, W. T. 1956. The Old Red Sandstone lavas of the western Sidlaw Hills, Perthshire. *Geol. Mag.*, **93**, 43–56.

—— 1958. The Old Red Sandstone lavas of the eastern Sidlaws. *Trans. Edinb. geol. Soc.*, **17**, 105–12.

HATCH, F. H., WELLS, A. K. and WELLS, M. K. 1949. *The petrology of the igneous rocks.* 10th edit. London.

MACGREGOR, A. G. 1939. The term 'plagiophyre'. *Bull. geol. Surv. Gt Br.*, No. 1, 99–103.

MACGREGOR, M. and MACGREGOR, A. G. 1948. The Midland Valley of Scotland. 2nd edit. *Br. reg. Geol.*

MACNAIR, P. 1908. *The geology and scenery of the Grampians and the valley of Strathmore*, vol. 2. Glasgow.

MYKURA, W. 1960. The Lower Old Red Sandstone igneous rocks of the Pentland Hills. *Bull. geol. Surv. Gt Br.*, No. 16, 131–55.

NOCKOLDS, S. R. 1941. The Garabal Hill–Glen Fyne igneous complex. *Q. Jl geol. Soc. Lond.*, **96**, 451–510.

PEACH, B. N., CLOUGH, C. T., HINXMAN, L. W., WILSON, J. S. G., CRAMPTON, C. B., MAUFE, H. B. and BAILEY, E. B. 1910. The geology of the neighbourhood of Edinburgh. 2nd edit. *Mem. geol. Surv. Gt Br.*

PIRSSON, L. V. 1915. Microscopical characters of volcanic tuffs. *Am. J. Sci.*, (4), **40**, 191–211.

READ, H. H. 1927. The western Ochil Hills. *Proc. Geol. Ass.*, **38**, 492–4.

RICHEY, J. E., ANDERSON, E. M. and MACGREGOR, A. G. 1930. The geology of north Ayrshire. *Mem. geol. Surv. Gt Br.*

ROBSON, D. A. 1948. The Old Red Sandstone volcanic suite of eastern Forfarshire. *Trans. Edinb. geol. Soc.*, **14**, 128–40.

SUMM. PROG. 1962. *Mem. geol. Surv. Summ. Prog.* for 1961.

TEALL, J. J. H. 1883. On hypersthene andesite. *Geol. Mag.*, (2), **10**, 344–8.

F

TOCHER, F. E. 1961. Microdiorite and other dykes of lower Glen Gairn, near Ballater, west Aberdeenshire. *Trans. Edinb. geol. Soc.*, **18**, 230–9.

WALKER, F. 1928. The plutonic intrusions of the Southern Uplands east of the Nith valley. *Geol. Mag.*, **65**, 153–62.

—— 1939. A quartz-diorite from Glenduckie Hill, Fife. *Geol. Mag.*, **76**, 72–6.

WENTWORTH, C. K. and WILLIAMS, H. 1932. The classification and terminology of pyroclastic rocks. *Bull. natn. Res. Coun. Wash.*, **89**, 19–53.

Chapter V

LOWER OLD RED SANDSTONE
UPPER DIVISION

INTRODUCTION

IN THE STIRLING district the upper part of the Lower Old Red Sandstone succession consists of sandstone with variable amounts of conglomerate and mudstone. These sediments crop out over most of the northern and western parts of the district and occupy in all nearly half the area covered by the one-inch map. They lie in an asymmetrical syncline which is a continuation of the *Strathmore Syncline* of Angus and Kincardineshire, and to which the same name is given in this account. The Strathmore Syncline has a steep north-western limb, a broad axial belt and a gently-dipping south-eastern limb. The north-western limit of the Lower Old Red Sandstone sediments is formed by the Highland Boundary Fault, the south-eastern by the emergence in the Ochil Hills of the underlying lavas (which are to some extent interbedded with the sediments). The southern limit of outcrop is formed partly by the Ochil Fault and partly by the uncon- formable junction with the Upper Old Red Sandstone.

Neither the top nor the base of the Lower Old Red Sandstone succession is seen within the Stirling district: the rocks below the lavas of the Ochil Hills and their presumed equivalents in the Keltie Water are not exposed and the topmost surviving beds form the core of the Strathmore Syncline with no certain evidence of an end to deposition. The Upper Old Red Sandstone follows the Lower unconformably, and the thickness of the latter removed by erosion during the break in sedimentation is unknown.

The total thickness of Lower Old Red Sandstone sediments is more than 10 000 ft on both limbs of the syncline (*see* Table 4). The successions exposed on the two limbs differ from one another and illustrate a type of lateral variation commonly found in the Lower Old Red Sandstone: the amount of conglomerate increases towards the north-west.

Previous research. The Lower Old Red Sandstone sedimentary rocks of the Stirling district have hitherto attracted little attention. Powrie (1861, p. 541), in his account of the Old Red Sandstone rocks of Forfarshire, alluded to the discovery of *Pteraspis* near Bridge of Allan. Harkness (1862) reported the occurrence of *Cephalaspis* at Wolf's Hole Quarry [NS 790981], Bridge of Allan, and Stonehill Quarry [NN 798008], Dunblane. He described the strata seen around Dunblane, Doune and Callander, and recognized most of the groups into which the succession can be divided; he also indicated that the beds lie in a syncline, and in a section across this fold he suggested a correlation which is basically similar to the one adopted here (*see* Table 4). Jack and Etheridge (1877) described some fossil plants discovered near Callander, and also added 'Geo- logical Notes on Horizon' which included a more detailed and accurate des- cription of the successions on the two limbs of the Strathmore Syncline than that of Harkness. Their correlation across the syncline is also basically similar to that now adopted by the Geological Survey. Further discoveries of plants from the same area were described by Henderson (1932). Allan (1940) described

TABLE 4

Lower Old Red Sandstone successions in the Strathmore Syncline in the Callander–Dunblane area

NORTH-WESTERN LIMB		SOUTH-EASTERN LIMB	
Uamh Bheag Conglomerate ..	400 ft		
Teith Formation	3000 ft		
Conglomerates of mixed volcanic and Highland materials..	3500 ft	Cromlix Formation	2500 ft
		Dunblane Formation	2600 ft
		Buttergask Formation	900 ft
Ruchill Formation (including Callander Craig Conglomerate)	3000 ft	Sheriffmuir Formation	1400 ft
Volcanic conglomerate with some basic lavas* ..	3000 ft	Volcanic conglomerate	0–1000 ft
Lavas of Keltie Water	1000 ft (base not seen)	Lavas of Ochil Hills	10 000 ft (base not seen)

*part of succession cut out by Highland Boundary Fault

SOUTH-WEST PERTHSHIRE CALLANDER	Feet	CENTRAL PERTHSHIRE COMRIE–CRIEFF (Allan 1940)	Feet	EAST PERTHSHIRE AND CENTRAL ANGUS DUNKELD–ALYTH–KIRRIEMUIR (Allan 1928)	Feet	SOUTH-EAST KINCARDINESHIRE HIGHLAND BORDER (Campbell 1913)	Group
Uamh Bheag Conglomerate	400	Sandstones	900	Sandstones	900	Sandstones	Strathmore
Teith Formation (mainly sandstone)	3000						
Conglomerates of mixed volcanic and Highland materials	3500	Conglomerates of mixed volcanic and Highland materials	2500	Quartzite conglomerates	1900	Conglomerates of Highland and acid volcanic materials	Garvock
Ruchill Formation, including Callander Craig Conglomerate	3000	Sandstones with suncracks and shale fragments	1700	Sandstones	1300	Sandstones with clay galls	
Volcanic conglomerates with some basic lavas*	3000	Volcanic conglomerates with some basic lavas*	3600	Volcanic conglomerates with some basic lavas	5600	Conglomerates of acid volcanic material and tuffs	Arbuthnott
Lavas of Keltie Water: basic andesites and basalts	1000	Lavas: pyroxene-andesites and olivine-basalts	600	Lavas: pyroxene-andesites	900		
		Conglomerates: mainly of Highland and mixed volcanic materials	500	Conglomerates of acid volcanic materials	2000	Conglomerates of Highland and acid volcanic materials	Crawton
		Lavas: acid andesites	1000	Lavas: acid andesites and dacites	1400	Lavas: acid andesites and dacites	
		Volcanic conglomerates	600	Lavas: biotite-andesites Conglomerates of Highland materials	2500	Conglomerates of quartzitic and volcanic materials	Dunnottar
		Lavas: olivine-basalts	200	Lavas: augite-andesites	700	Lavas: augite-andesites	
		Conglomerates of Highland and mixed volcanic materials	200			Quartzite conglomerate	

*part of succession cut out by Highland Boundary Fault

the ground immediately north of the Stirling Sheet. Recently White (1963) re-examined the ostracoderms from Wolf's Hole Quarry, and confirmed the occurrence of *Pteraspis mitchelli* Powrie, which he found particularly interesting in view of the rarity of pteraspids in Scotland. He also described from the same locality three new species of cephalaspids, *Cephalaspis scotica, Securiaspis waterstoni* and *S. caledonica.*

Classification. On the south-eastern limb of the Strathmore Syncline, the lavas which form the Ochil Hills are in many places overlain by volcanic conglomerate. The sequence above this has been subdivided into four formations each with a characteristic lithology which shows little significant variation when traced along the strike (*see* Table 4). There is generally an alternating passage between one formation and the next, and consequently the boundaries between them are not sharply defined. The lowest of these subdivisions, the *Sheriffmuir Formation*, consists mainly of grey and brown sandstones which in places interdigitate both with the lavas and the volcanic conglomerates; the thickness is about 1400 ft. These strata are succeeded by about 900 ft of mainly brownish-purple siltstones, shales and flaggy sandstones which constitute the *Buttergask Formation*. Next comes the *Dunblane Formation*, about 2600 ft thick, which is composed mainly of cross-bedded purple and brown sandstones; and finally the *Cromlix Formation*, which comprises about 2500 ft of dull reddish-purple silty mudstones.

On the north-west limb of the syncline the succession comprises three formations, two of conglomerates and an intervening one of much finer sediments. The lowest, about 3000 ft thick, is made up of volcanic conglomerates. These are overlain by, and to some extent interdigitated with, strata of the *Ruchill Formation*, which consists of some 3000 ft of interbedded purple shales and siltstones, and purple and grey flagstones. This formation has two main intercalations of conglomerate, the lower consisting of volcanic pebbles and the upper of mixed conglomerate (see below); this upper intercalation is referred to in the sequel as the *Callander Craig Conglomerate.*

The Ruchill Formation passes upwards, locally by alternation, into what are here termed 'mixed' conglomerates; these consist mainly of lava and quartz pebbles in varying proportions, with some of quartzite and other metamorphic rocks. These conglomerates pass locally into pebbly sandstone and in the Keltie valley, where they are some 3500 ft thick, they include a noteworthy lenticular band of sandstone and mudstone which dies out north-eastwards.

Much of the axial zone of the Strathmore Syncline is occupied by the *Teith Formation*, which is notably variable but consists essentially of purple, brown and grey sandstones, locally with some mudstones; the thickness is about 3000 ft. This formation overlies all the strata described above, and is in turn succeeded by the *Uamh Bheag Conglomerate*, about 400 ft thick, which forms the highest part of the Lower Old Red Sandstone sequence in the Stirling district. North-eastwards from Callander the Teith Formation is progressively replaced by conglomerate so that on Beinn Odhar the Uamh Bheag Conglomerate cannot be separated from the rest of the mixed conglomerates. This maximum of conglomerate development is doubtless responsible for the large amount of high ground stretching from Ben Clach to Uamh Bheag, which is the highest hill composed of Lower Old Red Sandstone sediments in the Midland Valley of Scotland.

The successions on the two limbs of the Strathmore Syncline cannot be equated with certainty but the correlation suggested in Table 4 is regarded as the most probable in the light of available evidence. It is based on the assumption that the base of the Teith Formation and the top of the volcanic conglomerate on each limb are at least approximately contemporaneous, and it takes into account the general similarity in lithology between the Ruchill and Buttergask formations.

Correlation with other areas. The only published correlation of the various local successions of Lower Old Red Sandstone strata on the north-west limb of the Strathmore Syncline is by Allan (1940) whose work is limited to the area north and north-east of the Stirling district. A suggested expansion of Allan's work to include this district is given in Table 5. If this is even approximately correct, it follows that the Uamh Bheag Conglomerate and much of the Teith Formation are younger than any other Lower Old Red Sandstone strata hitherto described in the Strathmore Syncline. It is not yet practicable to link up along the south-east limb of the syncline with the succession established in the Stonehaven area by Campbell (1913). Too little is known about the stratigraphy in the Perth district. In Angus, Hickling's (1908) classification is based on the succession on the south-east limb of the Sidlaw Anticline.

Conditions of deposition. The Lower Old Red Sandstone sediments of the Midland Valley of Scotland, which were described by Kennedy (1958, p. 116) as the '*molasse* of the Caledonian chain', were laid down in a broad depression flanked to the north by the mountainous Highland area and to the south by high ground in what is now the Southern Uplands. The great thickness of these deposits indicates that they accumulated in a subsiding area and it is probable that the flanking uplands were periodically rejuvenated by isostatic uplift.

The importance of the Highland Border as a control upon the deposition of the Lower Old Red Sandstone has been disputed. Allan (1940, pp. 186–7) regarded it as a pivotal line separating a northern area of periodic denudation from a southern one of fairly continuous accumulation, and suggested that during the Lower Old Red Sandstone period a monoclinal fold developed along it. Allan's hypothesis was endorsed by Waterston (*in* Craig 1965, pp. 275–6) and Kennedy (1958, p. 116) expressed similar views. According to Kennedy, the Midland Valley in Lower Old Red Sandstone times was essentially a graben limited by the Highland Boundary and Southern Upland faults. He considered that sedimentation was confined to the area of the graben and that it was only in a few exceptional areas that the rocks extended across the boundary fractures. On the other hand George (1960, p. 48) maintained that the outcrop of the Highland Boundary Fault 'was indifferently transgressed' by the Lower Old Red Sandstone strata, and found supporting evidence in Allan's own descriptions of the Crieff, Blairgowrie and Kirriemuir areas. He suggested that the Lower Old Red Sandstone rocks preserved north-west of the fault may well be the remnants of a much more extensive accumulation and gave 'the Highland Boundary Fault no important place as a control on deposition of the Lower Old Red Sandstone'.

There can be no doubt that in the Strathmore Syncline there is considerable lateral variation from south-east to north-west, involving marked increase in the amount of conglomerate in that direction, whereas lateral variation is much less marked from south-west to north-east. Thus there is an extensive belt of comparatively constant stratigraphy adjacent and parallel to the Highland Boundary Fault, and abrupt changes in stratigraphy occur as the strata are traced away from the fault. Furthermore some at least of the conglomerates of the Highland Border area are so coarse that the material cannot have travelled far from its source. These lines of evidence support the conclusions of Allan and Kennedy and strongly suggest that the Highland Boundary did act as an important control on the deposition of the Lower Old Red Sandstone by forming the approximate north-western limit to the subsiding basin. There is no doubt, however, that accumulation of Lower Old Red Sandstone rocks extended for some distance into the Highland area, but it is probable that as a result of periodic uplift and denudation much of the material was subsequently stripped off and redeposited in the subsiding basin to the south-east.

The area of the Strathmore Syncline is therefore envisaged as being low ground bounded to the north-west by a mountainous tract out of which flowed powerful streams carrying large amounts of detritus. The coarser detritus was laid down near the Highland Border and the finer sediments were carried further to the south-east. The environment is regarded as having been mainly fluviatile. The conglomerates derive from fluvial gravels which may have been deposited in alluvial fans locally coalescing to form a bajada along the Highland mountain front. Many of the sandstones, particularly in the Dunblane Formation, are demonstrably channel deposits; others probably accumulated on floodplains, the intercalated mudstones being deposited in flood-basins. These sediments provide abundant evidence of intraformational erosion in the common occurrence of argillaceous and calcareous inclusions derived from penecontemporaneous break-up of beds of mudstone with concretions.

The intercalation of the fine-grained and thinly-laminated sediments of the Ruchill Formation within the Highland Border conglomerates probably marks a period of peneplanation of the source areas. No undoubted lacustrine deposits are known in the Lower Old Red Sandstone of the Stirling district but it is not improbable that some of the finer sediments of the Ruchill and Buttergask formations may have been laid down in impersistent bodies of standing water. The succeeding mixed conglomerates, with both metamorphic and volcanic detritus, attain their maximum development for the Stirling district in the Uamh Bheag area, where they replace the sandstones of the Teith Formation. It is thought probable that a major river supplying detritus from the Highlands entered the basin there. The conditions of deposition of the Cromlix Formation remain problematical. This thick accumulation of poorly-bedded and poorly-sorted silty mudstones and muddy siltstones was laid down with no recognizable discontinuities under conditions which must have remained very stable over a large area for a lengthy period, while a few miles to the north-west the mixed conglomerates were being formed.　　　I.H.F.

SOUTH-EAST LIMB OF STRATHMORE SYNCLINE

VOLCANIC CONGLOMERATES

Lenses of volcanic conglomerate composed principally of well-rounded lava pebbles are commonly present at or intercalated near the top of the lava succession on the northern side of the Ochil Hills. They vary greatly in thickness. In the area south of Cauldhame [NN 825011] where great conglomerate wedges interdigitate with the lavas, the total thickness is probably not far short of 1000 ft. Elsewhere the thickness is much less than this and in places there is no conglomerate at all below the Sheriffmuir Formation. It appears that certain lenticular conglomerate bodies fill valleys or depressions in the underlying lava surface.

DETAILS

At the western end of the Ochil Hills volcanic conglomerate crops out over wide areas. It appears in crags overlooking the Carse south of Bridge of Allan Golf Course and can be traced north-eastwards to beyond Cauldhame and Loss Hill. Between these two localities a wedge of lava splits the main conglomerate mass and increases in thickness north-eastwards, the two remaining tongues of conglomerate dying out in this direction. An intercalation of lava within the conglomerate and another lava band overlying the conglomerate can be traced between Pendreich and Cauldhame.

The northern tongue of conglomerate is exposed for half a mile upstream from the bridge [NN 827013] over the burn north-east of Cauldhame. The overlying lava crops out between the bridge and a point 200 ft downstream where a north–south fault, throwing down to the east, brings up the conglomerate into the burn again for a short distance. The lava is visible at intervals along the Wharry Burn upstream from the bend south-south-east of Lynns. North-east of Cauldhame it coalesces with the main mass of the Ochil lavas as the northern tongue of conglomerate dies out. A younger bed of volcanic conglomerate overlying the lava is exposed on the south bank [NN 818010] of the Wharry Burn near Lynns. It extends north-eastwards and is exposed south of Sheriffmuir Inn at the road bridge [NN 827016] over that burn, where it is faulted down into the underlying lava between two faults trending about north–south. The northernmost outcrop of this conglomerate is on the hillside 2000 ft east of Lairhill.

A lens of volcanic conglomerate at the base of the Sheriffmuir Formation is well exposed in the burn just east of Carim Lodge [NN 862048] and can be traced north-eastwards in the burns draining the north-west slopes of Tambeth. One of these burns, 1350 ft north-east of Carim Lodge, exposes [NN 864051] a bed of sandstone within this conglomerate.

Volcanic conglomerate crops out in the streams on the hillside south of Banheath [NN 906078] but none is exposed between here and the Danny Burn 300 ft south-east of Burnside, where a few feet of volcanic conglomerate are visible under sandstones dipping north-west at 12°. The Danny Burn conglomerate is considered to be an intercalation in the Sheriffmuir Formation and the lavas to the south are probably separated from it by an east–west fault which may also throw the basal conglomerate against the lavas south-west of Banheath.

East of Bardrill [NN 912080] volcanic conglomerate is exposed in a burn upstream from a point [NN 917083] north-east of the farm. In the eastern branch of the burn, about 300 ft south of the junction with the western branch, the conglomerate terminates to the east against a steep plane trending N. 20° W. which probably marks a fault, there being some crushing in the conglomerate a little downstream from it. For about 350 ft to the south there are outcrops of brown amygdaloidal lava in the stream and in the quarries just west of it; beyond this conglomerate reappears, and persists upstream for a further half mile: the lava is regarded as being an intercalation in the conglomerate. In the western branch of the stream, conglomerate exposures extend upstream for 1100 ft from the junction, and are succeeded to the south by exposures of brown amygdaloidal lava. The conglomerate margin here lies much further north than in the eastern branch. This may be due to irregularity in the lava floor below the conglomerate. There is, however, some evidence of faulting and it is possible that a downthrow to the east contributes to the present anomalous disposition of the conglomerate margins.

Volcanic conglomerate with included blocks up to 1 ft in diameter crops out in the small burn south-west of West Mains.

Conglomerate exposed along the burn west of Cornhill is underlain by tuffs and lavas about half a mile upstream from the road bridge [NN 944102] west-north-west of Cornhill. On the flanking hillsides the junctions of the conglomerate with the underlying lavas are considerably further north than in the burn and it is suggested that the conglomerate was deposited on an irregular lava surface, and that on the line of the burn it occupies a former valley or depression in the lava. A quarry [NN 946097] west of the burn shows conglomerate succeeded to the west by brown vesicular lava, and it is possible that the quarry exposures mark the western edge of the conglomerate infilling of the supposed valley. The conglomerate is overlain by sandstone at the base of the Sheriffmuir Formation about 100 feet south of the road bridge.

There are a few outcrops of volcanic conglomerate in the stream south of Drummondsfold. In a small stream [NN 955111] north-west of Eind, conglomerate is overlain by coarse calcareous sandstones and siltstones of the Sheriffmuir Formation. The conglomerate contains thin bands of tough calcareous sandstone, for the most part deeply weathered.

South-west of Cloanden, there are exposures, by the roadside and in a small gully [NN 960113], of volcanic conglomerate, succeeded and presumably overlain to the north by lava. The conglomerate is here intercalated in the lavas, and must die out rapidly north-eastwards for it is not seen in the Cloan Burn. In a gully 500 ft to the west volcanic conglomerate and sandstone are exposed.

The only conglomerate bed in the area east of Auchterarder is exposed in the railway cutting north-west of Pairney and on Thorny Hill [NN 973132]. It lies in the fault block between the north-north-west fault crossing the Pairney Burn west of Pairney and the west-north-west fault which passes a little to the south of Tarnavie [NN 987131]. Near the east end [NN 977136] of the railway cutting the uppermost lava of the local volcanic sequence, a trachyandesite, is overlain by conglomerate which is well exposed along the cutting to the west. The conglomerate is composed of mainly angular fragments derived from the underlying lava and has a sparse finer matrix. There is little sign of bedding except at the west end of the cutting. Similar fragmental rocks and underlying lava are exposed on Thorny Hill, notably on the south side.

SHERIFFMUIR FORMATION

The Sheriffmuir Formation is composed mainly of grey and dull brown, cross-bedded, coarse to fine-grained sandstones with subordinate shale beds. Its outcrop crosses Sheriffmuir and the formation is named from this locality although exposures here are not good.

Locally at the base of the formation the sandstones interdigitate with the highest Ochil lavas and at the top they pass up into the fine-grained flaggy sandstones, siltstones and shales of the overlying Buttergask Formation. Between Dunblane and Auchterarder the estimated thickness of the Sheriffmuir Formation varies between 1000 and 1800 ft.

The sandstones of the Sheriffmuir Formation in places contain grey calcareous inclusions, commonly associated with shale fragments and quartzitic and igneous pebbles. The calcareous inclusions probably originated as concretions in calcareous shale beds which were eroded soon after deposition, the debris being incorporated in sandy sediment. The sandstones themselves are composed chiefly of quartz and quartzose material together with microcline, untwinned alkali-feldspar, plagioclase and micas. Fragments of basic lava are locally abundant. A calcite matrix is almost always present and the clastic grains are commonly replaced by this mineral.

Details

The lava band which immediately overlies the volcanic conglomerate between Pendreich and Cauldhame is farther to the south-west separated from the conglomerate by a wedge of sandstone at the base of the Sheriffmuir Formation. This sandstone is exposed in the Cock's Burn east-south-east of Drumdruills, and also at the notable locality of Wolf's Hole Quarry [NS 790981] which has yielded *Pteraspis mitchelli* and the holotypes of *Cephalaspis scotica, Securiaspis waterstoni* and *S. caledonica* (White 1963). In the lower part of the Cock's Burn south of Drumdruills there is a section of the sandstones above the horizon of the lava, and these are again visible in Kippenrait Glen above the lava on the upthrow (west) side of the fault which crosses this glen a little east of Wharry Bridge [NS 800996]. A higher lava horizon in these sandstones is exposed just south-west of the road [NS 798998] by Kiltane Farm.   M.A.

The Sheriffmuir Formation is well exposed on Knock and Gallow hills north of Bridge of Allan, particularly in Gallowhill Quarry [NS 782988]. The strata here consist of massive grey or purplish-grey sandstones, with mudstone bands. The Allan Water section provides almost continuous exposures from Bridge of Allan to the base of the Buttergask Formation west of Kippenross House. South of the confluence of the Cock's Burn with the main stream [NS 789986] the sandstones are mostly purple in colour.
                I.H.F.

Outcrops of sandstone with pebbly bands may be traced in the Wharry Burn for over half a mile upstream from the north-north-west fault a little east of Wharry Bridge [NS 800996].

Sandstones in the upper part of the Sheriffmuir Formation have been worked in the extensive quarries [NN 797008] west of Stonehill. These strata, said by Harkness (1862, p. 254) to have yielded ostracoderm fossils, consist of cross-bedded grey and brown sandstones. A quarry [NN 809016] north-east of Stonehill shows fine-grained brown and grey sandstones with brown mudstone bands. There is here also a 3-ft band of conglomerate consisting mainly of shale pebbles with a few small, rounded calcareous inclusions.

Thin-bedded sandstones at the top of the Sheriffmuir Formation crop out on a track [NN 799013] east of Dykedale and beside Sheriffmuir Reservoir [NN 808818].

Sandstones are well exposed in a quarry [NN 815015] north of Lynns and form small outcrops on the moorland extending northwards from Sheriffmuir Inn.

Red shales with calcareous nodules are exposed in a small burn [NN 840028] a little to the north of an outcrop of volcanic conglomerate on the hillside 2500 ft east of Lairhill. Red shales are also exposed in the lower part of the same burn just before it falls into the Wharry Burn.

Grey, cross-bedded calcareous sandstone near the top of the Sheriffmuir Formation crops out in Geordie's Burn, south-west of Head-dykes, and in old quarries nearby [NN 836047]. The sandstone contains quartz, jasper, lava and siltstone pebbles as well as grey and brown calcareous inclusions.

In the Millstone Burn south-east of Harperstone [NN 842043] there is no volcanic conglomerate and the Ochil lavas are succeeded downstream by mainly arenaceous strata at the base of which are red shales with calcareous nodules. Some 1900 ft north-north-east of Harperstone medium-grained and coarse sandstones exposed in the stream are succeeded to the north by tough grey and brown siltstones of the Buttergask Formation.

Red shales with calcareous nodules crop out in the burn west of the ruins of Carim Lodge. Overlying sandstones appear to the north along the Buttergask Burn as far downstream as Balgower, where they are faulted against finer-grained rocks of the Buttergask Formation.

Red shales with calcareous nodules occur among the strata a little above the volcanic conglomerate in the upper part of the Burn of Ogilvie by Carim Lodge, and further downstream there are numerous outcrops of sandstone dipping north-westwards. A lava intercalation in the sandstones is exposed in a small burn [NN 862054] and on the hillsides north-east of Cockplea. In a few places, as in an old quarry [NN 878073] on the south-east bank, the sandstone contains cross-bedded units full of calcareous and shaly inclusions. Grey, brown and yellow sandstones typical of the Sheriffmuir Formation are exposed both upstream and downstream from the road bridge [NN 891085] south-west of Mill of Ogilvie.

In the Danny Burn 300 ft south-east of Burnside, buff sandstones are underlain by a few feet of volcanic conglomerate which is thought to be an intercalation in the Sheriffmuir Formation and to be faulted against lava to the south. A little to the south-west of the last outcrop, sandstones containing pebbles dip at 12° north-west-wards and presumably also overlie the conglomerate. Downstream to Wauk Mill, at higher horizons, grey and brown sandstones with pebbles and grey calcareous (locally septarian) inclusions are exposed in a few places.

There are a few outcrops of north-westerly-dipping grey-brown cross-bedded sand-stones in the two small burns between Kinpauch and Drumhead.

Sandstone is exposed in the small burn just north of Bardrill and also in the Dama-kellis Burn and its western tributary south of Damakellis [NN 908084]. Quarries [NN 908080, 908082] on the east bank of the former reveal cross-bedded brown and grey micaceous sandstone with grey calcareous and shale inclusions and other pebbles. In the quarries and in the Damakellis Burn the beds dip north-westwards at about 12° but dip more steeply in the western tributary.

Cross-bedded brown and grey sandstones with north-westerly dip appear at intervals in the bed and banks of the Ruthven Water from just east of Lochside [NN 928093], at the foot of Glen Eagles, to the confluence [NN 949123] with the Lochy Burn south of Auchterarder. The sandstones commonly contain pebbles and shaly and calcareous inclusions. Tributary streams falling into the Ruthven Water from the south-east have cut steep ravines with waterfalls, in which the soft-weathering sandstones have been eroded into smooth rounded surfaces which bear little relation to bedding or jointing. The base of the Sheriffmuir Formation is exposed in the tributary stream west of Cornhill, about 100 feet south-east of the road-bridge [NN 945102], where coarse brown sandstone with a north-westerly dip is visible resting on volcanic conglomerate.

Sandstones, dipping north-westwards, crop out in the burn west of Drummondsfold downstream from a point 750 feet south-east of the road-bridge [NN 948106]. They contain lava pebbles, quartzose and calcareous pebbles and shale fragments. A bed of sandstone 390 ft south-east of the bridge contains many grey calcareous inclusions and another, 150 ft south-east of the bridge, is full of fragments of brown to grey laminated calcareous siltstone. North-west of the road-bridge the stream falls steeply into the valley of the Ruthven Water, and shows good exposures of brown sandstones cut by a dolerite dyke.

In the Ruthven Water west of Drummondsfold, almost opposite the foot of a tributary gully from the south [NN 944105], the sandstones contain a calcareous siltstone band 4 in thick, with calcareous nodules and lenses.

Siltstone and coarse sandstones at the base of the Sheriffmuir Formation overlie volcanic conglomerate in a small stream [NN 955111] north-west of Eind. Possible evidence of interdigitation of sediments and lavas at the base of the Sheriffmuir Formation is provided by a bed of brown calcareous rock with included lava fragments which forms a small crag [NN 962117] north-west of Cloanden. It apparently dips north-westwards at 28° and presumably lies stratigraphically beneath the lavas in the burn a short distance to the north.

In the large quarry [NN 938122] south-west of Auchterarder, buff and grey well-laminated sandstones with purplish bands contain a few shaly and micaceous layers. These rocks are near the top of the Sheriffmuir Formation. In the north-east corner of the quarry a one-foot layer of tough grey calcareous sandstone with many brown shale inclusions rests on siltstone. This calcareous band is very similar to one in the Buttergask Formation of the Millstone Burn which has yielded a fish fragment. The rocks in the quarry are intermediate in character between typical Sheriffmuir and typical Buttergask strata and exemplify the zone of transition between the two formations.

Coarse-grained sandstones are exposed in an old quarry [NN 964123] south-west of Coul and in the stream just to the west, with similar, somewhat higher, beds visible just south of the railway bridge west of Coul.

West of Pairney, sandstones are seen in the Pairney Burn east of the railway bridge [NN 969130]. They are pebbly, particularly the coarse band whose top crops out 450 feet east of the bridge. The sandstones are bounded to the east by the north-north-west fault which crosses the burn, unexposed, about 1000 feet east of the bridge, and which throws them down against agate-bearing lava exposed in the burn [NN 972131] just east of the presumed position of the fault. North of the bend in the Pairney Burn by the railway bridge grey and brown cross-bedded sandstones, in places coarse-grained and containing pebbles, crop out in the west bank, dipping north-west at 12°.

Medium- and coarse-grained, cross-bedded brown and grey sandstones with included shale fragments and quartz pebbles are exposed in the Ruthven Water on the bend by Nether Coul and at intervals for a little over half a mile downstream. About 1500 feet east of Nether Coul, a grey band in the sandstone cropping out on the south-east bank [NN 968138] has yielded carbonaceous plant impressions. In old quarries [NN 972143] on the north side of the stream, cross-bedded sandstones show a curious minute green mottling not known elsewhere in the area. At the eastern edge of the easternmost quarry a few feet of thin-bedded, grey calcareous micaceous sandstone and brown shale containing limestone nodules are disturbed by small faults, trending about north-east and probably throwing down to the north-west.

Coarse sandstone referable to the Sheriffmuir Formation is exposed in a largely overgrown quarry 500 feet south-east of Millhaugh.

BUTTERGASK FORMATION

The Buttergask Formation comprises an assemblage of dull grey and brown fine-grained sandstones, siltstones and shales which are readily distinguished in the field from the much coarser strata of the contiguous Sheriffmuir and Dunblane formations. The fine sandstones are generally calcareous and typically show micro-cross-lamination and ripple-marked bedding planes. In composition they resemble the sandstones of the Sheriffmuir Formation, with quartz, alkali-feldspars, plagioclase and micaceous minerals. Lava fragments, however, are inconspicuous or absent.

The formation attains a maximum thickness of about 900 ft. It is well exposed in the Buttergask Burn, the type locality, in the Millstone Burn south of Greenloaning and in the Allan Water south of Dunblane. It thins southwards and this is reflected in the narrowness of the outcrop south of Dunblane. North-east of Auchterarder a few intercalations of coarser sandstone with pebbles appear. A fragment of fish-bone was found in the strata exposed in the Millstone Burn (p. 76).

The strata of the Buttergask Formation in certain respects resemble those of the Ruchill Formation of the Highland Border, although the latter are in general somewhat coarser. The general stratigraphical equivalence of the two formations is probable and this is implied on the one-inch map where both carry the same symbol.   M.A.

DETAILS

Strata referable to the Buttergask Formation were not encountered in any of the Geological Survey (Stirling) bores nor were they recognized in the exposures in and near the River Forth around Drip Bridge. The outcrop has therefore been drawn west of these exposures and some distance east of No. 2 (Westwood Lane) Bore. It extends from there to the rather poor exposures in the back-feature of the post-Glacial raised beach south-east of Keir House. Thence the outcrop runs north-north-eastwards through almost unexposed ground to the exposures in the Allan Water immediately south of Dunblane, where sandstones, usually flaggy and silty, and silty mudstones, generally purple or purplish-red in colour, are well displayed. A good exposure of similar strata is seen at the north end [NN 783004] of the railway tunnel at Kippenross. Purple and grey micaceous flaggy sandstone is exposed in a small stream west of Dyke-dale [NN 798014], and a short distance to the north-east, in the Rylands Burn and one of its tributaries, there are sections of flaggy micaceous sandstones, mudstones and silty shales, usually purple but in places dark brown or grey.   I.H.F.

On Sheriffmuir one of the few available exposures is in a disused dolerite quarry [NN 814029] which has metamorphosed micaceous sandstone and siltstone in its walls. An unnamed stream [NN 824036], about three-quarters of a mile further north-east, provides a good section of the typical fine-grained sandstones and siltstones of the Buttergask Formation.

In Geordie's Burn north-west of Head-dykes [NN 837047] there are good exposures of tough, fine-grained flaggy sandstones, commonly calcareous, with interbedded siltstones and shales, dipping to the north-west at about 20°. Tough greyish-brown, fine-grained flaggy sandstones with bands of siltstone and shale, dipping to the north-west, are exposed in a disused quarry by the roadside east of Quoigs House and in the Millstone Burn [NN 843048–838066], where there is an almost complete section through the Buttergask Formation. A fragment of fish bone has been obtained from a lens, up to 1 ft 8 in thick, of tough calcareous sandstone, full of brown calcareous fragments, beside the stream 2000 ft S.S.W. of Greenhill. In the Blueton Burn immedi-ately east of Williamsfield [NN 852074] there are exposures of grey and purplish-brown, fine-grained flaggy sandstones and siltstones.

There is a good section of brown and grey, fine-grained, thinly-bedded sandstones, siltstones and shales, dipping to the north-west at about 20°, along the Buttergask Burn north-eastwards from Balgower [NN 868075].

North-east of the Buttergask Burn section, the Buttergask Formation is largely concealed by drift and the infrequent exposures are mainly in disused quarries. In one of these [NN 916112], by the stream south of Gleneagles Hotel, brown, micaceous very fine-grained sandstone is exposed. Two others, east and west of the road immedi-ately north of Tullibardine Cottage [NN 921118], are in greyish-brown, fine- to medium-grained sandstone with fine lamination; in the western one interbedded shale layers up to 1 ft thick can be seen low down in the north-east corner.

In an old quarry [NN 930128] east of Easthill, grey ripple-marked micaceous sand-stone is cut by tholeiitic veins. Brown sandstones with occasional pebbles appear in a stream between Castleton [NN 937133] and West Kirkton, and a bed of brown shale, at least 2 ft 6 in thick, is exposed in the same stream, 500 ft E.N.E. of Castleton. Buff sandstones crop out on a low ridge 250 yd south-east of West Kirkton.   M.A.

DUNBLANE FORMATION

The Dunblane Formation consists largely of the purple and brown, massive cross-bedded sandstones which are generally regarded as typical of the Lower Old Red Sandstone of the Midland Valley of Scotland. The thickness of the formation is about 2500 ft, and does not show a great deal of variation along the outcrop. The latter stretches from Craigarnhall and Keir by Dunblane, Ashfield, Greenloaning and Braco, to near Auchterarder. It forms a broad north-easterly-trending belt, complicated a little by faulting near Kinbuck and

Braco, and expanding slightly towards the north-east as the north-westerly dips of about 25° near Dunblane decrease to about 15°.

The best natural sections are in the cliffs near Craigarnhall; in the Allan Water at Dunblane, at Ashfield, and at Kinbuck; in the Millstone Burn at Greenloaning and in the River Knaik north of Braco. Sandstones of the Dunblane Formation were formerly wrought for building stone, and most of the quarries are still open and provide useful sections.

The sandstones are mostly fine- to medium-grained and well sorted. Pebbly sandstones and fine conglomerates have been recorded but are rare. Films of hematite round the grains have been noted in some slices. After quartz, the most abundant and widespread minerals are plagioclase, untwinned alkali-feldspar, microcline and muscovite, with biotite somewhat less abundant. Fine mosaics of quartz are also of frequent occurrence, but fragments of basic lavas and of schists are rare. Near the top of the formation north-west of Braco, however, there are some medium- to coarse-grained, rather poorly sorted sandstones which contain abundant lava grains.

The sandstones commonly occur in beds several feet thick, separated by generally much thinner bands of purple mudstone; many of the latter are more or less disrupted and fragments of mudstone are incorporated in the overlying sandstone.

The sandstones of the Dunblane Formation usually have a carbonate matrix, which is locally abundant, but only rarely does the carbonate become sufficiently abundant to justify the term 'cornstone' being applied. Fine-grained argillaceous and highly calcareous nodules and nodular ribs, purple or grey in colour, are locally found. The former occur particularly among fragments of disrupted mudstone near the base of a sandstone bed, but only one instance of a discrete bed of cornstone has been recorded (see p. 78).

Details

Some 80 ft of strata referred to the Dunblane Formation were encountered in Geological Survey Stirling No. 2 Bore (Westwood Lane). They consisted of sandstones, generally pale, dull purple in colour, with abundant mudstone fragments and a few thin mudstone bands.

The southernmost natural exposures of the Dunblane Formation occur in the cliffs [NS 752982–761982] which form the back-feature of the post-Glacial raised beach. These exposures constitute the most complete section of the upper part of the formation. The cliffs reach 40 ft in height and extend continuously eastwards for more than half a mile from the junction with the overlying Cromlix Formation. The dip is about 20° to slightly north of west, and about 1000 ft of strata are exposed, consisting mostly of purple cross-bedded sandstones. They include some mudstone bands, mainly thin, but locally as much as 10 ft thick. The lower parts of many of the sandstone beds are full of mudstone fragments, as a result of contemporaneous erosion of the preceding mudstone band. Some of the mudstones are calcareous and one or two include thin ribs of very argillaceous limestone. The lower part of the Dunblane Formation is not so well exposed in these cliffs, but where seen is generally similar. Purple sandstones are also seen in the Glen Burn [NS 764984].

Between these cliffs and the Allan Water at Dunblane, the Dunblane Formation is visible in a number of scattered exposures, mostly in disused quarries. The strata consist mainly of purple or chocolate sandstones, commonly cross-bedded. In one such quarry, 300 yd east of Greenyards [NN 761012], the sandstone is coarse-grained and contains pebbles.

The exposures in the Allan Water at Dunblane extend almost continuously for 500 yd and comprise the type section of the formation. The strata dip north-westwards at 20° to 25° and are mostly purple cross-bedded sandstones, with thin mudstone bands. The latter have usually been disrupted to some extent by the currents that brought in the overlying sandstones, which commonly contain near their bases small flat pellets of mudstone. The sandstones also contain pebbles of purple, argillaceous, fine-grained limestone probably derived from nodules in these mudstones. At the bend in the Allan Water by Auchinlay Cottage [NN 775019] a band of conglomerate is exposed. The basal beds are not seen in the Allan Water but form a small exposure of similar chocolate and purple sandstones in a ditch near Kippendavie Lodge [NN 794023].

The lower part of the Dunblane Formation, dipping north-west at about 25°, is seen in a number of streamlets and disused quarries about a mile N.E. of Barbush [NN 784024], where it consists of purple and chocolate sandstones, generally silty and flaggy, interbedded with some siltstone and mudstone.

The section in the Allan Water resumes west of Barbush and continues almost without interruption to Ashfield [NN 785039], exposing strata in the middle and upper parts of the formation. Similar strata are exposed locally in the nearby railway cuttings. They consist mostly of purple sandstone with occasional pebbly bands, and also bands of mudstone, commonly to some extent disrupted into pellets. About half a mile north of Barbush there is a disused quarry [NN 785032] where the effects of the intrusion of a quartz-dolerite dyke on the sandstones can be observed. As the dyke is approached the latter become hardened to a massive reddish-grey quartzitic sandstone and near the contact to a dark-grey quartzite.

The topmost beds of the Dunblane Formation are poorly exposed north-west of Dunblane in two small streams north-west of Lower Auchinlay [NN 776025] and in a disused quarry half a mile to the west. They consist of purple and brown flaggy sandstones with pebbly bands, and also some mudstones and sandy mudstones. They are, however, much better exposed in the Allan Water from Kinbuck village to Kinbuck bridge [NN 792054]. Here the alternation of purple flaggy sandstones with siltstones and mudstones, and the increase in amount of the latter towards the junction with the Cromlix Formation, are well displayed, in beds dipping W.N.W. at 16° to 20°. Apart from an old quarry [NN 793044] in purple sandstones, locally silty and pebble-bearing, the Dunblane Formation is very poorly exposed in the vicinity of Glassingall.

In a small gully [NN 807055] 1650 yd north-east of Kinbuck Station, the following section was noted:

	ft	in
Pebble bed, hard	2	0
Coarse-grained sandstone		6
Silty sandstone		2
Sandstone, hard, coarse-grained, with a few pebbles	1	3
Pebble bed, with pebbles of lava, felsite, quartz and quartzite ..	1	3
Cornstone (base not exposed)	1	6

There appears to be a small break in the continuity of sedimentation above the cornstone. Exposures in the vicinity are few and neither the cornstone nor the pebbly beds, which themselves are a most unusual lithology for the Dunblane Formation, are seen anywhere else. They lie near the top of the sequence.

The cornstone is a very hard, massive rock which weathers to a cream colour. The lower and middle parts are generally sandy and locally pass into highly calcareous sandstone. They are cut by a few fawn-coloured bands up to 0·2 in thick, and are overlain by a 3-inch pseudo-brecciated band, pale pink in colour. A 1½-inch band of pale-grey calcareous mudstone with scattered sand grains follows. The top band, 3 inches thick, is another pseudo-brecciated layer similar to the lower one, but generally fawn in colour and crossed by a horizontal band of finely laminated carbonate which has developed locally in concentric fashion round nuclei.

Microscopic examination shows that the sand grains are mostly between 0·1 and 0·5 mm in diameter. They include, in addition to abundant quartz, alkali-feldspar, muscovite, biotite, microcline, plagioclase, and also rare fragments of schist. The grains are often markedly angular, with ragged edges. Contacts with the matrix are generally sharp, but locally are very ill-defined. These features suggest replacement of the silica or silicate by carbonate, and this is confirmed by the occurrence of grains, particularly of biotite, which show partial replacement, and of pseudomorphs of grains now entirely composed of carbonate. This process has been discussed by Walker (1957, p. 267; 1956, p. 1828), who regarded it as more common and significant than is generally suspected, by Carozzi (1960, pp. 39–43) and also by Burgess (1961) who described similar phenomena in cornstones of Upper Old Red Sandstone age in Ayrshire.

The matrix of the sandy parts, the 1½-inch band of calcareous mudstone and the 'fragments' in the pseudo-brecciated bands all consist of turbid brown, microcrystalline carbonate. The 'matrix' in the pseudo-brecciated bands consists of recrystallized, clear macrocrystalline carbonate, which also occurs locally in the sandy parts. Between the two types of carbonate there is generally a thin rim of crystals intermediate in size, showing that the recrystallization took place in two stages. A similar rim surrounds some of the detrital grains. At the base of one of the fawn-coloured bands a series of thin laminae of microcrystalline carbonate similar to that noted near the top of the cornstone was observed. The latter is also affected locally by the recrystallization.

I.H.F.

Cross-bedded brownish sandstones and subordinate shaly beds of the Dunblane Formation are well exposed dipping west-north-west at about 20° in the burns draining north-westwards into the Allan Water south of Greenloaning. The sandstones contain pebbles and the characteristic calcareous inclusions. The base of the Dunblane Formation crosses Geordie's Burn north of Langbank. In the Millstone Burn it lies about 200 yd south of Dam of Quoigs, to the north of which typical brown sandstones with calcareous inclusions are exposed in the burn as far as Greenloaning Station.

Brown sandstones with included pebbles and shale fragments crop out in the Feddal Burn about Feddal House, in a small stream in a plantation to the south [NN 821082], and in the Bullie Burn north of Bridge of Keir [NN 833095]. In the last-mentioned stream, 1200 feet south of Nether Braco, the uppermost horizon seen, a grey calcareous sandstone, is brought against siltstones of the Cromlix Formation by a north-westerly fault.

This fault probably crosses the Bullie Burn again south-south-east of Braco Castle, and south-west of its probable position brownish sandstones, some coarse-grained with shaly and calcareous inclusions, are visible in the burn. Strata near the top of the Dunblane Formation are exposed farther upstream and in a disused quarry south-east of Blairmore; in the latter dull purplish and grey finely-laminated sandstones, containing shaly layers with associated mudcracks, dip W.N.W. at 6°.

North-westwardly-dipping sandstones in the River Knaik north of Braco are succeeded upstream by mudstones of the Cromlix Formation a little west of Mill of Ardoch. The top of the Dunblane Formation north-east of the river may be traced through the quarry [NN 842116] formerly worked for dolerite east-north-east of Over Ardoch, in which the sandstones and siltstones are metamorphosed. The small outcrops around the road junction south-west of Garrick show sandstones, succeeded by mudstones to the north-west. A similar change was visible in a trench section cut near the road west of Garrick in 1959. Metamorphosed sandstone is exposed in quarries [NN 849117 and 852117] opened for dolerite south of Garrick.

The above-mentioned sandstones in the River Knaik and in the ground to the north-east are commonly coarse-grained, with silty layers, and are dull brown and grey in colour. They appear in general to be poorly sorted, and are locally calcareous, although the calcareous inclusions so common lower down in the Dunblane Formation are inconspicuous here.

G

Over the heavily drift-covered area in Strathallan east of Braco there are a few small exposures of brown sandstone, occasionally with pebbles, e.g. in the old quarry and stream south-east of Redford, in the stream (Orchill Den) east of Berrydyke, in the old quarry [NN 873119] east of Orchill and in a small burn [NN 869123] north of Orchill.

Cross-bedded sandstones near the base of the formation are exposed in the Piner Burn south of Monkscroft where the easternmost outcrop [NN 938145] includes siltstone partings showing transition down into the Buttergask Formation.

Brown cross-bedded sandstones are exposed in the burn flowing through the wood south of the chapel near West Mains of Tullibardine. Metamorphosed sandstone is seen in the two dolerite quarries east of the chapel, and in the north wall of the eastern one [NN 915134] the strata dip north-west at angles of 14° to 18°.

Grey and brown sandstones crop out in the Sawmill Burn west of Tullibardine Mill. West of Monkscroft an old quarry [NN 928147] shows sandstone with barytes veinlets, and sandstone is also exposed in the burn to the north.

Strata referable to the Dunblane Formation crop out in the Buchany Burn east of Westpark and also upstream in the West Slack, its continuation south-west of the Crieff–Glen Eagles road. The sandstones in this neighbourhood are markedly cross-bedded. They contain shale fragments and occasional grey septarian calcareous inclusions, some of which weather to a red colour. Similar rocks crop out in the Buchany Burn south-west of Brackenhill and north of the railway.

An old quarry [NN 889138] by the ruin of Lucas is cut into dull brown and grey sandstones which are also seen in a small burn to the south-west. The Lucas Burn flows under the Crieff–Glen Eagles road close by and downstream from the road-bridge there are outcrops of sandstone, locally pebbly and usually coarse-grained, with north-westerly dip. These outcrops, which are of strata high in the Dunblane Formation, persist downstream to near Farmton Muir.   M.A.

CROMLIX FORMATION

The Cromlix Formation takes its name from Cromlix House [NN 782061], 3 miles north of Dunblane, which is situated in the middle of the outcrop and near a number of exposures. The formation is about 2500 ft thick between Doune and Dunblane but thins northwards to 800 ft north of Braco. It consists almost entirely of silty and sandy mudstones which pass locally into argillaceous siltstones. (For the sake of brevity the unqualified term 'mudstone' is generally used in this account.) These rocks present a strikingly uniform appearance and have a characteristic tendency to weather to a cuboidal rubble. In colour they range from dull brownish-red through maroon to purplish-brown. Bedding is very poorly developed except in the occasional shaly or sandy bands, the latter in many places forming hard ribs. In the absence of such bands, the dip of the mudstones may be difficult to determine. At the upper and lower boundaries of the Cromlix Formation the mudstones are interdigitated with the sandstones, usually flaggy and argillaceous, of the Teith and Dunblane formations respectively. In its typical development the Cromlix Formation is seen only on the south-eastern limb of the Strathmore Syncline, but a group of sandstones and mudstones, brown, purple or red in colour, which separates the A'Chrannach and Bracklinn Falls conglomerates north-east and south-west of Callander (Fig. 9), is tentatively regarded as the equivalent, on the north-western limb, of the lower part of the formation.

The outcrop of the Cromlix Formation forms a broad band about 1½ miles wide, extending in a north-north-easterly direction from near Gargunnock (where the formation was proved in Geological Survey Stirling Bore No. 3), across the Carse of Stirling, past Row [NS 742994] and Craigarnhall [NS 753986], to Kilbryde Castle [NN 756037] and Cromlix itself. North-east of Cromlix the continuity of the outcrop is broken by faulting, but it resumes again on the eastern slopes of Feddal Hill and across the Bullie Burn. It is again affected by faulting near Braco Castle and the River Knaik, beyond which it extends north-eastwards to the northern limit of the district. The mudstones are on the whole well exposed despite their generally soft and crumbling nature. Particularly good sections occur in the cliffs between Row and Craigarnhall and in the Ardoch Burn, and there are good exposures in the Muckle and Bullie burns and the River Knaik.

Several slices of the mudstones from the Cromlix Formation were examined by Mr. R. W. Elliot, who reports that the rocks are ferruginous and generally calcareous mudstones or muddy siltstones. The detrital material, whose abundance within any one slice is variable, is generally in the silt and very fine sand grades but includes a little coarser sand. The rocks are therefore not well sorted. Some evidence of replacement of feldspar grains by calcite was found. The detrital grains include quartz, feldspar (orthoclase, microcline.and plagioclase were all noted), rhyolite, an intermediate igneous rock and schist. Abundant flakes of mica are generally present, mainly muscovite with subordinate biotite and chlorite.

DETAILS

All the solid rocks encountered in Geological Survey Stirling No. 3 Bore (Low Wood) belong to the Cromlix Formation. The borehole pierced 78 ft of fine sandy and silty mudstones typical of the formation except that near rockhead they are somewhat redder in colour than is usual.

The most southerly natural exposures of the Cromlix Formation occur on a knoll 150 yd S.S.W. of Nyadd [NS 742974] where interbedded fine-grained flaggy sandstones and sandy mudstones, reddish-brown in colour, dip to the W.N.W. at 20° to 30°. In the cliffs between Row and Craigarnhall the lower part of the formation and its downward passage into the Dunblane Formation are very well displayed. Dips to slightly north of west varying between 20° and 24° have been noted. Mudstones are also laid bare in the stream by Easter Row [NS 751993], on the slopes above Greystone [NS 742998] and in a small stream which joins the River Teith [NN 736002] south of Inverardoch Mains.

The upper part of the Cromlix Formation is well exposed in the Ardoch Burn between Longbank [NN 736014] and Glenhead Cottage [NN 750014], where the presence of a number of sandstone bands was noted. The dip is about 20°, varying in direction from west to west-north-west. Above a sharp bend [NN 755016] in the Ardoch Burn the upper part of the Cromlix Formation is again revealed in a series of fine and almost unbroken exposures, with cliffs up to 50 ft high near Torrance and Kilbryde Castle. The strata dip to W.N.W. at between 15° and 20°. The upward passage into sandstones of the Teith Formation is clearly displayed. The mudstones are also well exposed in the Grainston Burn south of Nether Grainston [NN 758033]. The lower part of the Cromlix Formation is largely drift-covered in this area, but there are exposures of mudstones on the hillside about 400 yd north-east of Corsecaplie [NN 761023] and also in two small streams between there and Upper Auchenlay [NN 774032].

The next group of exposures towards the north are those round Cromlix House. Mudstone is seen in a number of places in the Lodge Burn, dipping to the W.N.W. at 10° to 15°, and in a few places in the Bracklinn Burn. Glacial drainage channels between Cromlix Lodge and Wester Cambushinnie provide a number of exposures of red and purple mudstones.

By a small stream south of Naggyfauld [NN 801054] purple and red silty mudstones of Cromlix type dip at 28° to the north-west. These exposures lie over half a mile east of the base of the formation as traced in the Lodge Burn close to its confluence with the Allan Water near Kinbuck. While it is possible that the mudstones form a very thick (at least 250 ft) intercalation in the sandstones of the Dunblane Formation, no other intercalation of this order of thickness is known. They are therefore interpreted as a downfaulted portion of the Cromlix Formation.

The upper part of the Cromlix Formation and the junction with the Teith Formation are well exposed, dipping W.N.W. at 10° to 15°, in the Muckle Burn and also in some of its tributaries around Cambushinnie [NN 790079]. Further downstream a downfaulted wedge of strata referred to the Teith Formation breaks the continuity of the outcrop of the Cromlix Formation. Strata probably referable to the latter were encountered in an old bore at Coupings Farm [NN 813077]. North of the faulted wedge of Teith strata, mudstones of the Cromlix Formation are well exposed on the southeastern slopes [NN 800090] of Feddal Hill, but there are few exposures on the northern slopes.   I.H.F.

The Bullie Burn provides an almost complete section of the Cromlix Formation, with particularly good exposures near its confluence with the Tochie Burn. The latter also provides a good section, as do other northern tributaries between it and Blairmore [NN 816106]. An intercalation of grey siltstones and shales near the base of the formation is exposed at the foot [NN 813103] of one of these tributaries. The dips in this area are generally below 10° to a little south of west.   I.H.F., M.A.

In the Bullie Burn near Nether Braco strata belonging to the Cromlix Formation are bounded to the south by the north-westerly fault, with downthrow to the north-east, which crosses the burn 1200 ft south of the farm. They are chiefly poorly-bedded mudstones containing coarse sand in places. The presence of fine-grained sandstone layers in the southernmost outcrops by the fault suggests proximity to the base of the formation.

Above Mill of Ardoch, mudstones and muddy sandstones are exposed in the bed and banks of the River Knaik for over a mile and are also seen in a number of small tributaries. Bedding is poorly developed, but a north-westerly dip of about 5° may be observed in places. The boundary between the Cromlix and Teith formations is drawn in the middle of transitional strata at the foot [NN 816122] of a ravine on the north bank.

Mudstones are exposed immediately north of Over Ardoch, and show contact alteration, with change in colour to grey, near the dolerite dyke which lies just north of the Mill Dam [NN 837116]. Towards the north-east there are occasional small outcrops of mudstone.

South-west of Muirhead [NN 853139] siltstone and mudstone dipping at low angles to the west or west-north-west crop out in the Aldonie Burn. Near Muirhead itself the burn cuts through grey and purple siltstones dipping northwards. Downstream towards Lurg siltstones and brown mudstones are exposed, and a small stream just east of Lurg shows outcrops of mudstones and silty sandstones.

Brown siltstones and muddy sandstones are exposed in the small stream east of Standingfauld, and in the stream which flows past Cairn on its north-west side brown, muddy, poorly-sorted sandstone is seen dipping N.W. at 10°. Some of these sandstones, which are near the bottom of the Cromlix Formation, are tough and calcareous.   M.A.

AXIAL REGION OF STRATHMORE SYNCLINE

TEITH FORMATION

The outcrop of the Teith Formation lies in the broad axial zone of the Strathmore Syncline and extends from Kippen in the south to the northern limit of the district, reaching a width of 7 miles between Callander and Doune. The succession consists of sandstones varying in colour from grey to purple and brown, with variable amounts of mudstone and shale, usually purple or brown in colour. In the Uamh Bheag–Ben Clach area the Teith Formation passes laterally into mixed conglomerates. Widespread lateral variation, prevalent low dips and low relief over all but the northern part of the outcrop, make it difficult to establish the full thickness and detailed order of succession of the Teith Formation. However, the maximum known thickness as developed east of Callander is at least 4000 ft, and the formation may be divided into three facies, a lower purple sandstone facies, a grey sandstone facies and an upper purple sandstone facies. All three are diachronous, and though they tend to occur in the order stated there is a considerable amount of lateral replacement of one by another. The lower purple sandstone facies consists of purple and purplish-brown sandstones with variable amounts of shale and mudstone. It forms the basal part of the Teith Formation on the south-eastern limb of the Strathmore Syncline, and on the north-western limb (Fig. 9) between Callander and Uamh Bheag where the amount of argillaceous sediment locally constitutes nearly half of the succession. The grey sandstone facies also includes subordinate mudstones and shales. It overlies the lower purple sandstone facies on the north-western limb of the syncline, and south of Callander replaces it as the basal member. On the south-eastern limb this facies is poorly represented, but occurs on Slymaback and persists as far as the Arrevore Burn. Elsewhere the two purple sandstone facies apparently come together.

The upper purple sandstone facies occurs in the axial zone of the syncline around Thornhill and Kippen and on the southern slopes of Uamh Bheag, Beinn Odhar and adjacent hills, where the sandstones are commonly coarse-grained. Rocks of this facies were encountered in Nos. 4 to 7 of the Geological Survey Stirling bores.

Exposures of the Teith Formation are largely confined to streams and a few disused quarries. The River Teith itself provides good sections of the lower purple sandstone facies between Doune and Lanrick and of the grey sandstone facies west of Drumvaich. The lower purple sandstone facies is also well exposed on the south-eastern limb and in the axial zone of the Strathmore Syncline in the Ardoch, Annet, Muckle and Arrevore burns and in the River Knaik. On the north-western limb the best exposures are in the Keltie Water, the Eas Uilleam and the Eas Fiadhaich. The grey sandstone facies is well exposed in the Sruth Geal and the Garvald Burn. There is no notable section of the upper purple sandstone facies near Thornhill, but good exposures are found in the Allt na Gaisge and the upper part of the Arrevore Burn.

Most of the sandstones in the Teith Formation are fine- to medium-grained and well-sorted except for those in the zone of transition to the conglomerates where the grain size increases and the degree of sorting decreases. A calcareous or argillaceous matrix may be present, but more commonly there is little or no cementing material. In most of the slices examined quartz grains are the most abundant constituent, followed usually by fragments of basic or intermediate lava; in a few cases the latter predominate. Muscovite, plagioclase and orthoclase come next in order of abundance, with microcline rather less common. Schist, slate and quartzite fragments are quite numerous, the last-named occurring particularly in the upper purple sandstone facies. Iron ore, chlorite, biotite, epidote and zircon all occur in small quantities in a number of slices.

DETAILS

Lower purple sandstone facies. The lowest strata in the Teith Formation east of Callander belong to the lower purple sandstone facies and consist of a series of sandstones and mudstones with some shales, generally purple or brown in colour but including some grey sandstones and red mudstones. An almost continuous section (Fig. 9) of these beds in the Brackland Glen stretch of the Keltie Water, immediately below the Bracklinn Falls, is magnificently exposed in cliffs up to 100 ft high. Good sections are also found in the Eas Uilleam and the Eas Fiadhaich. In the latter the proportion of mudstone, generally purple or red in colour, tends to increase upstream and the sandstone bands are generally grey. In the head-waters of the Brackland Burn (Allt Ruith an Eas and its tributaries) the sandstones and mudstones are intimately interbedded with pebbly sandstones and conglomerates which increase north-eastwards till most of the finer sediments are replaced.

Two bands of purple sandstone, generally coarse-grained and pebbly and containing some fine conglomerate, persist further north-east. One crops out round the north side of Meall Clachach, is well exposed on Sgiath Gorm [NN 693131] and probably dies out in Coire na Fionnarachd. The other crosses Meall Clachach, passes along the southern slopes of Coire na Fionnarachd and reaches the col [NN 708118] between Uamh Bheag and Beinn Odhar, but apparently does not persist as far as the north-west slopes of the latter, where the whole of the Teith Formation is replaced by mixed conglomerates.

Strata of the lower purple sandstone facies are 2000 ft thick in Brackland Glen, south-west of which they are not seen: there is a gap in the exposures for over a mile in this direction, beyond which the conglomerates are immediately overlain by strata of the grey sandstone facies.

On the south-eastern limb of the Strathmore Syncline strata of the lower purple sandstone facies are poorly exposed south of the River Teith. Some 15 ft of massive purple, grey and brown mottled sandstone are exposed in a disused quarry a quarter of a mile south-west of Meldrum [NS 719997], and similar strata are seen in another disused quarry 300 yd north-east of Mains of Burnbank [NS 706989]. The basal beds can be seen in the banks of the River Teith opposite Inverardoch, and in the Ardoch Burn by Doune Castle. They consist of purple sandstones, commonly flaggy and argillaceous, and purplish-red mudstones. The dip is westerly at about 25°. Above the Bridge of Teith, past Deanston, to Lanrick, there is an almost continuous section of purple sandstones with subordinate shales and mudstones. The westward dips decrease upstream from 10° to almost zero in places and the transition to the grey sandstone facies can be traced.

North of the river, exposures are almost entirely confined to the streams. The best sections are in the Annet Burn from above High Wood [NN 697064] to Milton of Cambus [NN 702044], where the top beds of the lower purple sandstone facies are seen, and in the upper Ardoch Burn downstream from Calziebohalzie [NN 724073]. In the latter section the basal beds and the transition from the Cromlix Formation are visible east of Nether Glastry [NN 748044]. The Annet Burn provides a splendid section, locally in cliffs as at Caldron Linn [NN 700049], through flat-lying purple sandstones with some shale bands. Beds of grey sandstone appear towards the northern end as the transition to the overlying grey sandstone facies begins. The Ardoch Burn section is less complete, particularly in the upper part, but it provides many exposures of purple, purplish-brown and pinkish-purple sandstones with bands of shale and mudstone. The last-mentioned increase in number down towards the junction with the Cromlix Formation. The westerly dips fall off westwards from 15° to about 5°. Small sections of similar strata are seen in the Buchany Burn [NN 712036], in the Lundie Burn [NN 716047, 718052], in a streamlet immediately west of Wester Lundie [NN 720041], and in the Argaty Burn [NN 725052–728046; 740033].

Towards the north-east the next good section of the lower purple sandstone facies is provided by the Muckle Burn [NN 772080–758083]. The section includes purple mudstones and shales, and grey and brown sandstones in addition to the purple sandstones. The strata dip to the west or west-north-west at angles of between 10° and 20°. Further down the Muckle Burn, between Altersie and Craighead, and also in the Crocket Burn, there are exposures of purple, pale-purple and purplish-brown sandstones, commonly flaggy, with some purple mudstones, which interrupt the continuity of the outcrop of the Cromlix Formation. As they resemble the lower purple sandstone facies rather than strata of the Dunblane Formation they are assigned to the Teith Formation and are interpreted as part of a downfaulted wedge. The dips in the inlier are generally normal, i.e. to the west-north-west at 10° to 15°, but in the vicinity of the line of one of the postulated faults there is a reversal of dip seen in the Crocket Burn.

Purple and brown sandstones with purple mudstones, especially towards the base, are exposed in the Bullie Burn and in the gorge through which the Tochie Burn flows to join it. On the steep northern slopes of Cromlet the sandstones become coarse-grained and carry some pebbles. They are interbedded with purple mudstones. I.H.F.

A long section, with few interruptions, through the lower purple sandstone facies of the Teith Formation is provided by the Arrevore Burn, below its confluence [NN 777126] with the Androhal Burn, and continued by the River Knaik. Purple and purplish-brown sandstones constitute most of the sequence, with bands of purple mudstone and shale common. Occasional bands of pebbly sandstone and fine conglo-merate occur, and initiate the north-westward transition from the lower purple sand-stone facies to the mixed conglomerates. A north-westerly fault cuts the section obliquely at a locality [NN 791131] east of Arrevore, where steep dips and broken strata can be seen. The same fault cuts [NN 794129] a section through generally similar strata in a tributary of the main stream, producing similar effects. The dip is less than 10° to the W.N.W. in the eastern part of the section, but swings to about 10° to the W.S.W. upstream in the Arrevore Burn. Exposures on Coire Odhar are rare, but purple and brown sandstones, generally coarse-grained, are visible in a few places, mostly in the streamlets which flow off the hill. I.H.F., M.A.

Grey sandstone facies. Grey, generally flaggy, sandstones are the dominant rock type over a considerable part of the outcrop of the Teith Formation from Braes of Greenock [NN 631054] and Lennieston Muir in the west, through Torrie Forest, past Drumloist, to the lower southern slopes of Uamh Bheag and over Slymaback as far as the Arrevore Burn. The sandstones locally have scattered quartz pebbles and there are occasional bands of fine-grained quartz-conglomerate. Locally, thin bands of grey mudstone or shale occur, in many places much disrupted by the currents which brought in the overlying sandstones. The strata are well exposed in the Tarr Burn by Ballanucater [NN 630023] and on a steep bank running east-south-east along the southern margin of Lennieston Muir to near Braendam House [NN 645019]. Other sections occur in the old quarry [NN 651024] by the Callander–Thornhill road, near Muir Dam and Brae of Boquhapple [NN 657018], and in two old quarries south of Daldorn [NN 669031]. In several of these exposures plant fossils, consisting of carbon-aceous films, have been recorded (Jack and Etheridge 1877; Henderson 1932).

North of Lennieston Muir, on which exposures are rare, there are several outcrops near the Glasgow–Callander road, south of Braes of Greenock. The grey sandstones are seen at intervals along the banks of the River Teith, the best sections being between a half and one mile west of Drumvaich. The Keltie Water provides a few short sections, e.g. by St. Mary's Well [NN 651056], 200 yd west of Cambusmore [NN 651062], and at its confluences with the Sruth Geal [NN 655077] and the Brackland Burn [NN 654078]. There are many exposures of the grey sandstones around Drumloist [NN 682061], particularly in the small stream which flows past the house on its west side. In this vicinity interbedding of grey with brown and purple sandstones is locally found.

The streams flowing southwards from Uamh Bheag mostly provide sections showing grey sandstones, those in the Sruth Geal and the Annet Burn being the best. Grey sandstones are the most abundant rock type exposed in the upper part of the Garvald Burn section, but purple and brown sandstones and grey mudstones also occur interbedded with them. The streams flowing southwards off the Slymaback ridge do not give good sections, but there are exposures, mostly of grey sandstone, in a few of them, e.g. the head-waters of the Muckle Burn, the Pole Burn, and the Froskin Burn. North of the Slymaback ridge grey flaggy sandstones are seen in some of the south-bank tributaries of the Arrevore Burn, and in the latter at and for several hundred yards above its confluence with the Androhal Burn [NN 777126]. There are very good exposures at the incised meander 450 yd west of this confluence.   I.H.F.

Upper purple sandstone facies. Around Thornhill exposures of the upper purple sandstone facies are almost entirely confined to streams flowing southwards to the Carse. The best sections are in the Tarr and Littlemill burns where mostly grey and purplish-grey sandstones with some purple mudstones are exposed, and in the Boquhapple and Cessintully burns where grey, brown and purple sandstones and purple and brown mudstones crop out. The only other notable section is found between Craighead [NS 690980] and Coldoch [NS 699982] where purplish-grey sandstones, rich in lava grains, and purple shales are exposed. The only natural exposure of the Teith Formation within the area of the Carse lies about half a mile to the south, in the Goodie Water [NS 690975], and consists of poorly-sorted purplish-grey sandstone rich in lava grains and containing fragments of purple shale.

South of the Carse, strata of the upper purple sandstone facies of the Teith Formation are exposed around Kippen, the best section being in the Broich Burn from a point 250 yd east of Claylands [NS 633942] downstream to the Broich Bridge [NS 641952]. The rocks are mostly purplish-grey sandstones, generally rich in lava grains and locally carrying small pebbles of volcanic or Highland origin, with some purple mudstones. The dip is to the north-west and is generally less than 10°. From 300 yd S.S.E. of Claylands upstream to the junction with the Upper Old Red Sandstone there are exposures of soft, crumbling, poorly-sorted, argillaceous, purplish-red sandstones, with lenses of conglomerate containing pebbles up to 8 mm in diameter, mostly of quartz, lava and sandstone. Red clay pellets also occur.

In both colour and texture these latter sandstones are unlike any other strata of the Teith Formation and they cannot be matched in any other part of the Lower Old Red Sandstone in the Stirling district. Similar strata have, however, been noted near the junction of the Teith Formation with the Upper Old Red Sandstone in the Cuthbertson Burn [NS 649944] near Kippen, in Geological Survey Stirling No. 7 (Claylands) Bore (*see* Appendix II), and at several localities just beyond the western limit of the district. A slice from the borehole showed much hematite staining. This, together with the fact that they only occur in the vicinity of the unconformity below the Upper Old Red Sandstone, suggests that these strata owe some of their characteristics to oxidation during Middle or early Upper Old Red Sandstone times.

The Claylands Bore entered the Teith Formation at a depth of 89 ft 2 in and continued in it to the final depth of 150 ft 6 in. The succession (*see* Appendix II) consists of sandstones interbedded with some mudstones. The sandstones are poorly-sorted, argillaceous and generally purplish-red. Some carry pebbles up to 7 cm in diameter, mostly of lava. The mudstones vary from dull purplish-red to bright red in colour and are generally sandy or silty.   I.H.F., W.A.R.

West of the Broich Burn there are sporadic small exposures, mostly in small streams and ditches, of sandstone and mudstone, purple, grey or brown in colour. The backfeature of the post-Glacial raised beach is steep but yields only a few exposures of grey sandstone with purple mudstone. The best exposures in this area are in an old quarry 200 yd south-west of Cloney [NS 625940], in which are exposed coarse-grained purplish-grey sandstones, rich in lava grains and containing small pebbles of lava and quartzite towards the top. The dip is to the west at 10°.   I.H.F.

East of the Broich Burn, purple and grey sandstones and purple and red mudstones are exposed in the Arngomery Burn for 250 yd upstream from the road-bridge [NS 643951]. In an old quarry [NS 647953] on the south side of the Stirling–Dumbarton road, 10 ft of dull purplish-grey argillaceous sandstone and sandy shale are visible, and intermittent exposures of sandstone occur for 250 yd eastwards along the back-feature of the post-Glacial raised beach.

The strata near the junction with the Upper Old Red Sandstone in the Cuthbertson Burn (see above) consist mostly of mudstone with some sandstone, dipping to the south-west at 10°. Further downstream, at Burnside, there are exposures of purple and grey, poorly-sorted, fine- to medium-grained sandstones, dipping at about 12° to the north-west or north. The stream flows past Glentirran [NS 655949] in a gorge 30 ft deep, cut in purple argillaceous sandstones, and then over the waterfall of Leckie's Loup, near which 60 ft of purplish-grey argillaceous sandstones are exposed, with thin mudstone bands in the upper and middle parts. The dip is to the north-west at 15°. In an old quarry [NS 653952] 30 ft of purplish-grey argillaceous sandstone, dipping to the north-west at 8°, are visible. For nearly a mile to the east, on and near the back-feature of the post-Glacial raised beach, there are scattered exposures of purple and grey argillaceous sandstones, with purple shales, dipping to the N.N.W. at about 10°.

Strata belonging to the upper purple sandstone facies of the Teith Formation were proved by Geological Survey Stirling Nos. 4 to 6 bores to extend beneath the Carse deposits for over a mile further east. Nos. 4 and 5 bores proved more than 50 ft of the beds, and No. 6 Bore more than 100 feet (see Appendix II). In all three bores the sequence consisted of an alternation of sandstones and mudstones, individual beds varying in thickness from a few inches up to about 10 feet. The sandstones are generally fine- to medium-grained and dull purple or purplish-grey in colour, except in No. 5 Bore where the greenish-grey colour locally found in the other two bores becomes dominant. The mudstones are generally micaceous, sandy and silty; in colour they vary from purplish-red to dull red and reddish-brown, with occasional bright red bands.

I.H.F., W.A.R.

On the southern slopes of Uamh Mhòr and Uamh Bheag, e.g. in the head-waters of the Annet Burn, the upper purple sandstone facies is represented by purple and brown sandstones, locally coarse and pebbly. These strata are partly replaced north-eastwards by the conglomerates and pebbly sandstones which form the eastern ridge of Uamh Bheag. Strata of the grey sandstone facies cropping out on the southern slopes of Slymaback are largely replaced on the northern slopes by sandstones of the upper purple sandstone facies which are generally flaggy and argillaceous; some of the sandstones are coarse-grained or pebbly and there are occasional bands of mudstone and shale. These beds are exposed in the Allt na Cuile, and the head-waters of the Allt na Gaisge and the Arrevore Burn, lying almost flat or with gentle dips to the south-west. Increased grain size and pebble content are notable in the exposures of the upper purple sandstone facies in the upper parts of the Allt na Cuile and the Allt a'Mhiadain as the overlying Uamh Bheag Conglomerate capping Beinn Odhar is approached. The sandstones remain purple in colour but the shales become bright red. Under Beinn Odhar these beds must be replaced completely by conglomerates, for they are not seen at all on the north-west slopes of the hill or on Creag Beinn nan Eun.

Coire Nochd Mòr is believed to be largely made up of strata belonging to the upper purple sandstone facies, except for the conglomerates on the northern slopes, but exposures are rare. Coarse-grained, pebbly, purple sandstones with shale bands are exposed in an almost unbroken section [NN 747113–770127] in the Arrevore Burn, dipping to the south-west at 10°. They appear to have replaced laterally strata of the grey sandstone facies, and to be themselves replaced by mixed conglomerates in the western part of Meall a'Choire Riabhaich. On the eastern part of the latter, replacement of the grey sandstone facies apparently becomes complete and purple-brown sandstones and mudstones with conglomerate bands are seen in two dry valleys on the eastern slopes.

The coarse-grained and commonly pebbly sandstones of the upper purple sandstone facies also crop out in the Corriebeagh Burn [NN 766140–782138], and are seen at intervals in the River Knaik above its confluence with the latter. The transition between the two purple sandstone facies can be traced in the River Knaik downstream from that confluence to just below the confluence with the Arrevore Burn, and also in streamlets flowing off Meall a'Choire Odhair east of Langside [NN 792138]. Purple pebbly sandstones, dipping slightly west of south at 10°, form a series of scarps at the western end of the same hill near the northern limit of the district.   I.H.F.

NORTH-WEST LIMB OF STRATHMORE SYNCLINE

VOLCANIC CONGLOMERATES AND SANDSTONES

The volcanic conglomerates, with their associated volcanic sandstones, are the lowest strata exposed in unfaulted succession on the north-west limb of the Strathmore Syncline. Their outcrop stretches from the western margin of the district, near Callander, across the Keltie Water (*see* Fig. 9) south of Braeleny, over Druim Meadhoin and across the Allt an Dubh Choirein. They reach a maximum thickness of 2800 feet north of Callander and gradually become thinner towards the north-east till the conglomerates disappear about a quarter of a mile south of Glenartney Lodge [NN 688155]. This disappearance seems to be caused partly by faulting and partly by thinning-out laterally, the conglomerates being replaced by volcanic sandstones with thin beds of conglomerate. In the western part of the outcrop of the volcanic conglomerates, there is an intercalation of lavas, near the base, all of a uniform type of porphyritic purplish-grey basalt with plagioclase phenocrysts. It extends for about $2\frac{1}{2}$ miles and reaches a thickness of over 200 feet. It seems unlikely that only one flow is involved in such a thickness, but no flow junctions have been detected.

Volcanic conglomerates similar to those which comprise the main outcrop occur in the zone between the Highland Boundary Fault and the Eas Dearg Fault. The lower part of the Ruchill Formation, which passes laterally into volcanic conglomerate north of Callander (*see* Fig. 9), contains thin beds of the latter in places, and one lenticular band about 150 ft thick.

The volcanic conglomerates are very coarse, some of the boulders reaching 2 ft in diameter. The stones are generally well-rounded, with a rather scanty matrix of volcanic sandstone. The stones are almost all of dark purple or brown basic or intermediate lavas, commonly porphyritic, which strongly resemble Old Red Sandstone basalts and andesites of the Ochil Hills and other areas. Occasional pebbles of quartzite and vein quartz are also present.

Throughout their outcrop the volcanic conglomerates are vertical or within 10° of verticality, but they are so massive that the dip can usually be measured only where a sandstone band occurs. These bands, generally of dull purple, coarse-grained sandstone, differ from the conglomerates only in grain size, for the grains are composed mostly of basic or intermediate lava, with a few of quartz, quartzite or quartz-schist. The grains are well-rounded and generally well-sorted, and the deposits bear every sign of being water-laid sediments and not tuffs. Each slice contains grains obviously derived from many different flows, with wide variety of grain size and texture. Similar beds of volcanic sandstone occur in the Ruchill Formation, particularly in the zone of lateral transition to the volcanic conglomerates north of Callander.

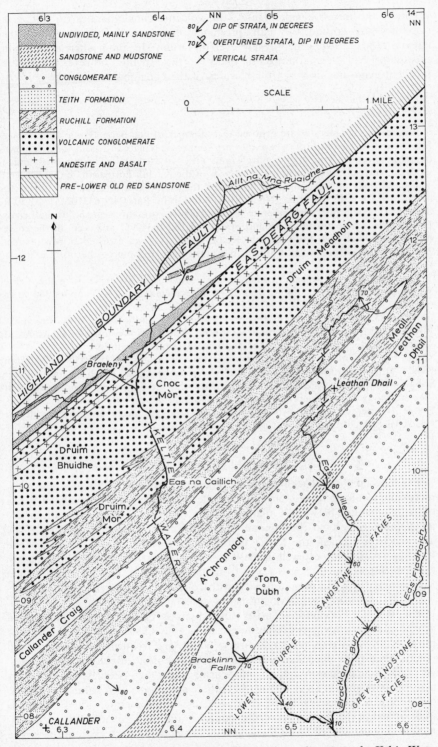

FIG. 9. *Sketch-map showing Lower Old Red Sandstone sediments in the Keltie Water area*

Unlike the mixed conglomerates, the volcanic conglomerates do not as a rule form high ground with many prominent exposures. Indeed away from the streams exposures are generally few, even on Druim Meadhoin where altitudes in excess of 1200 ft are attained. In many of the streams, however, there are excellent exposures in which the features of the conglomerates can be studied.

DETAILS

Volcanic conglomerates are exposed in a number of places on Druim Buidhe (*see* Fig. 9), and on Druim Mòr, where they are seen to be replaced towards the north-east by interdigitation with coarse purple and grey sandstones, frequently with much volcanic material, which form the basal beds of the Ruchill Formation in this vicinity. The basal beds of the conglomerate, below the basalt lava intercalation, form the hillocks of Cnoc an Fhuarain [NN 629104] and Druim Ban [NN 633107]. The 150-ft thick lens of volcanic conglomerate in the Ruchill Formation can be traced across Druim Mòr, where it forms a prominent outcrop [NN 634096], and is cut by the gorge of Eas na Caillich [NN 640101] in the Keltie Water. It is well exposed in the streamlet 200 yd north-east of Eas na Caillich, but apparently dies out to the north-east (*see* Fig. 9).

The main body of volcanic conglomerate is well exposed in places in the Keltie Water, particularly about 100 yd west of Thomasgreen and at a bend about 350 yd to the south. The basal beds are prominent where the stream passes Braeleny, on the north-west slopes of Tom a'Ghobhainn [NN 638112], and in some of the streamlets flowing north-westwards off Druim Meadhoin. There are a number of exposures of volcanic conglomerate on Cnoc Mòr, but few on Druim Meadhoin.

The top beds of the volcanic conglomerates are exposed in the Allt a'Chaltuinn [NN 674138], and most of the succession is seen in the Allt an Dubh Choirein. There are a few exposures on Monadh Odhar, mostly near the Callander–Comrie path, but the main body of conglomerate dies out about a quarter of a mile south of Glenartney Lodge. Isolated exposures of conglomerate do, however, occur among the volcanic sandstones which replace them towards the north-east.

RUCHILL FORMATION

The outcrop of the Ruchill Formation occupies a band about half a mile wide, increasing to about three-quarters of a mile where there are intercalated bands of conglomerate, between Callander and Glenartney Lodge. The strata are approximately vertical throughout, but show little evidence of faulting. They are well exposed near the Keltie Water (Fig. 9), rather poorly around Meall Leathan Dhail, and very well in the Water of Ruchill from which the formation takes its name. The thickness varies from 2500 to 3000 ft, and except on Druim Mòr, where the rocks are interleaved with volcanic conglomerates, the contacts with the conglomerates above and below are well-defined.

The Ruchill Formation consists for the most part of thinly interbedded purple and grey, fine-grained flagstones, micaceous siltstones and dull purple or purplish-brown shales and mudstones, which are frequently calcareous and commonly display micro-cross-lamination. Coarse-grained volcanic sandstones, generally dull purple in colour and bearing some lava pebbles, occur locally near the base and on Druim Mòr where there are intercalated bands of volcanic conglomerate. A lenticular band of volcanic conglomerate, 150 ft thick, is intercalated in the lower part of the sequence, and the Callander Craig Conglomerate (Fig. 9), 400 to 500 ft thick, occurs in the upper part, both in the Keltie

Water area. Interdigitation of the top beds of the Ruchill Formation with fine-grained quartz-conglomerates occurs on Leacann Buidhe and Auchnashelloch Hill. Thin bands of both volcanic conglomerate and quartz-conglomerate are seen in the section along the Water of Ruchill.

The sandstones in the Ruchill Formation are generally argillaceous, micaceous and fine- or very fine-grained, with a carbonate matrix. Apart from quartz and muscovite, the most abundant detrital minerals are plagioclase and iron ore, followed by biotite, orthoclase and microcline. Hornblende, zircon, epidote and chlorite occur more rarely. Fragments of schist are quite common, and there are a few of very fine quartz mosaics, but grains of basic lava are rare or absent.

DETAILS

North of Callander the lower part of the Ruchill Formation, below the volcanic conglomerate of Eas na Caillich (Fig. 9), consists largely of coarse-grained, purplish-grey volcanic sandstones with occasional pebbles of lava and quartz, and some red mudstone. On Druim Mòr they are seen to interdigitate with the underlying volcanic conglomerates. Between the volcanic conglomerate, which is very well exposed at Eas na Caillich, and the Callander Craig Conglomerate, there are some bands of volcanic sandstone, but most of the succession consists of purple and grey flagstones interbedded with purple and brown shales. The Keltie Water provides an almost complete section in which the beds are approximately vertical throughout, and there are good exposures on the slopes to the west. East of the Keltie Water the lens of volcanic conglomerate disappears and the lower and middle parts of the Ruchill Formation come together. Exposures are generally poor except in the head-waters of the Eas Uilleam, above Leathan Dhail [NN 654107], where grey sandstones, generally coarse-grained and with some pebbly bands, are associated with purple and red mudstones. On a small ridge 1000 yd W.S.W. of Leathan Dhail grey sandstone and red mudstone are seen in close association.

The upper part of the Ruchill Formation, above the Callander Craig Conglomerate, consists of purple and brown flagstones, locally coarse-grained and pebbly, with reddish-purple shales. The best exposures west of the Keltie Water are in a small disused quarry 200 yd north of Callander station, where the beds dip to the south-east at 70°, and there are other scattered exposures among the trees below the Craig and near the Callander–Braeleny road. Unlike the lower part of the formation the upper part is very poorly exposed in the Keltie Water.

East of the Keltie Water there are good exposures on the north-western slopes of A'Chrannach (*see* Fig. 9), where the protruding near-vertical slabs of purple flagstone are in strong contrast to the massive beds of A'Chrannach Conglomerate on the south-eastern slopes of the hill. There are several exposures of purple flagstones with purple and red shales in the Eas Uilleam and in a small tributary stream of the latter, by Leathan Dhail. The Callander Craig Conglomerate dies out north-eastwards on the north-west slopes of Meall Leathan Dhail, where there are exposures of red and purple flagstones and shales.

The left-bank tributary of the Allt a'Chaoruinn provides a long section [NN 669129–673132], mostly along strike, of the lower part of the Ruchill Formation, in which purple and grey flagstones and purple shales are exposed. In the Allt a'Chaoruinn itself there are exposures of similar strata which become mostly red in colour towards the top. Near the top an intercalation of fine-grained quartz-conglomerates appears, and the red flagstones and shales are interbedded with both these and the overlying main body of mixed conglomerates. The red beds between the conglomerates die out on the western slopes of Leacann Buidhe, but about a quarter of a mile further north-east strata typical of the Ruchill Formation reappear within the conglomerates, at a slightly higher horizon, and are seen to persist over the Allt Ollach and across Auchnashelloch Hill, to the Allt Mòr. They consist of purple flagstones and red shales interbedded with coarse-grained purple pebbly sandstones and fine-grained quartz-conglomerates.

Purple and grey sandstones, locally coarse-grained, and purple shales, at the base of the Ruchill Formation, are exposed in the Allt a'Chaltuinn and the Allt an Dubh Choirein. In both streams the abrupt nature of the change from the underlying volcanic conglomerates is well displayed.

The section from which the Ruchill Formation takes its name begins just below the confluence [NN 676137] of the Allt a'Chaltuinn and the Allt a'Chaoruinn and continues almost without a break down the Water of Ruchill for over a mile to below its confluence with the Allt Ollach. The strata, lying approximately vertical, are magnificently displayed by the sides of the stream, but, as the section is almost along strike, only the middle part of the formation is visible. However, the lower part is seen in the Allt an Dubh Choirein, as already noted, in exposures on the south-east slopes of Monadh Odhar, and at intervals further downstream in the Water of Ruchill; and the upper part is well displayed in the Allt Ollach and in a number of streamlets descending from Leacann Buidhe, including the Allt Eas nan Earb, so that a virtually complete section of the Ruchill Formation is available in this vicinity. The strata consist of flagstones and shales, generally dull purple in colour, but including some grey and brown sandstones and some red shales. They are finely interbedded, and locally contain yellow calcareous nodules. The sandstones are generally fine-grained and argillaceous, but include some coarse-grained beds and a few bands of volcanic conglomerate and of fine-grained quartz-conglomerate.

MIXED CONGLOMERATES

On the north-west limb of the Strathmore Syncline much, and in places all, of the upper part of the Lower Old Red Sandstone succession within the Stirling district is composed of conglomerates. These are called mixed conglomerates, primarily to distinguish them from the volcanic conglomerates. The term 'mixed' refers to the fact that they are composed partly of pebbles similar to the Lower Old Red Sandstone lavas of the Ochil Hills, etc., and partly of vein quartz, quartzite and other rocks for which a Dalradian source seems probable.

The mixed conglomerates are generally not as coarse as the volcanic conglomerates: they consist mostly of cobbles with some pebbles (*sensu stricto*) and a few small boulders. These are mainly of basic or intermediate lavas and vein quartz; quartzite comes next in abundance, and other metamorphic rocks are also represented. The proportions of the two main constituents vary widely and either may be absent in some beds. The lava fragments tend to be larger on the whole than the others, and are rare in the finer conglomerates and the pebbly sandstones into which the mixed conglomerates frequently grade laterally.

The mixed conglomerates (*see* Table 4) overlie the Ruchill Formation, and are thought to be approximately equivalent to most of the Dunblane, Cromlix and, in places, Teith formations. They also include the Uamh Bheag Conglomerate, the highest part of the Lower Old Red Sandstone succession in the district, and the lenticular Callander Craig Conglomerate within the Ruchill Formation.

In the Keltie Water area the junctions of the mixed conglomerates with the Ruchill Formation, the sandstone intercalations and the Teith Formation are generally clear-cut, with little evidence of transition, but in the Glen Artney area there is some interdigitation with the Ruchill Formation. The lateral transition north-eastwards from the Teith Formation into the conglomerates is highly complicated, much more so than can be shown on the map.

The mixed conglomerates are well exposed and generally form high ground, including the bulk of the high Uamh Bheag–Beinn Odhar–Ben Clach range, where there is a maximum of conglomerate development.

The total thickness of mixed conglomerate exposed in the Keltie Water is about 3000 ft, separated by fine-grained strata into three parts: the Callander Craig Conglomerate (500 ft), the A'Chrannach Conglomerate (1200 ft) and the Bracklinn Falls Conglomerate (1300 ft). In the Uamh Bheag–Beinn Odhar area conglomerates replacing the Teith Formation and the Uamh Bheag Conglomerate are continuous with the united A'Chrannach and Bracklinn Falls conglomerates but the total thickness of conglomerate remains more or less constant. If anything the incoming of conglomerates involves a decrease rather than an increase in the total thickness of the deposits. No evidence of minor unconformities within the conglomerate succession could, however, be obtained: on Creag Beinn nan Eun, which provides the best section of the mixed conglomerates in the Stirling district, the bedding is seen to be most regular with no evidence of intraformational unconformity.

DETAILS

Apart from a few thin beds of fine quartz-conglomerate in the Water of Ruchill, the lowest band of mixed conglomerate is the Callander Craig Conglomerate (Fig. 9). Its outcrop extends from beyond the western limit of the district for about 3 miles, the dip being vertical or nearly vertical throughout. It forms the spectacular cliffs of Callander Craig and a ridge which can be traced from the Keltie Water across the moors to Leathan Dhail [NN 654107], three-quarters of a mile north-east of which it apparently dies out. The pebbles are mostly of quartz with a certain amount of quartzite and lava.

Another band of fine conglomerate appears at a rather higher horizon at the northern end of Meall Leathan Dhail, is exposed in the Allt a'Chaoruinn [NN 675128], and coalesces with the main body of mixed conglomerate on Leacann Buidhe. Farther north-east, this band is again separable from the rest of the mixed conglomerates in the Allt Ollach, on Auchnashelloch Hill and in the Allt Mòr. In this area the interdigitation of conglomerates with the topmost strata of the Ruchill Formation is particularly intricate.

The A'Chrannach Conglomerate (Fig. 9) is exposed in the woods [NN 627074] on the south side of the Callander–Thornhill road and at a number of places in the Bracklinn Road area of Callander [NN 633078]. Many of the houses in the town are built partly at least of these fine-grained quartz-conglomerates, derived from now disused quarries nearby [NN 635082]. Bands of pebbly sandstone, sandstone and mudstone occur among the conglomerates in these quarries. Conglomerate is exposed at a number of places by the road to Braeleny, and in the north-west corner [NN 636082] of Callander golf course. The dip is to the south-east and varies in amount from 60° to 80°.

Exposures in the Keltie Water are comparatively poor, but the conglomerates are magnificently exposed on the south-west slopes of A'Chrannach, where a thin band of reddish-brown sandstones and mudstones is intercalated among them. The outcrop of this band is easily traced because it forms a gully between the massive slabs of more resistant conglomerate. Quartz-conglomerates are also well exposed on Tom Dubh and in the Eas Uilleam, north-east of which the A'Chrannach and Bracklinn Falls conglomerates come together.

Strata separating the A'Chrannach and Bracklinn Falls conglomerates were formerly exposed in Callander beside the railway [NN 634077] and by the roadside [NN 637076].

The exposures consisted of brown sandstones and shales but are now obscured. An intercalation of red and brown mudstones and sandstones, dipping at 80° to the south-east, is seen in a tributary [NN 644087] of the Keltie Water flowing south-westwards off Tom Dubh. The outcrop of these finer sediments forms a notable groove extending across the hillside between the massive exposures of conglomerates. Red mudstones with nodular bands of cornstone in the Eas Uilleam [NN 654099] form the most north-easterly exposures of this intercalation, which apparently dies out within about half a mile.

Similar strata reappear over a mile further north-east. The outcrop probably begins on the north-east part of Meall Leathan Dhail, where purple flaggy sandstone is seen at one place. In the Allt a'Chaoruinn [NN 677124] red mudstones with cornstone nodules are exposed. Red and brown sandstones and mudstones, dipping south-east-wards at 45° to 50°, occur in a small tributary of the latter, which flows south-westwards in a depression between the harder conglomerates on either side.

The Bracklinn Falls Conglomerate (Fig. 9) is well exposed on Cock Hill, south of Mollands [NN 630069], with a generally south-easterly dip of 60° to 70°. There is a gap of about 1½ miles between there and the exposures in the Keltie Water at and above the Bracklinn Falls. At the falls fine quartz-conglomerates and pebbly sandstones are magnificently exposed, dipping to the south-east at 70° to 80°. There are many exposures on the lower slopes of Tom Dubh, and the top of the Bracklinn Falls Conglomerate can be traced accurately as far as the Eas Uilleam, which plunges over a 40-foot water-fall at the junction with the overlying Teith Formation. North-east of the stream there are scattered exposures of conglomerates and pebbly sandstones, dipping to the south-east at about 70°.

The united A'Chrannach and Bracklinn Falls conglomerates form most of Meall Leathan Dhail, on whose eastern flanks they are well exposed, dipping to the south-east at about 50°. There are many exposures of conglomerate, mostly fine-grained, with some pebbly sandstones, in Coire Airidh Ailpein and the head-waters of the Allt a'Chaoruinn. Further downstream there is a group of fine-grained quartz-conglo-merates dipping at 70° to the south-east, separated from the main body of conglomerate by strata belonging to the Ruchill Formation.

There are continuous sections of fine-grained quartz-conglomerates in the upper part of the Allt Eas nan Earb and the unnamed streamlet adjacent to it. In the next streamlet to the north-east (also unnamed), however, Ruchill Formation strata reappear at about the same horizon and again separate a group of fine-grained quartz-conglo-merates and pebbly sandstones from the main body of conglomerate. This group is also exposed in the Allt Ollach, on the north-east slopes of Auchnashelloch Hill and in the Allt Mòr.

The main body of conglomerate is well exposed, with south-easterly dips of about 40°, in the three streamlets mentioned above which flow north-westwards off Leacann Buidhe. Together with their tributaries these streamlets have excavated a remarkable series of deep narrow gorges, presumably along major joints, mostly in fine-grained quartz-conglomerate with some pebbly sandstone and a few beds of purple sandstone and red shale. Repeated small-scale interbedding of the conglomerates with the generally pebbly sandstones is well displayed in the excellent series of exposures from Am Beannan [NN 693136] to Sgiath Gorm [NN 693131]. The conglomerates here contain more lava pebbles on the whole than the equivalent beds towards the south-west. The dip decreases southwards from 35° to 25° in a south-south-easterly direction. There are a number of exposures of these conglomerates in the Allt na Creige Duibhe and the Allt Ollach.

The highest beds of mixed conglomerate found in the Stirling district, and probably the youngest strata in the Strathmore Syncline, form the top parts of Uamh Bheag and Beinn Odhar and comprise the Uamh Bheag Conglomerate (see Table 4). They consist mostly of rather fine conglomerate with some pebbly sandstones and are 400 feet in thickness.

The Uamh Bheag Conglomerate lies in the broad axial zone of the syncline and consequently lies horizontal or dips very gently. Exposures are good, especially on the south-west face of Uamh Mhòr where there has been a certain amount of landslipping. On the east ridge of Uamh Bheag itself, the individual conglomerate beds form a series of scarps, visible from a considerable distance, which continue as far as the col at the source of the Garvald Burn [NN 708118].

West of Uamh Bheag and on Meall Clachach the replacement of the Teith Formation by conglomerates, best traced in the head-waters of the Allt Ruith an Eas, is almost complete, so that north of the summit only two thin bands of sandstone remain between the Uamh Bheag Conglomerate and the main body of mixed conglomerates described above. Creag na Craoibhe [NN 692126] consists mostly of lava-quartz-conglomerate with some pebbly sandstones and similar beds are well exposed in the head-waters of the Allt na Creige Duibhe. The cliffs on the south-east side of Coire na Fionnarachd are composed of lava-quartz-conglomerate with sandstone bands, dipping to the south-south-east at 10°, in which the Eas a'Mhonaidh has cut a deep cleft [NN 696126]. The cliffs west of the head-waters of the Allt Ollach are generally similar.

East of the Allt Ollach the intercalation of Teith Formation strata which in the Meall Clachach area separates the Uamh Bheag Conglomerate from the main body of mixed conglomerates apparently dies out. As the Uamh Bheag Conglomerate has no distinctive lithological features, its base cannot be mapped in this area, though clearly the group forms the highest beds on Beinn Odhar and on Creag Beinn nan Eun. Exposures are rare on the grassy slopes of Beinn Odhar, except on its steeper western flank where lava-quartz-conglomerate and pebbly sandstone are seen in several places. The Allt Mòr, however, provides an almost complete section through the mixed conglomerates, which show considerable variation in the proportions of basic or intermediate lava and vein quartz, the two principal constituents. Further east the Allt na Stainge provides another good section, much of it in a narrow gorge. On the southern slopes of Beinn Odhar there are a few exposures in the head-waters of the Allt Cuile and the Allt a'Mhiadain.

The best section of the mixed conglomerates is at Creag Beinn nan Eun, where nearly 1000 feet of these strata, dipping south-south-west at about 12°, are exposed in continuous section. Most of the succession consists of quartz-lava-conglomerate, a good deal of it fine-grained, with pebbly sandstone bands. The top 300 feet consist mostly of fine-grained quartz-conglomerates, with coarse-grained, usually pebbly, sandstones and some coarser conglomerate. The stratification is well-developed and exceedingly regular: there is no sign of lateral variation in a horizontal distance of more than half a mile nor is there any evidence of intraformational unconformity.

In the Findhuglen Water below Findhuglen Cottage there are several exposures of mostly fine-grained quartz-conglomerate, interbedded with a good deal of sandstone and some red shale. The south-easterly dips fall off rapidly upstream from 75° to 20°. Above the cottage for nearly a mile exposures are very few in this stream, but in its upstream continuation, the Allt na Gaisge, there are some exposures [NN 739135–740132] of quartz-lava-quartzite-conglomerate, dipping south-south-westwards at 20°.

The mixed conglomerates are well exposed on Sròn Odhar, particularly on the south-western and eastern slopes, and also on the eastern slopes of Cnoc nan Oighreag, with generally southerly dips of 15° to 20°. Exposures on the southern slopes of Ben Clach are scattered, but on the eastern side there is an almost continuous section of quartz-lava-quartzite-conglomerate, 800 feet thick, extending almost to the summit of the hill. The upper beds tend to be finer than the rest, and to have a higher proportion of pebbly sandstone. The regularity of the scarps of conglomerate is again noteworthy. The true dip is difficult to determine exactly because of the nature of the exposures, but is probably to the south-south-west at about 17°.

The relations between the mixed conglomerates and the Teith Formation south of the Uamh Bheag–Beinn Odhar–Ben Clach range are as follows. South of Uamh Bheag and Beinn Odhar the Uamh Bheag Conglomerate overlies the Teith Formation

H

which within these hills must be largely replaced by conglomerates. On Coire Nochd Mòr, on the other hand, Teith Formation strata overlie the fine conglomerates which are exposed on the northern slopes and in the Allt na Gaisge. They are not seen at all at Creag Beinn nan Eun where they must be replaced laterally by some of the conglomerates (except possibly for the lowest beds which may persist north-westwards for some distance under the peat and boulder clay east of the cliff).

On the western slopes of Meall a'Choire Riabhaich scarps of quartz-lava-conglomerate protrude in places from the peat. These gradually die out towards the south-east and it is thought that their disappearance more or less coincides with that of the conglomerates, none of which are seen in the Arrevore Burn to the south.

Conglomerate, with some pebbly sandstone, is exposed on the south bank of the Corriebeagh Burn [NN 742134–767141] and in a narrow band round the northern slopes of Meall a'Choire Riabhaich. This band is underlain by sandstones, commonly pebbly but including only thin bands of fine conglomerate, which are exposed in the stream. These strata have been assigned to the Teith Formation and the boundary between the latter and the main body of mixed conglomerates has therefore been drawn further north. Owing to lack of exposures the exact position of the boundary in this area is uncertain.   I.H.F.

REFERENCES

ALLAN, D. A. 1928. The geology of the Highland Border from Tayside to Noranside. *Trans. R. Soc. Edinb.*, **56**, 57–88.

―― 1940. The geology of the Highland Border from Glen Almond to Glen Artney. *Trans. R. Soc. Edinb.*, **60**, 171–93.

BURGESS, I. C. 1961. Fossil soils of the Upper Old Red Sandstone of south Ayrshire. *Trans. geol. Soc. Glasg.*, **24**, 138–53.

CAMPBELL, R. 1913. The geology of south-eastern Kincardineshire. *Trans. R. Soc. Edinb.*, **48**, 923–60.

CAROZZI, A. V. 1960. *Microscopic sedimentary petrography*. New York.

CRAIG, G. Y. (*editor*). 1965. *The geology of Scotland*. Edinburgh and London.

GEORGE, T. N. 1960. The stratigraphical evolution of the Midland Valley. *Trans. geol. Soc. Glasg.*, **24**, 32–107.

HARKNESS, R. 1862. On the position of the Pteraspis Beds and on the sequence of the strata of the Old Red Sandstone Series of south Perthshire. *Q. Jl geol. Soc. Lond.*, **18**, 253–8.

HENDERSON, S. M. K. 1932. Notes on Lower Old Red Sandstone plants from Callander, Perthshire. *Trans. R. Soc. Edinb.*, **57**, 277–85.

HICKLING, G. 1908. The Old Red Sandstone of Forfarshire. *Geol. Mag.*, (5), **5**, 396–408.

JACK, R. L. and ETHERIDGE, R., JUN. 1877. On the discovery of plants in the Lower Old Red Sandstone of the neighbourhood of Callander. *Q. Jl geol. Soc. Lond.*, **33**, 213–22.

KENNEDY, W. Q. 1958. The tectonic evolution of the Midland Valley of Scotland. *Trans. geol. Soc. Glasg.*, **23**, 106–33.

POWRIE, J. 1861. On the Old Red Sandstone rocks of Forfarshire. *Q. Jl geol. Soc. Lond.*, **17**, 534–42.

WALKER, T. R. 1956. Carbonate replacement of quartz and feldspar as a source of silica in silicified sediments. *Bull. geol. Soc. Am.*, **67**, 1828.

―― 1957. Frosting of quartz grains by carbonate replacement. *Bull. geol. Soc. Am.*, **68**, 267–8.

WHITE, E. I. 1963. Notes on *Pteraspis mitchelli* and its associated fauna. *Trans. Edinb. geol. Soc.*, **19**, 306–22.

Chapter VI

UPPER OLD RED SANDSTONE

INTRODUCTION

A LONG PERIOD during which earth movements and great erosion took place intervened between the deposition of the Lower and the Upper Old Red Sandstone and as a result the latter rests with marked angular unconformity upon the former within the Stirling district (p. 108). The beds included in the Upper Old Red Sandstone lie above this unconformity and below strata of Ballagan Beds facies. The top of the division, like the base, is probably diachronous (p. 101) and is generally difficult to define in a passage by alternation upwards into strata of Ballagan Beds facies. There is no palaeontological evidence for the age of the strata classed as Upper Old Red Sandstone in this district and it has recently been suggested by Waterston (*in* Craig 1965, p. 302) that the Upper Old Red Sandstone facies persisted in Scotland whilst marine Tournaisian was being deposited in southern England.

Within the Stirling district Upper Old Red Sandstone sediments are found, either at the surface or immediately below drift, in a western, a central and an eastern outcrop. The western, or main, outcrop is much the largest and best exposed of the three. It forms a strip three-quarters of a mile to one and a half miles wide which runs east-north-eastwards from the western limit of the district to about two miles west of Stirling, bounded to the north by the line of unconformity and by the Ochil Fault and to the south by the Carboniferous rocks at the foot of the Fintry, Gargunnock and Touch hills. The central outcrop is the smallest and least well exposed of the three and has been inferred from one small group of exposures at Causewayhead, north of Stirling. It has been mapped provisionally as lying between two branches of the Ochil Fault. The eastern outcrop is situated around Devonshaw at the eastern limit of the district. The strata in all three areas consist predominantly of sandstone. In the western and eastern outcrops they have been separated into a lower division characterized by red sandstones and an upper division containing cornstones. As the relationships between these two divisions are thought to differ in the two outcrops the latter are described separately.

WESTERN OUTCROP

The western, or main, outcrop is the only one of the three where both the unconformable base and the gradational top of the Upper Old Red Sandstone are known to crop out at the surface. As in the Campsie area immediately to the west (Clough and others 1925, p. 8), the topmost sandstones pass by alternation upwards into the cementstones, mudstones and shales of the Ballagan Beds facies. Within the western outcrop the upper boundary of the Upper Old Red Sandstone has been drawn arbitrarily at the top of the highest local cornstone or medium-grained sandstone. The outcrop is 1 to $1\frac{1}{2}$ miles wide in the west where both the base and top of the division crop out. Further east, however, where the bottom of the division is cut off by the Ochil Fault and the top is cut off locally by the Abbey Craig Fault, the width of outcrop narrows. West of the north–south National Grid line 68 the direction of dip varies between south-south-east and south, with dip values generally between 15° and 20° but locally steeper. East of this grid line the direction of dip swings to between south and south-south-west and the dip values are between 5° and 15°.

In addition to the Ochil and Abbey Craig faults the strata of the western outcrop are cut by some smaller faults and by a series of small dykes (p. 159).

The total thickness of Upper Old Red Sandstone strata decreases eastwards along the outcrop from about 2300 ft in the west to about 1900 ft south-east of Boquhan, beyond which it is impossible to estimate as the base of the division is faulted out. It is possible that some of this eastward thinning is due to overlap of the basal sediments, but there may also be variation in thickness due to differential subsidence, especially as the overlying Carboniferous sediments below the Clyde Plateau lavas also thin eastwards (p. 119).

The succession is generally similar to that in the Campsie area immediately to the west (Bailey *in* Clough and others 1925, pp. 6–8), but it has been found more convenient here to divide the Upper Old Red Sandstone into two rather than into three parts. The strata of the lower division are dominantly red sandstones which have been named the Gargunnock Sandstones (Read 1960, p. 41). The strata of the upper division, which were initially named the Transition Beds (Read 1960, p. 41) but are here referred to as the Cornstone Beds, are red and white sandstones with subordinate silty mudstones and numerous irregular beds, nodules and pebbles of cornstone. In the following account the terminology used in describing the carbonate rocks is that used by Phemister (*in* Muir and others 1956, pp. 66–74).

An account of the sedimentary structures, palaeocurrent directions and probable conditions of deposition of the Upper Old Red Sandstone west of Stirling has recently been published (Read and Johnson 1967).

GARGUNNOCK SANDSTONES

The Gargunnock Sandstones are approximately equivalent to the lowest division of the Upper Old Red Sandstone of the Campsie area, which consists of red sandstones with very subordinate marl beds. The base of the Gargunnock Sandstones is diachronous as it is an unconformity. The top is drawn arbitrarily at the base of the lowest local cornstone (p. 101), so that in this case too the mapped boundary does not occupy a constant stratigraphical horizon. Nevertheless the variations in the thickness of the division reflect those of the Upper Old Red Sandstone as a whole and the Gargunnock Sandstones thin eastwards from about 2000 ft in the west to about 1200 ft at Boquhan. East of this the base is cut out by the Ochil Fault.

Within the Stirling district the Gargunnock Sandstones may be divided into two parts, the lower consisting of red, or locally white, sandstones with beds of pebbly sandstone and conglomerate, and the upper of uniform, fine- and medium-grained brick-red sandstones. Both subdivisions contain rare thin beds of siltstone and silty mudstone. The lower subdivision crops out only in the western part of the main outcrop, where it seems to be about 700 ft thick, and is intermittently exposed south-west of Kippen. It is also known from Stirling No. 7

(Claylands) Bore (pp. 330–1). The beds within it differ from those of the upper, thicker, subdivision in coarseness, colour and nature of cement.

The pebbles in the pebbly beds may be as much as 15 cm or more long and the larger pebbles are commonly rounded. Most of them are of rock types that have probably been derived ultimately from the Southern Highlands. They include vein quartz, pebbly grit, glassy quartzite, schistose grit with interlocking quartz grains and greenish flakes of chlorite and muscovite, quartz-chlorite-schist, metamorphosed siltstone, greenish phyllite, slate and indurated mudstone, some of which show strain-slip cleavage, and rare fragments of chert. Although all of these could have been derived directly from the Highlands some of the rock types can be matched with pebbles in the pebbly sandstones of the Teith Formation immediately below the unconformity, and it is therefore possible that some at least were derived via the Lower Old Red Sandstone. Rock types that were almost certainly derived from the Lower Old Red Sandstone include specimens of rather decomposed fine-grained igneous rock, pebbles of which are abundant in the underlying Teith Formation, and pebbles of indurated 'volcanic siltstone' which can be matched with specimens from the Ochil volcanic rocks. Pebbles of very poorly sorted argillaceous sandstone were probably derived locally from the Teith Formation and some irregular pellets of chloritic silty and sandy mudstone, which seem to have been soft when incorporated in the sediment, may either be derived from the Teith Formation or else be pene-contemporaneous with the conglomerates.

The pebbles lie in a sandy matrix which is commonly rather poorly sorted but is generally medium-grained, coarse or very coarse. Quartz usually constitutes 80 per cent. or more of the detrital grains of the matrix. Up to 20 per cent. of the quartz grains are of metaquartzite and a high proportion of the remainder show undulose extinction, suggesting ultimate derivation from a metamorphic source. The roundness of the grains varies greatly but up to 5 per cent. of the grains fall into the rounded and well-rounded classes of Pettijohn (1957, p. 59). Feldspar generally constitutes less than 5 per cent. of the detrital grains and is rare in some specimens. It includes orthoclase, microcline, which is usually fresh, and plagio-clase, which is commonly weathered. Some of the plagioclase crystals show distorted laminae, suggesting a metamorphic source. Mica is rare but there are a few flakes of both muscovite and biotite, some of the latter being green. Some specimens show irregular streaks of greenish chloritic material which may have been derived from the underlying Teith Formation, in which it is common. Many of the rock types found in the pebbles are also represented in the grains of the matrix.

The cement in the pebbly beds, unlike that in the higher strata of the Gargunnock Sandstones, is generally carbonate which locally forms as much as 10 per cent. of the total rock. Chemical staining tests (Evamy 1963) give a positive reaction for calcite, unlike specimens from the Cornstone Beds (pp. 105–7). It is generally patchily distributed in irregular grains which vary greatly in size and some slices (e.g. S 46438) show large areas of carbonate in optical continuity enclosing numerous detrital grains which 'float' in the cement. This texture may be recognized in hand specimen by the lustre of the carbonate patches which may be as much as 1 cm across. Many of the grains of quartz, metaquartzite and feldspar within and adjacent to the carbonate cement have intricate outlines and seem to have been corroded, as in the cornstones and calcareous sandstones of the Cornstone Beds (p. 103). In places the carbonate cement may be masked by irregular patches of clayey material which may have been derived from the destruction of clay pellets. Locally hematite or limonite forms incomplete rims to quartz grains and stains the clayey patches.

The colour of the conglomerates and pebbly sandstones, as in the strata of the Cornstone Beds (p. 102), seems to be related to the proportion of carbonate cement present. Where carbonate is relatively abundant the rock is generally white or pale-red in colour, but where it is relatively small in amount the rock is a brighter red in colour.

The strata of the upper subdivision of the Gargunnock Sandstones are well exposed in the Boquhan and Gargunnock burns. They are more uniform than either the strata of the lower subdivision or the Cornstone Beds and are typically brick-red sandstones with occasional thin beds of siltstone and silty mudstone. Mudstone pellets are commonly found within the sandstones, especially where the latter overlie thin argillaceous beds, but pebbles are absent. Most of the sandstones are fine- or medium-grained and relatively well-sorted, but there are some beds of very fine-grained sandstone. The coarser sandstones generally show well-developed cross-stratification, mostly of the planar and trough types of McKee and Weir (1953, pp. 385–7). Some of the very fine-grained sandstones are ripple-laminated. The foreset dips indicate that the sandstones of the upper subdivision were deposited by currents flowing mainly from the north-west and north (Read and Johnson 1967, pp. 254–61), suggesting that the pebbles of the lower subdivision could have been derived directly from the Highlands (see above). Some of the sandstones include a high proportion of wind-rounded grains (see below) but water seems to have been the dominant agent of transport. The strata are almost entirely brick-red but there are irregular thin beds and spots which are buff or pale-greenish in colour and locally some large, irregular patches in the sandstones have been bleached to a white or buff colour, especially where the rocks are overlain by peat. The prevailing brick-red colour suggests oxidation after deposition or, possibly, derivation of part of the material from red detritus (Krynine 1949). Red beds of this type are found in arid and semi-arid areas but they are not necessarily confined to such environments (*see* Walker 1967).

Generally more than 85 per cent. of the detrital grains are quartz and many of these are either grains of metaquartzite or show undulose extinction. Grains of high sphericity and roundness are common and in some examples about half of the grains fall into the rounded and well-rounded classes of Pettijohn (1957, p. 59). The larger grains are usually more rounded and many of the most rounded grains are of metaquartzite. The high proportion of rounded grains does not necessarily imply that the sandstones are aeolian deposits as on the flood plains of rivers, even in humid climates, considerable quantities of sand may be blown about by the wind (*see* Allen 1965, pp. 161–3). Quartz overgrowths are found locally (S 44968, 44969) and rarely (e.g. S 44864) the quartz grains interlock to form an intricate mosaic. These features, however, are less common than in the Cornstone Beds (p. 103).

The proportion of feldspar is variable but it seldom exceeds 5 per cent. of the rock. It includes orthoclase, usually weathered, plagioclase, which occurs in both fresh and weathered grains, and microcline, which is generally fresh. Mica is uncommon, possibly because the flakes were destroyed by wind action, but sporadic flakes, mostly of muscovite, are found. Fragments of weathered, fine-grained acid or intermediate igneous rocks and of indurated argillaceous rock are also present, but these are less common than in the strata of the lower group.

Most of the sandstones of the Gargunnock Sandstones fall into the proto-quartzite category of Pettijohn (1957, p. 291) but some are subarkoses. In most of the sandstones the only cement is a thin pellicle of hematite or limonite coating the quartz grains, although in the finer laminae there is usually also some interstitial clayey material. Carbonate seems to be virtually absent. These rocks are for the most part soft and open-textured, and have a fairly high porosity which should make them good aquifers.

CORNSTONE BEDS

Both the base and top of the Cornstone Beds are defined arbitrarily, the former being taken at the base of the lowest cornstone and the latter at the top of the highest medium-grained sandstone. Both base and top are probably diachronous. The thickness of the division seems to decrease eastwards from about 1300 ft in the west to some 600 to 700 ft south of Boquhan and to only about 340 ft in the Gargunnock Burn where, however, the base is probably cut out by a small fault (p. 113).

The formation is characterized by the presence of cornstones, including irregular beds and nodules of concretionary cornstone and also pebbles of con-glomeratic cornstone (*see* Allen 1960). Carbonate is the dominant cement but, unlike that in the basal beds of the Gargunnock Sandstones, it seems to be dolomite rather than calcite (Table 6). The sandstones are usually coarser than the Gargunnock Sandstones and pebbly sandstones and conglomerates are fairly common. Beds of siltstone and silty mudstone are also much more common than in the latter division.

The bulk of the succession can be divided into a series of repeated sedimentary sequences or cycles (Read and Johnson 1967, pp. 252–4) similar in some respects to those in the Upper Old Red Sandstone of south Ayrshire (Burgess 1961, fig. 2) and the Dittonian of the Welsh Border (Allen 1962; Allen and Tarlo 1963). The cycles usually consist of an alternation of two broad lithological phases—one sandy and the other argillaceous. The sandy phase is generally a sandstone with a disconformable base which cuts down into the argillaceous bed below. The base is commonly pebbly, with abundant pebbles of white conglo-meratic cornstone which may be as much as 13 cm long. Pebbles of other rock types, usually less than 5 cm long, are also present but are less numerous. Quartz and quartzite are the most abundant of these but pebbles of quartz-porphyry are also found. Locally the carbonate cement at the base of the sand-stone may be so abundant that there is a greater proportion of cement than of clastic fragments (p. 103). In other places this basal sandstone is composed of a mosaic of closely interlocking quartz grains (p. 103). Upwards from the base the sandstone tends to become progressively finer and more red and generally grades upwards into the argillaceous phase. In some cycles, however, this junc-tion is fairly sharp. The sandstone phase ranges in thickness from only a few feet to as much as 30 ft, but is usually between 10 and 20 ft. The sandstones are almost invariably cross-stratified and both the planar and trough types of McKee and Weir (1953, pp. 385–7) are represented. The dips of foresets indicate that, like the Gargunnock Sandstones, the Cornstone Beds were laid down by currents flowing mainly from the north and north-west (Read and Johnson 1967, pp. 254–61).

The argillaceous phase consists of silty mudstone or siltstone but in the lower part of the division it may be represented by fine or very fine clayey sandstones. It is usually less than 5 ft thick, poorly stratified or unstratified, and reddish or purplish in colour. Locally an argillaceous phase may be completely removed by the disconformity at the base of the overlying sandstone phase. Most argillaceous phases contain irregular beds, nodules or veins of concretionary cornstone. In some cycles the beds of cornstone are more than 3 ft thick and the argillaceous material of the phase may even be reduced to thin streaks and pockets within the cornstone; in others only a few nodules of concretionary cornstone are present. The concretionary cornstones are not entirely confined to the argillaceous phase and it is not uncommon for nodules to be found in the upper part of the sandstone phase.

These sedimentary cycles seem to be very much more local and less persistent than the cycles of the Limestone Coal Group, Upper Limestone Group and Coal Measures and are probably of fundamentally different origin. It seems probable that all the Cornstone Beds sediments were deposited under fluviatile conditions and it is thought that the sandstones represent channel infillings whereas the argillaceous beds represent overbank deposits (Read and Johnson 1967, pp. 261–2).

Within the Cornstone Beds there is a gradual change in colour from below upwards. Near the base the sandstones are generally dull red but higher up they tend to become purplish-red, and buff and white patches appear. Finally, towards the top of the succession, the sandstones are white or buff with some purplish patches. The silty mudstones and siltstones are almost always redder than the sandstones in any given part of the succession and their colour changes from bright red near the base of the division to dull purple with greenish spots and patches towards the top. These changes in colour within the Cornstone Beds seem to be related to the increase in the proportion of carbonate within the rocks as the succession is traced upwards. In detail, the white or buff patches within a red sandstone, or the greenish spots, veins and patches within a reddish or purplish silty mudstone or siltstone, seem to be areas where there is a greater concentration of carbonate. A narrow greenish zone generally margins the irregular beds or nodules of concretionary cornstone within the silty mudstones and siltstones.

The proportions of mineral types in the detrital grains of the Cornstone Beds are similar to those in the Gargunnock Sandstones (pp. 99–101). There are, however, considerable differences in texture and cementation.

Quartz generally forms 85 per cent. or more of the detrital grains of the sandstones, most of which fall accordingly into the protoquartzite and subarkose categories of Pettijohn (1957, p. 291). The variations in grain size are much greater than in the Gargunnock Sandstones and many sandstones are coarse or very coarse in grain. Grains with undulose extinction and grains of metaquartzite are still common but the latter seem to be somewhat less abundant than in the Gargunnock Sandstones. Most of the grains are subangular or sub-rounded. The number of rounded and well-rounded grains is considerably less than in the Gargunnock Sandstones and they are generally larger. In many places, however, the shape of the quartz grains has been modified by secondary overgrowths of quartz in optical continuity and in some examples (e.g. S 44847) these take the form of euhedral outgrowths into carbonate, suggesting that some at least of the secondary enlargements are later than the carbonate cement (*cf.* Carozzi 1960, pp. 43–4). In places the bulk of the sandstone is composed of a mosaic of closely interlocking quartz grains and this texture is found locally at the base of the sandstone phase, immediately above the relatively impermeable argillaceous phase (e.g. S 46814). As it is not always easy to distinguish between the original detrital quartz grains and the secondary outgrowths it is not possible to determine whether these mosaics are entirely due to the growth of secondary quartz (*cf.* Greensmith 1957, p. 401; 1961, p. 54) or whether they may possibly be partly due to pressure solution of quartz grains (*cf.* Carozzi 1960, pp. 24–9).

Feldspars usually form less than 5 per cent. of the detrital grains. They include fragments of orthoclase, albite, microcline and microperthite. In some specimens the feldspar grains are much more angular than the quartz grains. Some traces of secondary feldspar outgrowth with clear rims of authigenic feldspar surrounding crystals of orthoclase have been found. Fragments of indurated argillaceous rock and of fine-grained acid or intermediate igneous rock seem to be less common than in the Gargunnock Sandstones. Micas are rare and are represented mainly by muscovite but some flakes of green biotite and turbid, decomposed brownish biotite are also present. Heavy minerals include zircon and apatite.

One of the most characteristic features of the sandstones of the Cornstone Beds is the presence of an abundant carbonate cement. This cement, unlike the carbonate cement in the basal part of the Gargunnock Sandstones, is dolomite rather than calcite in all the specimens examined. Locally the cement is so abundant that the rock consists dominantly of carbonate enclosing sporadic detrital grains (p. 101) and thus grades into concretionary cornstone. This is thought to be due partly to the carbonate forcing the detrital grains apart and partly to the replacement of the detrital grains (Carozzi 1960, p. 39), rather than to the contemporaneous deposition of clastic grains and carbonate (*cf.* Greensmith 1961, p. 59).

Many of the detrital grains of quartz and feldspar show minutely irregular boundaries with the carbonate cement and seem to have been corroded by it, indicating that some replacement certainly took place. Some muscovite flakes also seem to have been forced apart along the cleavage by veins of carbonate.

In some of the sandstones (S 44833) the cement is in the form of definite rhombs of micrograined and fine-grained carbonate (*see* Phemister *in* Muir and others 1956, p. 69 for grain size classification) but usually the carbonate is rather irregularly distributed in patches of anhedral crystals of fine- and medium-grained carbonate.

Cornstones. The cornstones that characterize the Cornstone Beds are similar in appearance to those of the Upper Old Red Sandstone of other parts of Scotland but staining tests and chemical analyses suggest that they differ sharply from most of the latter in that they are dolomites rather than limestones (see below).

The cornstones are mainly concentrated in the silty mudstone and siltstone phases of the cycle but they are quite common in the sandstone phases where there is, in places, a complete gradation between sandstones with a high proportion of carbonate cement and concretionary cornstones with a high proportion of detrital grains. Rocks of the latter type are found locally at the bases of channel-phase sandstones, immediately above the argillaceous phase. This is in the same position in the cycle as some of the mosaics of closely interlocking quartz grains but the two rock types have not been discovered in the same cycle. These carbonate rocks (S 46819) at the base of the sandstone phase grade upwards imperceptibly into normal sandstone and in texture they closely resemble the carbonate-rich sandstones. Elsewhere within the sandstones the concretionary cornstones form indefinite nodules of irregular shape. Texturally these resemble the concretionary cornstones of the argillaceous phase (see below).

The macro-textures of the cornstones vary greatly. Commonly the cornstone occurs as impersistent, irregular beds or layers of nodules which tend to lie at definite horizons within the argillaceous phase. The tops of the beds stay at about the same horizons but the bases are commonly highly irregular and grade downwards into nodules. The tops of these beds are harder than the bases, which tend to be more friable. Several beds at different horizons may be present within the same silty mudstone or siltstone and these may merge together as they are traced laterally.

In some cycles almost all of the argillaceous phase is occupied by cornstone. This may be in the form of numerous irregular lenses and veins which commonly tend to run roughly parallel to, or at a slight angle to, the bedding, leaving a series of angular argillaceous fragments enclosed in the cornstone. Elsewhere the cornstones form platy and nodular beds 3 ft or more in thickness with only scattered irregular argillaceous inclusions. Some beds of cornstone are also cut by numerous vertical veins of purer and more coarsely crystalline carbonate and in places irregular thin veins of pinkish authigenic baryte are also found (*cf*. Burgess 1961, pp. 143–4).

Polished specimens of concretionary cornstones commonly have a 'curdled milk' appearance, with irregular brecciated fragments of pale fine-grained carbonate in a darker, more coarsely crystalline matrix. There are also fragments of banded carbonate and spherules of carbonate, some showing concentric structure, but these seem to be rather uncommon, possibly as a result of recrystallization.

The cornstones are highly variable in micro-texture but most specimens can be matched with one or other of the examples described by Phemister (*in* Muir and others 1956, pp. 97–100) or Burgess (1961, pp. 143–7). Most specimens contain some detrital grains, mainly of quartz or feldspar, 'floating' in the carbonate matrix, and in some these grains, which are commonly corroded, are abundant. The size of the carbonate crystals varies greatly from specimen to specimen, ranging from pelitomorphic (S 44832) to medium-grained (S 47045, 47607). With increasing grain size there is a parallel gradation from the heterogeneous clotted textures that are typical of the finer cornstones (e.g. S 47048) to the almost equigranular mosaic of carbonate crystals that characterizes the coarser types. The changes in both grain size and texture appear to be due to progressive recrystallization, for almost all the intermediate stages are found; indeed the process of recrystallization from finer to coarser carbonate may be seen even in a single slice. Many of the cornstones have also been cut by numerous veins of coarser carbonate, both dolomite and calcite. In at least one (S 44832) most of the corroded grains of quartz and feldspar 'floating' in a matrix of turbid pelitomorphic carbonate are surrounded by rims of clear, more coarsely crystalline carbonate; other patches of clear carbonate probably mark the former positions of detrital grains which have been completely replaced.

It seems probable that the concretionary cornstones of the Stirling district are analogous to 'kankar' or 'caliche' and were formed *in situ* by pedological processes of leaching and redeposition in a sub-humid to arid climate as suggested by Maufe (1910, pp. 35–6) and Burgess (1961, pp. 151–5). Modern caliche deposits show corroded detrital grains of quartz and feldspar surrounded by rims of clear, relatively coarse-grained carbonate 'floating' in a matrix of finer turbid carbonate, and thin veins of authigenic baryte have been recorded (*cf*. Brown 1956, p. 7; Swineford and others 1958, p. 109, plate 2). Some cornstones (e.g. S 44832) have proved to be indistinguishable in thin section from modern kankar deposits from Nigeria. A profile with a hard compact top or 'caprock' passing down into a more friable rock which grades down into the underlying deposits is characteristic of modern caliche formed in the C, Ca horizon of a pedocal soil, and older horizons of caliche may underlie younger horizons in the soil (Brown 1956, pp. 3–5). The brecciated texture, with fragments of banded carbonate, of some cornstones and the vertical cracks in others can be matched in the dense caprocks of modern caliche (Bretz and Hornberg 1949, pp. 491, 498). Both structureless and banded caprocks are known and at least in some areas the former is more common (Brown 1956, p. 6), as is the case in the concretionary cornstones of the Stirling district.

The optimum conditions for the formation of caliche are: the presence of rocks that yield minerals rich in calcium carbonate; alternating arid and moderately wet periods; effective rock permeability; low to moderate relief; sufficient time for the process to take place; and a position above the level of permanent water table (Swineford and others 1958, p. 115). It seems probable that most, if not all, of these conditions were satisfied at the time of formation of the Cornstone Beds.

Pebbles of conglomeratic cornstone are found in most of the sandstones of the Cornstone Beds and they are in general especially numerous towards the base of the sandstone phase. The pebbles can usually be distinguished from nodules of concretionary cornstone by their regular, generally well-rounded shape and sharply defined edges. Locally, however, parts of the edge of a pebble may be blurred, either because of recrystallization of the carbonate of the pebble and of the cement in the adjacent sandy matrix, or because the pebble formed a centre around which further carbonate subsequently accumulated.

Sayre (1937, p. 65) has described modern beds with the appearance of a conglomerate composed of pebbles of calcium carbonate which may have been formed by the erosion and transport of previously existing beds of caliche or by precipitation from groundwater in place. Most of the cornstone fragments in the sandstone phases seem to be true pebbles which may be matched in texture and grain size with one or other of the concretionary cornstones of the argillaceous phase. Some, however, may have been modified by precipitation of carbonate from groundwater. No examples have been discovered of the 'cupped' pebbles found in some modern caliche deposits (Bretz and Hornberg 1949, p. 495).

The most puzzling feature about both the concretionary and conglomeratic cornstones of the Cornstone Beds is their chemical composition. Apart from three samples said to occur near the top of the division the analyses of Upper Old Red Sandstone cornstones from various parts of Scotland (Muir and others 1956, pp. 35–6) give ratios of CaO to MgO ranging from about 40/1 to more than 200/1. The three exceptions mentioned give ratios of less than one but of these the specimen from the Gargunnock Burn can be disregarded as re-examination shows it to be a cementstone. Thus the majority of analysed cornstones from the

TABLE 6

Partial analyses of carbonate rocks from the Upper Old Red Sandstone and the Calciferous Sandstone Measures

| | | UPPER OLD RED SANDSTONE | | | | CALCIFEROUS SANDSTONE MEASURES | | | | | | | | |
| | | CORNSTONE BEDS | | | | BALLAGAN BEDS | | | | DOWNIE'S LOUP SANDSTONES | | | | |
		I	II	III	IV	V	VI	VII	VIII	IX	X	XI	XII	XIII
Acid-soluble fraction	CaO	25·0	28·5	26·6	25·1	24·1	22·8	22·5	20·7	49·3	45·7	42·2	46·7	43·7
	MgO	14·8	18·7	18·0	15·1	12·7	10·8	9·5	10·7	0·7	1·4	0·7	0·8	1·0
	Fe_2O_3	0·2	0·2	0·1	0·2	0·3	0·5	0·7	0·2	0·4	0·8	0·2	0·0	0·0
	FeO	1·2	0·9	0·1	0·5	0·7	0·4	0·6	0·6	0·5	0·6	0·1	0·2	0·6
	MnO	0·6	0·5	0·2	0·2	0·3	0·2	0·2	0·1	0·6	0·4	0·2	0·1	0·3
	CO_2	36·8	43·2	40·1	35·9	32·3	28·4	26·2	27·2	39·2	37·2	33·7	36·1	35·1
Acid-insoluble matter		19·8	7·6	13·1	21·3	24·9	31·8	33·4	34·9	5·8	9·9	20·0	12·8	16·2
Ratio CaO/MgO		1·7/1	1·5/1	1·5/1	1·7/1	1·9/1	2·1/1	2·4/1	1·9/1	70·4/1	32·6/1	60·3/1	58·4/1	43·7/1

DETAILS OF ANALYSED ROCKS OF TABLE 6
(Analyses by W. H. Evans and R. E. Mortlock)

I.   Concretionary cornstone. Gargunnock Burn. 1000 yd S.3°W. of Gargunnock Church. [NS 70649342]. At 141 ft 6 inches in section on p. 112. S 47602. Lab. No. 1918.

II.   Conglomeratic cornstone pebble. Gargunnock Burn. 1035 yd S.3°W. of Gargunnock Church. [NS 70639336]. At 94 ft 0 inches in section on p. 111. S 47609. Lab. No. 1925.

III.   Concretionary cornstone. Gargunnock Burn. 1095 yd due S. of Gargunnock Church. [NS 70679332]. At 36 ft 4 inches in section on p. 111. S 47608. Lab. No. 1924.

IV.   Concretionary cornstone. Gargunnock Burn. 1100 yd due S. of Gargunnock Church. [NS 70679331]. At 12 ft 0 inches in section on p. 111. S 47607. Lab. No. 1923.

V.   Stratified cementstone. Boquhan Burn. 565 yd S.58°W. of Ballochleam. [NS 65229211]. S 47603. Lab. No. 1919.

VI.   Stratified cementstone. Gargunnock Burn. 1215 yd S.1°E. of Gargunnock Church. [NS 70709317]. At 353 ft 5 inches in section on p. 130. S 47601. Lab. No. 1917.

VII. Cementstone. Gargunnock Burn. 1335 yd S.1°E. of Gargunnock Church. [NS 70749308]. At 257 ft 8 inches in section on p. 130. S 47600. Lab. No. 1916.

VIII. Cementstone. Stirling No. 1 (Kaimes) Bore (1961). 220 yd N.67°E. of Kaimes. [NS 77209454]. At depth of 405 ft 6 in. S 47611. Lab. No. 1928.

IX, X. Limestone pebbles in conglomerate. Fintry Hills. 1135 yd S.54°W. of Stronend summit. [NS 62078887]. S 47604, 47605. Lab. Nos. 1920, 1921.

XI.   Calcarenite. Downie's Loup, Gargunnock Burn. 1350 yd S.1°E. of Gargunnock Church. [NS 70749307]. S 47606. Lab. No. 1922.

XII. Limestone pebbles in calcirudite. Stirling No. 1 (Kaimes) Bore (1961). 220 yd
XIII. N.67°E. of Kaimes. [NS 77209454]. At depth of 242 ft 0 in. S 47610A, S 47610. Lab. Nos. 1926, 1927.

Scottish Upper Old Red Sandstone, like modern caliche deposits, are known to be limestones rather than dolomites. As shown in Table 6, however, the partial analyses of three specimens of concretionary cornstone from argillaceous phases (Anals. I, III, IV) and a specimen of a pebble of conglomeratic cornstone (Anal. II), all from the Gargunnock Burn section, give CaO/MgO ratios of between 1·5/1 and 1·7/1 so that these rocks must be regarded as dolomites rather than limestones. Moreover, chemical staining tests (Evamy 1963) on slices of other cornstones from the Stirling district have so far failed to reveal calcite, except for sporadic occurrences in veins, even in pebbles of conglomeratic cornstone near the base of the Cornstone Beds. One possible explanation is that the cornstones were originally deposited as calcium carbonate but were subsequently altered to dolomite by groundwater rich in magnesia at the time of deposition of the Ballagan Beds. This might also account for the widespread recrystallization within the cornstones although the crystals rarely show the conspicuous rhombs that are frequently characteristic of dolomite.

DETAILS

GARGUNNOCK SANDSTONES

Outcrops west of the Boquhan Burn. The area west of the Boquhan Burn is the only part of the district where the lower part of the Gargunnock Sandstones is not cut out by the Ochil Fault. Quite large areas of both the lower and upper subdivisions are exposed, especially south-west of Kippen where numerous outcrops project through the drift.

In the Broich Burn a section [NS 63379369] near the base of the lower subdivision shows 7 ft of pale-red conglomerate with rounded and subangular pebbles up to 15 cm long, overlain by 19 ft of dull and bright red, cross-stratified sandstone with thin beds of conglomerate, pebbly sandstone and mudstone. These rocks dip south-south-eastwards and lie only 20 ft south of an exposure of strata belonging to the Teith Formation (Lower Old Red Sandstone) which dip in the opposite direction. The Geological Survey Stirling No. 7 (Claylands) Bore, sited about 45 yd to the south, penetrated 83 ft of brick-red and white conglomerates, pebbly sandstones and sandstones of the Upper Old Red Sandstone (*see* Appendix II) which rest unconformably upon somewhat reddened strata of the Teith Formation. This evidence implies that the 7 ft of conglomerate exposed in the Broich Burn form part of the Upper Old Red Sandstone basal conglomerate and, unless there is a small fault in the burn section, the basal unconformity in this locality must dip south-south-eastwards at 30° to 35°.

Further up the Broich Burn towards Loch Laggan there are sporadic exposures of sandstone, pebbly sandstone and conglomerate, mostly brick-red in colour. The best of these exposures is at the waterfall by the ruins of New Mill [NS 63069332] where 8 ft of bright red and brownish-red conglomerate and pebbly sandstone very similar to the basal conglomerate are exposed. North-eastwards along the strike pebbly beds thought to be part of the basal conglomerate are also exposed at Settie [NS 63909407] but they have not been found further east.

The sandstones of the upper subdivision form extensive outcrops along, and to the east of, the road from Loch Laggan to Kippen where they were formerly quarried extensively for building stone. The old quarries are small with the exception of Bloodymires Quarry [NS 63209310], where more than 20 ft of brick-red, medium-grained, massive sandstone are still exposed, and a quarry [NS 63749358] lower in the succession west-north-west of Gribloch House, where more than 30 ft of brick-red, medium-grained and coarse sandstone with thin beds of buff sandstone and red silty shale may be seen. Some of the sandstones high up in the quarry face at the latter locality seem to have irregular bottom structures (Read and Johnson 1967, p. 247). In some quarries [e.g. at NS 64109328], where the sandstones are overlain by peat or peaty soil, the brick-red colour has been bleached white or buff so that they are similar in colour to the Cornstone Beds sandstones.

Immediately west of the Boquhan Burn two tributary streams have cut down deeply into the sandstones near the base of the Gargunnock Sandstones, leaving an 18-ft pinnacle, known locally as Dugald's Tower, in the angle between the two streams. The sandstones, brick-red with buff lenses, are for the most part medium-grained and are cross-stratified.

Boquhan Burn section. Between Hole of Sneath [NS 65529307] and Boquhan Bridge [NS 67049455], the Boquhan Burn has cut a gorge, 20 ft to more than 100 ft deep, which provides an almost complete section through the upper part of the Gargunnock Sandstones. Unfortunately the section runs at an angle of only about 30° to the strike so that the total thickness of strata exposed is difficult to estimate, especially as parts of the gorge are inaccessible except when the stream is very low. The section shows a remarkably uniform series of fine- and medium-grained, cross-stratified sandstones with occasional thin beds of very fine-grained sandstone, siltstone and silty mudstone. Almost all the beds are brick-red in colour but there are thin buff beds and patches in some of the sandstones. Bleaching has been observed in red sandstones adjacent to dykes [e.g. at NS 66049350]. Many of the sandstones contain pellets of red silty mudstone but no pebbles have been found.

Outcrops between the Boquhan and Gargunnock burns. East of Boquhan the lower part of the Gargunnock Sandstones is cut out by the Ochil Fault. Outcrops are generally smaller and less common to the east of the Boquhan Burn than to the west. In the former area they are largely confined to old sea cliffs at the edge of the Carse, a few stream sections and sporadic, rather small, outcrops on the interfluves. In the old sea cliffs [NS 69139473–69999470] of Craigmakessoch, north of Watson House and Bield, more than 30 ft of pale-red and brick-red, cross-stratified, mainly medium-grained sandstone with red mudstone pellets and thin beds of greenish laminated siltstone are exposed. The stream sections at Bogle Glen upstream from Burntown [NS 67759454], in the lower part of the Leckie Burn, and in Wester Glen [NS 70359376–70549426], as well as the scattered outcrops between the streams, all show strata very similar to those exposed in the Boquhan and Gargunnock burns.

Gargunnock Burn. The section exposed in the Gargunnock Burn is less extensive but rather more accessible than that in the Boquhan Burn. Furthermore the Gargunnock Burn flows roughly parallel to the direction of dip. About 650 ft of the upper part of the Gargunnock Sandstones are exposed but the very top is cut out by a small south-south-easterly fault. Most of the strata exposed are typical cross-stratified, medium- and fine-grained brick-red sandstones with rare buff ribs and lenses. There are also, however, some massive beds of fine-grained, rather clayey, sandstone with indefinite traces of disturbed stratification (*cf.* Selley and others 1963). Thin beds of silty mudstone, siltstone and very fine-grained, ripple-laminated sandstone occur also throughout the succession and in places there is a suggestion of a two-phase cycle similar to that seen in a much more definite form in the Cornstone Beds.

Local bleaching of red sandstone to a whitish or pale-greenish colour is found where they are cut by dykes [e.g. at NS 70649387] but more extensive bleaching is seen in a cliff [NS 70669386] on the east bank of the burn. Here fine- and very fine-grained sandstones with thin beds of silty mudstone are overlain disconformably by soft, medium-grained sandstone which probably represents a channel infilling; the exposure is crossed by a series of minor faults. The original colour of the strata is brick-red but within an irregular area extending from the surface to a depth of 4 to 10 ft the sandstones have been bleached yellowish-white and the mudstones green. Above the bleached zone, however, is a reddish-purple zone. The coarser beds are more readily bleached than the finer and some of the mudstone bands remain dull red in colour although the sandstones above and below them are bleached. The bleaching must have taken place after the faulting as it extends downwards along the fault planes. There is now no trace of peaty soil above the exposure, however, and the bleaching is not necesssarily recent in origin.

The sedimentary structures are much more obvious within the bleached area where numerous grains of dark brownish iron oxide show the stratification clearly. Most of the beds are elongate shallow lenses with simple, gently dipping, cross-lamination. There are also some traces of ripple-lamination in the finer sandstone and of load-casts and flame structures where sandstones overlie silty mudstones (Read and Johnson 1967, p. 250).

Outcrops east of the Gargunnock Burn. East of the Gargunnock Burn the Gargunnock Sandstones are seen only in a series of small outcrops at the edge of the Carse. About a mile east of the burn the western end of the Abbey Craig Fault throws the Gargunnock Sandstones against Carboniferous lavas.

CORNSTONE BEDS

Outcrops west of the Boquhan Burn. The Cornstone Beds are not quite so well exposed as the Gargunnock Sandstones in the area west of the Boquhan Burn but nevertheless there are fairly numerous outcrops and the cornstones themselves have been worked opencast, probably for agricultural purposes, in numerous trench-like quarries which run east-north-eastwards parallel to the strike.

The sandstones exposed in these outcrops are mostly white and pale or dull red in colour but there are some brownish beds. They are usually medium-grained, coarse and very coarse and commonly contain mudstone pellets, conglomeratic cornstone pebbles and, less commonly, pebbles of quartz and sandstone. Beds of silty mudstone and siltstone and of concretionary cornstone are known to be present but these are less commonly exposed than in the area of the Loch Lomond (38) Sheet immediately to the west, where cornstones were more extensively worked for lime. A slice (S 46818) of a concretionary cornstone from a trench-like quarry [NS 60559088] on Balgair Muir, roughly a mile west of the western limit of the Stirling district, showed no trace of calcite when stained and seems to be a dolomite.

Boquhan Burn. The Cornstone Beds are less well exposed in the Boquhan Burn than are the Gargunnock Sandstones. Most of the exposures are of dull red and white, cross-stratified sandstones, generally medium-grained to very coarse, but there are beds of pebbly sandstone and conglomerate which include pebbles of conglomeratic cornstone and quartz, and also some thin red argillaceous beds with nodules of concretionary cornstone which seem to become more common in the upper part of the succession. At one locality [NS 65289236] the stratification of a sandstone containing nodules of concretionary cornstone has been disturbed.

Fairly typical Cornstone Beds cycles may be seen near the top of the formation at Sheep Linn [NS 65339234] where the following section is exposed:

	ft	in
Sandstone, white with dull red patches; mostly coarse and very coarse, with occasional small quartzes greater than 2 mm; cross-stratified; includes red mudstone pellets and some thin nodular beds of concretionary cornstone; disconformable base, cutting down into bed below	25	0
Mudstone, silty, red with greenish patches; includes nodules of concretionary cornstone	4	0
Obscured	5	0
Sandstone, brown, mostly medium- and coarse-grained; cross-stratified; disconformable base	8	0
Mudstone, silty, red with greenish patches; includes nodules of concretionary cornstone .. ..(seen)	2	0

Outcrops between the Boquhan and Gargunnock burns. Between the Boquhan and Gargunnock burns exposures are rather rare except in stream sections and these unfortunately are, for the most part, thickly overgrown with vegetation.

A section similar to that seen in the Boquhan Burn is exposed a short distance to the east in the outcrop at Garrique [NS 66069280] and in the stream flowing northwards from there to join the Boquhan Burn. Few argillaceous beds with concretionary cornstones are exposed but their presence may be inferred from an old limekiln and the traces of numerous old workings.

Cornstones were also worked about a mile to the east-north-east where a system of long trench-like excavations [NS 67679325] runs eastwards to Loch Logan. These old workings are almost entirely overgrown. Downstream from Loch Logan the Cornstone Beds are exposed in the deep valley of St. Colm's Glen, which is drained by the Leckie Burn. They are also seen in the valleys of the Easter and Wester Blackspout which flow northwards to join the Leckie Burn south of Watson House, and in Wester Glen immediately east of the Gargunnock Burn. All these sections are badly overgrown but the strata exposed seem to resemble those seen in the more accessible section of the Gargunnock Burn, with typical Cornstone Beds cycles, especially in the upper part of the formation.

Gargunnock Burn. Much of our knowledge of the Cornstone Beds comes from the Gargunnock Burn section [NS 70679329–70739365] which is better exposed and more accessible than most of the other sections and which also runs roughly parallel to the direction of dip. The details of this section, measured from south to north, are as follows:

	Thickness		Total thickness	
	ft	in	ft	in
Cementstone (lowest bed of Ballagan Beds facies) ..	–	–	–	–
Obscured .. .. ca.	12	0	–	–
Concretionary cornstone, nodular, very sandy		3		3
Siltstone and silty mudstone, sandy, mottled dark-red, light-green and buff	1	3	1	6
Sandstone, white, fine- and medium-grained, with cornstone concretions near top	3	0	4	6
Concretionary cornstone (S 44832): irregular bed with corroded detrital grains commonly rimmed by a zone of clear carbonate 'floating' in a matrix of turbid pelitomorphic carbonate (*see* p. 104)		6	5	0
Sandstone, white with purplish patches, mostly coarse-grained, cross-stratified. Disconformable base with pebbles of conglomeratic cornstone and quartz ..	4	0	9	0
Shale, silty and sandy towards base, purple with green laminae, containing irregular beds and concretions of cornstone (S 47045; 47607 analysed specimen: *see* Table 6, Anal. IV), split by several lenses of coarse sandstone up to 3 ft thick, some with pebbles of conglomeratic cornstone	6	0	15	0
Sandstone, white, fine- and medium-grained	3	6	18	6
Obscured	10	0	28	6
Sandstone, white with some purple patches, mainly medium-grained. Pebbly at top. Some sandy cornstone concretions lower down	6	0	34	6
Siltstone and silty mudstone, sandy, with irregular beds and concretions of cornstone (S 47608 analysed specimen; *see* Table 6, Anal. III)	3	0	37	6
Obscured (traces of white and purple sandstone)	22	0	59	6
Sandstone, white with purple patches, cross-stratified, mostly medium-grained, interbedded with thin beds of purplish siltstone and silty mudstone; irregular beds and concretions of cornstone in both the sandy and argillaceous beds	20	0	79	6
Concretionary cornstone, sandy, nodular, with angular clayey inclusions	1	0	80	6
Sandstone, white with purple patches, cross-stratified. Top mostly medium-grained, with irregular beds of concretionary cornstone. Base coarse-grained and pebbly with pebbles of conglomeratic cornstone (S 47609 analysed specimen; *see* Table 6, Anal. II). Mudstone pellets throughout	13	6	94	0
Concretionary cornstone, nodular		6	94	6
Sandstone, white, cross-stratified, mostly medium-grained but with coarser pebbly lenses containing abundant pebbles of conglomeratic cornstone (baked by dyke which crosses section at NS 70639337)	3	0	97	6
Mudstone, silty, purple with greenish patches .. (seen)		6	98	0

	Thickness		Total thickness	
	ft	in	ft	in
Obscured	6	6	104	6
Sandstone, white and purple, mainly cross-stratified, fine-grained to very coarse, with pebbly lenses containing mudstone pellets and pebbles of conglomeratic cornstone and quartz; disconformable pebbly base	18	0	122	6
Mudstone, mainly bright red, but greenish immediately below the overlying sandstone	2	0	124	6
Obscured (traces of red silty mudstones and purplish sandstone)	9	0	133	6
Sandstone, white and purplish-red, mainly medium-grained, with concretions and several irregular beds of cornstone (S 47602 analysed specimen; see Table 6, Anal. I). Stratification seems disturbed at base	16	0	149	6
Concretionary cornstone, very sandy, creamy-white with purple patches	3	6	153	0
Sandstone, purplish-red, fine- and medium-grained, with irregular nodules of concretionary cornstone	5	6	158	6
Mudstone, silty and sandy, purple with greenish patches		6	159	0
Sandstone, white, mainly coarse-grained, with beds and concretions of cornstone; irregular base	8	0	167	0
Mudstone, silty, purple with green patches, irregular cornstone concretions	4	0	171	0
Sandstone, purple and white, cross-stratified, mostly medium-grained	10	0	181	0
Mudstone, purplish-red with greenish patches. Irregular beds and concretions of cornstone towards base ..	4	0	185	0
Sandstone, buff, purple and dull red, mainly medium-grained. Some cornstone concretions	14	6	199	6
Sandstone, hard, siliceous, with closely interlocking quartz grains (S 46819), resting disconformably upon underlying beds and cutting across them	1	0	200	6
Cornstone, concretionary, sandy in places, with irregular streaks and patches of purplish-grey siltstone; traces of clotted texture (S 46818)	1	7	202	1
Sandstone, purplish and buff, clayey and fine-grained at top with coarse-grained disconformable base	2	0	204	1
Mudstone, silty, and siltstone, purplish and dull red, with irregular cornstone concretions towards top		11	205	0
Sandstone, reddish-purple at top, cross-stratified. Some cornstone concretions	7	6	212	6
Sandstone, buff, mainly coarse-grained, with abundant mudstone pellets	2	0	214	6
Mudstone, silty, and siltstone, purplish	1	0	215	6
Sandstone, purplish, very fine-grained at top grading down to buff, coarse-grained at base; irregular concretions of cornstone at top	11	0	226	6
Obscured	10	0	236	6
Sandstone, red with buff patches, medium-grained ..	1	6	238	0
Siltstone and silty mudstone, sandy in places, brick-red with greenish patches	4	0	242	0
Sandstone, purplish-red at top, buff at base, mainly medium-grained	3	6	245	6

	Thickness		Total thickness	
	ft	in	ft	in
Mudstone, silty, brick-red with green patches		6	246	0
Concretionary cornstone, irregular, sandy	3	0	249	0
Sandstone, dull red, mainly medium-grained, with abundant cornstone concretions	7	0	256	0
Silty mudstone and siltstone, dull red and purplish, grading down into soft clayey sandstone; all with irregular cornstone concretions	4	0	260	0
Sandstone, buff, coarse and very coarse, with red mudstone pellets; sharp disconformable base	2	0	262	0
Siltstone and silty mudstone, purple, with irregular beds and concretions of cornstone	3	6	265	6
Sandstone, white and buff, medium-grained and coarse, mudstone pellets at base	8	6	274	0
Sandstone, purplish-grey, clayey, mainly fine-grained, grading down into dull red siltstone and silty mudstone; cornstone concretions near top and lenticular, buff, coarse-grained sandstone near middle	5	0	279	0
Sandstone, dull red with buff patches towards base, fine- and medium-grained at top but coarser at base which includes mudstone pellets and may rest disconformably on beds below	7	0	286	0
Sandstone, mostly dull red, but with buff and greenish beds, cross-stratified, mainly fine- and medium-grained, clayey, with nodules of concretionary cornstone near top ..	23	6	309	6
Sandstone, buff with red patches, coarse, with greenish mudstone pellets	1	0	310	6
Sandstone, purplish-red, fine- and medium-grained, clayey	3	0	313	6
Obscured	10	0	323	6
Sandstone, coarse and very coarse, with lenses of conglomerate containing pebbles of sandy conglomeratic cornstone (S 48443) and some quartz pebbles	3	0	326	6
Sandstone, dull red, fine- and medium-grained, with irregular concretions of sandy cornstone	10	0	336	6

The bottom of the section is cut off by a fault throwing down to the east-north-east but the throw is thought to be small; the total thickness of the Cornstone Beds probably does not greatly exceed 340 ft in this locality.

Exposures east of the Gargunnock Burn. The only exposures of the Cornstone Beds east of the Gargunnock Burn are in two quarries. In the more westerly of these [NS 70249331], which lies immediately east of the burn, the following section of beds near the top of the division is exposed:

	ft	in
Sandstone, white, cross-stratified, medium-grained and coarse	5	6
Conglomerate, white, including pebbles of conglomeratic cornstone, quartz and possibly decomposed igneous rock	1	0
Sandstone, white, cross-stratified, coarse	2	9
Obscured	1	0
Sandstone, as above .. .. (seen)	4	6

In the other quarry, which lies about two-thirds of a mile east of the burn, about 20 ft of mottled pale reddish-brown and white, medium-grained sandstone are seen. These beds are thought to lie near the base of the division. Further east it seems probable that the whole outcrop of the Cornstone Beds is cut out by the Abbey Craig Fault which throws the Carboniferous lavas down against the Gargunnock Sandstones.

CENTRAL OUTCROP

The central outcrop of Upper Old Red Sandstone has been inferred from a small cluster of exposures at Causewayhead. A small quarry [NS 80479581], now partly obscured, beside the main road to Bridge of Allan, formerly showed 20 ft of white, cross-stratified sandstones with some red patches and subordinate beds of siltstone, and a bright red mudstone containing greenish and white concretionary cornstones, all dipping south-south-eastwards at 40°. An outcrop [NS 80509579] immediately to the south-east shows 3 ft of red and white, fine-grained, laminated sandstone overlain by 1 ft 6 in of white and greenish, very coarse-grained sandstone. Another exposure [NS 80419591] of red sandstone was formerly seen at the roadside north-north-east of the quarry. Dinham and Haldane (1932, p. 7) correlated these rocks with the middle division of the Upper Old Red Sandstone of the Campsie area, which is equivalent to all except the topmost strata of the Cornstone Beds.

W.A.R.

EASTERN OUTCROP

Rocks of Upper Old Red Sandstone age crop out in the River Devon, east of the Muckart Fault, at the eastern limit of the district, where they dip northwards on the flank of a major north-easterly anticlinal structure. The core of this structure comprises lavas of Lower Old Red Sandstone age, cropping out half a

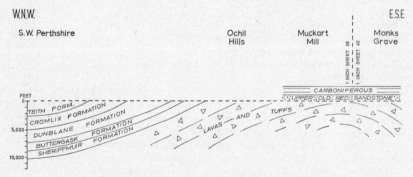

FIG. 10. *Diagram illustrating unconformity at base of Upper Old Red Sandstone*

mile to the south-east, in the Kinross (40) Sheet. The thickness of Upper Old Red Sandstone in this area was estimated as 500 ft by Geikie (1900, p. 31), but this figure may be more valid farther east than it is in the Devon where it may approach 1000 ft. Even so, this is a considerable reduction as compared with the Fintry area, farther west (p. 98). The lowest members overlying the lavas are not exposed, but the junction must mark a very considerable unconformity for a great thickness of volcanic rocks and sediments of Lower Old Red Sandstone age is missing (Fig. 10).

The succession can be subdivided into two parts which are somewhat similar, but not identical, in lithology to the Gargunnock Sandstones and Cornstone Beds of the western outcrop. The lower, or sandstone, subdivision is made up of about 800 ft of friable, cross-bedded, yellow, red and purple sandstones with thin bands of mottled grits and subsidiary beds of shale. It is well exposed in the Gairney Burn at and upstream from the railway viaduct.

The upper, or cornstone, subdivision consists of cornstones interbedded with sandstones and grits which have a mottled hue and, occasionally, a calcareous cement. One cornstone, 80 yd downstream [NT 00589853] from the viaduct, resembles in thin section some of the Cementstone Group rocks described by Dr. F. W. Anderson as desiccation breccias (p. 135), though in hand specimen it is paler and more pink in colour than the Carboniferous types. The topmost beds among the cornstones form the southern bank of the Gairney Burn for 200 yd above its confluence [NT 00389867] with the River Devon and make a spectacular erosional feature in the middle of the main stream for 350 yd to the west of the confluence. The same beds are poorly exposed abutting against the downthrow (western) side of the Muckart Fault [NS 99789851], 600 yd east of Muckart Mill.

The cornstone subdivision is 70 ft thick in the Gairney Burn, increasing to 170 ft half a mile to the west in the River Devon. This variation, taken in conjunction with the abrupt change in lithology marked at the base of the cementstones (p. 133), suggests some degree of unconformity towards the top of the subdivision. The cornstone lithology, on the other hand, is of a kind in which rapid lateral variation might be expected and since the topmost band appears to be persistent, the break, if there is one, must lie below it.   E.H.F.

REFERENCES

ALLEN, J. R. L. 1960. Cornstone. *Geol. Mag.*, **97**, 43–8.
—— 1962. Intraformational conglomerates and scoured surfaces in the Lower Old Red Sandstone of the Anglo-Welsh Cuvette. *Lpool Manchr geol. J.*, **3**, 1–20.
—— 1965. A review of the origin and characteristics of recent alluvial sediments. *Sedimentology*, **5**, 89–191.
—— and TARLO, L. B. 1963. The Downtonian and Dittonian facies of the Welsh Borderland. *Geol. Mag.*, **100**, 129–55.
BRETZ, J. H. and HORNBERG, L. 1949. Caliche in south-eastern New Mexico. *J. Geol.*, **57**, 491–511.
BROWN, C. N. 1956. The origin of caliche on the north-eastern Llano Estacado, Texas. *J. Geol.*, **64**, 1–15.
BURGESS, I. C. 1961. Fossil soils of the Upper Old Red Sandstone of south Ayrshire. *Trans. geol. Soc. Glasg.*, **24**, 138–53.
CAROZZI, A. V. 1960. *Microscopic sedimentary petrography*. New York.
CLOUGH, C. T., HINXMAN, L. W., WILSON, J. S. G., CRAMPTON, C. B., WRIGHT, W. B., BAILEY, E. B., ANDERSON, E. M. and CARRUTHERS, R. G. 1925. The geology of the Glasgow district. 2nd edit. revised by MACGREGOR, M., DINHAM, C. H., BAILEY, E. B. and ANDERSON, E. M. *Mem. geol. Surv. Gt Br.*
CRAIG, G. Y. (*editor*). 1965. *The geology of Scotland*. Edinburgh and London.
DINHAM, C. H. and HALDANE, D. 1932. The economic geology of the Stirling and Clackmannan Coalfield. *Mem. geol. Surv. Gt Br.*
EVAMY, B. D. 1963. The application of a chemical staining technique to dedolomitisation. *Sedimentology*, **2**, 164–70.

I

GEIKIE, A. 1900. The geology of central and western Fife and Kinross-shire. *Mem. geol. Surv. Gt Br.*

GREENSMITH, J. T. 1957. Lithology, with particular reference to cementation, of Upper Carboniferous sandstones in northern Derbyshire, England. *J. sedim. Petrol.,* **57,** 405–16.

—— 1961. The petrology of the Oil-Shale Group sandstones of West Lothian and southern Fifeshire. *Proc. Geol. Ass.,* **72,** 49–71.

KRYNINE, P. D. 1949. The origin of red beds. *Trans. N.Y. Acad. Sci.,* **2,** 60–8.

MCKEE, E. D. and WEIR, G. W. 1953. Terminology for stratification and cross-stratification in sedimentary rocks. *Bull. geol. Soc. Am.,* **64,** 381–90.

MAUFE, H. B. 1910. In *Mem. geol. Surv. Summ. Prog.* for 1909, 35–6.

MUIR, A., HARDIE, H. G. M., MITCHELL, R. L. and PHEMISTER, J. 1956. The limestones of Scotland: chemical analyses and petrography. *Mem. geol. Surv. spec. Rep. Miner. Resour. Gt Br.,* **37.**

PETTIJOHN, F. J. 1957. *Sedimentary rocks.* 2nd edit. New York.

READ, W. A. 1960. In *Mem. geol. Surv. Summ. Prog.* for 1959, 41.

—— and JOHNSON, S. R. H. 1967. The sedimentology of sandstone formations within the Upper Old Red Sandstone and lowest Calciferous Sandstone Measures west of Stirling, Scotland. *Scott. J. Geol.,* **3,** 242–67.

SAYRE, A. N. 1937. Geology and ground-water resources of Duval County, Texas. *Wat.-Supply Irrig. Pap., Wash.,* **776.**

SELLEY, R. C., SHEARMAN, D. J., SUTTON, J. and WATSON, J. 1963. Some underwater disturbances in the Torridonian of Skye and Raasay. *Geol. Mag.,* **100,** 224–43.

SWINEFORD, A., LEONARD, A. B. and FRYE, J. C. 1958. Petrology of the Pliocene Pisolitic Limestone in the Great Plains. *Bull. Kans. Univ. geol. Surv.,* **130,** 96–116.

WALKER, T. R. 1967. Formation of red beds in modern and ancient deserts. *Bull. geol. Soc. Am.,* **78,** 353–67.

Chapter VII

CALCIFEROUS SANDSTONE MEASURES

INTRODUCTION

WITHIN THE AREA of the Stirling Sheet the Calciferous Sandstone Measures fall naturally into three parts which differ sharply from each other in lithology. The lowest, which seems to succeed the Upper Old Red Sandstone conformably over the greater part of the outcrop, comprises the alternating cementstones, mudstones and shales of the Ballagan Beds, overlain by the Downie's Loup Sandstones. These sediments are succeeded by the volcanic rocks of the Clyde Plateau which are overlain in turn by sediments which are similar to those of the Lower Limestone Group. This threefold subdivision corresponds to that used in the Glasgow and Kilsyth districts (Clough and others 1925, pp. 10–31; Robertson and Haldane 1937, p. 9) and has been adopted in preference to the classification followed in the Stirling and Clackmannan Memoir (Dinham and Haldane 1932, pp. 7–11) in which the volcanic rocks and underlying sediments were assigned to a 'Lower (Cementstone) Group' and the sediments above the lavas to an 'Upper (Oil-Shale) Group'. While the sediments above the lavas are undoubtedly equivalent to the upper part of the Oil-Shale Group of the Lothians, it is not possible in the Stirling district to determine the stratigraphical level at which the base of the Oil-Shale Group, as defined in the Lothians (Tulloch and Walton 1958, pp. 8–16), should be drawn.

Only the top of the Calciferous Sandstone Measures, which is drawn at the base of the Murrayshall (Hurlet) Limestone, is known to be a definite stratigraphical horizon. The base and the boundaries between the three subdivisions are all thought to be diachronous. There is thought to be a large break between the top of the Clyde Plateau lavas and the overlying sediments. Currie (1954, p. 533) has drawn the base of the Upper Bollandian Stage (P_2) at the base of the Hurlet Limestone and it seems likely that the upper group of sediments belongs to the preceding Lower Bollandian Stage (P_1). There is, as yet, no satisfactory palaeontological evidence for the age of the two lower parts of the succession.

The remainder of this chapter is devoted to an account of the sedimentary rocks that lie beneath the volcanic rocks. Discussion of the latter, and the sediments that overlie them, is reserved for Chapter VIII.

SEDIMENTS BELOW THE VOLCANIC ROCKS

The sediments that lie between the Upper Old Red Sandstone and the Clyde Plateau lavas crop out either at the surface or below drift in the south-western part of the district and sediments of approximately the same age also appear in the extreme east. The western outcrops cover a much larger area than the eastern. They comprise the main outcrop, which forms a strip up to about a mile wide that skirts the western and northern lava scarps of the Fintry, Gargunnock and Touch hills, and a smaller outcrop that lies between the Ochil and Abbey Craig faults, immediately west of Craigforth and about 1½ miles west of Stirling. The main outcrop, which includes several stream sections, tapers out eastwards, partly as a result of thinning of the sediments but principally because the strata are progressively cut out in that direction by a major strike fault—the Abbey Craig Fault. The smaller outcrop, west of the lavas of Craigforth, is entirely covered by the superficial deposits of the Carse of Stirling and was proved by the Geological Survey Stirling No. 1 (Kaimes) Bore [NS 77209454] in 1961 (pp. 322–5).

The eastern outcrops lie in the vicinity of Muckart Mill, between the Ochil and Arndean faults. Here the sediments are not overlain by lavas and may include beds at a higher stratigraphical level than in the western outcrops.

The lower boundary is nowhere well exposed but seems to be a passage by alternation from the sandstones of the Cornstone Beds to the typical Ballagan Beds lithology (p. 97). Thus it has been drawn at a change in facies which is almost certainly transgressive and can therefore have no widespread time-stratigraphical significance (cf. Macgregor and others 1940, pp. 256–8), especially as a sandstone facies very similar to the Cornstone Beds appears higher in the succession (p. 124). The upper boundary of this division is also probably diachronous as it is drawn at the lowest lava of the Calciferous Sandstone Measures and this is almost certainly not the same flow over the whole area (pp. 143–4). Furthermore no lavas are known to be present in the eastern outcrop.

In the western outcrops, below the Clyde Plateau lavas, the succession is divisible into two parts, the lower made up of alternating cementstones, shales, mudstones and subordinate sandstones, and the upper, the Downie's Loup Sandstones, consisting dominantly of white sandstones similar to those of the Cornstone Beds. In the eastern outcrops, where no Calciferous Sandstone Measures lavas have been found, a lower and an upper division of alternating cementstones, shales, marls and thin sandstones seem to be separated by a middle division of calcareous sandstones which are lithologically similar to the Downie's Loup Sandstones.

For convenience in the following account, the western and eastern outcrops are described separately.

WESTERN OUTCROPS

In the western outcrops, the base of the Calciferous Sandstone Measures is drawn arbitrarily in any given locality at the highest cornstone or medium-grained sandstone of the Cornstone Beds and the upper boundary is drawn at the base of the lowest local flow of the Basal Group of lavas. South-west of the Fintry Hills, in the extreme west of the Stirling district, the Basal Group dies out and it is impossible to separate the sediments below the Calciferous Sandstone Measures lavas from the Slackgun Interbasaltic Beds which elsewhere lie within the lavas (p. 144).

The main outcrop skirts the northern edge of the lava scarp and varies in width from three-quarters of a mile to just over a mile in the west, where the sediments are thickest, but narrows towards the east and eventually disappears where the sediments are cut out completely by the Abbey Craig Fault. In the smaller outcrop, between the Abbey Craig and Ochil faults, the strike is thought to run roughly north-south, approximately parallel to the strike of the overlying lavas in the southern part of Craigforth.

The beds of the main outcrop generally dip south-south-eastwards at angles between 5° and 15°, although steeper dips are found close to faults; in the outcrop west of Craigforth the dip is eastwards at angles between 13° and 26°.

Apart from the Balmenoch Burn and Abbey Craig faults the sediments seem to be affected by only a few, comparatively small faults. They are, however, cut by the Dun intrusion, the Skiddaw sill, the Downie's Loup sill and a number of small dykes (p. 159). The sediments below the lavas thin eastwards from about 1600 ft immediately north-west of Stronend to about 950 ft north of Standmilane Craig, some 3½ miles towards the east-north-east. Beyond this it becomes difficult to estimate thickness because of the effects of the Abbey Craig Fault which runs parallel to the strike. It seems probable that the eastward thinning continues but only the top 219 ft were proved in Stirling No. 1 Bore. This bore proved, however, that Dinham was justified in questioning Peach's interpretation, implicit in the 1882 edition of the one-inch map, that the lavas overlap the underlying Calciferous Sandstone Measures sediments to rest directly upon rocks classed as Upper Old Red Sandstone (*see* Dinham and Haldane 1932, pp. 8–9; Dixon 1938, pp. 426–8). The lowest Calciferous Sandstone Measures sediments, like the underlying Upper Old Red Sandstone, seem to have been affected, during deposition, by the differential subsidence of a synclinal structure (*cf.* George 1958, fig. 26), which may possibly continue the line of the Strathmore Syncline (p. 240).

The lithological succession in the western outcrops closely resembles that around Ballagan of Strathblane (Bailey *in* Clough and others 1925, pp. 11–3) and comprises a lower division, of Ballagan Beds facies, which is characterized by alternating cementstones, mudstones and shales, and an upper division consisting dominantly of sandstones. The strata of the latter division seem to be approximately equivalent to the Spout of Ballagan Sandstone and have been named the Downie's Loup Sandstones as they are best exposed at Downie's Loup in the Gargunnock Burn (Summ. Prog. 1960, p. 41). The sedimentary structures and probable conditions of deposition of the Ballagan Beds facies and of the Downie's Loup Sandstones have been discussed respectively by Belt, Freshney and Read (1967) and Read and Johnson (1967).

Lower Division (Ballagan Beds Facies)

The lower division seems to pass by alternation down into the white, carbonate-rich sandstones of the Cornstone Beds (*cf.* Bailey *in* Clough and others 1925, p. 11) and up into the similar Downie's Loup Sandstones. Although there is no definite evidence within the outcrop, it is also quite probable that some strata of Ballagan Beds facies pass laterally as well as vertically into both groups of white sandstones (*cf.* Macgregor and others 1940, p. 257). The fossils that have been found in the western outcrops consist almost entirely of ostracods and fish remains. Pebbles of algal limestone similar to that found in the eastern outcrops occur in the Downie's Loup Sandstones, for which a north-westerly or westerly derivation is suggested (Read and Johnson 1967, figs. 1, 4).

Cementstones, shales, mudstones and occasional thin beds of sandstone are found throughout the lower division although the relative proportions differ in various parts of the succession (see below). The cementstones form beds, in some cases nodular, of micrograined to pelitomorphic dolomite (*see* Phemister *in* Muir and others 1956, pp. 69–74) with a varying proportion of angular detrital quartz and argillaceous material. The CaO/MgO ratio of specimens analysed ranges from 1·9/1 to 2·4/1 (Table 6, Anals. V–VIII); this is somewhat higher than the ratios for cementstones in the Ballagan Burn analysed by Young (1867,

p. 211) but is within the range of cementstones from other Scottish localities (Muir and Hardie *in* Muir and others 1956, pp. 37–41).

Individual beds of cementstone may be locally more than 2 feet thick but are generally less than 9 inches. The thickness of most of the beds remains more or less constant in most exposures, but some may be seen to decrease in thickness abruptly. In Stirling No. 1 Bore the cementstones frequently grade into the shales above and below and may have highly irregular bases (Plate IV, fig. 6). Some of these cementstones have a brecciated appearance with fragments of relatively pure carbonate in a more argillaceous matrix (Plate IV, fig. 7). The cementstones in the bore are generally more argillaceous than those in the outcrops to the south-west and are commonly nearer in composition to dolomitic mudstone than to cementstone. A similar northward change was noted by Bailey (*in* Clough and others 1925, p. 13) in the Campsie Fells.

A few of the beds show definite internal stratification which is brought out by aligned mica flakes and by laminae relatively rich in detrital quartz. These stratified beds also contain obscure thin-shelled spheroidal and vermiform bodies which are almost certainly organic (S 44830). The tops of at least two of these beds are broken by a rectilinear pattern of cracks which are filled with either more sandy carbonate or coarse-grained carbonate (Plate V, figs. 3a, 3b). As the cracks are generally vertical and taper downwards they are thought to be desiccation cracks formed when the top of the bed lay above water level,

---

PLATE IV

SEDIMENTARY STRUCTURES IN THE BALLAGAN BEDS

All specimens are from Stirling No. 1 (Kaimes) Bore (1961)

FIG. 1. 'Striped beds' (alternating laminae of pale coarse-grained siltstone and very fine-grained sandstone, and of dark greenish-grey silty shale) disturbed by a series of pre-consolidation 'faults' which seem to diverge from a point immediately beyond the left-hand side of the core. These 'faults' may reflect differential compaction in the adjacent or underlying strata. Core between 336 ft 7 in and 337 ft 0 in.

FIG. 2. 'Striped beds', similar to those in Fig. 1, with irregular carbonate nodules which seem to *replace* the clastic sediments by a gradual increase in the proportion of cement. The lamination within the clastic sediments may be traced into the outer parts of the carbonate nodules. Core between 346 ft 0 in and 346 ft 7 in.

FIG. 3. 'Striped beds' with ripple-drift cross-lamination. Core between 347 ft 4 in and 347 ft 7 in.

FIG. 4. Convolute lamination within 'striped beds'. Core between 366 ft 9 in and 367 ft 3 in.

FIG. 5. Irregular contact between pale-grey, very fine-grained sandstone with a high proportion of carbonate cement and slightly silty, dark greenish-grey mudstone with some red mottling. Irregular veins of sandstone cut the mudstone and enclose angular fragments of it. Core between 377 ft 8 in and 378 ft 2 in.

FIG. 6. Pale-grey, silty and sandy cementstone, with highly irregular base resting on greenish-grey mudstone. Core between 404 ft 6 in and 405 ft 3 in.

FIG. 7. Pale-grey cementstone passing down into cementstone breccia with fragments of pale-grey cementstone in a matrix of darker, purplish-grey, more argillaceous carbonate. Core between 433 ft 2 in. and 434 ft 0 in.

rather than synaeresis cracks formed under water while the carbonate mud was in a flocculated state (White 1961, pp. 561–7). It is thought that these stratified cementstones are primary beds. Some cementstone nodules displace the shales above and below them to an extent which is difficult to explain by differential compaction alone, and in Stirling No. 1 Bore irregular nodules of carbonate may be seen replacing alternating laminae of coarse-grained silt and micaceous silty shale, with the coarser quartzose laminae gradually fading out within the nodules (Plate IV, fig. 2). Thus both the displacive and replacive nodules are thought to be secondary. Similarly the highly irregular bases of some of the cementstones in the bore (Plate IV, fig. 6), and the presence of numerous minute, irregular streaks and patches of clay in carbonate and vice versa suggest that these cementstones also may be of secondary origin. In most cases it is very difficult to decide whether cementstones exposed at outcrop are primary or secondary; many of the cementstones that lie directly below thin red mudstones are however stained red and commonly decalcified and so must have been in existence before the oxidation of the red mudstones. As the latter are generally less than 3 ft thick and are thought to have been oxidized shortly after deposition, the cementstones below are likely to be primary or to have formed under only a few feet of muddy sediment. A few cementstones, however, which lie above instead of below red mudstones, have reddened bases which suggests that restricted migration of ferric iron may have taken place some time after deposition. In addition to the cementstones, almost all the clastic sediments contain carbonate which may, in places, be comparable in amount to the detrital minerals.

The mudstones are generally less than 3 ft thick but some are more than 6 ft. They are commonly micaceous and silty, and a few beds are sandy with quartz grains more than 1 mm long. Unlike the shales they lack any well-defined stratification. Their lack of fissility may indicate that the mudstones were deposited as flocculated mud (White 1961, pp. 264–5), possibly in water of higher salinity than that in which the shales were deposited. Salt pseudomorphs, however, seem to be found more commonly in the shales than in the mudstones and the lack of stratification in the latter may not necessarily be original. The proportion of mudstones seems to be higher in Stirling No. 1 Bore than in the stream sections of the main outcrop, but this difference may be due to traces of stratification being picked out by weathering at the outcrop. Some of the mudstones are a uniform greenish-grey or grey colour but many are mottled in shades of brown, purple and dull red; the most prominent beds are dull red, or, less commonly, bright red. As most of these red beds are thin they are thought to have been oxidized under conditions of low water table, possibly during recurring periods of desiccation.

In the main outcrop shales form a higher proportion of the lower division than any other rock type. They are generally greenish-grey or grey but some are brown or red mottled. Many are micaceous and silty and in some the presence of light-grey coarse silt or very fine-grained sand laminae mark a passage by alternation into sandstone. In Stirling No. 1 Bore these alternating coarser and finer laminae have been disturbed in places by convolute lamination, sag structures and pseudo-nodules (Plate IV, fig. 4; Dzulynski and Smith 1963; Kuenen 1958, pp. 17–21; Stewart 1963, pp. 205–11), small-scale pre-consolidation 'faults', burrows and polygonal cracks filled with the coarser sediment. Some beds also show ripple-lamination of a type characteristic of water laden with a high proportion of clay (Walker 1963, pp. 176–7).

Sandstones are rare and seldom more than 3 ft thick. Most of the beds are of uniform thickness within a given exposure but some are lenticular and may be local channel infillings. They may be pale-grey, brownish-grey or greenish-grey in colour and are almost always very fine-grained. Most of the sandstones are ripple-laminated, commonly with forms resembling small-scale trough cross-bedding (Hamblin 1961, pp. 390–5) and there are many good examples of ripple-drift (Plate IV, fig. 3) (*cf.* Sorby 1859, pp. 143–4; McKee 1939, pp. 72–5); there are also some massive, poorly sorted sandstones. Most of the quartz grains are angular, and undulose extinction and composite grains seem to be common. In some specimens the quartz grains may be closely interlocking (S 44863) but in others they seem to be entirely surrounded by an abundant carbonate cement (S 47220). Feldspar, including both fresh and weathered grains of plagioclase, is generally present, but seldom constitutes more than 10 per cent. of the sandstone. Mica is also generally present but is much less abundant than in rocks of similar grain size in the Upper Carboniferous. Almost all the sandstones contain argillaceous material in the matrix or concentrated into clayey micaceous laminae. The proportion of carbonate in the matrix is variable and in some sandstones it may be very high. It is generally micrograined or pelitomorphic and may locally be masked by clayey material in the matrix.

The sandstones, like those of the Ballagan Burn (Bailey *in* Clough and others 1925, p. 12), are intercalated without any recognizable relationship to the cementstone, shale or mudstone alternation, but are most common in the parts of the succession where the red mudstones are most prominent (see below).

Unlike the equivalent strata of Campsie Glen (Robertson and Haldane 1937, p. 10; Robertson 1948, pp. 145–7) the lithological types are not repeated in any obvious order and it is difficult to determine any characteristic sedimentary rhythm other than the alternation of carbonate and clastic sediments. Cementstones, mudstones, shales and sandstones may be found throughout the succession, but the relative proportions of these rock types vary in such a way that the succession may be divided into three facies types. Typical sections of these are illustrated in Fig. 11. The lower and upper facies are similar and are characterized by a relatively low proportion of cementstones and a relatively high proportion of red mudstones and sandstones, whereas in the middle facies cementstones are relatively abundant and red beds and sandstones are comparatively rare. Thus the passage by alternation down into the Cornstone Beds and up into the Downie's Loup Sandstones tends to be associated with a decrease in the proportion of carbonate rocks deposited and an increase in the number of horizons at which oxidation and, probably, desiccation are thought to have occurred.

Marine fossils have been found in rocks of somewhat similar facies in the Canonbie area (Peach and Horne 1903, p. 841), and George (1958, p. 304) has suggested that the cementstones are in part chemical precipitates derived from carbonates 'brought in by gentle marine infiltration across flats protected by bars, or sills, or merely by distance'. Possibly the cementstones may have been formed on a wide coastal flat by the concentration of groundwater, fed by percolation from the highly saline waters of coastal lagoons. Another possible mechanism is the precipitation of very fine-grained primary dolomite following a rise in pH caused by plant growth in shallow saline water, as described by Alderman and Skinner (1957) in South Australia. Thus it seems likely that the Ballagan Beds were laid down in a coastal flat environment which may have been adjacent both to a marine environment where algal limestones were being

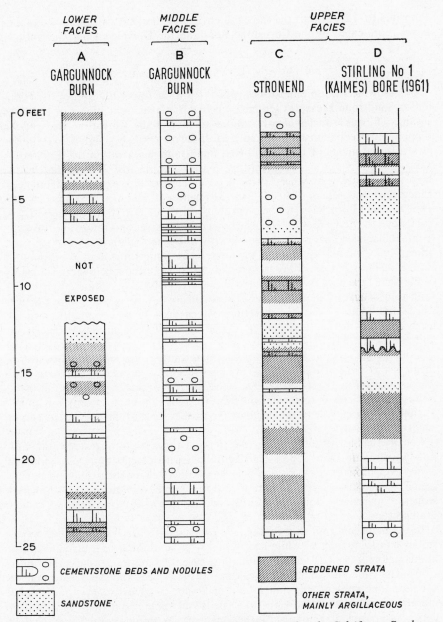

FIG. 11. *Comparative vertical sections of facies types within the Calciferous Sandstone Measures sediments below the Downie's Loup Sandstones*

A. Strata 10 to 35 ft above highest Cornstone Beds exposed in the Gargunnock Burn [NS 70689326]

B. Strata 113 to 138 ft above highest Cornstone Beds exposed in the Gargunnock Burn [NS 70739312]

C. Strata immediately below the Downie's Loup Sandstones at Stronend [NS 62288961]

D. Strata 370 to 395 ft from surface and 29 ft below the lowest limestone conglomerate in Stirling No. 1 (Kaimes) Bore (1961) [NS 77209454]

deposited (p. 127) and to the fluviatile environment of the calcareous sandstone facies represented by the Cornstone Beds and the Downie's Loup Sandstones.

Upper Division (Downie's Loup Sandstones)

The Downie's Loup Sandstones, which form the upper division of the Calciferous Sandstone Measures sediments below the lavas, represent a reversion to a sandy, fluviatile facies closely similar to that of the Cornstone Beds of the Upper Old Red Sandstone (Read and Johnson 1967, pp. 261–3). A similar return to sediments of Upper Old Red Sandstone facies within the Calciferous Sandstone Measures has been recorded in the Campsie area (Young 1860, p. 14; Bailey *in* Clough and others 1925, p. 8) and in other parts of Scotland (e.g. Macgregor and others 1940, p. 238; Mitchell and Mykura 1962, pp. 35–40). The Downie's Loup Sandstones are probably equivalent to the Spout of Ballagan Sandstone of the Campsie Fells which becomes coarser and thicker northwards from Ballagan Glen, but thins towards the east (Bailey *in* Clough and others 1925, p. 13). Both the Downie's Loup Sandstones and the Spout of Ballagan Sandstone may have been laid down in a restricted belt while sediments of Ballagan type were being deposited elsewhere. The cross-bedding of the former sandstones suggests that they were deposited mainly by currents flowing eastwards and south-eastwards—directions which seem to be compatible with the likely trend of the southern margin of the Spout of Ballagan Sandstone (Read and Johnson 1967, pp. 254–61, figs. 1, 4).

None of the streams which cross the main outcrop gives a complete section through the division but the total thickness seems to decrease east-north-eastwards from about 330 ft north of Stronend to 126 ft at Stirling No. 1 Bore where, however, the facies is somewhat different (p. 120). The western outcrops of the Stirling district may lie to the north of the thickest part of the postulated belt of sandstone.

Locally the base of the Downie's Loup Sandstones seems to rest abruptly and possibly disconformably upon strata of Ballagan Beds facies; the erosion implied is however thought to be confined to purely local channels as elsewhere there seems to be a passage by alternation, and the base of the Downie's Loup Sandstones is in general drawn arbitrarily at the lowest bed coarser than a fine-grained sandstone.

In the main outcrop, skirting the lava escarpment, the Downie's Loup Sandstones consist mainly of white sandstone, with subordinate pebbly sandstones and conglomerates containing abundant pebbles of limestone, quartz and mudstone. There are also some highly calcareous sandy beds and these, like some of the limestone pebbles, are similar in appearance to concretionary and conglomeratic cornstones of the Cornstone Beds but differ from them in chemical composition (pp. 105–7). Towards the top increasing amounts of volcanic detritus appear and the strata closely resemble parts of the Slackgun Interbasaltic Beds; indeed in the area south-west of Stronend, where the intervening basal lavas die out, it becomes almost impossible to separate the two sets of strata.

Stirling No. 1 Bore proved that the Downie's Loup Sandstones are present at outcrop west of Craigforth, but are of a somewhat different facies, characterized by abundant calcirudites, or limestone conglomerates, and calcarenites (Pettijohn 1957, p. 401). These are associated with white and greenish sandstones and subordinate grey shales and mudstones in the upper part of the succession but

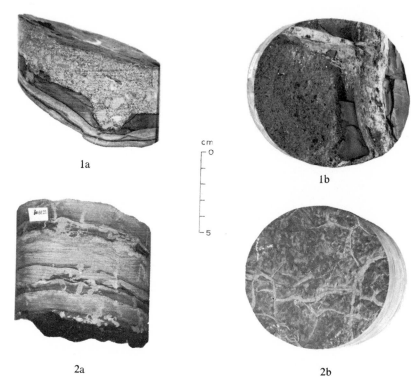

1a

1b

2a

2b

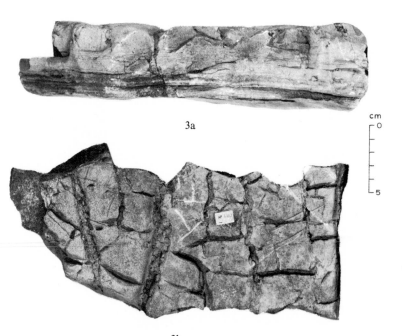

3a

3b

alternate with thick greenish-grey mudstones and shales lower down so that the Downie's Loup Sandstones grade down into strata of modified Ballagan Beds facies. The volcanic detritus at the top of the succession seems to be represented in the bore by purplish mudstones.

As in the Ballagan Beds facies, almost all the clastic sediments contain a greater or lesser proportion of carbonate in the matrix. In addition some pale nodular, highly calcareous beds are found in the sandstones and pale calcareous nodules are quite common in the mudstones and shales. These calcareous rocks are generally similar in appearance to the concretionary cornstones of the Corn-stone Beds and probably have a similar origin (pp. 104–5), but are less common. None has, as yet, been analysed.

Mudstones without any definite stratification are fairly common in the Downie's Loup Sandstones and are especially thick and abundant in the lower part of the succession in Stirling No. 1 Bore where they alternate with limestone conglomerates. Some are silty or even sandy. In the stream sections most of the mudstones are purplish and closely resemble the mudstones of the Cornstone Beds, but in the bore they are generally greenish-grey or grey and resemble some of the mudstones of Ballagan Beds facies.

Shales, most of which are greenish-grey, are generally less common than mudstones and many are silty and micaceous. Passages by alternation into very fine-grained sandstone are common and display sedimentary structures similar to those seen in strata of the same type in the Ballagan Beds.

Sandstones seem to make up the bulk of the succession in the main outcrop but constitute only slightly more than half of the succession in Stirling No. 1 Bore. Most of them are fine-grained or medium-grained but there are also very fine-grained sandstones, with sedimentary structures similar to those in the sandstones of the Ballagan Beds facies (Plate IV, fig. 1; Plate V, figs. 2a, 2b), as well as some coarse and very coarse varieties. Some local erosion seems to have taken place prior to the deposition of many of the coarser sandstones, some of which probably represent channel infillings. Most of the sandstones are white

---

PLATE V

Sedimentary structures in the basal Downie's Loup Sandstones and the Ballagan Beds

Fig. 1a. Load-casts at base of a thin calcirudite band overlying 'striped beds'. Downie's Loup Sandstones. Stirling No. 1 (Kaimes) Bore (1961). Core from between 269 ft 9 in and 269 ft 11 in.

Fig. 1b. Base of the same calcirudite bed showing two elongate load-casts at roughly 90° to each other.

Fig. 2a. Pale-grey, very fine-grained sandstone with even laminae of dark-grey silty mudstone cut by irregular sandstone veins thought to be desiccation crack infillings. Downie's Loup Sandstones. Stirling No. 1 (Kaimes) Bore (1961). Core between 280 ft 0 in and 280 ft 3 in.

Fig. 2b. Top of 2a showing rectilinear pattern of sandstone-filled cracks.

Fig. 3a. Stratified pale-grey cementstone with laminae of darker, more argillaceous material. The top of the bed is split by cracks which taper out downwards and are thought to be desiccation cracks. Ballagan Beds. Boquhan Burn [NS 65229211].

Fig. 3b. Top of 3a showing rectilinear pattern of cracks.

but many of the finer varieties are greenish, as are the sandstones towards the top of the succession, where the rocks grade into volcanic detritus. The sandstones usually show cross-stratification and both the planar and trough types of McKee and Weir (1953, pp. 385–7) are present.

Most of the quartz grains are angular or subangular and many show undulose extinction or are composite grains of metaquartzite, suggesting that they were probably derived ultimately from metamorphic rocks. In places the quartz grains form an intricate mosaic with closely interlocking grains and some grains show definite secondary enlargements (S 47209). In other sandstones, especially those with abundant carbonate cement, quartz has been partially replaced by carbonate. The proportion of feldspar among the detrital grains varies considerably but it may be higher than 10 per cent. in some beds. Plagioclase seems most common and both weathered and fresh grains are found. Orthoclase and microcline are generally subordinate. Feldspar grains may also be partially replaced by carbonate. Both muscovite and biotite occur, but micas are generally not abundant except in some of the finer-grained sandstones. Heavy minerals include zircon, garnet, tourmaline and possibly rutile.

Pebbly sandstones and conglomerates are fairly common and are especially abundant in Stirling No. 1 Bore. They generally fall into one or other of two categories. In the first, which is the type most commonly found in the main outcrop, limestone pebbles, some of which may be more than 15 cm long, are generally the most abundant but there are significant numbers of pebbles of other rock types including vein quartz, quartzite, and decomposed fine-grained basic igneous rocks in addition to abundant fragments of shale and mudstone. A few pebbles of calcareous sandstone, similar in type to some beds within the Downie's Loup Sandstones themselves, have also been found. In the second category, which is best represented in Stirling No. 1 Bore, although a bed of the same type is found at Downie's Loup, fragments of limestone ranging in size from 0·1 mm to more than 10 cm form the bulk of the rock. The carbonate pellets are normally rounded or subangular but where they are especially concentrated they have recrystallized into a closely interlocking mosaic of carbonate fragments (S 47214, 47216). In addition to the limestone conglomerates or calcirudites, there are some beds of calcarenite (Pettijohn 1957, p. 401) in which the average size of the carbonate pellets is less than 2 mm. The most common carbonate pellets are pelitomorphic and micrograined types (Phemister in Muir and others 1956, p. 69) which are very similar in appearance to some of the cementstones, but there are also pellets of fine-grained carbonate, comparable in grain size to some of the cornstones of the Cornstone Beds, and of calcarenite. Traces of recrystallization are common within the carbonate pellets, some of which are very difficult to distinguish from the carbonate matrix. Many of the pellets contain angular grains of detrital quartz. A few of the carbonate pebbles in Stirling No. 1 Bore show concentric and layered algal structures in pelitomorphic carbonate (cf. p. 135).

Despite the similarity in appearance of some of the carbonate pellets in the Downie's Loup Sandstones to cementstones and conglomeratic cornstones, partial analysis of carbonate pebbles from both categories of conglomerate and of a calcarenite (Table 6, Anals. IX–XIII) have all yielded CaO/MgO ratios between 32·6/1 and 70·4/1, all of which are much higher than any of the ratios for either the cementstones or the cornstones of the Cornstone Beds. Some of the pebbles may have been derived from concretionary cornstones formed within the sandy environment in which the Downie's Loup Sandstones were laid down but many of the pelitomorphic and micrograined pellets, including all those containing algal fragments, were probably derived by erosion from deposits of a different facies which included algal limestones. Although beds of similar type have been recorded in the eastern outcrops (p. 135), the cross-bedding suggests derivation from the west or north-west rather than the east (Read and Johnson 1967, figs. 1, 4).

DETAILS

Western slopes of the Fintry Hills. Strata of Ballagan Beds facies overlain by Downie's Loup Sandstones are exposed in the Illachan Burn [NS 62258788–62388804] and one of its tributaries [NS 61798822–62038839] on the slopes above Culcreuch. The Ballagan Beds belong to the upper facies and include sandstones up to 5 ft thick, which become more numerous and thicker as the Downie's Loup Sandstones are approached. The latter, which are exposed in the streams and also in scattered sections on the hillside, are mostly medium-grained to coarse and include abundant mudstone and limestone pellets in places. Many of the beds show good trough cross-stratification which has locally been disturbed and contorted.

Further north the Downie's Loup Sandstones are seen in scattered exposures below the crop of the Skiddaw sill. In one exposure [NS 61978891], which is thought to lie only a short distance above the base of the Downie's Loup Sandstones, strata reminiscent of the Ballagan Beds, including nodular beds of highly calcareous sandstones that weather out like cementstones, thin beds of grey shale and very fine-grained sandstone, are interbedded with the coarser white sandstones typical of the Downie's Loup Sandstones. Near the same locality, but higher in the succession [NS 62078887] is the exposure of conglomerate from which two of the limestone pebbles analysed (S 47604, 47605; Table 6, Anals. IX, X) were collected. The boundaries of some of the limestone pebbles with the matrix are locally very intricate, suggesting some secondary enlargement of the pebbles (cf. p. 105). Other pebbles are of vein quartz, up to 5 cm long, quartzite and calcareous sandstone; one of the latter shows a remarkable concentration of heavy minerals including zircon, tourmaline and garnet (S 47209). There are also abundant greenish clayey pellets, some of which may be pebbles of highly decomposed igneous rock. The matrix of the conglomerate is an ill-sorted greenish clayey sandstone which contains chloritic material also probably derived from volcanic detritus.

Northern slopes of the Fintry Hills. Sections in the Ballagan Beds may be seen in three gullies west and north-west of Stronend and there are scattered exposures of the Downie's Loup Sandstones on the hillside above. The following section [NS 62288961–62208965], in the middle gully, is the best exposed and shows a gradual change from the middle to the upper facies of the Ballagan Beds. The base of the Downie's Loup Sandstones here is sharp and probably coincides with a local disconformity but a passage by alternation between the two facies seems to take place only 600 ft to the south-south-west [NS 62208945].

	Thickness		Total thickness	
	ft	in	ft	in
Sandstone, white, mainly medium-grained, with abundant mudstone pellets, cross-stratified, sharp base	5	8	5	8
(Base of Downie's Loup Sandstones)				
Shales and mudstones, greenish-grey and red, silty and micaceous in places, with five beds of very fine-grained greenish sandstone, all less than 8 in thick. Nine cementstones up to 6 in thick, mostly decalcified and reddened, in addition to cementstone nodules (see Fig. 11, C) ..	18	3	23	11

K

	Thickness ft	in	Total thickness ft	in
Mudstones with subordinate shales, red, greenish-grey and grey, silty and micaceous in places, with a 6-in bed of very fine-grained sandstone near the middle. Ten cementstones in beds up to 8 in thick, five of which are reddened	23	2	47	1
Mudstones, mainly grey or red, with subordinate shales. Seven cementstones in beds up to 2 ft 1 in thick, two of which have reddened tops..	28	3	75	4
Sandstone, greenish, fine-grained and very fine-grained, with subordinate laminae of silty shale and thin beds of red-mottled mudstone	3	3	78	7
Obscured	18	0	96	7
Mudstones and shales, grey, greenish and red, silty and micaceous in places. Nine cementstones in beds up to 10 in thick, one of which is reddened	29	0	125	7
Alternating grey shale and cementstone in beds up to 3 in thick with a 10-in bed of grey fragmental clay-rock towards the top	2	7	128	2
Stratified cementstone with traces of shale partings ..	1	3	129	5
Grey shales with subordinate greenish and grey mudstones, which are silty and micaceous in places. No red mottling. Fourteen cementstones in beds up to 13 in thick, the two lowest of which are stratified with shale partings. Some cementstone nodules also found	20	2	149	7
Mudstone, pale greenish-grey, silty and sandy, with quartz grains up to 1·5 mm	3	0	152	7
Shales with some mudstones, greenish and grey with rare local red mottling, silty and micaceous in places. Six cementstones in beds up to 7 in thick in addition to numerous cementstone nodules	12	0	164	7

Higher up the slope [NS 62298953], near the top of the Downie's Loup Sandstones, white pebbly sandstones may be seen to grade up into yellowish and greenish volcanic detritus which locally contains plant impressions. The total thickness of the Downie's Loup Sandstones in this locality was found to be about 330 ft.

East-north-eastwards along the strike about 50 ft of cross-stratified white sandstones, which lie near the base of the Downie's Loup Sandstones, are exposed in crags immediately west of the Balmenoch Burn Fault. Most of the sandstones are medium-grained but they also include lenses of coarser sandstone with calcareous pebbles, finer greenish clayey sandstones and irregular beds of purplish-grey and greenish-grey shale and mudstone.

About a mile to the north-east more than 200 ft of Ballagan Beds, including occasional dull red mudstones and thin very fine-grained sandstones, are exposed in an overgrown stream [NS 64619125–64559147] which drains northwards into the Pow Burn.

The Ballagan Beds are poorly exposed in the Boquhan Burn and the Downie's Loup Sandstones are not exposed at all. One of the two stratified cementstones analysed (S 47603; *see* Table 6, Anal. V) crops out in the burn [NS 65229211] only a short distance above the topmost Cornstone Beds. The top of this cementstone shows a particularly good polygonal pattern of vertical cracks and lower down the bed is interleaved with occasional laminae richer in detrital quartz, mica and clay minerals. Obscure thin-shelled spheroidal bodies, probably organic, may be seen in thin section (S 47211, 47603).

Northern slopes of the Gargunnock Hills. Between the Boquhan and Gargunnock burns exposures are rather poor and are largely confined to gullies below the lava scarp. In one of the best of these gully sections [NS 67499242–67569226], which runs down from the foot of the steep scarp of Standmilane Craig, patchy exposures of greenish, very fine-grained sandstones and grey, purple and red mottled mudstones with carbonate nodules, which are thought to belong to the upper facies of the Ballagan Beds, are overlain by more than 100 ft of strata belonging to the lower part of the Downie's Loup Sandstones. The latter are mostly white, cross-stratified, fine, medium-grained or coarse sandstones with subordinate greenish, very fine-grained clayey sandstones and purple mudstones. Calcareous nodules found in the mudstones and some irregular highly calcareous beds within the sandstones both look similar to some of the concretionary cornstones of the Cornstone Beds. The total thickness of the Downie's Loup Sandstones here must be about 200 ft provided that neither the Skiddaw sill nor the Downie's Loup sill crops out in the drift-covered ground immediately above the gully.

The same part of the succession is rather less well exposed in the gully [NS 69169278–69169268] drained by the Easter Blackspout about a mile to the east-north-east, and 21 ft of dull red, greenish and yellowish mudstones and sandy mudstones belonging to the volcanic detritus at the top of the Downie's Loup Sandstones are exposed nearby [NS 68989260] between the basal lava and the Downie's Loup sill.

By far the best exposures of both the Ballagan Beds and the Downie's Loup Sandstones within the Stirling district may be seen in the Gargunnock Burn between the foot of the lava scarp [NS 70729295] and the highest Cornstone Beds [NS 70679331]. Unfortunately the section is incomplete as strata in the middle facies of the Ballagan Beds are thrown against Downie's Loup Sandstones by the western end of the Abbey Craig Fault (p. 249). The section is cut by several smaller faults, a dyke, and the Downie's Loup sill but the passage upwards from the lower to the middle facies of the Ballagan Beds may nevertheless be followed in detail. The actual junction with the Cornstone Beds is, however, obscured. A bed of dark reddish mudstone thought to be derived from volcanic detritus lies immediately below the lavas. This bed closely resembles a bed immediately below the lavas in Campsie Glen (Robertson and Haldane 1937, p. 10). The details of this sections are as follows:

	Thickness		Total thickness	
	ft	in	ft	in
Slaggy irregular base of lowest lava	–	–	–	–
Mudstone, grey at top but mostly dark red, with grains of feldspar, detrital quartz, pseudomorphs after olivine and fragments of decomposed lava	8	6	8	6
Obscured	33	0	41	6
Mudstone, reddish-brown with pale-grey specks	1	6	43	0
Obscured	12	0	55	0
Conglomerate with pebbles up to 15 cm long including limestone, vein quartz and white sandstone set in an unsorted matrix of calcareous sandstone	2	0	57	0
Obscured	130	0	187	0
Downie's Loup sill at the top of the waterfall	20	0	207	0
Sandstone, mainly white, medium-grained and coarse, cross-stratified, with limestone pebbles and clay pellets in places. Top of bed baked hard	10	0	217	0
Sandstone, fine-grained and very fine-grained, greenish, with a thin bed of purplish mudstone containing large rounded calcareous concretions	14	2	231	2
Sandstone, greenish-white, medium-grained	1	7	232	9

	Thickness ft	in	Total thickness ft	in
Laminae and thin beds of pale very fine-grained sandstone alternating with greenish micaceous shale and mudstone. A 2-in band of calcarenite (S 47606 analysed specimen; see Table 6, Anal. XI) lies 1 ft below the top	10	9	243	6
Obscured (Abbey Craig Fault)	8	6	252	0
Shales with subordinate mudstones, locally silty and micaceous, greenish and grey with local reddish-brown mottling. Some beds up to 1 ft 3 in thick of cementstone, the topmost of which has been analysed (S 47600; see Table 6, Anal. VII), and scattered cementstone nodules. Section cut by three minor faults	28	6	280	6
Obscured (probable fault)	4	6	285	0
Shale, greenish-grey with reddish mottling in places, with limestone nodules which seem to displace the shale laminae	4	3	289	3
Shale, silty and micaceous, grey and greenish-grey with rare reddish mottling. Abundant cementstone nodules and twenty-three beds up to 8 in thick of cementstone, two with traces of stratification. Traces of ostracods in shales 8 ft, above the base (see Fig. 11, B)	25	8	314	11
Shales, locally silty and micaceous, with subordinate mudstone, greenish-grey with red mottling in places. One 2-in bed of very fine-grained sandstone near the centre. Some nodules and seventeen beds of cementstone up to 9 in thick	37	5	352	4
Cementstone, stratified, with some laminae richer in detrital quartz and mica. Traces of a polygonal pattern of vertical cracks at the top. Fish remains and minute thin-shelled spheroidal and vermiform bodies. (S 47601 analysed specimen; see Table 6, Anal. VI)..	1	1	353	5
Shale, mainly silty and micaceous, mainly grey with purple and red mottling. One 3-in bed of silty cementstone and a layer of flattened cementstone nodules	3	7	357	0
Mudstone, silty, micaceous, massive, mostly dull red, but purplish-grey at top		6	357	6
Cementstone which becomes progressively reddened and decalcified towards the north		8	358	2
Mudstones and subordinate shales, commonly silty and micaceous, grey, greenish and red. A few nodules and three beds all less than 4 in thick of cementstone. Some salt pseudomorphs. Cut by a 6-ft fault and a basic dyke	33	0	391	2
Mudstones and shales, commonly silty and micaceous, mainly grey or red, with few thin, very fine-grained sandstones. Seven cementstones, the lowest five of which are partly reddened. Obscured for 5 ft near the centre. (Fig. 11, A)	26	4	417	6
Obscured	10	0	427	6
Cornstone Beds	–	–	–	–

Strata of Ballagan Beds facies are not exposed east of the Gargunnock Burn but there are a few outcrops of the Downie's Loup Sandstones between the Downie's Loup sill and the basal lavas. The sandstones in most of these outcrops have been baked and indurated by the sill.

Outcrop west of Craigforth. The sediments below the Craigforth lavas are known only from Stirling No. 1 Bore. This proved the presence of Downie's Loup Sandstones and strata of modified Ballagan Beds facies (pp. 322–5) but as it did not penetrate down to the Cornstone Beds the total thickness is unknown.

Below the Downie's Loup Sandstones the strata differ from the normal Ballagan Beds facies of the main outcrop further west in that they show a much more intimate association between the carbonate and the clastic sediments. Thus the cementstones are more argillaceous and commonly grade into the shales and mudstones above and below. Some have highly irregular bases and others are in the form of highly irregular nodules. In a few peculiar breccia-like beds rather angular fragments of cementstone lie in a mudstone matrix or vice versa.

Mudstones predominate over shales in the bore but this may be because incipient stratification has not been brought out by weathering as it would have been in surface exposures.

The chief difference between the Downie's Loup Sandstones in the bore and those in the main outcrop is in the high proportion of limestone conglomerates, or calcirudites, and calcarenites in the former. These are commonly interbedded with mudstones, especially in the lower part of the succession, and include pebbles of algal limestone. One thin bed of limestone conglomerate (at a depth of 268 ft 11 inches in the bore) shows peculiar load-casting effects, the conglomerate penetrating down into the underlying mudstone in two sets of elongate casts roughly at right angles to each other. A summary of the log of the bore is given in Appendix II.   W.A.R.

EASTERN OUTCROP

Only the lower part of the Calciferous Sandstone Measures succession is exposed in the eastern outcrop. There is no trace of the Clyde Plateau lavas which are so well developed in the western outcrops but it is not known whether this is because the rocks exposed are all below the stratigraphical level of the lavas or whether the lavas have died out (*see* Geikie 1900, p. 43; Dinham and Haldane 1932, p. 17).

The two facies types represented are closely similar to the Ballagan Beds and Downie's Loup Sandstones facies of the western outcrops, but in the eastern outcrop the sandstones which succeed the Ballagan Beds seem to be overlain in turn by more Ballagan Beds strata. It is possible however that the Ballagan Beds are repeated by faulting. The succession is as follows:

Upper cementstones	? 200 ft
Calcareous sandstones	300 ft
Lower cementstones	200 ft

DETAILS

Lower cementstones. The lowest subdivision displays a lithology of Ballagan type which consists mainly of red, green and grey-blue marls and shales with numerous thin ribs of cementstone whose combined thickness amounts to about one eighth of the total thickness of the subdivision. In the upper part thin cross-bedded lenticles of white, calcareous sandstone appear; there is evidence of erosion at the bases of some of these where they transgress the bedding of the underlying marls and cementstones. One rock obtained from the south bank of the River Devon, a third of a mile east

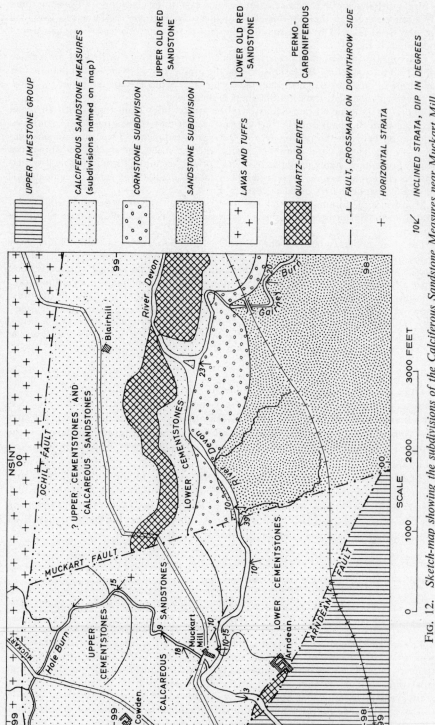

Fig. 12. *Sketch-map showing the subdivisions of the Calciferous Sandstone Measures near Muckart Mill*

of Muckart Mill, is described by Dr. F. W. Anderson as 'a pale-grey banded cement-stone with large botryoidal masses of dark-brown cementstone which usually have coarsely crystalline centres. These appear to be flattish, dome-like algal growths like those described by Anderson (1950, p. 24) from the Rosyth Bore as "*Shermano-phycus gouldi*" type. In thin section they are seen to be composed of bands of dark flocculent finely granular calcite alternating with lighter bands of crystalline calcite mosaic. The dark bands appear to be composed of badly preserved algal tubules of about 0·001 mm diameter.'

The lowest 120 ft of the subdivision form a cliff below the Cauldron Linn quartz-dolerite sill in the Gairney Burn (Fig. 12) and from silty mudstones 45 ft and 60 ft from the base of this cliff Mr. W. G. E. Graham obtained *Spirorbis sp.*, *Curvirimula sp.*, ostracods and fish scales and teeth. The following section in the River Devon, measured from the west side of the Muckart Fault [NS 99789851] to a cliff on the south bank [NS 99389853], 200 yd S.E. of Muckart Mill, is uninterrupted by faulting or intrusion and includes all but the topmost 20 ft or so of the subdivision, which are covered by the bed of the river.

	ft	in
Marl, red and green, with two 9-in cementstones	6	5
Sandstone, white, calcareous	2	6
Marl, red and green, with a few thin nodular cementstones ..	12	0
Sandstone, pale-green, calcareous, with micaceous partings ..	1	0
Marl, red and green, with six cementstones 4 in to 8 in thick..	15	9
Sandstone, green, calcareous, flaggy .. .. .. 1 ft to 2		6
Marl, mottled red and green, with six cementstones 5 in to 8 in thick, some with nodular tops	16	6
Marl, red and green, with thin nodular cementstone ribs ..	3	0
Sandstone, green, hard, micaceous		4
Marl with cementstones (partly inaccessible)	16	0
Sandstone, green, calcareous, flaggy		9
Marl, green, with five cementstones 4 in to 10 in thick ..	15	5
Sandstone, white, calcareous, cross-bedded, transgressive at base; concretionary with plant remains at top .. 7 ft to 15		0
Marl, mainly green, with about twenty cementstones 3 in to 7 in thick	40	0
Limestone, grey, sandy, micaceous	1	0
Marls and cementstones, poorly exposed	12	0
Limestone, grey, hard, sandy and micaceous, with plant and fish remains	1	0
Cementstone		10
Obscured (marl)	2	0
Sandstones and grits with cementstones (Upper Old Red Sandstone) near Muckart Fault	–	–

Calcareous sandstones. In the sandstone subdivision the dominant rock type is calcareous sandstone in beds varying in thickness between 6 in and 20 ft. Green marls and pebble beds or breccias are intercalated and towards the top of the subdivision there are also thin beds of mottled calcareous grit like those of the Upper Old Red Sandstone (p. 115).

The section extending from a point 350 yd up the Hole or Back Burn [NS 99339885] down to the north bank of the River Devon [NS 99369859], 150 yd east of Muckart Mill, is as follows:

	ft	in
Breccia, calcareous..	3	0
Obscured	15	0
Breccia, coarse, calcareous	2	0

	ft	in
Marl, green and red	4	6
Grit, calcareous, lenticular .. .. 1 ft to 3		0
Marl, red and green		8
Grit, calcareous, lenticular .. .. 3 in to		9
Marl, green above, blue-grey below	4	0
Breccia, calcareous, with intermittent blue-grey marly partings	3	0
Obscured (some green marls seen)	9	0
Breccia, calcareous, coarse, with a median 18-in band of green marl	2	8
Obscured	1	6
Sandstone, pale-green, calcareous	1	3
Obscured	4	0
Sandstone, pale-grey, with green shaly partings and calcareous brecciated bands..	15	0
Marl, soft, green		9
Sandstone, white, calcareous, cross-bedded	15	0
Obscured	3	0
Sandstone, calcareous, with a brecciated band	2	0
Marl, green		9
Sandstone, white, calcareous, hard	2	0
Marl, pale-green	6	0
Breccia, calcareous		6
Marl, grey, sandy, with thin layers of sandstone	11	6
Sandstone, white, calcareous, soft, with shaly partings ..	4	6
Marl, red	1	8
Sandstone, calcareous, gritty at base	1	6
Marl, green, with four bands of calcareous sandstone, 1 to 3 ft thick	20	0
Sandstone, white, calcareous, cross-bedded	20	0
Obscured (some sandstone seen)	6	0
Marl, green	3	0
Sandstone, white, calcareous, hard, with brecciated layers in the upper part .. .. about 20		0
Marl, green, sandy, with thin sandstone ribs	2	9
Sandstone, white, calcareous	3	0
Marl, green, brecciated		6
Sandstone, white, calcareous, massive except for one brecciated bed	15	0
Sandstone as above with thin partings of green marl	6	6

The lowest 20-ft sandstone of the above section crops out just above the bridge crossing the Hole Burn at Muckart Mill and continues into the cliff in the north bank of the River Devon 150 yd farther east, being disturbed by a fault which has a downthrow of about 10 ft to the north.

Five samples collected from the breccias or pebble beds at distances of 25, 225, 320, 330 and 370 yd up the Hole Burn from Muckart Mill have been examined by Dr. F. W. Anderson who reports as follows: 'They consist of angular and rounded fragments of cementstone in a very sandy calcite matrix. The colour of the rock may be grey, yellowfawn, green or pink, but the composition varies very little. The constituent fragments include the following range of rock types:

(a) limestone composed of dark, very finely granular calcite: it may contain small detrital quartz grains, be irony, uniform or flocculent in texture, or may be

septarian (i.e. with a radial and concentric crack system now filled with calcite mosaic)
(b) limestone composed of medium- or fine-grained calcite mosaic, often with detrital quartz
(c) calcareous sandstone
(d) large well-rounded quartz grains ($\pm$ 1·0 mm diameter)
(e) quartzite
(f) fine-grained chert
(g) basic feldspars.

Many of the fragments grouped under (a) appear to be of algal limestone. There are often traces of tubules of *Ortonella* type and possibly also of *Girvanella*, but the preservation is rarely good enough for positive identification of species. Other fossils are extremely rare and consist chiefly of small plant fragments.

In addition to the similar rocks already mentioned as occurring in the lower cementstones and the cornstone subdivision of the Upper Old Red Sandstone, fragmental rocks of this kind have been recorded from the Upper Old Red Sandstone and basal Carboniferous of Midlothian and of Ayrshire (Anderson 1940). They can be described as desiccation breccias which have all been laid down under similar conditions regardless of their age'.

Upper cementstones. In the Hole Burn the mottled grits are followed in upward succession by a gap beyond which 90 ft of alternating red and green marls and cementstones reappear with marked change of strike. It is possible that these belong to the lower cementstone subdivision here repeated by faulting (assuming, that is, that the Muckart Fault has a more westerly trend than that shown in Fig. 12). The marls and cementstones are succeeded by 20 ft of red and white mottled sandstones which include a few calcareous concretions and form a waterfall [NS 99429918] 100 yd below the junction of the Hole Burn with the Back Burn. Drift obscures the higher rocks until the Ochil Fault is reached 200 yd up the Back Burn [NS 99439936]. Sheared calcareous sandstones and cementstones appear there in juxtaposition with tuffs of Lower Old Red Sandstone age.   E.H.F.

References

ALDERMAN, A. R. and SKINNER, H. C. W. 1957. Dolomite sedimentation in the southeast of South Australia. *Am. J. Sci.*, **255**, 561–7.

ANDERSON, F. W. 1940. Algal limestones in the Calciferous Sandstone Series of east Fife. *Advmt Sci.*, **1**, No. 2, 259.

—— 1950. Some reef-building calcareous algae from the Carboniferous rocks of northern England. *Proc. Yorks. geol. Soc.*, **28**, 5–28.

BELT, E. S., FRESHNEY, E. C. and READ, W. A. 1967. Sedimentology of Carboniferous cementstone facies, British Isles and eastern Canada. *J. Geol.*, **75**, 711–21.

CLOUGH, C. T., HINXMAN, L. W., WILSON, J. S. G., CRAMPTON, C. B., WRIGHT, W. B., BAILEY, E. B., ANDERSON, E. M. and CARRUTHERS, R. G. 1925. The geology of the Glasgow district. 2nd edit. revised by MACGREGOR, M., DINHAM, C. H., BAILEY, E. B. and ANDERSON, E. M. *Mem. geol. Surv. Gt Br.*

CURRIE, ETHEL D. 1954. Scottish Carboniferous goniatites. *Trans. R. Soc. Edinb.*, **62**, 527–602.

DINHAM, C. H. and HALDANE, D. 1932. The economic geology of the Stirling and Clackmannan Coalfield. *Mem. geol. Surv. Gt Br.*

DIXON, C. G. 1938. The geology of the Fintry, Gargunnock and Touch Hills. *Geol. Mag.*, **75**, 425–32.

DZULYNSKI, S. and SMITH, A. J. 1963. Convolute lamination, its origin, preservation and directional significance. *J. sedim. Petrol.*, **33**, 616–27.

GEIKIE, A. 1897. *The ancient volcanoes of Great Britain*, Vol. 1, London.

—— 1900. The geology of central and western Fife and Kinross. *Mem. geol. Surv. Gt Br.*

GEORGE, T. N. 1958. Lower Carboniferous palaeogeography of the British Isles. *Proc. Yorks. geol. Soc.*, **31**, 227–318.

HAMBLIN, W. K. 1961. Micro-cross-lamination in Upper Keweenawan sediments of northern Michigan. *J. sedim. Petrol.*, **31**, 390–401.

KUENEN, P. H. 1958. Experiments in geology. *Trans. geol. Soc. Glasg.*, **23**, 1–28.

MACGREGOR, M., KENNEDY, W. Q. and EYLES, V. A. 1940. *In* Discussion on the boundary between the Old Red Sandstone and the Carboniferous. *Advmt Sci.*, **1**, No. 2, 256–8.

MCKEE, E. D. 1939. Some types of bedding in the Colorado River delta. *J. Geol.*, **47**, 64–81.

—— and WEIR, G. W. 1953. Terminology for stratification and cross-stratification in sedimentary rocks. *Bull. geol. Soc. Am.*, **64**, 381–90.

MITCHELL, G. H. and MYKURA, W. 1962. The geology of the neighbourhood of Edinburgh. *Mem. geol. Surv. Gt Br.*

MUIR, A., HARDIE, H. G. M., MITCHELL, R. L. and PHEMISTER, J. 1956. The limestones of Scotland: chemical analyses and petrography. *Mem. geol. Surv. spec. Rep. Miner. Resour. Gt Br.*, **37**.

PEACH, B. N. and HORNE, J. 1903. The Canonbie Coalfield; its geological structure and relations to the Carboniferous rocks of the north of England and central Scotland. *Trans. R. Soc. Edinb.*, **40**, 835–77.

PETTIJOHN, F. J. 1957. *Sedimentary rocks*. New York.

READ, W. A. and JOHNSON, S. R. H. 1967. The sedimentology of sandstone formations within the Upper Old Red Sandstone and lowest Calciferous Sandstone Measures west of Stirling, Scotland. *Scott. J. Geol.*, **3**, 242–67.

ROBERTSON, T. 1948. Rhythm in sedimentation and its interpretation: with particular reference to the Carboniferous sequence. *Trans. Edinb. geol. Soc.*, **16**, 299–306.

—— and HALDANE, D. 1937. The economic geology of the Central Coalfield of Scotland, Area I. *Mem. geol. Surv. Gt Br.*

SORBY, H. C. 1859. On the structures produced by the currents present during the deposition of stratified rocks. *Geologist*, **2**, 135–47.

STEWART, A. D. 1963. On certain slump structures in the Torridonian Sandstones of Applecross. *Geol. Mag.*, **100**, 205–18.

SUMM. PROG. 1960. *Mem. geol. Surv. Summ. Prog.* for 1959.

TULLOCH, W. and WALTON, H. S. 1958. The geology of the Midlothian Coalfield. *Mem. geol. Surv. Gt Br.*

WALKER, R. G. 1963. Distinctive types of ripple-drift cross-lamination. *Sedimentology*, **2**, 173–88.

WHITE, W. A. 1961. Colloid phenomena in sedimentation of argillaceous rocks. *J. sedim. Petrol.*, **31**, 560–70.

YOUNG, J. 1860. On the geology of the Campsie district. *Trans. geol. Soc. Glasg.*, **1**, 5–68.

YOUNG, J. W. 1867. On the Ballagan series of rocks. *Trans. geol. Soc. Glasg.*, **2**, 209–12.

Chapter VIII

CALCIFEROUS SANDSTONE MEASURES
(*continued*)

VOLCANIC ROCKS

INTRODUCTION

THE VOLCANIC ROCKS within the Calciferous Sandstone Measures are known only in the south-western part of the Stirling district, where the lavas of the Campsie Fells continue northwards to form the Touch, Gargunnock and Fintry hills, the most northerly part of the Clyde Plateau still preserved. These hills are characterized by a steep, relatively well-exposed lava escarpment. This starts roughly 2½ miles west of Stirling and runs west-south-westwards for about 8 miles to Stronend (1677 ft), the highest point of the Fintry Hills, where it turns southwards and then eastwards to run along the north side of the Endrick valley. The escarpment is backed by an undulating dip-slope inclined towards the south-east and east. This is relatively poorly-exposed owing to extensive deposits of peat and morainic drift. The Touch and Gargunnock hills form a continuous mass of high ground separated from the Fintry Hills to the west by a valley which runs south-eastwards from the deep corrie-like embayment in the scarp at the Spout of Ballochleam and is drained by the Backside Burn and the upper Endrick Water.

The isolated hill of Craigforth, which rises from the Carse about a mile west of Stirling, is thought to represent the western end of another outcrop of lavas that is cut off from the main lava outcrop by the Abbey Craig Fault and is bounded to the north by the Ochil Fault. The rest of this outcrop is concealed by drift.

The lowest lavas seem to rest without angular discordance upon the Downie's Loup Sandstones. The stratified volcanic detritus that is found towards the top of the sandstones (Summ. Prog. 1961, p. 44) is thought to be derived either from deposits of tuff marking an initial period of explosive activity or from the weathering and erosion of volcanic rocks earlier than the lowest lavas of this district. Peach, followed by Geikie (1897, p. 384, figs. 114, 122) and Dixon (1938, pp. 426–8) considered that the lowest lavas overstepped the Ballagan Beds and came to rest unconformably upon the Upper Old Red Sandstone at the eastern end of the Touch Hills. Dinham (*in* Dinham and Haldane 1932, pp. 8–9) on the other hand suggested that a strike fault would account more satisfactorily for the observed relationships and, in fact, it has recently been proved that the western end of the Abbey Craig Fault throws the lavas down against the Upper Old Red Sandstone (pp. 249, 251). In detail the base of the lava pile is, however, diachronous as different flows seem to form the base of the volcanic succession in different localities.

The top of the lava pile as it is now preserved seems to be more markedly diachronous than the base. A long period of weathering, probably accompanied by erosion, followed the cessation of volcanic activity and in consequence the overlying sediments rest unconformably upon the lavas (p. 165). Thus the highest lavas poured out in Calciferous Sandstone Measures times in this area are probably not now preserved.

Geikie (1861, pp. 642, 654) originally assigned the lavas of the Touch, Gargunnock and Fintry hills, together with those of the Campsie Fells, to the Upper Old Red Sandstone but subsequently (Geikie 1897, p. 366, fig. 122) he correlated them with the Oil-Shale Group of the Lothians, a correlation that was followed by Dinham (in Dinham and Haldane 1932, pp. 10–1). There is, however, no evidence for the implied correlation of the base of the lavas in the Stirling district with the base of the Oil-Shale Group, as defined in the Lothians (Tulloch and Walton 1958, p. 11).

In the east of the main outcrop the lavas generally dip eastwards and north-eastwards below the overlying sediments at angles between 5° and 15° but further west the dip swings round towards the south-east and south and is generally between 4° and 8°. Within the main outcrop there are local variations in direction and steepness of dip which are due partly to the proximity of faults, such as the Abbey Craig Fault, and partly to the fact that the original surface over which each lava flowed was somewhat irregular. In some localities the trap features form broad open folds (p. 145) but it is uncertain to what extent these reflect original topographic irregularities rather than subsequent tectonic activity. These open folds are illustrated in Plate VI where, however, the great exaggeration of the vertical scale makes them seem much more marked than they really are. Along the northern escarpment of the Gargunnock and Fintry hills the dips of the lower lavas seem to be greater than those of the higher flows. This may imply some measure of differential subsidence in the south during the formation of the lava pile or it may reflect the thickening of individual lavas in this direction (cf. Walker 1959a, p. 389).

The lavas in the outcrop of Craigforth dip eastward at angles of 15° to 20° but the dip may decrease further east, below the drift cover.

Apart from the Ochil Fault which throws the lavas of Craigforth down against the Lower Old Red Sandstone to the north and the Abbey Craig Fault which separates the Craigforth lavas from the main outcrop, the Calciferous Sandstone Measures lavas do not seem to be greatly affected by the large easterly-trending faults that characterize the coalfield area further east. Of those that cut the lavas the Wallstale and Auchenbowie faults are by far the largest. Both have large throws where they enter the lava outcrop from the east (pp. 252–3) but neither can be traced very deeply into the lava country and it seems probable that the throws of both decrease westwards. All the other known easterly-trending faults seem to be comparatively small.

Most of the remaining faults may be assigned either to a group trending between south-east and south-south-east or to a group trending between south-south-west and south-west. The throws of most of these faults are comparatively small but where they cross drift-free areas such as the northern part of the Touch Hills they commonly give rise to prominent gullies. The south-south-easterly Balmenoch Burn Fault which crosses the Fintry Hills is, however, known to have a throw of at least 100 ft down to the east-north-east where it cuts the northern escarpment and the throw may well increase further south (p. 254).

The lavas of the Touch, Fintry and Gargunnock hills are dominantly olivine-basalts of Markle and Jedburgh types, together with flows that are intermediate in character between these two types and composite flows in which the two types occur as separate components. There are also subordinate trachybasalts, including mugearites, and rare Dalmeny basalts. Thus the more mafic types of Carboniferous olivine-basalt are virtually unrepresented. Albitization is widespread and this makes it difficult to separate some albitized microporphyritic basalts from mugearites and other trachybasalts (*cf*. MacGregor 1928, p. 348). On the poorly-exposed dip-slope detailed subdivision of the lavas was found to be impracticable and in consequence the rocks mapped as microporphyritic basalts may in fact include some trachybasalts. The petrography of the lavas is discussed on pp. 159–65.

FIELD CHARACTERS

The various types of basalt differ appreciably in field characters (*see* MacGregor 1928). The Markle basalts, which are characterized by abundant macrophenocrysts of feldspar, are generally massive rocks without flow structure. The central parts of flows may show rough columnar jointing and spheroidal weathering. Markle flows are generally persistent but thin. Apart from one exceptional record of 110 ft, they range in thickness from 8 to 36 ft and approximately half of the flows are between 15 and 25 ft thick.

The Jedburgh basalts are commonly massive and show spheroidal weathering. Many, however, have a well-developed flow structure which is in general roughly parallel to the tops and bottoms of the flows and which gives them a platy fracture. Such rocks cannot readily be separated from trachybasalts in the field, especially as they are generally finer in grain than the more massive Jedburgh flows, and, as many of the platy rocks are decomposed and albitized, it is not always possible to distinguish between Jedburgh basalts and trachybasalts in thin section (p. 163). Jedburgh flows seem to be less persistent than Markle flows and are also generally thicker. Thicknesses range from 7 ft to more than 80 ft and most flows are 25 ft or more thick.

Rare phenocrysts of feldspar greater than 2 mm long may be found in many flows of Jedburgh basalt and such macrophenocrysts are more numerous in basalts transitional between the Markle and Jedburgh types. In such rocks the field characters are generally intermediate between those of Markle and those of Jedburgh flows. Thus they commonly show flow structure. The different components of composite flows show the field characters appropriate to their particular lava type.

The trachybasalts, including mugearites and basaltic mugearites, are generally finer in grain and more decomposed than the Jedburgh basalts. The great majority of trachybasalts have good planar flow structure which gives rise to the characteristic platy fracture of these lavas. Locally this platy structure may be steeply dipping or distorted into trough-like forms (p. 157; *cf*. Walker 1959a, p. 372). Trachybasalts range in thickness from 10 ft to about 60 ft and seem to be generally thicker than Markle basalts. They seem, however, to be commonly more persistent than Jedburgh basalts and at least one flow may be traced for more than four miles along the scarp.

Many of the lavas exhibit structures which are not characteristic of any single petrological type. For example, many flows show the tripartite division that characterizes aa lava, with a central massive portion overlain and underlain by a slaggy layer—the upper slaggy layer commonly much thicker than the lower (*cf*. Wentworth and Macdonald 1953, p. 61). In other flows, however, the central portion contains irregular lenticular masses of slaggy material and it is not uncommon to find flows in which large rounded bodies of massive lava with curving platy joints or concentric bands of vesicles near the margins are surrounded by envelopes of slaggy material. This structure is best developed in some of the Jedburgh basalts, in which the massive bodies may be as much as 30 ft wide and 10 ft high. It seems probable that these bodies represent sections through filled lava tubes, which are generally characteristic of pahoehoe lava (Macdonald 1953, pp. 171–2; Wentworth and Macdonald 1953, p. 45). Traces of massive arch-like tubes with radiating columnar joints have been found (p. 157). These resemble small-scale versions of the 'war-bonnet' lava tube filling described by Waters (1960, p. 354).

Vesicles and amygdales are common in and near the slaggy parts of most lavas and, especially in the Jedburgh basalts, may be scattered throughout the more massive parts of the flow as well. Most vesicles have the irregular distorted shapes characteristic of those in aa lava but some Jedburgh basalts have smooth spheroidal vesicles like those characteristic of pahoehoe (cf. Macdonald 1953, pp. 172, 179, fig. 2). Pipe amygdales are not commonly seen but this may be due in part at least to the paucity of exposures at and near the bases of lavas.

In contrast to the lateral persistence of the majority of trap features there are some which are impersistent. These may represent flow units (Nichols 1936) formed by the repeated breaking out of tongues of lava from the front of a pahoehoe flow. This phenomenon may also explain the presence of lenses of slaggy material within many of the flows. Some of the apparent lack of persistence of the Jedburgh basalts compared to Markle basalts and trachybasalts (pp. 146–7) may be due to the presence of flow units within the Jedburgh flows. This cannot be confirmed, however, for flows, even in modern lava fields, cannot easily be distinguished from flow units unless weathering and decomposition have produced an intervening soil (Wentworth and Macdonald 1953, p. 32).

The slaggy tops of many of the flows have been weathered and decomposed by penecontemporaneous subaerial processes, leading to the formation of bole—a reddish mudstone containing isolated fragments of decomposed lava. Weathering back of the decomposed slaggy lava and bole at the tops of flows has given rise to the well-developed trap features that characterize the northern parts of the Touch, Gargunnock and Fintry hills. The boles are relatively rarely seen except in gullies and excavations as they are generally covered by grass, scree and hillwash but, in some localities at least, they form quite a high proportion of the succession (p. 154).

Tuffs form a relatively small proportion of the total thickness of the volcanic pile and seem largely to be restricted to three horizons where, however, they form beds more than 100 ft thick. The non-committal term 'interbasaltic beds' has been used to describe the deposits at these three horizons because, in addition to undoubted tuff, they include thick deposits of highly decomposed bole-like material. Beds of water-transported volcanic detritus derived either from tuff or from weathered lava may also be present.

Composite flows. No fewer than eleven composite flows are known in the Touch, Gargunnock and Fintry hills and it is strongly suspected that there may be others. In the examples so far identified each composite flow is composed of a macroporphyritic component and a microporphyritic component. The former have generally been classed as Markle basalts, although some could be regarded as porphyritic basaltic mugearites, and are usually characterized by abundant macrophenocrysts of feldspar. The microporphyritic components are mostly

Jedburgh basalts but trachybasalts are also represented; on the map the latter have been grouped with the Jedburgh basalts. Within a single composite flow the composition of the microporphyritic component is usually closely similar to that of the groundmass of the macroporphyritic component. Commonly the actual contact between the two is obscured. In several localities where the contacts are exposed, however, the relationships between the two components seem to be rather more complex than in most of the composite flows described by Kennedy (1931; 1933), Walker (1959a; 1959b) and Gibson and Walker (1963). For instance, dyke-like bodies and irregular steeply dipping tongues of macroporphyritic basalt occur in places within microporphyritic basalt (pp. 150, 153). Furthermore, in some of the flows which contain the large rounded bodies of massive lava interpreted as filled lava tubes, some of the massive rounded bodies are of macroporphyritic and some of microporphyritic basalt, whereas all the enveloping slaggy material is of microporphyritic basalt (pp. 145, 150). This would seem to imply that the microporphyritic component was slightly earlier and that lava tubes formed within it were filled by the slightly later macroporphyritic type.

A thin transitional zone with sporadic large feldspar phenocrysts commonly blurs the contact between the two components (cf. Kennedy 1931, p. 169) but in one locality, just beyond the southern limit of the district (p. 157), there is an intimate intermixture of the two types, which seem to have behaved like two almost immiscible liquids. Under the microscope (S 46809) the macroporphyritic component seems to be intrusive and to decrease slightly in grain size towards the microporphyritic, although the exact contact is diffuse and there is no chilled margin. The groundmass feldspars of the former tend to be aligned parallel to the contact. These features all suggest that here also the macroporphyritic component is the later of the two.

An unusual composite dyke on the northern slopes of the Fintry Hills (p. 159) may possibly have been a feeder for a composite flow, although this cannot be proved. Within the dyke the macroporphyritic and microporphyritic components are not arranged symmetrically but are intimately intermixed as in the composite lava just described (cf. Kennedy 1931, pp. 174–5, 179).

Comparison with flood basalts. Tyrrell (1937, pp. 92–3) classed the lavas of the Clyde Plateau as 'multiple-vent basalts' and suggested that they arose 'from the confluence of lava flows from a large number of small and closely-spaced volcanoes'. The detailed mapping of flows in the Touch, Gargunnock and Fintry hills suggests, however, that in some respects at least these lavas resemble the flood basalts of areas such as eastern Iceland which are thought to have been derived largely from fissure eruptions (Walker 1959a, p. 390). Only two structures that may possibly be vents are known within the present area (p. 158). The closely spaced vents along the north of the Campsie Fells are only a short distance to the west of the Fintry Hills but the plugs associated with the vents are all composed of Jedburgh basalt, and apparently cut what are almost certainly the lateral equivalents of the only thick group of Jedburgh basalts represented in the Touch, Gargunnock and Fintry hills. Thus it seems probable that only the scattered flows of Jedburgh basalt in the higher part of the succession could have originated from the northern Campsie vents and even this cannot be proved.

The uniformity of the lava stratigraphy (pp. 142–4, Plate VI) and the lateral persistence of individual lavas are features which have more in common with the flood basalts of eastern Iceland (Walker 1959a, p. 387) than with a succession derived from a large number of closely spaced vents. Trap features may commonly be traced for two or three miles and some thin flows are known to persist for at least four or five. Bearing in mind that the limits to which individual flows can be traced are usually determined by the extent of the drift cover rather than by the lateral persistence of the flow, it seems probable that many of the flows are widespread sheets rather than the elongate tongues generally associated with lavas from individual vents (*see* Wentworth and Macdonald 1953, fig. 13). Furthermore, it seems unlikely that a whole series of such tongue-like flows could lie parallel to the present escarpment. The lateral continuity of flows exposed in the escarpment also implies that each lava flowed over a gently sloping surface formed by earlier lavas; such gentle slopes are said by White (1960, pp. 367–71) to be typical of the flood basalts of the Keweenawan of Lake Superior. Other features that link the lavas of the present area to flood basalts are the numerous intercalations of bole between the flows and the great preponderance of lavas over tuffs (*cf.* Tyrrell 1937, pp. 100–1).

Dykes similar in composition to the lavas are common (p. 159) and may have served as feeders, but they do not seem to form parallel swarms (Tyrrell 1937, p. 101) nor are they as numerous as in the typical flood-basalt areas of Iceland (Walker 1959a, pp. 383–6) or the Columbia River (Waters 1960, p. 350). In the latter area, however, the swarms are separated by wide areas with relatively few dykes. The lavas of the Touch, Gargunnock and Fintry hills are generally much thinner than the flood basalts of the Keweenawan of Lake Superior (White 1960, pp. 367–8) or those of the Columbia River Plateau (Waters 1960, p. 350) but are very similar in thickness to the flood basalts of eastern Iceland (Walker 1959a, pp. 370–1).

STRATIGRAPHY

The relatively good exposures along the escarpment and, to a lesser extent, on the upper part of the dip-slope of the Touch, Gargunnock and Fintry hills made it possible for the lavas there to be mapped in considerable detail. There are many good cliff sections along the escarpment and these can be linked together by tracing individual trap features across the intervening areas. The lateral persistence of the lowest of the interbasaltic beds (p. 146) has also greatly assisted correlation. The lava succession has proved to be much less variable than Dixon (1938, p. 429) supposed and in both the eastern and western parts of the area a definite eruptive sequence can be recognized. The flows can be divided into several petrographically distinctive groups (Table 7), some of which extend throughout the whole area. The groups interdigitate to a certain extent and the boundaries between them may be diachronous. Different types of lava were probably poured out simultaneously from different sources. Exposures are unfortunately too poor to allow the flows on most of the dip-slope to be grouped in this way.

The outcrops of the lava groups and the variations in thickness as determined from measured sections on the escarpment are shown on the sketch map in Plate VI. As may be seen from the section in Plate VI, the volcanic succession thins towards the east and the total number of flows tends to decrease in this direction. It is only in the Touch Hills, in the eastern part of the area, that the highest lava groups are preserved.

Although the lava pile as a whole thins eastwards each of the groups is subject to local variations some of which do not conform to the regional pattern. The variations in the lower part of the succession are particularly interesting. The trachybasalts and microporphyritic basalts of the Basal Group seem to thin and die out westwards in the western part of the Gargunnock Hills and the

TABLE 7

Lava groups in the northern part of the Touch, Gargunnock and Fintry hills

FINTRY HILLS	GARGUNNOCK AND TOUCH HILLS
	Touch House Group (Total thickness unknown). Only Markle basalts seen
	Black Mount Group (More than 80 ft). Mostly microporphyritic basalts with subordinate trachybasalts
—— Higher lavas removed by erosion —— Fintry Hills Group (More than 400 ft). Mostly Markle basalts but with a fairly high proportion of microporphyritic basalts, together with rare trachybasalts	Gargunnock Hills Group (300 to more than 500 ft). Dominantly Markle and composite basalts with subordinate microporphyritic basalts and rare mugearites
Shelloch Burn Group (130 to 200 ft). A varied assemblage including trachybasalts, microporphyritic and Markle basalts	Lees Hill Group (0 to 120 ft). Mostly trachybasalts
Spout of Ballochleam Group (200 to 300 ft). Mostly Jedburgh basalts with the Stronend Interbasaltic Beds intercalated in the west	Spout of Ballochleam Group (80 to 300 ft). Mostly Jedburgh basalts
Slackgun Interbasaltic Beds (150 to 260 ft). Tuff (possibly with volcanic detritus), bole and weathered lava resting unconformably on lavas below	Slackgun Interbasaltic Beds (0 to 150 ft). Tuff (possibly with volcanic detritus), bole and weathered lava resting unconformably on lavas below
Skiddaw Group (0 to 120 ft). Mostly Markle and composite basalts	Baston Burn Group (30–220 ft). Markle basalts
	Basal Group (100–150 ft). A varied assemblage including trachybasalts, Jedburgh and Markle basalts

PLATE VI

HORIZONTAL SECTION AND MAP OF THE NORTHERN PART OF THE FINTRY, GARGUNNOCK AND TOUCH HILLS, SHOWING DISTRIBUTION OF LAVA TYPES AND THE BOUNDARIES BETWEEN LAVA GROUPS

L

overlying Markle basalts of the Baston Burn Group increase in number and total thickness westwards as far as the Gargunnock Burn, but further west they are progressively truncated by the 'unconformable' base of the Slackgun Interbasaltic Beds. These Interbasaltic Beds themselves thicken progressively westwards and in the western part of the Fintry Hills the underlying lavas of the Skiddaw Group (which may possibly be equivalent to part of the Baston Burn Group) disappear altogether so that the Slackgun Interbasaltic Beds merge with the stratified volcanic detritus at the top of the Downie's Loup Sandstones.

Above the Slackgun Interbasaltic Beds there seems to be a general tendency for microporphyritic basalts and trachybasalts to become more abundant towards the west and for the proportion of Markle basalts to decrease. In the Gargunnock Hills Group of the Gargunnock and Touch hills, which is composed dominantly of Markle basalt, the total number of flows increases towards the south and the group as a whole presumably thickens in this direction. In this connexion it is interesting to note that Bailey (*in* Clough and others 1925, pp. 137–8) suggests a southern source for the Markle basalts of the southern Campsie Fells. Directional structures (*see* Waters 1960) are comparatively rare and generally poorly developed and it is not yet possible to determine with any degree of accuracy the sources of the various lava groups.

DETAILS

In the following account the Touch and Gargunnock hills, which are separated from the Fintry Hills by the valley of the Backside Burn, are discussed first. For convenience this area may be divided into a northern portion which includes that part of the Touch and Gargunnock hills shown in Plate VI (map), and a southern portion embracing the ground to the south of this. As the erosion of all but the lowest part of the lava succession in the valley of the Backside Burn and the relatively poor exposures in this area make it difficult to link the higher groups of the Gargunnock Hills with those of the Fintry Hills, the latter area is treated separately. This area may be divided into a northern and western portion which includes the ground west of the Balmenoch Burn Fault and that part of the Fintry Hills, east of the fault, which is shown on Plate VI (map), and a south-eastern portion covering the southern part of the area east of the fault.

NORTHERN TOUCH AND GARGUNNOCK HILLS

Basal Group. The Basal Group is a thin group of varied lava types with trachybasalt predominant. In the extreme east the outcrop is largely obscured by drift but the following succession [NS 73119352–73159340] is exposed:

	Thickness ft	Total thickness ft
7. Trachybasalt transitional to Jedburgh basalt, platy jointing towards base	26	26
6. *Obscured*	12	38
5. Jedburgh basalt, platy jointing	8	46
4. *Obscured*	17	63
3. Markle basalt, slaggy, vesicular	2	65
2. *Obscured*	5	70
1. Mugearite or albitized trachybasalt, platy jointing, top vesicular	32 seen	102

Both the succession and the total thickness vary remarkably little as the outcrop is traced westwards for more than three miles, but the group ceases to be recognizable in the west of the Gargunnock Hills (Plate VI). The lavas of this group generally form a series of cliffs at the foot of the escarpment and the basal trachybasalt forms a particularly prominent crag which may be traced, with some breaks where it is obscured by scree, etc., for more than four miles. This flow, which is locally more than 40 ft thick, is generally characterized by platy jointing but may be massive in places. By contrast the thin flow of Markle basalt immediately above is the least persistent of the group and is confined to the east where it is only sporadically exposed. The upper trachybasalt is generally rather more massive than the lower. It becomes obscured by scree and hillwash at Slackdown [NS 68409244] and cannot be recognized further west.

Baston Burn Group. The Baston Burn Group is almost entirely composed of Markle basalts and generally weathers back to form a wide step in the escarpment above the cliffs formed by the Basal Group.

In the extreme east [NS 73159339–73189331], the group seems to be only about 50 ft thick and comprises three flows, but it thickens westward and in a section [NS 72329320–72349297] south-east of Hillhead it is more than 90 ft thick and comprises five flows; these are all of Markle basalt except the thin middle flow which is of Jedburgh type and may possibly be the microporphyritic component of a composite flow. The group attains its maximum development in the Gargunnock Burn section [NS 70739292–70609267], where it lies in a shallow synclinal structure (p. 138). Here it is about 220 ft thick and comprises more than ten flows. All of these are of Markle basalt except the lowest and highest which are transitional between Jedburgh and Markle types. The lowest flow is known to be composite elsewhere and south of Hillhead its macro-porphyritic and microporphyritic components are exposed only 30 feet apart [NS 71549305].

As the group is traced westwards from the Gargunnock Burn it thins progressively as successive flows are truncated by the overlying Spout of Ballochleam Group so that where the first exposures of the Slackgun Interbasaltic Beds which are associated with this 'unconformity' appear, some two miles away, only the two lowest flows of the Baston Burn Group are preserved and the shelf formed by the group disappears. Still further along the strike [NS 66839176], the upper of these two remaining flows is reduced to a series of massive nodules lying within the thick bole at the base of the Interbasaltic Beds and the total thickness of the group is probably less than 40 ft. Beyond this the group cannot be identified with certainty.

Skiddaw Group. In the western Gargunnock Hills neither the Basal Group nor the Baston Burn Group can be recognized and here and farther west the only lavas seen between the Downie's Loup Sandstones and the Slackgun Interbasaltic Beds are a number of Markle basalts, composite basalt flows and microporphyritic basalts which constitute the Skiddaw Group. It is thought that the Skiddaw Group may be contemporaneous with parts of both the eastern groups, but it may possibly be equivalent to the lower part of the Baston Burn Group only.

The easternmost exposures are at Slackgun [NS 65729122] where the following section was measured:

	Thickness ft	Total thickness ft
Bole, dull red, resting on the irregular top of the lava below (p. 146)	15 seen	15
Transitional Jedburgh–Markle basalt, massive, traces of columnar jointing	15	30
Composite flow. Massive rounded bodies (mostly of Markle basalt but some near centre and top of flow are of Jedburgh–Dalmeny basalt) in a matrix of slaggy, highly vesicular microporphyritic basalt (*see* p. 141)	35	65

L*

	Thickness ft	Total thickness ft
Obscured	2	67
Markle basalt, slaggy and vesicular towards top	27	94
Obscured	4	98
Coarse-grained olivine-basalt, slightly decomposed ..	14	112

The Jedburgh–Markle flow immediately below the bole resembles the basal flow of the Baston Burn Group but there is insufficient evidence for a firm correlation.

Slackgun Interbasaltic Beds. As the Slackgun Interbasaltic Beds are soft they generally weather back to form a shelf on the escarpment and they have also given rise to a series of landslips (p. 289). The horizon of these beds coincides with the 'unconformity' between the Baston Burn and Spout of Ballochleam groups further east and they seem to rest on an irregular weathered surface which cuts across the underlying lavas. Although the upper part of these beds is composed of stratified tuff or volcanic detritus the lower part is characterized by thick deposits of bole probably formed by the decomposition, in situ, of the lavas below. Thus during the formation of the lower part of these interbasaltic beds the effusion of lavas probably ceased for a relatively long period and the earlier lavas were deeply weathered. The overlying stratified deposits may indicate the renewal of explosive volcanic activity prior to the effusion of the lavas of the overlying Spout of Ballochleam Group.

The interbasaltic beds are poorly exposed and are generally covered by landslip, scree, hillwash or vegetation. At the east end of Standmilane Craig [NS 67819220], and about 800 ft to the west, highly decomposed vesicular lava crops out through the hillwash and scree that obscure the strata between the Baston Burn and Spout of Ballochleam groups. Traces of bright red bole are seen immediately below the lowest exposed Jedburgh basalt of the latter group. About half a mile to the west-south-west [NS 66839173] there are several outcrops of thick bole (p. 145). The best exposures, however, are in the corrie-like scar of Slackgun, immediately north-west of Lees Hill, where the following section [NS 65769118–65779112] was measured up the scarp:

	Thickness ft	Total thickness ft
Lowest exposure of Spout of Ballochleam Group ..	–	–
Obscured	7	7
Tuff (or volcanic detritus): very evenly stratified beds, generally less than 2 in thick, of dull purplish-grey mudstone. many with rounded and angular fragments of decomposed basalt	27	34
Obscured	6	40
Dalmeny basalt, massive towards base but slaggy, vesicular and highly decomposed at top	21	61
Obscured	35	96
Bole, dull red, resting on the irregular top of the composite flow below	15	111

The lower part of the Dalmeny basalt is relatively fresh and it is possible that it may represent an isolated flow poured out during the period when the interbasaltic beds were being formed.

Spout of Ballochleam Group. The Spout of Ballochleam Group, which is the only lava group in the Touch and Gargunnock hills that is composed largely of Jedburgh basalts, usually forms the most prominent crags in the escarpment. In general the lavas are much less persistent than those of the other groups and it is commonly impossible to correlate the flows between measured sections. Some at least of the flows are divided into flow-units (p. 140). Many of the Jedburgh basalts are relatively coarse-grained and massive, with no clear distinction between the feldspar phenocrysts and the feldspars of the groundmass. The group also includes rare flows with affinities to Dalmeny basalt, generally near its base, and isolated flows of Markle, or transitional Jedburgh–Markle basalt higher in the succession. These may be the precursors of the abundant Markle basalts of the Gargunnock Hills Group which succeeds the Spout of Ballochleam Group directly in the east. In general the group tends to thicken westwards but it seems to fluctuate somewhat in thickness as it is traced along the escarpment (Plate VI).

North of Scout Head in the Touch Hills the group comprises only three or four flows with a total thickness of less than 100 ft but a section further west [NS 72339297–72409276] shows that in less than a mile the number of flows increases to five or more with a total thickness of more than 160 ft. Still further west, at the Gargunnock Burn, there are seven flows with a total thickness of about 150 ft. The lowest flow at the Gargunnock Burn shows affinities with Dalmeny basalt.

Westwards from here the group seems to swell abruptly to reach a thickness of more than 260 ft in the head-waters of the Easter Blackspout [NS 69129252–69119242]. The section here is complicated by a dyke but at least two flows seem to be more than 50 ft thick. The succession is well exposed, however, in the prominent gully in the steep cliffs at the east end of Standmilane Craig, where the following section [NS 67579210–67629200] was measured:

	Thickness ft	Total thickness ft
Trachybasalt at base of Lees Hill Group	–	–
Obscured	23	23
Jedburgh basalt, massive but with local platy jointing; slaggy lenses and slaggy vesicular base	19	42
Bole, dull red, with nodules of decomposed lava	1	43
Obscured	7	50
Jedburgh basalt, massive but with platy jointing; slaggy vesicular base	20	70
Bole, dark red..	1	71
Obscured	3	74
Transitional Jedburgh–Markle basalt, some platy jointing; slaggy vesicular base and top	33	107
Bole, reddish-purple, with nodules of decomposed lava ..	2	109
Jedburgh basalt, coarse-grained, massive, spheroidally weathered; slaggy, vesicular, decomposed top	26	135
Obscured	11	146
Jedburgh basalt, coarse-grained, massive, spheroidally weathered; traces of columnar jointing, sporadic amygdales throughout; slaggy base	60	206
Obscured	3	209
Jedburgh basalt, coarse-grained, massive; slaggy vesicular base, top similar but decomposed	25	234
Obscured	1	235
Jedburgh basalt, platy jointing; slaggy vesicular base, top similar but decomposed	34	269
Bole, bright red (? top of Slackgun Interbasaltic Beds) ..	1 seen	270

Towards the west-south-west the group seems to thin somewhat and then to thicken again as the scarp turns southwards towards the Spout of Ballochleam (p. 154).

Lees Hill Group. The Lees Hill Group generally forms the crest of the escarpment at the top of the cliffs formed by the Spout of Ballochleam Group. Unlike the Basal and Shelloch Burn groups it is composed almost entirely of trachybasalts but it does, however, include some rare Markle basalts which may be derived from the same general source as the Markle basalts of the Gargunnock Hills Group.

The group seems to be absent in the Touch Hills except in the extreme west. At the mostly easterly point where it can be recognized [NS 71849247], on the boundary between the Touch and Gargunnock estates, it comprises a single flow of trachybasalt within the Markle and Jedburgh–Markle basalts near the base of the Gargunnock Hills Group. In the Gargunnock Burn [NS 70659249–70599222], roughly three-quarters of a mile to the west, the group is much thicker and the following section is exposed:

	Thickness ft	Total thickness ft
Lowest exposure of Markle basalt of Gargunnock Hills Group	–	–
Obscured	5	5
Trachybasalt, fine-grained, massive; slaggy, highly vesicular base	35	40
Obscured (Markle basalt of this horizon exposed farther west [NS 69879223])	19	59
Trachybasalt, fine-grained, mostly massive but with platy jointing in places; vesicular base	70	129
Obscured	2	131
Topmost exposure of Jedburgh basalt of Spout of Ballochleam Group..	–	–

It is not known which of the two trachybasalts correlates with the single flow further east.

Further west the intercalation of Markle basalt dies out and the whole group consists of trachybasalts. The lowest flow of the group forms a persistent line of crags, locally more than 40 ft high, along the lip of the escarpment but as the upper part of the group is not well exposed total thicknesses are difficult to estimate. At Lees Hill the group is known to include at least two flows and its outcrop is two miles wide, but the width of outcrop decreases towards the south and the group cannot be traced through the drift-covered ground along the valley of the Backside Burn.

Gargunnock Hills Group. The Gargunnock Hills Group forms the greater part of the dip-slope of the Touch and Gargunnock hills. It is composed dominantly of Markle basalts but it also includes at least four composite flows, several microporphyritic basalts and rare mugearites. The total thickness of the group can be calculated only in the eastern part of the Touch Hills where it is rather more than 300 ft. The lower part, however, is known to thicken westwards (Plate VI) and the whole group therefore was probably considerably more than 500 ft thick in the Gargunnock Hills before its upper part was eroded away.

The topmost part of the group is composed of three flows of Markle basalt which are well exposed on Craigbrock Hill and also in the gorge of the Touch Burn downstream from the waterfall of Gilmour's Linn [NS 73959252] where the following section was measured:

	Thickness ft	Total thickness ft
Base of Black Mount Group	–	–
Bole	3	3
Markle basalt, massive	15	18
Bole containing nodules of decomposed, slaggy Markle basalt	3	21

	Thickness ft	Total thickness ft
Markle basalt, slaggy throughout (varies from 15 to 30 ft)	23	44
Bole	5	49
Markle basalt, rather slaggy..	20	69
Bole, dark red, forming cave below waterfall	7 seen	76

The remainder of the group is fairly well exposed on the northern and eastern slopes of Scout Head, where the following section was recorded [NS 73549337–73509313–73869301]:

	Thickness ft	Total thickness ft
Lowest exposure of the lowest flow of the Touch Burn section described above	–	–
Obscured	5	5
Transitional Jedburgh–Markle basalt, slaggy	5	10
Obscured	7	17
Jedburgh basalt, platy jointing; rather slaggy especially towards top	10	27
Obscured	7	34
Microporphyritic olivine-basalt (with affinities to Dalmeny basalt)	9	43
Obscured	15	58
Markle basalt trending towards trachybasalt with rather platy jointing	1	59
Obscured (occasional exposures of slaggy, vesicular basalt)	9	68
Microporphyritic olivine-basalt trending towards trachy-basalt, platy jointing (exposed on summit of Scout Head)	15	83
Obscured (Jedburgh basalt exposed at this horizon to the north-east)	22	105
Markle basalt, massive	9	114
Obscured (some exposures of vesicular Markle basalt) ..	5	119
Markle basalt, rather slaggy..	5	124
Obscured	10	134
Transitional Jedburgh–Markle basalt, some platy jointing, rather slaggy	11	145
Obscured	31	176
Transitional Jedburgh–Markle basalt, platy jointing, vesicular, decomposed	1	177
Obscured	12	189
Transitional Jedburgh–Markle basalt, massive, rather decomposed..	8	197
Obscured	14	211
Transitional Dalmeny–Markle basalt, some platy jointing at base but more massive towards top	10	221
Obscured	15	236
Transitional Jedburgh–Markle basalt, massive, rather decomposed and albitized..	5	241
Obscured	5	246
Top exposure of Spout of Ballochleam Group	–	–

The total number of lavas within the group seems to increase markedly to the west and south of Scout Head. Although some of the flows of microporphyritic basalt seem to die out westwards, additional flows, some composite, appear at slightly different horizons and there is a general tendency for microporphyritic basalts to increase in number westwards towards the Fintry Hills. In a composite flow about a mile south-south-west of Scout Head the microporphyritic component of transitional Jedburgh–Dalmeny basalt is cut by a dyke-like body of Markle basalt [NS 72929168]. North of this only the microporphyritic component is exposed but as the trap feature is traced southwards outcrops [NS 72949159] of Markle basalt very similar to that of the dyke-like body may be seen. Further south, exposures [NS 73199083] at the top of what seems to be the same flow have abundant large feldspars whereas those nearer the base show only sporadic large feldspars. Composite flows were also found at two other localities [NS 69039110, 68449123] on the dip-slope of the Gargunnock Hills and in both cases the microporphyritic components show affinities with mugearite. The more westerly flow contains bodies of massive basalt surrounded by platy and slaggy basalt. The macroporphyritic component is confined to some of the massive bodies, especially those towards the base of the exposure.

Trachybasalts seem to be rare but two or more flows of mugearite form quite a large outcrop on the top and eastern flanks of a rather indefinite hill [NS 709903] in the south-west of Touch Muir.

Black Mount Group. The Black Mount Group is preserved only on the eastern slopes of the Touch Hills. It is best exposed in the steep cliff that fringes the northern edge of Black Mount and forms the south side of the Touch Burn gorge where the following section [NS 74389244] was measured:

	Thickness ft	Total thickness ft
Jedburgh, or transitional Jedburgh–Markle, basalt with sporadic large feldspar phenocrysts, albitized, platy jointing .. .. seen	6	6
Obscured	18	24
Jedburgh basalt, albitized (varies from 15 to 20 ft) ..	18	42
Obscured (possibly bole)	6	48
Mugearite, very fine-grained, platy jointing, slaggy, rather decomposed..	8	56
Obscured	8	64
Jedburgh basalt, albitized, slaggy, vesicular, decomposed	12	76
Bole resting on Markle basalt at top of Gargunnock Hills Group	3	79

Touch House Group. The Touch House Group includes the remainder of the succession up to the eroded top of the lava pile. Only the Markle basalts which form the lowest part of the group are well exposed. These crop out near the edge of the Carse between Touch Saw Mill [NS 75189331] and Touch House [NS 75359276]. Because of the drift cover the total thickness of the group is difficult to estimate and little is known about its upper part. There is, however, a possibility that the Markle basalts north of Touch House may not lie far below those exposed only a short distance below the basal Volcanic Detritus in the head-waters of Johnny's Burn [NS 76269213] and also south-west of Murrayshall.

SOUTHERN TOUCH AND GARGUNNOCK HILLS

The southern slopes of the Touch and Gargunnock hills are largely covered by drift and in consequence the stratigraphy of the lavas is known only in a general way. It is possible, however, to recognize a lower division consisting predominantly of Jedburgh basalts, which crops out only in the south-west, and an upper division characterized by Markle basalts which covers the rest of the area. The lower division is thought to be roughly equivalent to the Spout of Ballochleam Group and the upper to the Gargunnock Hills, Black Mount and Touch House groups but precise correlation is impossible as the Lees Hill Group of trachybasalts seems to have died out towards the south.

The Cringate Interbasaltic Beds, which are at least 150 ft thick, lie close to the top of the lower division and are rather patchily exposed in the Endrick Water and in a left-bank tributary near Cringate. In the Endrick Water they seem to overlie highly decomposed microporphyritic basalt [NS 68078742]. An exposure in the north-east bank [NS 68008750] shows rather poorly stratified dull red tuff or volcanic detritus, with persistent beds of red mudstone, interspersed with lenticular masses of unsorted lava fragments set in a matrix of greenish clayey material. These masses may be as much as 5 ft thick and their lower surfaces seem to cut across the stratification of the finer beds. They contain fragments of decomposed basalt of all sizes up to 8 in across. These are commonly rounded but locally the outlines are irregular and seem to interlock. Under the microscope (S 46812) some of the basalt fragments are seen to be scoriaceous, with small irregular amygdales filled with chlorite or carbonate. The matrix includes carbonate and also contains some grains of quartz and feldspar.

In the left-bank tributary, about 130 ft of tuff or volcanic detritus, some of which is stratified, is seen to be overlain by 20 ft of microporphyritic basalt which forms a waterfall [NS 68588756].

Although the thickness of these beds approaches that of the Slackgun Interbasaltic Beds they seem to be much more local and cannot be traced through the poorly-exposed ground to the east and west.

The best section in the lower part of the upper division is in the deep valley of the Burnfoot Burn where it is exposed for about two-thirds of a mile upstream from the confluence with the Endrick. Here the succession consists predominantly of Markle basalts but it also contains three flows of microporphyritic basalt, the lowest of which may be the flow that overlies the Cringate Interbasaltic Beds. The highest part of the upper division, immediately below the Volcanic Detritus at the base of the overlying sediments (p. 165), is known from the North Third Reservoir puddle-trench section, continued by the Drumshogle Burn section, in the extreme east of the area. The former was described in some detail by Martin and Tyrrell (1908) who examined the section while the excavation was being made. This section was re-examined during the recent survey and it was found that most of the flows are still exposed. It seems probable that the softer beds between the lavas, which were described as tuffs by Martin and Tyrrell (1908, pp. 250, 253), may be either boles or stratified volcanic detritus derived from bole, for these authors also describe as tuff the undoubtedly non-tuffaceous volcanic detritus at the base of the sediments that overlie the lavas (cf. Martin and Tyrrell 1908, p. 245; Dinham and Haldane 1932, p. 11). The details of the section given by Martin and Tyrrell (1908, p. 250) are set out below, together with a revised interpretation based on a study of thin sections by Dr. J. Phemister and Mr. R. W. Elliot.

Bed	Original interpretation	Revised interpretation	Thickness ft	Total thickness ft
U	Trachytic mugearite	Probably trachybasalt	12	12
T	Tuff	Not seen	4	16
S	Trachytic mugearite	Probably trachybasalt	10	26
R	Tuff	⎫	17	43
Q	Mugearite, porphyritic	⎬ Not seen	10	53
P	Tuff	⎭	16	69
O	Mugearite, porphyritic	Albitized Markle basalt	110	179
N	Tuff	Not seen	4	183
M	Mugearite, porphyritic	Albitized Markle basalt	11	194
L	Tuff	Not seen	4	198

			Thickness ft	Total thickness ft
K	Mugearite, porphyritic	Albitized Markle basalt	21	219
J	Tuff	Not seen	6	225
I	Mugearite, porphyritic	Albitized Markle basalt	19	244
H	Slag	Not seen	6	250
G	Mugearite, porphyritic	Markle basalt	15	265
F	Slag	Not seen	3	268
E	Mugearite	Mugearite, coarse-grained	19	287
D	Slag	Not seen	15	302
C	Mugearite	Mugearite	29	331
B	Coarse tuff	} Not seen	8	339
A	Trachytic mugearite		27 seen	366

Unfortunately this section cannot be correlated in detail across the Wallstale Fault with the section seen in the north of the Touch Hills. The supposition by Martin and Tyrrell (1908, p. 242) that the section represents nearly the total thickness of volcanic material in this neighbourhood is known, however, to be incorrect. The mugearites at the base of the succession may be traced northwards to Berryhill [NS 75089000]. Here only a single flow of basalt intermediate between Jedburgh and Markle types seems to separate them from the lavas exposed at the top of the Drumshogle Burn section where the following succession [NS 74879030–74549010] may be seen:

	Thickness ft	Total thickness ft
Basaltic mugearite or basalt, albitized, with sporadic large feldspar phenocrysts; slaggy and vesicular at top and base	11	11
Obscured (traces of reddish-brown bole)	2	13
Bole, purplish-grey	2	15
Basaltic mugearite, albitized, platy jointing; slaggy top, rather decomposed..	6	21
Obscured	8	29
Jedburgh basalt, albitized, mostly massive with spheroidal weathering, but platy jointing in places	14	43
Obscured	3	46
Markle basalt, massive, decomposed	5	51
Obscured	5	56
Mugearite, platy jointing, slaggy, uneven base and slaggy top	17	73
Jedburgh basalt, albitized; slaggy base and slaggy, highly decomposed top with tongues of bole	23	96
Obscured	3	99
Jedburgh basalt, albitized, platy jointing; slaggy, irregular base	10	109
Markle basalt, slaggy, highly decomposed	1	110
Obscured	4	114
Markle basalt, massive, locally decomposed; irregular slaggy, vesicular base	12	126
Markle basalt, decomposed	6	132

Composite flows are not uncommon in the upper division and examples may be seen on the eastern part of the dip-slope north of the Wallstale Fault [NS 74889083, 74629062, 74079033], and between the Wallstale and Auchenbowie faults [NS 74978946,

74238862, 74558899]. In the last-mentioned exposure, which is in the King's Yett Burn, rounded masses of Markle basalt are surrounded and overlain by platy microporphyritic basalt with an intervening transitional zone containing sparse large feldspars in places. Further west another composite flow lower in the succession may be seen in the Earl's Burn [NS 70908788–71098759].

NORTH AND WEST FINTRY HILLS

Skiddaw Group. In the Boquhan Burn, downstream from the Spout of Ballochleam, the lower lavas of the Skiddaw Group are not exposed but the upper portion of the group is represented by more than 45 ft of Markle basalt, possibly in two flows. As the group is traced westwards along the strike, a composite lava, at least 25 ft thick, is exposed [NS 63689037] immediately east of the Balmenoch Burn Fault, which throws it down against the Skiddaw sill. The group reappears west of this fault and the following section [NS 63399011] is exposed below the thick bole at the base of the Slackgun Interbasaltic Beds:

Composite flow of Jedburgh and Markle basalt, albitized,
  vesicular top and base   ..   ..   20 ft
Markle basalt, vesicular and highly decomposed at top ..   10 ft seen

Within the composite flow the macroporphyritic component seems to be distributed in nodular masses which tend to be more concentrated towards the bottom of the flow. A highly irregular, steeply-dipping, tongue-like body of Markle basalt which tapers upwards is also seen (p. 141). From here the group may be traced by a series of scattered exposures of transitional Jedburgh–Markle, and possibly Jedburgh, basalts to Skiddaw, but south of this the whole group seems to have been largely removed by weathering and erosion at the time when the Slackgun Interbasaltic Beds were formed. A single exposure [NS 62508814] of Markle basalt north-east of Culcreuch may mark a local reappearance of the group in the southern part of the area.

The scattered exposures of decomposed microporphyritic lava and bole in a small stream [NS 63028745–62948743] on the hillside above the Dun intrusion may represent another residual mass of lava, lying below, or possibly within, the Slackgun Interbasaltic Beds. These lavas do not, however, resemble the Markle basalts and composite flows that are typical of the Skiddaw Group.

Slackgun Interbasaltic Beds. The Slackgun Interbasaltic Beds are well exposed in the Fintry Hills, where they are considerably thicker than in the area to the east. In the Boquhan Burn, immediately downstream from the Spout of Ballochleam [NS 65268994–65239014], the succession is as follows:

	Thickness ft	Total thickness ft
Base of Spout of Ballochleam Group	–	–
Tuff, or volcanic detritus, evenly stratified, mostly silt or clay grade; purplish-grey, with coarser laminae composed of minute grains of decomposed volcanic material	6	6
Obscured	10	16
Tuff, or volcanic detritus, evenly stratified, with alternating bands, up to 5 cm thick, of dull purplish-grey mudstone and coarser bands containing rounded and angular fragments of decomposed volcanic material with rare fragments of fresh microporphyritic lava and chalcedony, all set in a matrix of fine mudstone or, locally, calcite ..	75	91
Obscured .. .. (estimated)	60	151
Bole, mostly dull red, with nodules of highly decomposed Markle basalt	7	158
Top of Skiddaw Group	–	–

Microscopic examination of the stratified tuff or volcanic detritus (S 44879) reveals that the basalt fragments commonly contain chlorite-filled amygdales and xenoliths of quartz. Grains of quartz, including granulitized quartz, are commonly found in the clayey matrix together with grains of albitized plagioclase and rare microcline. Scattered exposures of both the bole near the base of the beds and of the stratified tuff or volcanic detritus higher up are seen along the northern slopes of the Fintry Hills and, on their western slopes, the beds have been eroded back to form a shelf about half a mile broad between the scarps formed by the Skiddaw sill and by the Spout of Ballochleam Group. South of Skiddaw, where the lavas of the Skiddaw Group die out, it is difficult to distinguish the Slackgun Interbasaltic Beds from the volcanic detritus at the top of the Downie's Loup Sandstones. Scattered exposures [e.g. NS 62398874] of greenish-brown mudstone with carbonaceous layers and of greenish, chloritic, argillaceous sandstone with plant impressions, which closely resemble the beds at the top of the Downie's Loup Sandstones, seem, however, to lie above the horizon of the Skiddaw Group and so to be part of the Slackgun Interbasaltic Beds. More typical deposits of bole and of stratified tuff or volcanic detritus are seen in scattered exposures on the shelf further south.

Perhaps the most striking exposures of the Slackgun Interbasaltic Beds are seen on the southern slopes of the Fintry Hills in the Cammal Burn, immediately downstream from the Spout of Balbowie [NS 64338697] and in the Balmenoch Burn downstream from the waterfall [NS 64828694]. In the Cammal Burn section, the basal lava of the Spout of Ballochleam Group is underlain by more than 90 ft of stratified tuff or volcanic detritus in alternating fine-grained and coarse-grained beds. The former range in thickness from 1 mm to 50 cm and are for the most part well-sorted and very evenly stratified. They contain fragments of greenish-grey decomposed basalt up to 1 mm in a dull reddish matrix of silt and clay grade. The coarser beds are between 5 mm and 30 cm thick and are generally better stratified and better sorted in the lower part of the exposure where they are also locally cross-stratified. They contain fragments of decomposed lava which are usually less than 2 cm but rarely as much as 15 cm across. Both the fine and coarse bands abut against large, rounded fragments of decomposed basalt which may possibly be volcanic bombs. Locally there are traces of sagging in the strata immediately below these large fragments but this may be due to differential compaction. In thin section (S 46802) some of the smaller igneous fragments are seen to be chloritized and glassy. The matrix is similar to that in the rocks of the Spout of Ballochleam (p. 153) and includes grains of quartz, granulitized quartz, orthoclase and microcline. Similar exposures of volcanic detritus are seen downstream and the total thickness of the Slackgun Interbasaltic Beds in this locality is probably more than 200 ft.

In the Balmenoch Burn section, which lies little more than a quarter of a mile to the east, a thick deposit of red, massive, bole-like material lies at the same stratigraphical horizon as the stratified tuff or volcanic detritus. This red bole-like material contains abundant fragments, of all sizes, of grey, vesicular, decomposed basalt. Most of these fragments are highly irregular in shape but some of the larger ones have a spindle-like shape which suggests that they may be volcanic bombs. At one locality [NS 64888686] more than 40 ft of reddish bole-like material are exposed. This has traces of a vague stratification dipping in a generally southerly direction and contains both fusiform and irregularly shaped fragments of grey vesicular decomposed basalt. These may possibly be equivalent to the fusiform and 'pancake' bombs described by Wentworth and Macdonald (1953, pp. 80–1). A few yards to the south the deposit is cut by an irregular dyke of highly vesicular decomposed basalt. Alternations of decomposed microporphyritic lava and reddish bole-like material containing irregular basalt fragments are somewhat poorly exposed farther upstream.

Spout of Ballochleam Group. The following section, the base of which lies at the foot of the Spout of Ballochleam waterfall, is exposed in the Boquhan Burn [NS 64908963–65268994]:

	Thickness ft	Total thickness ft
Jedburgh basalt, massive, but slaggy and highly decomposed at top	21	21
Bole, dull red	3	24
Obscured	5	29
Jedburgh basalt, rather massive; slaggy base; highly decomposed at top	17	46
Obscured	3	49
Jedburgh basalt with sporadic large feldspar phenocrysts, massive; rather decomposed at top	22	71
Jedburgh basalt, massive; slaggy vesicular base and top; top decomposed	24	95
Jedburgh basalt, massive; slaggy vesicular base and top; top decomposed almost to a bole	25	120
Jedburgh basalt, massive, platy jointing; irregular base; highly vesicular decomposed top	28	148
Jedburgh basalt, massive; platy jointing towards base; top decomposed almost to a bole	36	184
Jedburgh basalt with irregular lenticular bodies of massive basalt and slaggy basalt; slaggy, highly vesicular and rather decomposed at top	62	246
Obscured	15	261
Dalmeny basalt, massive, with sporadic vesicles; irregular slaggy vesicular base	17	278

The lowest flow of Jedburgh basalt seems to maintain its thickness as it is traced westwards round the northern escarpment of the Fintry Hills for it forms crags more than 60 ft high three-quarters of a mile west-north-west of the Spout of Ballochleam. At this locality [NS 64259047] it contains large rounded bodies of massive basalt, thought to be filled lava tubes, surrounded by envelopes of slaggy material (p. 141).

Almost the whole succession is exposed in the line of steep cliffs that fringes the western edge of the Fintry Hills, where the group is thought to be about 200 ft thick and to include at least eight flows. The Stronend Interbasaltic Beds, which lie above the middle of the group, have weathered back to form a prominent shelf but the beds themselves are largely obscured. At one locality [NS 62888885], about a third of a mile south of Stronend summit, more than 5 ft of bole, which lies near the base of the beds, is exposed and about a mile to the south-east more than 9 ft of bole, probably at the top of the beds, crops out [NS 63998764] in a tributary of the Cammal Burn. The Stronend Interbasaltic Beds seem to be relatively thin and local and may possibly be only an unusually thick bole.

The lower lavas of the Spout of Ballochleam Group continue to form a prominent line of crags along the southern slopes of the Fintry Hills. Upstream from the Spout of Balbowie [NS 64318700], the Cammal Burn and a left-bank tributary provide a section through the group, which here comprises at least 8 flows with a total thickness of more than 330 ft. Most of these flows are basalts of Jedburgh type but the third flow up from the base is transitional between the Jedburgh and Markle types.

Shelloch Burn Group. The Shelloch Burn Group is thought to be approximately equivalent to the Lees Hill Group of the Gargunnock Hills, but no detailed correlation can be made over the intervening valley. Unlike the Lees Hill Group it contains not only trachybasalts, including mugearites, but also Markle basalts, microporphyritic basalts and basalts transitional between these two types. The group is best developed in the north of the Fintry Hills and seems to die out towards the south-east. The following section through the upper part of the group is exposed in the Shelloch Burn [NS 65098913–65238924]:

	Thickness ft	Total thickness ft
Basal lava of the Fintry Hills Group	–	–
Bole, dull red	6	6
Obscured	5	11
Mugearite, fine-grained, platy jointing; slaggy vesicular base	15	26
Bole, dull red, grading down into highly decomposed basalt	2	28
Obscured	3	31
Microporphyritic (?Jedburgh) basalt, mostly massive; slaggy, vesicular and decomposed at top	21	52
Markle basalt, mostly massive but with traces of platy jointing in places; slaggy, vesicular and decomposed at top	12	64
Basaltic mugearite, slaggy, highly vesicular, decomposed..	4	68

The lower part of the group is best exposed in the Boquhan Burn [NS 64688967–64908963], about a third of a mile to the north, where the following section was measured. Any gap, or overlap, between these two sections is thought to be small.

	Thickness ft	Total thickness ft
Basaltic mugearite, massive but with platy jointing in places; slaggy, vesicular base	16	16
Bole, red	3	19
Trachybasalt, mostly with platy jointing; slaggy vesicular top and base; top decomposed	40	59
Top of Spout of Ballochleam Group ·..	–	–

West of the Balmenoch Burn Fault the group forms the highest part of the Fintry Hills but it is not particularly well exposed here and the correlation linking the eastern and western sides of the hills in Plate VI is hypothetical. A good section through all but the topmost lavas of the group may, however, be seen in the highest of the crags that form the western edge of the Fintry Hills. The following section [NS 62818910–63048870] was measured obliquely up these crags:

	Thickness ft	Total thickness ft
Trachybasalt, with platy jointing	1	1
Obscured	20	21
Basaltic mugearite, massive but with platy jointing in places; slaggy, vesicular top	25	46
Obscured .. .. (estimated)	15	61
Basaltic mugearite, massive but with platy jointing in places, with irregular slaggy, vesicular lenses	35	96
Trachybasalt, massive but with platy jointing in places; irregular slaggy, vesicular top	36	132
Transitional Jedburgh–Markle basalt with sporadic rounded bodies of massive basalt surrounded by slaggy vesicular material; top decomposed; zeolites towards base	13	145

	Thickness ft	Total thickness ft
Transitional Jedburgh–Markle basalt, slaggy decomposed top	23	168
Trachybasalt, with platy jointing that forms trough-like structures in places; slaggy, vesicular top and base; top decomposed..	30	198

Traces of a massive arch-like structure with radiating columnar joints are seen in the fourth flow from the base of this section [NS 62978874]. This structure resembles the 'war-bonnet' type of lava tube filling described by Waters (1960, p. 354).

Fintry Hills Group. The Fintry Hills Group is thought to be roughly equivalent to the Gargunnock Hills Group but, although it is composed dominantly of Markle basalts, it contains a higher proportion of microporphyritic basalts than the latter group. It is also known to include rare mugearites. Although the top is nowhere seen, the group is known to be considerably more than 400 ft thick in the east of the Fintry Hills. R. L. Jack recorded 'well-rounded ash' [NS 64098794] in a tributary of the Cammal Burn during the original geological survey in 1871. This exposure is now obscured but it seems possible that it represents a deposit of tuff or volcanic detritus, possibly at the same horizon as that of the Cringate Interbasaltic Beds.

SOUTH-EASTERN FINTRY HILLS

The succession on the eastern, downthrow, side of the Balmenoch Burn Fault cannot be matched with that on the western side and no more than a tentative correlation can be attempted. It is thought that the microporphyritic basalts with subordinate Markle basalts and composite flows that crop out in the lower part of the southern slopes of the Fintry Hills, immediately east of the fault, may be roughly equivalent to the Spout of Ballochleam Group. A composite flow in this part of the succession, exposed in the north bank [NS 66438614] of the Endrick Water just south of the limit of the district, shows an intimate intermixing of the two components and provides strong evidence that the macroporphyritic component was the later of the two (p. 141).

The trachybasalts that succeed the microporphyritic basalts may represent part of the Shelloch Burn Group and the remaining flows, which are mostly Markle basalts with subordinate microporphyritic basalts, seem to be roughly equivalent to the Fintry Hills Group. A mugearite from this upper part of the succession has been analysed (Clough and others 1925, p. 182).

CRAIGFORTH

The lavas that crop out on the isolated hill of Craigforth, about a mile to the west of Stirling, seem to be the only exposed part of a strip of Calciferous Sandstone Measures volcanic rocks that lies between the Ochil and Abbey Craig faults. The lavas are at least 150 ft thick and comprise the following sequence of flows in upward succession—albitized Jedburgh basalt; basalt transitional between Jedburgh and Markle types; albitized Jedburgh basalt; Markle basalt; albitized Jedburgh basalt; Markle basalt.

As Stirling No. 1 (Kaimes) Bore (1961), which was sited [NS 77209454] immediately west of Craigforth, passed into the stratified volcanic detritus at the top of the Downie's Loup Sandstones at a depth of 215 ft, it is thought that the lowest flow exposed at Craigforth may possibly lie some 200 ft above the base of the lava succession. Correlation between the Craigforth flows and the lava groups of the Touch Hills is not possible on the basis of the information at present available, especially as the whole volcanic succession seems to become attenuated progressively towards the north-east.

Intrusions associated with the Volcanic Rocks

Numerous minor intrusions cut the Upper Old Red Sandstone, Ballagan Beds, Downie's Loup Sandstones and Calciferous Sandstone Measures volcanic rocks. Many of them are of petrological types similar to those found among the Clyde Plateau lavas and as such intrusions are absent in the Carboniferous sediments above the lavas, it seems probable that they are related to the volcanic episode.

Irregular intrusions of uncertain origin. An irregular mass of unusually fresh Jedburgh basalt appears on the lower slopes of the Fintry Hills immediately north of the site of Craigton and forms the prominent minor hill known as the Dun [NS 62878726]. This mass, which appears abruptly within the soft boles, tuffs, volcanic detritus and highly decomposed lavas of the Slackgun Interbasaltic Beds, is composed of fresh, dark, massive Jedburgh basalt, commonly coarse-grained, which is readily distinguishable in the field from any of the lavas in this part of the succession. Vertical columnar jointing is common and forms almost perfect hexagonal prisms on the steep western face of the Dun. The contacts with the surrounding rocks are not exposed but they seem to be steeply transgressive in some localities yet roughly parallel to the regional dip in others. North of Craigton the mass crops out on the hillside over a vertical distance of more than 400 ft and this outcrop may be traced south-eastwards beyond the limits of the Stirling district. Thus the intrusive nature of this mass is no longer in doubt and its outcrop seems to be more extensive than was formerly supposed (*cf.* Clough and others 1925, fig. 6).

A mass of mugearite, probably intrusive, crops out immediately north of the Dun intrusion and in its northern part at least appears to be in the form of a sill. In hand specimen the rock differs from that of the adjacent Skiddaw sill (p. 159) and is fine-grained and brownish-weathering, with very rare large phenocrysts of feldspar.

Sills. Only two relatively thick sills are known to invade the rocks between the base of the Upper Old Red Sandstone and the top of the Calciferous Sandstone Measures lavas and both lie within the Downie's Loup Sandstones, almost immediately below the base of the lavas. They occur in different parts of the area, however, and are not known to overlap.

The Downie's Loup, or Dinning Quarry, sill is confined to the east where it lies at the foot of the northern escarpment of the Touch Hills and eastern Gargunnock Hills [NS 73089356–68959260]. It is composed of an unusual semi-mafic rock that differs from all the other Lower Carboniferous intrusions in this district (pp. 164–5). The sill seems to be subject to marked changes of horizon and of thickness. These changes are perhaps best illustrated by comparing the exposures in Dinning Quarry with those at Downie's Loup waterfall on the Gargunnock Burn [NS 70749308], only about 300 ft to the west. In the quarry, more than 60 ft of the sill are exposed. The lower half is coarse-grained and contains fairly abundant large phenocrysts of feldspar but these are absent in the upper half, which is finer in grain. The rough columnar jointing and the chilled top of the sill curve over towards the western part of the quarry face, suggesting that the sill transgresses downwards in that direction. At Downie's Loup, where the sill forms a waterfall, only 20 ft of igneous rock are exposed and the base of the sill seems to be lying at a lower stratigraphical horizon within the Downie's Loup Sandstones.

The Skiddaw sill is confined to the northern and western slopes of the Fintry Hills. In the field it closely resembles the Jedburgh basalt of the Dun intrusion but under the microscope is seen to be a trachybasalt which may be readily distinguished from the Dun intrusion, the Downie's Loup sill and the irregular intrusion of mugearite that seems to be intruded only a little higher up in the succession than the Skiddaw sill, north of the Dun (p. 163). The sill forms the crags of Skiddaw at the western end of the Fintry Hills where it is more than 35 ft thick and shows rough columnar jointing. It cannot be traced south of the Dun intrusion.

Thinner sills seem also to be rare. They include a 6-ft sill of decomposed basalt, probably of Markle type, which is intruded into strata near the top of the Cornstone Beds [NS 68579324], roughly a mile south-west of Watson House.

Dykes. More than fifty dykes, most of them only a few feet thick, have been recorded in the rocks between the base of the Upper Old Red Sandstone and the top of the Calciferous Sandstone Measures lavas. The majority are exposed either in the lava escarpment or else in stream sections in the underlying sediments; comparatively few have been found on the poorly-exposed dip-slope of the lavas. The dykes vary widely in trend and there is little indication of any preferred orientations. Locally two, three or even more narrow dykes are found running parallel to each other, only a few feet apart. The majority of the dykes are decomposed and have therefore been shown as 'mafic or semi-mafic rocks, unclassed' on the geological map. Many seem to be of rock types, such as Markle and Jedburgh basalt, trachybasalt etc., which are commonly found among the lavas, but there are a few which do not correspond to any of the lava types. These include a dyke of tholeiitic olivine-basalt [NS 70059242] trending roughly east-north-eastwards, and a dyke of decomposed olivine-rich dolerite or picrite with northerly trend, which is exposed in the Lernock Burn [NS 61599039] just beyond the western limit of the district.

An unusual composite dyke-like body of basalt is intruded into the Ballagan Beds low down on the north-western slopes of the Fintry Hills [NS 62388981]. This body, which trends roughly south-eastwards and is more than 30 ft wide, does not exhibit the parallel arrangement of the constituent members that characterizes many of the composite dykes of Arran (Tyrrell 1928, pp. 208, 220), but instead the macroporphyritic and microporphyritic components are intimately intermixed, as though the magmas had behaved as two almost immiscible liquids during intrusion. The boundaries between the two components are locally sharp but there is no definite chilling of one against the other and in places there is a transitional zone. The whole aspect of the rock closely resembles that of the composite flow exposed on the north bank of the Endrick Water (pp. 141, 157). The body contains numerous inclusions of baked shale and sandstone and, near the top of the exposure, one inclusion of sandstone seems to run horizontally almost across the body. No trace of the intrusion can be found higher up in the cliff face and it may have died out before reaching the surface.

W.A.R.

Petrography of the Volcanic Rocks and Associated Intrusions

The lavas of the Touch, Gargunnock and Fintry hills are principally olivine-basalts similar to those occurring in other outcrops of Calciferous Sandstone Measures lavas in the Midland Valley. The basalts are mainly of the felsic

Markle and Jedburgh types or intermediate between these types, and relatively few of the more mafic varieties occur. More felsic rocks including mugearites and other trachybasalts are important though less plentiful. Intrusions of basalt, of types similar to those occurring as lavas, and of mugearite and trachy-basalt also occur.

DETAILS

OLIVINE-BASALTS

The classification used in this account is that given by MacGregor (1928) which is based on the original classifications by F. H. Hatch (quoted by Geikie, 1892, pp. 129–30) and W. W. Watts (quoted by Geikie, 1897, p. 418) modified as found necessary by experience.

Markle type. The macroporphyritic basalt lavas of this area can be accommodated largely within the Markle type, which is characterized by plentiful large phenocrysts, over 2 mm in diameter, of plagioclase and, less commonly, of olivine, in a matrix of plagioclase, augite, iron ore and small olivines.

The feldspar phenocrysts, which may be as much as about 1·2 cm in diameter (S 40419), appear to be mainly bytownite (about An_{70} to An_{84} at core), albeit entirely albitized in some specimens, and are generally abruptly zoned to about labradorite and commonly margined by oligoclase. The zoning may be continuous or discontinuous and oscillatory zoning is seen in some specimens (S 44855). The full range of composition is not seen in all specimens and in one (S 40404) a maximum anorthite content of An_{60} was determined by measurement of extinction angles in albite–Carlsbad twins. It is possible, however, that this value represents an intermediate or outer zone of the phenocryst examined, due to the random intersection of the phenocryst by the thin section.

In some specimens of Markle type (S 40404, 44047–9) and of rocks intermediate between Markle and Jedburgh types (S 42651) the plagioclase phenocrysts contain inclusions of augite, iron ore and small pseudomorphs after olivine. Patches of chlorite may occur and some phenocrysts (S 44852) are sieved by chlorite and iron oxide. In several slices (S 42647, 44852) thin veinlets of augite, chlorite and iron ore cut the feldspar phenocrysts and locally connect the coarser inclusions and nests of groundmass which are enclosed in the feldspar. The veinlets are commonly controlled by the cleavages of the feldspar, particularly the {010} cleavage.

The groundmass feldspar is mainly zoned labradorite occurring as small laths, generally 0·1 to 0·3 mm long though up to about 0·6 mm long in coarser varieties. Anorthite contents ranging from about An_{54} to An_{68} have been determined though the full range of composition is not seen in all slices. Oligoclase is common, particularly in the rocks trending towards mugearites or trachybasalts, occurring interstitially in the matrix and investing the laths and phenocrysts of basic plagioclase. Alkali-feldspar also occurs interstitially in some specimens.

The plagioclase, both phenocrysts and groundmass, is in general partly or completely albitized (S 40406–7, 40419, 40616) and in a number of specimens (S 42637, 44049, 45009) patchy zeolitization of the feldspar occurs.

Fresh olivine has not been observed: it is replaced by a variety of alteration products including 'iddingsite', bowlingite, serpentine, quartz and iron oxide. In some rocks (S 44047, 44874) the pseudomorphs occur as phenocrysts, up to about 3 mm in diameter, but commonly the pseudomorphs are not larger than microphenocrysts (ca. 0·1 to 0·2 mm in diameter) and in some rocks are more or less restricted to the groundmass.

The augite is generally restricted to the groundmass as small prisms and grains, generally 0·02 to 0·05 mm in diameter, and is normally pale in colour though commonly with a pale purplish or brownish tint. A number of the lavas (S 44055, 44821, 44852)

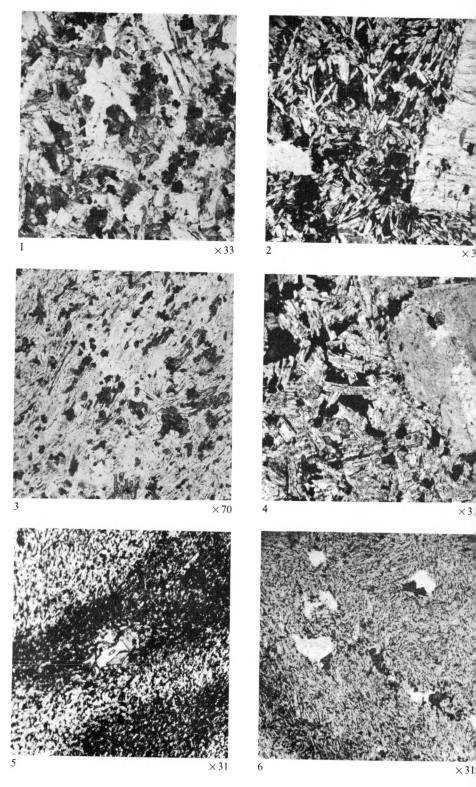

1 ×33

2 ×3

3 ×70

4 ×3

5 ×31

6 ×31

are characterized by purplish ophitic augite (Plate VII, fig. 2) and correspond to the 'Kilsyth type' defined by Watts (quoted by Geikie, 1897, p. 418) but later incorporated in the Markle type (Bailey *in* Clough and others 1925, p. 177; MacGregor 1928, pp. 330–1). These ophitic feldspar-phyric olivine-basalts are rather more mafic than normal for Markle type. MacGregor (1928, p. 331) refers to a record by Dr. J. Phemister of a persistent but thin development of basalts similar to the 'Kilsyth type' in the neighbourhood of Carnwath. In addition a number of specimens (S 42658, 44047, 44049, 44051, 44874) occur which are more mafic than normal but which are characterized by microlitic augite. The augite occasionally occurs as small microphenocrysts and in one rock (S 44046) which shows a stronger tendency towards the Dunsapie type a phenocryst of brownish augite occurs. In a zeolitized basalt (S 42637) the microlitic pyroxene adjacent to patches of fine-grained zeolite has a cinnamon colour and a microphenocryst of pale-purple augite has a cinnamon-coloured margin. In the more altered rocks the pyroxene is replaced by chlorite and carbonate.

Iron ore occurs throughout as small grains, often 0·02 to 0·05 mm in diameter, and as larger plates in the coarser rocks. Apatite also is a ubiquitous accessory in the form of small slender needles. Other constituents in interstitial patches and amygdales include chlorite and other viriditic material, locally oxidized, quartz, chalcedony, jasper, hematite, carbonate and zeolites. These minerals also occur in veinlets and in some specimens the matrix is locally patchily impregnated by hematite.

PLATE VII

PHOTOMICROGRAPHS OF CALCIFEROUS SANDSTONE MEASURES IGNEOUS ROCKS

FIG. 1.   Olivine-basalt (Jedburgh type). 3400 ft E.10°N. of Craigton. Lathy microphenocrysts of plagioclase in groundmass of plagioclase laths, ophitic augite, pseudomorphs after olivine and plates of iron ore. S 46801. Plane polarized light. Magnification × 33.

FIG. 2.   Olivine-basalt (Markle type). 1280 ft W.36°N. of Carleatheran summit. Phenocryst of bytownite in matrix of labradorite laths, ophitic augite, pseudomorphs after olivine, plates of iron ore and interstitial chlorite. S 44852. Plane polarized light. Magnification × 31.

FIG. 3.   Trachybasalt. Stronend, north cliffs about 420 ft N.15°W. of Stronend summit. Small fluxioned laths of feldspar, mainly potash-oligoclase zoned out probably to anorthoclase, shredded trachy-ophitic plates of augite, small plates of iron ore and small pseudomorphs after olivine. S 45319. Plane polarized light. Magnification × 70.

FIG. 4.   Feldspar-phyric rock, cf. trachybasalt. Old quarry, bottom of central face, about 4050 ft S.7°E. of Gargunnock Church. Phenocryst of patchily decomposed, albitized plagioclase in a matrix of laths of albitized plagioclase rimmed by alkali-feldspar, subhedral prisms of augite, small plates of iron ore and interstitial chlorite. S 44816. Plane polarized light. Magnification × 33.

FIG. 5.   Basaltic mugearite. Crag about 7650 ft S.13°W. of Gargunnock Church. Tiny fluxioned laths of plagioclase, about andesine in composition, invested by oligoclase, granular augite and iron ore and small pseudomorphs after olivine. Rock patchily impregnated by hematite. Hornblende crystals line chlorite-filled amygdales. S 44846. Plane polarized light. Magnification × 31.

FIG. 6.   Mugearite. Trap feature about 6850 ft N.32°W. of summit of Earl's Hill. Tiny fluxioned laths of oligoclase, granular iron ore and tiny pseudomorphs probably after augite and olivine. Crystals of sphene line quartz-filled amygdaloidal patches. S 45303. Plane polarized light. Magnification × 31.

Jedburgh type. The basalts of Jedburgh type are characterized, in general, by plentiful lathy microphenocrysts (less than 2 mm in diameter) of plagioclase in a groundmass of plagioclase laths, augite, olivine and iron ore; they commonly exhibit well-developed flow structure. Included within this type are basalts in which the feldspars show very poorly-developed microporphyritic character but which are more feldspathic than those of Dalmeny type (cf. MacGregor 1928, p. 337).

The plagioclase microphenocrysts and groundmass laths are labradorite (values ranging from about An_{50} to An_{65} have been determined in various slices) zoned out to about andesine. They are commonly at least partly albitized. Oligoclase occurs investing the more basic plagioclase and interstitially (S 44888, 46784, 46801), and alkali-feldspar is also present in some specimens.

Rare feldspar phenocrysts occur in some basalts of Jedburgh type and these may contain inclusions as in the basalts of Markle type. A small phenocryst in one specimen (S 44883) is sieved by augite which is patchily in optical continuity and is also sieved by chlorite.

The olivine is almost always completely replaced but some fresh olivine occurs in a sliced rock (S 46784) from the Dun intrusion (p. 158).

As in the basalts of Markle type the augite shows some variation in colour and texture. In many specimens (S 44068, 44837, 44859, 44883, 46801) it is purple and ophitic (Plate VII, fig. 1) but in others it is apparently colourless or pale in colour and microlitic (S 40412, 41181, 44851). Though the more deeply purple augite is normally ophitic the converse is not true and in one trachy-ophitic basalt (S 42644) the augite has only a faintly purplish tint. In decomposed varieties the augite is replaced by chlorite and carbonate, locally with some sphene.

In varieties which trend towards the mugearites and trachybasalts oligoclase and alkali-feldspar are more plentiful in the groundmass. In some of these rocks, as in the basaltic mugearites, rare small scraps of biotite (S 44851) occur, locally accompanied by hornblende (S 45298).

Dalmeny type. The basalts of Dalmeny type (MacGregor 1928, p. 341) are characterized by the presence of numerous microphenocrysts of olivine, which may be accompanied by a few microphenocrysts of augite and sporadic microphenocrysts of plagioclase, in a matrix of basic plagioclase laths with abundant augite and iron ore.

Relatively few rocks of this type occur in the lavas of this area. One (S 44880) contains numerous microphenocrysts, commonly about 0·3 mm in diameter, of bowlingite after olivine and sporadic microphenocrysts of labradorite in a matrix of laths of labradorite (An_{54} at core), small pseudomorphs after olivine, purple ophitic augite and grains of iron ore. Flow structure is moderately well developed. Another specimen (S 44878) containing plentiful pseudomorphs after olivine as microphenocrysts also contains numerous microphenocrysts of labradorite and the pyroxene of the matrix is microlitic. Though this rock is allied to the Dalmeny type it could be regarded, according to the proposals of MacGregor (1928, p. 350) as intermediate between this and Markle type.

Rocks intermediate between the olivine-basalt types. Olivine-basalt intermediate between the Jedburgh and Markle types occurs commonly in this district. This variety contains plagioclase phenocrysts which are normally only sporadic and never as plentiful as in the Markle type. The mineralogical characteristics are as in Markle and Jedburgh types.

Some of the olivine-basalts, particularly ophitic varieties (S 42832, 44875, 45311), are more mafic than the normal Jedburgh type and olivine pseudomorphs are more abundant. These rocks have been classed as intermediate between the Jedburgh and Dalmeny types. One specimen (S 42832) which, in view of its proportion of oligoclase and alkali-feldspar, is transitional between the basalts and trachybasalts contains some fresh olivine, and a few flakes of biotite and a crystal of hornblende have been observed in this rock.

A number of specimens of lava (S 42634, 44840, 46794, 46808) are characterized by numerous lathy microphenocrysts of plagioclase accompanied by many microphenocrysts of pseudomorphs after olivine. According to one of the alternative proposals of MacGregor (1928, p. 356) these may be grouped as intermediate between the Dalmeny and Markle types. One specimen (S 46794) is ophitic and in composition resembles those rocks grouped as intermediate between Jedburgh and Dalmeny types. The others have microlitic pyroxene and the presence of an appreciable proportion of oligoclase and alkali-feldspar indicates their affinities with the trachybasalts.

One unusual variety of basalt (S 42643) occurring in the Gargunnock Hills Group contains numerous laths, up to about 0·3 mm long, of labradorite with small pseudomorphs after olivine in a fine-grained matrix of abundant granular augite and iron ore and sparse small laths of labradorite. In appearance the groundmass is similar to that of the mafic basalts of Hillhouse type but the numerous feldspar microphenocrysts distinguish it from that type. In composition the rock is probably allied to the Dalmeny type.

MUGEARITES AND TRACHYBASALTS

The mugearites (S 44065, 44997, 45010, 45303, 46984) of this area are generally fine-grained rocks composed of fluxioned laths of oligoclase, much iron ore as small grains and plates, and small pseudomorphs in chlorite and iron oxide after olivine and augite. In many of the rocks the laths of oligoclase have irregular serrate edges at their mutual boundaries. Neither orthoclase nor anorthoclase was detected with certainty in the mugearites and one slice (S 13933A) which was treated with sodium cobaltinitrite after etching with hydrofluoric acid did not give a positive stain for potash. Amygdaloidal patches are filled by quartz and chlorite. A little sphene (Plate VII, fig. 6) occurs associated with amygdaloidal patches and in the matrix (S 45303).

An abnormal variety described by Bailey (*in* Clough and others 1925, p. 181) forms the small intrusion to the north of the Dun (p. 158). The rock (S 13933, 45327) is characterized by the presence of plentiful pseudomorphs after olivine.

Many of the mugearitic rocks in this area, both lavas and the less common dykes, are better described as basaltic mugearites. They (S 13934, 14130, 44846, 44848, 44850, 46806) differ from the mugearites in the presence of small microlites or laths of more basic plagioclase, at least as basic as andesine and apparently normally about labradorite in composition. These rocks have a more basaltic appearance with enrichment in augite and olivine. The olivine is generally completely decomposed but some residual fresh olivine was observed in one sliced rock (S 13934). Some specimens (S 47389) contain sporadic microphenocrysts of labradorite. In general the basaltic mugearites are very fine-grained and exhibit well-developed flow structure interrupted by lines of 'ruck'. Slightly coarser rocks occur which have increased content of labradorite (S 44890, 45324) and which more closely approach the basalts in composition. In general all transitions appear to occur between the mugearites and basalts.

Albitization is common and, as observed by MacGregor (1928, p. 348), 'rocks similar to mugearites in many respects are produced by the more or less complete albitization of some fine-textured basalts'. Difficulty is also encountered in distinguishing partly albitized basalts from partly albitized basaltic mugearites or trachybasalts in both of which residual basic plagioclase may occur.

Feldspar-phyric basaltic mugearites or trachybasalts occur containing numerous phenocrysts of basic plagioclase, commonly albitized. In one of the composite lava flows the aphyric member (S 44850) is a basaltic mugearite and the other member (S 44849) is similar but characterized by abundant feldspar phenocrysts. A number of the flows (S 44985, 44988) of feldspar-phyric basalt of Markle type in the North Third Reservoir puddle-trench section (pp. 151–2) contain an appreciable proportion of oligoclase and alkali-feldspar in the matrix. These rocks may be regarded as at least showing some approach to the mugearites or trachybasalts but the presence of albitization makes an estimation of the proportion of primary oligoclase difficult.

M

Other rocks have been grouped as trachybasalts since they differ somewhat in character from the mugearites. Like those rocks designated as basaltic mugearites they generally contain laths of oligoclase with a proportion of more basic plagioclase commonly as microlitic cores to the oligoclase. Alkali-feldspar appears to be more prominent in the trachybasalts. Some (S 42656) are allied to the basalts of Jedburgh type. Another variety (S 44045, 44824) contains pseudomorphs after olivine as small microphenocrysts as well as in the groundmass. In this variety the augite occurs as tiny prisms and grains generally about 0·02 to 0·04 mm in diameter and small fluidal laths, commonly 0·1 to 0·2 mm long, of labradorite occur invested by oligoclase and with interstitial alkali-feldspar.

The proportion of relatively basic plagioclase to more alkaline feldspar is somewhat variable though difficult to assess particularly in the fine-grained rocks. In one group of trachybasalts (S 45322, 45326) relatively little basic plagioclase occurs and the pyroxene is almost colourless or may have a pale greenish tint. Similar to this variety is the rock (S 45315) forming the Skiddaw sill (p. 159) which contains scattered pseudomorphs after olivine and rare microphenocrysts of labradorite in a groundmass of laths of oligoclase zoned out to more alkaline feldspar. Labradorite (An_{51}) occurs as scattered small laths and locally forms a slender core to the laths of oligoclase. Treatment of a slice (S 45315A) with sodium cobaltinitrite after etching with hydrofluoric acid stained the oligoclase yellow and it is probably best regarded as potash-oligoclase zoned out to anorthoclase.

One rather unusual variety grouped with the trachybasalts (S 45319, 46805, 48797) is characterized by the shredded trachy-ophitic texture (Elliott 1952, p. 928) of the pyroxene (Plate VII, fig. 3) which is pale-green in colour. This variety contains slender fluxioned laths or microlites, generally 0·1 to 0·2 mm long, of feldspar, apparently mainly potash-oligoclase zoned out probably to anorthoclase. Some laths of more basic plagioclase which did not react to the sodium cobaltinitrite stain for potash also occur (S 45319A, 46805A). Small pseudomorphs in viriditic material after olivine occur as tiny grains.

Hornblende and biotite, though always in small quantity, occur as late-formed accessory minerals in a number of the basaltic mugearites and trachybasalts (S 42656, 44846, 46806). They occur as small irregular, locally spongy, plates in the matrix and euhedral crystals of hornblende locally line chlorite-filled amygdales (S 44846, Plate VII, fig. 5). In some specimens (S 13934, 14130, 46806) these minerals appear more common in or near the planes of 'ruck' which interrupt the well-developed planar flow structure. The hornblende, like that described by Flett (1908, p. 123), is normally biaxial positive (+2V large; Z:c=26°) and pleochroic (α, almost colourless; β, peach; γ, reddish-peach). In one sliced rock (S 47389), however, the hornblende is optically negative. The biotite (−2E ca. 65°), which is pleochroic in shades of reddish-brown, peach and pale peach or yellow, commonly shows moderately strong dispersion ($r < v$).

Apatite is a common accessory mineral as colourless needles in the mugearites and trachybasalts. In addition, in a number of rocks prisms of dusky apatite occur containing dark inclusions arranged in striae parallel to the principal axis.

Probably best grouped with the trachybasalts is the distinctive but unusual feldspar-phyric rock (Plate VII, fig. 4) which occurs in the composite Downie's Loup sill (p. 158). The rock (S 32356, 42653, 44066, 44816) contains plentiful phenocrysts, up to about 5 mm in diameter, of turbid albitized plagioclase in a groundmass of laths of albite-oligoclase, generally small, subhedral, locally subophitic plates of pale-coloured clinopyroxene and small plates of iron ore. Chlorite is common in interstitial patches, accompanied, in one specimen (S 42653), by quartz. A few small rather shapeless patches of chlorite may represent pseudomorphs after olivine. The plagioclase of the phenocrysts and groundmass is largely turbid albite-oligoclase but remnants of more basic plagioclase in one specimen (S 44816) indicate that albitization has occurred. Some alkali-feldspar occurs as a thin rim to the plagioclase and in one specimen

(S 44066) clear glassy alkali-feldspar ($-2E$ ca. 50°), probably sanidine, is plentiful rimming the plagioclase and as squat tablets margining the interstitial patches of chlorite. Tiny crystals of alkali-feldspar also occur in the patches of chlorite in this specimen. A few scraps and blades of hornblende occur fringing the pyroxene in one specimen (S 44816). The amphibole differs in character from that of the basaltic mugearites and is pleochroic in shades of reddish brown and greenish yellow ($-2V$; $Z:c=21°$; strong dispersion $r<v$). Adjacent to chloritic patches (S 44816), the clino-pyroxene locally has a thin green selvage probably of aegirine-augite. The aphyric variety (S 32357, 46987) of rock from this intrusion is finer in grain and composed of laths of hematite-dusted albite-oligoclase, possibly at least in part albitized plagioclase, small pseudomorphs in chlorite after augite and perhaps after olivine, and small grains of iron ore. A thin selvage of clear alkali-feldspar mantles the plagioclase in one specimen (S 32357). Chlorite and quartz are common in interstitial patches.

R.W.E.

Sediments above the Volcanic Rocks

The sediments that lie between the weathered top of the lavas of the Clyde Plateau and the Hurlet Limestone were formerly classified as the Upper Sedimentary Group (Clough and others 1925, p. 14; Robertson and Haldane 1937, p. 9; Read 1959, pp. 4–5). They are probably equivalent to part of the Upper Oil-Shale Group of the Lothians but exact correlation between the two areas is not yet possible. The outcrop of these beds forms an irregular strip which runs southwards from Causewayhead to the southern limit of the district and varies in width from less than 300 ft to about half a mile, but in places it has been split into two by the outcrop of the Stirling sill. Much of the outcrop is covered by drift, but the sediments are well exposed in two sections in the Bannock Burn, one near Todholes (Figs. 13, 15) and the other near Touchadam Quarry, two-thirds of a mile north of the North Third Reservoir (Figs. 14, 15).

Generally the strata dip north-eastwards or eastwards at angles of 15° or less but anomalous dips are found close to some of the larger faults—for example in the Touchadam Quarry section where the beds have been folded to form a basin-like structure. The continuity of the outcrop is broken by several east–west faults including the Abbey Craig, Crook, Wallstale and Auchenbowie faults, the last-named being responsible for a shift of the outcrop amounting to as much as two miles. The Stirling sill has invaded the sediments between the Crook Fault and Cambusbarron and also south of the North Third Reservoir.

The beds above the lavas fall naturally into two lithological divisions. The lower of these was named the Volcanic Detritus by Dinham (*in* Dinham and Haldane 1932, p. 11) as it is almost entirely derived from the weathering products of the highest lavas. The upper is composed of strata which closely resemble those of the Lower Limestone Group and the equivalent beds further west were, in fact, formerly classed with that group (Neilson 1913, pp. 324–7).

LOWER DIVISION OR VOLCANIC DETRITUS

A prolonged period of weathering and erosion followed the extrusion of the highest lavas of the Touch Hills and as a result the succeeding sediments rest unconformably upon various members of the lava succession. This unconformity does not, however, necessarily imply any prior tectonic movement as the lavas were extruded subaerially. It is commonly quite difficult to define the exact

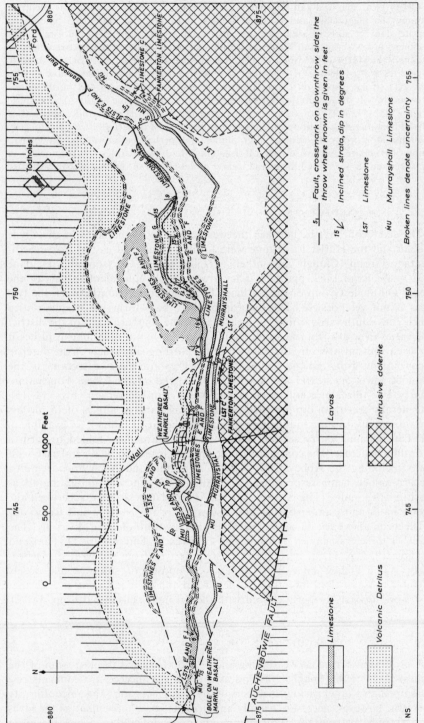

Fig. 13. *Sketch-map of the limestones exposed in the Bannock Burn near Todholes*

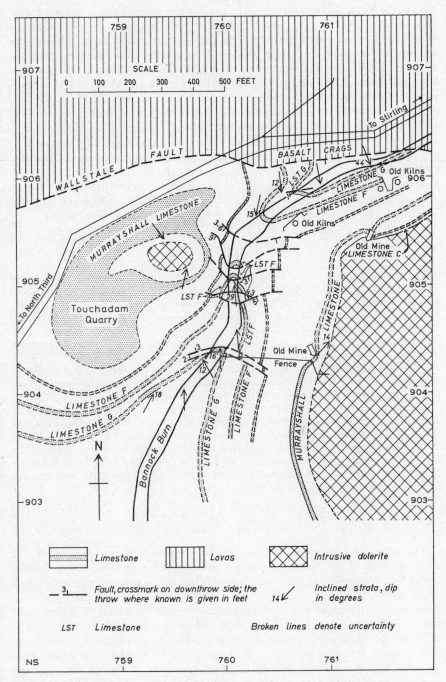

FIG. 14. *Sketch-map of the limestones exposed in the Bannock Burn near Touchadam Quarry*

base of the Volcanic Detritus in a given exposure as in many places the weathered lava grades upwards into bole which is in turn succeeded by bole material which has been re-sorted by water. The deposits are characteristically variable and include conglomerates with pebbles of weathered lava, arenites (Pettijohn 1957, p. 17) and mudstones, all largely composed of volcanic material and coloured dull red, purple, grey, green, yellow or brown. Most of the deposits were laid down as lenticular bodies and many are cross-stratified.

The Volcanic Detritus is also very variable in thickness, ranging from 7 ft to more than 200 ft; Dinham was almost certainly correct in regarding it as a transgressive marginal deposit laid down at the edge of an old volcanic land mass while sediments of Lower Limestone Group facies were being deposited farther out to sea. As the sea rose progressively the coast line with its fringe of volcanic detritus retreated until, at the time when the Murrayshall (Hurlet) Limestone was being deposited, all the lavas were probably submerged (Dinham *in* Clough and others 1925, pp. 16–7; Dinham and Haldane 1932, p. 10).

DETAILS

The best exposures of the Volcanic Detritus are in the Todholes section of the Bannock Burn where, in the south bank [NS 74688768], 7 ft of yellowish-green and greyish volcanic detritus with fragments of weathered basalt rest on an irregular surface of greatly weathered slaggy Markle basalt. About 300 ft due east [NS 74778769] the Volcanic Detritus swells to more than 12 ft and still further east [NS 75018768], where its base is not exposed, it is at least 22 ft thick. Some 200 ft farther downstream a disconformity between the lower and upper divisions is exposed [NS 75048773]; here cross-stratified volcanic detritus with south-westerly depositional dips is seen to be overlain, with an angular discordance of about 20°, by shales, mudstones and ironstones of the upper division, immediately below Limestone G.

Further north, the Volcanic Detritus seems to be considerably thicker in the Bannock Burn section immediately upstream from Touchadam Quarry; it is probably more than 200 ft thick here, but the exposures are smaller and more scattered than those in the Todholes section. There are also scattered small exposures below the crags of the Stirling sill, e.g. at the north-eastern corner [NS 76008926] of North Third Reservoir (Read 1959, p. 7), near Murrayshall [NS 76819121], near Gartur [NS 76409205] and in trench excavations immediately to the north.

UPPER DIVISION

The strata of the upper division are best exposed in two sections in the Bannock Burn. These can be correlated with each other and with the sections in the northern part of the Central Coalfield, but the scattered exposures which occur elsewhere along the outcrop are generally difficult to correlate.

In most of the exposures of topmost Calciferous Sandstone Measures sediments within the Stirling district, sandstones are poorly represented (Fig. 15), although they form a relatively large proportion of the Lower Limestone Group. Their place is taken by sediments of sand and clay grade which are largely composed of volcanic detritus derived from the remnants of the old volcanic land mass. Normal quartzose sandstones are found however in Canglour Glen and also in sections immediately to the south of the district (Dinham and Haldane 1932, pp. 16–7), where they seem to replace part of the shale, mudstone and limestone succession exposed in the Bannock Burn. Considerable lateral

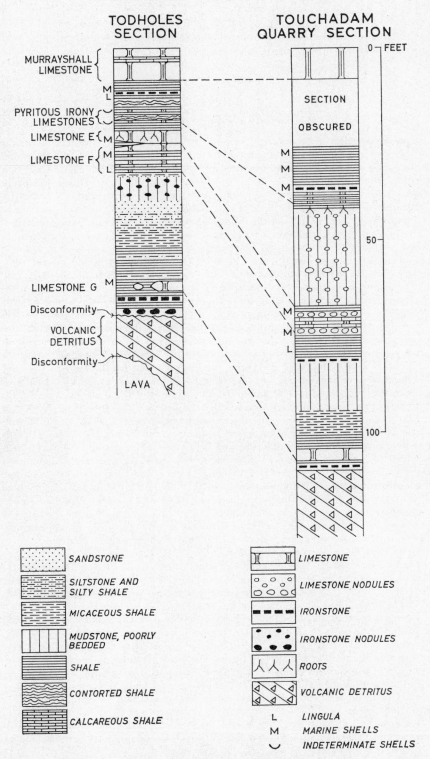

Fig. 15.   *Comparative vertical sections of Calciferous Sandstone Measures sediments above the volcanic rocks in the Bannock Burn*

variation of this sort is, in fact, typical of the top Calciferous Sandstone Measures sediments and is in marked contrast to the relative constancy of the succession above the Hurlet Limestone (Clough and others 1925, pp. 14–6).

DETAILS

BANNOCK BURN SECTIONS

Volcanic Detritus to Limestone G. The beds between the disconformity at the top of the Volcanic Detritus and Limestone G dip at the same angle as the limestone. They comprise 1 to 4 ft of shales, mudstones, silty shales and ironstones and generally include a thin bed of calcareous shale with marine shells immediately below Limestone G. In the Todholes section a thin band of irony nodules lies directly above the disconformity and a persistent thin bed of silty ironstone lies some 2 ft below Limestone G.

Limestone G. Limestone G or the *Productus* Limestone is generally a grey crystalline limestone with some argillaceous bands. It is characterized by a varied marine fauna which includes *Gigantoproductus* and simple and compound corals (p. 181). The character of this fauna suggests that Limestone G should be correlated with the Hollybush Limestone of the Paisley district (p. 181; Lee *in* Dinham and Haldane 1932, p. 14).

The abrupt thinning out of Limestone G towards the west may be traced in the Todholes section. About 750 ft south-south-east of Todholes the limestone [NS 75328779] is a continuous bed more than 2 ft 3 in thick but 500 ft upstream [NS 75208771] it is only 6 to 10 in thick; 550 ft farther to the west [NS 75038781] it is reduced to a band of calcareous nodules no more than 6 in thick. The limestone probably dies out altogether a short distance further west. At Touchadam, where the whole succession is thicker (Fig. 15), Limestone G is about 3 ft thick.

Limestone G to Limestone F. The interval between limestones G and F is about 30 ft in both the Todholes and Touchadam Quarry sections of the Bannock Burn. In the former section Limestone G is succeeded by a bed of dark grey shale containing brachiopods, which grades upwards into more silty beds containing only rare fragments of drifted plants. These beds become progressively more greenish in colour before passing upwards into yellowish-green and grey silty mudstones and chloritic clayey sandstones, capped by a pale-grey mudstone with ironstone nodules and a sandy, irony top. All these beds above the grey shales contain a high proportion of weathered igneous material which has almost certainly been derived from the old volcanic land mass to the west. Finally a thin bed of dark-grey shale with marine fossils lies immediately below the lowest leaf of Limestone F.

The succession in the Touchadam Quarry section is similar but less well exposed. Marine shells have not, as yet, been recorded here from the shale above Limestone G and the shale below Limestone F is thicker than that at Todholes.

Limestones F and E. One of the most striking lithological changes in the uppermost Calciferous Sandstone Measures is apparent when limestones F and E of the Todholes section are compared with the equivalent beds in the Touchadam Quarry section, where Limestone E is entirely missing.

Over much of the length of the Todholes section limestones F and E are combined to form a single bed with contrasting lithologies in its upper and lower parts. Upstream, however, a thin wedge of shale appears and progressively separates the dark-grey, argillaceous Limestone F from the distinctive white nodular Limestone E above. Dinham (*in* Dinham and Haldane 1932, p. 14) correlated Limestone F with the Blackbyre Limestone of the Paisley district and Limestone E with the White Coral Limestone of the Corrie Burn which it closely resembles both in lithology and fauna (pp. 181–2; Read 1959, p. 6).

Limestone F is almost always in leaves which are separated by partings of fossiliferous, and generally calcareous, shale. Its thickness, exclusive of partings, ranges from 1 ft 4 in at the western end of the section to 4 ft 4 in at the eastern end. The lowest leaf, which is 2 to 6 in thick, is usually darker in colour, more silty and possibly more irony than the higher leaves. It also contains *Lingula* alone whereas the rest of the limestone and the intervening shale partings contain a varied marine fauna, including bryozoa, brachiopods and lamellibranchs (pp. 181–2). The easternmost exposure [NS 75428778] of Limestone F in the Todholes section also contains abundant fragments of the goniatites that characterize this limestone in the Touchadam Quarry section.

The bed of fossiliferous, calcareous shale that separates limestones F and E may be as much as 2 ft 6 in thick in the western part of the section but thins eastwards to 4 in [NS 74568769] and finally disappears altogether.

Limestone E ranges in thickness from 3 ft 9 in to 5 ft 6 in and is split in places by thin beds of calcareous shale. It is generally pale-grey in colour but weathers whitish-yellow and is characterized by irregular streaks and patches of pale-grey calcareous mudstone and argillaceous fine-grained limestone set in a more coarsely crystalline groundmass, which give the bed an uneven nodular appearance when weathered. The limestone usually contains abundant fossils including crinoid columnals, bryozoa, brachiopods, gastropods and lamellibranchs, but in some of the upstream exposures it is almost barren and traces of carbonaceous roots may be detected in the top of the limestone. These roots seem to be the only traces of the seatclay and the Hurlet Coal which overlie the White Coral Limestone at the Corrie Burn, some eight miles to the south-west (Clough and others 1925, p. 29; Robertson and Haldane 1937, p. 18).

In the Touchadam Quarry section Limestone F closely resembles its analogue in the Todholes section except that the limestone leaves are thinner and locally become nodular; the total thickness of limestone, exclusive of shale partings, is commonly less than 1 ft 6 in. Goniatites are abundant, as in the easternmost exposure of the Todholes section (p. 182). Limestone E is absent in the Touchadam section and its position in the succession is occupied by more than 25 ft of pale-grey and greenish-grey calcareous mudstone with limestone nodules (Fig. 15). This mudstone is similar in lithology to some of the argillaceous streaks and patches found in Limestone E in the Todholes section. It is possible that the calcareous mudstone in the Touchadam Quarry exposures may represent clayey material, derived from weathered volcanic rocks, which was deposited near the edge of an area in which limestone was being formed in comparatively clear water.

Limestone E to Murrayshall (Hurlet) Limestone. The strata between Limestone E and the Murrayshall Limestone are best exposed [NS 74438767] in the Todholes section where they are 13 ft thick and consist almost entirely of shales. The shales in the lower part of the succession are very fissile, with crystals of selenite along some of the bedding planes. They contain two or more beds of nodular, well-jointed, pyritous limestone, each a few inches thick, and also a few thin ribs of clayband ironstone. Some beds of shale a few inches thick are intricately folded and contorted whereas the beds above and below are undisturbed. The contortions do not resemble those made by the pene-contemporaneous disturbance of unconsolidated beds (e.g. Kuenen 1953, pp. 1056–8; Ten Haaf 1956; Sanders 1960; Dott and Howard 1962; Dzulynski and Smith 1963) and may possibly be of tectonic origin (*cf.* Cope 1946; Williamson 1956, pp. 396–7), for locally some of the limestones are disturbed by small faults which are apparently associated with the contorted strata. In any given exposure however the contorted beds seem to remain at the same stratigraphical horizon. Fish debris and some poorly preserved shells, including brachiopods and lamellibranchs, have been found in the lower shales [NS 74138766].

The shales in the upper part of the sequence are less fissile, and are calcareous just below the Murrayshall Limestone where they contain *Lingula* and other brachiopods.

In the Touchadam Quarry section the strata between the calcareous mudstone described above and the Murrayshall Limestone are just over 30 ft thick. The lower part of the succession, as at Todholes, consists of fissile shales with crystals of selenite and ribs of argillaceous, pyritous limestone and ironstone towards the base. The limestone ribs are generally three in number, all less than 6 in thick, and the thickness of these and of the intervening shales varies considerably. Only root-like bodies have been found in the lowest shales immediately above the calcareous mudstone but both the limestone ribs and the shales above them contain marine shells.

OTHER SECTIONS

Polmaise No. 4 (Broadleys) Bore [NS 81159194] cut 39 ft of strata below the Murrayshall Limestone. The strata closely resemble the higher beds exposed in the Bannock Burn sections but a seatclay and a thin coal at the very bottom of the bore underlie the shales with thin calcareous ribs. This 3-inch coal may be equivalent to the thick Hurlet Coal of the Central Coalfield.

Scattered exposures of sandstones, siltstones and shales with marine fossils (Dinham and Haldane 1932, pp. 16, 27), which probably belong to the topmost Calciferous Sandstone Measures, are found below the Stirling sill about a mile south-south-east of Todholes, but as they have been disturbed by the Auchenbowie Fault and baked by the dolerite they cannot be correlated with the Todholes section.   W.A.R.

REFERENCES

CLOUGH, C. T., HINXMAN, L. W., WILSON, J. S. G., CRAMPTON, C. B., WRIGHT, W. B., BAILEY, E. B., ANDERSON, E. M. and CARRUTHERS, R. G. 1925. The geology of the Glasgow district. 2nd edit. revised by MACGREGOR, M., DINHAM, C. H., BAILEY, E. B. and ANDERSON, E. M. *Mem. geol. Surv. Gt Br.*

COPE, F. W. 1946. Intraformational contorted rocks in the Upper Carboniferous of the southern Pennines. *Q. Jl geol. Soc. Lond.*, **101**, 137–76.

DINHAM, C. H. and HALDANE, D. 1932. The economic geology of the Stirling and Clackmannan Coalfield. *Mem. geol. Surv. Gt Br.*

DIXON, C. G. 1938. The geology of the Fintry, Gargunnock and Touch Hills. *Geol. Mag.*, **75**, 425–32.

DOTT, R. H. and HOWARD, J. K. 1962. Convolute lamination in non-graded sequences. *J. Geol.*, **70**, 114–21.

DZULYNSKI, S. and SMITH, A. J. 1963. Convolute lamination, its origin, preservation, and directional significance. *J. sedim. Petrol.*, **33**, 616–27.

ELLIOTT, R. B. 1952. Trachy-ophitic texture in Carboniferous basalts. *Mineralog. Mag.*, **29**, 925–8.

FLETT, J. S. 1908. On the mugearites. *Mem. geol. Surv. Summ. Prog.* for 1907, Appendix I, 119–26.

GEIKIE, A. 1861. On the chronology of the trap-rocks of Scotland. *Trans. R. Soc. Edinb.*, **22**, 633–54.

—— 1892. The Anniversary Address of the President of the Geological Society. *Q. Jl geol. Soc. Lond.*, **48**, Proceedings, 38–179.

—— 1897. *The ancient volcanoes of Great Britain*, Vol. 1, London.

GIBSON, I. L. and WALKER, G. P. L. 1963. Some composite rhyolite/basalt lavas and related composite dykes in eastern Iceland. *Proc. Geol. Ass.*, **74**, 301–18.

KENNEDY, W. Q. 1931. On composite lava flows. *Geol. Mag.*, **68**, 166–81.

—— 1933. Composite auto-intrusion in a Carboniferous lava flow. *Mem. geol. Surv. Summ. Prog.* for 1932, Part II, 83–93.

KUENEN, P. H. 1953. Significant features of graded bedding. *Bull. Am. Ass. Petrol. Geol.*, **37**, 1044–66.

MACDONALD, G. A. 1953. Pahoehoe, aa, and block lava. *Am. J. Sci.*, **251**, 169–91.

MacGregor, A. G. 1928. The classification of Scottish Carboniferous olivine-basalts and mugearites. *Trans. geol. Soc. Glasg.*, **18**, 324–60.

Martin, N. and Tyrrell, G. W. 1908. A puddle-trench section at North Third, near Bannockburn, with notes on the geology of the surrounding district. *Trans. geol. Soc. Glasg.*, **13**, 240–54.

Neilson, J. 1913. Notes on the Geological Survey Memoir. *Trans. geol. Soc. Glasg.*, **14**, 324–7.

Nichols, R. L. 1936. Flow-units in basalt. *J. Geol.*, **44**, 617–30.

Pettijohn, F. J. 1957. *Sedimentary rocks.* 2nd edit. New York.

Read, W. A. 1959. The economic geology of the Stirling and Clackmannan Coalfield, Scotland: Area south of the River Forth. *Coalfld Pap. geol. Surv.*, No. 2.

Robertson, T. and Haldane, D. 1937. The economic geology of the Central Coalfield of Scotland, Area I. *Mem. geol. Surv. Gt Br.*

Sanders, J. E. 1960. Origin of convoluted laminae. *Geol. Mag.*, **97**, 409–21.

Summ. Prog. 1961. *Mem. geol. Surv. Summ. Prog.* for 1960.

Ten Haaf, E. 1956. Significance of convolute laminations. *Geologie Mijnb.* (NW Ser.), 18e Jaargang, 188–94.

Tulloch, W. and Walton, H. S. 1958. The geology of the Midlothian Coalfield. *Mem. geol. Surv. Gt Br.*

Tyrrell, G. W. 1928. The geology of Arran. *Mem. geol. Surv. Gt Br.*

—— 1937. Flood basalts and fissure eruption. *Bull. volcan.*, (II), **1**, 89–111.

Walker, G. P. L. 1959a. Geology of the Reydarfjördur area, eastern Iceland. *Q. Jl geol. Soc. Lond.*, **114**, 367–93.

—— 1959b. Some observations on the Antrim basalts and associated dolerite intrusions. *Proc. Geol. Ass.*, **70**, 179–205.

Waters, A. C. 1960. Determining direction of flow in basalts. *Am. J. Sci.*, **258A**, 350–66.

Wentworth, C. K. and Macdonald, G. A. 1953. Structures and forms of basic rocks in Hawaii. *Bull. U.S. geol. Surv.*, **994**.

White, W. S. 1960. The Keweenawan Lavas of Lake Superior, an example of flood basalts. *Am. J. Sci.*, **258A**, 367–74.

Williamson, I. A. 1956. A guide to the geology of the Cliviger valley near Burnley, Lancashire. *Proc. Yorks. geol. Soc.*, **30**, 375–406.

Chapter IX

LOWER LIMESTONE GROUP

INTRODUCTION

THE LOWER and upper limits of the Lower Limestone Group are the base of the Murrayshall (Hurlet) Limestone and the top of the Top Hosie Limestone, respectively. Currie (1954, pp. 534–5) allocated almost the whole of the group to the Upper Bollandian Stage (P_2), excepting only the Top Hosie Limestone and the shale immediately below it which she placed in the Pendleian Stage (E_1). Within the Stirling district the group appears at the surface only on the western limb of the Clackmannan Syncline, between Causewayhead in the north and Easterton, two miles west of Plean, in the south. As a result of displacement by the Abbey Craig, Crook, Wallstale and Auchenbowie faults the outcrop is discontinuous and from King's Park, Stirling, southwards to Milnholm it is further complicated by the intrusion of the Stirling sill. Fairly good exposures of the strata below the Fankerton (Blackhall) Limestone are found below the dolerite crags of the Stirling sill between the Wallstale and Auchenbowie faults, but the higher beds are not well exposed and most of the information available on the upper part of the succession comes from quarries and temporary exposures; there are also some bores, but only a few of these have been examined by a geologist.

The general dip at the outcrop is between 5° and 15° and is usually towards the east or north-east, but steeper dips and anomalous dip directions are found where beds have been disturbed by faulting or igneous intrusions.

The total thickness of the group has been proved in only two bores but there is nevertheless sufficient evidence to trace in some detail the thickness variations of the two parts of the succession above and below the base of the Fankerton Limestone (Fig. 16). Both parts show a marked increase in thickness eastwards, but this increase is especially abrupt in the lower part which more than doubles its thickness in less than three miles. The upper part also increases in thickness on the downthrow side of the Campsie Fault in the Denny area, immediately south of the Stirling district. These variations in thickness suggest that differential subsidence of both the broad basin-like structure known as the Kincardine Basin (Read 1961, p. 274), which was the forerunner of the Clackmannan Syncline, and of the flexure that later developed into the Campsie Fault was taking place whilst the Lower Limestone Group was being deposited. Possibly the thickening of the Lower Limestone Group on the western side of the Kincardine Basin may be linked with the eastward thinning of the underlying lavas (p. 142).

LITHOLOGY

Typical sections of the Lower Limestone Group are given in Fig. 17. These show that the succession cannot conveniently be divided into cycles of sedimentation as can the Limestone Coal and Upper Limestone groups (pp. 186, 195); this is mainly because of the absence of coals, which are few in number and rarely

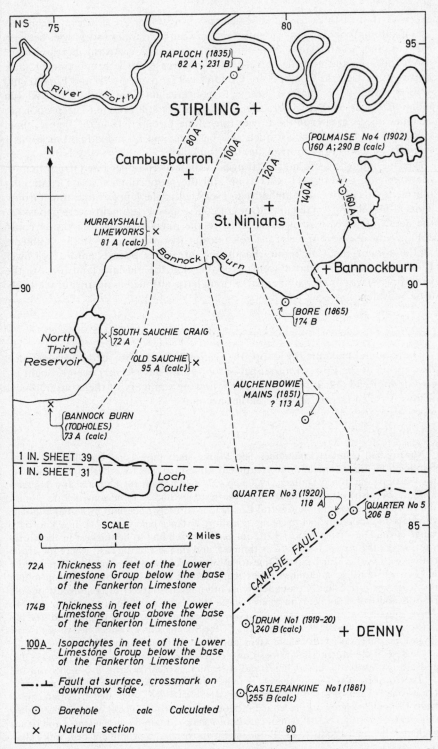

NS 75 80 95

RAPLOCH (1835)
82 A ; 231 B

River Forth

STIRLING +

80 A

100 A

POLMAISE No4 (1902)
160 A ; 290 B (calc)

Cambusbarron +

120 A

140 A

160 A

+ St. Ninians

MURRAYSHALL
LIMEWORKS
81 A (calc)

Bannock Burn

+ Bannockburn

90

N

North
Third
Reservoir

SOUTH SAUCHIE CRAIG
72 A

OLD SAUCHIE
95 A (calc)

BORE (1865)
174 B

90

AUCHENBOWIE
MAINS (1851)
? 113 A

BANNOCK BURN
(TODHOLES)
73 A (calc)

1 IN. SHEET 39
1 IN. SHEET 31

Loch
Coulter

QUARTER No3 (1920)
118 A

QUARTER No5
206 B

85

SCALE

0   1   2 Miles

CAMPSIE FAULT

72A   Thickness in feet of the Lower
      Limestone Group below the base
      of the Fankerton Limestone

174B Thickness in feet of the Lower
      Limestone Group above the base
      of the Fankerton Limestone

100A Isopachytes in feet of the Lower
      Limestone Group below the base
      of the Fankerton Limestone

⌐·⌐ Fault at surface, crossmark on
      downthrow side

⊙   Borehole   calc   Calculated

×   Natural section

DRUM No1 (1919-20)
240 B (calc)

+ DENNY

CASTLERANKINE No1 (1881)
255 B (calc)

80

FIG. 16.   *Variations in thickness of the Lower Limestone Group above and below the
Fankerton (Blackhall) Limestone*

exceed a foot in thickness, and seatearths. Sandstones are, however, relatively abundant and appear in all the intervals between limestones except that between the Top and Second Hosie limestones. In general the eastward increase in the proportion of sand and the corresponding decrease in the proportion of shale noted in the Central Coalfield by Goodlet (1957, p. 64, fig. 5) and Forsyth and Wilson (1965, p. 78, plate iv) seems to continue into the Stirling district but individual beds of shale more than 90 ft thick are still present. The proportion of limestone is greater in the Lower Limestone Group than in the Upper Limestone Group and may be as much as 7 per cent. but no individual limestone is definitely known to be more than 10 ft thick.

Marine influences are much stronger in the Lower Limestone Group than in the overlying Limestone Coal Group and the proportion of strata containing marine fossils is probably higher than even that in the Upper Limestone Group. Thus although appreciable quantities of coarse clastic sediments were deposited, the depth of water was rarely reduced to the point at which vegetation could colonize the area. No trace of the volcanic detritus which recurs in the sediments at the top of the Calciferous Sandstone Measures persists into the Lower Limestone Group so that it seems probable that the old lava land mass to the west (p. 168) was finally submerged, although it continued as an area of relatively little subsidence.

STRATIGRAPHY

Dinham and Haldane (1932, pp. 18–34) have already provided a very detailed description of the Lower Limestone Group, which has recently been brought up to date by Read (1959, pp. 7–10). The following summary of the stratigraphical details is based largely on these earlier accounts.

DETAILS

Murrayshall (Hurlet) Limestone. The Murrayshall Limestone, also known as the Bannock 'D' Limestone and the Northfield Limestone, has long been correlated with the Hurlet Limestone (Dinham 1920, pp. 37–8). Dinham (*in* Dinham and Haldane 1932, p. 24) also correlated it with the Charlestown Station Limestone of Fife. Unlike the Hurlet Limestone in the Central Coalfield it is rarely underlain by a coal although roots are found locally in Limestone E a short distance below (p. 171). It is known to range in thickness from 5 ft to 9 ft 2 in, generally tending to be thickest in the north-west, where the group as a whole is thinnest, and thinnest in the east, where the group is thickest. As the Murrayshall Limestone was worked very extensively for lime, both in opencast workings and mines, it has been removed along much of its outcrop so that no clear exposure is left. Consequently its lithology has largely to be judged from old records and from fragments in quarry waste (Dinham and Haldane 1932, pp. 19–24). These suggest that it is generally a blue-grey limestone which may darken and develop pyritous patches where it has been baked by the Stirling sill. An 8-inch bed of dark-grey crystalline limestone with calcite veins and crinoid columnals which is known to lie at the base of the Murrayshall Limestone is exposed in the Bannock Burn [NS 74438768] and a loose block of similar limestone, 3 ft thick, which contains a 2-inch band full of *Lithostrotion* was found nearby. Farther upstream the top of the Murrayshall Limestone is seen in a series of exposures [NS 74108765] separated by small faults. Here 1 ft of dark-grey argillaceous limestone with pyritous flecks and pyritized shell fragments is overlain by 1 ft 6 in of calcareous shale containing *Orbiculoidea* and bands packed with small Productoids. Immediately above this, a prominent bed, more than

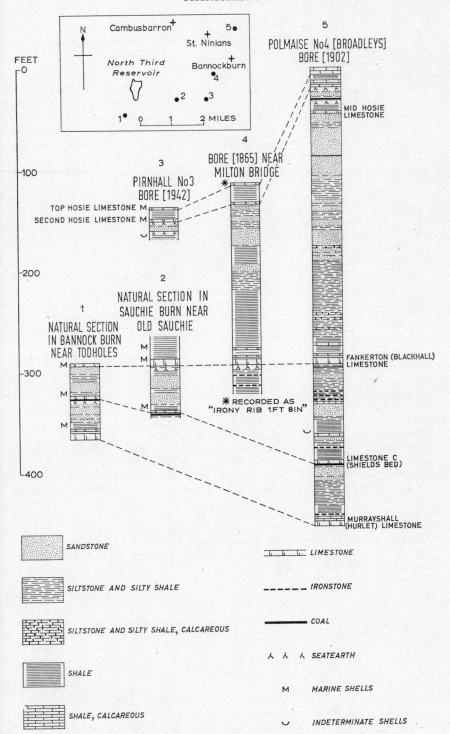

FIG. 17. *Comparative vertical sections of the Lower Limestone Group*

2 ft thick, of dark-grey, very argillaceous limestone runs across the stream; it is cut by occasional calcite veins and contains Productoids and gastropods.

Murrayshall Limestone to Limestone C. The strata between the Murrayshall Limestone and Limestone C thicken eastwards from just over 30 ft to more than 55 ft. This part of the succession approximates much more closely to a cycle of the type found in the Limestone Coal and Upper Limestone groups (pp. 186, 195) than do the strata in most of the intervals between the limestones of the Lower Limestone Group.

The shale roof of the Murrayshall Limestone varies in thickness from less than 10 ft to more than 25ft and is best exposed in the Bannock Burn [NS 74438768], where its lower part is calcareous and contains a 2-inch bed of argillaceous limestone. This shale is characterized by an abundant and varied marine fauna including crinoid and echinoid fragments, bryozoa, Productoids and other brachiopods, gastropods and lamellibranchs (p. 182; Dinham and Haldane 1932, p. 21). The shale grades upwards into a passage by alternation from silty micaceous shale to sandstone, this part of the succession being locally disturbed by roots. The sandstone is overlain by seatearth and a persistent coal which ranges in thickness from 5 in to 25 in but is usually only about 6 in. This seam has proved useful in identifying Limestone C, which lies almost immediately above.

Limestone C (Shields Bed). Limestone C ranges in thickness from 6 in to 3 ft 5 in and is generally between 2 and 3 ft thick. It is usually a dark-grey, rather argillaceous limestone which contains sporadic crinoid columnals and brachiopods. Local patches of pyrites occur and in some places, e.g. the Bannock Burn section (Dinham 1920, p. 36), the limestone has been decalcified. It is almost certainly equivalent to the Shields Bed of Campsie (Macnair and Conacher 1914, pp. 45, 47) which has recently been traced eastwards as far as Dumbreck No. 1 Bore, near Kilsyth (Forsyth and Wilson 1965, p. 70, plate iv), but it is more commonly underlain by a coal than the latter bed. Dinham (1924, pp. 119–20) also correlated Limestone C with the Craigenhill Limestone of the Wilsontown area and the Charlestown Green Limestone of Fife. Limestone C has been worked for lime to a much smaller extent than the Murrayshall Limestone but small-scale opencast workings are found at its outcrop [NS 749876] immediately south of the Bannock Burn and it also seems to have been worked at the Weatherlaw inlier [NS 764875] (Read 1959, p. 9).

Limestone C to Fankerton Limestone. The strata between Limestone C and the Fankerton Limestone are only about 30 ft thick at outcrop but are known to swell eastwards to about 95 ft. The proportion of sand, however, seems to be greater in the west than in the east (cf. Read 1961, p. 285). Limestone C is overlain by a bed of shale which contains a varied marine fauna (p. 182). This bed may locally be more than 15 ft thick in the bores to the east but its thickness at the outcrop is only a few feet. Some sections show two more beds of shale higher in the succession, separated by silty and sandy strata, and in Polmaise No. 4 (Broadleys) Bore [NS 81159194] calcareous ribs have been recorded at the bases of both beds of shale and shells in the lower bed. A thin coal underlies the Fankerton Limestone in the same bore but this seam is represented by only a seatearth in other sections. It lies at a rather higher horizon than the Wilsontown Smithy Coal (Macgregor and others 1923, pp. 46, 49) which is not known to be present within the area of the Stirling Sheet.

Fankerton (Blackhall) Limestone. Dinham (1920, p. 37) recognized that Limestones 'A' and 'B' of the Bannock were the upper and lower leaves of the Fankerton Limestone of the River Carron section west of Denny and the latter name has been adopted for this limestone within the Stirling district. The overlying Neilson Shell-Bed (p. 182) allows the Fankerton Limestone to be correlated with the Blackhall Limestone of the Glasgow area, the Foul Hosie Limestone of the Wilsontown area and Carriden No. 5 Limestone of the Bo'ness area. Dinham (1924, p. 119), Currie (1954, table i) and Wilson (1966, fig. 2) extended the correlation to the Charlestown Main Limestone of Fife. These correlations are supported by the fact that all the limestones named are overlain by an unusually thick bed of shale.

The Fankerton Limestone is almost everywhere the thickest limestone in the Lower Limestone Group and is known to range in thickness from about 4 ft to 10 ft. It is quite commonly in leaves and, along the outcrop, is generally in two leaves with different lithologies. The lower leaf—Limestone B—is a grey, argillaceous limestone containing nodules of a slightly darker colour; these have a concentric structure and weather out prominently. This feature has enabled the upper of the two limestones exposed at the Weatherlaw inlier to be correlated with Limestone B (Read 1959, p. 9). Limestone B is virtually unfossiliferous, unlike the lithologically similar lower leaf of the Blackhall Limestone in the Central Coalfield, which contains a non-marine fauna (Hinxman and others 1920, pp. 35–6; Clough and others 1925, pp. 38, 42, 45). Marine fossils have been recorded from the strata immediately below the limestone (Dinham and Haldane 1932, p. 28).

By contrast the upper leaf—Limestone A—is generally a hard, dark, bluish-grey limestone which contains numerous crinoid columnals and brachiopods.

In a recent trench excavation [NS 77908983] north-east of Sauchieburn House the Fankerton Limestone is represented by a decalcified ochre bed 5 ft thick. The only locality where the limestone seems to have been worked is at Easterton [NS 804864].

Fankerton Limestone to Second Hosie Limestone. The thickness of strata which separates the Fankerton and Second Hosie limestones varies from less than 150 ft to more than 260 ft. As there are comparatively few sections, none of which have been examined by a geologist, much less is known about this part of the succession than about any other part of the group.

The distinctive bed of shale that overlies the Fankerton Limestone is locally more than 90 ft thick and the lower part of this bed contains a varied marine fauna which closely resembles that of the Neilson Shell-Bed of the Glasgow area (p. 182; Wilson 1966). This fossiliferous shale is fairly well exposed in sections below Sauchie Craig [NS 76038898, 76038914] ,near Old Sauchie [NS 77958839] and north-west of Craigend in a section in the Canglour Burn [NS 78658800]. The upper part of the shale is not exposed but borehole sections show that it becomes progressively more silty and grades up into a succession of silty and sandy beds broken by a few thin beds of shale and, towards the east, by sporadic thin coals. Neither the Milngavie Marine Band (Forsyth and Wilson 1965, p. 71) nor the Main Hosie Limestone has, as yet, been recognized within the area of the Stirling Sheet, although the horizon of the latter may be identified in the Quarter and Denny areas immediately to the south. The Mid Hosie Limestone, however, is known to be 25 in thick in Polmaise No. 4 (Broadleys) Bore [NS 81159194] and 20 in thick in Polmaise No. 1 (Balquhidderock) Bore [NS 81079101], in both of which it is overlain by a bed of shale. The lower leaf of the Lillie's Shale Coal of the Glasgow area is probably represented in these bores by a thin coal that lies a few feet above the Mid Hosie Limestone and it is possible that a thin sandstone immediately above the coal may be equivalent to the Lillie's Sandstone. This thin sandstone is now thought to thicken abruptly westwards to form the coarse-grained Raploch Sandstone, formerly quarried at Raploch [NS 786942] immediately west of Stirling, which is known to be 26 ft thick at the nearby Raploch Bore (1835). An outcrop of more than 30 ft of coarse-grained, pebbly sandstone which was formerly exposed [NS 80709578] near Causewayhead was considered by Dinham (in Dinham and Haldane 1932, p. 32) to lie at the same horizon as the sandstone quarried at Raploch. The abrupt increase that seems to take place in the grain size and thickness of the Raploch Sandstone suggests that it may be a channel infilling. The upper leaf of the Lillie's Shale Coal may be represented by an 8-inch coal that was found below a 14-inch ochre bed, thought to be the Second Hosie Limestone, in a trench excavation [NS 78638873] south-west of Rodgerhead.

Top and Second Hosie limestones. On the west side of the Clackmannan Syncline the Top and Second Hosie limestones range in thickness from 13 to 20 in and from 12 to 26 in respectively. As they are separated by only 12 to 16 ft of fossiliferous shale with no intervening sandy or silty strata or coals they could be regarded, at least on

N

the western side of the Clackmannan Syncline, as two leaves of the same limestone, especially as they unite farther west in the Milngavie area (Forsyth and Wilson 1965, p. 72). On the eastern side of the Central Coalfield, however, their supposed correlatives at Carriden, the Upper and Middle Carriden limestones, are separated by strata which include sandstones and coals (Macgregor and Haldane 1933, fig. 5). The Second Hosie Limestone is generally a hard grey limestone with crinoid columnals and shell debris, whereas the Top Hosie approaches the argillaceous, cementstone type of lithology that characterizes it in the Central Coalfield (Clough and others 1925, p. 39; Dinham and Haldane 1932, pp. 31–2). Locally either or both limestones seem to pass laterally into calcareous shale. The shale between the two limestones may also be partly calcareous. It contains a varied marine fauna including crinoid columnals, bryozoa and brachiopods (pp. 182–3).

On the eastern limb of the Clackmannan Syncline the only reliable section in the Lower Limestone Group within the Stirling district comes from the bottom of Blair Mains No. 2 Bore [NS 97128604] where the Upper Kinniny Limestone, which is thought to be equivalent to the Top Hosie Limestone, was found to be 8 in thick (Francis 1956, p. 5).   W.A.R.

REFERENCES

CLOUGH, C. T., HINXMAN, L. W., WILSON, J. S. G., CRAMPTON, C. B., WRIGHT, W. B., BAILEY, E. B., ANDERSON, E. M. and CARRUTHERS, R. G. 1925. The geology of the Glasgow district. 2nd edit. revised by MACGREGOR, M., DINHAM, C. H., BAILEY, E. B. and ANDERSON, E. M. *Mem. geol. Surv. Gt Br.*

CURRIE, ETHEL D. 1954. Scottish Carboniferous goniatites. *Trans. R. Soc. Edinb.,* **62,** 527–602.

DINHAM, C. H. 1920. In *Mem. geol. Surv. Summ. Prog.* for 1919, 34–41.

——— 1924. In *Mem. geol. Surv. Summ. Prog.* for 1923, 114–26.

——— and HALDANE, D. 1932. The economic geology of the Stirling and Clackmannan Coalfield. *Mem. geol. Surv. Gt Br.*

FORSYTH, I. H. and WILSON, R. B. 1965. Recent sections in the Lower Carboniferous of the Glasgow area. *Bull. geol. Surv. Gt Br.,* No. 22, 65–79.

FRANCIS, E. H. 1956. The economic geology of the Stirling and Clackmannan Coalfield, Scotland: Area north of the River Forth. *Coalfld Pap. geol. Surv.,* No. 1.

GOODLET, G. A. 1957. Lithological variations in the Lower Limestone Group of the Midland Valley of Scotland. *Bull. geol. Surv. Gt Br.,* No. 12, 52–65.

HINXMAN, L. W., ANDERSON, E. M. and CARRUTHERS, R. G. 1920. The economic geology of the Central Coalfield of Scotland, Area IV. *Mem. geol. Surv. Gt Br.*

MACGREGOR, M., ANDERSON, E. M., HINXMAN, L. W. and LIGHTFOOT, B. 1923. The economic geology of the Central Coalfield of Scotland, Area VI. *Mem. geol. Surv. Gt Br.*

——— and HALDANE, D. 1933. The economic geology of the Central Coalfield of Scotland, Area III. *Mem. geol. Surv. Gt Br.*

MACNAIR, P. and CONACHER, H. R. J. 1914. The stratigraphy of the limestones lying immediately above the Calciferous lavas in the Glasgow district. *Trans. geol. Soc. Glasg.,* **15,** 37–50.

READ, W. A. 1959. The economic geology of the Stirling and Clackmannan Coalfield, Scotland: Area south of the River Forth. *Coalfld Pap. geol. Surv.,* No. 2.

——— 1961. Aberrant cyclic sedimentation in the Limestone Coal Group of the Stirling Coalfield. *Trans. Edinb. geol. Soc.,* **18,** 271–92.

WILSON, R. B. 1966. A study of the Neilson Shell Bed, a Scottish Lower Carboniferous marine shale. *Bull. geol. Surv. Gt Br.,* No. 24, 105–30.

Chapter X

LOWER CARBONIFEROUS PALAEONTOLOGY

THIS CHAPTER is restricted to an account of the fossils found in the Lower Carboniferous, comprising the Calciferous Sandstone Measures and the Lower Limestone Group, as the faunas of the Upper Carboniferous have already been published (Wilson and Calver *in* Francis 1956, tables 1, 2; Wilson *in* Read 1959, pp. 63–8).

The lower part of the Calciferous Sandstone Measures, of cementstone facies, is almost barren of fossils. In the Gargunnock Burn, 1300 yd S.2°E. of Gargunnock church, poorly preserved ostracods have been found and in the Gairney Burn, 630 yd N.33°E. of Devonshaw, *Spirorbis sp.*, *Curvirimula sp.*, ostracods and fish scales were collected.

Limestone G. Marine fossils are confined to the uppermost part of the Calciferous Sandstone Measures and the lowest level at which they appear is in Limestone G (p. 170) and the mudstones immediately above and below the limestone. Two exposures of these beds, namely (1) Bannock Burn near Touchadam Quarry, 1420 yd W.9°S. of Wallstale, and (2) Bannock Burn, 500 yd S.36°W. of Todholes, have yielded the following fauna; the numbers following the names refer to the localities as above.

Lithostrotion junceum (Fleming) (1), *L.* cf. *pauciradiale* (McCoy) (1, 2), crinoid columnals (2), *Avonia youngiana* (Davidson) (2), *Composita sp.* (1), *Dictyoclostus pinguis?* (Muir-Wood) (2), *Eomarginifera* cf. *setosa* (Phillips) (1), *Gigantoproductus sp.* (large) (1, 2), *G.* cf. *latissimus* (J. Sowerby) (1, 2), *Pugilis pugilis* (Phillips) (1, 2), *Rhipidomella michelini* (Léveillé) [common below limestone] (2), *Schizophoria* cf. *resupinata* (Martin) (1, 2), *Tornquistia* cf. *polita* (McCoy) (2), *Glabrocingulum sp.* (2), *Retispira sp.* (2), *Edmondia* cf. *maccoyi* Hind (2), *Pterinopectinella sp.* (2), *Schizodus sp.* (2), *Sedgwickia sp.* (2), goniatite? and nautiloid fragments (2).

The presence here of a species of *Gigantoproductus* allied to *G. latissimus* is noteworthy. This species is also found in the Hollybush Limestone in the Paisley area (Lee *in* Clough and others 1925, p. 121). The probable correlation of Limestone G with the Hollybush Limestone was suggested by Lee (*in* Dinham and Haldane 1932, p. 14).

Limestones E and F. Between the mudstones immediately above Limestone G and those below Limestone F, the strata are poorly exposed and appear to be unfossiliferous. For the purposes of this account, Limestone F, Limestone E and the accompanying mudstones can be treated as one unit. The two limestones are separated by only a few inches of mudstone and in places even this is absent (p. 170). Although the two limestones differ markedly in lithology their contained faunas are very similar. The fossils listed below have been collected at the following localities: (1) section in left bank of Bannock Burn at Touchadam Quarry, 1 mile east of Shielbrae, (2) Bannock Burn, 500 yd S.36°W. of Todholes, at first waterfall up from road, (3) Bannock Burn, 1010 yd S.69°W. of Todholes at third waterfall up from road, (4) Bannock Burn, 830 yd S.63°W. of Todholes. The numbers following the names refer to the localities at which they were collected.

Sponge (3), coral (2, 4), crinoid columnals (1, 2, 3, 4), Cidarid spines (2, 4), Fenestellid (2, 3, 4), trepostomatous bryozoa (2, 4), *Antiquatonia insculpta* (Muir-Wood) (2), *Avonia youngiana* (2, 3), *Buxtonia sp.* (1, 2, 4), '*Chonetes*' *dalmanianus?* de Koninck (1, 2, 3), *Crurithyris urii* (Fleming) (3), *Dielasma* cf. *hastata* (J. de C. Sowerby) (4), *Echinoconchus* cf. *punctatus* (J. Sowerby) (2, 3), *Eomarginifera setosa* (1, 2, 3, 4), *E. spp.* (2, 3), *Gigantoproductus sp.* (fluted trail, large) (2), *Lingula spp.* (1, 3, 4), *Orbiculoidea sp.*

181

(1, 4), Orthotetid (2, 3, 4), *Phricodothyris sp.* (1, 2, 4), *Productus sp.* (1, 2, 3, 4), *Pugilis pugilis* (2, 3, 4), *Rhipidomella michelini* (1, 2, 3, 4), *Spirifer sp.* (2, 3, 4), *Tornquistia* cf. *polita* (2, 4), *Euphemites urii* (Fleming) (1), *Retispira striata?* (Fleming) (1), *Actinopteria persulcata* (McCoy) (1, 2, 4), *Aviculopecten spp.* (1, 2, 4), *Cypricardella rectangularis* (McCoy) (1), *Edmondia* cf. *senilis* (Phillips) (1), *Euchondria sp.* (1), *Lithophaga lingualis* (Phillips) (2, 4), *Myalina spp.* (1), *Naiadites* cf. *crassus* (Fleming) (2), *Palaeoneilo mansoni* Wilson (1), *Pernopecten sowerbii* (McCoy) (1, 2, 3, 4), *Posidonia corrugata* (Etheridge jun.) (4), *Pterinopectinella sp.* (2, 3, 4), *Sanguinolites costellatus* McCoy (2, 3), *Solemya primaeva* Phillips (1), *Sulcatopinna flabelliformis* (Martin) (2), *Beyrichoceratoides truncatus?* (Phillips) (1), goniatite fragments (1, 4), orthocone nautiloid (1, 2, 4), trilobite pygidia (2, 3, 4), fish remains [common under Limestone F] (2).

In the section on the left bank of the Bannock Burn at Touchadam Quarry, Limestone D (Murrayshall) (pp. 171–2) has been removed by quarrying but immediately below the position of the limestone there is a thick bed of mudstone resting on an unfossiliferous limestone. In the lower part of the mudstone a marine fauna occurs with: *Eomarginifera setosa?*, *Euphemites urii*, *Retispira decussata* (Fleming), *Myalina* cf. *pernoides* (Portlock), *Posidonia corrugata?*, *Sanguinolites* aff. *clavatus* (Etheridge jun.), *S. costellatus*, *S. variabilis?* McCoy, *Beyrichoceratoides?*, orthocone nautiloid, *Euestheria?*. Above this a non-marine fauna is found containing: *Carbonicola?*, *Curvirimula* cf. *scotica* (Etheridge jun.), *Naiadites?*, *Euestheria sp.* Near the top of the bed marine fossils reappear including: crinoid columnals, *Eomarginifera* cf. *praecursor* (Muir-Wood), 'Linoproductus'?, *Productus sp.*, *Actinopteria?*, *Aviculopecten sp.*, *Posidonia corrugata* [common], and *Pterinopectinella sp.*

Limestone D. Limestone D, taken as the base of the Lower Limestone Group, is nowhere exposed in the area so that its fossil content is unknown. The roof-beds of the limestone can be seen, however, in the Bannock Burn, 1320 yd S.W. of Todholes where *Eomarginifera* cf. *setosa* and *Euphemites sp.* were collected.

Limestone C. The succeeding limestone in the succession is Limestone C (p. 178) which is exposed at Sauchie Craig (south), 810 yd E.4°N. of Greathill. The fossils obtained from the limestone and the associated mudstone are:

coral, crinoid columnals, *Fenestella sp.*, trepostomatous bryozoa, *Lingula spp.*, *Orbiculoidea sp.*, *Productus* cf. *carbonarius*, Rhynchonellid, *Spiriferellina sp.*, *Retispira sp.*, *Dentalium* s.l., *Actinopteria persulcata*, *Aviculopecten* cf. *plicatus* (J. Sowerby), *Dunbarella sp.*, *Edmondia sp.*, *Leiopteria thompsoni?* (Portlock), *Palaeoneilo mansoni*, *?Posidonia corrugata*, *Streblopteria ornata* (Etheridge jun.) [common], orthocone nautiloid, *Weberides mucronatus* (McCoy).

Limestones A and B. In the same section at Sauchie Craig, Limestone A and Limestone B (pp. 178–9) are exposed. These beds together with the two feet of intercalated mudstone are poorly fossiliferous but the mudstone forming the roof of Limestone A, although baked by the overlying Stirling sill, yielded the following fossils:

coral, crinoid columnals, *Crurithyris urii* (Fleming), *Eomarginifera sp.*, *Orbiculoidea sp.*, *Naticopsis sp.*, *Straparollus (Euomphalus) carbonarius* (J. de C. Sowerby), *Polidevcia attenuata* (Fleming), orthocone nautiloid, trilobite fragments. Although not rich, this fauna is correlated with that of the Neilson Shell-Bed which overlies the Blackhall Limestone of the Glasgow area, a correlation suggested by Dinham (*in* Dinham and Haldane 1932, p. 27) and Wilson (1966, pp. 107, 112). An exposure, in a small stream 390 yd W.40°N. of Craigend, of baked, fine-grained siltstone containing crinoid columnals, Chonetoid, *Crurithyris sp.*, and *Polidevcia attenuata* is also probably at this horizon.

Hosie Limestones. The Hosie limestones at the top of the Lower Limestone Group are not exposed in their full sequence in the area. In the excavation for the North Third Reservoir Pipeline at 1630 yd E.25°S. of Sauchieburn House, a mudstone, possibly the roof of the Second Hosie Limestone, contained: crinoid columnals, *Fenestella sp.*, *Productus sp.*, *Spiriferellina sp.* and ostracods. At Abbey Craig, 375 yd W.8°S. of the Wallace Monument, a limestone, 1 ft 3 in thick, is exposed with some associated mudstone and a thin nodular limestone. This locality, which is taken to be at some level in the Hosie limestones, yielded: *Avonia sp.*, '*Camarotoechia*' *sp.*, *Composita sp.*, *Lingula squamiformis* Phillips, *Productus concinnus, Pugilis kilbridensis?* (Muir-Wood), *Schizophoria* cf. *resupinata, Myalina* cf. *mitchelli* Wilson, *Streblochondria sp.*

R.B.W.

REFERENCES

CLOUGH, C. T., HINXMAN, L. W., WILSON, J. S. G., CRAMPTON, C. B., WRIGHT, W. B., BAILEY, E. B., ANDERSON, E. M. and CARRUTHERS, R. G. 1925. The geology of the Glasgow district. 2nd. edit. revised by MACGREGOR, M., DINHAM, C. H., BAILEY, E. B. and ANDERSON, E. M. *Mem. geol. Surv. Gt Br.*

DINHAM, C. H. and HALDANE, D. 1932. The economic geology of the Stirling and Clackmannan Coalfield. *Mem. geol. Surv. Gt Br.*

FRANCIS, E. H. 1956. The economic geology of the Stirling and Clackmannan Coalfield, Scotland: Area north of the River Forth. *Coalfld Pap. geol. Surv.*, No. 1.

READ, W. A. 1959. The economic geology of the Stirling and Clackmannan Coalfield, Scotland: Area south of the River Forth. *Coalfld Pap. geol. Surv.*, No. 2.

WILSON, R. B. 1966. A study of the Neilson Shell Bed, a Scottish Lower Carboniferous marine shale. *Bull. geol. Surv. Gt Br.*, No. 24, 105–30.

Chapter XI

LIMESTONE COAL GROUP

Introduction

THE LIMESTONE COAL GROUP includes the strata between the Top Hosie Limestone and the Index Limestone. Currie (1954, p. 532) provisionally placed the whole of the group in the Pendleian Stage (Lower *Eumorphoceras* Age, E_1) of the Namurian but, as yet, the only goniatite recorded in the group is a specimen of *Cravenoceras*? which was found in the Black Metals (p. 190) in a section just beyond the southern limit of the Stirling Sheet (*see* Read 1959, p. 63). This identification is, however, consistent with a position in the Pendleian Stage.

Within the Stirling district the group crops out only on the western limb of the Clackmannan Syncline where it extends southwards in an irregular belt, a third of a mile to $2\frac{1}{2}$ miles wide, from Abbey Craig to west of Plean. Exposures are rare within this belt, which is almost entirely covered by drift.

From the outcrop the group dips north-eastwards and eastwards at angles ranging from 5° to 30°, below an increasingly thick cover of younger rocks, towards the centre of the syncline; beyond this it rises on the eastern limb, where the dips are complicated by minor folding (p. 245), and comes to the surface a short distance beyond the eastern limit of the district. The strata are traversed by a number of major faults. As some of these have considerable displacement—over 900 ft in places—they have greatly affected the mining of coal.

No single bore or shaft section within the district gives an unbroken succession from top to bottom of the Limestone Coal Group, but it is estimated that the total thickness varies from about 700 ft west of Plean to about 1800 ft at the Parklands Bore (Plate VIII, 6).

As there are few sections in the lower part of the succession it has not been found possible to draw isopachytes for the whole group, but the variations in thickness of the greater part of the group may nevertheless be demonstrated by using the base of the Garibaldi Coal as a datum (p. 189). Isopachytes for the part of the succession that lies above this horizon are shown in Fig. 18 which

---

Borehole and shaft sections indicated on Fig. 18

1. Powis Mains Bore (1959). 2. Manor Bore (1910). 3. Westgrange No. 1 Bore (1905). 4. Steuarthall No. 3 Bore. 5. Polmaise No. 5 Pit (1939–58). 6. Tullibody No. 2 Bore (1934–37). 7. Polmaise No. 3 Pit Underground Bore (1937–38). 8. Polmaise No. 4 Pit Underground Bore (1946). 9. Gartarry Toll Bore (1953–54). 10. Solsgirth Bore (1941–62). 11. Saline No. 1 Bore. 12. Parklands Bore (1924–27). 13. Overton Bore (1933). 14. Balgonar Bore (1923). 15. Lethans No. 2 Bore. 16. Saline No. 3 Bore (1922). 17. Sunnyside Bore. 18. Shepherdlands Bore (1933–34). 19. Bannockburn No. 1 Pit (1892) and Underground Bore (1925–26). 20. Plean No. 4 Pit (1901–02) and No. 5 Underground Bore (1907). 21. Plean No. 3 Bore (1857). 22. Carbrook Mains No. 1. Bore (1909). 23. Carnock No. 1 Bore (1901–02) and Underground Bore (1933). 24. Mossneuk Bore (1950–52). 25. South Letham No. 1 Bore (1952). 26. Kincardine Bridge Bore (1952–53). 27. Tulliallan No. 1 Bore. 28. East Grange Bore (1902). 29. Righead Bore (1953–56). 30. Blair Mains No. 2 Bore (1955–56). 31. Culross No. 2 Bore (1957). 32. Blairhall No. 1 Bore (1898–99). 33. Blairhall No. 4 (Lord Bruce) Pit. 34. Langlees No. 2 Bore. 35. Valleyfield No. 3 Shaft. 36. Herbertshire No. 5 Pit (1937–39). 37. Little Denny No. 4 Bore (1857–64). 38. Cuthelton Greens No. 8 Bore. 39. Glenbervie No. 2 Bore (1925–26). 40. Orchardhead Bore (1956). 41. Grangemouth Dock Bore (1956–57). 42. Culross No. 3 Bore (1958). 43. East Salcoats Bore (1949). 44. Kinneil Colliery No. 24 Underground Bore (1945–46). 45. Kinneil Colliery No. 34 Underground Bore (1952–54). 46. Kinneil No. 1 Pit (1952–56).

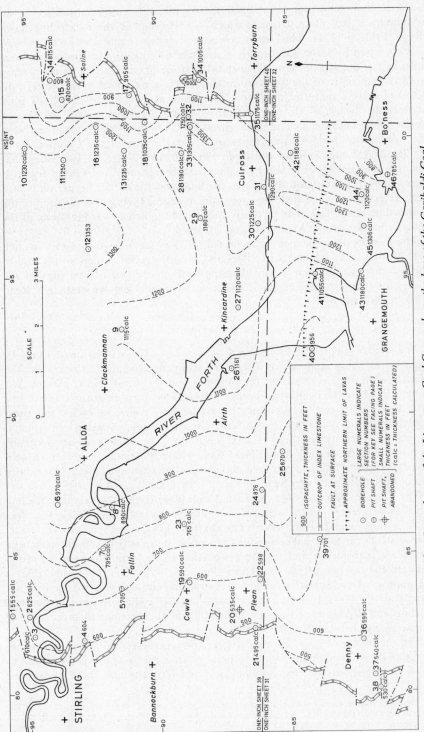

FIG. 18. *Isopachytes of the Limestone Coal Group above the base of the Garibaldi Coal*

indicates that deposition was controlled by the differential subsidence of an asymmetrical basin-like structure which has been named the Kincardine Basin (Read 1961, p. 274). This basin corresponds very roughly with the present Clackmannan Syncline but the axis of maximum deposition lies more than four miles east of the axis of the syncline and thicknesses increase much more abruptly towards the centre of the basin from the eastern side than from the western. In detail there is a centre of maximum deposition at or near the Parklands Bore and another south-south-west of Culross which are separated by an area of thinner sedimentation around the Righead Bore. On the western side of the basin the isopachytes bend sharply westwards over the line of the Campsie Fault (*cf.* Read 1959, fig. 5; Read and Dean 1967, pp. 151–2, fig. 3c), suggesting that this line was already followed by a flexure in Limestone Coal Group times. It seems quite probable that the line of the fault and the earlier flexure may have been determined by a Caledonoid structure at depth. Perhaps the position of the Kincardine Basin itself may be partly controlled by the eastward thinning of the Calciferous Sandstone Measures lavas at depth.

The pattern of isopachytes shown on Fig. 18 is not repeated exactly in each part of the succession and the centres and axes of maximum deposition tend to shift, commonly in such a way that the local thickening of one part of the succession is compensated by the local thinning of the overlying strata (*e.g.* Read 1961, p. 283, fig. 6).

LITHOLOGY

The greater part of the Limestone Coal Group of the Stirling district may be regarded as being made up of a series of sedimentary sequences or cycles. The limit of each cycle is drawn at the top of a coal, or, if no coal is present, at a seatearth, where the coal or seatearth is overlain by strata undisturbed by roots. Stratified mudstones[1] or siltstones lie at the bases of most cycles and these argillaceous beds commonly pass upwards by alternation into sandstone which is overlain in turn by another seatearth and coal. The sandstones are generally in a fine-grained or very fine-grained sheet phase but thicker, coarser channel phases (Hopkins 1958, p. 1) are not uncommon. These channel phases have sharp disconformable bases which cut down into the underlying strata.

The average thickness of cycles varies from place to place within the area and tends to be greatest in the areas of maximum subsidence. It is rarely less than 15 ft or more than 27 ft, however. The number of cycles between any two widespread stratigraphical markers tends to increase in direct proportion to the total amount of subsidence and thus in proportion to the total thickness of strata between the markers (Read and Dean 1967, pp. 147–8, fig. 2). This increase in the number of cycles in the thicker successions means that whereas sections are comparatively easy to correlate in directions parallel to the isopachs (e.g. between Stirling and Glasgow) it is much more difficult to correlate them across the isopachs (e.g. between Stirling and Culross).

The succession of coal-bearing cycles of the type described above was sometimes modified or interrupted by a general relative rise in sea-level which led to the deposition of mudstones containing a varied marine fauna. These mudstones,

---

[1]The term mudstone is here used as a synonym for the mining term 'blaes' as many of the records on which this account is based give no indication as to whether the bed in question was sufficiently fissile to be termed shale.

which are commonly thick and persistent, occur in the following parts of the succession: immediately above the Top Hosie Limestone, the Johnstone Shell-Bed, the Black Metals and at the top of the group, immediately below the Index Limestone.

Within the Limestone Coal Group marine influences become more marked towards the west. Thus *Lingula* is found more frequently in the west than in the east (Forsyth and Read 1962, p. 37, table 3). The effects of differential subsidence are, however, superimposed to some extent on this regional trend so that *Lingula* is found at a greater number of horizons in the thicker successions near the centre of the Kincardine Basin than it is in the thinner successions on the flanks. Coal swamp conditions are thought to have been more prevalent in the east as the total thickness of coal within the succession increases fairly uniformly in this direction (Read and Dean 1967, p. 153, fig. 4).

Volcanic Rocks

Contemporaneous volcanic activity is largely restricted to the east where both beds and thick intrusive bodies of tuff have been recorded (Francis 1957, pp. 71–3). Thin beds of kaolinized tuff are however more widespread and have proved useful for correlation within the group (Francis 1961). These beds are quite common in the east and more than 30 have been recorded in sections just south of the district but, surprisingly enough, only one such bed has been found to occur widely in the west, despite a careful search.

Stratigraphy

Most of the evidence relating to the Limestone Coal Group is derived from borings and cross-cut mines which are for the most part concentrated on the sides of the basin. In the wide central belt, where the succession is most variable, there are only a few scattered deep bores, some of which are cut by faults. For purposes of description, therefore, the basin may be divided into a western and an eastern area separated by a north–south line [National Grid line 925] which runs immediately west of Kincardine through the middle of the relatively poorly-known central belt (*see* Plate VIII). No attempt has been made to reproduce here all the detailed stratigraphical information which is already available in accounts by Dinham and Haldane (1932, pp. 35–87), Francis (1956, pp. 4–8), Read (1959, pp. 10–25) and Forsyth and Read (1962, pp. 45–50). For information on the palaeontology of the Limestone Coal Group the reader is referred to the faunal lists prepared by Dr. R. B. Wilson (*in* Francis 1956, tables 1, 2; *in* Read 1959, p. 63).

Several of the coals worked in the eastern area are known by names which were originally given to seams worked in the Dunfermline area, in the Kinross (40) Sheet. As correlation across the intervening ground is very difficult it should be emphasized that the seam names used in the following account are those generally used by the mining industry within the eastern area and that the implied correlation with seams of the same name further east has not necessarily been confirmed.

PLATE VIII

Comparative vertical sections of the Limestone Coal Group

Details

Top Hosie Limestone to Johnstone Shell-Bed. Little information is available on the strata between the base of the Limestone Coal Group and the Johnstone Shell-Bed as there are very few bore and mine sections through this part of the succession. Nevertheless it is possible to deduce a change in facies as the strata are traced eastwards, and possibly shorewards, from the sections around Stirling and Bannockburn, where coals are virtually absent and the proportion of mudstone is high, to the sections in west Fife, where several coals appear and the proportion of mudstone is lower.

In the western area, where this part of the succession is about 160 ft thick, the Top Hosie Limestone is overlain by a bed of mudstone 50 to 80 ft thick which contains occasional ribs and concretions of clayband ironstone. The upper part of this bed is commonly carbonaceous. *Posidonia corrugata* (Etheridge jun.) is generally abundant immediately above the limestone and an alternation of *Naiadites* and *Lingula* has been recorded higher up in the mudstone. These faunal alternations may possibly reflect the formation of coal-bearing cycles further east. The higher part of the succession includes sandstones, siltstones and mudstones but very few coals.

In the eastern area the strata between the Upper Kinniny Limestone and the Johnstone Shell-Bed may locally be more than 290 ft thick but the mudstone above the former is only about 30 to 50 ft thick. The overlying strata are similar to the equivalent beds in the western area but they are known to include one marine band, at least three *Lingula* bands and as many as seven coals. The topmost of these, the Smithy or Sulphur Coal, is generally in two leaves which may together total as much as 5 ft of coal.

Johnstone Shell-Bed. Within the area of the Stirling Sheet the term Johnstone Shell-Bed has been used to cover a group of two or more marine bands separated by sandy strata. Furthermore, marine shells have also been found in the mudstone roof of the Dunfermline Under Coal, slightly higher in the succession. As it is not known whether the Johnstone Shell-Bed of the type area, which seems to be a single bed of mudstone (Hinxman and others 1920, p. 42), is equivalent to one or more of these marine bands it is difficult to define the true limits of the Johnstone Shell-Bed within the Stirling district. In addition it is difficult to correlate in detail between the western and eastern areas. It is proposed, therefore, to follow previous practice and arbitrarily to restrict the term to the marine bands between the Smithy Coal and the thin coal that lies immediately below the Dunfermline Under Coal.

Only a few bores have cut the Johnstone Shell-Bed in the western area but these suggest that here the marine bands become further subdivided by sandy and silty strata and also tend to pass laterally into *Lingula* bands, in contrast to the general tendency within the Limestone Coal Group for marine influences to be most marked in the west. It is not possible to identify the Smithy Coal with certainty within this area but the base of the Johnstone Shell-Bed seems to lie some 70 to 130 ft below the Lower Knott Coal.

In the eastern area the Johnstone Shell-Bed is generally in two leaves separated by 10 to 40 ft of sandy strata but in some sections it may be further subdivided into as many as seven. The upper leaf is locally underlain by a thin coal. A thin tuffaceous bed which is commonly recorded in this leaf may be correlated with a similar bed in the Kinneil area, in the Airdrie (31) Sheet (Francis 1961, plate vi).

Johnstone Shell-Bed to Garibaldi Coal. In the western area the distance between the base of the Johnstone Shell-Bed and the Garibaldi Coal varies from about 100 ft to more than 150 ft and seems to increase eastwards into the Kincardine Basin. The beds below the Lower Knott Coal are very poorly known but they are thought to include at least two thin coals. One of these, which lies about 20 ft below the Lower Knott Coal, may be equivalent to the Dunfermline Under Coal of the eastern area as both seams are overlain by mudstone containing *Lingula*.

The Lower Knott, Kilsyth Coking or Milton Coal is the only seam of workable thickness, attaining a maximum thickness of 41 inches in the north-west where it is in a single leaf. Southwards and eastwards from here it thins and the lower part of the seam splits off to form a separate seam, which may possibly be equivalent to the Dunfermline Splint Coal of the eastern area. The Lower Knott Coal is generally overlain by a mudstone containing a persistent *Lingula* band. The Milton Rider Coal is a very thin and rather impersistent seam which lies between the Lower Knott and Garibaldi coals. It is overlain by a more persistent mudstone which commonly contains *Lingula* and it is now thought that this seam, rather than the Lower Knott Coal, is more probably the equivalent of the Two Foot Coal of the eastern area.

The thickness of strata between the Smithy Coal and the Five Foot Coal, which is thought to be the lateral equivalent of the Garibaldi Coal, ranges from less than 200 ft to more than 275 ft in the eastern area where, in contrast to the west, this part of the succession contains at least six relatively persistent coals. The lowest of these, a thin seam lying some 60 to 80 ft above the Smithy Coal, has a mudstone roof which locally yields *Lingula* and, rarely, marine molluscs. The Dunfermline Under Coal which lies between 80 and 95 ft above the Smithy Coal may be as much as 29 in thick. It is overlain by a thick bed of mudstone which almost always contains *Lingula* and, locally, marine lamellibranchs. The overlying Dunfermline Splint Coal, which lies 105 to 120 ft above the Smithy Coal, is generally the thickest seam in this part of the succession and attains a thickness of 40 in. *Lingula* has recently been discovered in the mudstone roof of this seam in the Solsgirth Bore [NS 99719483] but so far this is the only known record. The Wee Coal, which is next in the succession, is generally thin although locally it may thicken to 24 in. It is usually overlain by a mudstone which in places is separated from the coal by a cannel. Only non-marine lamellibranchs have been found in this mudstone within the Stirling district but *Lingula* has been recorded further south at what is thought to be the same horizon. Towards the centre of the Kincardine Basin one or two thin and less persistent coals occur between this seam and the Two Foot Coal which generally lies 20 to 30 ft below the Five Foot Coal. Although the Two Foot Coal seems to attain a thickness of 5 ft at the Gartarry Toll Bore [NS 93139126], it is rather impersistent and may be missing entirely in some sections. Its horizon may, however, be identified readily by the thick bed of mudstone containing a persistent *Lingula* band which overlies the coal. Locally a thin tuffaceous bed is also present (Francis 1961, plate 6).

Garibaldi and Five Foot Coals. In the western area the Garibaldi Coal is a persistent but generally thin seam which may be traced westwards to beyond Glasgow. It lies some 20 to 90 ft above the Lower Knott Coal and is overlain by a thick mudstone containing *Lingula* succeeded by non-marine lamellibranchs. The Five Foot Coal of the eastern area, which is thought to be equivalent to the Garibaldi Coal, is considerably thicker and reaches a maximum thickness of more than 6 ft. In some sections towards the centre of the Kincardine Basin the Five Foot Coal seems to split into two widely separated leaves, both of which are overlain by mudstones. Non-marine lamellibranchs have been recorded from both mudstones and there are also unconfirmed records of *Lingula* from both in the Saline No. 1 Bore [NS 99249340]. The upper leaf is commonly associated with blackband ironstone and a tuffaceous bed has been found in the overlying mudstone (Francis 1961, fig. 3). Further east near Valleyfield the two leaves of the Five Foot Coal seem to re-unite.

Garibaldi Coal to Banton Blackband Coal. In the western area the Garibaldi and Banton Blackband coals are generally separated by only 10 to 30 ft of strata, but in the eastern area their supposed correlatives—the Five Foot Coal and the Mynheer Coal—may be more than 60 ft apart. The intervening strata include a thin coal overlain by a mudstone which generally contains non-marine lamellibranchs only. *Lingula* was collected from this mudstone in Saline No. 1 Bore, however, suggesting that this horizon may possibly be equivalent to the *Lingula* band recorded immediately below the Banton Blackband Coal in the Glasgow region (Forsyth and Read 1962, p. 37).

Banton Blackband and Mynheer Coals. Within the western area the Banton Blackband Coal is a persistent but generally rather thin coal which, like the underlying Garibaldi

Coal, may be traced westwards to Glasgow and beyond. Only non-marine lamellibranchs have been recorded from the mudstone overlying this coal. As the latter is traced eastwards towards the centre of the basin some sections show that a wedge of sandy sediments appears at or near the top of the seam and separates the coal from its roof mudstone.

The seam known as the Mynheer Coal in the eastern area is certainly equivalent to the greater part, if not the whole, of the Banton Blackband Coal, as the same thick bed of mudstone containing non-marine lamellibranchs forms the roof of both seams. This coal, which is generally in two leaves, may be more than 5 ft thick but seems to thin out completely at the Gartarry Toll Bore [NS 93139126].

Banton Blackband Coal to Black Metals. The strata between the Banton Blackband Coal and the Black Metals range in thickness from about 50 to 115 ft in the western area and from about 110 to 170 ft in the eastern. Within this interval the horizons of the Banton Rider, Auchengree Four Inch and Torrance Four Inch coals (Forsyth and Read 1962, p. 32) can be traced throughout both areas; these three seams are now thought to be equivalent respectively to Coals E, D and C of Dinham and Haldane (1932, p. 73). Non-marine lamellibranchs have been recorded in the mudstone roofs of all three seams and, in addition, *Lingula* has been found in the roof of the Banton Rider Coal in both areas. A thin non-marine limestone containing *Spirorbis* and ostracods occurs in the mudstone roof of the Torrance Four Inch Coal at the Gartarry Toll Bore. The sandstones overlying the Mynheer, Banton Rider and Auchengree Four Inch coals all have local channel phases which may cut down into the underlying beds.

Black Metals. Over the greater part of the western area the Black Metals comprise a persistent bed of mudstone, ranging from 30 to 100 ft in thickness, which was deposited partly under marine conditions. East of a line drawn between Fallin and Airth, however, the bed of mudstone is split by wedges of sandstone which increase in number and thicken eastwards. In the eastern area, where the total thickness rises locally to as much as 220 ft, the whole succession becomes progressively more sandy and seatearths and coals appear, including the Torry Four Foot Coal (Coal A of Dinham and Haldane 1932, p. 73).

The complex lithological variations within the Black Metals of the area east of Stirling have recently been the subject of detailed studies by Read (1965) and Read and Merriam (1966).

Black Metals to roof of Bannockburn Upper Main Coal. The thick mudstone with non-marine lamellibranchs that forms the roof of both the Shale Coal of Glasgow and the undivided Bannockburn Main Coal of the western area has now been identified in the eastern area. It thus forms one of the most persistent marker bands above the Black Metals. The strata between it and the Black Metals include some of the thickest coals in the Limestone Coal Group of both the western and eastern areas but the upper part of this sequence is, unfortunately, one of the variable parts of the group. In general, where the lower part of this sequence, below the horizon of the base of the Bannockburn Main Coal, is thick the upper part is thin, and vice versa. It is thought that differential compaction of the lower part of the sequence gave rise, in the upper part, to local belts of subsidence where purely local cycles were formed (Read 1961, pp. 281–3, figs. 3–6).

The sequence in the western area falls naturally into two parts. The lower, which lies below the horizon of the base of the Bannockburn Main Coal, varies in thickness from about 50 ft to more than 130 ft but nevertheless retains a fairly constant stratigraphical succession which includes three relatively persistent coal horizons. The lowest of these is the Knott Coal, which attains a maximum thickness of 43 in and has been worked fairly extensively. A belt of unusually thin coal which runs southwards from near Steuarthall Farm [NS 822928] in this seam corresponds quite closely to the position of a thick channel phase in the sandstone immediately below. In addition a disconformity at the base of a channel phase in the sandstone above has removed the coal completely along a second belt which corresponds quite closely to the first

(Read 1959, fig. 6). This suggests that a channel in which sandy sediments were deposited may have persisted throughout the period during which the coal was formed. In localities beyond the influence of the washout the Knott Coal is commonly overlain by a bed of shale, which has yielded *Lingula* near Glasgow and also in one section just south of the Stirling district (Read 1959, pp. 18–9; Forsyth and Read 1962, table 3).

The horizons of the other two seams—the Knott Rider and the Knightswood Under coals—may be identified in most sections but the seams themselves are almost always thin and either may locally be absent. Each is commonly overlain by a thin mudstone.

The upper part of the sequence is occupied by the Bannockburn Main Complex (Read 1961, p. 276). In the vicinity of Bannockburn, Auchenbowie and Plean this is represented by a single thick seam known as the Bannockburn Main Coal. As this seam is traced eastwards towards the basin it becomes split progressively into leaves by wedges of clastic sediments and, within a distance of less than four miles, it passes laterally into a complex of strata which includes mudstones, sandstones, seatearths, and as many as fifteen coals. Over much of the area, however, there are only two principal leaves, named the Bannockburn Lower Main and the Bannockburn Upper Main or Bannockburn Steam Coal (Read 1961, p. 277). A *Lingula* band is found in the mudstone roof of the Lower Main Coal. This lower seam is still referred to in the mining industry as the 'Bannockburn Main Coal' although it represents only the lower part of the undivided Bannockburn Main Coal. A fuller discussion of the stratigraphy and sedimentation of this part of the succession has been given by Read (1961).

The mudstone roof of the Bannockburn Main Coal has now been correlated with the mudstone overlying the coal formerly worked at Valleyfield Colliery as the 'Diamond Coal', which is now generally called No. 1 Jersey Coal. The strata between the Black Metals and this mudstone are known to range in thickness from about 80 ft to more than 200 ft. Although they have not, as yet, been studied in as great detail as the equivalent strata in the western area, it is obvious that the coals in this part of the sequence, which together constitute the Main Group of coals, are uniformly thicker, and together total a much greater thickness of coal, than their equivalents in the west. These eastern seams are subject to considerable lateral variation and their nomenclature is extremely complex (*see* Dinham and Haldane 1932, pp. 75–82); consequently detailed correlation with the west is difficult. Nevertheless, the first seam above the Black Metals, formerly called the Jewel Coal at Valleyfield (Dinham and Haldane 1932, p. 75) but now generally known as the Lochgelly Splint Coal, may be correlated with the Knott Coal of the western area.

Roof of Bannockburn Upper Main Coal to Hartley Coal. Within the western area the strata between the Bannockburn Main and Hartley coals range in thickness from about 130 ft to more than 280 ft and include eight recognizable coal horizons. The two lowest, namely the Dumbreck Cloven Coal (known locally as the Smithy Coal of Fallin and the Wee Coal of Plean) and the Possil Main Coal, are both persistent and are both overlain by even more persistent beds of mudstone containing non-marine lamellibranchs. Both seams may split locally into two subsidiary coals. The Greenyards Coal may be locally as much as 4 ft thick and has been worked in several pits, but it is quite commonly less than 2 ft thick and is frequently split by thin partings of clastic sediments. The overlying Ashfield Coking, Ashfield Rider and Fourteen Inch Under coals are all less persistent and the sandstones that overlie each seam all have local channel phases which cut down through the mudstone roof, coal and seatearth into the sandstone below. The presence of a thick, composite sandstone in this part of the succession in some localities suggests either that disconformities have developed in two, or even three, successive sandstones or that channels carrying sandy sediment continued to exist throughout the periods when coals were being formed. By contrast the Fourteen Inch Coal (which may be as much as 23 in thick) is persistent, although locally it may be removed by a washout. In some sections it is interbedded with, or overlain by, a blackband ironstone, known locally as the Lower Denny Blackband Ironstone, and it is generally succeeded by a bed of mudstone, which contains non-marine lamellibranchs in places. The Lower Wee Coal is generally thin and is absent in places, but its horizon may readily be identified by the overlying mudstone, commonly more than 5 ft thick, which contains the distinctive Sub-Hartley *Lingula* Band towards its base and non-marine lamellibranchs at a slightly higher horizon. A thin calcareous bed that is found locally near the base of this shale may be tuffaceous in origin.

In the eastern area the mudstone roof of No. 1 Jersey Coal of Valleyfield (equivalent to the mudstone roof of the Bannockburn Main Coal) is separated from the Milton Main Coal (thought to be equivalent to the Hartley Coal) by 220 to 300 ft of strata. Correlation between the western and eastern areas is difficult in this part of the succession as, in general, there are rather more coal horizons in the east. It is, however, tentatively suggested that the Comrie Three Foot Coal, the Kelty Blackband Ironstone and the Comrie Two Foot Coal may be equivalent to the Dumbreck Cloven Coal (or to one of its leaves), the Greenyards Coal and the Ashfield Coking Coal respectively. The seam directly below the Milton Main Coal is almost certainly equivalent to the Lower Wee Coal as *Lingula* has been found in the overlying shale in at least four sections.

In Blair Mains No. 2 Bore [NS 97128604] strata below the Lower Wee Coal, which contain thin beds of tuffaceous material, have been intruded by thick veins of tuff and decomposed olivine-basalt; this suggests that a volcanic neck, probably of Limestone Coal Group age, lies at, or near, the site of this bore (Francis 1957, pp. 71–3, plate vi; 1960, p. 47).

Hartley Coal and Milton Main or Seven Foot Coal. The Hartley Coal, which is more than 3 ft thick in places, is one of the most widely worked seams in the western area. It is almost certainly equivalent to the Seven Foot or Milton Main Coal of Valleyfield as both are underlain by the Sub-Hartley *Lingula* Band. The latter coal, however, attains a thickness of about 5 ft, is frequently in leaves and is more commonly interbedded with, and overlain by, thick beds of blackband ironstone. The mudstone which usually overlies these coals has yielded non-marine lamellibranchs in the east.

Hartley Coal to Bo'ness Splint Coal. Seven coal horizons have been recognized between the Hartley and Bo'ness Splint coals in the western area, where the distance between these two seams ranges from about 110 ft to 200 ft. The thin Batchie Coal and the Upper Possil Coal, which are locally named the Lower and the Upper Wee Hartley Coals respectively, succeed the Hartley Coal. They are usually close together and the Batchie Coal locally combines with either the Hartley or the Upper Possil Coal. In one section all three seams are united. The Batchie and Upper Possil coals are both overlain by beds of mudstone but the bed above the latter seam is the thicker and more commonly contains non-marine lamellibranchs. A thin bed of tuffaceous material has been found in this upper mudstone in many sections.

The Possil Rider Coal is also thin and is typically overlain by a bed of mudstone in which non-marine lamellibranchs have occasionally been found. Locally either the coal or the mudstone may be absent and elsewhere clastic sediments split the coal into two leaves, each of which is overlain by a mudstone.

The Possil Rider Coal is generally missing in the western area but its horizon may easily be identified by the underlying seatearth, known as Fireclay A (Dinham and Haldane 1932, pp. 52, 59), and the overlying mudstone, both of which are thick and persistent. Fireclay A locally contains calcareous concretions (*cf*. Weller 1930, pp. 121–3), which are very rare in Limestone Coal Group seatearths, and *Lingula* has been recorded in the mudstone in the Kincardine Bridge Bore [NS 91648716]. Locally a thin wedge of sandy strata may split Fireclay A from the mudstone.

The Berryhills Coal is thin and rather impersistent but its position can almost always be identified by the overlying mudstone which contains the distinctive, non-marine Berryhills Limestone towards its base and a fairly persistent *Lingula* band at a higher horizon; non-marine lamellibranchs and ostracods have been found in the mudstone below the limestone. The limestone, which is generally thin and impure, and locally contains ostracods, is not found in every section but has been recorded in scattered localities throughout the western area. In some places a wedge of sandy and silty sediments, which may be rooty towards the top, separates the mudstone with non-marine fauna from the rest of the mudstone and locally seems to replace the Berryhills Limestone.

The Kilsyth No. 1 Blackband Under Coal and the Kilsyth No. 1 Blackband Coal are typically thin and both are underlain by seatearths and overlain by mudstones. Either coal may be cut out by local disconformities at the bases of the overlying sandstones and in places where both coals are missing a thick, composite bed of sandstone occupies most of the interval between the Berryhills Limestone and the Bo'ness Splint Coal.

In the eastern area the strata between the Milton Main and Blairhall Main coals range in thickness from about 160 to 240 ft. Although it has not yet been possible to study the beds in as much detail as in the west the successions are known to be similar, and the equivalents of the Possil Rider Coal, Fireclay A, the Berryhills Limestone and the Bo'ness Splint Coal may all be recognized. In addition *Lingula* bands have been found immediately above the last three horizons. The presence of a *Lingula* band above the Kilsyth No. 1 Blackband Coal is especially interesting as *Lingula* has not yet been recorded at this horizon in the western area, although it is known to be present in the Kilsyth and Glasgow areas (Forsyth and Read 1962, table 2). It is now thought that a thin calcareous bed which has been recorded in some sections, including the Righead Bore [NS 97178820] and Blair Mains No. 2 Bore [NS 97128604], is not the Berryhills Limestone but is at approximately the same horizon as Fireclay A. In the latter bore this calcare ous bed is known to be tuffaceous.

Bo'ness Splint and Blairhall Main Coals. The Blairhall Main Coal of the eastern area has long been known to be the same seam as the Splint Coal of Bo'ness (Macgregor and Haldane 1933, p. 54) and recently it has been found that this seam, together with the *Lingula* band in its mudstone roof, provides one of the best marker horizons in the upper part of the Limestone Coal Group and can be traced as far west as Glasgow (Forsyth and Read 1962, p. 41). In the western area it is thin and has been worked only around Manor Powis where it has combined with the underlying Kilsyth No. 1 Blackband Coal to form a seam, known locally as the 'Blairhall Main Coal', which may be as much as 3 ft thick. In the eastern area however the Blairhall Main Coal proper is quite commonly more than 3 ft thick and has been worked fairly extensively (Dinham and Haldane 1932, p. 85).

Bo'ness Splint Coal to Index Limestone. The strata between the Bo'ness Splint Coal and the Index Limestone range in thickness from about 55 ft to 190 ft in the western area, where this part of the succession is considerably more variable than the rest of the Limestone Coal Group. At least seven coals, or coal horizons, some of which are associated with unusually thick seatearths, may be distinguished in sections towards the centre of the basin. The lowest coal, which has been correlated with the Twechar Upper Coal, is generally thin. It is overlain by a thin mudstone which is quite commonly cut out by a washout at the base of the overlying sandstone. A coal near the middle of the succession, locally as much as 30 in thick, is thought to be equivalent to part at least of the Twechar Dirty Coal. It is overlain by a mudstone which contains *Lingula* but this bed is locally absent owing to erosion prior to the deposition of the overlying sandstone. The Index Limestone is generally underlain by 2 to 3 ft of mudstone which contains a varied marine fauna and usually rests on a thin coal.

In the eastern area the distance between the Blairhall Main Coal and the Index Limestone ranges from about 100 to 200 ft. Towards the south the succession is broadly similar to that in the western area and also includes at least seven coal horizons. One of the thickest of the coals is the Oakley Upper Coal (Dinham and Haldane 1932, p. 87), which may be the correlative of the Twechar Dirty Coal. In the northern part of the area the whole succession becomes progressively more sandy and the number of coals is reduced to one or two. The mudstone immediately below the Index Limestone is thicker in the eastern area than in the west and may be more than 20 ft thick.

W.A.R., E.H.F.

REFERENCES

CURRIE, ETHEL D. 1954. Scottish Carboniferous goniatites. *Trans. R. Soc. Edinb.*, **62**, 527–602.

DINHAM, C. H. and HALDANE, D. 1932. The economic geology of the Stirling and Clackmannan Coalfield. *Mem. geol. Surv. Gt Br.*

FORSYTH, I. H. and READ, W. A. 1962. The correlation of the Limestone Coal Group above the Kilsyth Coking Coal in the Glasgow–Stirling region. *Bull. geol. Surv. Gt Br.*, No. 19, 29–52.

FRANCIS, E. H. 1956. The economic geology of the Stirling and Clackmannan Coalfield, Scotland: Area north of the River Forth. *Coalfld Pap. geol. Surv.*, No. 1.

—— 1957. New evidence of volcanicity in Fife. *Trans. Edinb. geol. Soc.*, **17**, 71–80.

—— 1960. Intrusive tuffs related to the Firth of Forth volcanoes. *Trans. Edinb. geol. Soc.*, **18**, 32–50.

—— 1961. Thin beds of kaolinized tuff and tuffaceous siltstone in the Carboniferous of Fife. *Bull. geol. Surv. Gt Br.*, No. 17, 191–215.

HINXMAN, L. W., ANDERSON, E. M. and CARRUTHERS, R. G. 1920. The economic geology of the Central Coalfield of Scotland, Area IV. *Mem. geol. Surv. Gt Br.*

HOPKINS, M. E. 1958. Geology and petrology of the Anvil Rock Sandstone. *Circ. Ill. St. geol. Surv.*, **256**.

MACGREGOR, M. and HALDANE, D. 1933. The economic geology of the Central Coalfield of Scotland, Area III. *Mem. geol. Surv. Gt Br.*

READ, W. A. 1959. The economic geology of the Stirling and Clackmannan Coalfield, Scotland: Area south of the River Forth. *Coalfld Pap. geol. Surv.*, No. 2.

—— 1961. Aberrant cyclic sedimentation in the Limestone Coal Group of the Stirling Coalfield. *Trans. Edinb. geol. Soc.*, **18**, 271–92.

—— 1965. Shoreward facies changes and their relation to cyclical sedimentation in part of the Namurian east of Stirling, Scotland. *Scott. J. Geol.*, **1**, 69–92.

—— and DEAN, J. M. 1967. A quantitative study of a sequence of coal-bearing cycles in the Namurian of central Scotland. *Sedimentology*, **9**, 137–56.

—— and MERRIAM, D. F. 1966. Trend-surface analysis of stratigraphic thickness data from some Namurian rocks east of Stirling, Scotland. *Scott. J. Geol.*, **2**, 96–100.

WELLER, J. M. 1930. Cyclical sedimentation of the Pennsylvanian Period and its significance. *J. Geol.*, **38**, 97–135.

Chapter XII

UPPER LIMESTONE GROUP

Introduction

THE UPPER LIMESTONE GROUP includes the strata between the base of the Index Limestone and the top of the Castlecary Limestone. In certain parts of the area, however, the topmost beds of the group have been removed by erosion in early Passage Group times and where this has occurred the level of the erosion surface, in so far as it can be identified, has been taken as the upper limit of the group.

On the western limb of the Clackmannan Syncline the outcrop forms an irregular belt, 1 to 3 miles wide, which runs from Blairlogie in the north to Plean in the south. Along the eastern limb the group crops out at Culross, extending north-north-eastwards across the eastern margin of the district; it also forms two small inliers south and east of Dollar. Although there are continuous exposures in the River Black Devon and along the shore at Culross, most of our knowledge of the group is derived from borings and shaft sinkings through the cover of drift and of younger rocks.

The Upper Limestone Group ranges in thickness from about 1120 ft near Plean and 1140 ft at Cattle Moss to a maximum of at least 1940 ft at the Gartarry Toll Bore, $1\frac{1}{4}$ miles east-south-east of Clackmannan. An isopachyte map of the group (Read 1959, fig. 9) strongly suggests that in this district sedimentation in Upper Limestone Group times was chiefly controlled by the differential subsidence of the Kincardine Basin—a broad structure with maximum depression near Gartarry (p. 186). This structure coincides approximately with the Clackmannan Syncline.

Lithology

The cycles of sedimentation in the Upper Limestone Group (*see* Robertson 1948, pp. 154–5; Francis 1956, p. 9) are broadly similar to those of the Limestone Coal Group but the relative proportions of the various lithological types differ; for example, in the Upper Limestone Group there are fewer coals of workable thickness, but thick beds of mudstone containing marine shells are more numerous than in the underlying group. Calcareous mudstones and marine limestones reappear but the proportion of limestone to other sediments is much lower than in the Lower Limestone Group.

Ten marine limestones of varying thickness and persistence provide the primary basis for correlation (Plate IX). Four of these, namely the Index, Orchard, Calmy and Castlecary limestones, are in general relatively thick and persist over a wide area in the Midland Valley of Scotland, although the Castlecary is cut out locally by penecontemporaneous erosion; the other six, namely the Hunters-

---

PLATE IX

COMPARATIVE VERTICAL SECTIONS OF THE UPPER LIMESTONE GROUP

hill Cement, Lyoncross, Plean No. 1, an extra Plean and Plean Nos. 2 and 3 limestones, are generally thinner and less persistent. With the exception of the Castlecary, all the limestones are overlain by mudstones containing a varied marine fauna. In addition to the above-named limestones there are at least twenty-three other bands which have been found to contain a marine fauna, consisting usually of lamellibranchs and *Lingula*. The latter is the more persistent and bands which at one locality contain both marine lamellibranchs and *Lingula* may elsewhere contain only *Lingula* (*cf.* Plate IX). Faunal impoverishment of this kind is most marked as the bands are traced from the thicker successions to the thinner. The same is true of some of the major marine bands, such as the Lyoncross Limestone, which deteriorates on the flanks of the Kincardine Basin to such an extent that its identification amongst the minor bands is frequently difficult.

VOLCANIC ROCKS

Beds of tuff and tuffaceous siltstone occur at several levels throughout the Upper Limestone Group succession. They extend for distances of up to 10 miles from the originating small, short-lived vents in west Fife and consist mainly of comminuted sedimentary rock debris, usually, though not invariably, with some proportion of basaltic ejecta. The bands have been fully described elsewhere (Francis 1957; 1961).

The several small necks proved in west Fife are all of Upper Limestone Group age. There are three near East Grange, one at Valleyfield and another, which has recently been examined in detail, in the Bogside Mines (Francis 1959). The tuffs met in Bogside No. 4 Bore and Blair Mains No. 2 Bore (Francis 1957) are now reinterpreted as neck-fillings and at least two more necks are inferred to exist in the ground near Shires Mill.

STRATIGRAPHY

The following account is based mainly on earlier descriptions by Francis (1956) and Read (1959). Faunal details by Dr. R. B. Wilson are given in these publications and in a subsequent paper (Wilson 1967).

DETAILS

Index Limestone. The Index Limestone usually occurs in the lower part of a thick bed of mudstone, but occasionally it lies near the centre (e.g. in the Meadowhill and Righead bores). It varies in thickness from 1 ft to 4 ft 10 in, and in a few bores (Kincardine Bridge and Valleyfield) it consists of two leaves separated by a thin bed of calcareous mudstone. Normally the limestone is argillaceous and part of it may be shelly. *Gigantoproductus* cf. *latissimus* (J. Sowerby) is common and scattered crinoid columnals have been recorded in some sections.

Index Limestone to Lyoncross Limestone. The thickness of strata between the Index and Lyoncross limestones varies from about 230 ft near East Plean to nearly 500 ft at Gartarry Toll. The strata comprise a variable succession of sandy and argillaceous beds with a thin limestone and a number of thin coals. At the bottom and top of the succession there are mudstones with an abundant and varied marine fauna and in addition there are four intermediate bands with *Lingula* and marine molluscs or with *Lingula* alone.

The Index Limestone is succeeded by a bed of mudstone, with numerous marine fossils, which maintains a relatively constant thickness of 20 to 25 ft over most of the Clackmannan Syncline though it thickens locally to 30 ft or more. On the other hand it is less than 10 ft thick at some places in the south-western part of the syncline, where the thinning is probably due to erosion prior to the deposition of the overlying Bishopbriggs Sandstone (cf. Clough and others 1925, p. 76; Clough and others 1926, p. 23). Ironstone concretions are generally scattered through the mudstone.

The Bishopbriggs Sandstone in its type area north-north-east of Glasgow is a thick sandstone between the mudstone above the Index Limestone and the Huntershill Cement Limestone (Clough and others 1925, pp. 76–7; Clough and others 1926, pp. 23–4). It is represented in the Stirling district by a sandstone which is locally more than 60 ft thick, but thins progressively and becomes split by argillaceous partings towards the east until in the neighbourhood of Comrie the succession is so condensed that the Index and Huntershill horizons coalesce to form a 35-ft bed of mudstone in which the Index Limestone lies at the base and the Huntershill Cement is near the top. In the thicker succession farther south a minor cycle including a coal and a marine band occurs between the Index Limestone and the Huntershill Cement. The marine band may be the equivalent of an unnamed shelly limestone in the middle of the Bishopbriggs Sandstone in Glasgow (Clough and others 1925, pp. 76–7).

The Huntershill Cement Limestone of the Glasgow area has now been recognized in most parts of the Clackmannan Syncline. It is represented by a thin bed of shelly mudstone locally containing a limestone near the base. The limestone is thickest in the neighbourhood of Valleyfield where it varies from 12 to 21 in.

Between the Huntershill Cement and the Lyoncross limestones there are 220 to 430 ft of strata containing several marine bands and one or two thick sandstones. A sandstone which occupies the lower part of this interval in the southern part of the syncline seems to combine with the Bishopbriggs Sandstone below to form a thick composite bed so that the Huntershill Cement Limestone and its associated beds are entirely unrepresented. This composite sandstone may be traced south-westwards towards Denny, beyond the southern limit of the Stirling district. Coals, generally thin but some locally reaching a thickness of over 2 ft, are commonly found at various levels between the Huntershill Cement and Lyoncross limestones; they have been correlated with the Chapelgreen Coals of the Kilsyth area (Robertson and Haldane 1937, pp. 82–3). Lingula has been found in the roof of one of the lower coals of this group south of the Forth, but between Valleyfield and Blairhall there is a group of one to four Lingula bands or marine bands lying close above the Huntershill Cement, and somewhat higher in the succession there are beds containing non-marine lamelli-branchs and ostracods.

Above these non-marine beds a thick sandstone, the Cadgers Loan Sandstone, or Cadgers Loan Rock, appears south of the Forth. It is generally coarser than the Bishopbriggs Sandstone and pebbly bands and garnets have been recorded in some sections. In the Cadgers Loan area, west of Plean, the sandstone is about 90 ft thick; it maintains a thickness of roughly 100 ft around Fallin, Cowie and Carbrook and reaches its maximum thickness of about 155 ft in the Doll Mill Bore. North of the Forth, however, the Cadgers Loan Sandstone is not so thick and cannot readily be identified.

The Quarry Coal lies from 15 to 60 ft below the Lyoncross Limestone and over most of Stirlingshire it is the only coal in the variable succession between that limestone and the underlying Cadgers Loan Sandstone. In the area around Fallin, Cowie, Carnock and Plean it is generally in one leaf, usually over 15 in thick and locally up to 33 in thick. To the south and east of Plean, however, the Quarry Coal thins and is either absent or difficult to identify among several thin coals that are locally developed in this part of the succession.

Dinham and Haldane (1932, p. 104) state that the Crumpy Coal around Blairhall must lie at approximately the same horizon as the Quarry Coal, but evidence from recent borings suggests that the Crumpy Coal is, in fact, slightly higher in the succession. *Lingula*, in some cases accompanied by marine lamellibranchs, occurs in the roof. The lower of the two beds of tuff at Shires Mill occurs below the Crumpy Coal.

Lyoncross Limestone. The Lyoncross Limestone is much thinner than the Index, Orchard and Calmy limestones, its thickness varying from 4 to 17 in. Near outcrop along the eastern and western flanks of the syncline the limestone is represented by a bed of shelly, calcareous mudstone only. This normally contains a fauna which is rich enough to identify the horizon amongst the *Lingula* bands or marine bands immediately above and below, but north of Comrie the fauna is impoverished and correlation is uncertain.

Lyoncross Limestone to Orchard Limestone. The Lyoncross and Orchard limestones are separated by 100 to 250 ft of strata in which several minor cycles occur, some of them including thin coals. The succession also contains a *Lingula* band and four marine bands, the lowest of which lies directly above the Lyoncross Limestone and the highest directly below the Orchard Limestone. Persistent thick sandstones are uncommon.

The mudstone immediately above the Lyoncross Limestone is generally less than 10 ft thick and may thus be distinguished from the much thicker beds of mudstone which overlie the Index, Orchard and Calmy limestones; it generally contains numerous large concretions of clayband ironstone and marine fossils are common.

The strata between this mudstone and the Orchard Limestone include several thin, inconstant coals, two of which thicken northwards to become the Manor Coal and the Orchard Coal in the area north of the Forth. The Manor Coal is either too thin or too variable in quality to be of economic value. The Orchard Coal is usually absent south of the Forth, and is nowhere known to exceed 9 inches in thickness. This seam, which as a rule lies between 25 and 75 ft below the Orchard Limestone, is underlain by a thick seatearth, and overlain by a persistent bed of mudstone with many ribs and concretions of clayband ironstone. This bed may be more than 30 ft thick but in places its thickness is greatly reduced as a result of contemporaneous erosion and the base of an overlying sandstone descends to within a few feet of the Orchard Coal. *Lingula*, *Orbiculoidea* and marine lamellibranchs are found in the lower part of the bed and non-marine lamellibranchs in the upper part.

Between the mudstone and the Orchard Limestone the strata are generally sandy, but in places include one or two thin coals, the upper of which lies just below the limestone, from which it may be separated by a thin bed of mudstone with marine fossils; this coal may be as much as 18 in thick in the centre of the Clackmannan Syncline.

Graded tuffaceous siltstones associated with sandy tuffaceous limestones 5 to 9 in thick form the base of the mudstone immediately beneath the Orchard Limestone in Culross Nos. 2 and 3 bores.

Orchard Limestone. The Orchard Limestone is typically a hard, finely crystalline grey limestone which contains crinoid columnals and shell fragments. According to records its thickness ranges up to 3 ft 2 in but some of the greater thicknesses probably include beds of hard, calcareous, shelly mudstone that usually lie above and below the limestone proper. These calcareous mudstones are generally present in sections where the limestone is missing.

Orchard Limestone to Calmy Limestone. The thickness of strata between the Orchard and Calmy limestones ranges from about 160 ft to more than 300 ft. The Orchard Limestone is overlain by mudstones and siltstones which may be more than 75 ft thick. Numerous clayband ironstone nodules are scattered throughout the bed and marine fossils are common in its lower part. The remainder of the succession up to the Lower Hirst Coal consists very largely of sandy beds, and may be divided into two parts. Over most of the southern and central sectors of the syncline the lower part includes a thick sandstone, which has been quarried at several places, most extensively in the neighbourhood of Cowie, and which was named Cowie Rock by Dinham (*in* Dinham and Haldane 1932, p. 92). Traced northwards, however, this sandstone becomes split by argillaceous beds. Conversely a thick sandstone found in the upper part of the succession around Fallin and Carnock passes southwards and eastwards into a series of sandy and argillaceous beds with thin coals. Locally these two sandstones merge to form one continuous bed which occupies most of the interval between the Orchard Limestone and the Lower Hirst Coal and which, at Torwood in the Airdrie (31) Sheet to the south, may be as thick as 130 ft. It is probably to such a development that Dinham is referring when he speaks of the upward extension of the Cowie Rock (Dinham and Haldane 1932, p. 93). It is suggested, however, that the name be restricted to the sandstone in the lower part of the succession, which was worked at Cowie.

In the upper part of the succession abundant marine lamellibranchs and gastropods have been discovered at two horizons around Culross and, in addition, a *Lingula* band has been found a short distance above the marine bands there and farther north. Above these there is a group of coals including the most valuable seams in the Upper Limestone Group. The lowest of these in Stirlingshire is the Lower Hirst Coal, a seam which has been correlated with the Overton Gas Coal in west Fife. Both may have cannel, in some places with ironstone, at the top, but since in the Gartarry Toll Bore at about this horizon there are three such seams, each with a thickness of 18 in or more, within 25 ft of strata, the suggested correlation cannot be regarded as definite. Over most of the Clackmannan Syncline, these lower coals of the group are too thin to be of more than local importance, but west of Airth the Lower Hirst Coal locally attains a thickness of 29 in.

Graded tuffaceous siltstones up to 5 ft thick occur in the roof of the Overton Gas Coal in west Fife, and can be traced to a source near Solsgirth, just within the Kinross (40) Sheet.

The Upper Hirst Coal of Stirlingshire (Jenny Pate Coal of Fife) is the highest and thickest of the group of coals underlying the Calmy Limestone. Its thickness is known to vary from 18 in to as much as 101 in—the greatest thickness attained by any seam in this area. The Upper Hirst Coal is now mined extensively but until recently it was little worked, despite its thickness, because of its rather poor quality and tendency to occur in leaves.

The coal lies between 10 and 80 ft below the Calmy Limestone. Where the intervening strata consist wholly of shale and mudstone, as in the centre of the syncline, the lower part is carbonaceous, becoming cannelly with ribs of inferior blackband ironstone at the base, and contains fragments of fusain together with abundant fish remains. In the western part of the syncline the carbonaceous development is replaced by as much as 60 to 80 ft of sandstone (*see* Read 1959, fig. 10) and although sandstone occurs locally in the east, it is invariably thinner than in the west. Throughout the whole syncline the uppermost strata between the Upper Hirst Coal and the Calmy Limestone are mudstones containing a rich marine fauna and the well-known *Edmondia punctatella* Band (Haldane 1925; Wilson 1958) occurs consistently at the base of this phase.

Calmy Limestone. The thickness of the Calmy Limestone is usually more than 5 ft but is known to range from 2 ft 3 in to 11 ft 8 in. Although there are several records of the Calmy Limestone occurring as a single bed, it is generally divided into two by calcareous mudstone and in the south it is occasionally split into three or even four beds. In west Fife the lower of the two main leaves is parted by an inch or so of tuffaceous siltstone. The source of this volcanic material is probably beneath the Forth as it is thickest and coarsest in Culross No. 3 (Offshore) Bore. The limestone itself is typically fine-grained and argillaceous and is frequently rather light grey in colour; it commonly contains fragments of brachiopods and, in some localities, sporadic crinoid columnals.

Calmy Limestone to Plean No. 1 Limestone. Between 170 and 340 ft of strata separate the horizon of Plean No. 1 Limestone from the Calmy Limestone. Immediately above the latter is an argillaceous bed which is usually more than 50 ft and may be as much as 100 ft thick; this, like the bed above the Orchard Limestone, provides a useful lithological marker by reason of its thickness. The basal portion of this bed consists of calcareous mudstone but this passes up into dark, non-calcareous mudstone with abundant, fairly small, ironstone concretions. Towards the top the mudstone grades upwards into more silty beds with ironstone nodules. Abundant and varied marine fossils are found at the base of the mudstone, marine lamellibranchs and *Lingula* higher up and, in some sections, non-marine lamellibranchs at the top.

Evenly-laminated silty strata with ironstone nodules succeed the mudstone and grade upwards into a sandstone which is commonly evenly-laminated at its base. This sandstone has been quarried at several places (Dinham and Haldane 1932, p. 96). Marine fossils were recorded in a thin bed of siltstone in the lower part of this sandstone (about 80 ft above the Calmy Limestone) at the Kincardine Bridge Bore. In west Fife this sandstone passes upwards into silty beds which include several thin marine bands and *Lingula* bands with four local beds of tuff. A coal usually lies above these beds and almost immediately below Plean No. 1 Limestone. It is thickest in the east and south-east, reaching 60 inches at the Kincardine Bridge and Gartarry Toll bores, where it is split by several dirt partings. In north-eastern Clackmannanshire and adjacent parts of Fife the coal is thin and there is only one parting. This is 2 to 7 in thick and is bluish-green, brittle and sandy; it is believed to be volcanic in origin and to be derived from a source in the Saline area farther east.

Plean No. 1 Limestone. Of the several thin limestones that occur between the Calmy and Castlecary limestones, Plean No. 1 is the lowest and most constant. The horizon comprises a thick bed of shelly mudstone with thin ribs and lenses of limestone. In the south and west the limestone forms one or two leaves having a maximum recorded thickness of 3 ft 2 in. It is typically argillaceous and crinoidal, and in the northern part of the area is locally dolomitized. The limestone is usually overlain by a thick bed of mudstone containing an abundant marine fauna; the mudstone and the coal underlying the limestone are both more persistent than the limestone itself and, where the latter is absent, they serve to identify its horizon. Around Dollar, however, there is a minor unconformity at the base of a calcareous sandstone and both mudstone and limestone are cut out.

The limestone, together with an underlying limy, sandy tuff, crops out in the River Black Devon [NS 998941] where it was formerly identified by Dinham and Haldane (1932, p. 108) as the Castlecary Limestone.

Plean No. 1 Limestone to Castlecary Limestone. The strata between Plean No. 1 Limestone and the Castlecary Limestone range in thickness from about 200 ft to more than 400 ft. They may be divided into two distinct parts, the dividing line being taken at the top of the mudstone immediately above Plean No. 3 Limestone. The lower part contains three limestones and many thin coals with associated seatearths and mudstone beds; it includes also no fewer than eleven marine and *Lingula* bands. By contrast the upper part consists mainly of sandstones and seatearths with occasional thin coals and mudstone beds: no marine bands or *Lingula* bands have been recorded.

The succession between the mudstone above Plean No. 1 Limestone and Plean No. 2 Limestone contains at least twelve cycles, in a comparatively small thickness of strata. It is characterized by a series of thin coals which are underlain by thin seatearths and generally overlain by thin beds of mudstone containing bands and nodules of ironstone. Some of the coals are cannelly and are associated with blackband ironstone.

At least eight marine and *Lingula* bands—three of them passing upwards into *Curvirimula* bands—have been recorded from this part of the succession. The lowest of the bands is a marine band which generally has a more varied fauna than the others; it locally contains a shelly crinoidal limestone up to 9 in thick. Some of the bands may have been cut out locally by contemporaneous erosion, for there is no known section where all the bands are represented. Local unconformities occur beneath some of the sandstones throughout the area but erosion appears to have been most intense north of the Forth. Near Bogside Station some of the minor unconformities appear to coalesce and in Bogside No. 1 Bore (1955) most of the succession from beneath Plean No. 2 Limestone to No. 1 Marine Band in the Passage Group is replaced by sandstone.

In the area north of the Forth, a limy tuffaceous bed which forms a useful marker horizon occurs between 30 and 85 ft above Plean No. 1 Limestone, and apparently at a slightly higher horizon than the local crinoidal limestone mentioned above. This bed, which was originally described as a sandy limestone of obscure mode of formation (Francis 1956, p. 11), thickens appreciably north-eastwards (Francis 1961, fig. 5, p. 204), passing into basaltic tuffs. From its presumed source in the vicinity of Solsgirth, just within the Kinross (40) Sheet, it extends southwards and westwards for 5 and 10 miles respectively and, at different localities, is intercalated above, within or below a thin coal seam (Francis 1961, fig. 6, p. 205). The bed crops out at several localities in the Four Braes section of the River Black Devon [NS 997941].

Plean No. 2 Limestone lies between about 125 ft and 225 ft above the horizon of Plean No. 1 Limestone. It is in two leaves in bores around Throsk where it reaches its maximum known thickness of 1 ft 7 in, exclusive of the parting. It is typically an argillaceous, shelly limestone with crinoid columnals which passes laterally into calcareous mudstone in many places. The limestone generally lies at, or up to 10 ft above, the base of a bed of mudstone containing an abundant and varied marine fauna. Locally the mudstones underlying the limestone are cannelly near the base and are underlain by a thin coal which is, however, neither as thick nor as persistent as that directly below Plean No. 1 Limestone.

Plean No. 3 Limestone lies 20 to 40 ft above Plean No. 2 Limestone and about 50 ft to 140 ft below the Castlecary Limestone. Lithologically it resembles the other Plean limestones but it is less persistent than either of them. It has a maximum known thickness of 1 ft 2 in and is succeeded by a fairly thick bed of mudstone containing a marine fauna which seems to be rather less varied than the faunas associated with Nos. 1 and 2 limestones. Where Plean No. 3 Limestone is missing this mudstone often serves to identify its horizon.

The remainder of the succession up to the Castlecary Limestone is, in most parts of the area, largely composed of sandstones and seatclays with a few subordinate thin coals and mudstones. In some localities in the south and east there is a predominance of sandy beds, some of which have minor unconformities at their bases.

In many sections where the Castlecary Limestone is preserved there is a thin coal almost immediately below it and separated from it by a few inches of canneloid mudstone. Locally a thin bed of mudstone with marine fossils lies between the canneloid mudstone and the limestone.

Castlecary Limestone. In parts of the Clackmannan Syncline the Castlecary Limestone has been removed by erosion in early Passage Group times (Read 1959, fig. 9; Dinham and Haldane 1932, pp. 98–9, 115), but where it is preserved it is a very distinctive bed which differs in lithology and roof metals from the other limestones in the Upper Limestone Group. It ranges in thickness from 6 ft to almost 18 ft and is generally in two beds separated by a few inches of mudstone containing marine shells, though up to four beds have been recorded. The limestone is commonly dolomitic and parts of it, especially the top of the upper bed, are mottled light and dark grey and contain carbonaceous streaks; other parts are rather coarsely crystalline. Marine shells and crinoid columnals are scattered throughout the limestone.

As mentioned above, the limestone cropping out in the River Black Devon five miles north of Culross, which was identified by Dinham and Haldane (1932, p. 108) as the Castlecary, is now known to be Plean No. 1 Limestone.   E.H.F., W.A.R.

REFERENCES

CLOUGH, C. T., HINXMAN, L. W., WILSON, J. S. G., CRAMPTON, C. B., WRIGHT, W. B., BAILEY, E. B., ANDERSON, E. M. and CARRUTHERS, R. G. 1925. The geology of the Glasgow district. 2nd edit. revised by MACGREGOR, M., DINHAM, C. H., BAILEY, E. B. and ANDERSON, E. M. *Mem. geol. Surv. Gt Br.*

CLOUGH, C. T., HINXMAN, L. W., WRIGHT, W. B., ANDERSON, E. M. and CARRUTHERS, R. G. 1926. The economic geology of the Central Coalfield of Scotland, Area V. 2nd edit. with additions by MACGREGOR, M. *Mem. geol. Surv. Gt Br.*

DINHAM, C. H. and HALDANE, D. 1932. The economic geology of the Stirling and Clackmannan Coalfield. *Mem. geol. Surv. Gt Br.*

FRANCIS, E. H. 1956. The economic geology of the Stirling and Clackmannan Coalfield, Scotland: Area north of the River Forth. *Coalfld Pap. geol. Surv.*, No. 1.

—— 1957. New evidence of volcanicity in west Fife. *Trans. Edinb. geol. Soc.*, **17**, 71–80.

—— 1959. A volcanic vent in the Bogside mines, Fife. *Geol. Mag.*, **96**, 457–69.

—— 1961. Thin beds of graded kaolinized tuff and tuffaceous siltstone in the Carboniferous of Fife. *Bull. geol. Surv. Gt Br.*, No. 17, 191–215.

HALDANE, D. 1925. Notes on the discovery of '*Edmondia*' *punctatella* (Jones) in Fife. *Trans. Edinb. geol. Soc.*, **11**, 386–9.

READ, W. A. 1959. The economic geology of the Stirling and Clackmannan Coalfield, Scotland: Area south of the River Forth. *Coalfld Pap. geol. Surv.*, No. 2.

ROBERTSON, T. 1948. Rhythm in sedimentation and its interpretation: with particular reference to the Carboniferous sequence. *Trans. Edinb. geol. Soc.*, **14**, 141–75.

ROBERTSON, T. and HALDANE, D. 1937. The economic geology of the Central Coalfield of Scotland, Area I. *Mem. geol. Surv. Gt Br.*

WILSON, R. B. 1958. A revision of the Carboniferous lamellibranchs *Edmondia punctatella* (Jones) and '*Estheria*' *youngii* Jones. *Bull. geol. Surv. Gt Br.*, No. 15, 21–8.

—— 1967. A study of some Namurian marine faunas of central Scotland. *Trans. R. Soc. Edinb.*, **66**, 445–90.

Chapter XIII

PASSAGE GROUP

INTRODUCTION

THE PASSAGE GROUP, formerly known as the Scottish Millstone Grit (MacGregor 1960), has traditionally been taken to comprise the strata between the top of the Castlecary Limestone and the base of the Slatyband Ironstone of Crofthead, near Fauldhouse, in West Lothian. The Crofthead Slatyband Ironstone has always been difficult to recognize beyond the immediate vicinity of Crofthead and it is proposed here to use instead the base of the Lowstone Marine Band, only a few feet higher in the sequence, which is more easily identified and may be traced over a much wider area in the Midland Valley.

The group crops out in two faulted and sinuous tracts with general north–south trend, which flank the Coal Measures at the centre of the Clackmannan Syncline. The western tract is 1 to 2 miles wide and extends from the Ochil Fault west of Alva, in the north, to Rosehill in the south; the eastern outcrop, up to 3 miles wide, extends southwards from Dollar to the River Forth west of Culross.

In view of the stratigraphical details already in print (Dinham and Haldane 1932; Francis 1956; Read 1959) it is proposed to give here only a general account of the Passage Group, together with some previously unpublished data concerning the north-eastern part of the syncline. There recent boring and mining have proved attenuated successions amounting to no more than 745 ft near Broomhill and even less at Dollar (Fig. 20). These thicknesses compare with more than 1100 ft at Airth and Gartarry which must lie near the centre of a depositional basin (Fig. 19) not very different in its limits from that of Upper Limestone Group times (Read 1959, fig. 9).

LITHOLOGY

Up to and including No. 2 Marine Band the succession closely resembles that of the Upper Limestone Group. Above that band, however, it consists mainly of white, pale grey or yellow, feldspathic, locally pebbly sandstone, with subordinate, though in places thick, lenses of poorly-bedded clay-rock or seatearth, and thin stratified marine mudstones. Coals occur below many of the mudstones and elsewhere in the succession, but with the exception of the Netherwood and Bowhousebog coals they are thin and commonly impersistent.

According to Muir (1963, p. 479) the sandstones were derived from low-grade metamorphic rocks comparable with, and possibly a northern extension of, the Upper Dalradian beds north of the Highland Boundary Fault, though there were differences in source as compared with both Upper Limestone Group and Coal Measures. He also contends that there were differences in source between lower and upper parts of the group as indicated by the heavy mineral suites; within the area described here, however, both parts would seem to lie within the same sediment-petrographic province (Muir 1963, fig. 7). Indeed the difference in provenance between upper and lower parts of the group is much

203

less than that between the Stirling–Clackmannan area and other Midland Valley localities.

The most important clay-rocks are the Lower Fireclays between No. 2 Marine Band and the Netherwood Coal, which correspond in general terms to the seams worked as the 'Lower Fireclay' at Glenboig, Castlecary and Bonnybridge (Clough and others 1926, pp. 32, 37–9; Hinxman and others 1917, pp. 28–32). Of lesser importance are certain seatearths in the upper part of the Passage

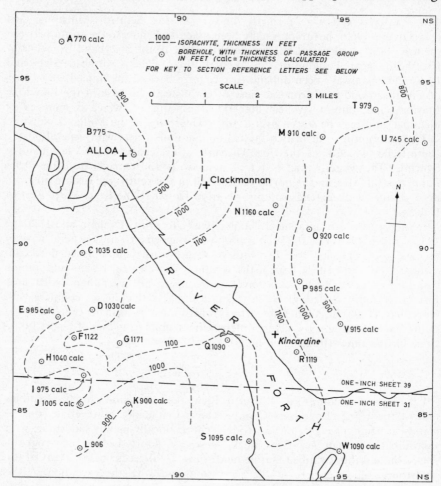

FIG. 19.   *Isopachytes of the Passage Group*

Borehole sections indicated on Fig. 19

A. Menstrie Yeast Factory Bore (1957). B. Younger's Brewery Alloa Bore (1892). C. Kersie No. 1 Bore (1903). D. Doll Mill Bore (1955). E. Carnock Estate No. 3 Bore (1916–18). F. Carnock No. 4 Bore (1918). G. Airth Estate No. 1 (South Westfield or Westfield) Bore (1918–22). H. Rosehill No. 1 Bore (1907). I. Mossneuk Bore (1950–52). J. Carronhall No. 36 Bore (1929). K. South Letham No. 1 Bore (1952). L. Carronhall No. 35 Bore (1928). M. Gartlove No. 1 Bore (1964). N. Gartarry Toll Bore (1953–54). O. Maggie Duncan's Hill No. 1 Bore (1964). P. Windyhill Bore (1964–65). Q. Kincardine Bridge Bore (1952–53). R. Tulliallan No. 2 Bore (1903). S. Orchardhead Bore (1956). T. Meadowhill Bore (1927). U. Solsgirth No. 1 Bore (1963). V. Longannet No. 1 Bore (1963). W. Grangemouth Dock Bore (1956–57).

Group which correspond in position to the 'Upper Fireclay' of the Central Coalfield. The Lower Fireclays and some of the clays at higher levels are rarely overlain by coals; they seldom contain any traces of roots and in many places they are variously mottled red, lilac, yellow and brown. From comparison with deltaic deposits in the Mississippi River (Fisk and McFarlan 1955, pp. 280–1, 296) it seems likely that this variegation is due to partial oxidation, leaching and other weathering processes under non-arid conditions during a period of low water table (Read 1959, p. 34).   E.H.F., W.A.R.

MARINE BANDS AND FAUNAS

Crampton (*in* Hinxman and others 1917, pp. 37–41) first described marine bands in the Scottish 'Millstone Grit' and numbered them in ascending order from 1 to 3, the top one comprising up to three separate marine horizons. Since then, other bands have been found by boring and the numerical scheme has been adapted to accommodate them (Dinham and Haldane 1932, pp. 111–2; Francis 1956, p. 13; Read 1959, p. 34). The names used at present are Nos. 0, 1 and 2 marine bands followed in ascending order by Nos. 3, 5 and 6 marine band groups. Some 16 or 17 separate marine horizons have been recorded in this district but some are of very local distribution (Fig. 20).

The faunas of the marine bands (Wilson *in* Francis 1956, pp. 13, 14, table 1; *in* Read 1959, pp. 66–8; Wilson 1967) are, in the main, a continuation of those present in the underlying Upper Limestone Group. The presence of *Anthracoceras paucilobum* (Phillips) and *Tylonautilus nodiferus* (Armstrong) in No. 0 Marine Band indicates an Upper *Eumorphoceras* (E_2) age for this band. The only other identifiable goniatites from the Passage Group are the recently discovered fragments of *Homoceratoides sp.* from No. 3 Marine Band Group in Maggie Duncan's Hill Bore (1964) [NS 94179054], about 2 miles north of Kincardine. Dr. W. H. C. Ramsbottom (*in* Neves and others 1965) considers that they indicate a horizon high in the Sabdenian (H) or low in the Kinderscoutian (R_1) stages. A depositional break between E_2 and Coal Measures times has been suggested (Macgregor and Pringle 1934, p. 6) but this new evidence indicates that in this area the break, if present, was not so great as was formerly supposed. Above No. 3 Marine Band Group the rich molluscan assemblages present in the lower part of the Passage Group are absent, the faunas of Nos. 5 and 6 marine band groups being poor in numbers and species. This suggests that in the upper part of the Passage Group the sea did not cover the area long enough for rich marine faunas to become established.

Torwood Glen, immediately south of the area, was one of the localities where Hind (1908) claimed to have identified a molluscan fauna with strong affinities to Upper Carboniferous faunas from Nebraska and Illinois. Wilson (1961) re-examined Hind's evidence, together with more recently collected specimens, and concluded that there was no necessity to invoke an influx of American species in Passage Group times as the forms present occur at lower levels in the Scottish Carboniferous.

An interesting feature is the presence of *Curvirimula* in the canneloid shale overlying the Castlecary Limestone at many localities. This genus is regarded as indicating non-marine conditions and its occurrence in the roof of a marine limestone is most unusual.   R.B.W.

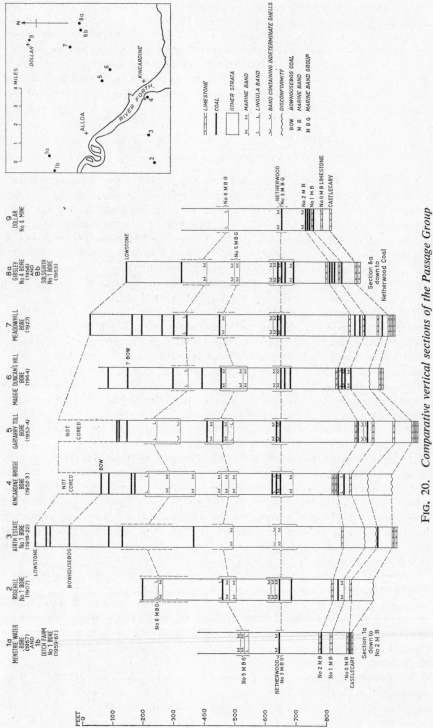

FIG. 20. *Comparative vertical sections of the Passage Group*

Unconformities

Penecontemporaneous erosion seems to have been a common occurrence in Passage Group times and is held to account for the fact that almost every marine horizon in the sequence is missing at one locality or another in the Stirling–Clackmannan area. The resultant unconformities, which are mostly of local significance only, occur below sandstones, the bases of which are commonly coarse and pebbly and may include eroded fragments of fine-grained sediments.

A more widespread unconformity of considerable magnitude was formerly inferred between Nos. 3 and 5 marine band groups (Dinham and Haldane 1932, pp. 113–8; Macgregor and Pringle 1934, pp. 5–6). This inference, which was based on the supposed break between 'Lower Carboniferous' and 'Upper Carboniferous' floras, seemed to be supported by a lithological change at about this level south of the Forth (Read 1959, pp. 33–4). Recent spore and goniatite evidence (see above; also Neves and others 1965) provides no evidence of a major break at this horizon, although there is the possibility of a break higher in the succession as spores indicative of the upper part of the Kinderscoutian (R_1) and the lower part of the Marsdenian (R_2) have not, as yet, been found. Neves suggests that, in terms of floral zones, the Passage Group ranges from Upper Namurian A below No. 2 Marine Band to Lower Westphalian A at the Bowhousebog Coal, with the Namurian–Westphalian boundary lying somewhere near the top of No. 6 Marine Band Group.

Stratigraphy

Most of the details of Passage Group stratigraphy have been obtained from borings, but a fairly complete succession is exposed along the north shore of the Forth west of Culross, and partial sections can be examined in the Devon gorge near Dollar.

Recorrelation of some of the inland exposures along the eastern margin of the district has become necessary as a result of recent borings. Marine bands in the Rough Cleugh Glen, $2\frac{1}{2}$ miles east of Forest Mill, were assigned to No. 3 Marine Band Group by Francis (1956, p. 16), but it is now quite clear that they are Nos. 1 and 2 marine bands. A short distance farther south, in the Four Braes section of the River Black Devon, the fossiliferous beds formerly equated (*loc. cit.*) with Nos. 0, 1 and 2 marine bands are now recognized as belonging to the Plean group of limestones at the top of the Upper Limestone Group (p. 200).

Details

Base of Passage Group to No. 0 Marine Band. The thickness of strata from the base of the Passage Group to No. 0 Marine Band is known to vary from less than 6 ft to 60 ft where the Castlecary Limestone is present and from 19 to 65 ft where that limestone is missing. Where present the Castlecary Limestone is succeeded by a distinctive bed of carbonaceous canneloid mudstone containing fish-scales and *Curvirimula*, though in some places a thin bed of mudstone with marine shells intervenes between it and the limestone. A local pale-grey unfossiliferous limestone 21 in thick occurs above the canneloid mudstone in Mains of Throsk No. 1 Bore (1959). Above the mudstone the strata are mostly sandstones and seatclays; the latter are usually subordinate, but at the eastern and western margins of the area north of the Forth they predominate. North-west of Alloa, where No. 0 Marine Band commonly lies less than 10 ft above the

Castlecary Limestone, the succession is almost entirely argillaceous, with a thin coal underlain by a few feet of grey, greenish or brown mottled clay-rock, the top of which may be rooty. In many places there is a minor unconformity at the base of the Passage Group and the Castlecary Limestone is missing (Francis 1956, fig. 4). In these localities, where sandstones overlie the unconformities they are commonly coarse-grained and may contain pebbly bands with fragments of mudstone.

No. 0 Marine Band. No. 0 Marine Band is a bed of mudstone 2 to 14 ft thick, which generally contains a limestone—No. 0 Marine Band Limestone. Unlike Nos. 1 and 2 marine bands, No. 0 Marine Band is not usually underlain by a coal. The limestone reaches a maximum known thickness of 3 ft 3 in (excluding some thin limestone ribs in the overlying mudstone) in a bore at Glenbervie, in the Airdrie (31) Sheet to the south; although it is generally fine-grained and argillaceous it is characteristically more crystalline and less impure than the limestones associated with Nos. 1 and 2 marine bands. Both the mudstone and the limestone of No. 0 Marine Band contain a relatively abundant marine fauna including goniatites which are more common than in any other marine band in the Passage Group.

No. 0 Marine Band to No. 1 Marine Band. The thickness of strata between No. 0 and No. 1 marine bands ranges approximately from 12 to 60 ft. Where the succession is thin, as at Cambus, it is made up entirely of seatclays, but where it is thick, as it is around Airth, Kincardine and north of Culross, it consists mainly of sandstones, some of them coarse and pebbly. A minor unconformity at the base of some of these beds transgresses well down into No. 0 Marine Band and in places cuts out the band altogether. A thin coal generally lies immediately below No. 1 Marine Band which may thereby be distinguished from No. 0 Marine Band.

No. 1 Marine Band. No. 1 Marine Band resembles No. 0 Marine Band in lithology and consists of 3 to 9 ft of mudstone with nodules of clayband ironstone and an impersistent, impure, shelly argillaceous limestone—No. 1 Marine Band Limestone—which rarely exceeds 12 inches in thickness and occurs at or near the base of the band. Marine fossils occur throughout the band, but the fauna is generally more abundant and varied above the limestone than below.

No. 1 Marine Band to No. 2 Marine Band. There are between 15 and 50 ft of strata, mainly sandstones, between Nos. 1 and 2 marine bands. Attenuated successions around Cattle Moss and Rough Cleugh Glen (p. 207) consist mainly of seatclays with a group of thin coals. Thicker successions towards the centre of the basin (Fig. 20) include two coals each with a mudstone roof. At Maggie Duncan's Hill Bore [NS 94179054] the lower mudstone contains *Lingula* and ribbed brachiopods and the upper mudstone *Lingula* alone. In many places there is minor disconformity near the base of the sandy beds that overlie No. 1 Marine Band and in bores between Carnock and Airth the marine band is cut out.

No. 2 Marine Band. No. 2 is the most persistent of the Passage Group marine bands. It consists of shelly mudstone 4 to 11 ft thick and commonly contains near the base an argillaceous limestone—the Roman Cement or No. 2 Marine Band Limestone. In the south and west of the basin this limestone is generally made up almost entirely of crushed Orthotetid shells. Although it persists over a remarkably large area in the Midland Valley of Scotland (Dinham and Haldane 1932, p. 112) it is locally absent around Saline and Dollar. It ranges in thickness up to 3 ft and, although generally in one leaf, may split into two or three. The limestone passes up into calcareous mudstones which are packed with brachiopods and other marine shells and which are in places overlain in turn by mudstones with clayband ironstone nodules.

No. 2 Marine Band to No. 3 Marine Band Group. The strata between No. 2 Marine Band and No. 3 Marine Band Group (where the base of the latter can be recognized) vary in thickness from some 60 to 250 ft, and are generally thickest in the centre of the area. They consist mainly of alternating beds of poorly-stratified clay-rock and cross-stratified sandstone, many of them of considerable thickness, but varying greatly from place to place; individual beds can rarely be traced for any great distance and it is not possible to identify any particular bed or beds of clay-rock as the precise equivalent of the seam or seams of fireclay known and worked as the 'Lower Fireclay' in the Central Coalfield (Clough and others 1926, pp. 32, 37–9; Hinxman and others 1917, pp. 30–2). These lower clay-rocks of the Passage Group differ from normal seatclays in that they contain relatively few traces of roots and are rarely overlain by coals; they are characteristically variegated, massive, unstratified rocks which may be as much as 60 ft thick in places: they are traversed in all directions by numerous polished surfaces and, at their outcrop, they frequently weather into small irregular cuboidal blocks. Locally they contain concretions of clayband ironstone which range from minute grains of spherosiderite to nodules some inches in diameter. North of the Forth, near the eastern and western margins of the basin, the clays form two thick seams directly overlying No. 2 Marine Band, but they are split by posts of sandstone into several thin leaves towards the centre of the basin.

The sandstones in this part of the succession vary greatly in lithology and thickness. Most of them are feldspathic and are whitish-grey or buff, but in some localities they are coloured green by chloritic material; locally they are clayey and grade into sandy clay-rocks. Individual sandstones are known to thicken greatly in very short distances and many of them have unconformable bases that cut down locally into the underlying clay-rocks to form washouts, probably along contemporaneous stream channels.

No. 3 Marine Band Group. Where fully developed No. 3 Marine Band Group includes four distinct marine bands, but there is only one known section in the district— Gibsley No. 1 Bore [NS 97949247]—in which all four have been recorded. In the sequel they are described from below upwards as the first, second, third and fourth marine bands of No. 3 Group.

The first and lowest marine band in the group has been recorded in only a few sections, but a thin coal that underlies it is more persistent and serves to identify its horizon where the band itself is missing. Crinoid columnals, brachiopods (including *Lingula*) and marine lamellibranchs have been recorded at this horizon, but the fossils seem to be rather less abundant than in the higher bands of the group.

Some 20 to 40 ft of strata separate the first from the second marine band of No. 3 Group. Most of the beds are clay-rocks or sandstones similar to those between No. 2 Marine Band and No. 3 Marine Band Group. Some of the sandstones contain abundant chloritic material which gives them a greenish colour.

A thin coal—the Netherwood Coal—underlies the second marine band of No. 3 Group. This seam is remarkably persistent over a very wide area and is a useful marker horizon for the underlying Lower Fireclays. Although the coal is usually thin in the area south of the Forth it comprises a 12-in lower and 9-in upper leaf separated by 27 in of coaly seatclay in Culross No. 1 Bore.

The second, third and fourth marine bands of No. 3 Group were formerly described collectively as 'No. 3 Marine Band' (Hinxman and others 1917, pp. 40–1; Dinham and Haldane 1932, p. 111). They all lie close together, the distance from the base of the second to the top of the fourth ranging approximately from 10 to 20 ft. Because of the rapid alternation of marine and coal-swamp conditions during the deposition of so small a thickness of strata, mudstones with marine shells have in places been invaded by roots penetrating down from an overlying coaly layer. The seatearths within this condensed succession have an unusual bluish colour which helps to make the group distinctive over most of the area north of the Forth.

The second marine band of No. 3 Group may be traced over almost as great an area as No. 2 Marine Band. It consists of a bed of mudstone 1 to 6 ft thick, the lower part of which is generally calcareous and packed with shells whereas the upper part is more sparsely fossiliferous and may contain ironstone concretions. The fauna of this marine band is more varied and abundant than those of the other three in the group: it includes several species of brachiopods, gastropods and marine lamellibranchs.

The third and fourth marine bands of No. 3 Group are thin beds of shelly mudstone. Each may be underlain by a thin coal but neither seam is as persistent as the Netherwood Coal. These marine bands cannot be recognized over as wide an area as the second of the group and the fossils in them seem to be rather fewer and less varied.

No. 3 Marine Band Group to No. 5 Marine Band Group. The thickness of strata between the top marine band of No. 3 Group and the bottom marine band of No. 5 Group is difficult to estimate, for in many sections these particular bands cannot be identified with any certainty; it is believed, however, to range from about 110 to about 170 ft. South of the Forth the succession may be divided into two parts, the lower including thick poorly-bedded clay-rocks and the upper consisting mainly of sandstones. The lower part shows the alternation of sandstones and variegated clay-rocks which is typical of the lower part of the Passage Group. The clay-rocks are lithologically similar to the Lower Fireclays but they are usually rather thinner and, up to the present, have not been worked as refractories. Most of the sandstones are relatively thin. A minor unconformity at the base of a sandstone low down in this part of the succession accounts for the absence of the three uppermost marine bands of No. 3 Marine Band Group at a bore approximately 1 mile east of Plean.

No. 5 Marine Band Group. No. 5 Marine Band Group—formerly No. 5 Marine Band (Dinham and Haldane 1932, p. 122)—contains at least three and probably four or more marine bands concentrated within about 70 ft of strata. Each of the bands may be cut out by penecontemporaneous erosion and it is very difficult to correlate them from section to section. The marine bands are beds of mudstone which range in thickness from a few inches to about 5 ft. They contain *Lingula* and other brachiopods, lamellibranchs and gastropods, but their faunas are distinctly poorer, both in numbers and variety, than those of the lower marine bands of the Passage Group. The intervals between the marine bands of No. 5 Group are largely occupied by sandstones but, commonly, a thin coal and seatearth lie beneath each bed of mudstone.

No. 5 Marine Band Group to No. 6 Marine Band Group. The strata between Nos. 5 and 6 marine band groups range in thickness from some 90 to 110 ft and consist mainly of sandstones with a few thin seatearths.

No. 6 Marine Band Group. South of the Forth No. 6 Marine Band Group is a much more arbitrary stratigraphical subdivision than either of the two lower groups. Whereas in No. 3 and No. 5 groups the marine bands are fairly close to each other, in No. 6 Group they may be distributed over as much as 150 ft of strata, possibly even more, and the interval between individual bands may be almost as great as that between Nos. 5 and 6 groups. North of the Forth the group is more condensed.

In all, four marine bands are known in No. 6 Group. Each of them may be missing owing to penecontemporaneous erosion and, as yet, they have not all been recorded in any one section. Each consists of a bed of mudstone, generally thin, but locally as much as 5 ft thick; their faunas are relatively poor and resemble those of the marine bands in No. 5 Group. The distance between the first and second marine bands of the group is of the order of 50 to 90 ft. The second and third are close together and cannot easily be differentiated where only one of them is present; they have been recorded together only in the Rosehill Bore where they lie no more than 6 ft apart. The fourth and highest of these bands lies about 60 ft above the second: it was first identified in the Kincardine Bridge Bore where, however, it yielded only *Lingula* and fish remains. The beds between the marine bands are mostly sandstones but they include some thin seatearths. A few thin coals have been found, usually just below the marine bands.

North of the Forth, around Alloa and Dollar, the group has not been found and in the thicker successions farther east few records show more than one or two bands.

No. 6 Marine Band Group to top of the Passage Group. The top marine band of No. 6 Marine Band Group and the horizon of the Lowstone Marine Band have not both been identified with certainty in any single section in the area, but the thickness of strata between them seems to range from about 190 ft to about 300 ft. The succession consists largely of sandstones but includes a number of seatearths and coals which are more common than in the underlying strata down to the base of No. 5 Marine Band Group.

South of the Forth relatively thick seatclays, which have been worked locally as refractories, are found above and below a fairly persistent coal which lies some 60 to 90 ft below the top of the Passage Group. These clays, and the coal associated with them, are respectively equivalent to the Upper Fireclay of the Bonnybridge area (Hinxman and others 1917, pp. 33–7) and the Bowhousebog Coal of the Hartwood area (Macgregor and Anderson 1923, pp. 68, 72, 75–6; Dinham and Haldane 1932, pp. 122–3). The Bowhousebog Coal ranges in thickness from a few inches to as much as 51 in. It is generally in leaves and, although of rather poor quality, it seems to have been worked under the name of 'Coal Moses' in the four old pits east and south-east of St. Andrew's Church, Dunmore (Dinham and Haldane 1932, pp. 168–9). The following section, probably of this coal, was measured in 1952 in a cellar at the north-eastern corner of Dunmore Estate kitchen garden, 1400 ft south-south-west of St. Andrew's Church: coal 6 in seen, fissile seatclay 6 in, fissile coal 5 in, seatclay 8 in, coal (fissile at top) 9 in seen.

The sandstones between No. 6 Marine Band Group and the top of the Passage Group are generally greyish-white or buff in colour, but red-stained sandstones, believed to lie a short distance below the 'Coal Moses', occur at Dunmore, where they are exposed in a series of small crags running west-north-west from St. Andrew's Church. The sandstones there are buff and brown in the most westerly exposures but farther east they are stained a deep red. This reddening may be due to oxidation penetrating downwards from a pre-New Red Sandstone land surface, following the plane of the neighbouring Dunmore Hill Fault in the same way as it has penetrated downwards along fault-planes in Ayrshire (Mykura 1960). This explanation, however, cannot be applied to similar staining at the top of the Passage Group south of Dollar, where there is no faulting. It has even less application in Midlothian where much of the Passage Group is red (Tulloch and Walton 1958) or in Fife where most or all of the group is reddened below an approximately constant horizon near the base of the Coal Measures and where a sub-Coal Measures unconformity or non-sequence has been suggested (Francis and Ewing 1962, p. 151). E.H.F., W.A.R.

REFERENCES

CLOUGH, C. T., HINXMAN, L. W., WRIGHT, W. B., ANDERSON, E. M. and CARRUTHERS, R. G. 1926. The economic geology of the Central Coalfield of Scotland, Area V. 2nd edit. with additions by MACGREGOR, M. *Mem. geol. Surv. Gt Br.*
DINHAM, C. H. and HALDANE, D. 1932. The economic geology of the Stirling and Clackmannan Coalfield. *Mem. geol. Surv. Gt Br.*
FISK, H. M. and MACFARLAN, E. 1955. Late Quaternary deltaic deposits of the Mississippi River. In *Crust of the Earth. Spec. Pap. geol. Soc. Am.*, **62**, 279–302.
FRANCIS, E. H. 1956. The economic geology of the Stirling and Clackmannan Coalfield, Scotland: Area north of the River Forth. *Coalfld Pap. geol. Surv.*, No. 1.
—— and EWING, C. J. C. 1962. Skipsey's Marine Band and red Coal Measures in Fife. *Geol. Mag.*, **99**, 145–52.
HIND, W. 1908. On the lamellibranch and gastropod fauna found in the Millstone Grit of Scotland. *Trans. R. Soc. Edinb.*, **46**, 331–59.
HINXMAN, L. W., CRAMPTON, C. B., ANDERSON, E. M. and MACGREGOR, M. 1917. The economic geology of the Central Coalfield of Scotland, Area II. *Mem. geol. Surv. Gt Br.*
MACGREGOR, A. G. 1960. Divisions of the Carboniferous on Geological Survey Scottish maps. *Bull. geol. Surv. Gt Br.*, No. 16, 127–30.
MACGREGOR, M. and ANDERSON, E. M. 1923. The economic geology of the Central Coalfield of Scotland, Area VI. *Mem. geol. Surv. Gt Br.*
—— and PRINGLE, J. 1934. The Scottish Millstone Grit and its position in the zonal succession. *Mem. geol. Surv. Summ. Prog.* for 1933, pt. 2, 1–7.

P

MUIR, R. O. 1963. Petrography and provenance of the Millstone Grit of central Scotland. *Trans. Edinb. geol. Soc.*, **19**, 439–85.

MYKURA, W. 1960. The replacement of coal by limestone and the reddening of Coal Measures in the Ayrshire Coalfield. *Bull. geol. Surv. Gt Br.*, No. 16, 69–109.

NEVES, R., READ, W. A. and WILSON, R. B. 1965. Note on recent spore and goniatite evidence from the Passage Group of the Scottish Upper Carboniferous succession. *Scott. J. Geol.*, **1**, 185–8.

READ, W. A. 1959. The economic geology of the Stirling and Clackmannan Coalfield, Scotland: Area south of the River Forth. *Coalfld Pap. geol. Surv.*, No. 2.

TULLOCH, W. and WALTON, H. S. 1958. The geology of the Midlothian Coalfield. *Mem. geol. Surv. Gt Br.*

WILSON, R. B. 1961. A review of the evidence for a 'Nebraskan' fauna in the Scottish Carboniferous. *Palaeontology*, **4**, 507–19.

—— 1967. A study of some Namurian marine faunas of central Scotland. *Trans. R. Soc. Edinb.*, **66**, 445–90.

Chapter XIV

COAL MEASURES

INTRODUCTION

IN SCOTLAND the Coal Measures are now classified as comprising Lower, Middle and Upper subdivisions (MacGregor 1960). The marine band containing *Gastrioceras subcrenatum*, which is taken as the base of the Coal Measures in England and Wales, is not known in Scotland, where the base is accordingly taken at locally convenient coal, ironstone or *Lingula*-bearing horizons which accord with the available faunal evidence (*see* p. 203). The boundaries between Lower and Middle and between Middle and Upper measures are more precisely defined by the base of the Queenslie Marine Band and the top of Skipsey's Marine Band respectively. Within the district described here the Queenslie Marine Band is well known, but there is no outcrop of Skipsey's Marine Band nor of any overlying strata, though it is calculated that both may be represented beneath the 'buried channel' of the River Devon between Alva and Tillicoultry.

This chapter is thus concerned almost entirely with the Lower and Middle Coal Measures. A generalized vertical section of the strata is given in Fig. 21, which also shows the distribution and zonal classification of non-marine lamellibranchs ('mussels') in the sequence. In the latter connexion it should be noted that although no mussels referable to the *Anthraconaia lenisulcata* Zone have been recorded in this district, the presence of the zone is nevertheless inferred on the indirect evidence provided by the Lowstone and Sub-Glenfuir marine bands (Calver *in* Francis 1956, p. 27). The Lowstone Marine Band has now been identified over a large part of the Central Coalfield as well as in Stirling and Clackmannan, and, as it is a more persistent and readily recognizable horizon than local ironstones correlated with the Crofthead Slatyband Ironstone of Fauldhouse, it forms a much more suitable marker horizon to use as the base of the Coal Measures (p. 203).

The strata crop out in a broad synclinal tract 2 to 4 miles wide, its axis extending from Alva and Tillicoultry in the north to Letham Moss and Airth in the south. With the exception of some local variations the plunge of this fold is northerly in the ground north of Clackmannan town and southerly to the south of it, and the whole syncline is broken by faulting. Most of the large faults trend from west to east, but there are a few big north-easterly fractures. There is also a group of small faults with north-westerly trend. The principal fracture, however, is the Ochil Fault which forms the northern limit of the Stirling and Clackmannan Coalfield and which has been estimated to have a displacement of several thousand feet between Menstrie and Dollar (p. 247). Carboniferous strata abutting against this fault and its subsidiary, the Arndean Fault, are everywhere turned down steeply towards the south. This abrupt reversal of the prevalent northerly dips has given rise to a series of asymmetrical basins of which the largest is superimposed on the main syncline at its northern extremity, between Alva and Tillicoultry. Smaller basins containing Coal Measures strata occur at Harviestoun, Dollar, Blairingone and Lambhill.

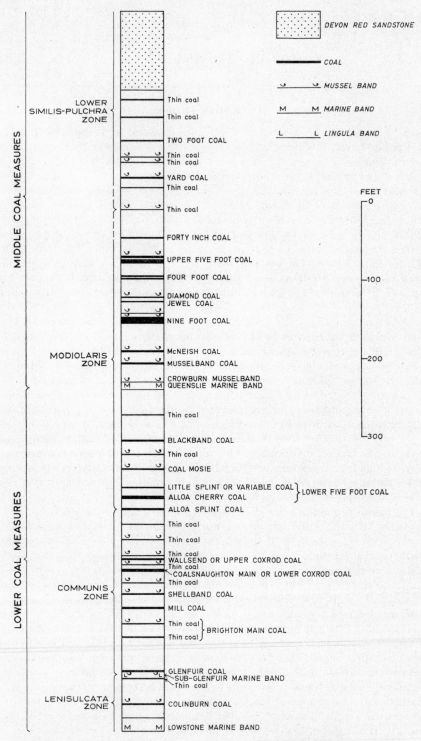

FIG. 21. *Generalized vertical section of the Lower and Middle Coal Measures*

The Coal Measures are thickest around Clackmannan town, from which area they become considerably attenuated towards the north and less so towards the south (Fig. 22). In Clackmannanshire the isopachytes of intervals between some of the lower coals (Francis 1956, figs. 9a, 9b) show that from the centre of the syncline there is further thinning eastwards towards Lambhill and westwards to the ground between Alva and Alloa. This variation in thickness is similar to that shown by the Passage Group and earlier formations and provides further evidence that the syncline was in process of formation in Carboniferous times.

None of the seams in the Coal Measures is now being mined: indeed it is true to say that in terms of present-day coalfield economics the measures are exhausted. One of the last mines to be abandoned was at Harviestoun, where some of the coals were found to be replaced by limestone in a zone of reddened, oxidized strata. These phenomena are discussed in a later section (p. 221).

STRATIGRAPHY

The stratigraphical details which follow are based to a large extent on the full accounts provided by Dinham and Haldane (1932), Francis (1956) and Read (1959). The palaeontology of this part of the succession has been described by Mr. M. A. Calver (*in* Francis 1956, pp. 25–31, table 2).

DETAILS

Base of Coal Measures to Colinburn Coal. The Lowstone Marine Band, overlying a coal up to 12 in thick, consists of a few feet of mudstone which has yielded *Lingula* and *Orbiculoidea* near Carronhall and foraminifera at Kincardine. The band has not been found farther north. In the south it is separated from the Colinburn Coal by 20 to 25 ft of strata which include a median seam of coal, up to 24 in thick, representing the Bonnyhill Craw Coal of Falkirk.

Colinburn Coal. The Colinburn Coal is a constant seam south of the Forth where it has a maximum thickness of 29 in and averages 22 in. This average is maintained as far north as Kincardine and the seam is still recognizable at Brucefield Colliery, near Clackmannan, but north and west from there its identification among the several thin seams which occur below the Glenfuir Coal is less certain.

Colinburn Coal to Glenfuir Coal. The Colinburn and Glenfuir coals are separated by 35 to 45 ft of strata consisting mainly of sandstone. In a boring near Kincardine *Curvirimula* and ostracods were obtained from the roof of the Colinburn Coal and provide the only faunal record from this horizon in the district.

In several other bores near Kincardine a thin coal lying 7 ft beneath the Glenfuir is overlain by a bed of pyritized mudstone varying in thickness from 2 to 6 in. Plant remains and *Curvirimula* have been obtained in each bore from the mudstone and in one bore *Lingula mytilloides* also was found in the lower part of the bed. *Lingula* has been seen at this position in only one other bore in this area, but it has been recorded 20 to 30 ft below the Glenfuir Coal in several bores at Tippethill, south-west of Bathgate, where it is associated with foraminifera. This horizon has been termed the Sub-Glenfuir Marine Band.

Glenfuir Coal. The Glenfuir Coal has been called 'Lower Splint' (at Brucefield), 'Hawkhill Main' (at Tulliallan), 'Lower Three Foot' (at Blairingone) and 'Ball' (at Tulligarth). Although the last name is the one which has been used most commonly in Clackmannanshire, 'Glenfuir' is preferred in this account, as it avoids confusion with the Ball Coal of Armadale—a seam rather higher in the succession—and accords with general usage in the area immediately south of the River Forth.

The seam is thickest in the neighbourhood of Kincardine where the several leaves into which it is split have a total thickness of 4 to 5 ft. Mining records in this area

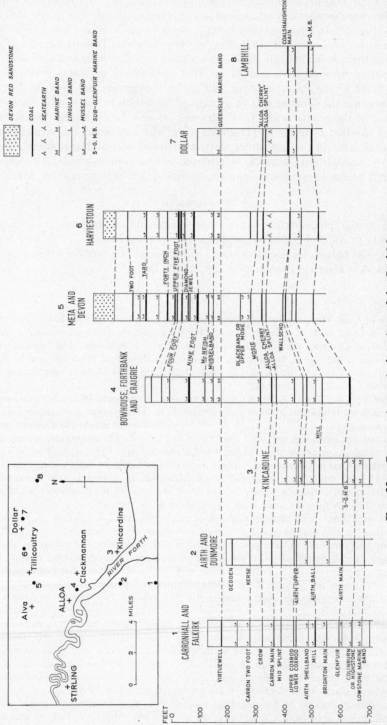

FIG. 22.   Comparative vertical sections of the Coal Measures

have been lost, but the coal must have been worked around the town and in the Tulliallan estate nearby. South of the Forth and northwards from Tulliallan the seam contains two or more partings and shows much local variation in thickness. For these reasons it has been extracted only over small areas though thicknesses of 3 ft or more have been recorded in bores around Gartmorn Dam, Tillicoultry Mains and Dollar.

The Glenfuir Coal crops out in the Kirk Burn, near Tillicoultry, and in Sheardale Glen, east of Sheardale House. It is exposed also in a tributary to the River Black Devon at Aitkenhead Farm where it was thought to be the Coalsnaughton Main Coal and was worked from a small drift mine.

Glenfuir Coal to Mill Coal. The strata between the Glenfuir and Mill coals vary in thickness from 54 ft at Dollar and Lambhill to 95 ft between Brucefield and Craigrie. They consist mainly of sandstone and seatclay and include a group of two or three thin coals. These probably represent the Brighton Main Coal of Falkirk which is thought to be, in part at least, identical with the Ball Coal of Armadale (Hinxman and others 1917, p. 69). A single specimen of *Carbonicola communis* Davies and Trueman has been obtained from the roof of the topmost of these coals in a boring near Collyland between Alloa and Alva.

Mill Coal. The Mill Coal is, on average, about 2 ft thick and reaches its maximum in the ground between Kincardine and Brucefield where it amounts to between 26 and 31 in. South of the Forth the topmost few inches of the seam consist of cannel, but farther north this lithology is represented by a cannelly bed at the base of the mudstone roof. The seam is exposed in Sheardale Glen, in Melloch Glen farther west and in the Black Devon, 450 yd downstream from Shawbernaig Bridge.

Mill Coal to Airth Shellband. In the southern part of the Clackmannan Syncline the Mill Coal is separated from the Airth Shellband by a sequence comprising mudstone overlain successively by sandstone, seatclay and coal, together amounting to a thickness of between 20 and 25 ft. The mudstone is about 6 ft thick, with clayband ironstone ribs and nodules, and has yielded fish scales from the cannelly band at the base: unlike the equivalent bed in the Falkirk area, however, the mudstone has nowhere been found to contain mussels. The coal at the top of the sequence—the Shellband Coal—is seldom more than 12 in thick and is, in places, absent. In the northern part of the syncline the sequence between Mill and Shellband coals is reduced to between 3 and 6 ft and it then consists merely of seatclay with ironstone nodules.

Airth Shellband. The Airth Shellband is a bed, 2 to 6 ft thick, of mudstone with clayband ironstone ribs and nodules. *Carbonicola communis* and *C. pseudorobusta* Trueman are particularly abundant in a thin layer, near the top of the bed, which remains persistently fossiliferous throughout the whole area and makes the Airth Shellband the most useful marker band in the Lower Coal Measures.

Airth Shellband to Coalsnaughton Main or Lower Coxrod Coal. The Coalsnaughton Main Coal is separated from the Airth Shellband by 20 to 30 ft of sandstone and silt-stone. About half way up, a thin band of cannelly mudstone containing *Curvirimula* has been found in borings in the Brucefield area and the same bed is exposed at the north end of the Hawkhill railway cutting, near Kincardine. The band does not continue, however, into the northern and western parts of the Clackmannan Coalfield, nor has it been recorded south of the Forth.

Coalsnaughton Main or Lower Coxrod Coal. The Coalsnaughton Main or Lower Coxrod Coal seldom exceeds 2 ft around Airth, Kincardine and Alloa, and is only 22 inches in the Tullibody mine, near its western outcrop. It thickens eastwards and north-wards to $2\frac{1}{2}$ ft at Brucefield, 3 ft around Gartmorn Dam, and up to 4 ft at Coals-naughton. A mile to the east of that village a washout 500 to 600 yd wide trends from north-west to south-east in the seam and farther east, around Sheardale, the coal is interleaved with so many dirt partings that it is unworkable. Still further east, however, in the Blairingone and Lambhill basins, these partings disappear and the seam has been worked. Near Blairingone a thickness of 3 ft of coal was recorded from a recent shallow bore in the western part of the basin and more recent bores at Lambhill have proved between 46 and 54 in of coal with a parting up to 2 in thick. Comparable thicknesses were found at Dollar in the recently abandoned mine there.

Coalsnaughton Main Coal to Wallsend or Upper Coxrod Coal. The strata between the Coalsnaughton Main and Wallsend coals vary in thickness from about 20 ft at Brucefield to as little as 3 ft in parts of the Dollar and Lambhill areas. They are equally variable in character, and have been found at Brucefield and Kincardine to include a thin bed of mudstone containing large non-marine lamellibranchs, the position of the bed varying from a few inches to 10 ft above the Main Coal. Traces of shells have been seen also at about the same relative position in two shallow bores near Sheardale.

Wallsend or Upper Coxrod Coal. The Wallsend or Upper Coxrod is the first seam lying above the Coalsnaughton Main or Lower Coxrod Coal. It shows a fairly uniform thickness of 18 to 24 inches in most parts of the area and was worked on a small scale from Devon Pit and from Dollar and Zetland mines. It was known as the 'Wee' or 'Gas' Coal at Brucefield but was not worked there.

Wallsend Coal to Alloa Splint Coal. The strata between the Wallsend and Alloa Splint coals decrease in thickness from 85 ft at Brucefield to 50 ft at Gartmorn Dam and, possibly, to an even lower figure farther north at Harviestoun, where both coals are only doubtfully recognized. Sandstone is the main rock type, forming about half of the succession in the south and an increasing proportion towards the north. There are also a few bands of poorly-bedded, pale-green clay-rock, containing spherosiderite, and five thin, inconstant coals. In addition, two mussel bands have been recorded. The lower of these occurs about a quarter of the way up the succession between the Wallsend and Alloa Splint coals. It has been observed at Carnock, at Kilbagie and near Kincardine where it consists of a bed of mudstone 3 ft thick, from which *Curvirimula* has been obtained. The upper of the two mussel bands lies about midway between the Wallsend and Alloa Splint coals. It is a thin bed of cannelly shale, containing *Curvirimula*, which forms the roof of one of the thin coals mentioned above. This upper band has been proved by borings to persist over the southern half of Clackmannanshire where it is exposed in a small stream at Chapelwell, south of Clackmannan town, and in the south bank of the Black Devon on both sides of the Clackmannan Woollen Mill. Its only record farther north is in a bore north of Gartmorn Dam.

Alloa Splint Coal. South of the Forth, where the equivalents of the Alloa Splint are the Carron Main of Airth and the New Main of Dunmore, the seam is between 3 and 4 ft thick. It retains this thickness to Tulliallan, north of the Forth, but is reduced to 30 or 33 in throughout most of the Clackmannan Syncline. North-eastwards in the detached basin of Harviestoun it dies out and it is absent in the Lambhill and Dollar basins (the 'Alloa Splint' of Dollar is now regarded as the Alloa Cherry).

Alloa Splint Coal to Alloa Cherry Coal. The Splint and Cherry coals of Alloa are separated by 12 to 36 ft of strata north of the Forth and by 40 to 56 ft south of the river. One or more thin coals are included in this interval and fish remains have occasionally been recorded from the beds immediately overlying the Alloa Splint Coal, but there are no mussels at this horizon as there are in the Falkirk area farther south.

Alloa Cherry Coal. Throughout the southern part of the area the Alloa Cherry Coal, equated with the Crow of Airth and the Old Main of Dunmore, is 3 to $3\frac{1}{2}$ ft thick. In the northern part of the Clackmannan Syncline it is joined by the Little Splint or Variable Coal and there becomes the Lower Five Foot Seam. In the Harviestoun Basin the coal varies in thickness from 63 inches in the centre to 46 inches in the west and to as little as 20 inches in the east. In the western part of the basin the variation may be due to erosion at the base of an overlying sandstone which rests directly on the coal; in the east, however, the sandstone is absent and the thinning of the seam in that direction is the result of normal attenuation. The 'Alloa Cherry' of the Dollar Basin should now be correlated with the Coal Mosie of the ground immediately south of Alva and Tillicoultry (referred to in the remainder of this account as the 'Main Basin'), the true Alloa Cherry at Dollar being the coal hitherto called 'Alloa Splint' (Fig. 22).

Alloa Cherry Coal to Coal Mosie. In most parts of the coalfield the Alloa Cherry is separated from the Coal Mosie by 35 to 40 ft of strata which include a median seam—the Little Splint or Variable Coal—12 to 24 in. thick. In northern and western localities the Little Splint joins with the Alloa Cherry Coal to form the Lower Five Foot seam and where attenuation is greatest, at Harviestoun and Dollar, the Lower Five Foot is separated from the Coal Mosie by only 5 to 6 ft of seatclay.

Coal Mosie. The Coal Mosie or Carron Two Foot Coal is a seam of inconstant thickness. Around Coalsnaughton alone, for example, it ranges from 18 to 43 in. At Dunmore, where it was called the Kerse Coal, it is $2\frac{1}{2}$ to $3\frac{1}{2}$ ft thick.

Coal Mosie to Queenslie Marine Band. The Coal Mosie is separated from the Queenslie Marine Band by 100 to 150 ft of strata. Immediately overlying the Mosie is a persistent bed of mudstone with ironstone ribs and mussels which serves to identify the seam throughout Clackmannanshire. There is another mussel band, in places underlain by a thin coal, about 30 ft higher in the sequence, but it does not persist as far north as Harviestoun or Dollar. Still higher, at about 25 to 50 ft above the Coal Mosie, there is an inconstant seam, 18 to 24 in. thick, which has been called the Blackband or Upper Mosie in Clackmannanshire. This coal, which may be equivalent to the Crow, or Craw, Coal of Dunmore, is overlain by a series of sandstones and unbedded greenish clay-rocks with a few thin coals. One of these coals is probably the Gedden of Dunmore.   E.H.F., W.A.R.

Queenslie Marine Band. In the Stirling district this important marker band forms the lower part of a 10-ft bed of mudstone with ironstone ribs and has yielded a fauna which includes *Rectocornuspira?*, cf. *Hyperammina*, *Conularia sp.*, *Lingula mytilloides* J. Sowerby, *Levipustula piscariae* (Waterlot), *Dunbarella?*, *Hollinella* cf. *bassleri* (Knight) and *Paraparchites?*.

Queenslie Marine Band to McNeish Coal. The Queenslie Marine Band is succeeded by a further few feet of mudstone—the Crowburn Musselband—which has yielded non-marine shells at Forthbank and Craigrie in the south. In the northern part of the area, however, this bed has so far proved to be barren. Some 20 to 25 ft above the mudstone and about midway between it and the McNeish Coal there is the Musselband Coal, a seam whose principal claim to importance is the occurrence throughout the area of abundant and distinctive non-marine shells in its roof (Calver *in* Francis 1956, p. 29).

McNeish Coal. The McNeish Coal varies considerably in thickness and is commonly split by numerous dirt partings, e.g. near the Devon Pit bottom where three partings are present in a seam 53 in. thick.

McNeish Coal to Nine Foot Coal. The roof of the McNeish Coal is formed by mudstone with ironstone bands and non-marine shells. Above the mudstone there is a post of sandstone, 10 ft thick at Devon and increasing to 50 ft at Forthbank and Ferryton. The sandstone, however, has an unconformable base and may rest directly on the McNeish Coal, as at Gartmorn Hill, or even on the seatclay below that seam, as it does in some of the borings at Harviestoun.

Nine Foot Coal. The Nine Foot Coal is the thickest of the Clackmannanshire seams and is subdivided into a lower 'cherry' leaf and an upper 'splint' leaf. In most places the parting between the leaves is thin and the seam, as a whole, varies in thickness from 9 ft in the south and at Devon Colliery to 5 ft at Clackmannan and Harviestoun. South of Alva and Tillicoultry the distance between the 'splint' and 'cherry' varies greatly, ranging from 1 in to 27 ft. At Dollar the seam is probably represented by the 'Dollar Three Foot Coal' which must have a very limited outcrop in the centre of that basin.

Nine Foot Coal to Upper Five Foot Coal. The strata which separate the Nine Foot and Upper Five Foot coals are 125 ft thick at Forthbank, but the thickness is reduced to 70 ft between Alva and Tillicoultry and to 45 ft at Harviestoun. In the Main Basin this part of the succession includes three worked seams named, in upward succession, Jewel Coal, Diamond Coal and Four Foot Coal. Because the correlation of these seams with coals lying between the Nine Foot and Upper Five Foot coals elsewhere in the coalfield is uncertain, the successions in the Main Basin, the Harviestoun Basin and the area around Craigie, Forthbank and Whinhall are described separately.

In the Main Basin the Jewel Coal lies 18 ft above the Nine Foot Coal and varies in thickness from 16 in to 32 in. The Diamond Coal lies 4 to 5 ft above the Jewel Coal and was 17 to 30 in thick at Meta Mine. Mussels have been collected from the mudstone overlying the Diamond Coal in the Meta Mine. The Four Foot Coal lies midway between the Jewel and Upper Five Foot coals. It consists of two leaves, the lower 1 to 2 ft thick separated by a 3-in to 9-in parting from the upper, 1 to 3 ft thick.

In the Harviestoun Basin the succession between the Nine Foot and Upper Five Foot coals contains no seam of workable thickness. It is probable that a thin coal lying a few feet above the Nine Foot at Devon has here become the top leaf of the Nine Foot Coal. A 6-in coal lying 15 ft above the Nine Foot is thought to be the Jewel, whilst a 9-in to 13-in coal underlying a mussel band 15 ft higher in the succession is correlated with the Diamond. Both these coals are exposed in an old quarry 350 yd south-east of Harviestoun Castle. It is believed that the Four Foot of Devon is equivalent to the lower two of the several leaves of the Upper Five Foot Coal in the Harviestoun Basin.

In the neighbourhood of Craigie, Forthbank and Whinhall the name 'Four Foot Coal' has been given to a seam, consisting of two leaves, which occurs midway between the Nine Foot and Upper Five Foot coals in the Great Mill, or Speedwell, Pit. In Bowhouse No. 4 Bore (1933–4) it was nearly 3 ft thick and was overlain by mudstone with mussels. It is probably the true equivalent of the Four Foot Coal of Devon and the two seams which occur next below it in this area are probably the Diamond and Jewel. An unnamed coal varying in thickness from 18 to 22 in has been recorded between the 'Four Foot' and Upper Five Foot Coals: it probably represents the lower leaf of the Upper Five Foot Coal at Devon.

Upper Five Foot Coal. The Upper Five Foot Coal is 48 to 50 in thick in the Craigie–Forthbank area and 32 to 34 in thick at Whinhall, near Alloa. Northwards from Whinhall it is joined progressively by lower seams. Thus the unnamed coal at Whinhall mentioned above forms the lower of the two leaves (totalling 72 to 96 in) of the Upper Five Foot Coal at Devon, whilst at Harviestoun the four or five leaves of the coal (totalling 91 to 110 in) include the equivalent of the Four Foot as well.

Upper Five Foot to Forty Inch Coal. In the Main and Harviestoun basins the strata between the Upper Five Foot and Forty Inch coals are 20 to 30 ft thick, and consist of sandstone with, at the base, a bed of mudstone with ironstone bands and a rich mussel fauna. Little is known of the equivalent measures farther south.

Forty Inch or Three Foot Coal. The Forty Inch Coal takes its name from its section in the old Devon (Furnacebank) Colliery, but is usually about 33 in thick in the Main Basin and 32 to 36 in thick at Harviestoun. It is correlated with a 17-in coal which occurs 24 ft above the Upper Five Foot Coal in Hilton No. 5 Bore and with a seam 12 ft above that coal in Bowhouse No. 4 Bore.

Forty Inch Coal to Yard, or Upper Three Foot, Coal. The Yard Coal is separated from the Forty Inch Coal by about 70 ft of mainly sandy strata, preserved only in the Main and Harviestoun basins. About 30 ft above the Forty Inch Coal in the Meta Pit and Mine there is a thin coal overlain by a bed of pale-grey mudstone with red hematitized ironstone bands. This bed contains a rich mussel fauna. The thin coal is missing at Harviestoun but the mussel band occurs there in Harviestoun No. 4 Bore and crops out in Blackhornduff Burn 130 yd south of the Harviestoun Home Farm–Whitehill-head road. It is also exposed in the next stream to the west at a locality 110 yd south of the same road. Fossils obtained from exposures in the Kelly Burn at the centre of the Dollar Basin show some agreement with the fauna of this mussel band but the measures above the Queenslie Marine Band are not well enough known at Dollar to ensure the correlation.

Yard, or Upper Three Foot, Coal. The Yard Coal is 44 in thick in the Meta Pit and 30 inches in the Devon Pit. At Harviestoun No. 4 Bore its thickness is 33 in.

Yard Coal to the base of the Devon Red Sandstone. A rich mussel band has been recorded in the roof of the Yard Coal both at the Meta Pit and at Harviestoun. About 20 ft above the Yard Coal at the Meta Mine there are two thin coals; both are overlain by mussel bands but neither the coals nor the mussels persist into the Harviestoun Basin. Some 20 ft higher in the Main Basin there is a group of three coals. The lowest of these has been worked locally as the Two Foot Coal; it lies 42 ft above the Yard Coal and 60 ft below the base of the Devon Red Sandstone. This group of three coals is represented at Harviestoun by two coals, 15 and 18 in thick, separated by 27 in of siltstone.

Devon Red Sandstone and Upper Coal Measures. The Devon Red Sandstone, which crops out near Devon Colliery, was formerly regarded as Upper ('Barren Red') Coal Measures lying unconformably on the older ('Productive') measures (Haldane 1925). Evidence subsequently advanced (Francis 1956, pp. 24–5, 30–1) runs counter to the concept of unconformity and suggests that the Devon Red Sandstone should be regarded as equivalent to the thick red sandstones which occur between the highest workable coal and Skipsey's Marine Band in the Coatbridge area (Clough and others 1926, p. 84) and in east Fife (Knox 1954, pp. 113–4). The sandstone is 120 ft thick in the Main Basin; at Harviestoun it is not completely represented. Although these beds are the highest seen in Clackmannanshire it is estimated that there are 600 to 700 ft of strata younger than the Devon Red Sandstone concealed beneath the 'buried channel' of the River Devon in the centre of the Main Basin. In that area, therefore, it is likely that some beds belonging to the Upper Coal Measures do occur and by analogy with the successions at Coatbridge and in east Fife their base has been drawn on the maps at 250 ft above the base of the Devon Red Sandstone.

OXIDATION OF GREY COAL MEASURES AT HARVIESTOUN

The first of the borings sunk near the centre of the basin at Harviestoun in 1954 encountered a group of intensely reddened strata devoid of coal seams, but containing four mussel bands indicative of the lower part of the *Anthracosia similis–Anthraconaia pulchra* Zone. Lithologically the group was so unlike the well-known succession beneath the Devon Red Sandstone that it was interpreted as being younger (Francis 1956, p. 24, figs. 8 and 10).

More recently Nos. 18 and 19 bores have shown that some of the coals beneath the Devon Red Sandstone become partly or wholly replaced by limestone and that the replacement is closely associated with reddening as it is in Ayrshire (Mykura 1960). This suggests possible alternatives to the concept of sequence and structure previously advanced.

No. 18 Bore, 115 yd west of No. 1 Bore (Figs. 23, 24), starts just above the base of the Devon Red Sandstone and continues through the Two Foot and Yard coals, with interbedded red and purple sandstones and siltstones. Analysis of the Two Foot Coal shows no abnormality. By contrast the Forty Inch Coal is missing and its position occupied by an 8-in limestone which is mainly buff-coloured, with red streaks. In thin section (S 42621) it is seen to consist of finely granular calcite with patches of platy dolomite and remnants of coal, many of them hematitized (*cf*. Mykura 1960, p. 83, plate v, fig. b). The limestone is immediately overlain by red sandstone which, at other localities, forms the roof of the coal also. In this bore the sandstone is traversed by veins of calcite dipping at 45° (the dip of the bedding is 18°). Lower in the bore the Upper Five Foot Coal, showing evidence of partial replacement by carbonate, has the following section: hard coal with lenses of grey carbonate 33 in, on sandstone 3 in, friable coal with carbonate veinlets 28 in, seatclay 2 in, hard coal with

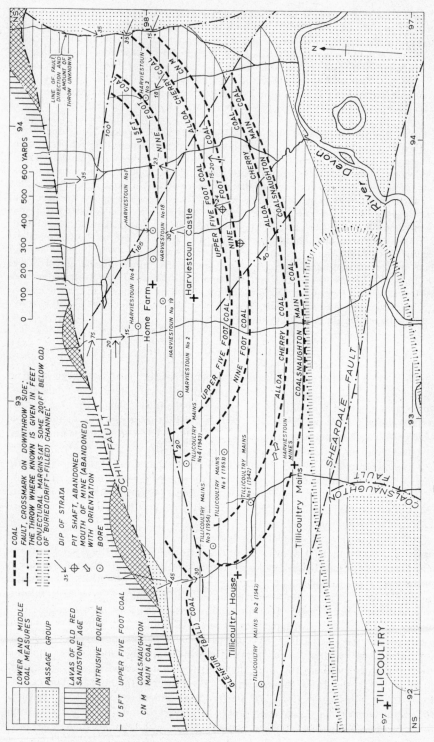

FIG. 23. *Geological map of Harviestoun Basin*

lenses of carbonate 10 in, cone-in-cone limestone 2 in, coal with inferior bands 29 in. According to the analyses made by the Coal Survey Laboratory of the National Coal Board the ash content of the leaves of the seam ranges from 11·5 to 16·9 per cent., averaging 15 per cent. for the whole seam excluding partings. The CO_2 value for the seam is 5·65 per cent., equivalent to about 10 per cent. $CaCO_3$. A thin section made from the top leaf (S 42622) shows the grey streaks to comprise a mosaic of fine platy calcite partly replacing cellular structures in the coal (cf. Mykura 1960, p. 92, plate vi, fig. a). The cone-in-cone limestone (S 42623) consists of fibrous carbonate aligned parallel to the surfaces of the cones which are 0·5 to 4·0 mm high. Fragments of coal, apparently broken and displaced during carbonate formation, appear between cones and also between layers of cones (cf. Mykura 1960, p. 94). The 16-in Diamond Seam (S 42624), 18 ft below the Upper Five Foot Coal, also contains wedges of grey carbonate causing cellular replacement of the coal (cf. Mykura 1960, p. 93, plate vi, fig. c). The replacement is similar to that of the Upper Five Foot Coal but is locally more advanced, though the seam as a whole has a lower ash content (12·7 per cent.) and a lower CO_2 value (1·74 per cent.). The Jewel and Nine Foot coals are cut out by a fault which has a calculated displacement of 185 ft. In contrast to the red strata above the fault those below are grey and the associated coals show no unusual features.

In No. 19 Bore there is an unbroken succession beginning in the Devon Red Sandstone and continuing down to the Nine Foot Coal. Above the Forty Inch Coal the strata are red, but below they are mainly grey with only occasional red patches. The Forty Inch is normal, but the Two Foot Coal is represented by a soft, friable, buff-coloured limestone 2 in thick. It consists (S 43161) of calcite, mainly finely granular, but also in platy aggregates, and is streaked through with black and brown remnants of coal. Lower in the bore, between the Yard and Forty Inch coals, two half-inch ribs of beefy limestone separated by an inch of sandstone occur in a coal position underlain by seatclay and overlain by a mussel band (Fig. 24). The limestone (S 43162) comprises a fine mosaic of calcite in contact with, and penetrating, the median sandstone. Streaks of carbonaceous material in the carbonate appear to represent unaltered coal. No other coal or limestone has been recorded at this position in Harviestoun bores, but an unnamed seam, 6 in thick, occurs there in the abandoned Meta Pit farther west. Local sequence and structure, as originally interpreted from Harviestoun No. 1 Bore (Francis 1956, p. 24, fig. 8), may be reconsidered in the light of the new evidence. In No. 1 Bore the highest 150 ft of strata, containing a fauna of lower similis–pulchra Zone age, were so reddened and so different from the known coal-bearing succession as to have been considered younger than the Devon Red Sandstone. The implication, therefore, was that the sandstone too must belong to the lower part of the similis–pulchra Zone and that the fault lower in the bore (as shown in Francis 1956, fig. 8) must have a displacement of about 300 ft. This interpretation may still be correct if it is assumed that the 300-ft fault has split into two components between Nos. 1 and 18 bores and that only one component appears in the latter bore.

An alternative interpretation is that the fault in No. 1 Bore is the same 185-ft fracture as that proved in No. 18 Bore. If so the 150 ft of strata at the top of No. 1 Bore should be equated with the measures between the Forty Inch Coal and the Devon Red Sandstone, though the lithology and distribution of fossil bands do not fit very well. Still another alternative is that the 185-ft fault in

No. 18 Bore does not cut No. 1 Bore at all and that the topmost 150 ft of reddened strata in the latter represent a completely oxidized sequence in which the thick Nine Foot, Upper Five Foot and Forty Inch coals have been destroyed. This fits the distribution of mussel bands better, though it is still not entirely satisfactory.

These alternatives weaken, but do not invalidate, the case for assigning the Devon Red Sandstone to the lower part of the *similis–pulchra* Zone of the Middle

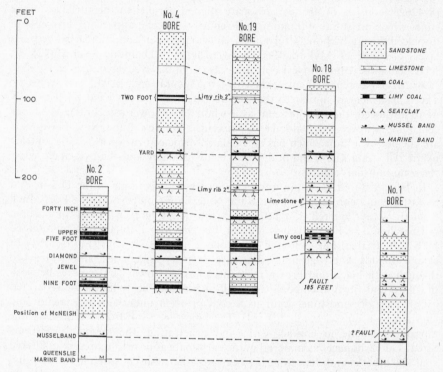

FIG. 24. *Comparative vertical sections showing distribution of coals altered to limestone at Harviestoun*

Coal Measures and the grounds for disregarding the supposed unconformity at the base of the sandstone are unshaken. In this connexion it may be noted that the alteration to limestone of the Two Foot Coal in No. 19 Bore supports the contention (Francis 1956, p. 25) that the 'burning' of that seam 2 miles to the south-west in the Main Basin of the Clackmannan Coalfield is related to reddening.   E.H.F.

REFERENCES

CLOUGH, C. T., HINXMAN, L. W., WRIGHT, W. B., ANDERSON, E. M. and CARRUTHERS, R. G. 1926. The economic geology of the Central Coalfield of Scotland, Area V. 2nd edit. with additions by MACGREGOR, M. *Mem. geol. Surv. Gt Br.*

DINHAM, C. H. and HALDANE, D. 1932. The economic geology of the Stirling and Clackmannan Coalfield. *Mem. geol. Surv. Gt Br.*

FRANCIS, E. H. 1956. The economic geology of the Stirling and Clackmannan Coalfield, Scotland: Area north of the River Forth. *Coalfld Pap. geol. Surv.*, No. 1.

HALDANE, D. 1925. The stratigraphical relations between the Devon Red Sandstone (probable Barren Red Measures) and the Productive Coal Measures of Clackmannanshire. *Mem. geol. Surv. Summ. Prog.* for 1924, 138–43.

HINXMAN, L. W., CRAMPTON, C. B., ANDERSON, E. M. and MACGREGOR, M. 1917. The economic geology of the Central Coalfield of Scotland, Area II. *Mem. geol. Surv. Gt Br.*

KNOX, J. 1954. The economic geology of the Fife coalfields, Area III. *Mem. geol. Surv. Gt Br.*

MACGREGOR, A. G. 1960. Divisions of the Carboniferous on Geological Survey Scottish maps. *Bull. geol. Surv. Gt Br.*, No. 16, 127–30.

MYKURA, W. 1960. The replacement of coal by limestone and the reddening of Coal Measures in the Ayrshire Coalfield. *Bull. geol. Surv. Gt Br.*, No. 16, 69–109.

READ, W. A. 1959. The economic geology of the Stirling and Clackmannan Coalfield, Scotland: Area south of the River Forth. *Coalfld Pap. geol. Surv.*, No. 2.

Chapter XV

CARBONIFEROUS–PERMIAN INTRUSIONS

INTRODUCTION

IN ADDITION to those intrusive rocks which are penecontemporaneous with the eruptive volcanic episodes described in previous chapters there are in this area, as elsewhere in the Midland Valley of Scotland, two important groups of basic intrusions. One consists of teschenite with basanitic variants, the other is represented by quartz-dolerite and tholeiite.

The teschenitic rocks are restricted to the south-eastern margin of the district where they form a sill-complex: dykes of this rock type are unknown locally. The quartz-dolerites and tholeiites are found throughout the district and take the form of a sill-complex, fault-intrusions and dykes. There is no direct evidence on the ages of the two rock types, but since the teschenites described here are not known to cut strata younger than Upper Limestone Group it is assumed that they are Carboniferous in age. Moreover, the highest level at which they are found (about the Orchard Limestone position) is only a little below the highest pyroclastic horizon (about the position of the Plean limestones). This lends support to Flett's (1931, p. 44) correlation between intrusion of teschenite and eruptive activity; a possible mechanism which might account for such a relationship has been suggested by Francis (1968). On stratigraphical evidence the quartz-dolerites and tholeiites have long been regarded as late Carboniferous or early Permian in age. Modern isotopic work on the co-magmatic Whin Sill of northern England supports this view without adding precision to it. Thus Holmes's (1959, p. 199) recalculated age of 280 m.y. agrees with Miller and Mussett's (1963) average figure of 281 m.y. and corresponds with the most recent estimate (Francis and Woodland 1964) of the Carboniferous–Permian boundary, whereas Fitch and Miller (1964, p. 169) by selective use of the same data infer an early Stephanian age of 295 ± 19 m.y.

TESCHENITE SILL-COMPLEX

In west Fife, towards the south-east margin of the district, teschenite and basanite have been intruded at various horizons in the Limestone Coal Group and Upper Limestone Group. Despite differences in horizon only one intrusion or intrusion-complex is involved. It reaches a maximum known thickness of 120 to 160 feet in the area between Valleyfield, Blairhall and Comrie collieries. One of the off-shoot sills is shown on borehole evidence to crop out south of Blairhall Colliery, but the main body of the intrusion crops out north of New Mills, in the Kinross (40) Sheet, to the east of the district described here. In general the teschenites are the coarser rocks forming the bulk of the thicker intrusions, while the basanites occur as fine-grained marginal rocks and as thin off-shoot sills.

QUARTZ-DOLERITE AND THOLEIITE SILLS AND DYKES

It is generally accepted that the quartz-dolerite sills of the Midland Valley are genetically connected with those dykes of quartz-dolerite and allied tholeiitic rocks which are aligned on approximately east–west lines. Moreover, to the south of the area described here at least one of the dykes is known to be a feeder to a sill (Clough and others 1925, p. 150). Around Stirling, however, the dykes and sills are geographically separate. The dykes cut Dalradian and Lower Old Red Sandstone rocks in the northern part of the district, whereas the sills are restricted to the Carboniferous rocks in the south. Between them quartz-dolerite has also been emplaced along the plane of the Ochil Fault.   E.H.F.

Sill-complex. The quartz-dolerite sill-complex crops out along the western limb of the Clackmannan Syncline where it is up to 300 feet thick and is known as the Stirling sill. Here it is known in some detail (Read 1959, pp. 53–9, figs. 13–15), occupying various positions in the Calciferous Sandstone Measures and the Lower Limestone and Limestone Coal groups, and changing from one horizon to another along dyke-like 'risers'. Towards the middle of the syncline all trace of the sill is lost except for 6-ft and 10-ft intrusions occurring within the lower leaf of the Black Metals in two deep boreholes, and it may be supposed that in this central area the main body of quartz-dolerite lies at some lower horizon, either in the Lower Limestone Group or Calciferous Sandstone Measures. It reappears on the eastern flanks of the syncline, occupying a position in the lower part of the Calciferous Sandstone Measures near Blairhill in the north and in the Lower Limestone Group and Limestone Coal Group farther south.

E.H.F., W.A.R.

Dykes. Two dykes are intruded entirely into Dalradian rocks and are aligned in an east-north-easterly direction, approximately parallel to the strike of these rocks. A third changes from a north-easterly to a more easterly trend as it passes from Dalradian to Lower Old Red Sandstone rocks across the Highland Boundary Fault. Most dykes, however, cut Lower Old Red Sandstone strata only and follow the east–west orientation which characterizes the quartz-dolerites and tholeiites throughout the Midland Valley. They nevertheless display more local deviations in trend than the dykes cutting Carboniferous rocks in the Central Coalfield to the south, and in further contrast they have a shorter linear extent. This is partly accounted for by the fact that, contrary to the opinion of Walker (1935, p. 137), many of the dykes are arranged *en echelon*.

The dykes are disposed in three main groups. These are:

(1) Gleann a'Chroin and Gleann an Dubh Choirein group, which comprises two dykes cutting Dalradian strata in the north-western part of the district. They belong to the group of dykes which extends from Loch Fyne to east of Perth;

(2) Callander–Auchterarder group, the biggest in the Stirling area and part of the larger group which extends from west of Loch Long to northern Fife;

(3) Callander–Dunblane–Dollar group, of which the dominant member is the Drumloist–Ashfield dyke.

The larger dykes range in thickness from 12 to 90 feet, but most fall within a median range of 40 to 70 feet. There are, in addition, a number of dykes 4 to 5 feet thick, most of them in the Callander–Dunblane–Dollar group and near the Drumloist–Ashfield dyke.

Although there is no exact relationship between dyke size and rock type the thicker intrusions are usually quartz-dolerites or coarse tholeiites, while the thinner ones are mainly fine-grained tholeiites.   I.H.F., M.A.

RELATION OF INTRUSION TO FAULTING

It is well known that the late Carboniferous or early Permian quartz-dolerites are younger than most of the faulting in this area. For example, the Ochil Fault-Intrusion, consisting of seven pod-like bodies of dolerite, has been emplaced along the main fracture and along the plane of the subsidiary Arndean Fault (Haldane 1927), and in the Stirling district there is abundant evidence that the sill-complex changes horizon by transgression as fault-planes are crossed (Read 1959, pp. 54–9).

At some places in the Stirling area the sill appears to cross a fault-plane without any change in geodetic level, but only at one locality is it known to be cut by a fault, and that of very small displacement (*op. cit.*).   E.H.F., W.A.R.

It is more difficult to explain how the teschenite changes horizon on the generally accepted premise that this sill-complex is Carboniferous in age and predates the main late Carboniferous–early Permian faulting. Some earlier system of fault or fracture planes must be postulated though this system cannot at present be distinguished from the later. In two instances, at Comrie and Blairhall collieries (*see* Details), there is an apparent coincidence of faulting with change of teschenite sill horizon, and in each case there is white trap or dolerite along the plane of the fault. Both trap and dolerite, however, are too decomposed for certain identification and the possibility cannot be excluded that they belong to the later quartz-dolerite suite.   E.H.F.

DETAILS

TESCHENITE SILL-COMPLEX

Throughout most of the Valleyfield and Blairhall colliery areas the teschenite varies in horizon between the Lochgelly Splint and Milton Main seams where it locally burns or destroys members of the Main Group of coals (Dinham and Haldane 1932, p. 75). It reaches a maximum thickness of 159 ft in Valleyfield Sea Mine and decreases to about 120 ft at the shafts and at Blairhall, locally splitting to form a thick lower and thin upper leaf. One of the several changes in horizon is seen on either side of a fault in Blairhall Colliery North Mine (Fig. 25). Here a 47-ft dyke lies along the fault-plane, but in contrast to the fresh teschenite of the sill obtained in the mine to north and south the dyke rock is decomposed and indeterminate. It remains uncertain, therefore, whether the dyke has acted as a 'riser' connecting the two levels of the sill or whether it is merely a representative of the younger quartz-dolerite suite.

A less important element of the sill-complex, 24 to 36 ft thick and lying at about the Lyoncross Limestone horizon, is shown on the basis of borehole evidence to crop out under drift between Valleyfield and Blairhall, though it is exposed only in Langleas Quarry [NT 012876] farther east (in the Kinross (40) Sheet). The complex becomes thinner towards the west. In Culross No. 3 Bore, immediately south of the district, it comprises three leaves, each about 25 ft thick. The two lower leaves, separated by 145 ft of strata, lie near the base of the Main Group of coals; the third lies more than 1400 ft higher in the bore, between the Index and Orchard limestones (Plate X). Still further west, in the Righead Bore, the complex is represented by a single 55-ft sill lying close below the Five Foot Coal. The petrographic affinity of the only available specimen of this sill at Righead is uncertain (p. 235) but teschenitic affinity is apparent in another specimen assumed to form part of the same body because it was obtained at the same stratigraphic horizon near the bottom of the Blinkeerie Bore only three-quarters of a mile to the north-north-west.

There is also attenuation towards the north. At Comrie Colliery and in the ground immediately to the south of it, the main body of teschenite is found at about the Mynheer Coal position, where it is still 120 ft or so thick. North of Comrie Colliery it lies near the Orchard Limestone where it persists in an area elongated east–west and corresponding closely with the belt between the Alloa and Abbey Craig faults. Here it has a maximum thickness of 84 ft in the Overton Bore and a minimum of 27 ft at its westernmost known extension in the Parklands Bore. Within this belt the dolerite crops out at Mains Quarry [NT 022920], about half a mile beyond the eastern limit of the district. The abruptness of the change of horizon from Mynheer Coal up to Orchard Limestone at about the position of the Alloa Fault is matched by an equally

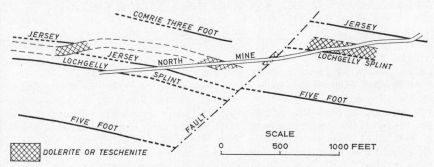

Fig. 25. *Horizontal section along Blairhall Colliery North Mine showing relationship of intrusions to structure*

abrupt change at or near the Abbey Craig Fault, north of which the sill is found between the Dunfermline Splint and Five Foot coals. It is at this horizon that it occurs in Saline No. 1 Bore (Flett 1931), where it is 62 ft thick, and also in Comrie North Mine [NT 016924]. At the latter locality, in the Kinross (40) Sheet, the plane of the Abbey Craig Fault contains blebs of white trap, and the sill, which crosses the mine nearby, was found by Mr. W. Manson to be only 29 ft 3 in thick, though it is thicker again in boreholes farther north.

It seems possible that the intrusion persists as far north as Dollar where the top of an indeterminate sill was met at the base of Nether Dollar Mains Bore (Francis 1956, p. 33).

E.H.F.

QUARTZ-DOLERITE SILL-COMPLEX

Western area: the Stirling sill. The Stirling sill, which is known from borehole evidence to be about 300 ft thick (Read 1959, pp. 54–7), is intruded at various horizons ranging from the top of the Calciferous Sandstone Measures to about the middle of the Limestone Coal Group. It crops out along the western limb of the Clackmannan Syncline and forms a striking series of westward-facing crags which extend south from Abbey Craig and Stirling Castle (Plate I, frontispiece). A full description of the sill, both at outcrop and underground in the coalfield immediately east of Stirling, was given by Read (1959, pp. 53–9).

The field characteristics of the Stirling sill and its offshoots are broadly similar to those of the quartz-dolerite sills of the Kilsyth area, described by Robertson (*in* Robertson and Haldane 1937, pp. 102–5). One minor difference that has been observed, however, is that coarse-grained dolerite with long feathery clusters of augite crystals is not confined, as it appears to be in the Kilsyth intrusions, to a zone in the top third of the sill, but also occurs locally in narrow zones a few inches wide fringing quartzo-feldspathic veins in the lower part of the sill. The Stirling sill commonly changes its geodetic and stratigraphical horizon by means of transgressive dyke-like bodies or 'risers' which form patterns of considerable complexity (Read 1959, figs. 13–15). Many, but not all, of these risers exploit the planes of pre-existing faults such as the Auchenbowie and Wallstale faults. The suggestion by Francis (1956, p. 33 and fig. 1) that the sill changes horizon along the plane of the Abbey Craig Fault has recently been confirmed by underground evidence.

More or less vertical belts of soft, highly decomposed dolerite run through the sill in directions roughly parallel to those of the major joints (Read 1956). They are thought to have been formed by post-consolidation hydrothermal activity, and their presence at a depth of some 1200 ft below O.D. in Manor Powis Colliery supports this conclusion.   W.A.R.

Eastern area. In the Righead Bore, about $2\frac{1}{2}$ miles E.N.E. of Kincardine, there are three sills, 55 ft, $4\frac{1}{2}$ ft and 159 ft thick, intruded respectively at levels above the Dunfermline Splint Coal, in the Mynheer Coal and below the Black Metals. From petrographic examination (p. 236) only the highest and thickest sill is certainly quartz-dolerite. The lowest is probably related to the teschenites (p. 235) while the $4\frac{1}{2}$-ft intrusion is a white trap of indeterminate affinity.

At Blairhall Colliery, two miles farther east, there are three sills of comparable thickness at roughly similar levels, but although the two lowest are of quartz-dolerite and tholeiite, the highest is teschenite (p. 228). There is evidence to suggest that the quartz-dolerite changes horizon nearer to the pit than to the bore. There is, for example, a 240-ft sill at the higher horizon in West Grange Bore (Plate X) and although no specimens are available this is so much thicker than the local maximum for teschenite as to be almost certainly a quartz-dolerite. Moreover, specimens obtained from a mine and underground bore nearby are of quartz-dolerite affinity, though decomposed (p. 236). It would seem to follow from this and from the continuity in the workings in the Five Foot and Lochgelly Splint coals to the west of Blairhall, that the quartz-dolerite must change to the lower horizon of the colliery shafts along the planes of two relatively small faults beneath Balgownie Wood [NS 990885]. A similar change must take place between the Righead and Blinkeerie bores (Plate X).

At Tulliallan No. 1 and Culross No. 1 bores only the highest element of the quartz-dolerite sill-complex has been proved. It is about 155 ft thick in two or more leaves lying at about the same horizon as at Righead. But farther south it lies lower in the succession. At the town of Culross it is wholly in or below the Lower Limestone Group for it is missing from Culross No. 2 Bore. Farther east it lies near the top of the Lower Limestone Group and is between 400 and 430 ft thick as measured at different sides of Valleyfield No. 3 Shaft, where both the lower and, more especially, the upper contacts transgress the sedimentary bedding planes.

North of Righead and Blairhall the quartz-dolerite sill-complex descends from the horizon of the Dunfermline Splint Coal to still lower levels in the succession and is seen again only in the Calciferous Sandstone Measures cropping out $2\frac{1}{2}$ miles E.N.E. of Dollar. Here the sill is exposed in the River Devon where it is perhaps 100 ft thick and forms the spectacular Cauldron Linn waterfall [NT 004988]. The lower part of the sill, underlain by baked cementstones and shales, can be traced southwards and eastwards from the waterfall into a high bluff in the north bank of the Gairney Burn (Fig. 12).

OCHIL FAULT-INTRUSION

The Ochil Fault-Intrusion comprises five irregular, discontinuous, pod-like bodies of quartz-dolerite intruded along the plane of the Ochil Fault between Alva and Dollar

---

PLATE X
RIBBON DIAGRAM ILLUSTRATING RELATIONSHIPS OF MAIN SILLS TO THE SUCCESSION IN
WEST FIFE

and two others along the Arndean Fault (Haldane 1927). Those exposed in Silver Glen, Mill Glen, Kirk Burn, Harviestoun Glen and the River Devon are small, ranging up to 400 ft in width and 1500 ft in length. The mass at Dollar, however, is over 2 miles long and has a maximum width of nearly 1000 ft; it is exposed almost continuously from Harviestoun to Lawhill. The Devonshaw intrusion on the Arndean Fault is 3200 ft long by 50 ft wide and is well exposed by quarrying [NT 006974]. The dolerite is still being quarried at the time of writing at Mill Glen, Tillicoultry, but working at Gloom Hill, Dollar, has ceased. E.H.F.

QUARTZ-DOLERITE AND THOLEIITE DYKES

Gleann a'Chroin and Gleann an Dubh Choirein group. The more north-westerly of the two big quartz-dolerite dykes which cross Gleann a'Chroin is about 50 ft thick and is conspicuously exposed on the south-west side of the glen, where its columnar jointing contrasts strongly with the irregular crags formed by the surrounding Ben Ledi Grits. It is not seen in place in the Allt a'Chroin, but discontinuous outcrops can be traced along a line running about E.30°N. on the north-east slopes of the glen as far as the northern limit of the district. In one streamlet [NN 639151] a small quartz-dolerite dyke at least 2 ft thick is seen 130 yd south of the main one.

The more south-easterly of the dykes is well exposed, trending approximately E.15°N., on the northern slopes of Sgiath an Dobhrain, in the Allt a'Chroin [NN 636142], on the southern slopes of Meall Odhar and the northern slopes of Tom Odhar. It is hidden by peat on the south-western side of Gleann an Dubh Choirein but reappears in the Allt an Dubh Choirein [NN 670151] where it cuts the Dubh Choirein diorite. From Sròn Aileach, where it invades the slates in complex fashion, it can be traced to the south and east of Glenartney Lodge.

Callander–Auchterarder group. A quartz-dolerite dyke crosses the western limit of the district about 1½ miles north of Callander. It follows the outcrop of the Leny Lime-stone and Shales for over a mile in a north-easterly direction before swinging gradually eastwards to cross the Upper Leny Grits and the ?Arenig shales. It cuts the Highland Boundary Fault immediately east of the Keltie Water, where it is 60 ft thick, and is exposed on the south bank of the Allt na Mna Ruaidhe [NN 653125]. It is thought to persist for at least a mile farther east, but there is no sign of it in the well-exposed ground extending for 3 miles still farther to the east and including Uamh Bheag.

A 2-ft dyke of tholeiite lies in the plane of the Highland Boundary Fault where it is exposed by the Keltie Water, and three others are intruded into the lavas on the down-throw side. One on the east bank [NN 644119] ranges from 6 to 18 inches in thickness. The other two, lying close together and following a north-easterly trend [NN 639114], are 1 ft and 15 ft thick, the latter being broken and slickensided. Another tholeiite dyke, 4 to 12 in wide, cuts lavas in a small stream about 300 yd south of Drumardoch [NN 631110].

A 4-ft dyke of tholeiite is exposed in the Allt Ruith nan Eas about 1000 yd W.S.W. of the summit of Uamh Bheag. Another 4-ft dyke of highly altered basic rock cropping out about 1¼ miles downstream [NN 667104] may also belong to this group.

The first member of the Callander–Auchterarder group to be exposed east of Uamh Bheag is in the Allt na Cuile [NN 718121]; in the Allt a'Mhiadain [NN 724122] there are at least 45 ft of highly altered dolerite which has disintegrated to a coarse yellow sand. The two exposures, 750 yd apart, are in an almost exactly west–east line, but the dyke does not appear to continue much farther to the east for no dolerite was noted in the almost continuous section in the Allt na Gaisge.

About half a mile to the east, however, a west–east quartz-dolerite dyke, at least 60 ft thick, is exposed in a runnel in the peat on the eastern slopes of Coire Nochd Mòr [NN 747118]. This dyke is seen again in the Arrevore Burn [NN 754117] and in one of its right-bank tributaries [NN 757117]. Another quartz-dolerite, at least 25 ft

Q

wide, trends eastwards across the Arrevore Burn, 300 yd to the south, but does not continue into the tributary where sandstones are exposed at its extrapolated position. More than a mile to the east in the Androhal Burn, two west–east dykes crop out. The southern, rather poorly exposed dyke, is in line with the more northerly dyke in the Arrevore Burn. The northern dyke is well exposed near a waterfall [NN 777124] and can be traced for about three-quarters of a mile round the northern slopes of Cromlet in a line which runs rather north of east. It is presumed to continue eastward beneath drift as far as an exposure in the River Knaik [NN 810123].   I.H.F.

Baked sandstone and siltstone lie close to the fine-grained southern edge of the dyke in a small quarry [NN 811123] on the slope just east of the River Knaik. Eastward from here the dyke has been traced by magnetic survey (p. 314) over nearly a mile of unexposed ground.

A west–east line of dolerite outcrops marks another dyke 1200 ft north of Beannie. This has been followed westwards by magnetic survey until it dies out just before reaching the River Knaik. A dolerite dyke, parallel to and north-east of the last, crops out 2500 ft north-east of Beannie [NN 833123] and still farther to the north-east two more dykes have been located by magnetic survey. The more northerly of these crops out [NN 853129] north-north-east of Garrick and was formerly exposed in a trench [NN 847128] north-north-west of Garrick. For three miles east of the outcrop the dyke has been traced by magnetic survey. It is exposed again, 90 ft wide, in the Buchany Burn [NN 903133] where the southern margin, trending eastwards, is seen in contact with sandstone; the dyke has been quarried immediately to the east of the burn.

East of West Mains of Tullibardine two quarries [NN 912134, 915134] have been opened in a dolerite dyke aligned slightly north of the dyke in the Buchany Burn. The dolerite in the south wall of the eastern quarry contains patches of pegmatitic material coarser than the normal rock and also finer basaltic patches. The north wall of this quarry is in indurated sandstones of the Dunblane Formation.

In a stream [NN 927135] west-south-west of Kirktonlees the northern edge of a dolerite dyke is separated from sandstone by a vein of barytes 2 ft 9 in wide. Other dykes north and north-west of Auchterarder have been mapped purely on the basis of magnetic survey (p. 314): none is exposed.

Sandstones in a disused quarry [NN 931127] west of Auchterarder are veined by thin tholeiitic intrusions and these may be related to a concealed dolerite dyke nearby.

From the north-west slopes of Blair Hill [NN 991129] a dyke can be traced over the top of the hill into the Bankist Burn [NN 995128] and for a further 1300 ft to the east. It is 16 ft wide between lava walls in the ravine of the Bankist Burn. Nearly parallel dykes on different alignments crop out farther east and constitute a good example of arrangement en echelon. The first [NO 002128] is west-north-west of Baadhead. The second crosses the small burn [NO 004128] north-west of Baadhead, continuing on a line a little north of east into old quarries 150 yards beyond the burn. The third crops out in the bottom of the ravine [NO 008129] south of Keltie Castle and can be followed for 170 yards eastwards to a small disused quarry where it is about 12 ft wide.

A west-north-westerly dyke of fresh quartz-dolerite has been quarried near Auchterarder Station (Walker 1934, pp. 113–5; 1935, p. 144). It is 55 ft wide and is intruded into sandstones.

A 65-ft west–east tholeiite dyke cuts amygdaloidal lavas in the Pairney Burn [NN 975115], about half a mile south of Upper Coul. For over a mile to the east it forms numerous outcrops, along a line about E.10°S., and is last seen on the north side of Simpleside Hill. South of the summit of Ben Effrey it is extensively rotted to brown sand [NN 980114].

West of the River Knaik the north wall of a dyke in contact with baked mudstone is exposed in a small stream [NN 825115] near Dunduff. To the east the dyke, 45 ft wide, crops out in the bed of the river and a 5-ft north–south dyke, which is probably an off-shoot, crosses the river 150 yards upstream. The main dyke and the baked mudstones south of it crop out [NN 837116] north of Over Ardoch and 500 yards to the east the dolerite has been quarried between walls of baked sandstone. On the same line and still farther east dolerite was formerly seen in a trench [NN 847117] south-south-west of Garrick.

A 45-ft dolerite dyke which is offset slightly to the south of the last has been quarried [NN 849116] south of Garrick, and in an overgrown quarry 250 yards to the east-north-east indurated sandstone indicates the proximity of the dyke. Eastwards to a point north of Shielhill it has been traced on the same alignment by magnetic survey.

A few hundred yards farther east another dyke, similarly offset to the south, has been located by magnetic survey and has been traced through disused quarries [NN 873119, 876118] near Orchill, where it is intruded into sandstones and has a thickness of about 20 ft. This dyke probably dies out about a mile east of Orchill.

Magnetic survey has located a dyke extending eastwards below the drift from just north of Seathaugh [NN 874108], across Gleneagles golf courses to the neighbourhood of Gleneagles Station.

Farther east a dyke on a more northerly line has been located by the same method near Muirhead [NN 941108]. It is at least 25 ft wide at outcrop in disused quarries [NN 946108] on the steep west side of the valley of the Ruthven Water. On the opposite side of the valley a dyke, offset slightly to the south of the last, forms an east–west ridge on the north side of a tributary ravine [NN 947107].

Still farther east, at about the same latitude, disconnected members of a dyke-*echelon* cut lavas and trend somewhat north of east. The first is exposed in the Cloan Burn [NN 965106] and in the disused quarry [NN 968107] south of Upper Cloan. The second, 42 ft wide, crosses the Pairney Burn [NN 978107] south-west of Beld Hill, and can be traced up both sides of the valley. The third crosses a small burn [NN 983107] south of Beld Hill. Dolerite outcrops south [NN 996108] and east [NN 999109] of the summit of Simpleside Hill probably mark two further members, similarly orientated.   M.A.

Callander–Dunblane–Dollar group. A west–east tholeiite dyke, 20 ft thick, follows the line of the Sruth Geal for about 100 yd a short distance east of its confluence [NN 655077] with the Keltie Water. About 750 yd further east an isolated exposure of dolerite in the former stream may belong to the same dyke.

West of Ballachraggan [NN 677065] a dyke of dark-grey, medium- to coarse-grained quartz-dolerite, about 50 ft wide, forms a prominent ridge, with west-north-westerly trend, up to 20 ft high and about 500 yd long. On the 1882 edition of the one-inch map this dyke was shown as being continuous with the Drumloist–Ashfield dyke (see below) but recent mapping suggests that this is unlikely, for any link would have to run at right angles to the main dyke trend and to cross an area where the superficial deposits are too thin to conceal a thick dyke.

The Drumloist–Ashfield dyke consists of dark-grey, rather coarse-grained dolerite and forms a ridge 1000 yd long and up to 20 ft high north and east of Drumloist [NN 682061]. It is also exposed west of, and in, the Annet Burn, where it is seen to side-step to the north by about its own breadth. Other good exposures occur along the southern margin of the High Wood, but eastwards from there the next exposure is in a ditch [NN 726050] over a mile away and almost exactly on the line of the dyke where last seen.

Argaty Quarry has been excavated along the sinuous line of the dyke for a quarter of a mile in a north-westerly direction. Because of flooding at the bottom of the quarry and extraction of some of the hardened country rock the dyke can now be seen only at the western end and at one or two places on the north face, where small apophyses have been intruded into the sandstones. The dyke is 60 to 70 ft wide and consists of dark-grey medium-grained dolerite. It can be traced south-east of the quarry for a further 200 yd but is then hidden by boulder clay for just over a mile, the next exposure being a small one [NN 750039] in the Craigingilt Burn.

In the Ardoch Burn [NN 756038] the dyke takes a small side-step similar to that in the Annet Burn. The line of the dyke hereabouts is almost due east but eastwards it must veer to east-south-east; it appears to have been quarried [NN 763035] beside the Grainston Burn where hardened mudstone and blocks of dolerite are seen. Other groups of dolerite blocks further east probably mark the approximate line of the dyke, which is nowhere exposed between the Ardoch Burn and the banks of the Allan Water.

The Drumloist–Ashfield dyke was quarried on the eastern side of the Allan Water [NN 785032] about half a mile south of Ashfield, where it consists of about 70 ft of coarse-grained grey dolerite with local pink mottling and calcite veining. The original one-inch map suggests that the dyke continued eastwards to link up with the dyke exposed on Sheriffmuir (see below). That it does not do so is almost certain as no dolerite is to be seen among the well-exposed sandstones along the extrapolated line of the dyke [NN 795031].   I.H.F.

A few scattered small dykes occur fairly near the line of the Drumloist–Ashfield dyke and may be considered to be members of the Callander–Dunblane–Dollar group. An olivine-basalt of possibly tholeiitic affinity (p. 237) forms a 3-ft north-westerly dyke exposed in the Eas Uilleam [NN 656091]. Minor intrusions of tholeiite more confidently identified with the group include a 5-ft west–east dyke seen in a small stream 750 yd S.E. of Calziebohalzie [NN 724073], a small highly altered intrusion immediately north of The Bows [NN 740065], two north-westerly dykes, 4 ft and 7 ft thick, lying close together in the Lodge Burn [NN 782055], another of 18 inches trending west–east in a small quarry [NN 789052] on the west bank of the Allan Water at Kinbuck and a 3-ft north-westerly dyke cutting the sandstones in Geordie's Burn [NN 822063].   I.H.F., M.A.

At its westernmost exposure, in a quarry [NN 815028] west of Lairhill, the Sheriff-muir dyke is 36 ft wide and cuts fine-grained sandstone and siltstone. From here it runs in an east-south-easterly direction and is exposed in other quarries [NN 836025, 837024] south-east of Lairhill. Dolerite was formerly seen in a right-bank tributary of the Old Wharry Burn [NN 849021], and on the east bank of the main stream [NN 854017] there is another isolated exposure. These two outcrops possibly mark a continuation of the Sheriffmuir dyke, though there is no sign of dolerite at the surface in the intervening ground.   M.A.

There are no exposures of quartz-dolerite between the Old Wharry Burn outcrop and a 30-ft dyke in the upper reaches of the Grodwell Burn [NN 910014], $3\frac{1}{2}$ miles to the east. The latter dyke trends W.25°N. and is spheroidally weathered at the centre. The country rock—a fresh grey lava—is slightly hardened at the contact. This dyke is the most westerly of a group of disconnected dykes, arranged en echelon, which extends for about 4 miles in a general easterly direction. About 1050 yd east of the Grodwell Burn outcrop a 15-ft dyke trending east crosses the Broich Burn [NN 920013] just below the Glenach Burn confluence. Dolerite is next seen nearly a mile to the south-east, near the head of the Burn of Sorrow [NN 935006], where it is at least 20 ft wide and trends W.27°N. along the south bank. A few yards upstream there are two thin west–east dykes which are probably off-shoots. The next dyke to the east is offset northwards and is exposed in three tributary streams on the southern slopes of Tar-mangie Hill. In the westernmost tributary [NN 943011] it is 15 ft broad, trending north-west and inclined to the south-west. Followed eastward into the adjacent streams [NN 946009, 948009] the dyke swings round to an easterly alignment and broadens to 50 ft. Occasional vesicles are seen in the chilled marginal rock. The most easterly member of this group of dykes is exposed [NN 963007] on the south-eastern flanks of Whitewisp Hill where it is about 12 ft wide; it has a northward inclination and is emplaced en echelon among crags of tuff and agglomerate. From there it follows a sinuous south-easterly course for about 1000 yd across Glen Quey and over the crest of Hillfoot Hill [NN 970004].

An east–west dyke, 1 to 2 ft wide, crosses the River Devon at its confluence with the Broich Burn [NN 911046]—a locality now under the waters of the Upper Glendevon

Reservoir. The trend of this intrusion suggests that it may be a member of the Carboniferous–Permian suite of quartz-dolerite and tholeiite dykes, but this is not wholly supported by its petrographic character (p. 237).   E.H.F.

PETROGRAPHY

TESCHENITIC ROCKS

As the petrographic characters of the Midland Valley teschenites are already well-known they merit only brief discussion here. In the district under review these rocks fall within the range of fine-grained teschenite and fine dense basanite; none is genuinely doleritic in grain size. They show no appreciable variation in accordance with geographical location or position in the sequence but individual intrusions generally show compositional zoning across their thickness. This is exemplified by the 62-ft sill in Saline No. 1 Bore (Flett 1931), where a central zone of picrite and picroteschenite, in which the olivines are decomposed, separates zones of much fresher, finer-grained teschenite.

The main feldspar is labradorite (An_{50-55}) in thin laths. Olivine forms phenocrysts up to 2·0 mm long though usually smaller. In the picritic zone this mineral is usually pseudomorphed in serpentine, chlorites or even in carbonate, but in most of the basanitic rocks it is fresh.

Augite is represented by a titaniferous variety which is typically paler at the centre and more highly coloured towards the rim. It forms phenocrysts up to 1·5 mm or more in the coarser rocks but in the finer varieties it occurs in granular aggregated form, occasionally (S 42625) giving rise to ocellar structures. Augite is usually fresh though in one particularly decomposed rock (S 43152) it is reduced partly to turbid material. Ophimottled and ophitic textures are uncommon, except in an aberrant specimen (S 41618) from the 55-ft sill in the Righead Bore. Because of this texture, and the absence of olivine, the inclusion of this sill with the teschenitic rocks is based on the identification of undoubted olivine-dolerite (S 51586) at the same horizon in the Blinkeerie Bore, only three-quarters of a mile to the north-north-west.

Iron ores are represented mainly by ilmenite, in some rocks partly altered to leucoxene. Most rocks contain interstitial analcime, either water-clear or turbid and faintly anisotropic. Some interstitial material which is isotropic and pale brown in colour may be glass. Partly decomposed nepheline was recorded from the sill in Saline No. 1 Bore by Flett (1931, p. 47) and from a very similar sill at Fordell, some 11 miles to the east-south-east (in the Kinross (40) Sheet), by Allan (1931). Accessory minerals are acicular apatite and small plates of biotite rimming olivines and iron ores.

The following slices are representative of the teschenitic rocks in west Fife: S 27839–43, 42435, 42625, 42661, 43152, 43701, 43703, 43787, 43793, 48279–82.   E.H.F.

QUARTZ-DOLERITE AND THOLEIITE

A comprehensive account of the petrography of the Scottish Carboniferous–Permian quartz-dolerites and tholeiites has been given by Walker (1935) who has also described some of the Perthshire dykes of this suite (1934) and dealt with differentiation in the upper part of the Stirling sill (1952). Other petrographic accounts of the Stirling sill are those by Goodchild (1892, pp. 252–3), Monckton (1895, pp. 480–91; 1897, p. 152) and Dinham (1927, p. 479).

Briefly, these rocks consist of plagioclase (labradorite-bytownite), augite, pigeonite, hypersthene, iron ores and a quartzo-feldspathic residuum with accessory olivine, hornblende, biotite, apatite and chlorophaeite. Olivine is commonly recognized in marginal rocks and is usually pseudomorphed in viriditic minerals. Hypersthene too is often replaced in this way.

Distinction is made between the quartz-dolerites and the tholeiites on textural grounds. In the former the augite is usually ophitic or subophitic to the plagioclase and the mesostasis consists mainly of quartz and micropegmatite. The tholeiites, however, have intersertal textures, with a fresh or devitrified glassy mesostasis, and elongated, intergrown laths of plagioclase form a stellate arrangement with granular to subophitic augite.

In general tholeiites occur as thinner dykes and sills or as marginal facies of thicker, quartz-dolerite intrusions, but there is no exact correlation between grain size and rock type. Many fine-grained marginal rocks, for example, retain quartz-dolerite characteristics, whereas some tholeiites approach dolerite in coarseness.

The pattern of finer and coarser zones established by Robertson (*in* Robertson and Haldane 1937, pp. 102–5) among quartz-dolerite sills in the Kilsyth area applies broadly to the sills described in this area, particularly regarding the location, a third of the way down from the top, of a coarse zone containing long feathery clusters of augite and pink quartzo-feldspathic patches.

E.H.F., I.H.F., W.A.R., M.A.

Sill-complex. In specimens of medium- to coarse-grained quartz-dolerite from Cambusbarron Quarry, Stirling, there are good examples of hornblende mantling augite (S 34643, 34837, 35979, 35980) and of reticulate skeletal iron ore patterns in the mesostasis (S 34731). A coarse rock from a quarry at St. Ninians (S 37759) contains unusually large (3·0 mm) phenocrysts of fresh hypersthene.

In the eastern area many of the rocks are decomposed. In specimens from the Cauldron Linn sill (S 23736–8, 38366) pyroxenes are partly or wholly replaced by carbonate and chlorite. Similar rocks come from Culross No. 1 Bore (S 48273, 48283–4), Culross No. 3 Bore (S 43529–31, 43786) and from a mine (S 43846, 48288) and underground bore (S 48286) between Blairhall Colliery and Righead Bore. In the Righead Bore the main sill (p. 230) is a typical ophitic quartz-dolerite with fresh augite (S 41513). A specimen from the thick intrusion in Valleyfield No. 3 Pit (S 43181) contains fresh ophitic augite mantled with hornblende and biotite and has patches of pink micropegmatite characteristic of Robertson's coarsest zone.

The 9-ft sill just above the Mynheer Coal in Blairhall Colliery (p. 230) is a tholeiite with abundant fresh glass (S 43700) and corresponds closely with dykes of Craigmakerran type described below.

Ochil Fault-Intrusion. Some of the coarse rocks obtained from Tillicoultry Quarry (S 37574) and at outcrop in the Kelly Burn, Dollar (S 38349) contain patches of pink micropegmatite resembling those from the coarsest zones of the sill-complex. A finer-grained rock from Gloom Hill Quarry, Dollar (S 17710) also contains abundant quartz and micropegmatite. Zoned augites and fresh hypersthene characterize other examples of fresh dolerite from Tillicoultry Quarry (S 17709, 31678, 38212) and Devonshaw Quarry (S 34730). Some marginal rocks are highly altered (S 23740, 38343) and occasionally show a tendency towards tholeiitic texture (S 38345, 38348).   E.H.F.

Dykes. Typical quartz-dolerites (S 43331, 43707, 44549 and 45221) contain quartz and micropegmatite. In other specimens the mesostasis includes devitrified glassy material, containing microlites, which shows low birefringence and spherulitic structure (S 43708, 45791, 46126). This type is represented (S 8936) in the Auchterarder Station dyke, the petrography of which has been described by Walker (1934, pp. 113–5). Rocks from the Drumloist–Ashfield dyke (S 25040, 34729) contain a mesostasis of finely granular quartz and alkali-feldspar with some viriditic material and carbonate.

I.H.F., M.A.

Most of the tholeiites fall broadly within the group described by Walker (1934, pp. 115–6) as the Corsiehill type, in which the mesostasis is a minor constituent consisting of brownish devitrified glass containing crystallites (S 40671, 43709, 43712, 44545); iron ores display good skeletal structures (S 45219). Pseudomorphs in serpentine and carbonate represent olivine or hypersthene or both. Coarse varieties (S 43710–11, 45521) contain laths of basic labradorite up to 3·0 mm long, though the overall grain size of the rock still falls below the lower limit for dolerite; the mesostasis in these coarser rocks is weakly birefringent and spherulitic.

Another type of tholeiite, finer in grain and containing more than 10 per cent. of glass, corresponds to Walker's (1934) Craigmakerran type. The abundant ilmenite in rocks of this type occurs in plates and in rods of two sizes, the smaller forming reticulate patterns in the mesostasis. Similar patterns are apparent in altered carbonate-rich fine-grained rocks (e.g. S 44553, 46780). The fresh rocks most resembling Walker's type rock are S 40655 and 46134, the former from Sheriffmuir along the same line of dyke as two coarser variants (S 40657, 40659). It is notable that along the line of the same impersistent dyke eastward towards Dollar there is a change first to tholeiite of Corsiehill type (S 40671) and finally to a quartz-dolerite (S 44195, 45287) of only faintly tholeiitic aspect.   I.H.F., M.A., E.H.F.

The narrow dykes at the confluence of the River Devon with the Broich Burn and in the Eas Uilleam (p. 234) are unlike any others of this suite. They contain microphyric basic plagioclase (An_{70}) in stellate intergrowths, abundant microphyric, idiomorphic olivine (up to 1·0 mm) and sub-ophitic augite with a little green, possibly chloritic, residuum. In the River Devon rock (S 38354) the olivine is almost entirely fresh, but in the Eas Uilleam specimen (S 43329) it is pseudomorphed in carbonate and serpentine. Petrographically the rocks have most affinity with some of the Tertiary intrusions of west Scotland which Tyrrell (1917) describes as 'tholeiitic basalts of Largs type' and which MacGregor (*in* Richey and others 1930) prefers to call olivine-basalt probably of tholeiitic affinities.   E.H.F., I.H.F.

REFERENCES

ALLAN, D. A. 1931. A nepheline-basanite sill at Fordell, Fife. *Proc. Lpool geol. Soc.*, **15**, 309–17.
CLOUGH, C. T., HINXMAN, L. W., WILSON, J. S. G., CRAMPTON, C. B., WRIGHT, W. B., BAILEY, E. B., ANDERSON, E. M. and CARRUTHERS, R. G. 1925. The geology of the Glasgow district. 2nd edit. revised by MACGREGOR, M., DINHAM, C. H., BAILEY, E. B. and ANDERSON, E. M. *Mem. geol. Surv. Gt Br.*
DINHAM, C. H. 1927. The Stirling district. *Proc. Geol. Ass.*, **38**, 470–92.
—— and HALDANE, D. 1932. The economic geology of the Stirling and Clackmannan Coalfield. *Mem. geol. Surv. Gt Br.*
FITCH, F. J. and MILLER, J. A. 1964. The age of the paroxysmal Variscan orogeny in England. *In* The Phanerozoic time-scale. *Q. Jl geol. Soc. Lond.*, **120s**, 159–73.
FLETT, J. S. 1931. The Saline No. 1 Teschenite. *Mem. geol. Surv. Summ. Prog.* for 1930, part 2, 44–51.
FRANCIS, E. H. 1956. The economic geology of the Stirling and Clackmannan Coalfield, Scotland: Area north of the River Forth. *Coalfld Pap. geol. Surv.*, No. 1.
—— and WOODLAND, A. W. 1964. The Carboniferous Period. *In* The Phanerozoic time-scale. *Q. Jl geol. Soc. Lond.*, **120s**, 221–32.
—— 1968. Effect of sedimentaton on volcanic processes, including neck-sill relationships, in the British Carboniferous. *Rep. 23rd Int. geol. Congr. (Czechoslovakia)*, *Sect. 2, Proc.*, 163–74.
GOODCHILD, J. G. 1892. Note on the specimens of calm, or camstone, and basalt collected at Sauchie by Sir James Maitland. *Proc. Geol. Ass.*, **12**, 252–3.
HALDANE, D. 1927. The Ochil Fault and its dolerite intrusion. *Mem. geol. Surv. Summ. Prog.* for 1926, 147–53.

HOLMES, A. 1959. A revised geological time-scale. *Trans. Edinb. geol. Soc.*, **17**, 183–216.

MILLER, J. A. and MUSSETT, A. E. 1963. Dating basic rocks by the potassium-argon method: the Whin Sill. *Geophys. J.*, **7**, 547–53.

MONCKTON, H. W. 1895. The Stirling dolerite. *Q. Jl geol. Soc. Lond.*, **51**, 480–92.

—— 1897. The Stirling district. *Proc. Geol. Ass.*, **15**, 152–6.

RANDALL, B. A. O. 1959. Intrusive phenomena of the Whin Sill, east of the River North Tyne. *Geol. Mag.*, **96**, 385–92.

READ, W. A. 1956. Channelling on the dip-slope of the Stirling sill. *Trans. Edinb. geol. Soc.*, **16**, 299–306.

—— 1959. The economic geology of the Stirling and Clackmannan Coalfield, Scotland: Area south of the River Forth. *Coalfld Pap. geol. Surv.*, No. 2.

RICHEY, J. E., ANDERSON, E. M. and MACGREGOR, A. G. 1930. The geology of north Ayrshire. *Mem. geol. Surv. Gt Br.*

ROBERTSON, T. and HALDANE, D. 1937. The economic geology of the Central Coalfield of Scotland, Area I. *Mem. geol. Surv. Gt Br.*

TYRRELL, G. W. 1917. Some Tertiary dykes of the Clyde area. *Geol. Mag.*, (6), **4**, 305–15, 350–6.

WALKER, F. 1934. A preliminary account of the quartz-dolerite dykes of Perthshire. *Trans. Proc. Perthsh. Soc. nat. Sci.*, **9**, part 4, 109–17.

—— 1935. The late Palaeozoic quartz-dolerites and tholeiites of Scotland. *Mineralog. Mag.*, **24**, 131–59.

—— 1952. Differentiation in a quartz-dolerite sill at Northfield Quarry, Stirlingshire. *Trans. Edinb. geol. Soc.*, **15**, 393–405.

Chapter XVI

STRUCTURE

INTRODUCTION

IN THE STIRLING district three main episodes of earth movement can be recognized, as follows:

(1) folding and metamorphism of the Dalradian rocks;

(2) folding of the Lower Old Red Sandstone rocks, accompanied by major movements along the Highland Boundary Fault, and probably by other faulting; and

(3) folding and faulting of the Upper Old Red Sandstone and Carboniferous rocks.

Each of these episodes was followed by uplift and erosion, and both the Lower and the Upper Old Red Sandstone must lie unconformably on the underlying rocks, though only in the latter case is the relationship demonstrable in this district.

During the Caledonian orogeny the Dalradian rocks of the southern Highlands were subjected to intense folding and deformation which may also have affected the rocks of supposed Arenig age. While precise dating of the various phases of the orogeny is not yet possible, it is generally agreed that the main tectonic activity took place in Lower Palaeozoic times and was over before the beginning of the Old Red Sandstone period. A detailed account of the structure of the Dalradian area north of Callander has been provided by Harris (1962; see also Chapter II).

The Lower Old Red Sandstone strata were folded in mid-Devonian times to form the Strathmore Syncline, with north-easterly Caledonoid trend, in what has been variously regarded (*cf.* George 1962, p. 21) as a late phase of the Caledonian orogeny or an anticipatory phase of the Armorican orogeny. This folding was accompanied by major movements along the Highland Boundary Fault, which resulted in a downthrow to the south-east, and probably by movements along the other faults which affect exclusively the Lower Old Red Sandstone rocks. The Ochil Fault (p. 247) may have been initiated at this time.

Downwarping of the Carboniferous sediments in the Kincardine Basin (*see* Chapters IX, XI–XIV) was certainly in progress during the Upper Carboniferous and was probably initiated during the Lower Carboniferous. The depositional basin coincides approximately with the north–south Clackmannan Syncline, which is the major fold affecting the Carboniferous rocks. Its formation is generally accepted as having been completed in late-Carboniferous or immediately post-Carboniferous times, during the Armorican orogeny.

Another major feature of the post- or late-Carboniferous structural activity is the formation of numerous west–east normal faults, of which the Ochil Fault (p. 246) is the largest. This fault, however, may already have been in existence during the Carboniferous or even earlier. These faults must reflect a period of north–south tension, presumably towards the end of the Armorican orogeny (Anderson 1951).

239

Strathmore Syncline

All the sediments of Lower Old Red Sandstone age in the Stirling district lie within the Strathmore Syncline, a major fold whose axis crosses the district in a north-easterly direction and eventually reaches the North Sea coast south of Stonehaven. The fold is markedly asymmetrical, with a steep north-western limb where, in a belt about a mile wide, the strata are nearly vertical and are locally overturned; the axial region is broad and ill-defined and on the broad gently-dipping south-eastern limb the inclination of the strata reaches a maximum of 30°. No subsidiary folds have been traced. On the south-east side of the syncline, the rocks of the Ochil Hills lie on the north-western flank of a broad complementary anticline, with dips almost universally to the north-west at about 15°, except for swings to the west or west-south-west in the Glen Devon area. The axis of this fold, which is the continuation south-westwards of the Sidlaw Anticline, crosses the eastern limit of the district at Muckart, but is abruptly cut off to the south by the Ochil Fault.

Details

The belt of vertical or inverted strata on the north-western limb of the syncline is well exposed both in the Keltie Water and in the Water of Ruchill. In the former it extends to the vicinity of the Bracklinn Falls, below which the marked decrease in inclination is well displayed: just over half a mile downstream, at the confluence [NN 654078] with the Brackland Burn, it has dropped to 10°. In the last-named stream there are extensive exposures of strata dipping at about 45°, and the transition to near-vertical dips is well exposed in its tributary, Eas Uilleam (Fig. 9).

The axial belt of the syncline is more than 4 miles wide. In the vicinity of the River Teith it extends from Cambusmore [NN 651062] to the eastern limits of Lanrick Estate. Locally, especially in the north, there are dips to the south-south-west of up to 18°, which appear to reflect the plunge of the synclinal axis in this area. This, together with the high relief, accounts for the preservation of the strata which are believed to be the youngest representatives of the Lower Old Red Sandstone in the Strathmore Syncline (*see* Chapter V).

The dips on the south-east limb increase gradually away from the axial belt: most of the strata in the Dunblane, Buttergask and Sheriffmuir formations have inclinations between 20° and 30°, except in the Braco–Auchterarder area where they tend to be lower (about 15°).

Highland Boundary Fault

The Highland Boundary Fault crosses the north-western part of the Stirling district, and separates Dalradian and ?Arenig strata from the Lower Old Red Sandstone. It is believed by George (1960, p. 43) to have originated as a normal tensional fracture with downthrow to the north in post-Dalradian, pre-Arenig times. This would account for the steepness of the hade, which is difficult to explain if the fault is regarded as having originated as a thrust in late Arenig times (Kennedy 1958, p. 111) or immediately prior to the Arenig (Anderson 1947, p. 508). Kennedy (*op. cit.*, p. 112) apparently regarded the thrust as continuing during the rest of the Lower Palaeozoic, but George (1960, p. 45), drawing mostly on evidence from Ireland, inferred that net movement along the Highland Boundary Fault 'was insignificant during later Lower Palaeozoic times'.

Whatever the ultimate origin of the fault, there is no doubt that the main movement, which occurred after Lower, but before Upper, Old Red Sandstone times, resulted in a downthrow of considerable magnitude on its south-eastern side. Allan (1940, p. 181) estimated this as being about 8000 ft in the Crieff area and at least 10 000 ft in the area between the rivers Tay and Noran (1928, p. 85). It is considered probable that the displacement in the Stirling district is of comparable magnitude. The fault is in places reversed and it appears at this stage to have acted as a thrust in response to N.W.–S.E. compressional forces which resulted in the north-western crustal block being carried forward over the sinking block to the south-east. Allan's (1940) hypothesis that this thrust developed from a major monoclinal fold along the Highland Border in Lower Old Red Sandstone times, probably along a pre-existing line of structural weakness, is accepted here. E. M. Anderson (1951, pp. 101–2) suggested that the Highland Boundary Fault might be a wrench fault and J. G. C. Anderson (1947, pp. 510–1) cited evidence which suggests that dominantly horizontal movements with sinistral displacement took place along the fault after the extrusion of the Clyde Plateau lavas and before the intrusion of the Permo-Carboniferous quartz-dolerite dykes; there is no evidence of such movements in the area under review, but the manner in which one of the above dykes crosses the fault virtually unaffected, and has sent an off-shoot along the actual fault-plane in the Keltie Water section, certainly demonstrates that no major movement post-dates its intrusion. Ramsay (1964, p. 228), from a study of deformed pebbles in the Old Red Sandstone, has concluded that the Highland Boundary Fault is 'a reverse fault of late Caledonian age rather than a Proto-Armorican wrench fault produced by N.N.E.–S.S.W. compression'.

DETAILS

In the south-western part of its outcrop within the Stirling district the Highland Boundary Fault zone includes three major components, as well as numerous minor ones. The most north-westerly of the major components divides the ?Arenig strata from the Upper Leny Grits. The middle one, the Highland Boundary Fault proper, separates these ?Arenig rocks from Lower Old Red Sandstone strata. The name 'Eas Dearg Fault' has been given to the south-eastern one: it is best exposed in the stream Eas Dearg immediately beyond the western limit of the district.

In this area the Highland Boundary Fault is exposed only in the Keltie Water [NN 645123], where the fault-plane dips at 54° towards N.40°W.: this is one of the places where the reversed nature of the fault can be demonstrated. Various directions of slickensiding in the fault zone testify to several directions of movement. Along the line of the fault there is a shatter belt about 1 ft wide into which a 2-ft tholeiite dyke has been intruded. The ?Arenig rocks on the north-west side are much sheared and brecciated, whereas the Lower Old Red Sandstone lavas to the south-east are generally less so. A number of shatter belts are seen to cut these lavas between the Highland Boundary and Eas Dearg faults, but their effects are very local and in general these rocks have not been greatly affected by the faulting.

Shearing and brecciation are very pronounced near the Eas Dearg Fault; the exposures in the Eas Dearg show that this fault also is reversed. Along it there is a broad belt of highly disturbed strata which is seen in the Keltie Water [NN 638112] and in one of its unnamed tributary streams [NN 631107]. It apparently joins the Highland Boundary Fault farther to the north-east [NN 658128]. The latter must pass through the valley between Druim nan Eilid and Druim Meadhoin, but there are no exposures either there or in the Allt an Dubh Choirein, where there is a gap [NN 677144] 150 yd wide between somewhat brecciated volcanic conglomerates and schistose grits.

North-east of the Allt an Dubh Choirein the Highland Boundary Fault apparently splits into four principal components, of which the most north-westerly separates the Dalradian from sandstones of the Lower Old Red Sandstone south of Glenartney Lodge [NN 688155]. Near the lodge another component diverges from this fault, and between them there is a belt of highly brecciated and carbonated rocks (see p. 45). Between the two south-easterly components there is a belt of much smashed and carbonated lava with some volcanic sandstones. None of these faults is actually exposed, and no information as to their hades is available.   I.H.F.

FAULTS CUTTING LOWER OLD RED SANDSTONE STRATA

A number of faults have been traced whose effects are confined to Lower Old Red Sandstone rocks and which are believed to pre-date the Upper Old Red Sandstone. They exhibit three principal trends, north-easterly, north-north-westerly and west-north-westerly. In the Ochil Hills some of these faults are mineralized (see Chapter XIX). Most of the known faults cutting Lower Old Red Sandstone rocks affect the lavas of the southern Ochil Hills: while this may indicate a greater concentration of faults there, it may be at least partly due to the easier recognition of faults in this area of high relief and good exposure, than in the northern Ochils and in much of the outcrop of the sediments to the north and west. It may be noteworthy that in the Craig Rossie area, where the exposures are good and the presence of distinctive acid lavas facilitates mapping, a number of faults have been recognized. On the other hand faults are conspicuously absent from the well-exposed sediments on the north-western limb of the Strathmore Syncline, suggesting that faults may in fact be more numerous in the lava terrain. The amount of displacement is generally difficult to estimate, but some of the faults cutting the sediments west of Braco must have throws of about 1000 ft.   I.H.F., E.H.F., M.A.

DETAILS

Braco area. Two faults are inferred to account for the interruption of the outcrop of the Cromlix Formation south-west of Braco by a wedge of strata referred to the Teith Formation. Neither fault is exposed but the course of the more southerly is probably indicated by high dips with anomalous directions which were noted in the Crocket Burn [NN 793082] and the Muckle Burn [NN 797079]. At their maxima about 3 miles west-south-west of Braco these faults both have throws of about 1000 ft, but they die out both westwards and eastwards in quite short distances, though one appears to displace the outcrop of the Buttergask Formation.

The one fault in the Braco area with a north-easterly trend is exposed on the eastern face of an old quarry [NN 793044] west of Glassingall, where it produces brecciation. This fault, with a downthrow to the east of about 1000 ft, accounts for the repetition of the outcrop of the Cromlix Formation indicated by the exposures of mudstones typical of the formation in a ravine [NN 801052] south of Naggyfauld.   I.H.F.

The distribution and attitude of the Cromlix Formation strata in the Bullie Burn and River Knaik suggest the existence of two faults in the area north-west of Braco. The first, trending west-north-west, has been detected in the Arrevore Burn, where dislocated strata extend for some 200 yd west of the footbridge [NN 792131], and also in a small tributary [NN 793129]. It probably passes between the exposures in the Bullie Burn west of Nether Braco to crop out further downstream [NN 832101] where

its effect is to bring sandy mudstones near the base of the Cromlix Formation on its
north-east side against grey sandstones of the Dunblane Formation. About a mile to
the west, the base of the Cromlix Formation is exposed in the Bullie Burn on the south-
west side of the fault and the shift of this horizon by the fault is taken to indicate a
north-easterly downthrow of about 500 ft.   I.H.F., M.A.

The second fault is believed to cross the River Knaik unexposed [NN 827116],
passing with north-north-west trend towards the neighbourhood of Braco. Its throw
is considered to be about 200 feet down to the west.

The strata of the Cromlix Formation near Nether Braco thus form a downfaulted
block which is pinched out south-eastwards as the two faults coalesce, giving an aggregate downthrow to the north-east. The dislocation must pass south of the sandstones
cropping out in the River Knaik near Braco, and is next detectable as a single fault in
the Buttergask Burn [NN 869075] near Balgower, where strata of the Buttergask Formation are thrown down to the north-east against sandstones of the Sheriffmuir Formation. Although the north-easterly downthrow is considerable (approaching 1000 ft)
there is no trace of faulting of comparable magnitude on the same line further south-
east. It is considered probable that the fault crosses the Burn of Ogilvie [NN 877073]
west of Knowehead to pass with diminished throw into an easterly-trending fracture
south of Burnside which brings volcanic conglomerate and the overlying pebbly
sandstones on its north side against lavas on its south side. Pebbly sandstone and lava
are exposed close together on the west bank of the Danny Burn [NN 888072] south
of Burnside and the fault probably passes between them.

Auchterarder area. The presence of a north-north-westerly fault crossing one of the
small streams [NN 918078] east of Bardrill is inferred from the rapid change from
volcanic conglomerate, crushed in places, to lava in the stream exposures and from
the presence of a steep plane, trending north-north-west, against which the conglomerate terminates eastwards. This fault is thought to throw down to the east and very
probably shifts the outcrop of the Buttergask Formation, although its precise course
northwards is unknown and the line shown on the map is hypothetical.

The volcanic breccia and lava in the railway cutting north-west of Pairney give place
westwards along the regional strike to sandstones of the Sheriffmuir Formation, an
effect probably attributable to a north-north-westerly fault which crosses the Pairney
Burn unseen [NN 972131] between lava and sandstone outcrops. The fault bounds the
upstanding rhyodacite mass of Kay Craig [NN 975128] along its western side and
recrosses the Pairney Burn to occupy the gully [NN 975127] south-west of Castle
Craig, where it throws down rhyodacite exposed on the south-west side against slightly
older amygdaloidal basalt. The fault crosses a small burn south-east of Upper Coul,
where it brings the rhyodacite against considerably older amygdaloidal lavas on the
north-eastern side. From the stream the fault may be followed south-south-eastwards
into the col east of the rhyodacite outlier on Ben Effrey [NN 980116], where its line is
crossed by a tholeiite dyke. It is likely that the fault continues as far as the head-waters
of the Pairney Burn [NN 988103] where agglomerate is separated from lava to the
east by a dislocation trending S.40°E.

Linear depressions trending between north-north-west and north-west on the slopes
of Craig Rossie mark small faults in the rhyodacite. One of these, throwing down to
the east, has been traced over the summit of Craig Rossie to the northern foot of the
hill [NN 980130] where there are signs of shattering.

North-west of Rossie Law it appears that a fault of west-north-westerly trend,
separating agglomerate to the south from autobrecciated lava to the north, has determined the position of a sharp inflexion in the course of the Banekist Burn [NN 995126].
West of this stream it is likely that the fault follows a west-north-westerly course,
probably throwing down to the north-east and shifting the outcrop of the local base
of the sandstone succession. This helps to account for the rapid dying out eastward of
the prominent feature formed by the lavas and volcanic conglomerate north of Pairney.

No fault on this line can be traced in the ground north of Rossie Law and it is thought likely that the fault abruptly changes direction east of the burn to pass along the south-west side of Rossie Law into a gully [NN 997122] trending north-north-westwards south of that hill.

A north-north-westerly fault is thought to occupy a gully [NN 998129] north of Rossie Law. It has been traced along the east side of the hill, where a quarry [NO 001123] reveals trachyandesite (presumably on the eastern, downthrow side of the fault) at a topographic level well below that of the base of the trachyandesite of Rossie Law. M.A.

Southern and central Ochil Hills. In the central and southern Ochil Hills the principal fault trends are north-westerly and north-easterly, with a subordinate group trending west–east. Mineralization has occurred along most faults and is generally believed to be late Carboniferous or early Permian and Tertiary in age (Chapter XIX). The west–east faults are also likely to be late Carboniferous or early Permian but are dealt with here for reasons of geographical convenience. The north-westerly and north-easterly fractures are dated by their association with the dykes as penecontemporaneous with the emplacement of the Lower Old Red Sandstone diorites, towards which the dykes are focussed (pp. 30–1).

At Blairlogie the surface traces of a group of faults trending between north-west and north are clearly discernible on the ground (Fig. 31). The main fault of this group is represented in the Blairlogie Burn [NS 827971] by a mineralized breccia 15 ft wide and at this locality it has a displacement of at least 800 ft down to the west as measured by the shift of a prominent pink felsitic sill (p. 41). The throw decreases northwards and north-westwards. This group of faults traverses the lavas, conglomerates and sand-stones at the top of the volcanic succession, and is well exposed around Pendreichmuir [NS 807993] and Wharry Bridge [NS 799997].

Another group of north-westerly and north-north-westerly faults is plainly delineated on the slopes between Menstrie and Balquharn where the Lipney trachyandesite is a useful indicator of displacement. The flanking fractures of the group have downthrows to the west of 250 to 300 ft, decreasing northwards in both cases until they die out a short distance after they converge about 2 miles north of Menstrie.

The middle reaches of the Alva Burn are aligned along a north-westerly fault which has a displacement of 200 ft down to west, but which dies out southward before reaching the Ochil Fault. The amount of movement along the extensively mineralized fractures of Silver Glen (Chapter XIX) seems to have been small.

Farther east, north-easterly faults become dominant and two are of particular importance: the planes of both are inclined to south-east, but the amount of displace-ment is unknown. One extends for 5 miles and is first seen about half a mile N.W. of Tillicoultry where it forms a gully feature on the eastern lobe of Wood Hill. Traced north-eastward it is seen to be a mineralized structure in the Daiglen and Gannel burns where it has been locally mined. The course of the Gannel Burn valley has been determined by the fault. A small parallel fault on the north-west side of the burn shifts a composite dyke (Fig. 6). The main fault is again exposed, partly mineralized, at several localities among the head-waters of the Burn of Sorrow and it continues north-eastwards into Glen Sherup which is another fault-controlled, deeply-incised valley. The fault appears to die out before reaching Glendevon.

The second large north-easterly fracture (Glen Quey Fault) is also intermittently mineralized (p. 300). It is exposed in the Burn of Care immediately west of Castle Campbell and forms a marked linear, partly gorge-like feature 3 miles long connecting the Burn of Care with Glen Quey. In the lower reaches of the Glenquey Burn a porphyrite dyke continues for half a mile further along the extrapolated line of the fault. About midway along Glen Quey [NN 971013] a north-westerly mineralized crush zone converges on the fault.

In the central part of the Ochils there is a group of north-westerly faults, with crush zones up to 15 ft wide, which are exposed in the upper reaches of the River Devon and its tributaries [NN 878026, 882035, 884038]. They appear to be of small vertical displacement. Mineralized sections of one of these faults crop out in Glen Bee and in the Muckle Burn (p. 301).

Some of the infrequent west–east faults also appear in the central part of the Ochils. One follows the River Devon on both sides of the Broich Burn confluence [NN 911046] and is now mainly covered by the Upper Glendevon Reservoir though exposures can still be examined in the south bank about 150 yd below the dam. During construction of the dam a crush zone 30 ft wide was exposed in the old bed of the river. Despite the size of this structure there was little apparent vertical displacement. It was also notable, from an engineering viewpoint, that the 30-ft crush itself was watertight though a good deal of leakage was encountered in minor parallel joints.

A smaller west–east fault is exposed in the head-waters of the Frandy Burn [NN 923030] and another follows a similar though more sinuous trend farther south, cropping out at two localities in the Grodwell Burn [NN 905018, 911016] and bringing lavas against tuffs in the Broich Burn [NN 920020] and Frandy Burn [NN 925021] before dying out eastward.

The most spectacular of the west–east faults, however, are in Dollar Glen, south of Castle Campbell. Here, in a 200-ft stretch of the Burn of Sorrow, near the confluence with the Burn of Care [NS 961992], the stream has cut along the plane of a southward-hading fault to form a narrow gorge with an overhanging wall. It is joined to the north by another southward-hading fracture which makes a gully feature extending midway up the cliff towards the ramparts of the castle.   E.H.F.

CLACKMANNAN SYNCLINE

The Clackmannan Syncline is the major structural feature on the south side of the Ochil Fault. It is a very broad and gentle fold with dips which rarely exceed 25° and are less than 10° over wide areas. The axis runs approximately southwards from between Alva and Tillicoultry, passing east of Alloa and immediately west of Airth. The syncline was initiated at least as early as Lower Limestone Group times as the depositional Kincardine Basin (see Chapters IX, XI, XII). In the northern part of the area the syncline plunges towards the north, but about four miles from the Ochil Fault there is a reversal of plunge over the northernmost of a group of west–east folds. The eastern limb of the syncline is complicated by minor folding along north-easterly axes.

On the south side of the Ochil Fault and its subsidiary, the Arndean Fault, there are several asymmetrical basins whose long axes are parallel to the fault. On their northern limbs dips are steep, ranging from 45° near the axes to 90° or more within the zone of contorted strata near the fault. These basins include one superimposed across the axis of the Clackmannan Syncline between Alva and Tillicoultry (in which Upper Coal Measures are preserved), two others related to the Ochil Fault at Harviestoun and Dollar (where small areas of Middle Coal Measures occur amongst Lower Coal Measures and Passage Group strata) and two at Blairingone and Lambhill which are aligned with the Arndean Fault (see Fig. 26).   E.H.F., W.A.R., I.H.F.

DETAILS

Two west–east anticlines cross the axis of the main syncline between Clackmannan and Kincardine. The axis of the northernmost is almost coincident with the Kilbagie Fault (p. 252), giving rise to southerly dips in the long-abandoned Ferryton and Craigton Coalfield (Dinham and Haldane 1932, pp. 153–6). Dips in Passage Group strata exposed east of Peppermill Dam and in workings in Bogside Mine and Blairhall Colliery indicate that the structure continues eastwards as a broad arch.

The southward-dipping Coal Measures at Craigton are cut off by the Craigton Fault which trends approximately along the axis of a syncline. Farther south, however, there is a further reversal of dip over a second west–east anticline. This runs sub-parallel with the Hawkhill Fault for a short distance before swinging towards the south-east and dying out between Kincardine and Culross.

East of Culross a sharply folded anticline plunging to the south-west is well exposed on the coast. Its axis can be traced north-eastwards, broken by faulting, until it converges with the Kilbagie Anticline south of Blairhall Colliery. Flanking this structure to the east a parallel syncline plunging to south-west is exposed on the coast and continues inland to a point south-east of Blairhall Colliery. The anticline is traversed by a group of north-westerly faults, the largest of which has a displacement of 300 ft.

The most unusual example of minor north-easterly anticlines, however, is found at Muirmealing [NS 998923], a mile to the north-west of Comrie Colliery. In this area a fault having a downthrow to south of about 300 ft has been proved in workings in the Diamond Coal and also in the Cattle Moss (1941) Bore [NN 99779164]: the fault is probably one of the several components of the Alloa Fault which splits as it dies out abruptly nearby (p. 251). During 1956 an endeavour was made to prove the surface trace of this component by means of an intensive programme of shallow borings into recognizable horizons in the Upper Limestone Group and Passage Group. No fault was found near the surface, however. Instead the borings revealed a minor dome elongated in a north-easterly direction and flanked to the east by a complementary syncline. Dips taken on strata exposed in the Bluther Burn confirm the structural interpretation of the boreholes which implies an upward transition from fault to anticline.

The Upper Old Red Sandstone (*see* Chapter VI) and Calciferous Sandstone Measures on the north-east side of the Arndean Fault lie on the north-western flank of another north-easterly anticline, whose axis, however, is cut off by the fault beyond the eastern limit of the Stirling district. E.H.F.

OCHIL FAULT

The Ochil Fault, the most important fault in the Stirling district, was formerly thought to extend right across Scotland from the Firth of Clyde between Helensburgh and Dumbarton to the Firth of Forth near Leven. It certainly continues beyond the eastern limit of the district but recent work strongly suggests that it dies out westwards within the area of the Stirling Sheet. Information obtained during the resurvey of the Kippen area, from investigations carried out by the Geophysical Department under Mr. R. McQuillin, and from the Geological Survey Stirling Bores (1961–2) has made it possible to plot the position of the fault west of Stirling much more accurately than before. The new evidence shows that the fault does not continue as a major dislocation west of Boquhan, about 8 miles west of Stirling, and it is therefore shown on the one-inch map and on Fig. 1 as terminating in that vicinity. East of Boquhan, the fault separates the Lower Old Red Sandstone to the north from the Upper Old Red Sandstone and Carboniferous to the south.

The southerly downthrow of the Ochil Fault is at its maximum near Alva, where Coal Measures strata have been brought against Lower Old Red Sandstone lavas. An accurate estimate of the throw is not possible but an approximate figure may be obtained by estimating the vertical displacement of the top of the Lower Old Red Sandstone volcanic pile. On the south side of the fault this horizon lies beneath a considerable thickness of Carboniferous and Old Red Sandstone sediments. In the scarp immediately north of the fault (Plate I, frontispiece) some 2000 feet of lavas are still preserved and the top of the pile must have been at a still higher level as an unknown thickness of lavas has been removed by erosion since the fault movements. The Lower Old Red Sandstone sediments deposited on top of the lavas can safely be excluded from the calculation as they were almost certainly eroded away before the Upper Old Red Sandstone was laid down. Thus the latter can be seen to lie unconformably on the underlying lavas on the south side of the fault near Monk's Grave, just beyond the eastern limit of the district, and the same relationship exists on the north side of the fault farther to the north-east, in the Kinross and Bridge of Earn areas.

The Coal Measures, Passage Group and Upper Limestone Group all decrease markedly in thickness northwards from their maxima in the Kincardine Basin towards the line of the Ochil Fault (Francis 1956). Similar thinning in the Limestone Coal Group and the Lower Limestone Group is suspected but has not yet been proved. The total thickness of all these measures in the area immediately south of the fault is very tentatively estimated to be of the order of 4000 to 4500 feet. If an estimated thickness of 1000 feet each for the Calciferous Sandstone Measures and the Upper Old Red Sandstone in the ground east of Dollar is added, the probable total for the Upper Old Red Sandstone and Carboniferous just to the south of the fault is fully 6000 feet. With the addition of 2000 feet for the lavas visible in the scarp and an allowance for post-fault erosion of the lavas the final figure must be of the order of 10 000 feet. This agrees with the estimate made by Geikie (1900, p. 175).

Not all the displacement may be attributable to the post-Carboniferous or late-Carboniferous movements. The Ochil Fault may have originated prior to the deposition of the Upper Old Red Sandstone, and probably acted, perhaps in the form of a monoclinal fold, as a control on subsidence and deposition during much of the Carboniferous. The Clackmannan Syncline was in process of formation during the Upper Carboniferous and at least the latest stages of the Lower Carboniferous. There is no evidence of any northward continuation of the structure in the Ochil Hills, and this together with the rapidity with which the throw of the Ochil Fault decreases both east and west of its maximum suggests that during the latter period the fault line separated a relatively positive area of slow and possibly intermittent subsidence to the north from a negative one of much greater and more continuous subsidence to the south.

E.H.F., W.A.R., I.H.F.

The Ochil Fault, as noted by Haldane (1927, p. 152), is seen in three places to be inclined to the south. From seismic evidence, however, Davison (1924, p. 150) concluded that the hade was to the north, i.e. that the fault was reversed. The apparent conflict between the geological and the seismic evidence has been discussed by Haldane (1927, p. 153), who suggested that the observed seismic effects might have been produced by movement, not of the Ochil Fault, but of another fault—possibly one which is too small to be detected on the ground or which meets the plane of the Ochil Fault below the surface—or by simultaneous movements along the Ochil Fault and the series of north-north-westerly faults on its northern side. It may perhaps be significant that these latter faults are most abundant in the area of greatest seismic activity, which lies between Stirling and Tillicoultry and is centred on Menstrie. Davison (1924, pp. 123–51) listed over

R

200 tremors along the Ochil Fault between 1736 and 1916, with maximum intensity 7 on the Rossi-Forel Scale. He found that the epicentres lie north of the outcrop of the fault, and inferred from the limited extent of the areas affected that the seismic foci were comparatively shallow. Between 1916 and 1940 Dollar (1951) recorded 5 earthquakes, with maximum intensities of 3 or 4 on Davison's modification of the Rossi-Forel Scale, in the Bridge of Allan–Dollar sector of the fault. He also recorded a number of shocks affecting particularly Stirling during 1940, including two of intensity 6, but did not indicate whether or not they were believed to arise from movements along the Ochil Fault.   I.H.F.

DETAILS

Stirling No. 7 (Claylands) Bore [NS 63359366] proved that the Upper Old Red Sandstone lies unconformably on the Lower Old Red Sandstone with an angular discordance of 30° to 40°. This unconformity has been traced by means of the basal pebbly sandstones east-north-eastwards as far as Settie [NS 639941], and thence must follow a somewhat sinuous line between outcrops of Upper and Lower Old Red Sandstone towards Boquhan. As already indicated, the Ochil Fault cannot therefore extend as a major dislocation separating Upper from Lower Old Red Sandstone west of Boquhan, but it is possible that it continues westwards for a short distance as a small undetectable fault in the Lower Old Red Sandstone, or that it turns abruptly to run west-south-westwards for a short distance as a fault or flexure in the Upper Old Red Sandstone. In the latter connexion it may perhaps be significant that a belt of relatively steep dips [NS 638936–630932] which could be associated with either a fault or a flexure runs west-south-westwards through the Gargunnock Sandstones south-west of Kippen.

From near Boquhan the Ochil Fault must run eastwards in order to pass between Stirling Nos. 6, 4 and 3 bores (which all encountered Lower Old Red Sandstone strata at rockhead) and the outcrops of Upper Old Red Sandstone that fringe the Carse only a short distance to the south. East of Westwood it was traced for about a mile [NS 745948–761949] by means of a gravity survey. This part of its course was confirmed by Stirling No. 2 Bore [NS 74619508] which encountered the Dunblane Formation of the Lower Old Red Sandstone, thus proving that the fault must lie to the south. The fault was traced by a magnetic survey for a further $1\frac{1}{2}$ miles to the east, passing between the Calciferous Sandstone Measures lavas of Craigforth Hill and the outcrops of Lower Old Red Sandstone a short distance to the north at Hill of Drip and in the River Forth.

The outcrop of red sandstones and green marls at Causewayhead (p. 114) has been interpreted as part of a thin slice of Upper Old Red Sandstone lying between two branches of the Ochil Fault, which apparently come together north of Abbey Craig.   W.A.R.

Between Abbey Craig and Alva the Ochil Fault is hidden by drift, but in Alva Glen and farther east the quartz-dolerite fault-intrusion is exposed in nearly every stream cutting the south face of the Ochils. A detailed account of the fault and of the intrusion is given by Haldane (1927), who recorded the plane of the fault as inclined southwards at 72° and 63° from the horizontal at Castle Craig Quarry, Tillicoultry and Gloom Hill Quarry, Dollar respectively. These readings should be regarded only as a general indication, however, for they are taken on the dolerite contact and are highly localized. At the time of writing, for instance, the plane of the fault as represented by the dolerite margin in Castle Craig Quarry does not lie at a simple angle of 72°. It makes a sigmoidal trace on the back wall of the quarry and illustrates how the plane of the fault is distorted by the emplacement of the pod-like bodies of intrusive dolerite.

A wide belt of complex faulting and folding in Coal Measures strata brought down on the south side of the fault is well exposed in Mill Glen, Tillicoultry, near the Castle Craig Quarry.   E.H.F.

FAULTS CUTTING UPPER OLD RED SANDSTONE AND CARBONIFEROUS STRATA

South of the Ochil Fault, most of the normal faults, which are especially abundant in the Stirling and Clackmannan Coalfield, fall into three groups, with easterly, north-easterly and north-westerly trend respectively (*see* Fig. 26). The faults of the first group are the most numerous and may all be regarded as relatively minor adjustments in response to the stresses that produced the Ochil Fault, even although in some cases the displacement locally approaches 1000 ft. Most of them, including all those within 4 miles of the Ochil Fault, throw down to the south.

The north-easterly faults, of which the Carnock Fault has by far the largest maximum throw (950 ft), are probably structural adjustments related to move-ments along the large Campsie Fault, which terminates north-eastwards before reaching the southern limit of the Stirling district. Like the latter, most of these faults throw down to the south-east.

The north-westerly faults are mostly small and unimportant, but include two branches from the Ochil Fault, the Sheardale and Arndean faults, the latter of which has a throw of several thousand feet.

No one group of faults can be proved to be altogether earlier or later than either of the others (*cf.* Read 1959, p. 46). On the most recent geological maps of the Stirling and Clackmannan Coalfield the north-easterly faults are generally shown as being earlier than the easterly ones, but the evidence on this point is inconclusive. The north-westerly faults are shown on the maps as the most recent of all, as Anderson (1951, pp. 34–7) has suggested that faults of similar trend in the Central Coalfield of Scotland may be of Tertiary age.

Except along the outcrop of the Stirling sill and in the lava country to the west, where drift cover is thin or absent, very few faults can be detected from surface evidence. In the mining areas, however, the information obtained from boreholes, mine sections and plans of underground workings has allowed the surface positions of the numerous faults to be plotted with considerable accuracy. The accuracy of the mapping has increased with the progress of mining operations and as a result many of the lines of faulting shown on the earlier published maps have had to be modified, in some cases to an important extent. Details of such changes are provided by Francis (1956) and Read (1959) and are not repeated in the following discussion of individual faults. In a few cases, however, informa-tion obtained since these two papers were published has been taken into account.

DETAILS

WEST–EAST FAULTS

Abbey Craig Fault. Evidence obtained during the resurvey shows that along the northern margin of the Touch Hills a strike fault throws the Downie's Loup Sandstones and the Calciferous Sandstone Measures volcanic rocks down to the south against Upper Old Red Sandstone. The possible existence of this fault was first suspected by Dinham, who suggested that the lavas do not rest unconformably upon the Upper Old Red Sandstone as Peach's mapping implied (*see* 1882 edition of the one-inch map), but are faulted against them (Dinham and Haldane 1932, pp. 8–9; Dixon 1938, pp. 426–8). The recent geophysical survey carried out under Mr. R. McQuillin has proved that this fault is the westward continuation of the Abbey Craig Fault.

The fault is now known to extend westwards at least as far as the Gargunnock Burn, where the type section of the Downie's Loup Sandstones is faulted against cement-

R*

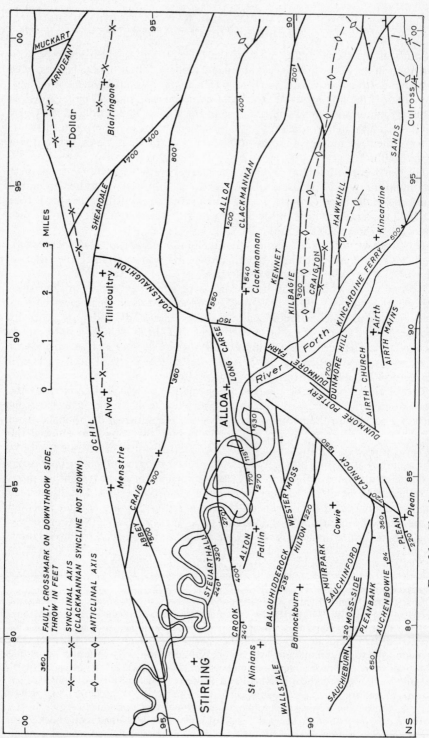

FIG. 26.　Sketch-map showing principal faults and folds in the Carboniferous strata

stones and shales. The throw of the fault probably increases fairly abruptly eastwards, for only two miles to the east an exposure [NS 740938] in the Gargunnock Sandstones lies no more than 700 ft north of lavas near the base of the Spout of Ballochleam Group. East of Craigniven the fault has been traced for nearly two miles by gravity and magnetic surveys [NS 752937–780942]. Further east, it must pass between the Ladyneuk Farm Bore [NS 80509464] and the southern end of the dolerite escarpment of Abbey Craig, beyond which it was encountered in stone mines in Manor Powis Colliery [NS 82949514 and 83039517] at a depth of about 1200 ft below O.D.; here the throw is about 500 ft and the fault plane is known to have been followed by a dyke-like body of dolerite (p. 230).   W.A.R.

The throw was found to have been reduced to about 300 ft in Tullibody No. 5 Bore [NS 85899508] and to about 360 ft north of Alloa, but in the Meadowhill Bore [NS 96169418] it had increased to fully 800 ft. During the resurvey an exposure of the fault was noted in a ditch 450 yd west of Saline Shaw [NS 994936].

Steuarthall Fault. The Steuarthall Fault has been encountered in several seams south of Upper Taylorton [NS 818935] where it has a throw of about 240 ft down to the south. East of the Bannock Burn, workings in the Bannockburn Main Coal have proved that the fault turns towards the east-north-east for a short distance as suggested by Dinham (in Dinham and Haldane 1932, p. 225), and its throw increases to 320 ft [NS 829932]. It swings to an east-south-eastward trend a short distance beyond Black-grange No. 2 Bore [NS 84059362], in which its throw is 180 ft, and joins the Bandeath Fault [NS 855932].

Crook Fault. The Crook Fault, with southerly downthrow, is not definitely known west of Stirling, but its presence is inferred and the Stirling sill is believed to have changed its horizon along the line of the fault. The Crook Fault cuts through the workings of Polmaise Nos. 1 and 2 pits where its throw increases from 240 ft north-west of Broadleys [NS 807921] to 400 ft south-west of Steuarthall [NS 828929]. Its eastward continuation is not known for certain, but it appears to be connected to the Bandeath Fault by means of a fault encountered in workings beneath Lower Polmaise [NS 834926]. This is supported by the fact that a recent exploratory mine from the Hartley Coal proved a fault with east-north-easterly trend [NS 84079268] and a throw of about 270 ft, which is similar to the throws of the Crook and Bandeath faults.

Bandeath Fault. The name 'Bandeath Fault' is now restricted to a fracture proved in the vicinity of Bandeath, e.g. in Polmaise No. 3 Bore (1901) [NS 849927], which probably connects the Crook Fault to the Alloa Fault.

Longcarse Fault. The Longcarse Fault appears as a sinuous fracture with downthrow to the south in the workings of the Hartley Coal beneath Alton [NS 845918]. Its displacement increases abruptly towards the east so that it reaches 170 ft in about a third of a mile. It continues east-north-eastwards and was proved in workings beneath the River Forth to have a throw of about 115 ft. It probably runs beneath Alloa to join the Alloa Fault a little east of the town.

Alloa Fault. This fault reaches its maximum displacement down to the south of about 540 ft a mile east of Alloa. Eastwards the throw decreases to about 200 ft in Gartarry Toll Bore [NS 93139126] but increases to 400 ft at Gibsley No. 3 Bore (1941) [NS 97759209]. About a mile east of the latter it turns abruptly south-eastwards and divides into two branches, both of which die out.

Alton Fault. The Alton Fault commences as a small fracture, with west-north-westerly trend and southerly downthrow, in the Bannockburn Main Coal [NS 81869231]. Its displacement increases towards the east and reaches 270 ft near Alton [NS 845918]. Workings on the north side of the fault have shown that it runs roughly eastwards from here, passing north of Throsk and through the northernmost part of South Alloa. The throw continues to increase in this direction and is known to reach 630 ft underground [NS 85929131]. This fault continues north of the River Forth as the Clackmannan Fault.

Clackmannan Fault. This fault runs through Clackmannan where it has a downthrow to the south of about 540 ft, decreasing to about 100 ft at Gartarry Toll Bore. Further east it has not been proved, but it is believed to continue, with a throw of about 200 ft, beyond the eastern limit of the district.

Wallstale Fault. The westernmost part of the Wallstale Fault is now thought to run from Touchadam Muir eastwards to cross the Drumshogle Burn [NS 74849022] where it seems to throw flows of mugearite down to the south against Markle basalt. Immediately north of Touchadam Quarry [NS 759905] the fault throws strata near the base of the Lower Limestone Group on its southern side against lavas to the north. Between there and Wallstale [NS 774908] the fault-plane appears to have been followed by a dyke-like body of dolerite which links two outcrops of the Stirling sill (Read 1959, p. 57). Beyond Wallstale the line of the fault is less certain, but it is believed to join up with the Balquhidderock Fault.

Balquhidderock Fault. The throw of the Balquhidderock Fault in Polmaise No. 1 (Balquhidderock) Bore (1871) [NS 81079101] is 235 ft down to the south. Underground workings on its north side indicate that the fault runs from there to Lower Greenyards [NS 821907], east of which it continues as either the Hilton Fault or, less probably, the Wester Moss Fault.

Wester Moss Fault. It is uncertain whether the Wester Moss Fault crosses the Balquhidderock Fault or is a continuation of it (*see* Read 1959, p. 48). Its throw increases eastwards from about 180 ft down to the south at the southern end [NS 837907] of Wester Moss to about 330 ft about a third of a mile to the east. This stretch of the fault has been traced underground in the workings in the Bannockburn Main Coal. Recent workings in the Hartley Coal have provided evidence that further east the Wester Moss Fault turns east-south-eastwards and splits into two branches, neither of which is known to cross the Carnock Fault.

Hilton Fault. The Hilton Fault, which trends east-south-eastwards, is known to cross the west–east Muirpark Fault, but the age-relation between the two faults is uncertain. There is no evidence of the Hilton Fault crossing the Carnock Fault. It has a maximum throw down to the south of about 220 ft.

Kilbagie Fault. South of Clackmannan the Kilbagie Fault has a throw of about 300 ft down to the south. It is believed to be the fault that is known to lie between Bogside Nos. 3 and 4 bores. In the former [NS 95278957] it has a throw of between 350 and 450 ft. Further east the Kilbagie Fault alters its trend and runs east-south-eastwards. It crosses an east-north-easterly fault north-west of Righead [NS 972887], whence it continues as far as the eastern limit of the district, though with much diminished throw.

Sauchinford Fault. The Sauchinford Fault is the most northerly fault in the western part of the coalfield to throw down to the north. It has a west-north-westerly trend and a maximum throw of about 270 ft west of Sauchinford [NS 825881]. At its eastern end it dies out abruptly without reaching the Pleanbank Fault.

Pleanbank Fault. The Pleanbank Fault runs east-south-eastwards and crosses the line of the Sauchieburn and Moss-side faults. As shown by Read (1959, p. 49) it must also intersect the Auchenbowie Fault underground. Its throw has been shown underground [NS 83878731] to be between 450 and 650 ft down to the south. Further east it appears to turn sharply north-eastwards to pass into the Carnock Fault.

Sauchieburn Fault. The name Sauchieburn Fault has been given (Read 1959, p. 50) to an inferred east-south-easterly fault with northerly downthrow, believed to run from near Sauchieburn House [NS 774893] to the vicinity of Howietoun Fishery.

Moss-side Fault. Workings in the Lower Knott Coal provide evidence of the westward continuation of a fault shown [NS 80438838] in a plan of workings with a 48-ft downthrow to the north, and borehole records indicate that the throw increases markedly westwards to reach 320 ft [NS 79668849]. This fracture crosses the Pleanbank Fault but its age-relationship with the latter is not known. It may continue westwards as the Sauchieburn Fault.

Auchenbowie Fault. The Auchenbowie Fault is one of the west–east faults that throw down to the north. It runs eastwards across the northern slopes of Drummarnock, where it throws Calciferous Sandstone Measures and Lower Limestone Group sediments down against Calciferous Sandstone Measures lavas, and continues eastwards along the northern side of Canglour Glen and south of Milnholm and Craigend. Beyond the last-named place it turns east-south-eastwards to run between Auchenbowie House [NS 799874] and Auchenbowie Mains. The Stirling sill seems to have risen to the south along the fault-plane (Read 1959, p. 55). South of Auchenbowie House the throw may be as much as 650 ft but eastwards it diminishes considerably, being only 84 ft west of Gartwhinnie [NS 821869]. Farther east the Auchenbowie Fault is joined from the north-west by a fault with a downthrow to the north of about 110 ft; east of the junction the throw of the combined fault is about 180 ft. It decreases to 65 ft immediately north of Plean No. 4 Pit [NS 82918775], but increases again to about 360 ft underground [NS 83908775] (*see* Read 1959, pp. 49–50). The fault may continue eastwards (as shown in Fig. 26) to join up with the 50-ft fracture proved underground a quarter of a mile south of Whitehill [NS 852878], in which case it must intersect any continuation of the Carnock Fault that may extend south-west of Gallamuir [NS 843879].

Plean Fault. The western end of the Plean Fault was found in underground workings [NS 82368621] below Blackcraig Quarry, where it has a small throw down to the south. Eastwards from there the displacement grows considerably to reach about 220 ft [NS 82888646] and 360 to 420 ft [NS 83498657]. The fracture is continued east-north-eastwards by a 145-ft fault encountered in workings about 300 ft north of Plean No. 5 Shaft [NS 83948622]. This abrupt reduction in throw may be due to the splitting of the Plean Fault into two branches (*see* Fig. 26), one of which runs north-eastwards to join the Carnock Fault (*cf.* Dinham and Haldane 1932, p. 179), but it may simply imply that the Plean Fault dies out to the east as abruptly as it does to the west.

Dunmore Hill Fault. The Dunmore Hill Fault throws Coal Measures of the North Dunmore Coalfield on its north side down against Passage Group to the south. Its maximum displacement of more than 700 ft exceeds that of any of the other west–east faults with downthrow to the north. It is shown in Fig. 26 as curving south-eastwards to continue as the Kincardine Ferry Fault (see below) but it may possibly intersect the latter. Its relation to the Dunmore Pottery and Dunmore Farm faults is also uncertain.

A number of west–east faults east of the Dunmore Pottery and Dunmore Farm faults (*see* Fig. 26) have been inferred (*see* Read 1959, p. 51), mainly from borehole evidence, though some information on the positions of the Airth Church and Airth Mains faults has been obtained from mine workings.

NORTH-EASTERLY FAULTS

North of the River Forth the throws of the north-easterly faults are comparatively small: the Coalsnaughton Fault has a maximum recorded throw of 160 ft, but as a rule they are much smaller than this. The courses of most of them can be followed closely in mine workings. South of the river, however, the amounts of displacement are locally much greater.

Carnock Fault. The Carnock Fault is known (Read 1959, p. 52) to pass immediately south-east of Gallamuir [NS 843879] with a throw down to the south-east of about 720 ft. In Carnock No. 1 Bore (1901–02) [NS 86028900] its throw is about 950 ft. The extent of its further prolongation north-eastwards is uncertain, but it is believed that it does not cross the River Forth. Uncertainty also exists about its south-western end: the whole fault possibly swings westwards to become the Pleanbank Fault (see above), or alternatively, as shown in Fig. 26 and the published maps, a fracture with much reduced throw may continue south-westwards to join the Plean Fault.

Dunmore Farm Fault. The Dunmore Farm Fault is known to form the north-western boundary of the North Dunmore Coalfield and is believed to have a maximum displacement down to the south-east of more than 400 ft. The Dunmore Pottery Fault, on the other hand, is inferred from borehole evidence (*see* Read 1959, p. 52).

E.H.F., W.A.R.

NORTH-WESTERLY FAULTS

Balmenoch Burn Fault. The Balmenoch Burn Fault is grouped for convenience with the faults of north-westerly trend although it runs more nearly north-north-west. On the northern scarp of the Fintry Hills [NS 637903] it displaces the Skiddaw sill and the overlying lavas by about 100 ft down to the east-north-east. From here it may be traced by air photographs across the dip slope of the Fintry Hills to the head of the Balmenoch Burn. On the southern scarp of the Fintry Hills the exposures of bole and highly weathered lava in the Slackgun Interbasaltic Beds are seen to be faulted against trap features of microporphyritic basalt a short distance east of the burn and air photographs reveal that the alignment of the fault corresponds with that of the fracture in the northern scarp.

W.A.R.

Arndean Fault. The Arndean Fault diverges southwards from the Ochil Fault [NS 981991] and throws Passage Group and highest Upper Limestone Group strata down to the south-west against Calciferous Sandstone Measures and Upper Old Red Sandstone. Its trend is E.40°S. and the amount of the throw is certainly in excess of 3000 ft and possibly approaches 4000 ft. The fault is exposed in the River Devon [NS 990984], where it is seen to consist of a number of fractures in a crush zone 100 ft wide. Other, presumably associated, fractures occur for about a further 250 ft downstream.

Sheardale Fault. The Sheardale Fault diverges from the Ochil Fault near Tillicoultry and is joined at Sheardale by a south-easterly fracture proved to have a 185-ft displacement in the Harviestoun Coalfield (p. 223). Near the junction the combined fault has a throw of about 700 ft down to the south-west. South-east from Sheardale changes have been made in the mapped course of the fault as a result of recent borings sunk to the west of Saline, in the Kinross (40) Sheet. It is now clear that the trend is to the south-east rather than east-south-east and that the fault joins with the Abbey Craig Fault, not with the fracture recorded in the Roughcleugh Burn (Francis 1956, p. 31). The displacement of the latter is now thought to be insignificant.

E.H.F.

Kincardine Ferry Fault. Whether or not the Kincardine Ferry Fault is a continuation of the west–east Dunmore Hill Fault is uncertain (see above). The former is believed to follow a south-easterly line below the River Forth near Kincardine and to separate the Airth and Kincardine coalfields. It has a throw of 600 ft in Tulliallan No. 2 Bore [NS 93818681] and 450 ft in Culross No. 1 Bore [NS 96428596].

E.H.F., W.A.R.

REFERENCES

ANDERSON, E. M. 1951. *The dynamics of faulting*. 2nd edit. Edinburgh.

ANDERSON, J. G. C. 1947. The geology of the Highland Border: Stonehaven to Arran. *Trans. R. Soc. Edinb.*, **61**, 479–515.

ALLAN, D. A. 1928. The geology of the Highland Border from Tayside to Noranside. *Trans. R. Soc. Edinb.*, **56**, 57–88.

—— 1940. The geology of the Highland Border from Glen Almond to Glen Artney. *Trans. R. Soc. Edinb.*, **60**, 171–93.

DAVISON, C. 1924. *A history of British earthquakes*. Cambridge.

DINHAM, C. H. and HALDANE, D. 1932. The economic geology of the Stirling and Clackmannan Coalfield. *Mem. geol. Surv. Gt Br*.

DIXON, C. G. 1938. The geology of the Fintry, Gargunnock and Touch Hills. *Geol. Mag.*, **75**, 425–32.

DOLLAR, A. T. J. 1951. Catalogue of Scottish earthquakes, 1916–1949. *Trans. geol. Soc. Glasg.*, **21**, 283–361.

FRANCIS, E. H. 1956. The economic geology of the Stirling and Clackmannan Coalfield, Scotland: Area north of the River Forth. *Coalfld Pap. geol. Surv.*, No. 1.

GEIKIE, A. 1900. The geology of central and western Fife and Kinross. *Mem. geol. Surv. Gt Br.*

GEORGE, T. N. 1960. The stratigraphical evolution of the Midland Valley. *Trans. geol. Soc. Glasg.*, **24**, 32–107.

—— 1962. *in* COE, K. (*editor*). *Some aspects of the Variscan fold belt.* Manchester.

HALDANE, D. 1927. The Ochil Fault and its dolerite intrusion. *Mem. geol. Surv. Summ. Prog.* for 1926, 147–53.

HARRIS, A. L. 1962. Dalradian geology of the Highland Border near Callander. *Bull. geol. Surv. Gt Br.*, No. 19, 1–15.

KENNEDY, W. Q. 1958. The tectonic evolution of the Midland Valley of Scotland. *Trans. geol. Soc. Glasg.*, **23**, 106–33.

RAMSAY, D. M. 1964. Deformation of pebbles in Lower Old Red Sandstone conglomerates adjacent to the Highland Boundary Fault. *Geol. Mag.*, **101**, 228–48.

READ, W. A. 1959. The economic geology of the Stirling and Clackmannan Coalfield, Scotland: Area south of the River Forth. *Coalfld Pap. geol. Surv.*, No. 2.

Chapter XVII

PLEISTOCENE AND RECENT
INTRODUCTION

PLEISTOCENE AND RECENT HISTORY

MOST of the glacial deposits in the Stirling district are believed to be no older than the Weichsel drifts of North Germany. The effects of older Pleistocene glaciations cannot be distinguished and no interglacial deposits have been identified. The Highland source of the ice is indicated by the wide distribution of Highland erratics, the ice movement being in general towards the south and east.

It is probable that the last ice-sheet completely to envelop the area under description also covered most of central Scotland. The distribution and form of subsequent retreat features, which may perhaps be assigned to more than one phase of deglaciation separated by ice readvance, indicate eastward escape of meltwater and westward ice-front recession.

Drumlin alignment suggests that in general the bottom ice followed the lines of the major valleys. Thus in the Teith valley and on the Teith–Forth interfluve the flow was dominantly to the east or east-south-east. On the southern slopes of Strathearn near Auchterarder it was towards the east-north-east. In the south-western part of the district the flow of bottom ice was split by the escarpment of the Fintry Hills so that part flowed south-eastwards up the Endrick valley and part east-north-eastwards and eastwards along the foot of the lava scarp of the Gargunnock Hills. East of the constriction in the Forth valley at Stirling the bottom ice fanned out, flowing south-eastwards on the south side of the valley and eastwards on the north side.

Erratic blocks and glacial striae indicate that the direction of flow at higher levels in the ice-sheet may have differed markedly from that of the bottom ice (*cf.* Hollingworth 1931). Thus in the south-west the higher ice flowed south-east-wards over the lava scarp of the northern Fintry Hills and the Gargunnock and Touch hills. Similarly, a south-easterly direction of ice movement over high ground south-east of Auchterarder (p. 269) differs considerably from that indicated by drumlin orientation on the adjacent low ground.

Simpson (1933) claimed to recognize an extensive late-Glacial ice readvance, chiefly on the basis of superposition of 'morainic' gravels on marine clays, at certain localities in the Earn and Almond valleys, north and north-east of the Stirling district. This resurgence of the ice he named the Perth Readvance. He envisaged that after a glacial retreat at least as far west as the Teith valley (Simpson 1933, p. 640), the ice reached Perth and possibly extended even further east on the south side of the Ochil Hills (Simpson 1933, pp. 638–9). He attributed most of the glacial retreat features in Strathallan and the Teith valley to the melting of this readvance ice.

Sissons and Smith (Sissons 1963b; Sissons and Smith 1965b) accepted Simpson's basic concept, and sought to trace the limits of the readvance through-out central Scotland, largely on the basis of the relative freshness of morainic deposits. In the Forth valley the line was drawn at the 'down-valley limit of the irregular type of raised beach' (Sissons 1963b, p. 152)—said to be characterized by kettle-holes and other features caused by the melting of buried glacier ice— and passes near Bridge of Allan, Tillicoultry, Kincardine, Airth and Plean (Sissons 1963b, fig. 1, p. 154; Sissons and Smith 1965b). The validity of this line is perhaps questionable, however, for the change in type of topography is by no means obvious and smooth spreads of 'raised beach' deposits exist well to the west of it.

The best evidence of readvance, as Sissons himself states (1963b, p. 152), would be the widespread occurrence of two distinct boulder clays separated by thick and extensive stratified sediments. No such definite evidence has, however, been discovered in the Stirling district. In the Forth valley only one boulder clay is known west of Stirling; east of Stirling a fairly small proportion of the numerous bore records (pp. 269–70) can be interpreted as showing stratified sediments within or below boulder clay, but these sediments appear to be discontinuous and are rarely thick. No frontal moraines associated with the Perth Readvance have been recognized in the Stirling district, although remnants might have been expected to survive on the interfluves at least, particularly east of Stirling. The moundy sands and gravels of the Berry Hills, near Cowie, are largely water-sorted and it is difficult to regard them as part of a frontal moraine (cf. Sissons 1963b, p. 156).

In the absence of such evidence of readvance, Sissons (1963b, p. 152) cites 'the extensive development of outwash gravels and sands over thick deposits of clays and silts'. Although this type of succession could be indicative of a re-advance, it might also result from the progressive seaward extension of a late-Glacial marine delta (see Scruton 1960) associated with a prolonged pause in the retreat of the ice-front near Stirling.

No incontrovertible evidence is therefore known for a readvance of the ice within the district on the scale envisaged by Simpson, although there are indications of more limited oscillations of the ice-front eastwards from Stirling (pp. 270, 278). The possibility of more extensive movements of the ice-front is not excluded, but most of the retreat phenomena in the Stirling district are provisionally described in this account as being in continuous sequence consequent on the melting of the last main ice-sheet. The lack of clear evidence of widespread readvance in the Forth valley stands in sharp contrast to the situation in the Glasgow district where such evidence has long been known (e.g. Geikie 1863).

During the down-wasting of the last general ice-sheet it is probable that the first emergent area of high ground was part of the Ochil Hills. The presumed sub-glacial channels in the neighbourhood of Corb Glen, north of Glen Devon Forest, were probably cut at an early stage. Corb Glen itself carried ice-impounded waters eastwards from the head of the Coul Burn valley and there is evidence that it may have functioned sub-glacially.

A later significant stage is marked by the conspicuous gravel terrace in Glen Quey. This deposit is composed of material of southerly derivation (p. 272) carried by meltwater through the Dollar–Glen Quey gap. The height of the gap, 1100 ft O.D., is therefore a minimum for the ice surface south of the Ochils at this stage. Contemporaneous ice filling the Devon valley below the foot of Glen Quey must have attained at least the level of the terrace, 890 ft O.D. The terrace level is matched by the height of the gap at the head of Glen Eagles and it seems highly probable that the latter functioned as a meltwater outlet to the north, thus controlling the depositional level in Glen Quey. The existence of such an outlet to the north would suggest that the ice in the Dollar area at this stage extended higher than contemporaneous ice north of the Ochil Hills in the neighbourhood of Glen Eagles (*cf.* Simpson 1933, p. 638).

The deposition of the Glen Quey gravel terrace was followed by further ice-recession during which a meltwater escape route to the east was opened by way of Coulsknowe. This phase is marked by flat tops in the glacial gravels of Glen Devon, and a gravel terrace in Glen Dey, all at about 800 ft above O.D. and corresponding to the level of the outlet at Coulsknowe.

An important feature of the deglaciation north of the Ochil Hills in ground which falls within the supposed limits of the Perth Readvance was the cutting of the large Kincardine Glen channel, which runs north-eastwards from the mouth of Glen Eagles, by meltwaters flowing eastwards over the Earn–Allan watershed. A somewhat earlier esker system, deposited by sub-glacial meltwaters along the northern slopes of Strathallan, and terminating near the foot of Glen Eagles in a single gravel ridge, was breached during the initiation of the spillway.

The Kincardine Glen channel controlled water levels within the ice occupying Strathallan and therefore influenced the levels to which sand and gravel accumulated within the ice on the floor of the strath. Thus a fall westward in the elevation of conspicuous flat kame tops in upper Strathallan is interpreted as an indication of progressive downcutting of the outlet. These flat-topped kames, attaining levels in excess of the present level of the watershed at the head of Strathallan (415 ft O.D.), persist westwards to the general neighbourhood of Braco and it is clear that the influence of the Kincardine Glen spillway was felt at least as far west as this.

The channel could have continued to function only as long as the ice in lower Strathallan remained an effective barrier to southward drainage into the Forth valley. Eventually the meltwaters found their way to the Forth valley through channels in or beneath the ice and the course of this southward drainage is probably marked by the line of gravel ridges and mounds from near Mid Cambushinnie by Kinbuck and Ashfield to Dunblane. South of Dunblane there is no evidence that the waters escaped along the depression now followed by the main road, and they may instead have initiated the deep gorge across the western extremity of the Ochil Hills, now occupied by the Allan Water. The somewhat irregular sand and gravel deposits around Airthrey Castle were probably formed at least in part by the Strathallan meltwaters skirting the Forth glacier near Bridge of Allan before entering the late-Glacial sea (*cf.* Dinham 1927, p. 487). The Kincardine Glen spillway was probably finally abandoned by Strathallan meltwaters about the time the retreating ice-front in the Forth valley reached the vicinity of Stirling.

The Knaik valley was still full of ice after the high ground on either side of it had emerged. Gradually the ice wasted down and became locally detached from the south side of the valley where two kame-terraces accumulated. Later a third, more extensive kame-terrace of gravel accumulated immediately below Glenlichorn. At this time ice probably still filled a good deal of Strathallan, and the Kincardine Glen spillway is presumed to have been in operation. After the stagnant ice in the upper part of the Knaik valley had melted, a terrace, composed at least in part of gravel, was laid down between Glenlichorn and Tighnablair. (The latter is a short distance beyond the northern limit of the district.) It appears probable that meltwaters from Strathearn and Glen Artney crossed the watershed there and deposited their load on an alluvial plain with temporary lakes which were subsequently drained as the Strathallan ice melted and southward drainage was no longer impeded. The age-relationship between this terrace and the eskers that rise above it is doubtful but it appears likely that the eskers pre-date the terrace.

South of the River Forth deglaciation probably involved early clearance of some of the higher ground on the Fintry, Gargunnock and Touch hills. Northward ice retreat in the hollow between the scarp of the Stirling sill and the dip-slope of the lavas of the Touch Hills is marked by gravel spreads and by melt-water channels near Touch. South of the Fintry, Gargunnock and Touch hills the wasting ice left behind masses of morainic drift as it receded into the Endrick and Carron valleys. It is uncertain how the deglaciation of the Fintry, Gargunnock and Touch hills proceeded relative to the retreat of the main Forth glacier and to its apparent stillstand at Stirling.

The patches of moundy sands and gravels east of Stirling are thought to have been deposited during the westward retreat of the ice. The best examples of these moundy deposits are found in the Cunninghar ridge at Tillicoultry and the Berry Hills near Cowie. Sissons (1963b, fig. 1) draws his limit of the Perth Readvance close to both these localities but it is possible that the deposits there were formed during a pause in the retreat as suggested by Dinham and Haldane (1932, p. 207). As the deposits are largely water-sorted they cannot be regarded as parts of a terminal moraine. Some of the moundy deposits pass laterally into spreads of outwash that slope gently down to merge with the complex assemblage of late-Glacial estuarine and deltaic sediments which were formerly grouped together as the 'High Raised Beach' deposits. These can best be regarded as the deposits of successive deltas of fluvio-glacial outwash derived from the front of a glacier which occupied the Forth valley (cf. Dinham 1927, pp. 486–7). The depositional surfaces at the tops of these deltas probably shelved gently down from just above to just below the contemporary sea-levels, which stood considerably higher than the level of the present-day sea. Some of the sandy sediments south-east of Stirling may, however, have been derived from material dumped as lateral moraines or irregular kame-terraces, etc., in or at the edge of the ice when the latter lay east of Stirling. This material would have been re-sorted and re-distributed by streams, waves and currents after the ice had retreated eastwards to the neighbourhood of Stirling (cf. Dinham 1927, p. 486; Dinham and Haldane 1932, p. 210).

From detailed levelling of these deposits and their equivalents lower down the Forth valley, Sissons and Smith (1965b) concluded that there are at least three terrace features, which they associate with former shorelines. They also found that the levels of the two uppermost terraces rise westwards and attributed the rise to rapid isostatic updoming shortly after the retreat of the ice. An eastward depositional slope of the original delta tops may, however, also contribute to the present gradient. Synge and Stephens (1966, pp. 115–7) have recently suggested that the feature mapped by Sissons and Smith as the marine limit is not synchronous but diachronous. They believe that isostatic recovery was more gradual and claim (p. 116) that in many cases 'a series of deltas or shorelines deposited at the edge of a retreating ice front tend to be aligned diachronously on the same tilted plane'.

Around Stirling the deltaic spreads of sand and gravel pass abruptly into moundy deposits with kettle-holes. These are thought to have been associated with an ice-front which lay near Stirling for some considerable time (*cf.* Dinham 1927, p. 487) and may have moved eastwards for a few miles on one or more occasions.

In the Forth valley west of Stirling the late-Glacial estuarine and deltaic deposits are much less extensive than to the east and their margins lie at a perceptibly lower level. This suggests that the final retreat of the ice from Stirling may have been rapid and that it was preceded by a distinct fall in sea-level (*cf.* Sissons and Smith 1965b).

Westward retreat of the ice-front from Dunblane to Doune was probably contemporaneous with the formation, on the slopes to the north, of a group of sub-glacial channels and associated eskers, of which the Argaty esker (p. 273) is the most prominent. Continued westward retreat up the Teith and Forth valleys allowed the meltwaters to escape into the Forth valley along the line of the River Teith. Large volumes of water were clearly available, and they laid down near Doune an extensive terrace of outwash gravel as the ice retreated towards Callander. This terrace, at about 125 ft above O.D. at Doune, is graded to the level of deltaic or estuarine deposits at about 100 ft above O.D. at Blair Drummond, indicating that the level of the late-Glacial sea at this time was about 100 ft above present sea-level. Another large gravel terrace accumulated in the Teith valley below Callander at about the time when the ice retreated beyond the western limit of the district.

An Allerød layer (Donner 1958) in the alluvium of Loch Mahaick, east of Callander, provides the earliest evidence of plant colonization following deglaciation. The last extensive ice-cover of the district is therefore clearly pre-Allerød, but no more precise statement than this can at present be made.

A restricted readvance of the ice, the Loch Lomond Readvance (Simpson 1933), took place during Zone III of the pollen zonation (*see* Table 8) in the Loch Lomond area (Donner 1957) and in the upper Forth valley, where Simpson placed the eastward limit of the ice at a terminal moraine just east of the Lake of Menteith, a short distance beyond the western boundary of the Stirling district. By this time the sea must have fallen considerably and in Simpson's opinion (1933, pp. 644–5) it was no more than about 50 ft above O.D. shortly after the start of ice recession. Sissons and others (1965, p. 122) suggest, from borehole evidence, that sea-level could not have been higher than 37·8 ft above O.D. when glacier ice still existed immediately west of the Lake of Menteith moraine.

It is probable that the ice also advanced into the Teith valley at the time of the Loch Lomond Readvance and comparison with the size of ice lobe postulated by Simpson in the Forth valley suggests that it might have extended to the vicinity of Drumvaich, midway between Callander and Doune. No terminal moraine exists in this area, but there is a noticeable change in the form of the gravel mounds, which have a fresher appearance towards the west. In that direction many of them are roughly aligned to form an esker chain up the middle of the valley with a branch to the northern side. The relation of these ridges to the gravel terraces south-east of Callander is not clear, but it seems unlikely that the ridges could have survived if the surrounding terrace gravels had been deposited later. More probably the ridges were formed in ice which, at the time of the Loch Lomond Readvance, had overridden the terrace gravels, the latter being deeply frozen and therefore resistant to erosion. The fresh moundy moraine on and around Lennieston Muir was probably formed at this time and some of the alluvial terraces further down the valley may also be related to the readvance.

TABLE 8

Approximate ages of late-Glacial and post-Glacial pollen-zone boundaries
(after Godwin 1961, pp. 294, 308)

		English pollen-zones	Age of zone-boundaries years B.C.	years B.P.
Post-Glacial	Sub-Atlantic	VIII		
			500	2500
	Sub-Boreal	VIIb		
			3000	5000
	Atlantic	VIIa		
			5500	7500
	Boreal	VI		
			7000	9000
	Pre-Boreal	V		
			7600	9600
		IV		
			8300	10 300
Late-Glacial	Upper Dryas	III		
			8800	10 800
	Allerød	II		
			10 000	12 000
	Lower Dryas	I		

It also appears probable that ice again occupied the valleys in the Highland Border area north of Callander. A glacier coming down Gleann a'Chroin, between Sgiath an Dobhrain and Meall Odhar, may have dammed the valley of a right-bank tributary (the Allt Breac-nic) and caused the accumulation of the gravel terrace near Sròn Eadar a'Chinn [NN 632132]. A stage in the retreat of the ice in Glen Artney is probably marked by the gravel terrace, with ice-contact slopes to the north, near the head of the glen.

Small corrie glaciers probably formed at the time of the Loch Lomond Readvance in the corries north-east of Uamh Bheag [NN 692119] and below the Spout of Ballochleam [NS 653900].

The ensuing Pre-Boreal period saw a return of milder conditions. It is probable that peat growth began in many parts of the district about this time, and over much of the ground this has continued until the present day. Durno (1956) reported the possible occurrence of Pre-Boreal peat at Flanders Moss and this has been confirmed by Newey (1966). Deposits of Pre-Boreal age have also been identified, at Loch Mahaick, by Donner (1958, p. 183). Boreal peat (Erdtman 1928; Godwin and Willis 1961) has been identified below younger marine deposits at many widely scattered localities in the Forth valley, and Sissons (1966) has shown that the peat grew on an earlier surface, associated with Zone III outwash, on which he detected three marine terraces. This implies that as a result of a fall in sea-level the sub-peat surface had emerged to form part of the land surface before peat growth began. According to Sissons (1966, p. 2) the emergence probably culminated about 8500 years ago.

The Atlantic period was characterized by an extensive marine transgression which may have begun in the Boreal period (*see* Newey 1966). As a result, the

Forth valley was flooded up to a height of more than 45 ft above O.D. The sea, however, must have been excluded from part of the Flanders Moss area where, as Durno (1956) and Sissons and Smith (1965a) have shown, peat growth continued without a detectable break through the period of the transgression up to the present day. Elsewhere at this time the Boreal peat was either removed by erosion or was covered by the silts and clays of the Carse (hence the term 'Sub-Carse Peat'). The Carse Clays closely resemble modern tidal flat deposits, and contain Mesolithic antler implements, found in association with whale remains, which indicate the colonization of the area by man. Radiocarbon dating of the peats above and below the deposits proves that they were laid down between 8421 ± 157 B.P. and 5481 ± 130 B.P. (Godwin and Willis 1961). East of Stirling, particularly on the north side of the Forth, the Carse is divided into two terraces by a definite feature (Read 1959, p. 62). Sissons (1963a, fig. 4) has proved by instrumental levelling that the upper terrace has been isostatically tilted.   M.A., W.A.R., I.H.F.

GLACIAL EROSION FEATURES

The topography of the Stirling district has suffered extensive glacial modification (*see* Forsyth, in press). Linton (1962, pp. 256–7) has estimated that, over an area of 100 square kilometres on the Old Red Sandstone outcrop in the Forth valley, no less than 100 metres of rock have been removed by the ice, and there is no doubt that this figure has in places been considerably exceeded.   M.A.

Corries and deep U-shaped glaciated valleys are conspicuous in the Highland Border area. Creag Beinn nan Eun is probably the western remnant of a corrie later modified by glacial transfluence (*see* Linton 1949), a process which is believed also to have caused breaching or modification of other watersheds in the Uamh Bheag range, e.g. between Callander Craig and Tom Dubh.   I.H.F.

In the Ochil Hills the steep-sided glaciated trough of Glen Eagles differs markedly from the other valleys. In the opinion of Linton (1949, p. 10, fig. 6) the pre-existing valley here has been greatly modified by a lobe of ice forced southwards into the hills from an ice mass occupying Strathallan and Strathearn.   M.A.

The lava scarp of the Fintry and Gargunnock hills and the southern scarp of the Ochil Hills have been steepened by glacial erosion. The crest of the former scarp is smoothed and rounded where it was overridden by ice, especially towards the east; it is deeply indented by a corrie at the Spout of Ballochleam. Ice also eroded the deep hollows, now concealed beneath drift, in the Forth and Devon valleys. Along the top of the escarpment formed by the Stirling sill only the lowest part of the zone of coarse-grained patchy dolerite is preserved; as the base of this zone might be expected to lie near the bottom of the top third of the sill (Robertson *in* Robertson and Haldane 1937, p. 103) it seems probable that almost a third of the total thickness of the sill has been removed by erosion.   W.A.R.

Ice-moulded spurs on both sides of Strathallan near Braco bear witness to an east-north-eastward movement of ice which here has largely destroyed the pre-Glacial drainage pattern (Linton 1962, pp. 249–50, 254; Forsyth, in press). The rock-cored drumlins which exist in various parts of the Stirling district, e.g. north-east of Auchterarder, may be partly erosional features.

Glacial striae are not commonly preserved on the rocks of the district and the present-day lack of working quarries restricts the opportunity to see freshly uncovered bedrock. The map of glacial striae in Scotland compiled by J. Geikie (1877, plate xvii) gives a fair indication of the general direction of ice movement; this agrees with the south-eastward carry of erratics in the Stirling district, but differs in places from the drumlin orientation, a circumstance explained on p. 256.   M.A.

Great thicknesses of drift have been proved by mining and boring in the Forth and Devon valleys. Cadell (1913, pp. 86–93) thought that this drift filled pre-Glacial channels of the Forth and Devon, graded to a sea-level about 500 ft below the present one. Dinham (1927, pp. 482–3) and Dinham and Haldane (1932, p. 205) questioned this hypothesis and indicated that although depths of 330 ft and 570 ft below O.D. had been proved at Menstrie and Bo'ness, only two of the 50 or 60 borings in the intervening ground showed rockhead levels more than 170 ft below O.D. They therefore suggested that the greater depths to rockhead might be due to glacial over-deepening of the valleys, though they admitted that Cadell's concept had not been entirely disproved.

A rockhead contour map (Fig. 27) of the lower Devon and Forth valleys east of Stirling, based on all available borehole and outcrop records, shows that the deep drift-filled trench in the lower Devon valley does not continue below the drift of the Forth valley in the manner envisaged by Cadell (1913, plate facing p. 92). The map also shows that the deepest hollows in the Devon valley, and possibly also in the Forth valley, do not form a continuous channel but are in the form of isolated basins. It is noteworthy that the rockhead information obtained from a line of bores across the Forth at Kincardine disproves the existence here of the deep channel postulated by Cadell (1913, plat facing p. 92). This is particularly significant in that Cadell realized from the data at his disposal that there was no other possible position for such a channel in this part of the Forth valley. In view of the large amount of new information which has become available, Cadell's concept of deeply buried pre-Glacial river channels is no longer tenable, and while comparatively shallow, possibly post-Glacial, buried channels could be present in both valleys there can be no doubt that the deep hollows in the bedrock surface must be due to glacial over-deepening (*cf.* Vincenz 1954; Parthasarathy and Blyth 1959; Soons 1960).   W.A.R., I.H.F., M.A.

The results of a recent gravity survey by Mr. R. McQuillin of the Geophysical Department of the Institute of Geological Sciences, and recent Geological Survey bores, can be interpreted as supporting the suggestion of Dinham (1927, p. 483) that a glacially deepened rock basin exists below the Carse west of Stirling. If this is true the Forth valley at Stirling must have been the locus of intense glacial erosion, both east and west of the constriction caused by the quartz-dolerite sill.   W.A.R.

DETAILS

Forth valley. Low values found during gravity traverses over the Carse west of Stirling suggest the presence of one, or possibly more, deep drift-filled hollows elongated roughly west to east (p. 317; Figs. 37, 38). Borehole evidence further east does not support the idea of a continuous buried river channel going down to more than 350 ft below O.D. and it therefore seems probable that the low gravity values west of Stirling indicate a system of ice-eroded drift-filled hollows in the rockhead

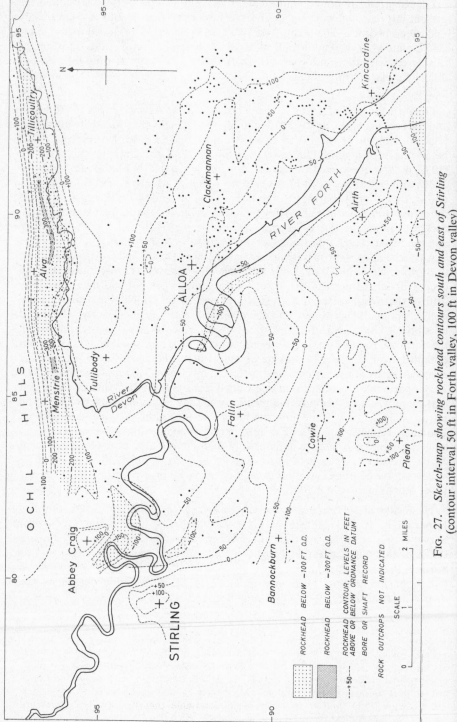

Fig. 27. *Sketch-map showing rockhead contours south and east of Stirling*
(contour interval 50 ft in Forth valley, 100 ft in Devon valley)

surface. Stirling No. 5 (Greenfoot) Bore [NS 69509614], sited near the low point on gravity traverse 'F' (Figs. 37, 38), encountered rockhead at a depth of −358 ft O.D. Stirling No. 1 (Kaimes) Bore [NS 77209454], sited a short distance east of the low point on gravity traverse 'A' and only 150 ft west of the screes at the edge of the steep lava crags at Craigforth, proved rockhead at a depth of 181 ft below O.D. This suggests that the cliff continues downwards below the drift into a deep ice-gouged hollow. Deepening immediately in front of an obstruction to the ice flow may also account for the 216 ft of drift recorded at Causewayhead, immediately west of the cliffs of Abbey Craig.

East of Stirling and south of the Forth rockhead is rarely known to sink below −100 ft O.D. (Fig. 27) within the Stirling district. In the Grangemouth area, a short distance beyond the southern limit of the district, however, rockhead was encountered at a depth of more than 140 ft below O.D. at Powfoulis and at 442 ft below O.D. in the East Salcoats Bore [NS 95138223].   W.A.R.

GLACIAL DRAINAGE CHANNELS

Glacial drainage channels occur in great numbers in the Stirling district and are particularly numerous in Strathallan and the Teith valley. Their general easterly trend is consistent with formation by meltwaters escaping from an ice-sheet which thinned away from the Highlands.

The oblique course of many of these channels down the main valley sides is strongly suggestive of some relation to the contemporary ice-margins. Most of them are regarded as sub-marginal (Mannerfelt 1945) although Sissons (1961, pp. 15–7) has suggested that the pattern of channels in the Greenloaning area may reflect control of the drainage in part by structures within the ice. In the Bullie Burn area, however, there is a group of parallel channels which may be truly marginal. These are very gently inclined and are locally one-sided, the missing downhill side having presumably been cut in ice.

Channels which run more directly downhill and generally have steeper gradients appear to be sub-glacial chutes (Mannerfelt 1945). They occur both as individual channels and as the steep downhill terminations of oblique channels of low gradient. In places they link successive oblique channels and presumably carried the waters from them directly below the ice.

In the area north of Doune certain channels have up-and-down longitudinal profiles. It is probable that these channels were cut beneath thick ice by waters flowing under hydrostatic pressure (cf. Sissons 1958).

Certain very large channels, such as Corb Glen north of Glen Devon Forest, Kincardine Glen near Auchterarder and the Findhu Glen–Corriebeagh through-valley some seven miles north of Doune, carried ice-controlled drainage eastwards over important watersheds. The two first-named probably functioned at least in part sub-glacially.   M.A., I.H.F.

South of the Forth certain deep, steep-sided channels, some still occupied by streams, were cut by meltwaters beyond the contemporary ice-margins. They include the gorges along the Touch Burn and part of the West Burn, Canglour Glen [NS 770874] on the Auchenbowie Burn, Windy Yet [NS 764895] and the breach where the Bannock Burn cuts through the Stirling sill at Wallstale.

W.A.R.

Two steep-sided channels, cut in rock to depths of up to 40 ft, commence abruptly near the summit [NN 771134] of Meall a'Choire Riabhaich and run almost straight down the eastern slopes. They are clearly sub-glacial in origin, formed at a time when this 1200-ft hill was completely covered by ice, and it seems most probable that they were cut by a powerful englacial stream which, in the vicinity of the channel intakes, descended abruptly to the base of the ice by way of a shaft or crevasse. I.H.F.

REFERENCES

CADELL, H. M. 1913. *The story of the Forth.* Glasgow.

DINHAM, C. H. 1927. Stirling district. *Proc. Geol. Ass.*, **38**, 470–92.

—— and HALDANE, D. 1932. The economic geology of the Stirling and Clackmannan Coalfield. *Mem. geol. Surv. Gt Br.*

DONNER, J. J. 1957. The geology and vegetation of Late-glacial retreat stages in Scotland. *Trans. R. Soc. Edinb.*, **63**, 221–64.

—— 1958. Loch Mahaick, a Late-glacial site in Perthshire. *New Phytol.*, **57**, 183–6.

DURNO, S. E. 1956. Pollen analysis of peat deposits in Scotland. *Scott. geogr. Mag.*, **72**, 177–87.

ERDTMAN, G. 1928. Studies in the Postarctic history of the forests of north-western Europe. I. Investigations in the British Isles. *Geol. För. Stockh. Förh.*, **50**, 123–92.

FORSYTH, I. H. Glacial modification of the drainage pattern in south-west Perthshire. *Bull. geol. Surv. Gt Br.*, No. 31 [in press].

GEIKIE, A. 1863. On the phenomena of the Glacial Drift of Scotland. *Trans. geol. Soc. Glasg.*, **1**, 1–190.

GEIKIE, J. 1877. *The Great Ice Age.* 2nd edit. London.

GODWIN, H. 1961. Radiocarbon dating and Quaternary history in Britain. The Croonian Lecture. *Proc. R. Soc.*, **B**, **153**, 287–320.

—— and WILLIS, E. H. 1961. Cambridge University natural radiocarbon measurements III. *Radiocarbon*, **3**, 60–76.

HOLLINGWORTH, S. E. 1931. The glaciation of western Edenside and adjoining areas and the drumlins of Edenside and the Solway Basin. *Q. Jl geol. Soc. Lond.*, **87**, 281–359.

LINTON, D. L. 1949. Watershed breaching by ice in Scotland. *Trans. Inst. Br. Geogr.*, **17**, 1–16.

—— 1962. Glacial erosion on soft-rock outcrops in central Scotland. *Biul. peryglac.*, **11**, 247–57.

MANNERFELT, C. M. 1945. Nagra glacial morfologiska formelement. *Geogr. Annlr*, **27**, 2–239.

NEWEY, W. W. 1966. Pollen analysis of Sub-Carse Peats of the Forth Valley. *Trans. Inst. Br. Geogr.*, **39**, 53–60.

PARTHASARATHY, A. and BLYTH, F. G. H. 1959. The superficial deposits of the buried valley of the River Devon near Alva, Clackmannan, Scotland. *Proc. Geol. Ass.*, **70**, 33–50.

READ, W. A. 1959. The economic geology of the Stirling and Clackmannan Coalfield, Scotland: Area south of the River Forth. *Coalfld Pap. geol. Surv.*, No. 2.

ROBERTSON, T. and HALDANE, D. 1937. The economic geology of the Central Coalfield of Scotland, Area I. *Mem. geol. Surv. Gt Br.*

SCRUTON, P. C. 1960. Delta building and the deltaic sequence. In *Recent sediments, Northwest Gulf of Mexico*, 56–81, Am. Ass. Petrol. Geol., Tulsa.

SIMPSON, J. B. 1933. The Late-Glacial readvance moraines of the Highland Border west of the River Tay. *Trans. R. Soc. Edinb.*, **57**, 633–46.

SISSONS, J. B. 1958. Sub-glacial stream erosion in southern Northumberland. *Scott. geogr. Mag.*, **74**, 163–74.

—— 1961. Some aspects of glacial drainage channels. *Scott. geogr. Mag.*, **77**, 15–36.

—— 1963a. Scottish raised shoreline heights with particular reference to the Forth valley. *Geogr. Annlr*, **45**, 180–5.

—— 1963b. The Perth Readvance in central Scotland. Part I. *Scott. geogr. Mag.*, **79**, 151–63.

—— 1966. Relative sea-level changes between 10 300 and 8300 B.P. in part of the Carse of Stirling. *Trans. Inst. Br. Geogr.*, **39**, 19–30.

—— CULLINGFORD, R. A. and SMITH, D. E. 1965. Some pre-carse valleys in the Forth and Tay basins. *Scott. geogr. Mag.*, **81**, 115–24.

—— and SMITH, D. E. 1965a. Peat bogs in a Post-glacial sea and a buried raised beach in the western part of the Carse of Stirling. *Scott. J. Geol.*, **1**, 247–55.

—— and SMITH, D. E. 1965b. Raised shorelines associated with the Perth Readvance in the Forth valley and their relation to glacial isostasy. *Trans. R. Soc. Edinb.*, **66**, 143–68.

SOONS, J. M. 1960. The sub-drift surface of the lower Devon valley. *Trans. geol. Soc. Glasg.*, **24**, 1–7.

SYNGE, F. M. and STEPHENS, N. 1966. Late- and post-Glacial shorelines and ice-limits in Argyll and north-east Ulster. *Trans. Inst. Br. Geogr.*, **39**, 101–26.

VINCENZ, S. A. 1954. A resistivity survey in Scotland. *Colliery Engng*, **31**, 157–63.

S

Chapter XVIII

PLEISTOCENE AND RECENT DEPOSITS

BOULDER CLAY AND ERRATICS

BOULDER CLAY or till, originating as the ground-moraine of an ice-sheet, covers much of the low ground in the Stirling district and is present also beneath thick accumulations of later deposits in the Forth and Devon valleys. In the Highland Border area it is generally confined to the valleys and lower slopes of the hills but on the south-east of the Uamh Bheag range exposures in the numerous streams that dissect the peat cover show that it also mantles the high ground to heights of up to 2000 ft above O.D. It extends well up the northern face of the Ochils and whereas the hills themselves are largely free of drift, most of the valleys have a bottom-filling of boulder clay which in places reaches a height of 2000 ft. It occurs on the southern slopes of the Fintry, Gargunnock and Touch hills but appears to be absent over much of the high ground.

On the slopes of the hills and on the higher ground generally, the boulder clay produces a rather subdued, featureless topography but at lower levels, below about 800 ft, it is characterized by irregular low mounds and hog-backed ridges (drumlins) elongated in the direction of movement of the bottom ice. Tracts of ice-moulded drumlin topography occur west of Dunblane, south of Kippen and east of Stirling and, to a lesser extent, north of Auchterarder. In the Ochil Hills the valley-bottom deposits form well-defined terrace-like features.

The thickness of the boulder clay sheet is very variable, ranging from a mere skin which barely conceals the underlying solid rocks, as on the watershed between Strathallan and Strathearn, to over a hundred feet. It is usually thinnest on the high ground but in many of the valleys, as on the low ground in general, thicknesses of 40 to 60 ft are not uncommon. The greatest thicknesses have been recorded where boreholes have penetrated drumlins: in one such case, north of Alloa, 185 ft of boulder clay were encountered.

The composition and texture of the boulder clay vary considerably and while far-travelled resistant boulders are present nearly everywhere, the matrix of the deposit usually reflects the nature of the underlying solid rocks. Thus in the Highland Border area the clay is generally fawn or pale-grey, with much slate debris. Over the Lower Old Red Sandstone the deposit is sandy, with a reddish-brown or purple colour. The boulder clay on the Ochil Hills is commonly pale-grey and is sandy in places; its boulder content is relatively high, with much lava debris. M.A., I.H.F., E.H.F., W.A.R.

A particularly close relation between matrix and bedrock exists west of Stirling where the bottom ice has moved for some distance along the strike of solid formations of differing lithology. The matrix of the boulder clay overlying the outcrop of the brick-red Gargunnock Sandstones is generally brick-red and very sandy. Over the Cornstone Beds it is sandy, but is commonly brown rather than red, and on the outcrops of the Ballagan Beds it is much more clayey and is generally grey or brownish-grey. On the dip-slopes of the Carboniferous lavas too the deposit is, for the most part, a fairly sticky brownish-grey clay, though

268

part of the clay content may have been derived from the mudstones and cement-stones which underlie the lavas in the scarp face rather than from the lavas themselves. East of the escarpment of the Stirling quartz-dolerite sill the matrix of the boulder clay is fairly sandy and, where fresh, is commonly mottled grey, buff and purplish-red. The grey and buff coloration almost certainly derives from the local Carboniferous mudstones and sandstones respectively, but the red colour may indicate partial derivation from the Upper Old Red Sandstone further west.

W.A.R.

Transported blocks which occur within the boulder clay and as isolated erratics furnish the most important evidence of glacial transport. They comprise rocks from the Highlands, of which the most characteristic is schistose grit; conglomerate and pebbly sandstone of Lower Old Red Sandstone age, largely from outcrops near the Highland Border; Lower Old Red Sandstone and Carboniferous lavas; and quartz-dolerite. The Highland blocks are found in the boulder clay throughout the Stirling district and large erratics of schistose grit are quite common. One of the latter lies near the summit of Uamh Bheag and others have come to rest high on the Ochil Hills. A notable erratic of pebbly sandstone occurs near Tullibardine Station. M.A., I.H.F.

Fragments of the distinctive rhyodacite of Craig Rossie are found in quantity in the boulder clay exposed in a small burn half a mile east of the summit of the hill. Large blocks of this material lie just north of the highest point of Simpleside Hill. These occurrences clearly indicate an ice-movement towards the south-east.

The Carboniferous lavas seem to have had little resistance to glacial abrasion and are not commonly represented in the boulder clay east of the outcrop of the Stirling sill. Fragments of dolerite derived from the sill seem to have been much more resistant than the lavas, but even so they do not appear to have travelled far from their source. Drifted dolerite blocks are locally common as erratics and as constituents of the boulder clay in the neighbourhood of the dolerite dykes and of the Ochil Fault-Intrusion. Fragments of the softer sandstones of the Lower and Upper Old Red Sandstone and of the Carboniferous sedimentary rocks are locally abundant in the boulder clay, but only near their source-beds, and they become progressively less common the further they have been transported from their original outcrop. M.A.

In the course of opencast working at Blairingone [NS 987967] during 1945, a very large mass of coal, folded and transported by ice, was seen within the boulder clay overlying the Alloa Cherry and Splint coals at outcrop. E.H.F.

In some sections, e.g. in the Ochil valley deposits and in the Callander area, the boulder clay contains layers of stratified sediments. In exposures [NN 642081] east of Callander these consist of sand, silt and fine gravel, and are similar to the deposits attributed by Carruthers (1939) to undermelting of an ice-sheet. I.H.F., E.H.F.

Stratified sediments beneath boulder clay have not been found in natural sections in the Stirling district but a fairly large proportion of the numerous borehole and shaft records from the Forth and Devon valleys refer to the presence of sand, gravel or clay beneath what might possibly be interpreted as boulder clay. In some cases these deposits appear to be underlain by a second 'boulder clay'. Unfortunately many of the records are relatively old and only the drillers' descriptions, often inadequate, are available. In such cases there is

S*

considerable doubt as to the true nature of the 'boulder clay', or indeed of the associated sediments which may in any case be englacial or sub-glacial in origin. Consequently such evidence, which might be taken as suggesting readvance (or at least oscillation) of an ice-front, must be treated with extreme caution in interpreting the glacial history of the area, particularly as neither stratified deposits beneath undoubted boulder clay, nor a second boulder clay, have been recorded in any borehole examined by a geologist. Indeed, the Geological Survey Stirling No. 5 (Greenfoot) Bore (1961), in which the drift was cored, encountered only one boulder clay although it was sited above a particularly deep drift-filled hollow where optimum conditions for the preservation of an earlier boulder clay might have been expected. Nevertheless there is a small number of records, perhaps about 25, all sited east of Stirling, which might reasonably be taken to show stratified sediments within or below boulder clay (e.g. Fig. 28, sections 1, 2). These do not by themselves indicate a readvance of the ice—indeed other explanations are equally possible—but it may be significant that about half of them relate to sites which lie within three miles of Stirling. These and several others further east are within the limit postulated by Sissons (1963b, fig. 3, p. 154) for the Perth Readvance in the Stirling area, but about 10 lie beyond it, in the Plean–Kincardine area.   W.A.R., I.H.F.

MORAINIC DRIFT

Morainic drift, like boulder clay, consists essentially of glacially deposited debris but it is usually distinguishable from boulder clay by its markedly hummocky topography and by its lithological characteristics. It is a loose, poorly consolidated deposit of unsorted rock debris, mainly angular or sub-angular, in a sandy to clayey matrix which varies greatly in amount. Although it consists largely of material which has been dropped directly from glacier ice, it frequently contains beds of stratified sediments which may include both re-sorted morainic material and the deposits of meltwater streams. In consequence it is locally difficult to distinguish from moundy glacial gravels, although the latter are commonly well-sorted and are generally stratified throughout.

I.H.F., W.A.R.

Moundy deposits of morainic drift occur on the floors and lower slopes of many of the valleys in the north-western part of the district, the spread on the south-west side of Gleann an Dubh Choirein being particularly extensive. In many places there is a distinct tendency for individual mounds and ridges to be elongated parallel to the valley axes. This is well seen on the east side of the Ollach valley where there is an exceptionally fine development of small, rounded mounds with northerly elongation parallel to the line of the valley; at the northern margin of this spread there is a large morainic ridge [NN 705140] with east-south-easterly trend. In Gleann an Dubh Choirein a conspicuous line of elongate mounds extends along the valley floor. A similar train of large mounds, composed mainly of gravelly material but locally including laminated sand, silt and clay, occurs in Findhu Glen and extends some distance southwards along the Allt na Gaisge as far as a large mound of gravelly moraine [NN 739130]. These deposits are continuous with the moraine and gravel accumulations in the dry valley between the head of Findhu Glen and the Corriebeagh valley. It appears that the latter deposits were laid down in front of a lobe of ice occupying Findhu Glen at a late stage in the deglaciation of the area.

The moundy drift which extends down the Teith valley from Callander to within two miles of Doune forms striking topographic features, particularly on Lennieston Muir. The material generally appears to be quite unsorted, and includes much locally derived angular debris. Much of this spread, including the Lennieston Muir moraines, is considered to have accumulated during a late valley glaciation contemporaneous with the Loch Lomond Readvance (Simpson 1933) but downstream from Drumvaich the deposits may be older (*see* p. 260). In the latter area the spread is less conspicuously moundy, although it includes the prominent hill of Knockmelly [NN 692039]. A certain amount of gravel and sand is generally present in these deposits but it is mixed with angular sandstone debris. The wide tract of morainic drift on the high ground (between 400 ft and 1200 ft above O.D.) east of Callander is likewise believed to be older than the late valley glaciation and was probably formed during the retreat of a much more extensive ice-sheet. This spread extends from the Brackland Burn eastwards to Severie [NN 704080] and includes some very large mounds with a south-easterly elongation near the stream Sruth Geal.   I.H.F.

South of the Forth, morainic drift is largely confined to a rather patchy spread on the southern slopes of the Fintry, Gargunnock and Touch hills, most of it below the 1250-ft contour. Other patches lie beneath the escarpments of these hills, in the corrie at the Spout of Ballochleam and east of Fintry between Stronend and Double Craigs.

The deposits on the south side of the hills were probably formed during the waning of the last extensive ice-sheet, at a time when the crests of the lava hills had emerged and separated a Forth glacier from the ice occupying the upper Endrick catchment. In the higher parts of the spread the drift is in the form of parallel elongate ridges which extend along the hill-slopes without appreciable fall in level. These are interpreted as successive lateral moraines deposited at the retreating margin of active ice. At lower levels the drift spread shows the irregular topography characteristic of ablation deposits from dead ice (Flint 1948, p. 131), with numerous, now mostly peat-filled, kettle-holes separated by mounds, short ridges and some longer, esker-like ridges. This lower zone probably marks a phase when the ice in the Endrick basin had become stagnant.

An isolated patch of morainic material around Todholes is moulded into parallel ridges trending south-eastwards. These may represent lateral moraines formed at the edge of a lobe of ice which lay between the dip-slope of the lavas and the scarp of the Stirling sill at a late stage in the deglaciation of the Touch Hills.

Moraines in the embayments of the lava scarp north-east of Fintry and at the Spout of Ballochleam were probably formed by corrie glaciers and are similar to those described by Bailey (*in* Clough and others 1925, p. 228, fig. 24) in the Corrie of Balglass in the Campsie Fells. The period of corrie glaciation is considered to be equivalent in age to the Loch Lomond Readvance.   W.A.R.

GLACIAL AND FLUVIO-GLACIAL SAND AND GRAVEL

Deposits of glacial and fluvio-glacial sand and gravel, products of a melting ice-sheet, are widespread in the Teith valley and in Strathallan, and cover lesser areas in the Forth, Devon and Knaik valleys. They are characteristically water-borne stratified deposits varying from coarse gravel to fine sand and silt, although some of the areas mapped as sand and gravel may include poorly-sorted material not readily distinguishable from morainic drift.

The glacial sands and gravels commonly owe their form to deposition in contact with ice and are usually markedly moundy, although they include flat-topped kames and kame-terraces, notably in Strathallan and Glen Devon. Subsequent melting of the ice has resulted in collapse and slumping, of which abundant evidence remains in the form of small faults and folds affecting the deposits. In places, as in the neighbourhood of Gleneagles Hotel and in the valley of the Teith, glacial sands and gravels take the form of eskers, prominent narrow ridges which probably mark the courses of sub-glacial or englacial streams.

The fluvio-glacial sands and gravels are terrace-like in form and have originated as outwash deposits. They have been distinguished between Cowie and Bannockburn House where they appear to grade into late-Glacial estuarine or deltaic deposits (Read 1959, pp. 60–1). In the valley of the River Teith they form two prominent terraces, one near Callander which falls downstream from 250 ft to 200 ft O.D. and another near Doune which slopes downstream from a level of about 145 ft O.D. The Doune terrace appears to grade into the late-Glacial estuarine or deltaic deposits near Blair Drummond, indicating that a high sea-level persisted after the lower Teith valley became free of ice. The fluvio-glacial deposits of the Teith valley are younger than those at Cowie, and are graded to a lower sea-level, the late-Glacial marine limit being appreciably lower to the west of Stirling than to the east (pp. 260, 274).   M.A., I.H.F., W.A.R.

DETAILS

The glacial and fluvio-glacial sands and gravels of Strathallan and the Knaik and Teith valleys, which are briefly discussed in this section, will be described in greater detail in a paper, now in preparation, by Armstrong and Forsyth.

Devon valley. Near Glendevon village there are two well-marked terraces of sand and gravel. The higher of these fills the lower part of Glen Quey, forming a flat-topped mass, partly covered by peat and having a back-feature just below the 900-ft contour; the sand and gravel contains appreciable amounts of coaly debris. The lower terrace has a back-feature just below 800 ft above O.D. and extends on both sides of the Glendey Burn as far as its confluence with the River Devon.

Both deposits can be explained by postulating that during the westward retreat of a Forth–Devon glacier, ice temporarily blocked the Devon valley south-east of Glendevon village; the presence of such ice is evidenced by a north–south esker, 800 ft long near Nether Auchlinsky [NT 002028]. The two terrace levels mark successive stages of deglaciation. At first Glen Devon was dammed to a height of about 900 ft, at which level the impounded drainage would have overflowed northwards into Glen Eagles four miles or so to the north-west. Simultaneously sand and gravel coming through the Dollar–Glen Quey gap would have been deposited up to the 900-ft level as a delta at the foot of Glen Quey. Later, as the ice receded down the Devon valley, the drainage was able to escape through the Glendey valley into the valley of the South Queich (in the Kinross (40) Sheet) by way of an outlet, just below 800 ft, near Coulsknowe, which controlled the level of the Glendey terrace.

Further down the Devon valley, deposits of sand and gravel form a moundy spread, mainly on the north side of the river, extending continuously from Muckart to Dollar and thereafter discontinuously to Tillicoultry where they end in the Cunninghar sand ridge which crosses, and originally blocked, the valley.   E.H.F., M.A.

Strathallan. The extensive deposits of glacial sand and gravel in Strathallan lie for the most part below the 450-ft contour. Upstream from Ashfield they form wide tracts with typical kame-and-kettle topography—particularly well seen on the north side of the Allan Water east of Braco—which flank the alluvial spread on the valley floor. Flat-topped kames and terraces are conspicuous in places, notably near Nether Braco, Ardoch House, Westerton and Blackford. The gravels extend well above the 450-ft contour on the northern slopes of Strathallan, where a system of branching eskers extends from Muir of Orchill to the neighbourhood of Gleneagles Station.

East of Auchterarder there is an extensive spread of glacial sand and gravel around Thorn and isolated gravel mounds occur along the north face of the hills towards Millhaugh.   M.A.

At Kinbuck a large transverse ridge, at least 60 ft high, almost blocks the valley. Immediately to the north, a large beaded esker of clayey gravel, 200 yd wide and 50 ft high, extends along the east side of the Kinbuck–Braco road for a distance of three-quarters of a mile. Below Ashfield the glacial sand and gravel is largely concentrated in a prominent ridge which can be traced along the floor of the valley for 1½ miles from Kinbuck to the Knock of Barbush [NN 786027]. The latter is a large mound, almost 100 ft high, which has been extensively quarried; it consists mainly of sand, much of it fine and silty, with some gravel, locally coarse. In Dunblane there are several large mounds of sand and gravel, including Laigh Hill and Holme Hill.

Knaik valley. Three kame-terraces, composed largely of gravel, have been recognized on the south side of the Knaik valley between Arrevore [NN 782132] and Glenlichorn [NN 797126]. They slope down to the east, indicating an escape of meltwaters towards Strathallan. Moundy gravel deposits on the south side of the valley include a north–south esker near Glenlichorn. Three other eskers rise above the floor of the valley north of the Corriebeagh Burn. A spectacular group of gravel mounds on the south side of the Findhu Glen–Corriebeagh through-valley extends up to a height of about 1250 ft above O.D., almost to the watershed between the Corriebeagh and Arrevore burns.

Teith valley. In the Teith valley the lower of the two fluvio-glacial terraces extends for about 2 miles on each side of Doune and grades down from about 145 ft to about 100 ft above O.D. at Blair Drummond where it merges with late-Glacial estuarine or deltaic deposits. The higher terrace lies immediately south and east of Callander and is best developed between the Teith and the lower Keltie Water. Its top is between 200 and 250 ft above O.D. This terrace is traversed by two series of esker-like ridges, including the very sinuous Roman Camp esker at Callander, the supposed Roman origin of which was refuted by Robertson (1794). A single series of ridges and mounds of gravel, with kettle-holes, extends as far as Drumvaich, west of which there is an area of spectacular kame-and-kettle topography on the north side of the Callander–Stirling road. East of Drumvaich the gravel belt is wider and includes eskers, prominent mounds and another area with marked kame-and-kettle topography south of Milton of Cambus [NN 702044]. North of Doune the gravels tend to be scattered round the large drumlins, except near Argaty House [NN 737032], where there is an area of moundy gravel bounded to the east by the Argaty esker. This is one of the most spectacular glacial features in the Stirling district and consists of a narrow gravel ridge which extends north-north-westwards for over a mile from a prominent mound of gravel near Netherton [NN 740020]. The latter encloses two distinct kettle-holes and has steep banks 40 ft high.

Glen Artney. A widespread and largely peat-covered terrace, consisting mainly of gravel with some sand and silt, occupies the head of Glen Artney and extends north-westwards as far as the Callander–Comrie path, where it is banked against mounds of moraine. At the mouth of Gleann an Dubh Choirein its northern limit is a steep slope overlooking lower, moraine-covered ground. This slope probably represents a former contact of the terrace with ice in Gleann an Dubh Choirein.

Isolated flat-topped mounds of gravel form an incipient kame-terrace for almost a mile down the north-west side of Glen Artney, the levels of their tops gradually decreasing downstream to just below 900 ft above O.D.

Keltie valley. A kame-terrace, composed mainly of fine gravel with some sand and a little silt and clay, extends across the mouth of Gleann Breac-nic at Sròn Eadar a'Chinn [NN 632132]. A solitary mound of gravel rises above it.

There are several gravel hillocks on both sides of the valley above Braeleny [NN 637111]. The two on the east side both have flat tops at a height of just over 800 ft above O.D. and are composed of sand and fine gravel; they probably form an incipient kame-terrace. The mounds on the west side, which do not have flat tops, are scattered along a line which follows closely the Highland Boundary Fault. The south-westerly ones are made of sand with some gravel, the north-easterly ones mostly of gravel.   I.H.F.

Area south of River Forth. North of the Fintry Hills two small patches of glacial sand and gravel lie immediately north of the Pow Burn south-west of Knowehead. Both were probably deposited against the southern edge of the waning Forth glacier.

An extensive deposit of moundy sand and gravel has been mapped on the north-eastern slopes of the Touch Hills, extending from below 100 ft up to more than 400 ft above O.D. There are smaller scattered patches of moundy material extending south-eastwards towards Wallstale up the valley between the dip-slope of the lavas and the dolerite crags of Gillies Hill, and also south of King's Park, Stirling. All these deposits are believed to have been laid down on the southern flank of ice occupying the Forth valley as it shrank off the higher ground.

Scattered patches of glacial sand and gravel are found east of the outcrops of the Stirling sill, above the level of the late-Glacial estuarine and deltaic deposits. These have been discussed by Dinham (*in* Dinham and Haldane 1932, p. 206) and by Read (1959, pp. 60–1).   W.A.R.

LATE-GLACIAL MARINE, ESTUARINE AND DELTAIC DEPOSITS

The deposits that were laid down on the seaward side of the Forth glacier in late-Glacial times comprise a complex assemblage of marine, estuarine and deltaic sediments. They underlie the post-Glacial Carse Clays throughout most of the area covered by the latter and also occur at the surface as patches of varying size on both sides of the Carse. West of Stirling these patches are mostly small and isolated, except for a broad tract between Thornhill and Blair Drummond. East of Stirling, however, they form almost continuous flat spreads, one on the south side of the Carse between Stirling and Plean, and another, north of the Carse, extending from Tullibody to Culross. Smaller tracts occur in the valley of the Bluther Burn and along the River Devon between Tillicoultry and Dollar.

The morphology of these deposits is complex and the terms '100-ft Raised Beach' and 'High Raised Beach' which were formerly applied to them are misleading as few of the sediments are undoubtedly littoral (*cf.* Thompson 1937; McKee 1957, pp. 1706–18). Indeed over much of the area, as Dinham (1927, pp. 486–7) pointed out, the deposits are largely of fluvio-glacial origin and were laid down near the margins of the estuary in a series of deltas. The mapping of such deposits presents considerable problems for it is virtually impossible in places to separate the marine arenaceous sediments laid down at, or just below, contemporary sea-level from spreads of fluvio-glacial outwash which slope gently down to this level. Consequently the mapped boundary between marine and fluvio-glacial deposits is in places a somewhat arbitrary line, as for instance near Plean and near Blair Drummond. East of Stirling this boundary has been taken at a level of between 130 and 135 ft above O.D., but west of Stirling it is drawn locally below 100 ft.

Since the mapping of the Stirling district was completed, Sissons and Smith have instrumentally levelled the features associated with these deposits and in places have detected breaks in slope, at somewhat lower levels, which they interpret as corresponding to the contemporary shoreline (Sissons 1963a; Sissons and Smith 1965b). In this connexion it is interesting to note that Morris (1931) suggested that the '100-ft Raised Beach' includes features of somewhat different ages, lying at slightly different levels. According to Sissons and Smith (1965b, pp. 152–7), features marking three main shorelines can be identified in a tidal delta near Larbert (a short distance south of the district under review), at levels of 84·3–87·7, 107·8–109·2 and 116·0–119·5 ft above O.D. They trace the highest of these features northwards to Plean where it rises to a level of 121·4 ft O.D. and merges with a more steeply sloping spread of outwash material. The next highest feature has been traced further up the Forth valley and at Bannockburn it is said to lie at a height of between 120·5 and 122·9 ft above O.D.; at St. Ninians, near Stirling, the deposits of this terrace too merge into an outwash fan. A slightly lower outwash spread at Stirling itself is thought to be related to a somewhat lower sea-level. Sissons and Smith (1965b, p. 164) postulate a considerable fall in sea-level whilst the ice lay at Kincardine, the limit they draw for the Perth Readvance, and a similar fall in sea-level during a rather later stillstand or minor readvance of the ice near Stirling. As evidence of these changes in sea-level they cite the absence of 'raised beach' deposits at levels higher than 75 ft O.D. in the area west and north-west of Kincardine and at levels above 76 ft O.D. west of Stirling. This evidence, however, seems to be contradicted by the presence, in both areas, of deposits which are believed to have been laid down near the contemporary sea-level at heights of about 100 ft above O.D. The presence of kettle-holes with rims below 100 ft O.D. in the deposits at King's Park, Stirling, and at 85 ft O.D. near Airthrey Castle (Sissons and Smith 1965b), was taken by these authors to provide evidence for a considerable relative fall in sea-level while the ice-front lay near Stirling. Synge and Stephens (1966, pp. 103–4), however, drawing upon evidence in Finland, have suggested that the presence of kettle-holes is no proof that the area was not completely overswept by the sea after all the ice had disappeared. It may be, therefore, that the sea-level had not fallen as much as Sissons and Smith postulated before the ice finally retreated westwards from Stirling.

The deposits are very variable in lithology and include gravel, sand, and laminated clays and silts. The latter are generally thought to have been laid down offshore in comparatively quiet water (Dinham 1927, p. 487) and they may be compared, in general terms, to the outer pro-delta deposits of modern deltas (cf. Fisk and others 1954, pp. 86–7). Within the Stirling district they have so far yielded only marine shells but further east in the Forth valley similar clays are said to contain Arctic mammalian faunas (Cadell 1883, p. 15; Peach and others 1910, pp. 335–49; Tait 1934, pp. 61–5). Isolated stones within the clays (Plate XI) may have been derived from floating ice (cf. Jamieson 1865, pp. 175–7). The sands and gravels were probably deposited close to the ice-margin at first but were subsequently built out progressively over the underlying clays and silts. Sissons and Smith (1965b, p. 145) have suggested that gravels are comparatively rare within the 'raised beach' deposits as opposed to the spreads of glacial outwash but in fact beds of gravel have commonly been recorded in boreholes, well below the levels of the contemporary shorelines.

West of Stirling remnant patches of sand and gravel are found along the margins of the old estuary and the few boreholes that are available have proved pinkish laminated clays and silts of the offshore facies which are locally overlain by sand. Similar clays and silts are widespread in the Forth and Devon valleys, east of Stirling, where they are, in general, overlain by arenaceous deposits. The laminated silts and clays west of Stirling may be considerably later in date than those to the east and may well have been deposited after the final retreat of the ice from Stirling. East of Stirling there are many local exceptions to the general rule that argillaceous deposits are overlain by arenaceous deposits. Beds of pinkish clay may be found in the upper part of the sequence and beds of sand and gravel in the lower part. Many of these beds are probably lenticular and borehole evidence strongly suggests that argillaceous and arenaceous beds were being deposited contemporaneously in close proximity. A bed of boulders which was found at the junction between the argillaceous and arenaceous deposits at Bo'ness Dock (Cadell 1883, p. 16) has been recorded at only a few places in the Stirling district.

Where the margin of the sediments has been exposed by excavations they are seen to be banked up against the underlying solid rock or boulder clay with little trace of erosion (Dinham 1927, pp. 486–8). The exact margin has generally been blurred by hillwash and solifluction deposits.

PLATE XI

CARSE CLAYS AND LATE-GLACIAL ESTUARINE CLAYS

All specimens are from Stirling No. 2 (Westwood Lane) Bore (1962)

Carse Clays

FIG. 1. Brownish-grey silty clay with laminae of pale coarse-grained silt and very fine-grained sand. Lamination disturbed by 'faults' and by numerous burrows, including U-shaped and vertical types. Burrowing organisms have completely destroyed the stratification at the base of the specimen, which contains specks of a bright blue mineral, probably vivianite derived from fish bones. Core between 19 ft 2 in and 20 ft 2 in.

Late-Glacial estuarine clays

FIG. 2. Alternating diffuse bands of reddish-brown silty clay and paler brownish-grey clayey and sandy silt, all disturbed by abundant nearly-horizontal burrows which have almost completely destroyed the original lamination. Some traces of this lamination may, however, be seen some 3 cm above the base of the specimen. A few small isolated stones are scattered through the specimen. Core between 104 ft 0 in and 104 ft 7 in.

FIG. 3. Alternating very even laminae of reddish-brown silty clay and paler brownish-grey coarse-grained silt with some very fine-grained sand. The contacts between laminae are slightly diffuse but there is no definite graded bedding and the sediments cannot be considered as varved clays. The lamination is interrupted by isolated stones, mostly of Highland grit, which were probably dropped from floating ice. There are many nearly horizontal burrows but these have not affected the original lamination to the same extent as in Fig. 2. Portion of incomplete core recovered between 116 ft 6 in and 130 ft 0 in.

PLATE XI

Geology of Stirling *(Mem. Geol. Surv.)*

1

2

3

DETAILS

Forth valley west of Stirling. The deposits between Thornhill and Blair Drummond are poorly exposed but appear to consist largely of sand and fine gravel.

The moundy spread of glacial sand and gravel south of Touch House slopes down to a rather poorly defined terrace at a level of over 100 ft above O.D. which seems to be composed largely of clayey gravel and sand but also includes traces of pink, stoneless clay. Another patch at a similar level stretches westwards from Cambusbarron (*see* Dinham and Haldane 1932, p. 211).   W.A.R., I.H.F.

In the absence of good sections at the surface, most of our knowledge of the superficial deposits between rockhead and the Carse Clays has been obtained from the Geological Survey Stirling bores, the sites of which are shown on Fig. 37. As no trace of the Sub-Carse Peat was found in any of these bores it was not possible to draw a satisfactory boundary between the late-Glacial deposits and the overlying Carse Clays. Furthermore, there is a possibility that in some places sub-aqueous sedimentation may have continued from the end of late-Glacial times (Zone III) into the Pre-Boreal (Zones IV and V) and even Boreal (Zone VI) periods.

Boulder clay appears to rest directly on bedrock in the six bores that were sited on the Carse, with the exception of No. 4 (Watson House) from which no samples of the superficial deposits were obtained. In four of the bores—No. 2 (Westwood Lane), No. 3 (Low Wood), No. 5 (Greenfoot) and No. 6 (Inch of Leckie)—the boulder clay is succeeded by late-Glacial clays. In cores obtained from Nos. 2 and 5 bores, these are reddish-brown or pinkish-brown silty clays with laminae of pale-grey silt or very fine-grained sand. The red coloration is attributed to the presence of iron which, in the absence of decaying organic matter, is in the ferric state. The laminae are commonly very thin and even but much of the stratification has been disturbed by horizontal burrows which are different from the burrows found in the Carse Clays (*see* Plate XI). The lamination is also interrupted by sporadic isolated stones. These clays differ from varved clays in that they show little trace of graded bedding and it is probable that they were deposited in water which was too saline to allow varves to develop (Frazer 1929, p. 59).

The pinkish-brown silty clays encountered in the boreholes closely resemble the late-Glacial clays which are exposed at the surface and which have also been seen beneath the Carse Clays in bore and shaft sections, east of Stirling, but they are not necessarily of exactly the same age (p. 276).

In Nos. 2, 3 and 6 bores, the pinkish-brown clays are succeeded by sands with some clayey laminae, all containing fragments of marine molluscs and barnacles; in No. 1 Bore, similar sands rest directly on boulder clay. These sands are overlain by definite Carse Clays and there are traces of an upward passage by alternation from sand to clay in No. 2 Bore. The exact age of the sands is uncertain but it is possible that they may ultimately have been derived from outwash from the ice-front near the Lake of Menteith during the Loch Lomond Readvance (Zone III).

These sands are absent in No. 5 Bore where the pinkish-brown laminated clays are overlain, at a level of 248 ft below O.D., by brownish-grey silty clays with subordinate pale laminae of silt and sand. The change from a reddish to a greyish colour is accompanied by the appearance of abundant organic remains and it is possible that this marks a transition to less rigorous climatic conditions. Apart from the presence of sporadic layers of pebbles, the general appearance of these beds is similar to that of the more sandy parts of the Carse Clays, into which they grade imperceptibly at the top of the bore. They contain layers of broken shells and numerous complete shells were obtained from the washings. The fauna, identified by Mr. A. Rodger Waterston of the Royal Scottish Museum, is as follows: *Balanus crenatus* (Bruguière), *Lacuna vincta* (Montagu), *Littorina littorea* (Linné), *L. saxatilis* (Olivi), *Natica pallida groenlandica* (Moller), *Lora trevelliana* (Turton), *Nuculana pernula* (Müller), *Mytilus edulis* (Linné), *Astarte? borealis* (Schumacher), *A. montagui* (Dillwyn), *Thyasira flexuosa* (Montagu), *Macoma balthica* (Linné), *Abra prismatica* (Montagu). Mr. Waterston states that the association of *Nuculana*, *Macoma*, *Mytilus* and *Natica* is a common one in the deposits of the post-Glacial drifts and that *Nuculana pernula* and *Astarte borealis*, now extinct in British waters, still occur in the Arctic, whereas *Balanus crenatus* is still found in Scottish waters. The balance of evidence would seem to suggest a post-Glacial rather than a late-Glacial age but this is difficult to reconcile with the great depth of the base of the deposits, especially as the Sub-Carse Peat is not known to fall much below 10 ft above O.D. in this area. A possible explanation is that in the deep rock-basin on which the bore was sited, sedimentation may have continued without a break from late-Glacial times into the Pre-Boreal and Boreal periods.

Forth valley east of Stirling. On the south side of the Forth, sections in both the sands and gravels and the laminated clays and silts were formerly exposed in gravel pits and temporary excavations; these were recorded in detail by Morris (1922) and Dinham (*in* Dinham and Haldane 1932, pp. 207–12). W.A.R.

North of the river spreads of sand and gravel occur, e.g. around Tullibody and Tulliallan, but the main deposits are the brown and pink 'gutta-percha' clays which generally extend up to between 90 and 110 ft above O.D. Augering in the deposits near Tullibody and Tulliallan and in the valley of the Bluther Burn shows that the spreads of sand and gravel overlie the clays and this relationship is seen in a section [NS 97718976] on the north bank of the Bluther Burn.

Borehole evidence in the Clackmannan area shows that clays of the same type as the late-Glacial estuarine clays occur at heights in excess of 75 ft O.D. (*cf.* Sissons and Smith 1965b). Thus the Brucefield Colliery No. 2 Bore (1954) [NS 92559110], which has a surface level of 103·0 ft O.D., encountered, beneath 2 ft of soil, 9 ft of chocolate-coloured plastic clay resting on boulder clay.

A large number of commercial bores and shafts have been sunk into the superficial deposits below the Carse Clays in the Forth valley east of Stirling, and for some 300 of these reasonably detailed logs are available. Unfortunately the horizon of the Sub-Carse Peat can be identified in only about 30 of the sections (p. 283) and the late-Glacial sediments cannot everywhere be separated easily from the Carse Clays. Differences in colour and lithology are however of some assistance in distinguishing the two sets of deposits: the late-Glacial clays are predominantly pinkish-brown and locally contain beds of sand and gravel, whereas in the Carse Clays, which are characteristically greyish in colour, sand and gravel are virtually absent. From the evidence of logs that can be interpreted with confidence, the thickness of the deposits between either rockhead or the top of the boulder clay and the base of the Carse Clays seems to range up to more than 120 ft in this area. I.H.F., E.H.F., W.A.R.

Graphic sections of twelve of the more detailed bore and shaft sections east of Stirling are shown in Fig. 28. The abrupt variations in the deposits encountered in adjacent sections is immediately apparent. In the sections nearest Stirling the sediments are generally more sandy and include intercalations of boulder clay which suggest possible local oscillations of the ice-front (p. 257). Further east most sections show a basal layer of sand and gravel, which may mark an initial period of ice melting east of Stirling, resting on boulder clay or directly on solid rock. This is usually succeeded by pinkish-brown laminated clays which contain scattered stones and shells and may represent sedimentation in quieter water more remote from the ice front (Dinham 1927, pp. 487–8). In most sections these clays are succeeded in turn by more sandy beds which may possibly be equivalent to the sands in Stirling Nos. 2, 3 and 6 bores west of Stirling (p. 277). These upper sandy beds locally pass upward into more argillaceous sediments immediately below the Sub-Carse Peat or the Carse Clays. There are many exceptions to this general succession however and the abrupt variations in the proportions of the sands and clays, combined with the striking differences between closely adjacent sections, suggest a sedimentary environment in which sharply contrasted arenaceous and argillaceous phases were being deposited contemporaneously in

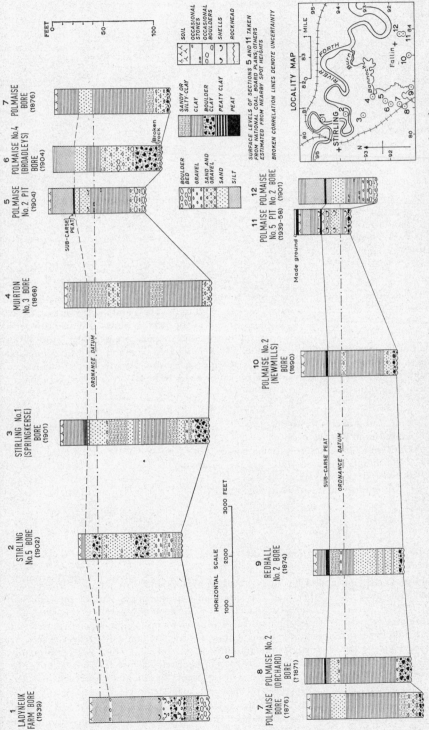

FIG. 28. *Comparative vertical sections of the superficial deposits in the Forth valley east of Stirling*

close proximity to each other, as in the modern Mississippi delta (Fisk and others 1954).

The only section that has been examined in detail by a geologist is Polmaise No. 5 Pit (1939–58) at Fallin [NS 83739142] where Mr. W. Manson recorded the following succession (*see* Fig. 28, section 11):

	Thickness		Depth from surface	
	ft	in	ft	in
(Sub-Carse Peat: base at 18·3 ft above O.D.)	–	–	–	–
Clay, sandy, greenish and grey, with rootlets and twigs ..	2	0	28	3
Clay, sandy, grey, bedded, with *Macoma*				
Sand, fine-grained, grey, with abundant *Macoma* and *Cardium*	18	6	46	9
Clay, reddish, laminated, tenacious, with worn boulders up to 9 in across	1	0	47	9
Clay, reddish, with sandy laminae. Two specimens of *Yoldiella arctica* (Gray)	5	9	53	6
(Boulder clay)	1	11	55	5

W.A.R.

Devon valley. In the 'buried channel' of the Devon (*see* Fig. 27) the deposits believed to be late-Glacial in age commonly exceed 200 ft in thickness and locally exceed 300 ft, but the paucity of records of the Sub-Carse Peat (pp. 283–4) makes it difficult to establish with certainty that most of the infilling of the 'channel' predated the latter. As in the Forth valley, the deposits consist largely of laminated clays and silts with some sand and gravel. Flett (1930, p. 35) summarized the sections of the late-Glacial deposits in the three deepest of the series of Devon valley bores near Alva (one of which is reproduced as section 5 in Fig. 29) as follows:

	ft	in
Sand and gravel (?fluvio-glacial)	5	0
Clayey sand with layers of clay	21	0
Dark grey 'gutta-percha' laminated clays	64	0
Reddish and brownish 'gutta-percha' laminated clays ..	120	0
Brown clay with layers of sand	18	0
Clean reddish sand, stones at base	12 to 42	0
Total thickness	240 to 270	0

Cores or samples were examined by Mr. W. Manson, and the section is therefore well-authenticated.

Further east, around Tillicoultry, the borer's logs more frequently mention silt, sand and sandy clay rather than clay, especially in the upper part of the sequence (*cf.* Fig. 29, section 7). The late-Glacial clays are generally more or less silty, and although to some extent this apparent eastward coarsening of the deposits may result from differences in human observation, it appears probable that it also reflects a genuine increase up the Devon valley in the amounts of silt and sand which were presumably derived mainly from the north and east. Records of red clay are few and occur in the lower parts of the sections concerned. Gravel occurs locally and the records usually, but not always, show it at the base of the late-Glacial deposits.

West of Alva there is only one really satisfactory record of the late-Glacial deposits in the deeper part of the 'buried channel' of the Devon, at Blair Mains Bore (1910)

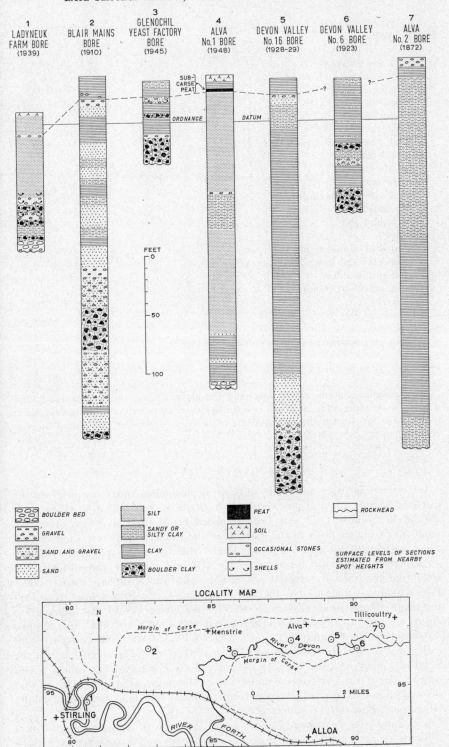

FIG. 29. *Comparative vertical sections of the superficial deposits in the Devon valley*

[NS 82789632] where the following section (Fig. 29, section 2) was recorded by the late H. M. Cadell:

	ft	in
Sand and gravel	4	6
Fine sand	12	0
Laminated clay	21	0
Fine sand	13	0
Muddy sand	7	0
Hard sand	10	0
Sand with plies of clay	5	0
Laminated clay	10	0
Muddy sand	7	0
Sharp sand	20	0
Sand with muddy plies	10	0
Laminated clay	5	0
Firm sand	18	0
Gravel	7	0
Sand with bands of clay and stones	26	0
Sandy clay and stones (?boulder clay)	38	0
Sand and boulders	15	0
Sand, gravel and boulders	31	0
Gravel	2	0
Laminated clay	5	0
Sand	13	6
Sandy clay with stones and boulders (?boulder clay)	7	3
Total thickness	287	3

This sequence contains much more sand and gravel than in the bores around Alva, which is to be expected from its position further west and therefore, presumably, nearer to the ice-front. It also shows a possible occurrence of boulder clay within the succession.

I.H.F.

SUB-CARSE PEAT

In commercial bore and shaft sections at more than thirty localities on the Carse of Stirling a bed of peat resting on rooty beds, generally at levels between 10 and 30 ft above O.D., has been recorded below the Carse Clay. The peat seems to be higher towards the margins of the Carse, but its restricted vertical range suggests that it grew on a fairly level surface of earlier sediments, possibly on a depositional plain formed in Zone III times or later and subsequently somewhat modified by erosion (cf. Sissons and Smith 1965a; Sissons 1966). Pollen analysis suggests that the age of the Sub-Carse Peat ranges from Pre-Boreal to Boreal times (Zones IV to VIc: see Newey 1966). By radiocarbon dating the age of the peat was found to be 8690 ± 140 years B.P. near Kippen (Sissons 1966, p. 27) and 8421 ± 157 years B.P. at Airth Colliery in the Forth valley east of Stirling (Godwin and Willis 1961, p. 63). The significance of the Sub-Carse Peat, which in the seaward parts of the Forth and Tay valleys passes below present sea-level, was pointed out by Jamieson (1865, pp. 183–5) who showed that it marks an important emergence of the land between the late-Glacial and post-Glacial submergences.

The Sub-Carse Peat attains a maximum thickness of at least 6 ft, but it is commonly only a foot or less. It occurs only locally and its absence over much of the area is probably due partly to erosion before the overlying Carse Clays were laid down and partly to non-deposition (Sissons 1966). In the upper Forth and Teith valleys beds with drifted plant material, probably contemporaneous with the peat and at about the same level, are known from several sections.

It appears that peat formation was not everywhere terminated in the Carse area by the Atlantic marine transgression, since a peat succession embracing pollen zones V to VIII has been recognized by Durno (1956, fig. 3c) in part of Flanders Moss. Recent boreholes put down by Sissons and Smith (1965a) proved that the Sub-Carse Peat here rests on a surface between about 30 and 36 ft above O.D. and that the wedge of Carse Clays which separates this peat from the surface peats tapers out so that they merge into a single bed. Sissons (1966) has subsequently discovered that the surface on which the Sub-Carse Peat rests north of Kippen may be subdivided into three distinct terraces at levels between 36·0 and 40·4 ft, 28 and 38 ft, and 21 and 28 ft above O.D.

Details

West of Stirling. Several sections through a plant-bed, possibly at the horizon of the Sub-Carse Peat, occur in the banks of the River Forth south of Flanders Moss [e.g. NS 628960, 632961, 635961 on the north bank; 633961 on the south bank]. The plant material is mostly drifted and includes leaves, twigs and branches, but traces of roots in the underlying beds indicate some plant growth in place. The bed lies between 8 and 10 ft below the surface of the Carse and is up to 2 ft thick.

Near Littleward Wester the plant-bed is exposed in the north bank of the Forth [NS 655969] where it is overlain by 5 ft 6 in of Carse Clays. The bed is 4 ft thick and contains abundant drifted plant debris, including woody twigs and branches in a matrix of grey, micaceous, silty clay with laminae of pale silt and very fine-grained sand. There are faint traces of roots in the underlying silty clays.

At Heathershot the plant-bed is exposed in the north-western bank of the Teith [NS 763972]. The section is as follows:

	Thickness		Total thickness	
	ft	in	ft	in
Clay, silty, grey, with brownish mottling (Carse Clays) ..	6	6	6	6
Clay, silty, grey, with pale laminae of silt and very fine-grained sand. Some leaf impressions	3	6	10	0
Clay, silty, grey, with carbonaceous layers packed with leaf impressions and twigs	1	6	11	6
Gravel, stones up to 10 mm in a matrix of clayey sand ..	1	0	12	6
Clay, grey, with fragments of wood (below river level) ..	1	0	13	6

In a 14-ft trench section [NS 764923] very close to the southern edge of the Carse immediately north-west of Gartur, brown woody peat was found below Carse Clays.

East of Stirling. The horizon of the Sub-Carse Peat has been recorded in only 32 of the many mineral and water bores and shafts that have been sunk through the Carse Clays east of Stirling (Fig. 30). In 30 of the sections the peat probably rests on earlier stratified superficial deposits and in all but two of these its base lies between 10 and 30 ft above O.D. Sissons, Smith and Cullingford (1966, p. 15) have suggested that the surface below the Sub-Carse Peat east of Stirling is divided into two terrace features which may be correlated with the two lower terraces discovered by Sissons (1966) near Flanders Moss. The peat, which ranges in thickness from 2 in to 6 ft, is probably the eroded remnant of a much more extensive bed. The sections where the peat is preserved are rather scattered but show a tendency to be concentrated in three areas which, probably, were relatively sheltered from erosion during the Atlantic transgression. In the Forth valley, twelve of the sections, all less than a mile from the edge of the Carse, occur between Stirling and Throsk. Further down the valley a second group, comprising twelve records, occurs between the western margin of the Carse and the isolated hills of Dunmore and Airth, which formed islands in Carse Clay times. In the Devon valley the Sub-Carse Peat was found in four sections near Alva.

W.A.R., I.H.F.

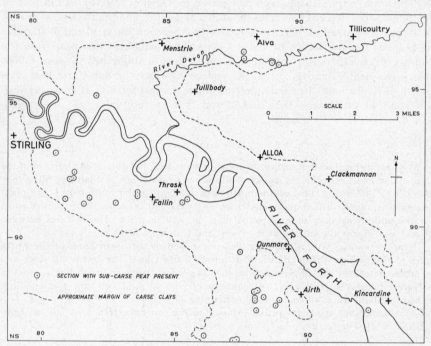

FIG. 30.   *Sketch-map showing distribution of records of Sub-Carse Peat south and east of Stirling*

POST-GLACIAL MARINE AND ESTUARINE ALLUVIUM

Post-Glacial marine and estuarine deposits, locally known as Carse Clays, form the broad plain of the Carse of Stirling (Dinham 1927, p. 490). They comprise marine clays, silts and, rarely, sands. An Atlantic age was suggested for these deposits by Erdtman (1928, pp. 181–2) on the basis of palynological dating of the overlying peat, and of the Earn valley correlative of the Sub-Carse Peat. Recently, however, Newey (1966, p. 59) has suggested that west of Stirling the deposition of the Carse Clays commenced in Zone VIa to VIb (Boreal) times. Recent radiocarbon datings of the peats in the Forth valley (Godwin and Willis 1961, p. 63; 1962, p. 67) show that deposition of the Carse Clays took place between 8421 ± 157 and 5481 ± 130 years B.P.

The Carse Clays bear a strong resemblance to modern tidal flat deposits. Layers with numerous shells, mostly cockles, oysters, mussels and periwinkles, are common. In the Alloa area there are a number of records of shells at or near the base of the clays. Specimens from Forthbank No. 2 Mine [NS 89069147] and

Bowhouse No. 3 Bore [NS 89429183] were identified by Mr. A. Rodger Waterston of the Royal Scottish Museum as follows: *Buccinum undatum* Linné, *Littorina littorea* (Linné) juv., *Thais* (*Polytropa*) *lapillus* (Linné), *Turritella communis* Risso, *Chlamys distorta* (da Costa), *Macoma balthica* (Linné), *Modiolus modiolus* (Linné), *Nucula nucleus* Linné, *Ostrea edulis* Linné, *Venerupis pullastra* (Montagu). Skeletons of seals have been recorded and the remains of stranded whales have been discovered in sixteen localities. Mesolithic antler implements (Forest Culture Period III) have been found in association with the whales in four places and it is probable that they were used in cutting up the carcasses (Lacaille 1954, pp. 169–75, figs. 64–66).

The landward margin of the Carse Clays is usually marked by a distinct feature cut in either boulder clay or, locally, solid sandstone; the cliff-line cut in Old Red Sandstone rocks between Row and Bridge of Allan is particularly prominent. A re-assessment of the literature on the raised beaches of the Forth area led Sissons (1962) to postulate that this shoreline is tilted towards the east, as Jamieson (1865) and many later workers recognized. Earp, Francis and Read (1962) questioned the validity of this conclusion but subsequently Sissons (1963a, fig. 4) was able to show by precise instrumental levelling that tilting has undoubtedly taken place. Thus the shoreline is now known to fall eastwards very gradually from just over 48 ft above O.D. at the western limit of the Carse (in the Loch Lomond (38) Sheet) to just under 42 ft near Stirling, a distance of more than 13 miles. This range of levels is in close agreement with that previously postulated by Dinham (1927, p. 490). East of Stirling, particularly on the north side of the Forth, the Carse in places is divided into two distinct terraces by a definite feature which interrupts the otherwise gentle slope towards the middle of the old estuary. The base of this feature is at about 30 ft above O.D. Read (1959, p. 62) has suggested that instead of the gradual fall in the landward margin of the Carse plain between Carnock [NS 865882] and Grangemouth (in the Airdrie (31) Sheet), as envisaged by Dinham (1927, p. 490), there may be a more abrupt change of level from the back-feature of the higher terrace to that of the lower, somewhere between Kinnaird House and Grangemouth.

Durno (1956, fig. 3c; 1958, p. 47) and Sissons and Smith (1965a) have shown that peat growth was taking place at Flanders Moss throughout the period of deposition of the Carse Clays. This, however, appears to be a local phenomenon.

W.A.R.

DETAILS

West of Stirling. Core samples were obtained from the Carse Clays in Geological Survey No. 2 (Westwood Lane) and No. 5 (Greenfoot) bores. These were partially dried and then sliced open for detailed examination under a binocular microscope; thin sections of some of the sediments were also made. As may be seen from the photographs (Plate XI), the Carse Clays contrast sharply with the late-Glacial marine or estuarine clays. Where unweathered they are typically dark-grey, silty clays with pale laminae of coarse-grained silt or very fine-grained sand. The junction between the coarser and finer material is generally sharp and graded contacts are rare. The laminae are generally sub-lenticular and the deposits are rarely as evenly laminated as the late-Glacial clays, but the specimens from the top 29 ft of No. 2 Bore suggest that this may be partly due to disturbance by burrowing organisms. These have disturbed the lamination with U-shaped and vertical burrows up to 1·5 cm deep and, in patches, much of the coarser and finer material has been so mixed that all trace of lamination has been destroyed. Specks of a bright blue mineral, probably vivianite replacing fish bones, are found in some of the burrowed and mixed horizons. Inorganic disturbances seen in the specimens include minor faulting and contortion of the laminae, but these effects may be partly due to the process of coring.

In thin section the sediments from Stirling No. 2 Bore resemble the modern tidal flat deposits of the Wadden See in the relatively high minimum grain size and well-sorted nature of the coarser material and in the relatively poor orientation of flaky minerals in the clayey laminae. Further parallels may be found in the sub-lenticular nature of the laminae, in the presence and nature of the burrows and in the destruction of lamination and mixing of sediment by the burrowing organisms. The specimens from No. 2 Bore seem most closely to resemble sediments deposited in a low tidal flat environment (Van Straaten 1954).

The topmost deposits in Stirling No. 5 Bore are similar, but below 8 ft from the surface they are mostly black, probably because any iron present is in a mono-sulphuric state, suggesting anaerobic conditions (Van Straaten 1954, p. 40). In surface exposures the Carse Clays are commonly oxidized to a brownish or even yellowish-grey colour and brownish tubes are formed around recent roots.

In the absence of the Sub-Carse Peat it is impossible to estimate the total thickness of the Carse Clays and in Stirling No. 5 Bore these grade down into rather similar deposits of uncertain age with a thin-shelled molluscan fauna (pp. 277–8). It may be possible, however, to distinguish the Carse Clays radiometrically, by their lower gamma intensity (p. 332).

The back-feature at the edge of the Carse is locally blurred by alluvial cones deposited by streams, and by slipped material and gently-sloping aprons of sandy, stony clay derived from boulder clay. In addition to steep boulder clay slopes at the Carse margin there are also prominent cliffs of solid rock, especially in the Gargunnock Sandstones north and north-east of Watson House [NS 69259460]. W.A.R.

The back-feature is also very prominent for considerable distances along the north side of the Carse, between Thornhill and East Coldoch [NS 704984], and between Row [NS 742994] and Bridge of Allan. In the latter stretch it is particularly well-marked, with cliffs which reach 50 ft in height, cut in Lower Old Red Sandstone strata.

I.H.F.

East of Stirling. Numerous boreholes penetrate the Carse Clays east of Stirling and south of the Forth, but where the Sub-Carse Peat has not been preserved or recorded it is not always easy to separate these clays from earlier marine and estuarine deposits. The records suggest, however, that the Carse deposits were laid down on a slightly uneven, eroded surface of earlier sediments, that they may be as much as 50 ft thick in a few localities and that their base may lie as low as 8 ft below O.D. In the neighbourhood of Carnock House [NS 866883] and the hills of Dunmore and Airth the drift is very thin and it seems probable that over much of this area the Carse Clays rest directly upon solid rock. A similar relationship appears to exist locally around Kincardine on the other side of the Forth. The clays are generally grey, bluish-grey, brownish-grey or black in colour, but in many borehole records the top few feet are said to be yellow (Dinham and Haldane 1932, p. 213).

On the south side of the Forth the break in slope near the back-feature of the Carse Clays slopes down from 42·2 ft O.D. at Stirling to just below 40 ft O.D. on the southern margin of the Stirling district (Sissons 1963a). The second feature at about 30 ft O.D. is best preserved between the hills of Dunmore and Airth (Read 1959, p. 64). North of the river, on the other hand, the lower feature is more persistent and it has been traced almost continuously from Kincardine to Tullibody. Only the higher feature, however, is found along the lower Devon valley.

Reclaimed land. Extensive areas of salt marsh and tidal flats have been reclaimed since the late 18th century on either side of the Forth downstream from Stirling by inducing rapid deposition of mud in slack water behind artificial barriers and so progressively raising the level (Cadell 1929, pp. 18–22). W.A.R., E.H.F.

FRESHWATER ALLUVIUM

Fluviatile alluvium, in the form of flood-plain deposits and terraced spreads, is found along many of the streams and rivers, the most extensive tracts being in upper Strathallan and in the Devon valley between Tillicoultry and Dollar. In places, gently sloping alluvial cones are developed where steeply graded tributary streams emerge on the floors of the main valleys; conspicuous examples occur in the lower Devon valley, at the base of the Ochil escarpment. In many parts of the district, isolated patches of alluvium in enclosed hollows mark the sites of lakes or tarns which have been silted up. Such deposits are generally composed of silt or mud, commonly peaty, whereas the fluviatile sediments are characteristically more variable in character, consisting of silt, sand and gravel, any one of which may be locally predominant. Much of the material mapped as alluvium is of Recent age but as it is not always easy to distinguish fluvio-glacial sand and gravel from normal river alluvium it is probable that some of the deposits date back to late-Glacial times.   M.A., E.H.F., I.H.F., W.A.R.

DETAILS

Forth valley. Upstream from the limit of tidal action, alluvium in the Forth valley is restricted to fairly narrow strips on either side of the river. The alluvium generally consists of brownish clayey sand which is easily distinguishable from the Carse Clays.

Isolated patches of sand and gravel occur above the feature at the southern margin of the Carse on the sides of the Gargunnock, Leckie and Boquhan burns. These are thought to be the eroded remnants of alluvial cones which may possibly have been graded to a late-Glacial sea-level. Another series of sandy alluvial cones is found at a lower level where these streams flow out on to the surface of the Carse and there is a similar cone north-east of Kippen.   W.A.R.

Devon valley. The River Devon flows through two large alluvial stretches. One extends up Glen Devon for two miles above Glendevon village and includes three gravelly terraces. These are graded downstream and seem clearly to be related to the downcutting of the gorge of the Devon below the village. The highest terrace may possibly be of the same age as some of the glacial sand and gravel south of Glendevon village and in the valley of the Glendey Burn (p. 272). The other alluvial area, about half a mile broad and flanked by a series of small alluvial cones at the foot of tributary streams, extends for three miles between Tillicoultry and Dollar and for a further mile east of Dollar where a higher terrace appears to the north. A little further upstream, above Vicar's Bridge [NS 986980], the river flows through a rock-cut gorge which opens out to a limited extent just below Muckart Mill to show terraces at five levels.

Other stretches of alluvium, each about two miles long and containing a single higher terrace, extend along the Black Devon above Forest Mill and along the Bluther Burn between Brucefield House and Bogside Station.   E.H.F.

Auchterarder area. There are several alluvial terraces along the Ruthven Water east of Auchterarder. Higher and more extensive areas of alluvium east of Shinafoot and east of Rossiebank are probably graded to the level of late-Glacial terraces in Strathearn.

Strathallan. The broad alluvial tract flooring upper Strathallan descends from a height of over 400 ft above O.D. at Blackford and over 350 ft at Braco to about 325 ft near its downstream termination at Kinbuck, where a ridge of glacial gravel constricts the valley. Natural sections along the Allan Water and River Knaik show the alluvium to consist of silt, sand and gravel. On the east side of the River Knaik east of Keirallan, a trench cut in 1960 exposed at least 6 ft of brown laminated clay. This material may have been deposited, during the last stages of deglaciation, in a lake impounded in upper Strathallan by the gravel ridge of Kinbuck.   M.A.

T

Between Kinbuck and Ashfield the Allan Water traverses another broad belt of alluvium, composed largely of sand and silt, at about 300 ft O.D. with a higher terrace in places. This tract is believed to have been the site of a temporary lake dammed by glacial gravel deposits near Ashfield.

At Dunblane there are four alluvial terraces along the Allan Water. The highest falls from about 240 ft at Dunblane to about 170 ft near Kippenross House. It was probably deposited when the sea in the Forth valley stood at a higher level in late-Glacial times, and may therefore be contemporaneous with terraces mapped as fluvio-glacial sand and gravel in the valley of the River Teith.

Knaik valley. Narrow strips of flood plain and two terraces lie along the River Knaik in its upper reaches. A broad terrace, composed mainly of gravel, extends from Tighna-blair (half a mile beyond the northern limit of the district) to near Glenlichorn and occupies the interfluve between the Corriebeagh and Arrevore burns in their lower reaches and the River Knaik. This tract, largely peat-covered north of the Corriebeagh Burn, descends from 750 ft near Tighnablair, where it is little higher than the Knaik flood plain, to 650 ft near Glenlichorn, where it is 20 to 30 ft above the river. It is thought to have accumulated during deglaciation when ice still lay in Strathallan and the lower part of the Knaik valley. It is younger than the group of kame-terraces on the hillsides near Glenlichorn and is probably contemporaneous with certain glacial gravel deposits in Strathallan. The extent of the deposit suggests that it was laid down by meltwaters from the Strathearn or the Glen Artney ice, which must therefore still have been thick at this period.

Corriebeagh Burn and Findhu Glen. A terrace of gravel on the east bank of the Findhuglen Water at the western end [NN 739135] of the through-valley from Findhu Glen to the Corriebeagh Burn is continuous eastwards with the alluvium of the Corriebeagh Burn.

The extensive stretch of alluvium flooring Findhu Glen for about a mile above Findhuglen Cottage [NN 727152] probably marks the site of a temporary moraine-dammed lake.

Teith valley. Between Callander and Drumvaich, the River Teith and the Keltie Water are bordered by extensive alluvial spreads, including two prominent gravel terraces and a more restricted flood plain. Between Drumvaich and Doune the alluvial belt is narrow and impersistent. Three terraces, composed mainly of gravel, occur above the level of the flood plain. Below Doune the alluvial belt is broader and includes up to three terraces of sand and gravel. The two lower terraces, which tend to merge downstream, are both graded to the level of the Carse, and pass into the post-Glacial marine deposits near Blair Drummond. The flood plain, built of silt, sand and clay, is graded to a level below that of the Carse.

There is a considerable area of alluvium in the neighbourhood of Loch Mahaick. Donner (1957; 1958) has made a pollen analytical study of this locality, and has detected deposits of Allerød age and also representatives of pollen-zones IV and V. Loch Mahaick is rapidly silting up and is at present half the size it was a century ago.

I.H.F.

PEAT

The following account relates to the deposits of peat which occur at the surface in many parts of the Stirling district; the thin peat layer of Boreal age known as the Sub-Carse Peat, which underlies the Carse Clays in many places, is discussed on pp. 282–4.

Hill peat covers wide expanses of high ground in the Fintry and Gargunnock hills, in the Ochil Hills and between Callander and Braco. At lower levels, many poorly drained areas are occupied by deposits of basin peat, the largest of which lie on the carse lands by the River Forth. These low-level deposits, which include

Flanders Moss and the mosses of Ochtertyre, Dunmore and Letham, were formerly more extensive, much of the peat having been stripped off in the 18th and 19th centuries (Cadell 1913, pp. 10–4).

The peat has accumulated over a long period and although there is no actual proof it seems possible that peat of Allerød age may exist in the district. Alluvium of this age, undisturbed by glacial action, has been found at Loch Mahaick (Donner 1958) and at other places (Donner 1957) outside the limits of the Loch Lomond Readvance ('Highland Readvance' of Donner).

On the basis of pollen analysis of samples from Ochtertyre Moss Erdtman (1928, pp. 181, 186) concluded that the peat mosses overlying the Carse Clays are of Sub-Boreal and Sub-Atlantic age. Radiocarbon datings of peat at various levels above the Carse Clays at Flanders Moss (Godwin and Willis 1962, pp. 66–7) range from 5492 ± 130 to 1858 ± 110 years B.P. These values are in accord with Erdtman's palynological datings.

In part of Flanders Moss the peat base descends to about 30 ft above O.D. which is appreciably lower than the general level of the Carse surface in the area. Within this thicker peat Durno (1956, fig. 3c) identified pollen-zones V to VIII (Pre-Boreal to Sub-Atlantic), thus demonstrating that the Carse Clays, of Atlantic age (Zone VIIa), are locally missing, presumably because continuously growing peat excluded the estuarine muds of the period. In this area, therefore, the Sub-Carse Peat and surface peat are physically continuous.   M.A.

Landslips

Fintry, Gargunnock and Touch hills. The greater part of the lava escarpment of the Fintry, Gargunnock and Touch hills is fringed by landslips which extend outwards as a series of lobes, for distances of as much as 2000 ft. Most of the landslips belong to one or other of two types: (1) slips composed almost entirely of large angular blocks of rock, generally lava, and backed by steep amphitheatre-like scars in the cliffs above, and (2) apron-like masses derived from clayey beds such as weathered volcanic detritus, shales or boulder clay, which have flowed out in broad lobes carrying massive blocks of rock upon them or within them. Many landslips of the second type have smaller landslips of the first type superimposed on them and locally the relation between the two types becomes so confused that it is almost impossible to separate them. In addition it is in places impossible to separate the landslips from the locally-derived morainic debris of corrie glaciers, especially in localities where the morainic material itself has slipped.

It is thought that many of the landslips are related to glacial and periglacial conditions in the late Pleistocene when the lavas were shattered by frost action and the clayey beds were saturated with water. Possibly the retreat of the main Forth glacier left an oversteepened rockface in a highly unstable state. Land-slipping may also have taken place under periglacial conditions during the Loch Lomond Readvance. Some movement is known to have taken place, however, in recent times.   W.A.R.

Uamh Mhòr. Incipient rock slips have been observed on the south side of Uamh Mhòr, where portions of the flat-lying conglomerates have become detached from the main body of the mountain, with deep clefts opening up behind them.   I.H.F.

Craig Rossie. The east side of Craig Rossie, near Auchterarder, is noteworthy for the extensive landslipping of the rhyodacite lava. The unmoved mass of the hill terminates in a cliff facing eastwards. A huge slice of the lava has broken off and slid downhill to form a second rocky scarp at a lower level. Joints, formerly nearly vertical, now dip away from the hill, and the upper surface of the slipped mass is tilted backwards towards the hill, both effects presumably being caused by rotation during movement. Rocky irregularities of the upper surface reflect differential movement of individual parts of the slipped mass. To the north other prominent lava masses have travelled further downhill and they become more and more disorientated in this direction, resulting in a scene of chaotic disarray. Towards the bottom of the hill near Tarnavie the landslip terminates in completely broken material with large blocks of the Craig Rossie lava carried forward on lobate projections probably consisting in part of drift at the extreme limit of movement. The east side of the slipped area is marked by ridges presumably heaved up in response to the movement, while at the head of the landslip, just east of the summit of Craig Rossie, a large hollow probably represents the former position of some of the slipped material.

It appears that the rock has slid on planes discordant to the base of the rhyodacite, possibly fault-planes, and that the slipping must have involved the immediately underlying rock, though no exposures of this have been recognized in the area. It seems probable that the slipping is largely of late-Glacial age.

M.A.

REFERENCES

CADELL, H. M. 1883. Notice of the surface geology of the estuary of the Forth round Borrowstounness. *Trans. Edinb. geol. Soc.*, **4**, 2–33.
—— 1913. *The story of the Forth*. Glasgow.
—— 1929. Land reclamation in the Forth valley. *Scott. geogr. Mag.*, **45**, 7–22, 81–100.
CARRUTHERS, R. G. 1939. On northern glacial drifts: some peculiarities and their significance. *Q. Jl geol. Soc. Lond.*, **95**, 299–333.
CLOUGH, C. T., HINXMAN, L. W., WILSON, J. S. G., CRAMPTON, C. B., WRIGHT, W. B., BAILEY, E. B., ANDERSON, E. M. and CARRUTHERS, R. G. 1925. The geology of the Glasgow district. 2nd edit. revised by MACGREGOR, M., DINHAM, C. H., BAILEY, E. B. and ANDERSON, E. M. *Mem. geol. Surv. Gt Br.*
DINHAM, C. H. 1927. Stirling district. *Proc. Geol. Ass.*, **38**, 470–92.
—— and HALDANE, D. 1932. The economic geology of the Stirling and Clackmannan Coalfield. *Mem. geol. Surv. Gt Br.*
DONNER, J. J. 1957. The geology and vegetation of Late-glacial retreat stages in Scotland. *Trans. R. Soc. Edinb.*, **63**, 221–64.
—— 1958. Loch Mahaick, a Late-glacial site in Perthshire. *New Phytol.*, **57**, 183.
DURNO, S. E. 1956. Pollen analysis of peat deposits in Scotland. *Scott. geogr. Mag.*, **72**, 177–87.
—— 1958. The dating of the Forth valley Carse Clay (a note). *Scott. geogr. Mag.*, **74**, 47–8.
EARP, J. R., FRANCIS, E. H. and READ, W. A. 1962. Discussion on J. B. Sissons' paper on Late-glacial shorelines [Sissons 1962]. *Trans. Edinb. geol. Soc.*, **19**, 216–20.
ERDTMAN, G. 1928. Studies in the Post-arctic history of the forests of north-western Europe. I. Investigations in the British Isles. *Geol. För. Stockh. Förh.*, **50**, 123–92.
FISK, H. N., McFARLANE, E., KOLB, C. R. and WILBERT, L. J. 1954. The sedimentary framework of the modern Mississippi delta. *J. sedim. Petrol.*, **24**, 76–99.
FLETT, J. S. 1930. In *Mem. geol. Surv. Summ. Prog.* for 1929, pt. 1.

FLINT, R. 1948. *Glacial geology and the Pleistocene epoch*. New York.

FRAZER, H. J. 1929. An experimental study of varve deposition. *Trans. R. Soc. Can.*, **23**, 49–60.

GODWIN, H. and WILLIS, E. H. 1961. Cambridge University natural radiocarbon measurements III. *Radiocarbon*, **3**, 60–76.

—— and WILLIS, E. H. 1962. Cambridge University natural radiocarbon measurements V. *Radiocarbon*, **4**, 57–70.

JAMIESON, T. F. 1865. On the history of the last geological changes in Scotland. *Q. Jl geol. Soc. Lond.*, **21**, 161–203.

LACAILLE, A. D. 1954. *The Stone Age in Scotland*. London.

MCKEE, M. D. 1957. Primary structures in some recent sediments. *Bull. Am. Ass. Petrol. Geol.*, **41**, 1704–48.

MORRIS, D. B. 1922. Geological section at Dumbarton Road. *Trans. Stirling nat. Hist. archaeol. Soc.* for 1921–22, 151–3.

—— 1931. Three geological sections at St. Ninians. *Trans. Stirling nat. Hist. archaeol. Soc.* for 1930–31, 124–8.

NEWEY, W. W. 1966. Pollen-analyses of Sub-Carse peats of the Forth valley. *Trans. Inst. Br. Geogr.*, **39**, 53–9.

PEACH, B. N., CLOUGH, C. T., HINXMAN, L. W., WILSON, J. S. G., CRAMPTON, C. B., MAUFE, H. B. and BAILEY, E. B. 1910. The geology of the neighbourhood of Edinburgh. 2nd edit. *Mem. geol. Surv. Gt Br.*

READ, W. A. 1959. The economic geology of the Stirling and Clackmannan Coalfield, Scotland: Area south of the River Forth. *Coalfld Pap. geol. Surv.*, No. 2.

ROBERTSON, J. 1794. Parish of Callander. *The [Old] Statistical Account of Scotland*, **11**, 574–627.

SIMPSON, J. B. 1933. The Late-glacial readvance moraines of the Highland Border west of the River Tay. *Trans. R. Soc. Edinb.*, **57**, 633–46.

SISSONS, J. B. 1962. A re-interpretation of the literature on Late-glacial shorelines in Scotland with particular reference to the Forth area. *Trans. Edinb. geol. Soc.*, **19**, 83–99.

—— 1963a. Scottish raised shoreline heights with particular reference to the Forth valley. *Geogr. Annlr*, **45**, 180–5.

—— 1963b. The Perth Readvance in Central Scotland. Part I. *Scott. geogr. Mag.*, **79**, 151–63.

—— 1966. Relative sea-level changes between 10 300 and 8300 B.P. in part of the Carse of Stirling. *Trans. Inst. Br. Geogr.*, **39**, 19–29.

—— and CULLINGFORD, R. A. 1966. Late-glacial and Post-glacial shorelines in south-east Scotland. *Trans. Inst. Br. Geogr.*, **39**, 9–18.

—— and SMITH, D. E. 1965a. Peat bogs in a Post-glacial sea and a buried raised beach in the western Carse of Stirling. *Scott. J. Geol.*, **1**, 247–55.

—— and SMITH, D. E. 1965b. Raised shorelines associated with the Perth Readvance in the Forth valley and their relation to glacial isostasy. *Trans. R. Soc. Edinb.*, **66**, 143–68.

SYNGE, F. M. and STEPHENS, N. 1966. Late- and Post-glacial shorelines and ice limits in Argyll and north-east Ulster. *Trans. Inst. Br. Geogr.*, **39**, 101–25.

TAIT, D. 1934. Braid Burn, Duddingston and Portobello excavations. *Trans. Edinb. geol. Soc.*, **13**, 61–71.

THOMPSON, W. O. 1937. Original structure of beaches, bars and dunes. *Bull. geol. Soc. Am.*, **48**, 723–52.

VAN STRAATEN, L. M. J. U. 1954. Composition and structure of recent marine sediments in the Netherlands. *Leid. geol. Meded.*, **14**.

Chapter XIX

ECONOMIC GEOLOGY

An account of the mineral resources in the Stirling and Clackmannan coalfield has been given by Dinham and Haldane (1932) supplemented by Francis (1956) and Read (1959). Coal, refractory materials, limestone and building stone in the strata above the Calciferous Sandstone Measures lavas have been considered in some detail in these publications and are largely omitted from the following account.

Mineral Veins

Introduction. Mineralization in the Stirling district is largely confined to Old Red Sandstone rocks of the Ochil Hills and is associated with faults with three main trends, namely east–west, north-east and north-north-west.

The east–west faults generally follow the trend of the Ochil Fault and the mineralization associated with them is characterized by copper, iron (principally pyrite) and silver, with subordinate lead and arsenic ores, together with the gangue minerals calcite, quartz, and very minor barytes. Metals associated with the north-easterly fractures are dominantly iron (principally oxides of iron as ferruginous gouge) and silver, with minor cobalt, lead and copper contained in gangue composed mainly of calcite, with subordinate quartz and barytes.

The north-north-westerly fractures, by contrast, have copper mineralization, with very minor iron, in a gangue composed mainly of pinkish or, less commonly, white barytes, with calcite and subordinate quartz. There is no obvious genetic connexion between the various types of mineralization and country rock. It may, however, be significant that lead and silver are closely associated with quartz-dolerite intrusions along the Ochil Fault, for it has previously been observed (Wilson 1921, p. 61) that lead and silver occur in an east-north-easterly vein closely associated with much altered and decomposed quartz-dolerite at Hilderstone in West Lothian. Outside the area of Old Red Sandstone volcanic rocks, barytes occurs as the main mineral in veins with north-north-westerly trend which traverse lavas of Lower Carboniferous age near Burnside [NS 76758713]. Barytes is also associated with lead and copper ores in a west-north-westerly vein in the quartz-dolerite quarry at Northfield, about 5 miles south of Stirling, in the Airdrie (31) Sheet. North and west of the Ochil Hills barytes mineralization extends into the Lower Old Red Sandstone sedimentary rocks.

Age of mineral veins. Evidence has been advanced (MacGregor 1944, p. 5) to suggest that 'in central Scotland the formation of barytes and other mineral veins occurred at two epochs; the first in late Carboniferous or early Permian times mainly in conjunction with a fault system comprising fractures with E.–W., E.N.E. and possibly N.N.E. trends, and the second in Tertiary times mainly in conjunction with a W.N.W. to N.N.W. fault system'.

Interpretation of the sequence of mineralization in the Ochil Hills area must necessarily be somewhat tentative owing to the paucity of exposures and the inaccessibility of underground sections in abandoned mines within the crucial

292

area proximate to the Ochil Fault. But our observations confirm those of MacGregor in that they indicate that the ores of copper, lead, silver and iron, with minor cobalt and arsenic ores and subordinate barytes gangue were introduced into east–west and north-easterly fault fractures, as one or more phases of mineralization, during the period from the middle Carboniferous to the Permian; while the mineralization characterized by dominant barytes with subordinate copper ores which is associated with north-north-westerly faults may be as late as Tertiary in age. E.H.F., J.D.

Radioactivity survey. Former mining properties, sites of mineral trials, and numerous mineralized structures located in the southern sector of the Ochil Hills, between Bridge of Allan and Dollar, were examined for the occurrence of radioactive minerals by the Atomic Energy Division during the latter part of 1959. Weak radioactivity was recorded only on argentiferous veins exposed in accessible workings in Airthrey Hill Mine, Airthrey Silver Mine, Carnaughton Glen Silver Mine, Alva Silver Mine, and Tillicoultry Burn Mine. Highest ratemeter readings were obtained on mineralized structures with north-easterly trend. No discrete radioactive mineral has as yet been identified, the weak activity being associated with minute botryoids of hydrocarbon irregularly and sparsely disseminated throughout the veins. Mineral specimens containing smoky quartz were obtained from debris derived from Alva Silver Mine.

On available evidence there is little prospect of any mineralized structure containing an economic amount of radioactive minerals being discovered in the Ochil Hills area, though sufficient may be found to enable the mineralizations to be dated by uranium-lead methods. J.D.

Mining. Silver was mined at Airthrey, Alva, Tillicoultry and Carnaughton Glen during the 18th century. The lode found at Alva (p. 297) was particularly profitable, and even when the silver became exhausted the mine gained a further lease of life from the discovery of cobalt ore.

Copper and iron ores with subordinate amounts of lead ores were raised in the Ochil Hills from a small number of mines which were worked intermittently from the 17th to the 19th century.

Numerous shallow excavations into barytes veins in the Ochil Hills represent, in the majority of cases, trials for copper, which, at the time they were driven, yielded values too low for profitable extraction. On the other hand, for present-day requirements, the associated impurities are rather high to encourage exploitation of these veins for barytes.

DESCRIPTION OF MINES, TRIALS AND MINERAL VEINS

Burnside [NS 76758713]. A vein of white barytes 750 yd E.N.E. of Burnside was first noted by Peach (Dinham and Haldane 1932, p. 194). It is 13 to 16 in wide and trends N.30°W. A 6-in vein of pink and white barytes occurs 440 yd to the west [NS 76388712].

Allan Water [NS 787983]. About half a mile upstream from Bridge of Allan, sandstones and grits of the Sheriffmuir Formation are cut by a mineralized breccia 2 to 3½ ft wide, trending W.10°N. and dipping south at 70°. There are 2 to 3 ft of vuggy quartz and pink barytes on the hanging wall and 6 to 8 in of ferruginous clay gouge stained by copper ones (including malachite) on the footwall. Adits have been driven into the structure on both east and west banks of the Allan Water. The eastern one may be the drive reputed to extend here from Airthrey Hill Mine (see below). There are signs nearby of opencast working and of an infilled shaft, while a short distance to the east there is an area, 400 square yards in extent, of overgrown rock and mineral debris.

Airthrey Hill Mine [NS 795978]. The old Airthrey Hill Mine, in Mine Wood, just above Bridge of Allan, was worked intermittently between 1661 and 1815 (*see* Wilson 1921, p. 141 for historical references). Chalcopyrite and 'grey copper ore' (chalcocite and tetrahedrite) were the main minerals worked and they were accompanied by pyrite and arsenopyrite. More recently quartz, calcite and traces of hydrocarbon have also been noted. The following analysis of the rough ore is given by Heddle (1901, p. 39): iron 51·0 per cent., copper 19·2 per cent., arsenic 15·7 per cent., sulphur 14·4 per cent.

The vein now exposed at the minehead adit portal cuts volcanic conglomerate and is 2 to 3 ft wide, trending W.40°N. and dipping N.E. at 70° to 80°. It consists of pink barytes with a marginal zone of copper ores and is medially traversed by a 1-in vein of white barytes. About 30 ft from the minehead adit portal the vein bifurcates and the original W.40°N. drive terminates only 30 ft or so beyond this point. The west vein, however, is 4 ft thick and continues due west, dipping south at 80°, towards a partly walled-off shaft 20 ft beyond the fork. There is a drainage channel extending northwards from premises in Henderson Street, Bridge of Allan, to an adit level below Lesser Westerton Wood and thence as an adit to a shaft, 116 ft deep, in the grounds of the Allan Water Hotel. Mine workings between the hotel and the minehead are reported to be extensive. Ventilation shafts are located in the garden of the Provost's House and at the base of the escarpment west of Mine House. An infilled shaft is recorded 50 yd N.W. of the minehead.

Pendreich [NS 80659922]. Two mineralized breccias are exposed in an old quarry in lava 280 yd N.W. of Pendreichmuir Cottages. One is a vertical vein of barytes, quartz and calcite, 1 to 4 in wide, trending N.10°W. The other, in which there has been a small trial opencast working, has a similar trend and dips east at 70°. At the northern end of the exposure it is 2 ft wide and contains barytes, quartz, calcite and traces of copper ores, but 30 ft to the south it pinches to 8 in of calcite-filled breccia.

Airthrey Silver Mine [NS 81529720]. Between the years 1760 and 1764 about 12 tons of ore valued in London at £60 per ton were raised from Airthrey Silver Mine, the undertaking ending with the bankruptcy of the consignee. The exact site of the mine has been lost (Dinham and Haldane 1932, p. 194) but it is now tentatively identified with workings recently located 20 yd north of a hairpin bend in the Blairlogie–Sheriff-muir road. The adit portal is on the east side of a small stream and the drive extends for 50 ft on a mineralized breccia, 6 to 10 in wide, which trends W.10°N. and dips north at 70°. The minerals include calcite, quartz, chalcopyrite, iron ores and galena. From the terminal of this east drive there is a trial drive, 50 ft long, to the north and this intersects two thin structures. One is a vein of white barytes and calcite 2 to 4 in wide, and the other is of ferruginous clay gouge with traces of copper ore; both trend W.20°N. There is a trial opencast working on a thin vein of red jasper and calcite trending W.10°N. across the east bank of the stream about 20 yd north of the adit portal.

Blairlogie Trials. The steep scarp slope above Blairlogie is traversed by a group of sub-parallel faults trending north or north-north-west and these have provided access for the most intensive mineralization in the Ochil Hills. The gangue mineral is always barytes with traces of iron ores and such copper minerals as chalcocite, tetrahedrite, malachite and chrysocolla. Impurities of silica and fragments of country rock are normally present. Several trials for copper have been made, but none of the veins has been worked for barytes, though some are of workable thickness. The account below may be followed by reference to Fig. 31.

The largest fault of the area follows the Blairlogie Burn for part of its course and from about 100 yd north of Blairlogie Castle a mineralized zone (A) can be followed upstream for about 250 yd. In places pink and white barytes shows over a width of as much as 15 ft, but there are pockets of colloidal silica and country rock impurities as well as traces of ore minerals. An adit has been driven into the vein on the west side of the burn. Barytes stringers following a north-north-easterly trend at B may link this vein with the next to the east which forms at C a zone, up to 12 ft wide, of material similar to that at A. Farther south, at D, an adit has been driven on a north-westerly vein showing up to 2 ft of pink barytes. Lower down the hill, the fault carrying the mineralization at C reappears and shows values up to 4 ft wide though the barytes is a darker pink in colour and impure; adits have been driven into it at E and F. A short distance north-north-east of E a further trial at G has been driven north along a 2-ft

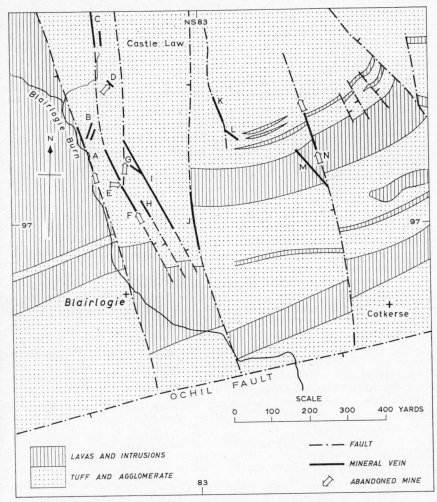

FIG. 31. *Sketch-map showing distribution of mineralization near Blairlogie*
Letters A to N refer to localities mentioned in the text

vein of barytes with copper ores and gangue minerals, and this vein may be continuous downhill with irregular minor mineralization at H. A 2-ft vein (I) of pink and white cockscomb barytes with copper ores and concentrations of granular quartz lies along a parallel north-westerly fault and joins with the north-trending vein a short distance above the adit at G.

Mineralization at J trends N.10°W. and forms a vertical vein, 1 to 3 ft wide, of pink and white cockscomb barytes with a little quartz and copper ores; it has not been opened up. To the north-east, cumulative thicknesses of 1 and 2 ft of barytes can be seen at K and L respectively, but it is distributed in the form of stringers. The north-westerly vein at M is 18 in thick, but wedges out upwards: it joins to the south-east with the more valuable vein at N. The latter is 2 to $3\frac{1}{2}$ ft thick, pinching to 1 ft as it is traced for 100 yd along a trend of N.30°W.; it dips west at 70°. The mineralization is of pink and white cockscomb barytes with copper ores, quartz and country rock debris. It has been opened at two levels, the adit at N being 30 to 40 ft long.

Jerah Mine. The old Jerah copper mine, of which no written records are available, follows a mineralized fault structure, 2 to 3 ft wide, on the lower slopes of Loss Hill, about half a mile north-west of Jerah farm. The vein consists of pink barytes with small strings of chalcocite and staining from malachite and chrysocolla, together with quartz, calcite and traces of galena. One adit level, blocked by collapse at the portal, and flanked by about 400 square yards of partly overgrown mine debris, is located near the southern base of the hill [NS 83239949]. From there the vein, trending N.20°W. and dipping at 80° to the west, can be traced for some distance up the hill along an overgrown opencast which is 4 ft wide and 2 to 3 ft deep. Still farther north-west, about 1150 yd from Jerah, there is a second adit [NS 83009982], and this has been driven back towards the first on a bearing of E.40°S. Near the portal there has been a little stoping and there are signs of opencast working close by.

Loss Burn [NS 84209870]. A mineralized fault structure is exposed for 250 yd along the northern bank of the Loss Burn just above its confluence with the Third Inchna Burn. It comprises a vein of pink barytes with traces of copper ore, 6 to 8 in wide and having several thin subparallel offshoots. The trend is about N.30°W. and the dip varies around 70°. There has been no working.

Third Inchna Burn [NS 84409890]. From a point about 200 yd up from its confluence with the Loss Burn, the Third Inchna Burn follows a mineralized fault structure for 400 yd upstream as far as Red Brae. The trend of the structure is at first N.30°W., veering to N.4°W. as it is traced upstream. A maximum thickness of 3 ft of pink and white cockscomb barytes can be seen wedging out upwards near the southern end of the exposure. At the northern end two close-set veins 5 and 18 in thick are contained in a crush zone altogether 30 ft wide. Elsewhere blebs of barytes extend beyond the veins into the country rock lavas and conglomerates. There are no signs of mining.

Second Inchna Burn [NS 85359980]. About a mile up from Menstrie Glen the Second Inchna Burn follows for 350 yd a west-dipping mineralized fault trending N.5°W. Green copper ores show prominently in a matrix of quartz and barytes ranging up to 6 ft in thickness. About 300 yd south-east [NS 85529949], in an east tributary stream, there is a 'float' of similar mineral assemblage probably derived from an extension of the same structure which there may be at least 5 or 6 ft thick. At neither locality is there evidence of mining.

Menstrie. Stringers of barytes up to 4 in wide are emplaced along north-west and north-north-westerly faults above Menstrie [NS 85139727; 85179721] and in a stream on the east slope of Dumyat [NS 84429789].

Myreton Hill. About half a mile north-east of Menstrie there are several mineralized fault structures in which the principal mineral is pink calcite with subordinate amounts of quartz, red jasper and white barytes and with traces of copper and iron ores. A mining prospectus dated 1907 lists 'mountain haematite' from this area. An adit 40 ft long has been driven on the southernmost vein which is 2 to 3 ft wide and trends at N.30°E. with a dip of 80° to south-east [NS 85649747]. The vein is cut medially by a red calcite–jasper stringer 1 to 2 in wide and traces of barytes and copper are exposed along the margins of the structure in the drive. A number of calcite–barytes stringers exposed at the adit portal have a N.20°W. trend parallel to a nearby fault which is mineralized at two localities to the north-west. At the lower of these [NS 85489762] there are about 10 ft of crush in which two calcite veins, 1 to 2 ft thick, are separated by a medial 'horse'. Farther up the hill [NS 85379783] similar pink calcite in a vein 10 ft wide has been tried in an opencast.

Balquharn Burn Trials. The lower reaches of the Balquharn Burn are crossed by several veins of pink barytes with quartz and calcite and with copper and iron ores. About 100 yd north of Balquharn itself the burn runs along a 1-ft east-dipping vein which pinches out along a bearing of N.20°E. About 50 yd upstream an adit has been driven for 30 ft along a W.10°N. trend in a vertical vein which is 2 ft wide at the portal, narrowing to 18 in at the terminal. Calcite–barytes veinlets trending N.30°E. and dipping N.W. at 80° are exposed in the adit walls. Still farther upstream, about 80 yd above the junction with the Lethen Burn [NS 86539782], there is a vein, 2 to 3 ft wide, trending N.47°W. along a large fault and dipping N.E. at 70°. An adit 150 ft long has been driven north-west and stoping has been carried out up to a height of 15 ft in the level. About 50 yd to the west another adit, 30 to 40 ft long, has been driven along a 2-ft vein trending N.20°W.

Carnaughton Glen Silver Mine [NS 87819754]. At Carnaughton Glen, west of Alva, there is a vertical fault structure, 2 to 4 ft wide, trending W.5°N. subparallel to, and only 50 yd north of, the Ochil Fault. It has been mineralized by red and white calcite and quartz with argentite, chalcopyrite, jasper, pyrite, ferruginous gouge, hydrocarbon and traces of galena. Adit levels have been driven on both sides of the burn. In the west drive, which is 100 ft long, the mineralized structure is still exposed in the terminal of the drive. Ten feet back, there is a cross-cut drive extending for 15 ft along a second fault structure trending N.20°W. and containing a zone of calc-ferruginous clay gouge 4 to 8 in wide. A water-filled shaft 4 ft square stands on the north side of the west drive about 20 ft from the adit portal.

The east drive is 40 ft long and is crossed 4 ft from its terminal by a 15-ft drive along a structure containing 4 to 6 in of calc-ferruginous gouge trending N.20°W. The mineralized structures are still exposed at the terminations of the drives.

Despite the extent of the workings and their designation on the older Ordnance Survey maps as an abandoned silver mine there is, surprisingly, no record as to output nor any previous mention of this locality in the literature.

Alva Glen. For much of its course Alva Glen follows the line of an impressive fault structure which is impersistently mineralized. A number of calcite veinlets having a maximum width of 6 in and trending at N.30°E. are emplaced in a 3-ft breccia zone [NS 88589770] about a quarter of a mile north of Alva. Farther upstream, from about a mile to a mile and a half above the town, the mineralization reappears, mainly on the east bank of the Alva Burn, following a trend of between N.40°W. and N.20°W. and comprising pink and white cockscomb barytes, calcite, quartz and copper ores. Barytes attains a maximum thickness of 14 in, including a thin medial zone of copper ores, at a locality [NS 87919917] about 200 yd downstream from the Strabanster Burn confluence.

A 4-in vein marks the continuation of the structure across the Strabanster Burn itself, about 100 yd up from the Alva Burn. Further mineralization is seen on parallel lines of disturbance in higher tributaries such as West Cameron Burn [NN 86860070] and Middle Cameron Burn [NN 87540103], the latter showing values up to 18 in of pink and white barytes with traces of copper ores.

In the Silver Glen, north-east of Alva, levels have been driven into a barytes vein trending at N.20°W. and having a maximum width of 2 ft: these, however, were probably in search of silver.

Alva Silver Mine. In 1711 thin stringers of silver ore were found in a glen, now called Silver Glen, half a mile east of Alva, and shortly after mining was begun a large mass of ore was struck; it contained native silver which yielded 85·7 per cent. pure metal. Some of the ore was pilfered by miners (Duncan 1796, p. 141), but even so the weekly output from the mine averaged £400 and totalled between £40 000 and £50 000 before the silver was exhausted, giving place to lead and copper. The mine was re-opened in 1759 when a large mass of cobalt ore (mainly erythrite) was discovered. This was mined and, together with ore recovered from the older spoil-heaps, was used in the manufacture of pottery at Prestonpans. An analysis of the cobalt ore (Wilson 1921, p. 144) gives the following percentages: Co 31·85, Fe 10·24, Cu 9·77, As 33·3, PbS (galena) 7·53.

The main workings are sited on a mineralized fault breccia trending W.15°S. and dipping south at 80°, which contains calcite, quartz (including nests of smoky quartz), pyrite, chalcopyrite, arsenopyrite, argentite, galena, erythrite, ferruginous gouge and botryoids of hydrocarbon. Galena also forms thin veins in an altered 5-ft basic dyke cropping out on the north wall of the vein on the eastern bank of Silver Burn.

Adits have been driven along the vein from both sides of the burn. The west drive (A on Fig. 32) follows a mineralized breccia 2 to 3 ft wide for 40 ft until it is blocked near the bottom of a partly-infilled shaft (B) which is, in turn, linked with an access

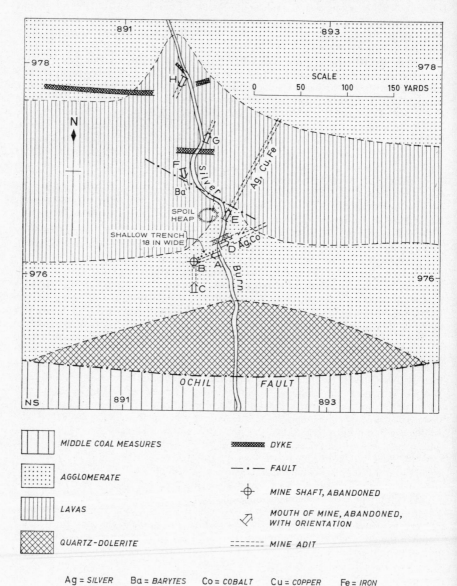

FIG. 32. *Sketch-map showing distribution of mineralization and mining in the Silver Glen, Alva*
Letters A to H refer to localities mentioned in the text

adit (C) driven in country rock from a point 100 ft to the south. A shallow trench, about 18 in wide, leads back from the shaft to the burn and probably marks the outcrop of the vein. The east drive (D) opens, 10 ft from the adit portal, into a chamber measuring 20 ft by 12 ft. A shaft 8 ft square descends for about 40 ft from the south-west sector of the chamber and a level leads off about 30 ft down from the east side of the shaft. From the east side of the chamber a winze descends westward at an angle of 60° towards the shaft. A drive leads off from the south-east corner of the chamber, following for 100 ft the mineralized breccia which still persists at the terminal of the drive. Another drive, 30 ft long, leads off from the south-east corner of the chamber following a mineralized structure, 4 to 8 in wide, along a trend of N.50°E. A ventilation shaft is sited in the north-east corner of the chamber and an inaccessible adit level drive, trending possibly north-east, leads off from the east side of the shaft.

From the description given by Wilson (1921, p. 144) it seems likely that the chamber is the site of the original rich lode of silver ore. The older accounts further indicate that the cobalt was recovered from a lower part of the vein approached from the chamber by the shaft and winze. These led to an intermediate level which was connected by a 66-ft winze to a still lower level. An unlocated adit 'on the burnside lower down the glen' (*loc. cit.; see also* Duncan 1796, pp. 140–4) provided further access to this lowest level.

Higher up Silver Glen there are several trials for silver which follow north-west and north-north-east trends. About 100 ft north of the silver vein, on the eastern side of a small waterfall, an adit (E on Fig. 32) has been driven on a bearing of N.30°E. along a mineralized fault breccia 2 ft wide and containing calcite, ferruginous gouge, quartz, pyrite, chalcopyrite, argentite and hydrocarbon. About 20 ft from the adit portal the level leads into a rock chamber 8 ft square. In the north-west quadrant of the chamber a shaft 4 ft square is flooded to adit level. A drive leading off from the north-east corner of the chamber follows the vein for 300 ft without coming to the end of the mineralized structure. There are signs of small-scale opencast working of the vein east of the stream.

A mineralized fault containing pink barytes with calcite and traces of copper ores is exposed in workings on the west bank of the burn (F on Fig. 32). It has a maximum width of 2 ft and trends N.10°W. From a small opencast working exposing 20 ft of the vein, a level blocked 5 ft from the portal leads off southwards (barytes mineralization along this strike is intersected in the west drive of the Silver Mine). An inaccessible level leads off from the north sector of the opencast working along the barytes vein. About 100 ft north-east a mineralized breccia 2 to 3 ft wide and trending N.20°E. is exposed on the east bank of the burn. A trial level (G) has been driven north-north-east for 30 ft, and still shows calcite, pyrite and ferruginous gouge at the terminal of the drive. About 200 ft upstream a subparallel structure, 3 ft wide, containing a vein of calc-ferruginous gouge 8 to 18 in thick, trends N.30°E. across the burn (H). A level, partly blocked at the portal, has been driven south-west for some 30 ft and overhead stoping to a height of 12 ft has been carried out along two 12-ft sections exposed in the roof of the adit level. Beyond the second section the level is almost completely blocked by stope debris. A short distance upstream, on the west side of the valley, a level has been driven south-westwards for some 40 ft on a fault breccia, 2 to 3 ft in width, containing an 18-inch zone of calcite and ferruginous gouge. There is evidence of former trial pits and trenches over the hillslope up to 100 yd west of Silver Glen, but these workings are now overgrown.

Tillicoultry Burn. The lower reaches of the Tillicoultry Burn and its main tributaries are crossed by a series of faults with north-westerly and north-easterly trends. Near the margin of the diorite, 150 yd north of the Ochil Fault [NS 91249780], a drive follows a disturbance for about 15 ft, where it intersects a 2-ft mineralized breccia trending N.20°W. and containing a calc-ferruginous vein 4 to 10 in wide. Drives to north and south have been made for about 20 ft along this vein and overhand stoping to a height of 10 ft has been carried out.

A fault structure 250 yd up the Daiglen Burn [NS 91069834] was mined, principally for copper, in the mid-eighteenth century. According to Osburn (1795, p. 196) veins up to 18 in thick yielded four different kinds of copper ore together with a little silver and cobalt, the dressed ore being worth £50 per ton. Fifty men were employed, but mining was unprofitable and ceased after a few years. The adit now visible on the west bank (Fig. 6) has been driven for 40 ft on a bearing of S.50°W. along a mineralized section of fault breccia 2 to 3 ft wide, dipping south at 80° and containing calcite, pyrite, chalcopyrite, argentite and ferruginous gouge. About 20 ft in from the adit portal there is a shaft, 4 ft square, flooded to adit level, in the line of the drive. At the shaft a breccia structure 2 to 3 ft wide follows a N.30°W. course across the S.50°W. level and drives have been made for 60 ft to the north-west and over 100 ft to the south-east. A second vein following a N.30°W. trend crosses the S.50°W. drive 15 ft in from the shaft; it contains 2 to 6 in of white barytes with copper ores and dips south-west at 70°.

The line of mineralization followed on the S.50°W. bearing in the adit continues for 400 yd to the north-east (Fig. 6), where it reappears in the Gannel Burn [NS 91309857]. Two other north-easterly mineralized faults [NS 90919857] cross the Daiglen Burn 300 yd upstream from the mine and one of these may be continuous with mineralization flanking a dyke in the Gannel Burn [NS 91409888] 500 yd to the north-east. Sporadic mineralization also appears along margins of north-westerly dykes in the Gannel Burn near the Daiglen confluence and for 300 yd upstream. About 300 yd north of Castle Craig Quarry the Tillicoultry Burn itself follows 4 to 5 ft of mineralized crush trending slightly east of north over a distance of nearly 100 yd. A north-north-westerly vein consisting of a foot of pink barytes is exposed on the hill west of the burn near the termination of a diorite dyke [NS 90919786].

Kirk Burn [NS 92349812]. About half a mile north-east of Tillicoultry, traces of mineralization follow an east-north-easterly fracture across the Kirk Burn, about 130 yd upstream from the Ochil Fault. A trial adit has been driven for about 10 ft along the structure from the east bank of the burn.

Dollar Burn. Three north-east to north-north-easterly mineralized faults cross the Dollar Burn and its tributaries. The lowest is exposed in the Burn of Sorrow [NS 96059930] 70 yd west of Castle Campbell where it forms a crush zone 3 ft wide with two thin calcite veins trending N.30°E., which contain barytes and ferruginous material. To the north-east it reappears following the west bank of the Burn of Care [NS 96239970], consisting there of a breccia 3 to 6 ft wide traversed by thin calc-ferruginous veinlets dipping south-east at 70°. According to Watson (1795, p. 161) the vein also contains silver, though in quantities too small to work profitably.

A mile or so west-north-west the Burn of Sorrow is crossed by a second north-north-easterly vein [NN 94550021] and this was worked for copper and, possibly, lead early in the 18th century. The vein is 2 to 3 ft wide and consists of breccia containing pyrite, chalcopyrite and galena as primary minerals, with accessory chalcocite, malachite, azurite, limonite, chrysocolla and traces of hydrocarbon. The gangue minerals are pink and white barytes with calcite and a little quartz. The vein was opened up on both sides of the burn, but the adit levels are now collapsed. Rock and mineral debris cover an area of about 2000 square yards over a distance of 100 yd downstream from the vein. There is evidence of a collapsed or infilled winze or shaft on the north bank of a tributary about 100 yd north-north-west of the old north adit.

At the head of the Burn of Sorrow [NN 93000070] stringers of barytes and silica follow two north-easterly fault lines. One of these is the north-easterly continuation of the mined fault structure in the Daiglen Burn (see above).

Danny Burn. Near the headwaters of the Danny Burn, between Mickle Corum and Sauchanwood Hill, signs of mineralization appear at three localities. The highest, near the confluence of three tributaries [NN 86500304] consists of a block of pink barytes, 18 inches in diameter; field relations are obscure and the block may not even be *in situ*, but it can nevertheless be taken to indicate mineralization nearby. Between 400 and 500 yd downstream there are two north-north-westerly fault structures showing mineralization. The southernmost [NN 86890311] is a crush rock containing traces of copper ores; the other, 100 yd below [NN 86900321], consists of ferruginous gouge.

River Devon. A 15-ft wide north-westerly fault breccia containing ferruginous material crosses the River Devon between Fin Glen and Glen MacDuff [NN 88170347]. Farther downstream, on the east bank of the Glen Bee Burn a few yards north of its confluence with the River Devon [NN 90460471], a large mass of pink barytes indicates proximity to a vein at least 3 ft thick. The field relations are obscured, but the mineralization almost certainly lies along the same line as a 3-ft vein of barytes trending between N.20°W. and N.40°W. across the Muckle Burn [NN 90970380], half a mile south-east. Another barytes vein, of indeterminate thickness, follows a north–south trend across the Muckle Burn 300 yd upstream [NN 90810359]. About a mile to the south of the latter there are stringers of quartz in an east–west crush zone, 3 ft wide, following the north bank of a tributary to the Grodwell Burn [NN 90610179].

Frandy Burn. Near the head of the Frandy Burn [NN 92580208] there are signs of barytes mineralization along an east–west fault and some distance downstream, about 200 yd south of Frandy farmhouse [NN 94150404], there is a pocket of barytes not obviously related to any fault structure.

Glen Sherup. The continuation of the major north-easterly fault structure already described as showing mineralization in the Daiglen and Gannel burns and Burn of Sorrow (p. 300) is followed also by Glen Sherup. On the north bank of the Glensherup Burn [NN 95090284], about 100 yd upstream from the entry of the Roughcleugh Burn, barytes stringers dip south-east in fault breccia. Halfway up the Rough Cleugh itself silica stringers are exposed within a north-westerly fault breccia 2 to 3 ft wide.

Glen Quey. Glen Quey, like Glen Sherup, follows a north-easterly fault line—the same structure as that seen in the Burn of Care and Burn of Sorrow (p. 300). Traces of barytes and quartz are exposed in the fault crush about 100 yd up the tributary Meadow Burn [NN 97630255] and similar mineralization is seen in a wide zone of breccia [NN 97070134] formed by a north-westerly fault which intersects the Glen Quey Fault on the south bank of the Glenquey Burn half a mile above the reservoir.

E.H.F., J.D.

Area north and west of the Ochil Hills. Calcite–barytes veinlets occur in association with a fault trending N.30°W. which cuts sandstones and siltstones in the Millstone Burn [NN 84010513] north of Harperstone. Large pieces of barytes ploughed up in a field [NN 836051] a quarter of a mile to the west may indicate the presence of yet another mineralized fault. These occurrences are probably related to the larger north-westerly dislocation which crosses Strathallan in this neighbourhood.

In a small stream near Kirktonlees, north-west of Auchterarder, a barytes vein 2 ft 9 in thick is exposed between sandstone and the north wall of an east–west quartz-dolerite dyke [NN 927135]. M.A.

In the Dunblane area barytes mineralization has been detected in the sedimentary rocks as far north as Ashfield [NN 785038] and as far west as the Cessintully Burn [NS 673993], near Thornhill. The veins, some of which occur in obvious crush zones, are generally less than one foot thick, but a thickness of 1 ft 6 in has been recorded [NN 762009]. The trend of the veins varies between west and north-west. I.H.F.

SHALE AND CLAY FOR BRICKMAKING

Shale has not, as yet, been worked for brickmaking within the Stirling district but some of the thick shales in the Carboniferous, particularly the Black Metals and the shales above the Murrayshall, Fankerton, Top Hosie, Index, Orchard and Calmy limestones, might prove useful for this purpose in localities where the drift cover is sufficiently thin to make extraction economic. The calcareous shales immediately above the limestones might be more difficult to utilize but these could possibly be used for the manufacture of light-weight concrete aggregate (Ehlers 1958, pp. 97–8).

Other possible sources of brickmaking material are the late-Glacial laminated clays, and the post-Glacial Carse Clays. The late-Glacial clays were at one time worked for brick and pottery manufacture at Hilton, near Alloa, and also in the Dollar area. The Carse Clays were formerly worked at the Boquhan Tile Works [NS 664958], at the Throsk Tile Works [NS 852915] (Dinham and Haldane 1932, p. 213), and at a site [NS 714984] near Blair Drummond.

W.A.R.

LIMESTONE AND DOLOMITE

In addition to the extensive working of the Murrayshall Limestone and, to a considerably smaller extent, Limestone C for agricultural lime (Dinham and Haldane 1932, pp. 19–26; Read 1959, p. 9; Robertson and others 1949, p. 177) some of the cornstones of the Cornstone Beds have been worked opencast (p. 110), also presumably for agricultural purposes, and there are traces of old horseshoe-shaped limekilns along the outcrop of these beds south-west of Kippen.

W.A.R.

BEDDED IRON ORES

During the 18th and early 19th centuries iron ore was widely sought in the area in order to meet the demands of local ironworks. One works was established at Furnacebank (Devon) about a mile south-east of Alva; others, outside the present district, were at Oakley (Forth) west of Dunfermline and, most important, at Carron near Falkirk. Some of the richest ores were obtained from the Limestone Coal Group. In the south the Banton Clayband in the Black Metals was considered to be of workable thickness in the Auchenbowie, Bannockburn and Plean area, and at East Plean a clayband ironstone in the roof of the Greenyards Coal was extracted together with the coal (Dinham and Haldane 1932, p. 42; Macgregor and others 1920, pp. 98–101). To the east the rich blackband ironstones of Comrie (including the Success and Inzievar seams) were wrought extensively around Blairhall and Oakley—first for the Carron Company and later for the local Forth Ironworks (Lee in Macgregor and others 1920, pp. 146–55; Haldane and Allan 1931, pp. 49–51, 60–3; Dinham and Haldane 1932, pp. 84–7).

In the Passage Group, nodular ironstones at the horizon of No. 3 Marine Band Group were extensively worked at Vicar's Bridge, near Dollar, for the Devon Ironworks; old ironstone pits near Blair Quarry, between Kincardine and Culross, were probably sunk to nodular bands near the top of the group (Dinham and Haldane 1932, pp. 125–8).

The only productive ironstone horizon in the Lower Coal Measures is above the Mill Coal, formerly exploited at Airth and near Tillicoultry (Anderson 1845, p. 69; Dinham and Haldane 1932, pp. 135, 165). Several ironstones in the Middle Coal Measures were worked in the Devon Colliery alongside the ironworks (Dinham and Haldane 1932, pp. 145–7).

E.H.F.

BUILDING STONE

The Lower Old Red Sandstone does not yield much good building stone, and many of the buildings in its area of outcrop have door and window surrounds of Upper Old Red Sandstone freestone brought from a distance. Nevertheless the sandstones, mainly in the Sheriffmuir, Dunblane and Teith formations, have been quarried in many places for local use (see Chapter V). The largest workings, now disused, are Gallowhill Quarry [NS 781989], Wolf's Hole Quarry [NS 790981], Stonehill Quarry [NN 798009] and Auchterarder Quarry [NN 939122], all in sandstones of the Sheriffmuir Formation. At Callander some of the less coarse mixed conglomerates have been quarried [NN 635082] for building stone.

The Gargunnock Sandstones were formerly worked extensively for building stone in a large number of small quarries south-west of Kippen (p. 108), and Culcreuch [NS 62028767] is said to have been built of rock from the Downie's Loup Sandstones. The best sandstones, however, are found in the Carboniferous sediments above the Clyde Plateau lavas; many of them were worked, some on a large scale, but there are no quarries now in operation (Dinham and Haldane 1932, pp. 195–202).

Craigton [NS 62908683], now demolished, is said to have been built from rock quarried from the Dun intrusion.   M.A., I.H.F., W.A.R.

ROADSTONE, ETC.

The quartz-dolerite intrusions provide the most reliable source of good material in the Stirling district. The quartz-dolerite of the Stirling sill is used extensively for road metal, concrete aggregate and kerbstones. It is at present being worked at Cambusbarron Nos. 1 and 2 quarries [NS 771921; 772922] and Murrayshall Quarry [NS 772912] and was formerly worked at several other localities. There is an active quarry in the Ochil Fault-Intrusion at Mill Glen, Tillicoultry. The working at Gloom Hill, Dollar, is disused. An intrusion on the Arndean Fault has been quarried [NT 006974] near Devonshaw. The quartz-dolerite dykes have been worked in the past in many localities, e.g. near Over Ardoch [NN 841116], south of Garrick [NN 849116], west of Tullibardine Station [NN 915134], at Auchterarder Station [NN 956122], north of Drumloist [NN 683063], at Argaty Quarry [NN 732049], on the east bank of the Allan Water south of Ashfield [NN 785032], and at two localities [NN 815028, 836025] on Sheriffmuir.

The Downie's Loup sill was formerly worked for road metal in Dinning Quarry (p. 158) but the crushing strength of the upper, non-porphyritic part of the sill is reported to have been poor.

Many of the lavas of the Calciferous Sandstone Measures are somewhat decomposed and these rocks have not been quarried to any great extent. The Old Red Sandstone lavas have been utilized in a number of places, e.g. near Pairney where both trachyandesite and rhyodacite have been quarried.

M.A., E.H.F., I.H.F., W.A.R.

FULLER'S EARTH

Material used as fuller's earth was formerly extracted from a bed of decomposed agglomerate of Lower Old Red Sandstone age on the east bank of the Keltie Burn [NO 009128] south of Keltie Castle.   M.A.

U

NATURAL GAS

A strong flow of gas was encountered in Culross No. 2 Bore [NS 98268587] while it was being drilled through Limestone Coal Group strata. According to the driller, the flow of gas tended to increase successively as each coal seam was cut, until a column of gas and water rose to a height of 30 ft above ground level. The gas, believed to be mainly methane, burned with a hot, yellow, non-smoky flame.

E.H.F.

SAND AND GRAVEL

There are extensive deposits of sand and gravel in the Stirling district, particularly in Strathallan and the Teith valley. They take various forms, including kames, kame-terraces and fluvio-glacial spreads. In places river alluvium makes a sizable contribution to the total quantity present. In the Teith valley and locally elsewhere, much of the most accessible material has already been quarried, but considerable reserves still remain, especially in Strathallan north-east of Kinbuck, where great quantities of sand and gravel await exploitation.

DETAILS

Teith valley. The fluvio-glacial terrace south-east of Callander consists largely of gravel, as do the alluvial terraces. Some of the ground north of the Callander–Stirling road or between the Callander–Thornhill road and the river might provide suitable sites for quarrying, but much of the ground is not likely to be available, e.g. because it is afforested. Several large gravel mounds and ridges near Ballachallan [NN 654056] and Cambusbeg [NN 661052] have likewise been planted with trees.

A quarry has recently been opened at the northern end of the large area of mounds and ridges between 3 and 3½ miles south-east of Callander (Anderson 1946, p. 41). It has provided quantities of gravel and coarse-grained sand, but morainic material and fine-grained silty sand also occur in places. This bears out Anderson's inference that the small pit showing 20 ft of soft sand is not typical of these mounds. This moundy spread extends eastwards on the north side of the railway between Drumvaich and Milton of Cambus, and locally there may be sufficient reserves to make quarrying economic.

South-east of Drumvaich on the north bank of the River Teith there are fluvio-glacial and alluvial terraces, largely made of gravel, which are at present being quarried and yield faces up to 25 ft high. The area is restricted by its proximity to the main road, which, however, provides easy access.

The fluvio-glacial terrace between Buchany and Doune has been very extensively quarried south of the main road at Wood of Doune and also north of the railway at Doune Station. Both quarries have now been abandoned, but an extension [NN 710023] of the former quarry has been opened up further west and shows a 20-ft face of rather coarse-grained gravel with some sand. One of the alluvial terraces nearby is yielding a 10-ft face of rather coarse gravel. Large reserves still remain north of the road and railway between the existing quarries and Doune Lodge. A few drumlins of boulder clay rise above the level of this terrace, and others may be concealed beneath its surface.

Two small quarries [NN 717012, 719009] have been opened in the same terrace on the south side of the river and west of the main road. Both show at least 10 ft of sand with some fine gravel; neither is now in use and the reserves in the vicinity are not large. The location of Gartincaber Pit (Anderson 1946, p. 41) is uncertain but it is thought that it may be one of the two above-mentioned quarries. Large amounts of sand and gravel exist in both the fluvio-glacial and the alluvial terraces on the west side of the River Teith between Doune and Blair Drummond, but here again there is a possibility of encountering hidden drumlins of boulder clay. Similar terraces occur on the east side of the river but they are much more limited in extent.

There is a great deal of gravel in the ground north of Doune, but most of it is thinly spread. Locally, however, there are deposits of considerable thickness, e.g. south of Argaty House [NN 737031]; south-east of Mansfield [NN 723034], where a quarry was recently opened but within a short period was abandoned; and around Netherton [NN 740020] where the thickness is at least 40 ft in places and quarrying began a short time ago.

Big quantities of sand and gravel are present in the through-valley between Doune and Dunblane, especially immediately east of the road junction [NN 756015] near which two quarries have been opened. One, now abandoned, on the south side of the main road (Anderson 1946, p. 42) shows a 20-ft face of sand with a little fine gravel. The other, on the north side of the road, is still in operation and shows a 20-ft face of mainly fine-grained sand with some coarser sand and a little gravel. Between this pit and the road junction there is a recently abandoned pit showing faces, generally less than 10 ft high, of coarse sand with some fine gravel. From this area eastwards to Dunblane there appear to be considerable reserves in mounds and ridges of sand and gravel, to which the main road gives easy access.

Lower Strathallan. Large quantities of sand and gravel have been deposited in a narrow belt in the centre of Strathallan between Dunblane and Ashfield. The deposits are especially thick near Dunblane, and have been extensively quarried at the Knock of Barbush [NN 786027] where work is still proceeding. The northern and eastern pits here have yielded mainly fine-grained and locally silty sand which towards the south and west passes into coarse-grained sand in which lenses of gravel appear. Considerable reserves remain at the Knock and also south of Barbush Farm, but within Dunblane itself the deposits are largely built over or lie within the public park. Considerable reserves also exist in mounds and ridges between Barbush and Ashfield, near which a bore [NN 78840385] passed through 53 ft of sand and gravel. Between Ashfield and Kinbuck there is some sand and gravel on both sides of the alluvial tract by the Allan Water, but the quantities are not so great. At Kinbuck, however, a ridge of gravel almost blocks the valley and must be almost 100 ft high in places. A disused quarry in this deposit, on the east side of the railway by Kinbuck Station, has recently been reopened. It shows a 60-ft face, mostly gravel towards the top and mostly medium- to coarse-grained sand in the lower part, with some gravel. Considerable reserves, easily accessible, are available here.

On the eastern side of the Kinbuck–Braco road, for about half a mile northwards from the bridge over the Allan Water, there is a 50-ft high ridge in which a small quarry [NN 795061] has been opened, showing rather argillaceous gravel, coarse in places. Between Mid and Nether Cambushinnie thick deposits of sand and gravel extend along the north side of the alluvial tract by the Allan Water.

Considerable quantities of sand and gravel occur on the south side of the Knaik valley, mainly west of Glenlichorn [NN 797126] and south of the Arrevore Burn, but extending across the latter in the vicinity of Arrevore. Access is, however, difficult and no attempt has been made to quarry these deposits.

Large amounts of sand and gravel in mounds also exist in the Corriebeagh valley, mainly on the south side of the through-valley to Findhu Glen, but access is very difficult, probably least so by way of Findhu Glen.   I.H.F.

Upper Strathallan. The extensive and accessible deposits of sand and gravel in upper Strathallan, between Braco and Auchterarder, have as yet been exploited only on a small scale. There are large reserves here, especially in the big kames east of Ardoch House, around Westerton and north of Blackford. The pebbles in these deposits comprise Highland rocks (schistose grit, quartz, epidiorite, etc.) and Old Red Sandstone rocks, both igneous and sedimentary. Sand and gravel are at present being worked in a pit [NN 834095] south-west of Braco and in another [NN 902096] north of Blackford.

U*

Coarse gravel, probably typical of the esker deposits along the north side of the strath, is intermittently dug at Loaninghead crossroads [NN 926098].   M.A.

Stirling area. Glacial sands and gravels occur in rather small isolated patches between Cowie, south-east of Stirling, and the eastern foot of the Touch Hills. These deposits were formerly exploited at several localities but are now worked only in the Berry Hills, immediately west of Cowie. The sandy and gravelly deposits associated with the high sea-level of late-Glacial times, which form an extensive tract between Stirling and Plean, have been worked in many places (*see* Dinham and Haldane 1932, pp. 206–9). Working, however, is rendered difficult by the heterogeneous nature of the deposits and by the presence of thin beds and lenses of silty and clayey material. In the area east of Stirling the presence of minute fragments of coal in the sand and gravel is an undesirable feature.   W.A.R.

Devon valley. Sand and gravel is at present worked in a pit at Arndean, two miles east of Dollar. In this general area between Dollar and Muckart there appears to be considerable scope for further exploitation of the deposits, most of which contain coal debris. The workings at Cunninghar Sand Pit [NS 925972] near Tillicoultry, now disused, were in sand with gravel lenses (p. 272).   E.H.F.

PEAT

Of the deposits of peat within the Stirling district, the raised mosses that overlie the Carse Clays in the Forth valley are most suitable for commercial exploitation. The eastern part of Flanders Moss, which lies largely within the area of Sheet 39, has been examined in detail by the Moss Survey Group of the Scottish Peat Committee and the following data are taken from their report. The depth is fairly uniform and averages about 4·5 metres (14·8 ft) over the area, except for the hollow in the north-east, where the depth may be as much as 7·5 metres (24·6 ft), and round the edges of the moss, where consolidation has taken place as a result of drainage and the depth is usually about 3·0 metres (9·8 ft). The total net volume of the peat is 39 776 000 metric tons and, taking the average moisture content as 92·7 per cent., the total amount of solids in the deposit is about 2 900 000 metric tons. The degree of humification varies from H_2 to H_8 on Von Post's Scale and the bulk of the peat is of the order of H_4 to H_5.

Further east much of the peat that formerly covered the Carse was stripped off in the 18th century (Cadell 1913, pp. 262–83; 1929, pp. 7–16) in order to reclaim the area for agriculture and some of this peat was sold as fuel. In more recent times peat has been worked on a fairly small scale for fuel and for horticultural purposes on Dunmore Moss and Letham Moss, two of the residual patches of peat on the Carse east of Stirling (Dinham and Haldane 1932, pp. 215–6; Read 1959, p. 62).   W.A.R.

Immense quantities of peat lie on high ground north-west of Strathallan. Between Uamh Bheag and Cromlet the average thickness is at least 6 ft over about 18 square miles. The ground, however, is difficult of access. Lesser, but still considerable, peat mosses occur in the Keltie valley, in Gleann an Dubh Choirein, on Meall Leathan Dhail, on Lennieston Muir, on Meall a' Choire Odhair and at Red Moss north-west of Langside. The peat has been worked at the last two localities. In Strathallan the peat of Shelforkie Moss, west of Carsebreck, has been extensively worked, but the bulk of the deposit remains. Extensive deposits of peat are also found in the Ochil, Fintry, Gargunnock and Touch hills but there has been little or no exploitation in these relatively inaccessible areas.

M.A., I.H.F., W.A.R.

WATER SUPPLY

Water supply in the Stirling district is obtained mainly from surface sources. Reservoirs collecting run-off from the volcanic rocks of the Touch, Gargunnock and Fintry hills supply Stirling, Grangemouth, Larbert and Falkirk. In the Ochil Hills there are reservoirs in Glen Quey, Glen Sherup and in upper Glen Devon at Frandy and Backhill. The Hillfoot towns, Menstrie, Alva, Tillicoultry and Dollar, draw supplies from the rapid streams descending the Ochil scarp.

Water is also obtained from boreholes in the Lower and Upper Old Red Sandstone, Upper Limestone Group, Passage Group and Coal Measures. Details of water supply from underground sources within the area of Sheet 39 are given by Robertson and others (1944) and by Colleran (1965).

M.A., W.A.R.

REFERENCES

ANDERSON, J. G. C. 1946. Sands and gravels of Scotland; Glasgow and west central Scotland. *Wartime Pamphlet geol. Surv.*, No. 30, pt. 3.

ANDERSON, M. 1845. Parish of Tillicoultry. *The new statistical account of Scotland*, Vol. 8, 66–75. Edinburgh.

CADELL, H. M. 1913. *The story of the Forth*. Glasgow.

—— 1929. Land reclamation in the Forth valley. *Scott. geogr. Mag.*, **45**, 7–22.

COLLERAN, NAN P. D. 1965. Records of wells in the areas of Scottish one-inch Geo-logical Sheets Loch Lomond (38), Stirling (39) and Crieff (47). *Water Supply Papers geol. Surv., Well Catalogue Series.*

DINHAM, C. H. and HALDANE, D. 1932. The economic geology of the Stirling and Clackmannan Coalfield. *Mem. geol. Surv. Gt Br.*

DUNCAN, J. 1796. Parish of Alva. *The [old] statistical account of Scotland*, Vol. 18, 125–48. Edinburgh.

EHLERS, E. G. 1958. The mechanism of lightweight aggregate formation. *Bull. Am. Ceram. Soc.*, **37**, 95–9.

FRANCIS, E. H. 1956. The economic geology of the Stirling and Clackmannan Coalfield, Scotland: Area north of the River Forth. *Coalfld Pap. geol. Surv.*, No. 1.

HALDANE, D. and ALLAN, J. K. 1931. The economic geology of the Fife Coalfields, Area I. *Mem. geol. Surv. Gt Br.*

HEDDLE, M. F. 1901. *The mineralogy of Scotland*. Edinburgh.

MACGREGOR, A. G. 1944. Barytes in central Scotland. *Wartime Pamphlet geol. Surv.*, No. 38.

MACGREGOR, M., LEE, G. W. and WILSON, G. V. 1920. The iron ores of Scotland. *Mem. geol. Surv. spec. Rep. Miner. Resour. Gt Br.*, **11.**

OSBURN, W. 1795. Parish of Tillicoultry. *The [old] statistical account of Scotland*, Vol. 15, 189–216. Edinburgh.

READ, W. A. 1959. The economic geology of the Stirling and Clackmannan Coalfield, Scotland: Area south of the River Forth. *Coalfld Pap. geol. Surv.*, No. 2.

ROBERTSON, T., MACGREGOR, A. G. and LAWRIE, T. R. M. 1944. Water supply from underground sources of Glasgow and adjacent Lowlands and Highlands (Quarter-inch Geological Sheets 13 and 14). Part II. Well catalogues for one-inch Sheets 38 (Loch Lomond and Aberfoyle) and 39 (Stirling and Clackmannan). *Wartime Pamphlet geol. Surv.*, No. 39.

—— SIMPSON, J. B. and ANDERSON, J. G. C. 1949. The limestones of Scotland. *Mem. geol. Surv. spec. Rep. Miner. Resour. Gt Br.*, **35.**

WATSON, J. 1795. Parish of Dollar. *The [old] statistical account of Scotland*, Vol. 15, 155–72. Edinburgh.

WILSON, G. V. 1921. The lead, zinc, copper and nickel ores of Scotland. *Mem. geol. Surv. spec. Rep. Miner. Resour. Gt Br.*, **17.**

Appendix I

GEOPHYSICAL INVESTIGATIONS

BY

R. McQuillin

Geophysical methods were used by the Geophysics Department to study a wide range of geological problems in the Stirling district, problems which include mapping the course of a 'buried channel' and locating or delimiting, beneath superficial deposits, fault lines, dolerite dykes and diorite intrusions.

In 1960, a survey was made of the flat, drift-covered land (the Carse) west of Stirling between the rivers Teith and Forth, bounded to the west by Flanders Moss. Both the Ochil and Abbey Craig faults pass from the east under this cover of drift, and it was hoped to interpret their positions from detailed gravity, magnetic and electrical curves. Results provide clear indication of the position of the Abbey Craig Fault, but geophysical results alone were not sufficient to establish with certainty the line, west of Craigforth [NS 774949], of the Ochil Fault. This failure was partly due to complication of the gravity field by anomalies associated with a hitherto unknown deep 'buried channel' which can be traced gravitationally between Craigforth and Flanders Moss and probably extends farther west. The first aim of the surveys in this area was to assist in siting a number of Geological Survey boreholes to obtain information about major faults west of Stirling and this was successfully achieved.

In 1961, more than 4000 magnetic measurements were made in the Keltie Water–Allt an Dubh Choirein area north of Callander to study the lateral surface extent of diorite intrusions, and in the country around Auchterarder to follow between surface exposures the concealed courses of a number of dolerite dykes. As the intrusive rocks were in both cases considerably more magnetic than the country rock this information was obtained without difficulty, except where strongly magnetic dykes occur at or near the margins of the diorite intrusions. Where this happens, the anomaly patterns interfere and the geophysical evidence is inconclusive. At this time, a number of the Geological Survey boreholes near Stirling were being drilled, and electrical tests were made in two of them.

Aeromagnetic survey of the district represented by the Stirling (39) Sheet was made as part of a larger survey of parts of Scotland and the adjacent sea areas, flown in 1962 for the Geological Survey by Hunting Surveys Ltd. (Summ. Prog. 1963, p. 67). Regional gravity coverage of the district is obtained by a compilation of surveys by the Geophysics Department and by Dr. W. Bullerwell and Dr. J. Phemister.

Magnetic Surveys

Magnetic measurements were first made in this area between 1885 and 1892 (Rücker and Thorpe 1890; 1896), at stations near Stirling in 1885, Callander in 1891, Dunblane in 1892 and Crieff Junction (now Gleneagles Station) in 1892. Rücker and Thorpe (1896) recognized from their survey the relationship between disturbances of the magnetic field in this area and abundance of basic igneous rocks. Recent surveys expose this relationship in much greater detail.

Aeromagnetic surveys. Flights were made 1000 ft above land with east–west traverses 2 km apart and north–south tie-lines every 10 km. Total force magnetic anomalies were reduced against first-order equations of regional magnetic variation over the British Isles for the epoch 1955·5, equations which were calculated from magnetic measurements on the ground, made during 1955, at an open network of 28

308

stations. Results of the aeromagnetic survey are shown on the anomaly map (Plate XII, fig. 1).

In parts of the area where surface rocks are mainly sedimentary but with a few igneous dykes, the magnetic gradients are low, whereas in other parts where igneous rocks predominate the magnetic field is disturbed by large-amplitude fluctuations. Major faults which cross the district are the Highland Boundary Fault and the Ochil Fault and both show associated magnetic anomalies of parallel trend.

Magnetic rocks occur on both sides of the Highland Boundary Fault; to the north-west a diorite intrusion crops out close to the fault and is probably intersected by it at depth, and to the south-east Old Red Sandstone lavas are exposed in steeply dipping beds. The diorite produces a positive anomaly exceeding +250 gammas, and anomalies due to the lavas, though less well defined, probably contribute to the magnetic gradient normal to the fault.

Between Dollar and Stirling, the area immediately south of the Ochil Fault is shown on the anomaly map to be associated with mainly negative magnetic values, but north of the fault, the anomaly, though irregular, is mainly positive. A peak value larger than +450 gammas was recorded over the diorite intrusion north-east of Tillicoultry, and, although at the surface this intrusion seems to exist only north of the fault, the area of positive anomaly extends well south of the fault, completely annulling the negative trough elsewhere developed on this side of the fault. It is suggested therefore that diorite may exist also south of the fault, but under a cover of sedimentary rocks. Because of the complex relationship between anomalies due to magnetic rocks on each side of the fault, it is not possible to give a reliable estimate of depth to the top of the postulated diorite south of the fault.

West of Stirling, anomalies associated with the Ochil Fault give way to anomalies associated with the Stirling sill and Carboniferous lavas of the Fintry and Gargunnock hills. A negative magnetic anomaly over the Carse with minimum below −550 gammas is more prominent than are the positive anomalies over the hills to the south, and this suggests normal (or if reversed, relatively weak) remanent magnetization of the lavas. Palaeomagnetic measurements have proved both normal and reversed remanent magnetization in British Carboniferous rocks, with inclination of the axis approaching the horizontal (*see* Belshé 1957; Clegg and others 1957; Cox and Doell 1960; Everitt and Belshé 1960; Everitt 1960; 1961). Lavas of the Fintry and Gargunnock hills are thought to correlate with the lower Rashiehill lavas which form the lower part of a succession which was sampled for magnetic measurements by Professor S. K. Runcorn and Dr. J. Hospers. Their specimens were taken from the cores of the Rashiehill Borehole [NS 83867301], sited south of the district, and they were unorientated. Results of their experiments were reported by Anderson (1963) who said that they had found the lavas to be strongly magnetized at 30° inclination.

East of the area of exposed Carboniferous igneous rocks, smaller magnetic anomalies may relate to displacement, by transgression or faulting, of these same rocks at depth. Best developed are the anomalies across the Muirpark Fault shown by a small magnetic high centred over Bannockburn [NS 813902], and a low to the south over Sauchinford

---

PLATE XII

MAGNETIC AND GRAVITY ANOMALY MAPS OF THE STIRLING DISTRICT

FIG. 1. *Map showing total force magnetic anomalies from aeromagnetic survey*
Contour interval 10 gammas except in areas of high gradient
Areas of positive anomaly shaded

FIG. 2. *Bouguer anomaly gravity map*
Contour interval 1 milligal
Broken line encloses area of detailed gravity survey

[NS 820882]. The maximum magnetic gradient is normal to the fault and almost directly over it. A possible cause of these anomalies is the transgression of a quartz-dolerite sill along this fault. Displacement of a sill by the fault is unlikely because quartz-dolerite sills in this area were intruded after movement of the major faults (p. 228).

The only conspicuous anomalies observed over the country between the Carse and the Highland Boundary Fault are those associated with dolerite dykes. These produce positive anomalies of up to +40 gammas with, in some cases, small subsidiary negative anomalies to the south.

Detailed surveys. Magnetic methods were extensively used in all parts of the district selected for special study, two proton magnetometers, measuring total force, being used. For convenience, results for each restricted locality were reduced to a local base without any regional correction though diurnal variations were allowed for.

On and around the Carse west of Stirling a close network of stations was observed before surveying twelve traverses along which stations were read at 30-ft intervals. Positions of these traverses are shown on Fig. 33 as well as a typical example of the magnetic profiles. Also shown on Fig. 33 are interpreted sub-drift positions of faults or other boundaries between magnetic and non-magnetic rock beneath drift. The Abbey Craig Fault is traced from near Stirling to where it is exposed at the foot of the Gargunnock Hills, but magnetic anomalies due to the Ochil Fault disappear west of Craigforth. The boundary between the exposed lavas at Craigforth and the non-magnetic sedimentary rocks to the west was investigated by two east–west traverses, and was discovered close to the line of the western edge of the Craigforth crags. Geological evidence suggests that this is a normal boundary.

West of Craigforth, anomalies due to a magnetic dyke were traced south-west from its exposure on the bank of the Forth [NS 76989539], near Drip Bridge, to a sudden termination close to the extrapolated line of the Ochil Fault. It is suggested that this dyke is cut off by the fault, and that the position where the anomaly disappears fixes the position of the fault. The course of the dyke is shown on Fig. 33.

Prior to geophysical investigations in the Keltie Water–Allt an Dubh Choirein area, north of Callander, diorite was known to crop out in three localities, in the Allt an Dubh Choirein [NN 670150], on Druim nan Eilid [NN 660135], and on Meall Odhar [NN 648146] and the geophysical work aimed to assess whether these were exposed parts of a single intrusion. When large magnetic anomalies were found over the exposed diorite, it was decided to use only the magnetic method, difficult terrain making detailed gravity surveys less practical. The results of the investigations are shown on the magnetic anomaly map (Fig. 34) and the positions of the thirty-nine detailed traverses from which this was compiled are indicated on Fig. 35.

Besides the diorites, there are within the area three distinct groups of magnetic rocks: dykes of Caledonian age, Lower Old Red Sandstone lavas and volcanic conglomerates, and quartz-dolerite dykes of late Carboniferous or early Permian age. Magnetic anomalies due to these rocks would be important if they could be confused with those from the diorites. Fortunately, in this area Old Red Sandstone lavas and conglomerates do not produce large anomalies. On the other hand, anomalies associated with the quartz-dolerite dykes are very large. Over northern margins of the dykes maximum values reach +2000 gammas with in some cases large negative troughs to the south. These same dykes were surveyed in more detail in the Auchterarder area. Unfortunately, in some places the dyke anomalies do interfere with those associated with the diorites. Dykes of Caledonian age comprise both basic and acid types, and some, if not all, are magnetic. In general it would seem that they are characterized by fairly symmetrical positive anomalies of up to about 1000 gammas, with negative anomalies either absent or small. Some or all of the anomalies north-east of the Allt an Dubh Choirein may be due to these dykes, and the geophysical evidence for the existence here of near-surface diorite (*see* Fig. 35) is therefore inconclusive. Evidence from field exposures shows that the outcrop of the diorite does not in fact extend for more than about a hundred yards to the north-east of the stream.

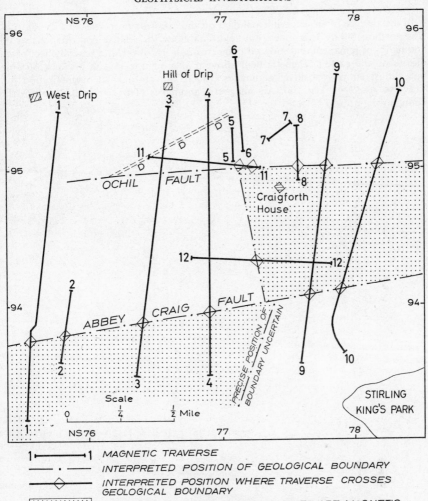

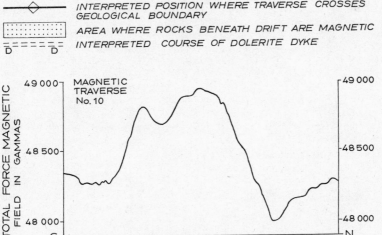

FIG. 33. *Sketch-map showing magnetic traverses in the Craigforth area, and a magnetic profile across the Ochil and Abbey Craig faults*

In the absence of any experimental data on the magnetic properties of these diorites, it is not possible to determine from field data alone the relative contributions to the anomalies of remanent and induced magnetization. However, the general effect of the diorite on the earth's magnetic field above it at ground level is to produce variable, but almost entirely positive, anomalies, which indicate normal magnetization (*see* Traverse A–A′ on Fig. 36). Aeromagnetic anomalies (Traverse B–B′) confirm this deduction.

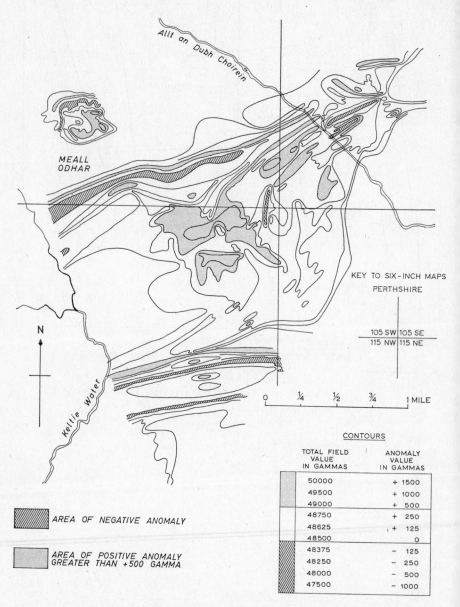

FIG. 34. *Total force magnetic anomaly map of the Keltie Water–Allt an Dubh Choirein area*

Large magnetic variations over the diorite are not necessarily associated with in-homogeneity of the diorite itself though this may be a contributory factor; similar large variations were noted over an exposed granite by Hawes (1952) and these were not related to variations in composition or mineralogy. In the present case variations probably relate to variable thickness of drift cover, irregularities in the top surface of the body, post-intrusive structural discontinuities within the body, and super-imposed dyke anomalies.

Both the amplitude and width of these anomalies are of use in estimating the depth below surface at which diorite occurs. The area shown as 'diorite at or near surface'

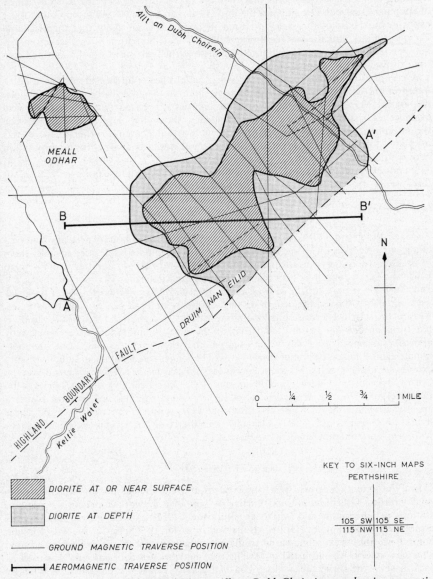

FIG. 35. *Sketch-map of the Keltie Water–Allt an Dubh Choirein area showing magnetic traverse positions and interpreted occurrence of diorite*

on Fig. 35 is the area within which diorite is expected at rockhead or beneath a very thin cap of Dalradian rocks. Similar and broader surrounding anomalies, indicated on Fig. 35 as 'diorite at depth', are thought to originate from diorite at depths of up to about 300 ft. The interpreted positions of the sides of the diorites, marked C on the ground magnetic profile shown on Fig. 36, coincide with the high positive magnetic gradient at the edge of regions of high anomaly. They are considered reliable except on the northern edge of the diorite on Meall Odhar, where magnetic effects of a quartz-dolerite dyke interfere, and in the area north-east of the Allt an Dubh Choirein mentioned above. The absence of anomalies between the diorite on Meall Odhar and the southerly intrusion indicates that they are not connected, whereas the continuity of anomalies between Druim nan Eilid and Gleann an Dubh Choirein shows that these exposures are part of the same intrusion. It does not seem likely that the Highland Boundary Fault cuts the surface diorite exposure, but the region of smaller anomalies between fault and near-surface diorite suggests that the fault may form the south-eastern limit of the body at depth.

A comparison between Fig. 35, in which geophysical evidence alone was used to interpret the lateral extent of the diorites, and the Solid Edition of the one-inch Geological Map, in which the diorite boundaries are based partly on geophysical evidence and partly on geological field evidence, shows the close agreement between the interpretations. Local divergencies can be attributed mainly either to the effects of quartz-dolerite and Caledonian dykes, or to uncertainties arising from interpolation between magnetic traverses.

Quantitative interpretation of the inclination of the margins cannot be made, but the absence of a negative anomaly along the north-western margins of the diorites indicates that this contact is not vertical, but dips outwards at the angle of the Earth's field (approximately 60°), or less. The peripheral zone of small anomalies further supports this suggestion.

Quartz-dolerite dykes in the Keltie Water–Allt an Dubh Choirein area are members of a group of important dykes which cross the district, and it was decided to study them in an area where they intrude sedimentary rocks, in order to ascertain the extent to which they are continuous between widely separated outcrops. Between Auchterarder and the River Knaik, north-west of Braco [NN 837098], nine north–south traverses were surveyed of individual length up to $2\frac{1}{2}$ miles as well as over forty short traverses. Results show that dykes are intruded along parallel fissures which are not continuous but form an *echelon* pattern; and that at the ends of individual fissures magnetic anomalies disappear in a way which suggests that the dykes thin out, rather than terminate against faults, or plunge downwards. The longest, seemingly continuous, fissure extends for about 4 miles. Magnetic curves are similar in shape to those observed over the Lornty dyke by McLintock and Phemister (1931) and over dykes near Glasgow by Powell (1963). Positive anomalies range up to +3000 gammas and in most places a negative anomaly of much smaller amplitude exists south of the positive peak. These dykes are known to dip nearly vertically, and therefore the anomalies are consistent with near-horizontal permanent magnetization.

GRAVITY SURVEYS

In 1950, gravity stations were observed by the Geological Survey at Kincardine, Auchterarder, Greenloaning and Stirling as part of a network connecting pendulum stations at Edinburgh and Aberdeen (Bullerwell 1952). A new gravity station was established at Stirling by Dr. W. Bullerwell and Dr. J. Phemister in 1953 (private communication) because increased traffic made the previous station difficult to occupy. This new station was adjusted in their gravity network for Scotland and was used as local-base in the surveys now described. All gravity values are presented as Bouguer anomalies reduced to a sea-level datum, corrected to the International Gravity Formula and referred to a gravity datum of 981·26500 cm/s² at Pendulum House, Cambridge.

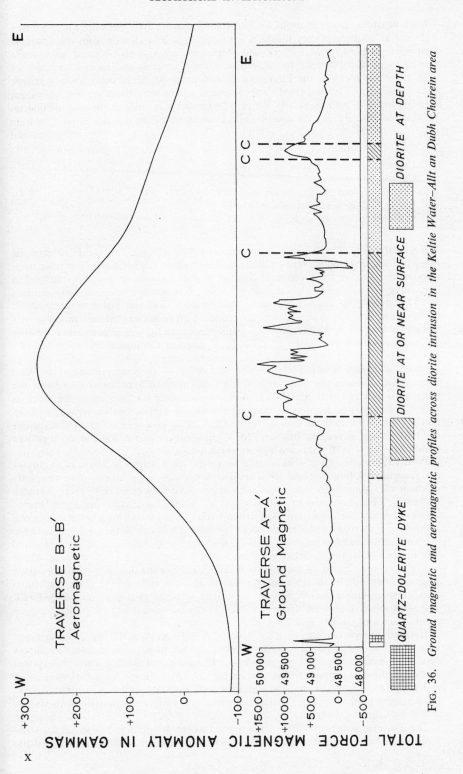

Fig. 36.   *Ground magnetic and aeromagnetic profiles across diorite intrusion in the Keltie Water–Allt an Dubh Choirein area*

Rock densities. Interpretations are based on published rock densities for specimens collected at Midland Valley localities outside the district. Rocks from the Glasgow area were sampled by McLintock and Phemister (1929) who obtained an average density value of 1·72 g/cm³ for superficial clays and sands and an average value of 2·38 g/cm³ for rocks of the Limestone Coal Group. Scattered outcrops in Ayrshire were sampled by McLean (1961) whose density values were based on 600 laboratory measurements as well as gravity meter measurements in mine-shafts and over topographic features. Results obtained by him include the values:

Formation	Density in g/cm³
Carboniferous sediments	2·54
Carboniferous lavas	2·72
Upper Old Red Sandstone sediments	2·41
Lower Old Red Sandstone sediments	2·60
Old Red Sandstone lavas	2·66

Regional survey. The Bouguer anomaly map (Plate XII, fig. 2) is compiled from the results of unpublished surveys by Bullerwell and Phemister (Bullerwell, private communication) and by the Geological Survey. Within the area enclosed by the broken line, surveyed in detail by the Geological Survey, contours are based on measurements at 347 stations, but outside this area, where values from the earlier reconnaissance survey alone are available, contours are based on 26 points so that only broad gravity features are established. To calculate topographic corrections Bullerwell and Phemister assumed a mean rock density of 2·67 g/cm³ whereas Geological Survey results are computed using a density of 2·65 g/cm³.

Near Tillicoultry, a broad negative anomaly occurs on the southern side of the Ochil Fault close to where the axial zone of the Clackmannan Syncline abuts against the fault. It is inferred that the thickness of lower-density Carboniferous sediments is greatest here despite northward thinning within the Upper Carboniferous (p. 247). North of the fault, over the Lower Old Red Sandstone lavas of the Ochil Hills, the few available readings, ranging from +3 to +7 milligals, indicate that the north-eastern quadrant is an area of restricted gravity variation.

Positive anomalies are also associated with the Carboniferous lava area of the Fintry and Gargunnock hills, but over these lavas an approximately southerly positive gravity gradient of 3–4 milligals/mile persists for approximately 4 miles from their northern boundary. This gradient is probably due to a continued southerly dip of the base of the lavas, and if the density in the Carboniferous lavas exceeds by 0·10 to 0·20 g/cm³ that in the underlying sedimentary rocks the interface is calculated to dip at between 10° and 20°. A narrow gravity trough occurs over the Carse north of the Fintry and Gargunnock hills; this is discussed in the following section.

The persistent feature of the north-western quarter of the map is a regular decrease in gravity towards the north-west at a rate of about 1 milligal/mile. This gradient is part of an extensive gravity feature associated with the Highland Boundary Fault, and must relate to a major density contrast at considerable depth (Bullerwell, private communication).

Detailed surveys. The area enclosed by a broken line on Plate XII, fig. 2 was surveyed with a station density of approximately two observations per square mile. This survey revealed the narrow gravity trough over the Carse west of Stirling which was further investigated on traverses A to J shown on Fig. 37. On Traverse A stations were 200 ft apart and on others the interval was increased to 300 ft. Profiles for nine of the traverses are plotted on Fig. 38 and interpretation is based on analytic methods described by Lustikh (1944).

The Traverse A gravity curve is interpreted as the gravitational effect of the Ochil Fault, with Lower Old Red Sandstone rocks on its northern side and the less dense

Lower Carboniferous and Upper Old Red Sandstone rocks on its southern side. Mean density contrast across the fault is probably between 0·1 g/cm³ and 0·2 g/cm³ and calculations show that to the south of the fault the base of the Upper Old Red Sandstone is probably at a depth of between 700 ft and 1000 ft. The interpreted position of the fault is shown on Fig. 37. Fault anomalies on Traverses B and C are complicated by anomalies due to a 'buried channel', but the large gradient on the northern part of the Traverse B curve is thought to be due to the combined effects of fault and 'channel' anomalies, and the interpreted fault position is thought to be reliable. It is possible to interpret the fault on Traverse C curve only by comparing it with the curves for A and B. Curves for Traverses B and C show also a strong gravity gradient over the Abbey Craig Fault, and the interpreted position of this fault is plotted on Fig. 37.

The remaining curves, for Traverses D to J, show anomalies that relate to the 'buried channel'. The interpreted course of the centre of this 'channel' is shown in Fig. 37. Depth to the base of the 'channel' can be estimated from the gravity anomalies and the main limitation to the accuracy of this estimate is unknown depth to rockhead outside the 'channel'. In places the latter depth is known from borehole evidence and the traverses which give the most reliable estimate of rockhead depth are therefore those that are sited near the boreholes. Density contrast between superficial deposits and Old Red Sandstone rocks is assumed to be between 0·6 g/cm³ and 0·8 g/cm³. Between Traverse B and Traverse E, depth to rockhead at the centre of the 'channel' is estimated to be about 300 ft. Farther west, Geological Survey No. 5 (Greenfoot) Bore was sited at the centre of the gravity trough and proved 396 ft of drift deposits. The 'channel' under Traverses F to J is calculated to be about 250 ft deep; thus if superficial deposits outside the 'channel' are 100 to 150 ft thick, rockhead at the centre of the 'channel' can be expected at a depth of about 400 ft (p. 265).

ELECTRICAL SURVEYS

Ground surveys. In the Carse west of Stirling, standard methods of electrical-resistivity surveying were used in an attempt to measure variations in thickness of superficial deposits, and to find out if resistance changes could be detected across the Ochil Fault in places where it cannot be positioned by other geophysical methods. Results of these surveys were inconclusive, probably because of lateral variations in drift deposits and because low-resistivity deposits immediately below the soil were found to overlie a higher-resistivity layer, conditions which greatly restrict the depth of exploration.

Vincenz (1954) used similar methods to study the extent and depth of unconsolidated deposits in the Devon valley between Alva and Tillicoultry in an area where a considerable amount of borehole information was available. His survey was in much greater detail and he was able to relate resistance values to variation of depth to rockhead across the 'channel'.

Surveys in boreholes. Single-point resistance and spontaneous potential (hereafter termed SP) logs were obtained in Geological Survey boreholes No. 6 (Inch of Leckie) and No. 7 (Claylands) using a Widco Electrical Logger. Site-positions of these boreholes are shown on Fig. 37.

In Borehole No. 6 (Inch of Leckie), only the section from 0 to 43 ft was tested. Below soil, clay to a depth of 24 ft produces low resistance values which increase with depth. The SP log shows a sharp negative deflection at 24 ft depth at the boundary between clay and the underlying sands. Sands, 24 to 31 ft, produce highest resistance values and this layer may be the high-resistance layer encountered during the ground electrical surveys. As depth increases beyond 31 ft, resistances gradually reduce to values lower than in the uppermost clay, indicating gradation with depth to a clayey sediment. Radiometric measurements were made in this borehole by Mr. J. Taylor and these are discussed in Appendix III.

x*

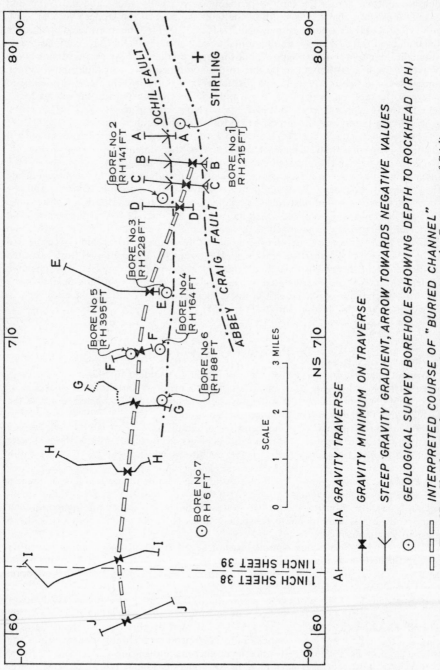

Fig. 37. *Sketch-map showing gravity traverses across the Carse west of Stirling*

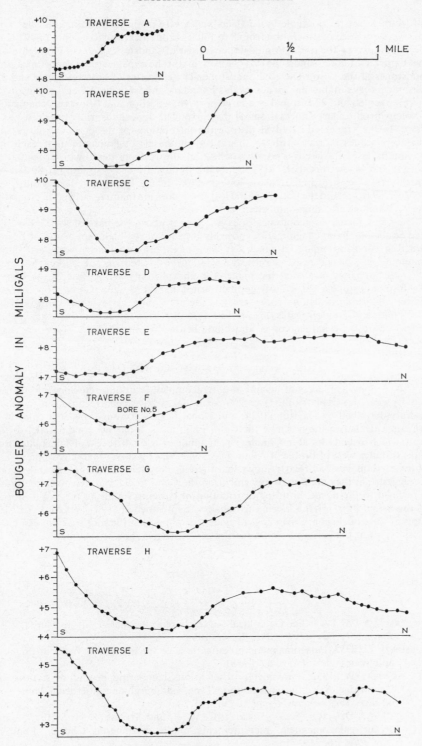

FIG. 38. *Gravity profiles over the Carse west of Stirling*

Electrical tests in Borehole No. 7 (Claylands) were made when drilling finished and logs were obtained of the section from 8 to 150 ft. From rockhead to a depth of 89 ft 2 in the strata, except for one thin mudstone, consist of sandstones and conglomerates of the Upper Old Red Sandstone. At 89 ft 2 in the hole passes into sandstones and mudstones of the Lower Old Red Sandstone. The character of both resistance and SP logs undergoes notable change across this boundary. Above it the SP curve is inactive, but between 86 and 89 ft it makes a large positive deflection and below this changes in lithology produce large fluctuations of the curve. The opposite is true of the resistance curve. In the Upper Old Red Sandstone the fluctuations of the curve are large and resistance values increase with depth until in the basal conglomerate they reach the maximum; at 81 ft there is a negative deflection towards considerably lower resistance values; and below this sharp deflection values gradually decrease until at 89 ft 2 in resistance values are similar to the lowest values in the Upper Old Red Sandstone. Between 89 ft 2 in and the bottom of the log, low values are maintained, and fluctuations due to lithological changes are small.

The main change in geophysical logs is 2 to 4 ft above the base of the Upper Old Red Sandstone basal conglomerate, possibly because of the high proportion of Lower Old Red Sandstone material which has been incorporated in the lowest part of the conglomerate. Nevertheless, electrical variations exhibited on the curves relate to lithological change in a way that makes the unconformity at the base of the Upper Old Red Sandstone a particularly good electrical marker horizon. Cores show that the Lower Old Red Sandstone rocks are considerably more clayey than the overlying sandstones and conglomerates (see pp. 330–1), and it is on this lithological change that differences in the electrical curves above and below the unconformity depend.

SEISMIC ACTIVITY OF THE OCHIL FAULT

This geophysical account would not be complete without reference to seismic activity near the Ochil Fault. Over 200 earthquakes have been recorded in the area and are described by Davison (1924) and Dollar (1950). Results show that epicentres are concentrated to the north of the Ochil Fault along a narrow zone parallel to the fault, which extends for about 9 miles, from a mile or two north-east of Tillicoultry to a short distance west of Bridge of Allan. Davison (1924, pp. 149–51) discusses the origin of the earthquakes and clearly shows that there is considerable seismological evidence to suggest that they are due to movement on the Ochil Fault, and that this great fault is inclined to the north. Both the distribution of epicentres and the relative positions of isoseismal lines for the larger earthquakes (September 21, 1905 and May 3, 1912) support this conclusion. Seismological evidence implies that the southerly dip exhibited by the fault at the surface is not a feature of the deeper zone of the fracture.

REFERENCES

ANDERSON, F. W. 1963. The Geological Survey bore at Rashiebill, Stirlingshire (1951). *Bull. geol. Surv. Gt Br.*, No. 20, 43–106.

BELSHÉ, J. C. 1957. Palaeomagnetic investigations of Carboniferous rocks in England and Wales. *Adv. Phys.*, **6**, 187–91.

BULLERWELL, W. 1952. Gravimeter observations comparing pendulum stations at Cambridge, York, Newcastle-upon-Tyne, Edinburgh and Aberdeen. *Mon. Not. R. astr. Soc. geophys. Suppl.*, **6**, 303–15.

CLEGG, J. A., DEUTSCH, E. R., EVERITT, C. W. F. and STUBBS, P. H. S. 1957. Some recent palaeomagnetic measurements made at Imperial College, London. *Adv. Phys.*, **6**, 219–31.

Cox, A. and Doell, R. R. 1960. Review of palaeomagnetism. *Bull. geol. Soc. Am.*, **71** 645–768.

Davison, C. 1924. *A history of British earthquakes.* 1st edit. Cambridge.

Dollar, A. T. J. 1950. Catalogue of Scottish earthquakes, 1916–1949. *Trans. geol. Soc. Glasg.*, **21**, 283–361.

Everitt, C. W. F. 1960. Rock magnetism and the origin of the Midland basalts. *Geophys. J. R. astr. Soc.*, **3**, 203–10.

—— 1961. The magnetic properties of three Carboniferous sills. *Phil. Mag.*, **6**, 689–99.

—— and Belshé, J. C. 1960. Palaeomagnetism of the British Carboniferous System. *Phil. Mag.*, **5**, 675–85.

Francis, E. H. 1956. The economic geology of the Stirling and Clackmannan Coalfield, Scotland: Area north of the River Forth. *Coalfld Pap. geol. Surv.*, No. 1.

Hawes, J. 1952. A magnetic study of the Spavinaw granite area, Oklahoma. *Geophysics*, **17**, 2–25.

Lustikh, E. N. 1944. On the use of gravitational survey data of reconnoitring nature. *Dokl. Akad. Nauk S.S.S.R. for. Lang. Edn.*, **43**, 242–3.

McLean, A. C. 1961. Density measurements of rocks in south-west Scotland. *Proc. R. Soc. Edinb.*, B, **68**, 103–11.

McLintock, W. F. P. and Phemister, J. 1929. A gravitational survey over the buried Kelvin valley at Drumry, near Glasgow. *Trans. R. Soc. Edinb.*, **56**, 141–55.

—— and Phemister, J. 1931. On a magnetic survey over the Lornty dyke, Blairgowrie, Perthshire. *Mem. geol. Surv. Summ. Prog.* for 1930, pt. 3, 24–9.

Powell, D. W. 1963. Significance of differences in magnetization along certain dolerite dykes. *Nature, Lond.*, **199**, No. 4894, 674–6.

Rücker, A. W. and Thorpe, T. E. 1890. A magnetic survey of the British Isles for the epoch January 1, 1886. *Phil. Trans. R. Soc.*, **181A**, 53–328.

—— and Thorpe, T. E. 1896. A magnetic survey of the British Isles for the epoch January 1, 1891. *Phil. Trans. R. Soc.*, **188A**, 1–661.

Summ. Prog. 1963. *Mem. geol. Surv. Summ. Prog.* for 1962.

Vincenz, S. A. 1954. A resistivity survey in Scotland. *Colliery Engng*, **31**, 157–63.

Appendix II

RECORDS OF THE GEOLOGICAL SURVEY BOREHOLES

DURING 1961 and 1962 seven boreholes were drilled under contract for the Geological Survey to assist in the mapping of the Stirling (39) Sheet. These were sited on drift-covered ground in the Forth valley west of Stirling and the programme was designed to obtain evidence of the course of the Ochil and Abbey Craig faults in this area, to locate concealed formational boundaries and to investigate the nature of the superficial deposits and underlying solid rocks. The drilling contractors were Messrs. John Thom Ltd., Walkden, Lancashire (now Cementation Exploration Ltd., Bentley Works, Doncaster, Yorkshire).

In all the boreholes the solid rocks were cored throughout and in three of the holes (Nos. 2, 5 and 7) cores of the superficial deposits were also taken. Cores were examined by Messrs. W. A. Read and I. H. Forsyth. The sites of the boreholes are indicated on Fig. 37.

Stirling No. 1 (Kaimes) Bore (1961)

Nat. Grid Ref. NS 77209454. Surface level 34·3 ft above O.D.

	Thickness ft	Thickness in	Depth ft	Depth in
RECENT AND PLEISTOCENE				
Not cored (description of strata based on washings)				
Clay, silty, brownish-grey and grey, with abundant fragments of marine shells including *Cardium*. (Carse Clays)	12	0	12	0
Sand, rather dark grey, clayey, with fragments of marine lamellibranchs, barnacles, etc.	56	0	68	0
Sandy boulder clay with indurated Highland grits, vein quartz and basalt	57	0	125	0
Ditto with large blocks of basalt	12	0	137	0
Cored from 137 ft				
Basalt, including microporphyritic and Markle types with slaggy tops and bottoms and boles. Cores commonly broken. Probably a buried landslip from the Craigforth scarp..	55	0	192	0
Boulder clay, brownish, with fragments of vein quartz, greenish indurated Highland grits, purplish Lower Old Red Sandstone and basalt..	23	0	215	0
CALCIFEROUS SANDSTONE MEASURES				
DOWNIE'S LOUP SANDSTONES				
Mudstone, sandy and silty, unsorted, massive and purplish with yellow mottling, passing down into greenish-grey, alternating laminae of very fine-grained sandstone and micaceous silty shale with numerous clastic grains of carbonate and traces of mudstone pellets. May be partly derived from volcanic detritus. Dip 23°–26°	8	0	223	0

	Thickness		Depth	
	ft	in	ft	in
Calcarenites and sandstones, pale-grey, poorly-sorted, with grains of carbonate and quartz mostly less than 2 mm in diameter set in a clayey matrix. Locally the carbonate grains are packed close together and distorted to form an interlocking mosaic. Greenish mudstone pellets throughout and a 5-in bed of crushed mudstone near the base	10	1	233	1
Limestone conglomerate with pebbles, mostly sub-angular, of limestone up to 10 mm long including some fragments of algal limestone and greenish mudstone pellets, all set in a calcareous clayey matrix with some sand. Some of carbonate fragments form an interlocking mosaic. Sharp base. (S 47610, 47610A, analysed specimens of limestone pebbles; see Table 6, Anals. XII, XIII)	9	5	242	6
Shale, dark-grey, calcareous, crushed at base. Possibly a small fault		7	243	1
Limestone conglomerate, similar to bed at 242 ft 6 in. Irregular top and base		7	243	8
Mudstone, massive, mostly dark-grey with rare dull-red mottling. Sporadic limestone concretions	8	2	251	10
Limestone conglomerate. Angular limestone pebbles up to 15 cm long, some with algal structures. Sharp base ..		9	252	7
Mudstone, massive, greenish-grey, with dark-grey limestone concretions	1	8	254	3
Sandstone, mainly very fine- and fine-grained, greenish, with sporadic thin layers of silty mudstone, some cut by polygonal patterns of vertical sand-filled cracks ..	6	6	260	9
Limestone conglomerate with pebbles up to 5 cm long, including some of algal limestone. Some thin beds of mudstone and shale and some greenish mudstone pellets. Dip 18°	8	8	269	5
Mudstone, dark-green, with beds of calcarenite and limestone conglomerate up to 1 in thick. The base of one bed at 269 ft 11 in shows elongate load-casts in two sets, roughly at right angles (Plate V, figs. 1a, 1b)		8	270	1
Limestone conglomerate with pebbles up to 3 cm and mudstone pellets. Some thin beds of alternating greenish and grey silty shale and very fine-grained sandstone which are locally disturbed by irregular sand-filled pipes about 5 mm in diameter	7	5	277	6
Sandstone, mainly greyish-white, fine- and medium-grained but with some greenish very fine-grained beds. Some irregular patches and thin beds of silty mudstone which are locally disturbed by sand-filled cracks. (Plate V, figs. 2a, 2b)	38	10	316	4
Shale, silty in places, greenish, with abundant granules of pyrite	1	2	317	6
Mudstone, silty towards the base, mainly greenish-grey, with irregular calcareous nodules. Sporadic beds of limestone conglomerate up to 1 ft thick and rare thin beds of fine-grained sandstone. Some plant scraps near base	17	6	335	0

	Thickness		Depth	
	ft	in	ft	in
Alternating laminae and thin beds of greenish-grey silty shale and paler very fine-grained sandstone. Rare calcareous nodules and plant scraps	5	9	340	9
Limestone conglomerate with pebbles up to 2 cm long in a sandy matrix		3	341	0

BALLAGAN BEDS

	Thickness		Depth	
Mudstone and shale, mostly greenish-grey, but with local red mottling, interspersed with thin layers of pale coarse-grained siltstone or very fine-grained sandstone, some of which show ripple-drifting (Plate IV, fig. 3). Irregular carbonate concretions throughout, some of which seem to replace stratified clastic sediments (p. 121, Plate IV, fig. 2)	7	0	348	0
Shale, micaceous, dark greenish-grey		8	348	8
Cementstone with irregular carbonate veins and segregations, grading into argillaceous beds above and below..	1	8	350	4
Mudstone, pale greenish-grey, with irregular small cementstone concretions	2	10	353	2
Sandstone, mainly very fine- and fine-grained, whitish, with a 7-in bed of greenish silty shale and a carbonate nodule 7 cm long towards the base	6	10	360	0
Shale with some mudstone, greenish-grey, with rare nodules and two thin laminae of cementstone. Passes by alternation into the bed below	3	0	363	0
Sandstone, mostly very fine-grained, whitish-grey. Base disturbed by load-casts and pseudo-nodules (Plate IV, fig. 4)	4	8	367	8
Shale, greenish-grey, with a 3-in bed of very fine-grained sandstone near the middle and irregular cementstone nodules in places	3	10	371	6
Cementstone, greenish-grey with reddish-brown mottling, grading into beds above and below	3	1	374	7
Mudstone, mottled greenish-grey and reddish-brown, with an irregular base from which mudstone veins run down into the bed below		3	374	10
Sandstone, mainly fine-grained, whitish-grey	1	6	376	4
Mudstones with subordinate shales, greenish-grey and dull red, silty and micaceous in places with rare thin beds, patches and irregular veins of very fine-grained sandstone (Plate IV, fig. 5). The mudstones are crushed in places. Nodules and six beds, all less than 1 ft thick, of cementstone (S 47611 analysed specimen from the lowest bed; see Table 6, Anal. VIII). Some of the cementstones, including the analysed bed, have highly irregular bases (Plate IV, fig. 6)	31	10	408	2
Alternating laminae of pale coarse siltstone and very fine-grained sandstone with greenish silty shale. Micro-cross-lamination in places	2	1	410	3

	Thickness		Depth	
	ft	in	ft	in
Mudstones, and subordinate shales, silty in places, mostly grey and brown with widespread red and purple mottling. Crushed at about 422 ft. Traces of rare cementstone nodules and three very hard beds which could be considered as very argillaceous cementstones. Dip 15° ..	16	1	426	4
Mudstones, mostly grey and greenish with widespread dull red and purple mottling. Nodules and three beds, all no more than 4 in thick, of cementstone, together with two very hard beds of mudstone resembling those in the item above. Lowest cementstone has an irregular base with carbonate veins penetrating downwards. Fish scales at base	6	9	433	1
Cementstone, grey, passing down into a breccia with grey, angular cementstone fragments in a darker, more argillaceous, matrix. Slightly purplish tint at base		11	434	0

Stirling No. 2 (Westwood Lane) Bore (1962)

Nat. Grid Ref. NS 74619508. Surface level 32·6 ft above O.D.

	Thickness		Depth	
	ft	in	ft	in
Cored from surface				

RECENT AND PLEISTOCENE

	Thickness		Depth	
Clay, silty, micaceous, brownish-grey, with laminae of pale coarse-grained silt and very fine-grained sand which tend to become more abundant towards the base. Stratification disturbed by modern roots in top 6 ft and by burrowing organisms lower down (Plate XI). Rare shell fragments. (Carse Clays)	27	9	27	9
Sand, mainly fine-grained, clayey, with fragments of lamellibranchs, gastropods and barnacles	74	3	102	0
Clay, silty, reddish-brown, with rare isolated stones. Evenly laminated but disturbed by horizontal burrows. (late-Glacial clays)	28	0	130	0
Boulder clay. Fragments include Highland schists and Lower Old Red Sandstone clayey sandstones	11	0	141	0

LOWER OLD RED SANDSTONE

DUNBLANE FORMATION

	Thickness		Depth	
Sandstone, mainly brownish-white or brownish-red, medium-grained but coarse-grained locally, cross-stratified; bands and flakes of brownish-red mudstone ..	7	8	148	8
Sandstone, purplish-brown and white mottled, medium- or coarse-grained, cross-stratified; clay pellets locally abundant	12	4	161	0
Sandstone, fine- or very fine-grained, brownish-purple, cross-stratified	2	11	163	11

	Thickness		Depth	
	ft	in	ft	in
Sandstone, brownish-purple and white mottled, medium- or coarse-grained; mudstone pellets locally abundant..	10	1	174	0
Sandstone as above, shattered	11	5	185	5
Shale, micaceous, silty, reddish-brown, shattered ..		5	185	10
Sandstone, medium- or coarse-grained, purplish-brown and white mottled, cross-stratified; mudstone pellets locally abundant; shattered at top	11	5	197	3
Mudstone, silty, sandy, micaceous, purplish-brown ..		3	197	6
Sandstone, mainly medium- to coarse-grained, purplish-brown, cross-stratified; mudstone pellets locally abundant; small pebbles (up to 1 cm) between 201 ft 6 in and 204 ft	13	11	211	5
Sandstone, dull pinkish-purple, mainly fine- to medium-grained; micaceous, argillaceous partings	6	0	217	5
Sandstone, medium- to very coarse-grained, with pebbles up to 1·5 cm in diameter; brownish-purple and white mottled; mudstone pellets locally abundant	3	1	220	6
Mudstone, silty, micaceous, reddish-brown		9	221	3
Sandstone, dull pinkish-purple, medium-grained, cross-stratified	1	11	223	2

Stirling No. 3 (Low Wood) Bore (1962)

Nat. Grid Ref. NS 71579498. Surface level 37·4 ft above O.D.

	Thickness		Depth	
Not cored (description of strata based on washings)	ft	in	ft	in

RECENT AND PLEISTOCENE

Clay, silty, brownish-grey (Carse Clays)	8	0	8	0
?Clay, as above, not seen	35	0	43	0
Sand, pinkish-brown to bluish-grey, with traces of pinkish silty clay. Sporadic boulders. Fragments of thick-shelled molluscs including *Mytilus* and gastropods, also fragments of barnacles	137	0	180	0
Late-Glacial clays	28	0	208	0
Boulder clay	20	0	228	0

Cored from 228 ft

LOWER OLD RED SANDSTONE

CROMLIX FORMATION

Sandstone, red	2	0	230	0
Mudstone, brick-red, micaceous, sandy and silty; calcite veins locally abundant; occasional green spots and patches	34	0	264	0

	Thickness		Depth	
	ft	in	ft	in
Mudstone, dull brownish-red, micaceous, sandy and silty	12	0	276	0
Mudstone, purplish-brown, silty and sandy (locally very sandy)	15	6	291	6
Mudstone, very sandy, silty, micaceous, dull brownish-purple or purplish-brown	14	8	306	2

Stirling No. 4 (Watson House) Bore (1961)

Nat. Grid Ref. NS 69589516. Surface level 36·5 ft above O.D.

	Thickness		Depth	
	ft	in	ft	in

Not cored

RECENT AND PLEISTOCENE

Superficial deposits	164	0	164	0

Cored from 164 ft

LOWER OLD RED SANDSTONE

TEITH FORMATION

Sandstone, mainly argillaceous, dull purplish-grey, fine-grained; locally with inclusions of dull reddish-brown mudstone	15	0	179	0
Mudstone, dull red, generally silty and locally sandy ..	3	11	182	11
Sandstone, argillaceous, purplish-grey, fine-grained ..	1	10	184	9
Sandstone, argillaceous, dull red, fine-grained, interbanded with mudstone, red, mainly silty and micaceous ..	8	1	192	10
Mudstone, mainly dull red, silty and micaceous	2	9	195	7
Sandstone, mainly argillaceous, purplish-grey, fine-grained, locally with many fragments of dull red mudstone ..	4	5	200	0
Sandstone, argillaceous, fine-grained, mainly dull red but locally pale greenish-white and calcareous, interbanded with mudstone, red, silty and micaceous	3	9	203	9
Sandstone, argillaceous, fine-grained, mainly purplish-grey but with 6-in greenish-white calcareous band	11	3	215	0

Stirling No. 5 (Greenfoot) Bore (1961)

Nat. Grid Ref. NS 69509614. Surface level 37·0 ft above O.D.

	Thickness		Depth	
	ft	in	ft	in

Cored from surface

RECENT AND PLEISTOCENE

Clay, silty, micaceous, top 8 ft brownish-grey but remainder blackish-grey with brown patches, mostly soft and plastic. Traces of pale, even laminae of coarse-grained silt in places. (Carse Clays)	50	0	50	0

	Thickness		Depth	
	ft	in	ft	in
Alternating, even laminae of dark-grey, silty, micaceous clay and subordinate pale brownish-grey coarse-grained silt and very fine-grained sand. Occasional layers with pebbles, including Lower Old Red Sandstone clayey sandstones and Highland grits. Sporadic layers of broken shells seen in core and abundant complete shells obtained from washings. (For faunal list see pp. 277–8)	235	0	285	0
Clay, silty, reddish-brown, with subordinate pale, very even laminae of coarse-grained silt and fine- and very fine-grained sand. Sporadic stones at base include fragments of vein quartz and Lower Old Red Sandstone sandstones. (late-Glacial clays)	49	0	334	0
Boulder clay with fragments of Highland schistose grits and mica-schists, vein quartz, Lower Old Red Sandstone conglomerates, sandstones and porphyrites	62	0	396	0

LOWER OLD RED SANDSTONE

Teith Formation

	Thickness		Depth	
Sandstone, grain size variable from very fine to coarse, mainly grey, locally argillaceous	2	6	398	6
Mudstone, sandy, micaceous, brownish-red, with sandstone bands	2	6	401	0
Sandstone, very fine-grained, pale-grey, with argillaceous partings showing ripple-lamination, and a few thin bands of mudstone	2	10	403	10
Mudstone, dull reddish-brown, sandy and silty near the base	2	2	406	0
Sandstone, very fine-grained, pale-grey, with argillaceous partings showing ripple-lamination		6	406	6
Mudstone, dull red, locally silty towards the top; some crushing, possibly indicative of a small fault	6	3	412	9
Sandstone, pale-grey, fine-grained, with partings and bands of dull red silty micaceous mudstone	3	2	415	11
Mudstone, dull red, silty, micaceous, with sporadic sandstone laminae	2	9	418	8
Sandstone, generally fine-grained, varying in colour from dull red to pale-grey, locally with clay pellets	7	0	425	8
Sandstone, mainly fine-grained, varying in colour from greenish-grey to reddish-brown, interbanded with mudstone, dull reddish-brown, micaceous	2	11	428	7
Mudstone, dull reddish-brown, micaceous, locally silty and with sandy laminae	2	7	431	2
Sandstone, mainly fine-grained and brownish-grey, but greyish-white and calcareous at top; shale laminae locally; many dull red and green clay galls near base..	6	6	437	8
Mudstone, dull red, silty, micaceous, with bands of fine-grained sandstone	4	11	442	7
Sandstone, very fine-grained, brownish-grey, ripple-laminated	2	1	444	8
Mudstone, reddish-brown, silty, micaceous	1	4	446	0

Stirling No. 6 (Inch of Leckie) Bore (1961)

Nat. Grid Ref. NS 67779512. Surface level 44·3 ft above O.D.

	Thickness		Depth	
	ft	in	ft	in

Not cored

RECENT AND PLEISTOCENE

Description of strata based on washings

	ft	in	ft	in
Soil	1	0	1	0
Clay, silty, micaceous in places, brownish-grey (Carse Clays)	23	0	24	0
Sand, slightly clayey, mainly fine- and medium-grained, pinkish at top becoming brownish lower down, with fairly abundant shell fragments (apparently of thin-shelled lamellibranchs)	26	0	50	0

No samples: description of strata from borer's log

	ft	in	ft	in
'Silty clay with few boulders' (?late-Glacial clays) ..	35	0	85	0
'Silty clay with boulders' (?boulder clay)	3	2	88	2
(See also Appendixes I and III for interpretation of geophysical and radiometric logs of the superficial deposits)				

Cored from 88 ft 2 in

LOWER OLD RED SANDSTONE

TEITH FORMATION

	ft	in	ft	in
Mudstone, mainly sandy and silty; locally crushed, colours variable and include dull red and dull purplish-grey ..	3	8	91	10
Sandstone, dull purple, medium-grained	1	4	93	2
Mudstone, purplish-red, locally silty and micaceous ..		10	94	0
Sandstone, argillaceous, fine-grained, dull purple.. ..	2	0	96	0
Mudstone, reddish-purple, locally silty and sandy, rather crushed	3	6	99	6
Sandstone, dull purplish but mainly discoloured to greenish-grey, medium-grained, and mudstone, dull purple, silty, micaceous	2	6	102	0
Mudstone, generally silty, dull maroon with greenish patches	4	6	106	6
Sandstone, medium-grained, greenish-grey, with disrupted bands of purple mudstone	2	4	108	10
Mudstone, sandy and silty, dull purple, with sandstone laminae	1	11	110	9
Sandstone, mainly brown, medium-grained and argillaceous; with sandy and silty mudstone	6	5	117	2
Mudstone, generally dull red	4	4	121	6
Sandstone, fine- and medium-grained; dull purplish-brown, with laminae of generally disrupted mudstone	4	7	126	1
Mudstone, dull red, mainly micaceous and silty or sandy	1	11	128	0
Sandstone, fine-grained, greenish-grey, with mudstone laminae		9	128	9

	Thickness ft	in	Depth ft	in
Mudstone, generally dull red, silty and micaceous; occasional sandstone patches	8	10	137	7
Sandstone, mainly fine-grained, grey and argillaceous, with bands of dull red mudstone	22	2	159	9
Mudstone, red, locally silty and micaceous, with thin beds of sandstone	8	5	168	2
Sandstone, medium- and coarse-grained		10	169	0
Mudstone, dull red, micaceous, interbanded with sandstone, fine-grained, purplish-grey..	3	4	172	4
Mudstone, dull red, mainly sandy, silty and micaceous ..	2	4	174	8
Sandstone, purplish-grey, fine- and medium-grained, with bands of dull red mudstone, locally silty and micaceous	13	4	188	0
Mudstone, dull red, generally silty, sandy and micaceous, with bands of fine-grained sandstone	3	10	191	10
Sandstone, argillaceous, dull red, fine-grained	3	2	195	0

Stirling No. 7 (Claylands) Bore (1961)

Nat. Grid Ref. NS 63359366. Surface level 406·3 ft above O.D.

Cored from surface	Thickness ft	in	Depth ft	in
RECENT AND PLEISTOCENE				
Soil	3	0	3	0
Boulder clay; abundant fragments of local sandstone and smaller pebbles of greenish Highland grits all set in a matrix of brick-red sandy clay	3	0	6	0
UPPER OLD RED SANDSTONE				
Sandstone, mainly medium-grained, brick-red and white mottled. Abundant dull red clay pellets..		6	6	6
Mudstone, silty and sandy, bright red with pale-green spots		6	7	0
Conglomerate, with pebbles up to 30 mm, mostly of quartz, in a matrix of brick-red fine- and medium-grained clayey sandstone	1	6	8	6
Sandstone, mainly medium-grained and coarse, brick-red with some white mottling and greenish spots, cross-stratified in places. Sporadic laminae of mudstone and bands of red clay pellets. Local bands of pebbles which are generally less than 15 mm but may be up to 50 mm, mostly quartz and schist. Detrital grains are set in calcite cement and are locally corroded (*see* p. 99). S 46438 at 15 ft 0 in, S 46439 at 25 ft 0 in	44	9	53	3
Sandstone, mainly coarse- and very coarse-grained, brick-red with greenish-white streaks. Abundant dull red clay pellets and pebbles. The latter are up to 30 mm and include quartz, greenish schist and rare fragments of decomposed fine-grained igneous rock	29	9	83	0

| | Thickness | | Depth | |
	ft	in	ft	in

Conglomerate, pale-red and white. Abundant dull red clay pellets and pebbles. The latter are up to 120 mm, mostly angular and subangular and include vein quartz, quartzite, schistose grit, greenish phyllite, argillaceous sandstone and, more rarely, decomposed fine-grained igneous rocks, all set in a matrix of coarse- and very coarsegrained calcareous sandstone. Irregular, gently dipping base with no trace of faulting .. .. — 6 — 2 — 89 — 2

LOWER OLD RED SANDSTONE

TEITH FORMATION

Sandstone, argillaceous, dull purplish-red (pale-green at top); poorly-sorted, with grain size varying from very fine to very coarse; pebbles up to 2 cm in diameter, mostly of lava, and also red clay galls .. .. .. — — 7 — 89 — 9

Sandstone, argillaceous, dull purplish-red, poorly-sorted, mainly fine-grained, but with quartz pebbles up to 1 cm in diameter; sporadic mudstone laminae .. .. — 1 — 5 — 91 — 2

Mudstone, dull purplish-red, locally reduced to pale-green; silty and sandy in places .. .. — 4 — 0 — 95 — 2

Sandstone, argillaceous, dull purplish-red, poorly-sorted, mainly medium-grained, but with coarse bands, and sporadic lava pebbles up to 2·5 cm in diameter .. — 8 — 0 — 103 — 2

Mudstone, red, silty, micaceous, locally sandy .. .. — 6 — 0 — 109 — 2

Crushed rock (probably small fault) .. .. .. — — 8 — 109 — 10

Sandstone, argillaceous, dull purplish-red, poorly-sorted, mainly medium-grained, with some coarser layers .. — 5 — 3 — 115 — 1

Pebbly sandstone, dull purplish-red, very coarse-grained, argillaceous, with pebbles, mostly of lava, up to 7 cm in diameter .. .. — 1 — 1 — 116 — 2

Sandstone, argillaceous, dull purplish-red, poorly-sorted, mainly coarse- or very coarse-grained, with lava pebbles up to 3 cm in diameter and clay pellets locally .. — 9 — 8 — 125 — 10

Pebbly sandstone, dull purplish-red, argillaceous; pebbles up to 8 cm in diameter include sandstone, lava, clay galls and metamorphic rocks .. .. — 1 — 10 — 127 — 8

Sandstone, dull purplish-red, coarse- or very coarse-grained, argillaceous; clay galls and a few lava pebbles up to 3 cm in diameter .. .. — 7 — 1 — 134 — 9

Mudstone, dull red, sandy, silty, micaceous .. .. — 1 — 1 — 135 — 10

Sandstone, argillaceous, dull purplish-red, poorly-sorted, medium-grained .. .. — 1 — 0 — 136 — 10

Mudstone, red, locally silty, sandy and micaceous .. — 8 — 2 — 145 — 0

Sandstone, argillaceous, medium- to very coarse-grained, purplish-red; a few lava pebbles up to 3 cm in diameter and clay pellets .. .. — 5 — 6 — 150 — 6

Appendix III

GAMMA LOGS OF
THE GEOLOGICAL SURVEY BOREHOLES

BY

J. TAYLOR

THE RADIOACTIVITY of boreholes 2, 3, 5 and 6 was measured by scintillation counter and it is evident that the lithology of the drift is fairly clearly expressed in the variation in radioactivity and in the form of the radiometric profile (Plate XIII). The drift was not cored in boreholes 3 and 6 and was deduced from washings only; the successions at these localities were verified respectively by comparison with the cored succession in Borehole No. 2. As there was some core loss in the latter borehole and an even greater loss in Borehole No. 5 the gamma logs may give a rather more accurate estimate of levels of the lithological contacts than was obtained from the cores.

The radioactivity of the various lithological units is given in the following table. The values for each unit in the different boreholes are in fairly close agreement but a reduction in absolute value of 15 to 20 per cent. has taken place because of the shielding effect of the casing.

| Borehole | Radioactivity mr/h | | | |
	No. 2	No. 3	No. 5	No. 6
Carse Clays	0·007–0·010	0·007–0·009	0·007–0·008	0·007–0·010
Weakly radioactive bed..	0·002–0·004	–	–	0·003
Fine- or fine- to medium-grained clayey sand ..	0·005–0·008	0·005–0·009	–	0·005–0·010
Clay with subordinate coarse silt and very fine sand	–	–	0·005–0·008	–
Late-Glacial clay ..	0·008–0·010	0·008–0·010	0·008–0·012	0·008–0·011
Boulder clay	0·003–0·006	0·004–0·007	0·006–0·010	0·005–0·008

The Carse Clays are distinguished from the sandy or clayey beds below by their higher radioactivity, sometimes by a definite radiometric low at their base and by another band of rather lower radioactivity 12 to 13 ft above this horizon. The weakly radioactive bed at the base of the Carse Clays is particularly prominent in boreholes 2 and 6 but there is no clear indication of its identity. The low radioactivity suggests a sandy bed, and this is to some extent confirmed by the surface resistivity survey of the area (see Appendix I), but there is no evidence of it at this point in the cores of Borehole No. 2.

The fine- to medium-grained clayey sand below the Carse Clays in boreholes 2, 3 and 6 has a characteristically lower radioactivity than the late-Glacial clay on which it lies. The latter is distinguished in boreholes 3 and 6 by more frequent minor peaks superimposed on the general level of the radiometric profile. Comparison of the radiometric profiles of these boreholes with that of Borehole No. 2 (Plate XIII) indicates that the base of the clayey sand is at 180 ft and 50 ft respectively in boreholes 3 and 6. In Borehole No. 5 the sandy and silty clay is defined by lower gamma intensity

PLATE XIII

RADIOMETRIC PROFILES AND INTERPRETED LITHOLOGY OF THE DRIFT DEPOSITS IN GEOLOGICAL SURVEY BOREHOLES

relative to the Carse Clays above and the late-Glacial clay below; its top and base have been pinpointed at 59 and 283 ft respectively.

The transition from late-Glacial clay to boulder clay is marked by a considerable reduction in radioactivity, in accordance with the higher clay content of the former. Their contact is sharp in boreholes 2 and 3 but transitional in Borehole No. 6. A sandy bed of low radioactivity (316 to 321 ft) intervenes between the late-Glacial clay and boulder clay in Borehole No. 5. The slightly higher radioactivity of the boulder clay at this locality compared with the others may be caused by an increase in the clay fraction or in the radioactivity of the coarser components, e.g. mica-schists and porphyrites.

The main rock types in the Old Red Sandstone bedrock are sandstone, commonly containing a varying proportion of mudstone or clayey material in the form of flakes or pellets, and mudstone which is more or less silty or sandy. The radioactivity ranges exhibited by the two lithologies overlap to some extent and are therefore not diagnostic in themselves (see table below). Nevertheless, where sandstone and mudstone, or their variants, occur immediately adjacent to one another, they can usually be separated by their differing radioactivities, which depend on the proportion of argillaceous material in the particular rock type. The effect of carbonate veining is not constant, as it may either slightly increase or decrease the radioactivity of the rock in which it occurs, relative to the radioactivity of the same rock where barren of carbonate veins.

	Dose rate mr/h
Sandstone	0·006–0·010
Sandstone with clayey or mudstone impurities	0·005–0·020
Mudstone, silty, sandy or calcareous	0·014–0·018
Mudstone	0·013–0·020

Appendix IV

LIST OF GEOLOGICAL SURVEY PHOTOGRAPHS
(ONE-INCH SHEET 39)

Taken by Messrs. R. Lunn, W. Manson and W. D. Fisher

COPIES of these photographs are deposited for public reference in the library of the Institute of Geological Sciences, South Kensington, London, S.W.7, and in the library of the Scottish office, 19 Grange Terrace, Edinburgh, 9. Prints and lantern slides are supplied at a fixed tariff on application to the Director.

Series C are half plate and Series D are 5 in by 4 in.

GENERAL

General views eastwards from Stirling, showing the Ochil Hills and the Carse .. .. C 3042–4 D 20–1

General view south-eastwards from the Knaik valley, showing Strathallan and the Ochil Hills .. .. D 437

General view north-westwards from the Gargunnock Hills, showing the Carse, Flanders Moss and the Highland Border hills .. D 767–8

General views north-eastwards from the Gargunnock Hills, showing the Ochil Hills, the Carse and the basalt lavas of the Touch Hills D 777–8

General view north-eastwards from the Touch Hills, showing the Ochil Hills and the Carse .. .. D 788

General view southwards from Dumyat, showing Abbey Craig, the Carse, Stirling and the Kilsyth Hills .. .. D 1008

General view south-westwards from Bridge of Allan, showing the Carse and the Touch and Gargunnock hills .. .. .. D 1007

General view south-westwards from Abbey Craig, showing the Carse, Craigforth and the Touch and Gargunnock hills .. D 1011

RECENT AND PLEISTOCENE

Erosional features

Findhu Glen–Corriebeagh through-valley .. .. D 411–3

Glacial drainage channels. Braco .. .. D 160–1, 179–181, 433–4, 436, 438, 442–3

Glacial drainage channel. Corb Glen, Ochil Hills .. .. .. D 1018–9

Glacial drainage channels. Corriebeagh Burn .. .. .. D 175

Glacial drainage channels. Doune .. .. D 61–2, 72, 74–76

Glacial drainage channel. Kincardine Glen, Auchterarder .. .. D 427

Glacial drainage channel. Meall a'Choire Riabhaich .. .. D 168–9

Glacial drainage channels. Strathallan .. .. D 13–4, 430–1, 1016

Glacial striae. Bogside .. .. C 3092

Glacial striae. Pleanbank .. .. C 3034

Glaciated valley. Glen Eagles .. .. D 423–4

Incised stream channel. Corriebeagh Burn .. .. D 166–7

334

Depositional features

Landslip. Craig Rossie, Auchterarder..	D 1020
'Saltings'. Airth	C 3040
Alluvial plain. Strathallan .. .. ..\	D 12
Alluvial plain. Knaik valley	D 165
Alluvial plain. Findhu Glen	D 406
Peat moss overlying 'Carse' clays. Dunmore..	C 3037
Plain of post-Glacial marine alluvium ('Carse'). Stirling	C 3006–8, 3029–31, 3042–3, D 17–8, 20–2, 779–80, 793, 839
Plain of post-Glacial marine alluvium ('Carse'), showing meander of River Forth. Stirling	D 1010
Plain of late-Glacial marine and estuarine alluvium. Cowie ..	C 3032–3
Plain of late-Glacial marine and estuarine alluvium. Stirling ..	D 19, 30
Late-Glacial alluvium and boulder clay. Stirling	C 3026–8
Fluvio-glacial sand and gravel. Glen Dey	C 3936–7
Kame terrace. Gleann a'Chroin	D 403–5
Kame-terrace with peat on top. Glen Artney	D 396–400
Glacial sand and gravel. Bannockburn .. ..·	D 29
Glacial sand and gravel. Braco	D 160–1, 435
Glacial sand and gravel. Callander	D 149–51
Glacial sand and gravel. Corriebeagh Burn	D 170–4
Glacial sand and gravel. Doune	D 71
Glacial sand and gravel. Dunblane	D 7
Glacial sand and gravel. Glen Devon..	D 1012–3
Glacial sand and gravel. Glen Eagles	D 1014
Glacial sand and gravel. Kinbuck	D 11, 15
Glacial sand and gravel. Strathallan	D 416–8, 425, 428–9, 439–441
Glacial sand and gravel. Teith valley	D 84–8, 90–1
Glacial gravel ridges. Strathallan	D 421
Kame-and-kettle topography. Strathallan .. .. ..· ..	D 419–20
Eskers. Doune	D 63–4
Eskers. Callander	D 192–4
Kettle-holes in glacial sand and gravel. Teith valley	D 69–70, 77, 83
Morainic drift. Findhu Glen	D 408–10
Morainic drift. Gleann an Dubh Choirein	D 391, 394–5, 401
Morainic drift. Glen Artney	D 177
Lake dammed by boulder clay. Loch Coulter	C 3063
Drumlin. Thornhill	D 187–8

Deposits

Fluvio-glacial sand and gravel. Callander	D 195–6
Fluvio-glacial sand and gravel. Doune	D 65–7, 95–7
Fluvio-glacial sand and gravel. Tillicoultry	C 3047–8
Glacial sand and gravel. Braco	D 432
Glacial sand and gravel. Cambusbarron, Stirling	C 3009–12
Glacial sand and gravel. Doune	D 68
Glacial sand and gravel. Dunblane	D 8–10, 157–8

Y

Glacial sand and gravel. Kinbuck .. .. D 16
Glacial sand and gravel. Strathallan .. .. D 414–5, 426
Glacial sand and gravel. Teith valley .. .. D 82, 89
Morainic drift. Callander .. .. D 147–8
Sand and silt in boulder clay. Callander .. .. D 152–3
Boulder clay. Muckle Burn, Braco .. .. D 182–4
Glacial erratic of dolerite. Tullibody .. .. C 3062
Glacial erratic of Lower Old Red Sandstone. Dunmore .. .. C 3039
Glacial erratics of conglomerate. Doune .. .. D 93–4
Ice-transported mass of coal. Blairingone .. .. C 3816–9

CARBONIFEROUS

Devon Red Sandstone (Coal Measures). Alva .. .. .. C 3061
Coal Measures strata. Clackmannanshire .. .. C 3056–60
Opencast coal workings. Dollar .. .. C 3831–5
Escarpment of Passage Group sandstone. Castleton .. .. C 3035
Volcanic vent of Upper Limestone Group age. Bogside .. .. C 3090
Limestones in Calciferous Sandstone Measures and Lower Limestone
  Group. Bannock Burn .. .. C 3019–21
Basalt lavas of Calciferous Sandstone Measures age. Craigforth,
  Stirling .. .. C 3007, D 17
Basalt lavas of Calciferous Sandstone Measures age, showing trap
  features. Touch Hills .. .. D 22, 770–2,
                                                         775–8, 781
Basalt lavas of Calciferous Sandstone Measures age, showing trap
  features. Gargunnock Hills .. .. D 779–80, 789–
                                                         799
Basalt lavas of Calciferous Sandstone Measures age. Fintry Hills.. C 2116–20,
                                                         D 800–12
Interbasaltic beds and basalt lavas of Calciferous Sandstone Meas-
  ures age. Fintry Hills .. .. D 815–22
Downie's Loup Sandstones (Calciferous Sandstone Measures).
  Gargunnock Burn .. .. D 830–1
Ballagan Beds (Calciferous Sandstone Measures). Gargunnock Burn D 786
Marls and cementstones (Calciferous Sandstone Measures). Dollar C 3051

UPPER OLD RED SANDSTONE

Cornstone Beds. Gargunnock Burn .. .. D 784–5, 787,
                                                         827–9
Gargunnock Sandstones. Gargunnock Burn .. .. .. D 823–4

LOWER OLD RED SANDSTONE

Sandstone escarpment (Teith Formation). Thornhill .. .. D 189
Sandstones of Teith Formation. Arrevore Burn .. .. .. D 164
Sandstone scarps (Teith Formation). Braco .. .. D 162
Steeply-dipping strata of Teith Formation. Eas Fiadhaich, Callander D 143–6
Strata of Teith Formation. Annet Burn, Doune .. .. .. D 78–9
Strata of Teith Formation. Bracklinn Falls, Callander .. .. D 137
Mudstones of Cromlix Formation. Ardoch Burn, Doune .. .. D 92
Mudstones of Cromlix Formation. Braco .. .. D 159, 185–6,
                                                         444
Quarry in Buttergask Formation. Auchterarder .. .. .. D 422

DALRADIAN

INTRUSIONS

Ochil Fault-Intrusion (quartz-dolerite), showing hade of fault to
south. Dollar .. .. C 3049–50
Ochil Fault-Intrusion (quartz-dolerite). Tillicoultry .. .. C 3045–6
Quartz-dolerite dyke. Doune .. .. D 73, 80–1
Downie's Loup sill. Dinning Quarry, Gargunnock .. .. .. D 779–80, 782
Downie's Loup sill. Downie's Loup waterfall, Gargunnock Burn.. D 783
Felsite sheet. Allt an Dubh Choirein .. .. D 386–7
Felsite sheet. Keltie Water .. .. D 388–9
Porphyrite sheet. Allt Breac-nic .. .. D 390

INDEX

Aa, 139–40

Abbey Craig, 182, 184, 229, 251, 265

—— —— Fault, 2, 98, 109, 114, 117–9, 129–30, 137–8, 157, 165, 174, 229–30, **249–51**, 254; fault plane followed by dolerite, 251; traced by gravity and magnetic surveys, 249, 251, 308, 310–1, 317–8

Aberfoyle fold, 7, 9

—— Slates, 5, 7, 9, 11; metamorphism, 11

A'Chrannach, 89, 91, 93

—— Conglomerate, 89, 91, 93

Acid porphyrite, 8, 13–5, 22, 30, 38, 41–3, 48, 50, 61–2; analysis, 48, 50; petrography, 22, 61–2

Aeromagnetic anomalies, 312, 315

—— survey, 308–10, 312–3, 315

Agates, 34

Agglomerate, 25, 35–6; *see also* tuff and agglomerate

Airth, 2, 190, 199, 203, 208, 213, 216–8, 257, 286, 302

—— Ball Coal, 216

—— Church Fault, 250, 253

—— Colliery, 282

—— Estate No. 1 Bore, 206

—— Main Coal, 216

—— Mains Fault, 250, 253

Airthrey Castle, 258, 275

—— Hill Mine, 293, **294**

—— Silver Mine, 293, **294**

Airth Shellband, 216, **217**

—— Upper Coal, 216

Aitkenhead Farm, 217

Albitization, 46–7, 52–4, 56–7, 60, 62, 139, 144, 149–53, 157, 160–1, 163–5

Aldonie Burn, 82

Algae, 119, 122, 126–7, 133, 135

Allan Water, 1–2, 73, 75–8, 234, 258, 287–8, 293, 305

Allerød, 260–1, 288; layer in alluvium of Loch Mahaick, 260, 288

Alloa, 1–2, 210, 215, 217–8, 220

—— Cherry Coal, 214, 216, **218**, 219, 222

—— Fault, 229, 246, 250, **251**

—— Splint Coal, 214, 216, **218**

Allt a'Chaltuinn, 90, 92

—— a'Chaoruinn, 91–4

—— a'Chroin, 231

—— a'Mhiadain, 87, 95, 231

Allt an Dubh Choirein, 7, 11–5, 48, 50, 88, 90, 92, 231, 242, 308, 310, 312–5

—— Breac-nic, 15, 261

—— Eas nan Earb, 92, 94

—— Mòr, 92–5

—— na Creige Duibhe, 94–5

—— na Cuile, 87, 95, 231

—— na Gaisge, 83, 87, 95–6, 231, 270

—— na Mna Ruaidhe, 44, 54, 89, 231

—— na Stainge, 95

—— Ollach, 92–5

—— Ruith nan Eas, 84, 95, 231

—— Srath a'Ghlinne, 45

Alluvial cones, 287

Alluvium, freshwater, 3, **287–8**

——, marine: *see* Carse Clays, late-Glacial marine, estuarine and deltaic deposits, post-Glacial marine and estuarine alluvium

Alton Fault, 250, **251**

Alva, 3, 26, 41, 203, 215, 218–9, 280, 282, 284, 307

—— Burn, 34, 244, 297

—— Glen, 37, 41, 45, 49, 51, 53, 248, 297

—— No. 1 Bore, 281

—— No. 2 Bore, 281

—— Silver Mine, 293, **297–9**

Am Beannan, 94

Analyses, chemical: Calciferous Sandstone Measures rocks, 106–7, 119–20, 126; Caledonian and Lower Old Red Sandstone igneous rocks, 48–51; Coal Measures coals, 223; Upper Old Red Sandstone rocks, 105–7

——, modal: Caledonian igneous rocks, 16

ANDERSON, F. W., 115, 133–5

Andesite: bosses, 42; lavas, 25–6, **32–4**, 44, 47, 49, 51–2, 54; minor intrusions, 30, 39, 41–2, 49, 51, 60–1

——, hornblende-: analysis, 49, 51; dyke, 39; lavas, 25–6, **33**; petrography, 45, 52, 61

——, hypersthene-: analysis, 49, 51; petrography, 45, 60–1; sill, 41–2

——, pyroxene-: dykes, 30; lavas, 25–6, 32, 33, 44; petrography, 45, 47, 52, 54, 60–1

Androhal Burn, 86, 232

Annet Burn, 83–5, 87, 233

Y* 339

Wallsend Coal, 214, 216, 218
Wallstale, 252, 265
—— Fault, 138, 152, 165, 174, 230, 250, **252**
Washouts: in Limestone Coal Group coals, 190–3; in Passage Group clayrocks, 209
Water of Ruchill, 90–3, 240
WATERSTON, A. R., iii, 277, 285
Watson House, 286
Wauk Mill, 74
Weatherlaw Inlier, 178–9
Wee Coal, 189
—— —— of Plean, 191; *see also* Dumbreck Cloven Coal
West Burn, 265
—— Cameron Burn, 41, 297
Wester Blackspout, 110
—— Cambushinnie, 81
—— Glen, 109–10
—— Kirk Craig, 41
—— —— —— diorite, 28, **37–8**, 39–40, 48, 50, 57; *see also* Tillicoultry diorites
—— Lundie, 84
—— Moss, 252
—— —— Fault, 250, **252**
Westerton, 273, 305
West Grange Bore, 230
—— Kirkton, 76

Westphalian, 207
Westplace Burn, 33, 39, 42
Westrig Burn, 42, 48, 50, 57, 62
West Slack, 80
Wether Hill, 25, 42, 62
Wharry Burn, 36, 45, 71, 73; *see also* Old Wharry Burn
Whinhall, 220
White Creich Hill, 29, 38–9
—— Hill, 36
Whitewisp Hill, 33, 42, 62, 234
Williamsfield, 76
WILSON, R. B., iii, 196, 205
Windy Yet, 265
Wolf's Hole Quarry, 65, 68, 73, 303
Wood Hill, 244
—— of Doune, 304

Yard Coal, 214, 216, **220**, 221, 223
Yellowcraig Wood, 42, 60

Zeolites, 156, 161
Zeolitization, 160–1
Zetland Mine, 218
Zones, faunal, 117, 174, 184, 205, 207, 213–4, 217, 221, 223–4
——, floral, 207

Printed in Scotland by Her Majesty's Stationery Office Press, Edinburgh
Dd. 569064 K12 (5996)